History of Augusta County, Virginia

HISTORY

—OF—

AUGUSTA COUNTY,

VIRGINIA;

—BY—

J. LEWIS PEYTON,

Author of "The American Crisis, or Pages from the Note Book of a State Agent during the Civil War;" "Over the Alleghanies and Across the Prairies, or Personal Recollections of the Far West one-and-twenty Years Ago;" "A Statistical View of the State of Illinois," etc.

STAUNTON, VIRGINIA:
SAMUEL M. YOST & SON.
MDCCCLXXXII.

FRANK PRUFER & SON,
Binders.
Staunton, Va.

INTRODUCTION.

A county remote from the first scenes of European settlement in Virginia; hot visited by whites until 1716; uncolonized till 1732, and organized less than a century and a half ago, appears to offer few materials for history. The Valley of Virginia, in the heart of which Augusta lies, was unknown to the whites for more than a hundred years after the landing at Jamestown. During this long period no effort was made to penetrate into what was supposed to be an impenetrable region lying beyond high and inaccessible mountains. No one ventured to overcome these obstacles of nature, and to enter a dismal solitude of irremediable barrenness and perpetual gloom, whose air was said to be infectious and mortal, the ground covered with serpents, the forests infested by wild beasts, and· the indigenous inhabitants a race of fierce and brutal savages, hating strangers and implacable in their cruelty. It was only after the return of the "Knights of the Golden Horseshoe" from their successful expedition over the mountains and into the Valley, that all previous accounts were discovered to be fabulous, and what was hitherto considered an accursed land, was found to be a delightful region, blessed with a delicious climate, rich fields, groves, shades and streams. From this period many persons seriously considered the question of making their homes in these hesperian regions, and within less than twenty years of Spotswood's return the Valley became the permanent home of Europeans. The early history of the discovery and occupation of the country west of the great mountains, so far as the present County of Augusta is concerned, is illustrated by few traditionary legends or incidents of border warfare, beyond the ordinary privations attending a new settlement, but when the entire territory which bore her name from 1738 to 1790, comes under view, it is eminently worthy of historical relation. A small remnant only of the adventures of our western pioneers is preserved. Much of the information, collected here and there from tradition, is uncertain and some of it absurd, yet we know enough as to their patient perseverance in subduing the wilds of nature; of their dauntless valor in their wars with the savages, (whose native courage was improved before these wars began, by the use of arms and the knowledge of discipline,) and of the events of those bloody struggles, to render their history both interesting and instructive.

A strong wish to preserve, in a permanent form, a record of the past, that it may no longer be clouded by ignorance nor perplexed by fiction; to rescue from unmerited oblivion the memories of our founders, whose heirs we are, with respect to civil and religious laws, language, science and territory; to keep alive in their descendants a love and veneration for their memories and a spirit of patriotism, has been the chief incentive to this work. It has been well said that a love of country and its institutions and distinguished benefactors is as natural to man as is the love of those who are endeared to him by his earliest, his most pleasing and permanent associations. And this sentiment inspires a deep sense of obligation to benefactors, and to that Being who, in His infinite mercy, is the bestower of every blessing enjoyed by man. It cannot be denied that to our forefathers we owe much of the happiness and prosperity we now enjoy, and every worthy descendant of those gallant and adventurous spirits must feel a strong desire to become intimately acquainted with their characters and history. A remembrance of what is past, and an anticipation of what is to come, seem to be the two faculties by which man differs from most animals. Though beasts enjoy them in a limited degree, yet their whole life seems taken up in the present, regardless of the past and the future. Man, on the contrary, endeavors to derive his happiness, and experiences most of his miseries, from these two sources.

That every existing history of Virginia is incomplete, is generally admitted and regretted. The student must still have recourse to Hening's Statutes at Large as the best record of the intellectual and moral advancement in our Commonwealth. When a complete history of Virginia is written, it will contain not only a full account of her political, civil and military transactions, but a clear and concise exposition of the character of her authors, scholars, statesmen, jurists and warriors, and also a view of her physical resources. Before such a comprehensive work can be composed, it is necessary to obtain true and precise details of private and preliminary transactions. In history, it is not the great and striking events that are instructive, but the accessory facts or the circumstances that have prepared or produced them. This is evident, because it is only by a knowledge of the preparatory circumstances that we can be enabled to avoid or to obtain similar results. It is not from the issue of a battle that we receive instruction, but from the different movements that led to its decision, which, though less splendid, are, however the causes, while the event is only the effect. Such is the importance of those details that, without them, the term of comparison is vicious, and has no analogy with the object to which we would apply it. The history of a county should abound in details, so necessary to the elucidation of the different parts of a general history; and if a complete history of each county cannot be now written, all the fragments, at least, should be collected and put in order, as necessary to just conclusions, as to the formation of society, the mechanism of government, and a correct view of the habits, manners, opinions, laws, internal and external regimen of each community or state. The gathering together of this material for a history of Virginia, its preservation in a convenient shape for reference—(it has been well said to know where you can find a thing is, in fact, the greatest part of learning)—is one of the duties which the present owes to the future.

With these views, the writer has undertaken the task of preparing a history of his native county. In the scope of his design, he could only aim at a brief sketch or outline of the subject previous to 1790, when the county assumed its present confines. He has endeavored to exhibit the principal events which belong to the history of the Valley and the western country,—or that part of Augusta without the existing limits of the county,—in the most general and simple terms, confining himself, for the most part, in the case of Indian depredations, murders, massacres, &c., to those which occurred within a certain area, or territory, not too remote from the present county. He has made free use of the works of various authors; he pretends to no originality, and offers his production to the public in the hope that it may prove useful and acceptable.

Under the head of Excerpts, Ana, &c., it has been found convenient to insert, at the close of several chapters, anecdotes, incidents related by living persons, genealogical memoranda, extracts from public records, original deeds, etc. Such matters could not be included in the text without interfering too much with the thread of the narrative. He has not sifted the evidence as to the authenticity of all these anecdotes, etc., but where there was a probability, from the story itself and the circumstances of the times that it was true,—where the matter was not inconsistent with nature and reason,—he has given them as he has found them in the newspapers or as they have been related to him. In this, the author has but followed the course of Herodotus, the father of profane history. History had its commencement in traditions, or narratives transmitted from mouth to mouth, from generation to generation. Indeed, before the art of printing was invented there was little else than these traditions. Such was the difficulty of multiplying books when writing was the only means by which they could be produced. While, therefore, implicit confidence may not always be placed in the stories handed down to us, we are not irreverently to reject them, unless irrational, contrary to nature and sound judgment. These scattered traditions, anecdotes and reminiscences are so many living monuments of antiquity, and serve at once to instruct and amuse.

It may, perhaps, be proper to make a further remark. In a work of this nature the author could not, without swelling the volume to unreasonable proportions, seek to minutely detail the policy or exhibit the springs and motives of government. He has, therefore, in general restricted himself to a plain exhibition of facts and events. It would be vain to attempt to unravel the tangled maze of British, French and Spanish politics in their connection with each other and their American colonies, within the limits necessarily assigned to the present volume. The intricacies of the complex machinery of government form a difficult study in themselves, and are therefore left, with other grave matters, to more competent hands.

In the appendix he has brought together all the information he could procure, or which was supplied to him by friends, as to the families of the pioneers or early settlers, and to this has been added a third part made up of biographical notices. These biographies are given, because biography is the hand-maid of history, portrait-painting for posterity, and the memory of our pioneer fathers and distinguished men is passing away, and will soon be forgotten unless some attempt be made to rescue it from impending oblivion. The heroes, who flourished before Agamemnon, says the Roman poet, passed into forgetfulness for want of a recording pen. Cicero eloquently remarks, the life of the dead is retained in the memory of the living, but a lethean wave will soon obliterate the remembrance of both living and dead, without the biographer's pen. If an apology is needed for his course it will be found in the remark of Lord Macaulay, who has justly observed: "A people, which takes no pride in the noble achievements of remote ancestors, will never achieve anything worthy to be remembered with pride by remote descendants."

The writer solicits indulgence for such errors, omissions or imperfections as may be found in his work, and will endeavor to render a second edition, if one should be called for, more worthy of public favor. In the progress of the work he has had frequent occasion to seek in various quarters for information, but has not thought it necessary to weary the reader by crowding his pages with references. All those interested in preserving facts worthy of being transmitted to posterity were invited through the Staunton papers to communicate them to him. He regrets that much apathy exists on the part of the general public, and that information was frequently received too late to be always introduced where it properly belonged. Notwithstanding this apathy, he has received from many so kind and ready a response to his appeal for information as to have excited his deep gratitude. He cannot forbear mentioning, in this connection, the spontaneous kindness of the following gentlemen, which has enabled him to enrich the work in many particulars: Rev. William T. Price, R. A. Brock, Joseph A. Waddell, Judge William McLaughlin, Hon. A. H. H. Stuart, Judge J. H. McCue, Wm. Withrow, Rev. J. S. Martin, Wm. E.

Craig, T. S. Doyle, Mathew Pilson, Chas. Campbell, Dr. C. Berkley, Dr. J. T. Clark, William M. Tate, George M. Cochran, jr., A. G. Christian, Marshall Hanger, J. H. Wayt, Maj. H. M. Bell, Hon. Absolom Koiner, J. W. Crawford, William Frazier, Hon. R. W. Thompson, Col. D. S. Young, J. N. Ryan, J. S. Gilliam, W. H. Peyton, W. A. Burnett, Joseph B. Woodward, Rev. John McVerry, Hon. Thomas Barry, D. A. Kayser and A. H. Davies.

To the people of Augusta, who love their native land, and who will peruse the work with interest, he commends the volume.

J. L. P.

STEEPHILL, NEAR STAUNTON, VA.,
November, 1882.

THE HISTORY

— OF —

AUGUSTA COUNTY.

CHAPTER I.

ANCIENT LIMITS.

The County of Augusta was ushered into existence the 12th year of the reign of George II., as one of the shires of the colony of Virginia. No reason appears in the act establishing the county for the name, but it is believed to have been selected in honor of the Princess Augusta, wife of Frederick Lewis, Prince of Wales, and daughter of Frederick II. Duke of Saxe-Gotha. Frederick county was created at the same time, and it is said, with good reason, to have derived its name from the Prince of Wales himself. From the act, which we quote in full from Hening's Statutes, vol. 5, pp. 78–79, it will be seen that Augusta and Frederick are twin sisters:

ACT FOR ESTABLISHING THE TWO COUNTIES PASSED BY THE GENERAL
ASSEMBLY OF THE COLONY OF VIRGINIA NOV. 1ST, 1738.

I. Whereas, great numbers of people have settled themselves of late upon the rivers of Sherrando*, Cohengoruto and Opeckon, and the branches thereof, on the N. W. side of the Blue Ridge mountains, whereby the strength of this colony, and its security upon the frontiers, and H. M.'s revenue of quit rents are like to be much increased and augmented : For giving encouragement to such as shall think fit to settle there.

II. Be it enacted by the Lieutenant-Governor, Council and Burgesses of this present General Assembly, and it is hereby enacted by the authority of the same, That all that territory and tract of land, at present deemed to be part of the county of Orange, lying on the northwest side of the top of the said mountains, extending from thence northerly, westerly and southerly, beyond the said mountains, to the utmost limits of Virginia, be

---

*Sherrando, or Shenandoah, signifies, in the Indian tongue, Beautiful Daughter of the Stars.

separated from the rest of the said county and erected into two distinct counties and parishes ; to be divided by a line to be run from the head spring at Hedgman river to the head spring of the river Potomack. And that all that part of the said territory lying to the northeast of the said line, beyond the top of the said Blue Ridge, shall be one distinct county and parish, to be called by the name of the County of Frederick and parish of Frederick ; and that the rest of the said territory, lying on the other side of the said line, beyond the top of the said Blue Ridge, shall be one other distinct county and parish, to be called by the name of the County of Augusta and parish of Augusta.

III. Provided, always, That the said new counties and parishes shall remain part of the County of Orange and parish of Saint Mark until it shall be made appear to the Governor and Council, for the time being, that there is a sufficient number of inhabitants for appointing justices of the peace and other officers, and erecting courts therein for the due administration of justice, so as the inhabitants of the said new counties and parishes be henceforth exempted from the payment of all public county and parish levies in the County of Orange and the parish of St. Mark ; yet, that such exemption be not construed to extend to any of the said levies laid and assessed at or before the passing of this act.

IV. And be it further enacted. That after a court be constituted in the said new counties respectively, the court for the said County of Frederick be held monthly upon the second Friday ; and the court for the said County of Augusta be held upon the second Monday in every month, and that the said counties and parishes, respectively, shall have and enjoy all rights and privileges and advantages whatsoever belonging to the other counties and parishes of this colony. And for the better encouragement of aliens, and the more easy naturalization of such as shall come to inhabit there,

V. Be it further enacted, That it shall and may be lawful for the Governor or Commander-in-Chief of this colony, for the time being, to grant letters of naturalization to any such alien, upon a certificate from the clerk of any county court, of his or their having taken instead of the oaths of allegiance and supremacy ; and taken and subscribed the oath of adjuration, and subscribed the test, in like manner, as he may do upon taking and subscribing the same before himself.

VI. And for the more easy payment of all levies, secretary's clerk, sheriff's and other officers' fees, by the inhabitants of the said new counties, Be it further enacted, That the said levies and fees shall and may be paid in money, or tobacco at three farthings per pound, without any deduction.—And that the said counties be and are hereby exempted from public levies for ten years.

VII. Provided, nevertheless, That from and after the passing of this act no allowance whatsoever shall be made to any person for killing wolves within the limits of the said new counties. Any law, custom, or usage to the contrary hereof, notwithstanding.

VIII. And for the better ordering of all parochial affairs in the said new parishes, Be it enacted by the authority aforesaid, That the freeholders and housekeepers of the same, respectively, shall meet at such time and place as the Governor or Commander-in-Chief of this dominion, for the time being, with the advice of the Council, shall appoint, by precept under his hand, and the seal of the colony, to be directed to the sheriffs of the said new counties, respectively, and by the said sheriffs publicly advertised; and then and there elect twelve of the most able and discreet persons of their said parishes, respectively: which persons so elected, having taken the oaths appointed by law and subscribed to be conformable to the doctrine and discipline of the Church of England, shall to all intents and purposes be deemed and taken to be the vestries of the said new parishes respectively."

The "utmost limits of Virginia," as expressed in this act for the western boundary of Augusta County, was the Mississippi river, beyond which were situated the French possessions known as Louisiana. This region was explored by the French in 1512 and partly colonized by them in 1699. In the year 1717 it was granted by the Crown to the Mississippi Company, but three years later was resumed by the Crown, and in 1763 was ceded to Spain, but was recovered by Napoleon in 1800. New Orleans was the southern and St. Louis the northern capital of these vast territories. The French claimed that their possessions extended from the Gulf of Mexico to the St. Lawrence, a claim that ignored the rights of English colonists to any portion of the western territory, or country lying beyond the Ohio river. In support of their pretensions, the French erected forts and blockhouses at intervals from the great Lakes through the western part of Pennsylvania to the Ohio, then along the banks of that stream to its junction with the Mississippi, whence their chain of military posts followed the course of the latter river to its mouth. The English colonists, more particularly the people of Augusta, found themselves by these proceedings of the French, hemmed in—prevented all expansion westward. A conflict, then, between the two races, the French and the English colonists of Augusta, Pennsylvania and New York, was, under these circumstances, sooner or later, inevitable. A conflict in fact took place as early as 1753, on the banks of the Ohio, between some English settlers and the garrison of one of the forts already referred to. Both parties hastened to lay the story of their injuries before their respective governments. The consequence was a long and sanguinary war between England and France, in which half of Europe became involved.

In this war Braddock's defeat temporarily delayed, but could not avert, the final catastrophe. The superior numbers and indomitable resolution of the Anglo-Saxon in the end prevailed. Canada was conquered and the forts on the Ohio were necessarily abandoned. France, it is true, still retained Louisiana, which comprehended not simply the present area of that State, but, as we have said, a vast tract of territory extending from the Gulf to the 49° of north latitude, and from the Mississippi river on the east to the Mexican frontier on the west. The territory embraced within the French claim is now known as Arkansas, Missouri, Kansas, Nebraska, Iowa, Minnesota, Montana, Wyoming, Idaho, Oregon and Washington. To the eastern limits of this vast region, the Mississippi river, the western boundary of Augusta county, extended under this act, and from its ancient territory were subsequently carved the present States of West Virginia, Kentucky, Ohio, Indiana, Illinois, Michigan, and part of Pennsylvania. It is not our purpose to write the history of this extensive region, now the seat of many great and prosperous Commonwealths. Its history, however, cannot be altogether omitted in our work. It was part of Augusta county for over fifty years subsequent to 1738, was the native land of many of the savage tribes who harassed the border, the scene of the French and Indian war, and the wars of 1764, 1774, and of many civil and military expeditions, and, in fact, of continual Indian hostilities for forty years previous to 1794, when the brilliant victory at the Rapids of the Maumee by Gen. Wayne brought permanent peace to the frontier.

All the events occurring in this region from the first settlement of Augusta had more or less influence upon the fortunes of the people of the Valley, and the inhabitants of Augusta and the Valley were so involved in them that they form in some measure a part of our history.

ABORIGINAL POPULATION.

At the period, 1716, of Col. Spotswood's discovery of the Valley, it was the camping, hunting-ground or residence of numerous tribes of Indians. These tribes, while wandering in pursuit of game from place to place during a considerable part of the year, possessed a few scattered villages, comprising a limited number of habitations, of the most imperfect construction, where they were in the habit of passing their winters and where they left their wives, children and old men during their absence. Round about these rude villages some feeble and ill-directed attempts at agriculture announced the more frequented and permanent haunts of savage life.

Many learned disquisitions exist as to the origin of these red men, and it cannot be denied that the origin, history, languages, and condition of the aborigines present ample materials for speculation. Among the Central and South American nations, notably in Mexico and Peru, many evidences exist of a regular, but limited civilization, but for the most part the tribes of both North and South America were, on the discovery of Columbus, composed of roving savages in a brutal state of abasement. Notwithstanding the greater progress among some of the aborigines, and certain physical differences, the Patagonians being generally over six feet high and the Esquimaux less than five feet,—a race of deformed and diminutive savages who tremble at the sound of arms,—the varieties of complexion, etc., those scholars whose opinions are entitled to most respect are agreed that there are sufficient points of general resemblance in all the nations of North and South America to justify the belief that they are sprung from one primitive pair. Religion, philosophy, geology, history and tradition combine to teach that man was created in Asia, and that his home after the flood continued in the high lands and lofty mountain regions of the Eastern continent.

While much obscurity rests on the question of the origin of the American tribes, it may be stated as the settled opinion that our continent was peopled from different quarters of the old world. Space will not permit us to enter into an examination of this subject, of the causes which drove the Asiatic tribes from their native seats, which impelled their march towards the northeastern portion of the Eastern continent, and finally brought them to the shores of the New World. In their route to America there was no particular obstacle. Behring's Straits, the water they are believed to have crossed, is only 39 miles wide; in it there are two islands, and in winter it is frozen over, so that quadrupeds as well as man can pass. And it has been well said that water is the highway of the savage, to whom, without an axe, the jungle is impervious. Even civilized man migrates by sea and rivers, and has ascended 2,000 miles above the mouth of the Missouri, while interior tracts in Virginia, New York and Ohio are still a wilderness. To the uncivilized man, no path is free but the sea, the lake and the river.

On supposed analogies of customs and language, some have thought the aborigines of the Tennessee Valleys and the plains of the Cordilleras were the descendants of the lost tribes of Israel, "who took counsel to go forth into a further country, where never mankind dwelt."—[II Esd. c. xiii, v. 40-45.]

Dr. Lang suggests the possibility of an early communication between the Polynesian world and South America, and while it is possible that it may have taken place, the better opinion is, as mentioned, that it was by Behring's Straits that America received her first inhabitants.

The following is a list of the various tribes who resided in or resorted to the Valley of Virginia in 1716-32, and they all spoke the same language or a dialect of it. This was the mother tongue of the natives from North Carolina to Massachusetts. This mother tongue received from the French the name of Algonquin, and under it all the wild tribes of this region were grouped:

I. The Shawanese, the most considerable of the Algonquin tribes, had their principal villages east of the Alleghanies, near the present town of Winchester, but their possessions extended west to the Mississippi river. Foote asserts (Second Series, p. 159) that the Shawanese owned the whole Valley of Virginia, but had abandoned it. He gives no authority for the statement, and we have found none in our researches. Of all the Indian tribes with whom our ancestors came in contact, the Shawanese were the most bloody and terrible, holding all other men, as well Indians as whites, in contempt as warriors in comparison with themselves. This estimate of themselves made them more restless and fierce than any other savages, and they boasted that they had killed ten times as many white people as any other Indians did. They were a well-formed, active and ingenious people, capable of enduring great privations and hardships, were assuming and imperious in the presence of others not of their own nation, and sometimes very cruel.

II. The Tuscaroras, whose villages were near Martinsburg, in the present county of Berkeley.

III. The Senedos, who occupied the north fork of the Shenandoah until 1732, when it was exterminated by hostile natives from the South.

IV. The Catawbas, whose headquarters were on the Catawba river in South Carolina.

V. The Delawares, who frequented the Susquehanna river in Pennsylvania.

  · VI. The Susquehanoughs, who originally occupied the headwaters of the Chesapeake bay, but were driven out by the Cinela tribe and took up their residence on the upper waters of the Potomac, supposed to be one of their favorite places of residence, as the remains of their villages are more numerous in this region than elsewhere in the Valley.

VII. The Cinelas, on the Upper Potomac.

VIII. The Pascataway tribe, on the headwaters of the Chesapeake.

IX. The Cherokees, who occupied the Upper Valley of the Tennessee river and the high lands of Carolina, Georgia and Alabama. The Cherokees were the tallest and most robust of the Southern tribes, their complexions brighter than usual with the red men, and some of their young women were nearly as fair and blooming as European women. They owed allegiance to the Muscogulges, who stood at the head of a confederacy composed of Cherokees, Seminoles, Chickasaws, Choctaws and Creeks, and it is probable that bands from all of these tribes, or at least warriors, accompanied the Cherokees in their annual visits to the Valley. Without exception, these Southern Indians were proud, haughty and arrogant, brave and valiant in war, ambitious of conquest, restless and perpetually exercising their arms, yet magnanimous and merciful to a vanquished enemy when he submitted and sought their friendship and protection.

These vagrant tribes camped or resided at great distances from each other, were widely dispersed over a vast country, and any connection between them and particular localities was of so frail a texture that it was broken by the slightest accident.

The different tribes or nations were small in number as compared with civilized societies in which industry, arts, agriculture and commerce have united a vast number of individuals whom a complicated luxury renders valuable to each other.

No accurate information exists as to the numbers composing these tribes, but it is most probable they did not exceed a few hundred warriors each. At the landing of the Pilgrims in 1620, the number of Indians in New En-

gland did not exceed 123,000, and a few years later the number was greatly
reduced by a plague. It is probable that the Indian population of Virginia was larger at this time, as the climate of our Valley and State is generally better adapted to the wants of man than that of New England.
Bancroft, however, ventures the opinion that the whole Indian population
east of the Mississippi and south of New England did not, in 1620, exceed
180,000.

Detached parties of armed barbarians from the Northern and Western
tribes occasionally came to the Valley, and the Massawomees penetrated
to Eastern Virginia and were a terror to the low-land tribes Armed parties also visited the Valley from the five nations situated on the rivers and
lakes of New York—the Mohawks, Oneidas, Onondagas, Cayugas and
Senecas.

There was little difference in character and person between these wild
men of whatever tribe, and the remark of Capt. Jno. Smith in his general
history, Vol. 1. p 120, that the Cinelas were of gigantic size, is now rejected
as incredible—a statement as little to be believed as the fabulous origin
assigned by the Goths to their enemies, the Huns, namely: that the witches
of Scythia had copulated in the desert with infernal spirits, and that the
Huns were the offspring of this execrable conjunction.

We distrust whatever is marvelous, but it is proper to mention in this
connection that the historian of the Valley gives an account, in his second
chapter, of the discovery, in Hardy county, of the under jaw bone of a human being of great size, with eight teeth in each side of enormous size, and
the teeth standing in the jaw bone transversely! What is repugnant to
experience and common sense we discredit, and consequently have little
faith in this story, though given upon the authority of a gentleman who
represented that he had himself seen the jaw bone. Within the present
year mastodon bones have been excavated on the Kentucky Central railroad. The supposed human jaw bone found in Hardy, was doubtless the
fossil remain of some extinct animal of the genus mammiferous.

That portion of the Valley now embraced within the County of Augusta,
is not known to have been the home or fixed residence of any tribe of
Indians at the period of its settlement, nor is it known that it was not the
home of some tribe or branch of a tribe. Such red men as Lewis met on
entering Augusta, in 1732, were friendly, and so continued for over twenty
years.

That the country had been, previous to 1732, permanently occupied, is indicated by the remains of barrows, cairns and ramparts, composed of mingled earth and stones, found at different points in the county
—notably near Waynesboro, on Lewis creek, a few miles below Staunton;
on Middle river near Dudley's mill, and at Jarman's Gap, north of Rockfish. The cairn at Jarman's Gap is probably sepulchral, and may have

been intended and uscd as a place of worship. In the lower Shenandoah Valley and the country west of the Alleghanies—in fact over every part of North America, especially in the Mississippi Valley—there are remains of fortifications, mounds and other monuments of a primitive race, bearing marks of great antiquity, which "whisper mysteriously of a shadowy race, populous, nomadic, not altogether uncivilized, idolatrous," worshipping "in high places." It does not come within the scope and design of this volume, however, to investigate the question whether they were the work of the progenitors of the Indians or of a race long since extinct. That and all similar matters must be left to those who have taste and leisure for such abstruse enquiries. We may remark, however, that no remains exist in the Valley which indicate labor on a large scale or which were worthy, in Jefferson's opinion, tò be styled Indian monuments. He would not dignify with that name their stone arrow-points, pipes, &c.

The Valley of Virginia was, in 1716, when visited by Spotswood, without extensive forests, but the margins of streams were fringed with trees; there were pretty woodlands in the low grounds, and the mountain sides were densely covered with timber trees. The wood destroyed by Autumnal fires was replaced by a luxuriant growth of blue grass, white clover and other natural grasses and herbage. The spontaneous productions of the earth were everywhere numerous and abundant, and there were many varieties of game and wild animals. The luxuriance of the vegetation evinced the fertility of a soil which required only the hand of art to render it in the highest degree subservient to the wants of man. But the nomads of the Valley were averse to improvement; their indolence refused to cultivate the earth, and their restless spirit disdained the confinement of sedentary life. To prevent the growth of timber and preserve the district as pasture, that it might support as much game as possible, and that the grass might come forward in the early Spring, the savages, before retiring into Winter quarters, set on fire the dry grass and burnt over the country. The absence of trees in an extensive quarter of the county N. W. of Staunton led our ancestors to style it "The Barrens," a name that it still bears, though it is interspersed at this time by handsome woodlands, the growth of the last eighty years.

As we shall speak in a subsequent page of the physical character and resources of the present county, nothing further need be now said beyond this, that the climate of the region west of the mountains was found by the first settlers to be mild and agreeable, the winds light and bracing, the rain fall ample, storms and mists rare, the soil fertile, producing trees and grass, and the earth apparently rich in ores, as indicated by mineral springs.

The two principal non-resident tribes who frequented this fine country in 1716-1745, were the Delawares from the North and the Catawbas from the South. At the time Augusta was settled, 1732, a bloody war was progressing between these tribes, and the Valley was the theatre of action. In this war other tribes now and again participated as the allies of one or the other party, and it was at a battle on the North fork of the Shenandoah, in the county now bearing that name, that the Senedos tribe was exterminated. There is a burial place there eighteen to twenty feet high and sixty feet in circumference, filled with human bones, which testify to the truth of this tradition.

Wars between the tribes who frequented the Valley were of constant occurrence, and much speculation has been indulged in as to their origin —some inclining to the opinion that there is a natural state of hostility of man against man. It is more probable, that these wars resulted from the restless and turbulent nature of mankind, the ambition of leaders and disputes as to the hunting grounds. Such, indeed, was the red man's martial and independent spirit, his love of arms, that he considered war and rapine as the pleasure and glory of mankind. It was the wars of the Iroquois and Massawomies, on the Ohio, which gave that beautiful stream its significant name of the "River of Blood." The war-paths conducting into the Valley were through Rockfish and Jarman's gaps, thence by the present site of Staunton and down the Valley, branching at different points.

Armed parties during this period constantly passed and repassed the white settlements without disturbing them. Sometimes they spent the night near the whites, and, when in need, asked for food and other supplies, which were always given them. If in want of provisions, and no white was near to supply them, they would kill pigs or cattle running at large, which they considered lawful game. The settlers were too few and too wise to resent these liberties, and continued on amicable terms with both Catawbas and Delawares when those tribes were, in 1732, and for many years subsequently, at war with each other. And it is worthy of remark that neither tribe sought to involve the colonists in their quarrels. When a single Indian, or a party of two or three, called at the hut of a white for victuals, rest or social conversation, he confidently approached the door and said, "I am come." Soon the whites set before them food and drink. After eating and drinking they lit their pipes, and while smoking conversed. This over, they arose and said, "I go," and off they walked, to stop without an introduction or invitation at the next habitation the appearance of which they liked. The sententious brevity with which they announced their arrival and departure may be ascribed to their limited English vocabulary rather than rudeness, though it must be allowed that the easy and graceful manners of a gentleman are not innate. The gradual process by which they are arrived at are summarized in Pope's line: "He marries, bows at court and grows polite."

The Indian villages in the Valley were principally on the upper waters of the Potomac, near the present towns of Martinsburg and Winchester, but at some period previous to the settlement of Augusta. villages had existed at numerous points on the banks of the streams East and West of the mountains. The spots can now be identified in Eastern Virginia by the deposits of oyster and muscle shells, these bivalves constituting a part of their food, and in the Valley by ashes, charred wood, arrow points, toma-hawks, pipes and other remains. Their huts or wigwams were built by uniting poles at the top and inserting them at regular distances in the ground. An aperture was left at the top for smoke, and the ribs or rafters were covered with bark, the skins of wild beasts or with the boughs of trees. A small opening was left on one side, and in front of this in warm weather their fires were lit. In Winter the fire was made in the centre of the wigwam, and the savages ranged themselves round it on skins, mats and the leaves of trees. It was their custom, and a wise one it was, to sleep with their feet to the fire. Each family had its own hut, but occasionally they allowed others to enjoy its shelter. Their villages were always located near pure water, and if possible under the protection of a hill or forest. Their wigwams were unfurnished, except a covering of leaves and skins, for the dirt floors on which they slept. They ate without table, chairs, knives or forks.

Their clothing consisted of skins—their feet being encased in a kind of sandal made of deer skin or other soft leather, called moccasin. It was, unlike the sandal, with a soft sole, and was ornamented on the upper side. They took fish with hooks made of fish bones or the spear, or caught them in nets. For hunting and in war they used clubs, bows and arrows and tomahawks headed with stone. After the settlement of the whites the heads of tomahawks were made of metal for their use by the English, with the hammer-head hollowed out to suit the purpose of a smoking pipe, the mouth-piece being in the end of the shaft. The tomahawk was the Indian's most valuable weapon. He used it in time of peace for cutting his firewood, and in war wielded it with deadly effect. Their arrow-points and scalping-knives were made of flint stone, and many of these are constantly picked up near Staunton and in other parts of the county.

For passing streams the Indians used canoes, which were made of birch bark, sewed together with fibres, or roots. Their treatment of females was cruel and oppressive. They were considered as slaves and treated as such. To the squaw was assigned the labors of the field and the ser-vices of domestic care. Chastity was not one of the virtues of the wo-men, but when married, they did not dispense their favors without the consent of their husbands. We have no account of the marriage cere-mony, if such a ceremony existed among them. and imagine the associa-tion of the sexes was a voluntary union, which might be terminated at any time by consent of the parties. As, however, in all ages and among all people, religion of some kind has prevailed, and a reverence and awe of a Divinity existed, and our red men paid honor and homage to the Great Spirit, we do not feel at liberty to declare that such unions were altogether without religious character. We shall not dwell upon these matters of marital infidelities, as we are not called upon to represent human nature in such colors and lineaments as dishonor her, and do not wish to familiarize the minds of our readers with vice. A slight allusion to them was important to historic truth, which renders it necessary to speak of the vices and failings as well as the virtues of a people. We shall be content with touching thus lightly upon them. The men, who were occupied procuring the means of a precarious subsistence, were not, as may be readily imagined, of a lively disposition. Indeed, much gaiety of temper or a high flow of spirits was altogether inconsistent with their surroundings. These red men were, therefore, in general, grave even to sadness ; had nothing of that giddy vivacity peculiar to some nations of Europe, and they despised it. Though usually silent and gloomy, their aged chiefs and the squaws were, on occasion, fond of conversation, and amused the children with tales of war and hunting. There were professional story-tellers also among them, who imitated the actions of their heroes, and thus increased the interest of their narratives and excited the liveliest interest in their hearers. When tales of bloody fights, or the incidents of buffalo hunts were recounted, the narrators imitating the actors in the scenes, the audience listened with breathless attention. When they related amusing stories, acting out the parts, the groups would break into wild shouts of laughter and applause.

The diseases of the Indians were not numerous ; their remedies few and simple, their physic consisting mainly of the bark and roots of trees.

For music they used rude drums, rattles made of gourds, and a cane on which they piped. They were hospitable, and grateful for benefits; brave, but wayward and inconstant. To sum up their character in a few words: They were distinguished in council for gravity and eloquence ; in war, for bravery and address. When provoked to anger they were sullen and retired, and when determined on revenge no danger would deter them : neither absence nor time could cool them. If captured by an enemy, they never asked life nor betrayed emotions of fear.

For over a hundred years after the settlement at Jamestown the colonists from Virginia to Massachusetts were harassed by the Indians. The friendly relations, which existed for a short time after the landing of the English, soon changed, and the Indians became hostile and relentless in their enmity. During their wars with the whites they practiced every possible cruelty, burnt their houses, shot them down in their fields when at work, and now and again met them hand to hand in battle. They were entirely unreliable, neither respecting in peace the faith of treaties nor in war the dictates of humanity. They tortured their prisoners to death, and some of the tribes notably. the Miamis, ate the flesh of their captives.

War, if not brought on by an accidental rencontre, was preceded by a formal declaration of hostilities. This was made with great ceremony. The chief, having determined on fighting, sent wampum, or belts of beads, to his allies, inviting them to come and destroy their enemies, and to the enemy a belt painted red, or a bundle of bloody sticks, as a defiance. A great fire was then lit and the war dance took place. These ceremonies observed, the braves issued forth singing to the women a farewell hymn. If they surprised a village of their foes, while the flower of the nation was absent, they massacred the women, children and helpless old men, or made prisoners of such as had strength to be useful to them. Their prisoners were treated with inconceivable barbarity, thus exhibiting to what an extremity men's passions lead them when unrestrained by reason and uninfluenced by the dictates of Christianity. These savage acts make us more sensible, too, of the value of commerce, the arts of civilized life, and the lights of literature, which, if they abate the force of some of the natural virtues by the luxury which attends them, have taken out likewise the sting of our natural vices and softened the ferocity of the human race.

The Indians were not without a certain species of government, which prevailed, with little variation, over the continent. Though free, they did not despise all sorts of authority. They were attentive to the voice of wisdom, which experience had conferred on the aged, and they enlisted under the banners of their chiefs with child-like confidence—chiefs in whose valor and military address they had learned to repose their trust. His power, however, was rather persuasive than coercive; he was reverenced as a father, rather than feared as a monarch. He had no guards, no prisons, no officers of justice; but, relying upon the respect, confidence and esteem of his people, he lived unthreatened by Nihilist cabals and unterrified by dynamite and infernal machines. Few modern European rulers do this. The elders in every tribe constituted a kind of aristocracy, and were always consulted on grave occasions by the chief and people. They possessed no power except the influence they exerted by reason of their age and experience, and the further fact that they constituted a kind of hereditary nobility. Among the Indians age alone acquired respect, influence and authority, because age brings experience, and experience is the chief source of knowledge among a people without literature.

Their religious belief consisted of traditions mingled with many superstitions. They believed in two Gods, the one Good, who was the superior, and whom they styled the Great Spirit; the other Evil. They worshipped both, but principally the latter, the Good Spirit, in their opinion, needing no prayers to induce him to aid and protect his creatures. Besides these, they worshipped various other deities, such as fire, water, thunder,—anything which they supposed to be superior to themselves and capable of doing them injury. They believed in a future state, in a tranquil and happy existence with their ancestors and friends, spending their time in those exercises in which they delighted when on earth.

From the picturesque situations of their villages, they are supposed to have admired the grand and beautiful in Nature. That they possessed to a considerable degree the poetic sentiment, is inferred from the names given to the rivers and mountains, their war songs, and the speeches of some of their chiefs.

Such, in short, were the wild red men of the forest, on whose lands the early settlers pitched their tents. The barbarian heroes of our border wars have been depicted with so much fidelity and graphic power by one of our greatest writers, that in the defect of materials strictly historical, they may to a certain extent supply their place. Nowhere can the moody, taciturn and sententious red man be more delightfully studied than in the pages of Fenimore Cooper. These delineations of Cooper should not be rejected because given to the world in his fictitious writings. Historical facts are often rendered the more agreeable by being conveyed in a story of adventure designed for the entertainment of the reader. Novels frequently approach to the nature of history, and history often partakes of the character of romance. Histories, in general, are full of chimerical and extravagant details, especially as they ascend to periods of great antiquity and are connected with the origin of nations, and it has been oftener than once said that even Livy is but a romance. Yet who would give up such histories? We read them with deep interest, though we feel that they are but a compound of truth and fiction. We linger over the harangues which the characters in history never made, and delight in the eloquence of Logan, though persuaded that the author of his eloquence was an educated white man.

A succinct résumé of Virginia's colonial history, from the landing at Jamestown to the year 1750, will be given in the next succeeding chapter, as an interesting, if not necessary preliminary to the history of Augusta.

CHAPTER II.

The following outline of colonial history, from the first landing at Jamestown to the year 1750, and slight reference to French explorations and settlements in the West, will enable the reader to understand the condition of
affairs in the colony and western country generally at the period Lewis
entered, took possession of, and settled Augusta. It exhibits also the
position of Virginia in her connection with the various colonies which afterwards united together to resist the tyranny of Great Britain and found the
United States, and will enable the reader to understand any points of general history which may be touched upon in the progress of this work.

The closing years of the fifteenth century saw the theatre of history suddenly enlarged. The history of the world, as embracing all parts of the
globe, commenced with the discoveries of Columbus and Vasco da Gama.
To within a century of the end of the Moorish kingdom in Spain, and of
that ten centuries of mediæval times, the first six of which are known as
the "dark ages," the settlement of Virginia carries us back. The earliest
incidents in her career belong to that European era which witnessed the
massacre of St. Bartholomew, the independence of the United Provinces
under William of Orange, the destruction of the Spanish Armada, and the
persecution of the Puritans in England. They belong also to that Eliza-
bethan era of English history so remarkable for literary taste and for the
spirit of commercial adventure which pervaded all classes. It was from
the England of Raleigh, Gilbert, Marlowe, Shakespeare, Burleigh, Wal-
singham, Essex, Leicester, Sidney and Francis Bacon that came the men
who undertook to found colonies on our shores and to build up political communities in the New World. The most remarkable of these men
was the "learned and valiant" Sir Walter Raleigh, whose name is indissolubly associated with the first efforts at English colonization in America.

Upon the unsuccessful efforts of Raleigh to make a settlement on Roanoke Island, we cannot dwell. He had undertaken a task beyond the
strength of a single individual, and met the common lot of enthusiasts.
His failures did not deter others, and a few years later James I granted
charters to the London and Plymouth companies for " deducing colonies
and making habitation and plantation in that part of America commonly
called Virginia." Under these charters all the coast was embraced lying
between Florida and Nova Scotia.

These charters are long and tedious documents, which possess no intrin-
sic merit—are just such stupid papers as one might expect from the narrow

mind of James. By virtue of them a complicated form of government was framed. For each colony separate councils, appointed by the King, were instituted in England, and these councils were in turn to name resident councillors for the colonies. Thirteen members constituted the resident council. They had power to choose their own president, to fill vacancies in their numbers, and, a jury being required only in capital cases, to act as a court of last resort in all other causes. Religion was established in accordance with the forms and doctrines of the Church of England. The adventurers, as the company were called, had power to coin money and collect a revenue for twenty-one years from all vessels trading to their ports, and they were also freed from taxation for a term of years. One article, and only one, in the most general terms, provided for the liberty of the subject. Another clause provided for community of goods.

A worse system of government could not have been devised. Two arbitrary and irresponsible councils—one in England and the other in America—the legislative power reserved to the King—the governing body commercial monopoly, and the chief principle of society a community of property. Such was the government elaborated in the charter. With such a frame of government the first colonists, composed of men who cared little for forms of government, set forth for Virginia.

The colony consisted of 105 persons, who sailed from the Downs, Jan. 1, 1507, for Virginia under command of Capt. Newport, who landed them at Jamestown on the 13th May, 1607. The men composing the expedition were wretched material for founding a State. There were seventy men in the party, of whom fifty-four were gentlemen, four carpenters and twelve laborers—or, as Capt. Smith describes them, "poor gentlemen, tradesmen, serving men and libertines." The first President of the Colony, appointed in London, was Wingfield, a man of wealth and social position, but incapable and unfit for governing. He was soon superceded by the strongest man among the colonists—a man to whose name a romantic interest attaches—the celebrated Capt. John Smith. Smith has been described as an adventurer of a high order in an age of adventurers. He had all the faults of his time and class in full measures, but he had also their virtues, and it was here that he surpassed his companions. He was arbitrary, jealous of power, quarrelsome and despotic, ready to lie audaciously to serve his own ends, and rashly overconfident. But he was also brave, energetic, quick-witted, and full of resource. By his energy and wisdom he preserved the colony from impending ruin and improved its condition. What we would call now-a-days a many-sided man, he made himself familiar, by repeated explorations, with the country and its products, became well acquainted with the aborigines, with whom he opened a trade, and in various ways displayed his superior qualities, and an earnest desire to promote the interest of the colony.

A small fort was erected, and a few log huts, and in these the colonists were kept together by Smith for two years, in the presence of a subtle and ferocious enemy, who, within a fortnight of the first landing, made an attack upon them, evidently with a view to their extermination. This attack of the Indians was repelled by the colonists under Wingfield, who was an old soldier, having served many years in the European wars. Notwithstanding Smith's efforts, the colony languished, and matters grew so much worse that the settlement was abandoned, and the colony would have been broken up but for the arrival of Lord Delaware, as Governor, with five hundred fresh men and supplies, in 1609—1610.

Lord Delaware, who received the appointment of Governor for life, surrounded himself with stately officers and liveried servants, and assumed the demeanor of the ruler of an opulent empire. He was an able man, and might have rendered valuable service, but unfortunately was forced, by disease brought on by the climate, to return to England. He committed the government to Mr. Percy, who was supplanted by Sir Thomas Dale in 1611, to whom the government granted authority to rule by martial law. Dale exercised his arbitrary powers with prudence and moderation, and to him Virginia is more indebted than to any of her early Governors. He established and maintained order, and extended the settlements into the interior, forming a colony of 350 men at a point up the James river, called Henrico. But the chief good of his administration consisted in breaking up the system of community of property and introducing individual proprietorship. On his departure, in 1616, he left the colony firmly established and under the protection of Sir Thos. Yeardley, whose administration was not unlike that of his predecessors, but he was soon superceded by Capt. Samuel Argall, a rough sea captain, accustomed to command respect, of a cruel, covetous and tyrannical disposition, with a decided taste for piracy. He made an energetic and active Governor, carrying out the military code in the spirit of a buccaneer. He oppressed and robbed the colonists, his greed lighting especially on the friends of Lord Delaware. Complaints went to England, and the Virginians awakened to the fact that they were shockingly misgoverned; that they were left at the mercy of one man's rule, and that man a tyrant; that their rights were unknown. The period of political development had, however, now began.

The indignation in London at Argall's misconduct led to a new and representative government in Virginia, granted under the influence of the Earl of Southampton, Sandys, Digges, Selden and others. Argall was recalled, and a new form of political organization was granted to the colonists. The Governor's power was in future to be limited by a council, and the assemblage of a representative body was authorized. Under this new order of things the first General Assembly was held at James City in

June, 1619, and in May, 1620, a second Assembly convened.   In order to give the reader, better than an elaborate disquisition would do, an idea of the spirit and character of the early settlers and of their sufferings and difficulties, more particularly with the Indians, we append the commission to Sir Francis Wyatt, Governor, and the Council, of date July 24, 1621. The object of the assembly was " to assist the Governor in the administration of justice, to advance Christianity among the Indians, to erect the colony in obedience to his Majesty, and in maintaining the people in justice and christian conversation, and strengthening them against enemies.   The said Governor, Council, and two burgesses out of every town, hundred or plantation, to be chosen by the inhabitants to make up a General Assembly, who are to decide all matters by the greatest number of voices ; but the Governor is to have a negative voice, to have power to make orders and acts necessary, wherein they are to imitate the policy of the form of government, laws, customs, manner of trial, and other administration of justice used in England, as the company are required by their letters patent.   No law to continue or be of force until ratified by a quarter court to be held in England, and returned under seal.   After the colony is well framed and settled, no order of quarter court in England shall bind till ratified by the General Assembly."

From the first, the Burgesses sought to obtain equal rights for all men before the law, by praying the company not to violate that clause in the charter by which they were guaranteed.   After passing various sumptuary and police laws, laws for the government of ministers and raising taxes on tobacco, &c., they adjourned.   But this year marks an era in Virginian annals—the dawn of representative government and constitutional freedom.   It is memorable also for the introduction of the first slaves in America, and of a forced class of immigrants—boys and girls seized by the press gang in the streets of London, and shipped, as if they were felons, to Virginia.

At this Assembly eleven boroughs were represented by twenty-two Burgesses, and this constituted the great State of Virginia in 1619.   But the prospects of the future were bright.   Immigration increased, and was now composed, not of adventurers, but of "prudent men with families," and in 1623, under the governorship of Sir Francis Wyatt, the population consisted of 4,000 persons, and the massacre of 350 by the Indians did not destroy the colony.   Under the system which prevailed in Virginia, freedom of debate and love of independence were fostered.

To the form of government established by the colony July, 1621, was added the proviso, as mentioned above, that no order of the Council in England should bind the colony, unless ratified by the General Assembly of Virginia.   Thus early in our country's history was introduced those principles of republicanism which eventually secured to us our present government.

James became jealous at what he considered an invasion of prerogative, and denounced the Company which gave a democratic constitution to Virginia "as a seminary for a seditious Parliament," and also said he would rather they "chose the devil as treasurer than Sir Edwyn Sandys." The Company was firm, and refused his claim to nominate their officers, and from the struggle and the feelings it excited, the colony derived solid advantages.

But the Company was doomed. James pursued them unrelentingly. A royal commission was sent to Virginia to gather material for its destruction. The commissioners, reaching Virginia, demanded the records of the Assembly, which were refused. The clerk was bribed to give them up by the commissioners. The Assembly stood their clerk in the pillory and cut off his ears. The patriotic resistance of the colonists was fruitless. A *quo warranto* was tried in the King's Bench, and the charter was annulled. The dissolution of the London Company was a distinct benefit to the colonists, by relieving the settlers from the cumbrous, complicated and uncertain government of a mercantile corporation, and placing them in the same relation to the King as his other subjects.

The five years which now followed of Sir Francis Wyatt's continuance in office were characterized for their legislative activity, for the formation of political habits, and for the first opposition to the home government, which strengthened and confirmed the independent spirit of the colonists. During the session of 1623–24, Royal Commissioners came to Virginia to assist in ruining the Company. This period is marked in the statute book by the definition and declaration of certain guiding political principles which were never afterwards shaken. The Governor's power was limited. He was not "to lay any taxes or impositions upon the colony, their lands, or other way than by the authority of the General Assembly, to be levied and employed as the said Assembly shall appoint." The Governor was not to withdraw the inhabitants from their labors for his own service, and the Burgesses attending the Assembly were to be free from arrest. These were the great and fundamental principles for which patriotic men were then contending in England. James I died March 25, 1625, and Charles I succeeded him and took the government in his own hands. He granted large plantations in Virginia to his favorites, Lords Baltimore and Fairfax. Shortly afterwards Wyatt departed, and George Yeardley was appointed his successor. He lived but a short time, when the Council chose Francis West as Governor. Subsequently, John Pott was appointed, who was soon superceded by Sir John Harvey. The latter quarreled with the colonists, was thrust out of the government, was reinstated by the King, and in 1639 the King reappointed Sir Francis Wyatt.

Two important events occurred during Harvey's administration—the settlement of Maryland by Lord Baltimore, an l the rise of the Puritan party in Virginia. The Virginia colonists considered Maryland as a part of Virginia, and resented the course of Lord Baltimore. Quarrels about jurisdiction soon broke out, and all parties suffered. Attached to the Church of England, Virginia was not a promising field for Puritans, but a community of them had settled in Virginia years before.

Wyatt was replaced in 1642 by Sir William Berkeley, who governed well at first, but his accession brought no increase of political freedom to Virginia. The first step toward federation was taken about this time, in the passage of an act ratifying and regulating commerce with Maryland. The prosperity of the colony increased rapidly, interrupted only by a second outbreak of Indians, which was quickly quelled.

The execution of Charles I, 1649, filled Virginians with horror and indignation, and the well-known sympathy of Virginia with the unhappy King drew many exiled cavaliers to America. The Governor invited Charles II to come to and be King of Virginia, but on the eve of his embarking from Holland for Virginia, in 1660, he was recalled to the throne of England. After he ascended the throne, Charles II, desirous of giving a substantial proof of the profound respect he entertained for the loyalty of Virginia, caused her arms to be quartered with those of England, Ireland, and Scotland, as an independent member of the Empire. This fact, and because Virginia was the first of the English settlements in the limits of the British colonies, led to her being styled "The Old Dominion."

During the administration of Cromwell, Virginia enjoyed a free and independent government under three Governors—Bennet, Digges, and Mathews—all Puritans, who were chosen by the Assembly. An old historian tells us that Mathews was "a most deserving Commonwealth's man, who kept a good horse, lived bravely, and was a true lover of Virginia." Under these three men the political rights of the people were firmly established and their commercial interests protected and extended by the commencement of treaties with New England, New York, and the cultivation of closer relations with Maryland. General prosperity consequently prevailed.

After the Restoration, the Virginia Assembly elected Berkeley Governor, an address was voted to the King, and Berkeley was sent to England to protest against the enforcement of the Navigation Act; the Church of England was re-established, and severe laws passed against Dissenters.* The Navigation Act was enforced; tobacco fell in price, and im-

---

*As the word Dissenter occurs frequently in these pages, we may as well state at this point that it is a vague word, which, in its full latitude, is applied to all who differ from the Church of England, which was the Established Church of Virginia down to 1776. Originally it meant in England only the Presbyterians, who rather differed from the discipline and polity, than the opinions of the Episcopal Church.

ports rose. The return of the Royalist party to power soon led to trouble, and as early as 1663 an outbreak, led by some of Cromwell's soldiers, occurred, which, however, miserably failed, and four of the conspirators were executed.

Under the profligate government of Charles II, the trade of Virginia was almost extinguished; the titles of the colonists were endangered, if not destroyed. by royal grants to Lords Arlington and Culpepper; the justices levied taxes for their own emolument; the Indians were treated with severity; the Church fell into contempt; the rectors and curates were licentious and incompetent; and corruption and extortion prevailed.

A second outbreak threatened in 1674, but partial reforms and the want of a leader quieted the people, though everything was in a combustible condition.

The unwise policy of severity towards the Indians led to a war, and Berkeley, for some unknown reason, disbanded the force which ought to have been used to repel the enemy.

. At this moment, the leader, whom the people had before wanted, appeared in Nathaniel Bacon, a young, popular, wealthy, brave and patriotic man. Bacon was aided, if not instigated, by two planters, Drummond and Lawrence, who evidently wished to effect a general reform of all abuses, as well as put down the Indians. Bacon, having vainly sought a commission, marched against the Indians at the head of a few brave volunteers, which gave Berkeley the opportunity to proclaim them rebels. The Governor started in pursuit of Bacon—not the Indians—with troops, but the revolt becoming general in his rear, he retreated. Aware now of the rising storm, the Governor issued writs for a new Assembly, to which Bacon was elected. On his way to James City, Berkeley caused his arrest, but released him on parole, and Bacon read at the bar of the house a written confession and apology, and was thereupon pardoned and readmitted to the Council, of which he had previously been a member. Shortly after, Bacon fled on a suspicion that his iife was threatened, and ret rned to Jamestown with a large force. He appealed to the Assembly, who made him their General, vindicated his course, and sent a letter to England approving him. While the Assembly was engaged in the correction of abuses, Berkeley dissolved them. Bacon, now too strong to be resisted, extorted the necessary commissions from the Governor, and again marched against the Indians. Availing himself of his absence, Berkeley proclaimed him a rebel. On hearing this news, Bacon retraced his steps, when Berkeley fled to Accomac, thus leaving Bacon supreme. Bacon immediately summoned a convention of all the principal men to replace the House of Burgesses, pledged them to his support, and even to resistance to England, if their wrongs were not redressed. Bacon now again moved against the Indians, but in his absence, the fleet, which he had sent to capture Berkeley, was betrayed, and the Governor returned to Jamestown at the head of his would-be captors. Bacon's friends in Jamestown made terms with the Governor, and Bacon returned a second time. Berkeley fled again to Accomac, and Bacon captured and burnt Jamestown. About this time he became ill of fever, and died shortly afterwards in Gloucester county. The hero dead, his followers scattered. The leaders were caught in detail and executed. Thus ended the so-called Rebellion.

Nothing was gained by Bacon's course, and for a hundred years the people sunk into apathy. Berkeley was recalled, and died soon after his return to England. He was a covetous, dishonest, bloodthirsty, cowardly impotent, whose life was stained with crime. He was succeeded by Col. Herbert Jeffreys who died a year later, in 1677, and was followed by Sir Henry Chicheley, and he by Lord Culpepper, upon whom the Governorship was conferred for life in 1675. Culpepper arrived in Virginia in 1680. His administration was, on the whole, one of simple greed and violent exactions. He came to Virginia to make his fortune, and stopped at no act to accomplish his purpose. He was one of the most cunning and covetous men in England. He was succeeded by Lord Howard, of Effingham. He also came to make his fortune, and as he became richer, Virginia became poorer. During his time immigration almost ceased. Howard returned to England to find James driven from the throne, which ended the Stuart domination. The reign of Charles was contemptible for its meanness and corruption, and that of James the basest and most barren in English history. Charles debauched and debased England, and Culpepper and Effingham degraded their governments and almost ruined Virginia.

The only political events of these times of any significance were the sending of delegates, in 1684, from Virginia to Albany to meet the Governor of New York and certain agents sent from Massachusetts to discuss Indian affairs. This was a move in the direction of confederation.

Virginia derived little benefit from the revolution of 1689, which placed William and Mary upon the throne, and shortly after that event, a war breaking out between the allied powers and Louis XIV of France, the colony was ordered to place itself in the best posture for defence.

The continued complaints of the Virginia Legislature led to the recall of Howard, and Sir Francis Nicholson succeeded him. Nicholson was an arbitrary man. and practiced the arts of a demagogue, but was not a corrupt man. His administration is marked for the establishment of William and Mary College, under Dr. James Blair, an active and energetic Scotchman, who became one of the most serviceable men in Virginia.

Sir Edward Andros came after Nicholson, and was actuated in his government by a sound judgment and a liberal policy. In 1698, Andros retired and Nicholson was reappointed and served seven years without accomplishing any good except what grew out of his own negligence. From his indifference, the Burgesses made the treasurer of the colony an officer of their own, and thus obtained control of the public purse.

In 1704, Edward Nott became deputy governor under the Earl of Orkney, but the history of Virginia, more particularly Eastern Virginia, from this time, is little more than a list of Governors.

The period from 1704 to 1776, barren as it is in political events, was socially a period of great importance. The social elements, which had gathered in Virginia from its foundation, crystalized, and the fabric of society, as seen in 1776, was built up.

In 1710, Alexander Spotswood became Governor. He was an accomplished and enterprising man,—the best of the eighteenth century Governors. He thus describes in his day the state of affairs in Virginia: "This government is," says he, "in perfect peace and tranquility, under a due obedience to the Royal authority, and a gentlemanly conformity to the Church of England."

The Virginians at this day were living in the forests, but were men who had inherited the culture and intelligence of the seventeenth century. They cherished personal freedom, secure possession, and legislative power. They soon manifested at the polls some uneasiness at royalist principles and the prospects of an aristocracy. "The inclinations of the country," says Governor Spotswood, "are rendered mysterious by a new and unaccountable humor, which hath obtained in several counties, of excluding gentlemen from being Burgesses, and choosing only persons of mean figure and character." From this it appears that in 1710–23, no less than in 1882, the post of honor was the private station; that instead of political positions being conferred upon the good and wise, they were, in Spotswood's day, as now, more frequently the rewards of greed and incompetency.

Many reforms were introduced by Spotswood, and among his benevolent schemes was one for civilizing and christianizing the Indians. With this view he undertook his expedition to the interior in 1716, of which we shall anon speak more freely.

In 1723, Spotswood was succeeded by Sir Hugh Drysdale, and he, in 1727, by William Gooch, who, during his term, commanded the expedition against Carthagena. This expedition was the most important event of Gooch's administration, as, taken in connection with the other colonies, it was another step in the development of union.

Gooch was a man of firmness and moderation, and ruled Virginia for twenty-two years much to the satisfaction of the people. During his time, wealth and population increased, printing was introduced, education became diffused, and its improving effects were felt in all, particularly the upper classes. But the loose and licentious character of the clergy made the Established Church but a feeble bulwark against the tide of religious enthusiasm which swept in with Whitfield, and the old cry was raised against Dissenters by those who conformed from habit or worldly interest to the Established Church. Gooch attempted to suppress heterodox opinions by all the powers of the State, and there was much petty persecution, which left the Church weaker and more unpopular even than before. In April, 1745, in his charge to the Grand Jury of the General Court, he said of the Presbyterians and other religious sects, "that false teachers had lately crept into this government, who, without order or license, or producing any testimonial of their education or sect, professing themselves ministers under the pretended influence of new light, extraordinary impulse, and such like satirical and enthusiastic knowledge, lead the innocent and ignorant people into all kind of delusion." And he called upon the jury to present and indict the offenders.

While England was colonizing in Virginia, New England, and at other points on the Atlantic coast, and sending into the interior hardy pioneers, the descendants of her two earliest colonies, the French were making explorations along the coast and into the backwoods. As far back as 1534, Jacques Cartier, at the head of a French expedition, entered the St. Lawrence and claimed the territory on both sides for France. In 1608, Quebec was founded by the French, and French immigrants arrived in succeeding years, until the dominion claimed by the French extended, as previously mentioned, from the St. Lawrence to the Gulf of Mexico. In 1673, the Upper Mississippi was discovered by Father Marquette, a monk of the reformed order of Franciscans, called Recollects. In 1679, the French sent a second expedition to the West under La Salle. It reached through the lakes the Chicago river, passed down the Illinois to where Peoria now stands, and there La Salle erected a fort called Crève Cœur, or broken heart, on account of the hopeless difficulties he encountered. In 1682, La Salle sailed down the Mississippi to the Gulf, and called the country Louisiana, in honor of Louis XIV.

In 1700, the population of Virginia was 22,000, and in 1716 did not exceed 30,000. It was principally seated on the rivers and streams of Eastern Virginia and the Atlantic coast. No county had been organized west of the 78° of longitude, nor were there any white settlements further west. The exploring party which discovered the Valley made its way from Germanna over a hundred miles through a trackless forest.

The progress of the population in the colony is indicated by the figures below: In 1607 it was 105; in 1609 it was 490; in 1617 it was 400; in 1622 it was 3,800; in 1628 it was 3,000; in 1632 it was 2,000; in 1644 it was

4,812; in 1645 it was 5,000; in 1652 it was 7,000; in 1700 it was 22,000; in 1748 it was 82,000.

From these matters of colonial history, so briefly recapitulated, the reader will understand the causes of the subsequent conflicts between the French and English colonists, the progress of the colony of Virginia, and its actual condition in 1716, when the Valley was discovered, and became a few years later the seat of an English settlement.

CHAPTER III.

The first passage of the Blue Ridge, or discovery of the Valley, was effected by Spotswood at the head of a troop of horse in August, 1716. The party consisted of about fifty persons, who had a large number of riding and pack-horses, an abundant supply of provisions, and an extraordinary variety of liquors. The expedition proceeded from Williamsburg by Chelsea, King William county, to Beverly's in the county of Middlesex, where the Governor left his chaise and continued on horseback to Germanna. There, on the 26th of August, he was joined by the rest of the party, among whom were four Meherrin Indians and two small companies of rangers. The party marched thence to Todd's, on Mountain Run, then to the Rappahannock, which they crossed at Somerville's ford, thence by the left bank to near Peyton's ford, on the Rapidan. Here they turned south, recrossed the river and proceeded to where Stanardsville now stands; thence through Swift Run gap to the Valley, crossing the Shenandoah river at a point about ten miles north of the present town of Port Republic. The popular belief, down to Bishop Meade's time, that the party had reached the Valley by Rockfish gap is thus shown to have been a popular error.

In commemoration of this event Spotswood is said to have been knighted, and to have presented each of the party with a golden horseshoe, on which was inscribed: "Sic jurat transcendere montes." (Thus he swears to cross the mountains.)

The glowing accounts given by Spotswood's party—or, as they were afterwards styled, the "Knights of the Golden Horseshoe"—of the fertile and beautiful valley beyond the mountains, excited the spirit of enterprise and adventure in the people of Eastern Virginia and Pennsylvania. Though the approach to the upper country was difficult either from the North or East, from the want of roads and bridges, and the hills were infested with roving tribes of savages, each tribe asserting certain rights in and to the country, many plans were now considered by families and little communities for changing their residence to these favored regions. The Knights of the Golden Horseshoe, who encountered no Indians on their entry into the Valley, spread abroad reports that the mountains east and west, which enclosed this lovely and fruitful Valley, presented an almost insurmountable obstacle to the entrance of savages, and that defenceless families might there live in security and plenty, enjoying not only the necessaries but the luxuries of life without labor and without price. They represented the verdant plains as sparkling with streams filled with fish, and covered with herds browsing in quiet joy. The trees which fringed the banks were festooned with vines, and both vines and trees were bending under their weight of luscious fruit. It is not surprising that an adventurous population, many of whom had already given evidence of their spirit by severing the ties binding them to friends and native land, should be seized with a desire to occupy such a country. Accordingly, in 1732, sixteen families from Pennsylvania crossed the Potomac and settled near the present town of Winchester.

Among those whose attention was now directed to our Valley was John Lewis, who had been for some time in Pennsylvania, quietly awaiting the arrival from Europe of his wife and children. This remarkable man was born in the north of Ireland, descended from a French-Protestant family, and was educated in Scotland. In Ulster, where he resided until fifty years of age, he commanded the confidence, respect and esteem of the people, and occupied that position of influence, and took that leading part in society and county affairs, which had been traditionally the role of the O'Donnells, Chichesters and O'Doghertys. In youth he was of impetuous temper, but the varied experience of an active life had taught him to control his spirit. He was endowed with a high order of intellect, a valorous soul, and soon became noted for his virtuous principles. A deplorable affair, but one alike honorable to his spirit and manhood, terminated his career in Ireland. He had been some time in America, when, in 1732, Joist Hite and a party of pioneers set out to settle upon a grant of forty thousand acres of land in the Valley, which had been obtained, in 1730, by Isaac Vanmeter and his brother, by warrant from the Governor of Virginia. Lewis joined this party, came to the Valley, and was the first white settler of Augusta.

The circumstances which led to the emigration of Lewis and his settlement of Augusta are detailed in the Virginia Historical Register for 1851, and in Howe's History. The accounts differ sufficiently to make both agreeable reading. The Register narrative, published some years after his death, was written by Hon. Jno. H. Peyton from information derived orally from Wm. I. Lewis, of Campbell, M. C. for that district from 1817 to 1819, and is as follows:

"Col. Lewis stated that the account given by the 'Son of Cornstalk,' in his essays, of the native country and the causes of the removal of his family to the Colony of Virginia, was incorrect. That the true history of the matter, as he had obtained it from his father, the late Col. William Lewis, of the Sweet Springs, who died in the year 1812, at the age of 85 years, and long after Col. Wm. I. Lewis had arrived at manhood, was this: John Lewis, his grandfather, was a native of Ireland, and was descended of French-Protestants, who emigrated from France to Ireland in 1685, at the revocation of the Edict of Nantes, to avoid the persecutions to which the Protestants, to which sect of religion they belonged, were subjected during the reign of Louis XIV. John Lewis intermarried with Margaret Lynn, also a native of Ireland, but descended of Scottish ancestors—the Lynns of Loch Lynn, so famous in Scottish clan legends. John Lewis, in Ireland, occupied a respectable position in what is there called the middle class of society. He was the holder of a free-hold lease for three lives upon a valuable farm in the County of Donegal and Province of Ulster, obtained upon equal terms and fair equivalents from one of the Irish nobility, who was an upright and honorable man, and the owner of the reversion. This lease-hold estate, with his wife's marriage portion, enabled the young couple to commence life with flattering prospects. They were both remarkable for their industry, piety and stern integrity. They prospered and were happy. Before the catastrophe occurred which completely destroyed the hopes of this once happy family in Ireland, and made them exiles from their native land, their affection was cemented by the birth of four sons, Samuel, Thomas, Andrew and William. About the period of the birth of their third son, the Lord from whom he had obtained his lease—a landlord beloved by his tenants and neighbors—suddenly died, and his estates descended to his eldest son, a youth whose principles were directly the reverse of his father's. He was proud, profligate and extravagant. Anticipating his income, he was always in debt, and to meet his numerous engagements he devised a variety of schemes, and among them one was to claim of his tenants a forfeiture of their leases upon some one of the numerous covenants inserted in instruments of the kind at that day. If they agreed to increase their rents, the alleged forfeiture was waived; if they refused, they were threatened with a long, tedious and expensive law suit. Many of his tenants submitted to this injustice, and raised their rents rather than be involved, even with justice on their side, in a legal controversy with a rich and powerful adversary, who could, in this country, under these circumstances, devise ways and means to harrass, persecute and impoverish one in moderate circumstances. Lewis, however, was a different man from any who thus tamely submitted to wrong. By industry and skill he had greatly improved his property, his rent had been punctually paid, and all the covenants of his lease had been complied with faithfully. To him, after seeing all the others, the agent of the young Lord came with his unjust demands. Lewis peremptorily dismissed him from his presence, and determined to make an effort to rescue his family from this threatened injustice by a personal interview with the young Lord, who, Lewis imagined, would scarcely have the hardihood to insist before his face upon the iniquitous terms proposed by his agent.

Accordingly he visited the castle of the young Lord.   A porter announced his name.   At the time the young Lord was engaged in his revels over the bottle with some of his companions of similar tastes and habits.

As soon as the name of Lewis was announced he recognized the only one of his tenants who had resisted his demands, and directed the porter to order him off.   When the porter delivered his Lord's order, Lewis resolved at every hazard to see him.   Accordingly he walked into the presence of the company—the porter not having the temerity to stand in his way.   Flushed with wine, the whole company rose to resent the insult and expel the intruder from the room.   But there was something in Lewis' manner that sobered them in a moment; and, instead of advancing, they seemed fixed to their places, and for a moment there was perfect silence, when Lewis calmly observed: " I came here with no design to insult or injure any one, but to remonstrate in person to your Lordship against threatened injustice, and thus to avert from my family ruin; in such a cause I have not regarded ordinary forms or ceremonies, and I warn you, gentlemen, to be cautious how you deal with a desperate man."   This short address, connected with the firm and intrepid tone of its delivery, apparently stupefied the company.   Silence ensuing, Lewis embraced it to address himself particularly, in the following words, to the young Lord : " Your much-respected father granted me the lease-hold estate I now possess.   I have regularly paid my rents, and have faithfully complied with all the covenants of the lease.   I have a wife and three infant children whose happiness, comfort and support depend, in a great degree, upon the enjoyment of this property, and yet I am told by your agent that I can no longer hold it without a base surrender of my rights to your rapacity.   Sir, I wish to learn from your lips whether or not you really meditate such injustice, such cruelty as the terms mentioned by your agent indicate; and I beg you before pursuing such a course to reconsider this matter coolly and dispassionately, or you will ruin me and disgrace yourself."   By the time this address was closed, the young Lord seemed to have recovered partially, (in which he was greatly assisted by several heavy libations of wine,) from the effects produced by the sudden, solemn and impressive manner of his injured tenant.   He began to ejaculate : " Leave me!   Leave me!   You rebel!   You villain!"   To this abuse Lewis replied calmly, as follows: " Sir, you may save yourself this useless ebullition of passion.   It is extremely silly and ridiculous.   I have effected the object of my visit; I have satisfied my mind, and have nothing more to say.   I shall no longer disturb you with my presence."   Upon which he retired from the room, apparently unmoved by the volley of abuse that broke forth from the young Lord and his drunken comrades as soon as he had turned his back.   After they had recovered from the magical effect which the calm resolution and stern countenance of Lewis produced, they descanted upon what they called the insolence of his manner, and the mock defiance of his speech, with all the false views which aristocratic pride, excited by the fumes of wine, in a monarchial government were so well calculated to inspire.   During the evening the rash purpose was formed of dispossessing Lewis by force.   Accordingly, on the next day, the young Lord, without any legal authority whatever, proceeded at the head of his guests and domestics to oust Lewis by force.   Lewis saw the approach of the hostile array, and conjectured the object of the demonstration.   He had no arms but a shelalah, a weapon in possession of every Irish farmer at that period.   Nor was there any one at his house but a brother, confined to bed by disease, his wife and three infant children; yet he resolved to resist the lawless band and closed the door. The young Lord, on reaching the house, demanded admittance. which, not being granted, the posse attacked the house, and after being foiled in several attempts to break down the door. or to effect in other ways an entrance, one of the party introduced the muzzle of a musket through an aperture in the wall and discharged its contents—a bullet and three buckshot—upon those within. Lewis' sick brother was mortally wounded, and one of the shot passed through his wife's hand. Lewis, who had up to this time acted on the defensive, seeing the blood stream from the hand of his wife, and his expiring brother weltering in his blood, became enraged, furious, and, seizing his shelalah. he rushed from the cottage, determined to avenge the wrong and to sell his life as dearly as possible. The first person he encountered was the young Lord, whom he despatched at a single blow, cleaving in twain his skull, and scattering his brains upon himself and the posse. The next person he met was the steward, who shared the fate of his master; rushing, then, upon the posse, stupefied at the ungovernable ardour and fury of Lewis' manner, and the death of two of their party, they had scarcely time to save themselves, as they did, by throwing away their arms and taking to flight. This awful occurrence brought the affairs of Lewis in Ireland to a crisis. Though he had violated no law, human or divine; though he had acted strictly in self-defence against lawless power and oppression, yet the occurrence took place in a monarchial government, whose policy it is to preserve a difference in the ranks of society. One of the nobility* had been slain by one of his tenants. The connexions of the young Lord were rich and powerful, those of Lewis poor and humble. With such fearful odds it was deemed rash and unwise that Lewis should, even with law and justice on his side, surrender himself to the officers of the law. It was consequently determined that he should proceed, on that evening. disguised in a friend's dress, to the nearest sea-port, and take shipping for Oporto, in Portugal, where a brother of his wife was established in merchandize. Luckily he met a vessel just ready to sail from the Bay of Donegal, in which he took passage. After various adventures, for the ship was not bound for Portugal, in different countries. he arrived at Oporto in the year 1729. Upon his arrival there, he was advised by his brother-in-law, in order to elude the vigilance of his enemies, to proceed to Philadelphia, in Pennsylvania, and there to await the arrival of his family, which, he learned, was in good health, and which his brother-in-law undertook to remove to America.

Lewis, following this advice, proceeded at once to Philadelphia. In a year his family joined him, and learning from them that the most industrious efforts were being made by the friends of the young Lord to discover the country to which he had fled, he determined to penetrate deep into the American forest. He moved then immediately from Philadelphia to Lancaster, and there spent the Winter of 1731 and 1732, and in the Summer of 1732, he removed to the place near Staunton, in the County of Augusta. Virginia, now called "Bellefonte," where he settled, brought up his family, conquered the country from the Indians, and amassed a large fortune. At the time he settled at this place, Augusta county was not formed. The country was in the possession of the Indians, and Staunton

---

*The man killed by Lewis was Sir Mungo Campbell, Lord of the Manor, and hence commonly called "The Lord." He was not a Baron or peer of the realm.

was not known. After establishing himself here, his family was a nucleus for new settlers from the East side of the Blue Ridge and Ireland, and the number had so increased by 1745, that the County of Augusta was organized, when John Lewis was appointed a magistrate, and assisted in the organization."

From this narrative it appears that our early historians, among them the late Dr. Ruffner, whose MS. is quoted in Howe, have incorrectly stated that Lewis came from Williamsburg. It is not surprising that such errors should have crept into our history, which, for nearly a century, was mere tradition : and the reader will not have been surprised to learn that Spotswood was believed to have entered the Valley by Rockfish gap until within a few years past, when the line of his march was ascertained by the publication of Fontaine's journal. The mistake as to Lewis may have arisen from the fact that a number of emigrants reached America about this time in her Majesty's men-of-war Blandford, Wolf and Hector—the latter under command of Sir Yelverton Peyton, Baronet R. N., and the transports accompanying them. These emigrants were for the most part Protestants from Salsburg and bound for Georgia. But some of them came to Virginia, in 1732, and were at Williamsburg, and thence made their way into the interior. Lewis may have been supposed to have belonged to this party.

Howe's account, p. 181, is as follows, and was written by Charles H. Lewis, late Minister Resident to Portugal :

" John Lewis was a native and citizen of Ireland, descended from a family of Huguenots, who took refuge in that country from the persecutions that followed the assassination of Henry IV of France. His rank was that of an Esquire, and he inherited a handsome estate, which he increased by industry and frugality, until he became the lessee of a contiguous property, of considerable value. He married Margaret Lynn, daughter of the Laird of Loch Lynn, who was a descendant of the chieftains of a once powerful clan in the Scottish Highlands. By this marriage he had four sons, three of them, Thomas, Andrew, and William, born in Ireland, and Charles, the child of his old age, born a few months after their settlement in their mountain home.

The emigration of John Lewis to Virginia was the result of one of those bloody affrays, which at that time so often occurred, to disturb the repose and destroy the happiness of Irish families. The owner of the fee out of which the leasehold of Lewis was carved, a nobleman of profligate habits and ungovernable passions, seeing the prosperity of his lessee, and repenting the bargain he had concluded, under pretence of entering for an alleged breach of condition, attempted, by the aid of a band of ruffians hired for his purpose, to take forcible possession of the premises. For this end, he surrounded the house with his ruffians, and called upon Lewis to evacuate the premises without delay, a demand which was instantly and indignantly refused by Lewis, though surprised with a sick brother, his wife and infant children in the house, and with no aid but such as could be afforded by a few faithful domestics. With this small force, scarce equal to one-fourth the number of his assailants, he resolved to maintain his legal rights at every hazard. The enraged nobleman commenced the affray by discharging his fowling-piece into the house, by which the invalid brother of Lewis was killed, and Margaret herself severely wounded. Upon this, the enraged husband and brother rushed from the house, attended by his devoted little band, and soon succeeded in dispersing the assailants, though not until the noble author of the mischief, as well as his steward, had perished by the hands of Lewis. By this time the family were surrounded by their sympathizing friends and neighbors, who, after bestowing every aid in their power, advised Lewis to fly the country, a measure rendered necessary by the high standing of his late antagonist, the desperate character of his surviving assailants, and the want of evidence by which he could have established the facts of the case. He therefore, after drawing up a detailed statement of the affair, which he directed to the proper authorities, embarked on board a vessel bound for America, attended by his family and a band of about thirty of his faithful tenantry. In due time the emigrants landed on the shores of Virginia, and fixed their residence amid the till then unbroken forests of West Augusta. John Lewis' settlement was a few miles below the site of the town of Staunton, on the banks of the stream which still bears his name. It may be proper to remark here, that when the circumstances of the affray became known, after due investigation, a pardon was granted to John Lewis, and patents are still extant, by which his Majesty granted to him a large portion of the fair domain of Western Virginia.

For many years after the settlement of Fort Lewis, great amity and good will existed between the neighboring Indians and the white settlers, whose numbers increased apace, until they became quite a formidable colony. It was then that the jealousy of their red neighbors became aroused, and a war broke out, which, for cool though desperate courage and activity on the part of the whites, and ferocity, cunning and barbarity on the part of the Indians, was never equaled in any age or country. John Lewis was, by this time, well stricken in years, but his four sons, who were now grown up, were well qualified to fill his place, and to act the part of leaders to the gallant little band who so nobly battled for the protection of their homes and families. It is not my purpose to go into the details of a warfare, during which scarcely a settlement was exempt from monthly attacks of the savages, and during which Charles Lewis, the youngest son of John, is said never to have spent one month at a time out of active and arduous service. Charles was the hero of many a gallant exploit, which is still treasured in the memories of the descendants of the border riflemen, and there are few families among the Alleghanies where the name and deeds of Charles Lewis are not familiar as household words. On one occasion, Charles was captured by the Indians while on a hunting excursion, and after traveling two hundred miles barefoot, his arms pinioned behind him, goaded on by the knives of his remorseless captors, he effected his escape."

It is unnecessary to give more of Howe's account. It is composed of matter which will find a more appropriate place in the history of the Lewis family.

At a point a mile east of Staunton, remarkable for the singular beauty and freshness of the scenery, on the estate owned in 1882 by D. C. McGuffin, Mrs. J. A. Harman, and Capt. John N. Opie, Lewis pitched his tent, calling the place " Bellefont," which a portion of it still bears, from a bold bright spring issuing from the hill side. He was the first to occupy the scene; no axe had ever before rung through that forest; no spade had ever turned up that soil; nature had delivered it into his hands in its untouched virginity, and it was for him to say where, and how, and to what extent labor should mingle with it, and art adorn and enrich it. Here this man, nurtured in high civilization, but by sinister fortune deprived of his position and banished from his country, planted himself—making a home which became his tomb—delighting in the tranquility and independence of his secluded retreat. Here, amidst the deep shadows of the wilderness, he built a stone dwelling, which, with its flanks, formed one side of Fort Lewis, and in this half dwelling, half fortress, he maintained a long struggle with the savages, and under its stout walls the infant colony grew in time strong enough to defy every foe. A portion of this old fort still remains in 1882, and is occupied as a dwelling by the proprietor. It is the oldest house in the Valley, and though without architectural beauty or pretensions, is one of the most interesting of our historical relics.

In this hitherto unvisited region, amidst beautiful landscapes and grand points of scenery, the old hero spent the remaining years of his life, finally closing his eyes upon a country blooming in cultivated fertility and enlivened by the arts of civilization.

Having pursued the fortunes of Lewis and his family to their settlement in the wilderness, we shall give in the next succeeding chapter a brief sketch of the early settlers, their manners and customs, modes of life, etc., or historical outline of the little colony from its foundation to the year 1749-'50, when Gov. Gooch sailed for England, in the flowery language of an old historian, "amidst the blessings and tears of the people, among whom he had lived as a wise and beneficent father."

Such poetical extravagance on the part of writers would shock the understanding but for its frequency. It certainly distorts the facts of history, and fills her pages with absurdities. Gooch was a moderate and sensible man, who reaped the benefits of Spotswood's administration, and governed Virginia generally in an acceptable manner. But he made mistakes—committed errors—as what man does not?—granted lands with lavish prodigality to his favorites, and incurred the hostility of those whom he did not fancy; indulged in much petty persecution of Dissenters, made enemies, and was far from escaping censure. It is probable, then, that this "wise and beneficent father" of the old historian left as many dry as weeping eyes in Virginia, and was followed to England by as many curses as blessings.

CHAPTER IV.

—

No census is extant of the population on Lewis creek at the period when the County of Augusta was formed. It is evident from the preamble of the act of 1738 that there had been a considerable increase of the inhabitants west of the great mountains, and it was to give these pioneers the benefits of civil government that the county was established. The County of Augusta, thus formed from Orange, which had previously embraced all the country west of the Blue Ridge, was not organized until some years later. Meanwhile the legal business of the people west of the Blue Ridge continued to be transacted at Orange Court-House. The expense, inconvenience and delay caused by this state of affairs, led to the organization of the county, at Staunton, in 1745, when there was a sufficient number of inhabitants for appointing justices of the peace and other officers, and erecting courts therein. The first court-house was erected on the site of the present County Clerk's office, as near as may be, and the first court was held on the 9th of Dec., 1745, when the following magistrates, previously commissioned by the Lieutenant-Governor, took their seats on the bench—viz.: John Lewis, John Brown, Peter Schall, John Pickens, Thos. Lewis, Hugh Thompson, Robt. Cunningham, James Keer, and Adam Dickinson.

John Patton was appointed High Sheriff, and Jno. Madison clerk.

The following gentlemen qualified as attorneys-at-law: Gabriel Jones, William Russell, James Porters, John Quin, Th. Chew. Gabriel Jones was appointed deputy attorney of the county, April 14, 1746, "as a fit person to transact his Majesty's affairs in this county," and qualified the following May. He was a learned lawyer, and married a Miss Strother, of Stafford county, a sister of Mrs. Thomas Lewis and Mrs. Madison, mother of Bishop Madison, and has, in 1882, a grandson living in Frederick county, namely, Mr. Strother Jones.

On the second day of the court, a commission from William Dawson, President of William and Mary College, was read, appointing Thomas Lewis surveyor.

From a motion now made by the Sheriff, it appears that up to this time there had been no prison in the settlement or county,—that for a period of nearly fifteen years this pious little community of Scotch and Irish Presbyterians had lived without bolts and bars.

Lewis, and we must speak much in this chapter of him, though not unmindful of the miserable weakness of mankind, which causes them to look with admiration upon persons glorious for mischief, and to be better pleased when reading of the destroyer than the founder of a state; who had entered the wilderness alone, or, at most, with a single companion, and whose family afterwards joined him, must be presumed to have given law to those who subsequently assembled around him. When the number increased, these freemen, no doubt joined together and framed a society as best pleased themselves, in which, we are sure, while they may have, and doubtless did, recognize the founder as head, they took care that such rules as they adopted were for the good of the governed and not the governor. We have a fine picture of freemen, living according to their own will, in the case of Abraham and Lot: they went together into Canaan, continued together as long as was convenient for them, and parted when their substance did not increase, and they became troublesome to each other. The men who collected in Augusta agreed together and framed a society, and thus became a complete body, having all power in themselves over themselves, subject to no other human law than their own. All those who composed the society being equally free to enter into it or not, no man could have any prerogative above others, unless it was granted by the consent of the whole, and nothing obliging them to enter into this society but the consideration of their own good; that good or their opinion of it must have been the rule, motive and end of all that they did ordain. It is lawful for such bodies to set up one or a few men to govern them, and he or they who are thus set up have no power except what is conferred upon them by the multitude, and should exercise those powers according to the ends for which they were given. That the Founder was thus constituted the leader of the community until 1745, cannot be doubted. In '45, he was placed at the head of the court, and continued in this position until he went down, nearly twenty years later, in peace to the grave.

In William I. Lewis' narrative, he speaks of the "industry, piety, and stern integrity of the young couple, John Lewis and Margaret Lynn," and we see in the significant fact that there was no prison in Augusta for nearly fifteen years after the Founder set down on the banks of Lewis creek, the legitimate fruit of their characters and example.

The people took their tone from the heads of the colony, and thus lived in the enjoyment of greater order and quiet than is commonly the lot of communities furnished with a regular system of laws and administration.

Such facts enable us to understand better the people themselves and the state of society in those days than would otherwise be possible. It must not be inferred, because the early colonists lived in the wilderness, beset with Indians and wild beasts, that they themselves lacked cultivation—partook of the nature of their surroundings. It was an infant colony, composed of grown men—a settlement in the wilds of the new world made up of men trained in the schools and civilization of the Old World. There were men of learning among them, and means were early applied for educating the rising generation. A general taste for literature prevailed, as is obvious from the attention paid to the erudite men who, from time to time, came among them as clergymen; from the collections of books in their houses—the libraries of the King's counsel, Gabriel Jones, and that of Hon. Thomas Lewis being famous—and from the early period at which schools, and particularly the Augusta Academy, were established.

Col. and Mrs. Lewis were indeed persons of gentle blood, of education, refinement and independent fortune. They were not adventurers, who came to America seeking wealth or social or political position. They were the innocent victims of adverse circumstances, of sinister fortune, and had crossed the sea and changed their climate, but not their characters. And what is true of them is true of others. Lewis, himself, was a man endowed with many noble qualities. Of a martial spirit and heroic courage, he was formed to excel in war; the ardent friend of progress, of public improvements, of trade and commerce, wise in his conceptions and persevering in his plans, he was equally adapted for peace. Irreproachable in his public and private morals; courteous, affable, and eloquent; fond of society and excelling in conversation, he excited the love and admiration of the people who adhered to him and the policy he pointed out, as well from their attachment to his person as because of their respect for his talents and his character. Had he continued in Europe his abilities and accomplishments, which had already given him a high local reputation and position, could not have remained long unknown and unrewarded by his Sovereign. He was destined, however, for another career, a more appropriate theatre for his ardent and restless genius. Providence ordained him to become a pioneer of civilization—to erect the standard of the Cross in the wilderness. In the colony which he founded the Church anticipated the town and the county. Before either was established the Gospel was preached in the houses of the settlers or under the shade of the trees. In Col. Lewis' house, indeed, the first sermon ever delivered in the county was preached by Mr. James Thompson, in 1739. A little later, log buildings were erected for the worship of God, called, in the language of the day, "meeting-houses." There was no settled pastor, no organized church, but the rude walls of the meeting-house resounded to the bold, zealous, impassioned and enthusiastic words of the old-school ministers, who, from time to time, passed through the settlement.

Lewis was not one of those men of overweening vanity, who fancy they can do without other men. He felt that he needed the counsel of others, and was not able to manage and direct all things alone. Accordingly, he early associated with himself in his labors persons of merit, employing each of these according to his talents, and left to them the management of minor matters, which only consume time, and deprived him of the liberty of mind so necessary in the conduct of important affairs. He thus prevented envy and jealousy, by dividing a power which is apt to be offensive when united in a single person, as if all merit centred in him alone. This wise course facilitated the execution of affairs, and made their success more certain. The value of a man of such rare parts—such disinterested soul—in a primitive community, cannot be exaggerated. Men, as Iago says, are but men. They must be treated, ministered to, provided for, and governed as such. In the Augusta settlement, they were freer than freedom, and in danger of running into licentiousness. Lewis saw, what universal experience has proved to be necessary, namely: that for prosperous self-government, a moral tone must pervade the community, a sound public sentiment prevail, and laws, though rude and unwritten, must exist, and are best upheld by it. He and his leading associates, by word and deed, accomplished the great task of moulding the opinions and forming the character of the people between 1732 and 1745. Without the aid of civil, military, or ecclesiastical establishments, by their wisdom and firmness, their humanity and justice, they maintained law and order in the colony, cultivated in all a respect for the rights of others, restrained vice, and asserted the majesty of moral virtue. Liberty is precious and dear to all men, and no people were more jealous of theirs than these pioneers, who had tasted the bitter fruits of slavery in their native lands. To preserve liberty—the rights and liberties of all—was the great motive principle of their actions, and became, in a manner, the soul of their laws, customs, and whole frame of government, as they afterwards existed, and as we see them to-day in America.

These grand men of the frontier, our primitive colonial fathers, not only rescued their fields from the forest, but cultivated them with their own hands, performing, without reluctance, the offices of domestics. Thus the colony soon became, and naturally enough, noted for its prosperity and honored for its citizens. Possessing an ample fortune, Col. Lewis dispensed much hospitality, especially to strangers. While entertaining with generosity, he was careful that his establishment should not degenerate into luxury. The spirit of hospitality extended to all, and when any stranger happened to pass through Augusta, he was not only received, lodged, and maintained everywhere, but the inhabitants disputed with each other the honor of having him for their guest. This inviolable regard to hospitality is still preserved among our rural population.

Each returning season brought accessions to the population from abroad. Many were good and true men, and many were turbulent spirits, impatient of control, and the enemies of law and order. The difficulties of the

Founder's position increased, but he and his associates exercised an irresistible influence in behalf of all measures for the public good. The men
who, after 1745, (as many had done before,) united with him in his
labors and exertions, were the Madisons, Pattons, Prestons, Browns, Keers,
Dickinsons, Pickens, Breckenridges, and others. Many of those early settlers founded families which have since become famous in the land. Madison was the father of the Right Rev. James Madison, DD., Bishop of Virginia, the first bishop consecrated in America by the three American bishops previously consecrated in Great Britain, of whom the first was Dr.
Seabury, of Connecticut, consecrated by the Scotch Episcopal Church,
who admitted him to the Scotch Episcopate 1784, by the hands of the
Bishops of Aberdeen, Ross, and Moray. The second and third bishops
were Drs. White and Prevost, the elect respectively of the conventions of
Pennsylvania and New York, who were consecrated at Lambeth Palace,
1787, by Archbishops Moore and Markham, and Bishops Moss, of Bath
and Wells, and Hinchcliff, of Peterborough.

John Preston and Robert Breckenridge were the founders of the distinguished families of their names in Virginia and Kentucky, and from other
early settlers are descended the extensive and highly respectable families
bearing their names in this county, the State, the West and South.

The Augusta colony, which was soon noted for its enterprising popula-
lation, its good order, its industry and progress, was thus physically and
socially in advance of other frontier settlements. It must be remembered,
however, that all the settlers in this community were not worthy men.
Augusta was not, as we have mentioned, thus signally blessed.

The subject of public improvements soon engaged the attention of the
leading men, and they quickly discovered difficulties, besides those of nature, in their way. In every population there are two orders of men—one,
who with little difficulty are open to a conviction that improvements are
desirable, and another, who either from excess of ignorance or perversity,
can tolerate no change whatever. With the former of these, the Founder
had no difficulty. They readily came into his plans and appreciated his
general policy, even acknowledging, with gratitude, the benefits and blessings that had already arisen from the schemes he had introduced of public
improvement, elementary education, etc. They anticipated other and
greater benefits from those he now proposed. The enemies of innovation
and improvement, the suspicious, the prejudiced, the grumblers, were
harder to manage, but they were, for the most part, in time, skillfully won
over, and in the end he was supported by a large majority of even these.

Though the Founder, from the early years of the colony, called to his
aid, as we have observed, the best men in it, there were such difficulties to
encounter in executing his wise and benevolent plans, that only the most
unwearied patience and self-denying virtue could have surmounted them.

One of the chief wants of the community was good roads, and particularly of a road communicating with the more improved parts of Eastern Virginia, whence their supplies were drawn. Lewis perceived this on his difficult journey into the wilderness, and every day satisfied him more fully that there could be no solid improvement or prosperity among them while this was the case. It was difficult to communicate any news or treat of affairs with other settlements far and near, being obliged to send a courier at great charge and loss of time, or wait for the departure of some person going north or east of the mountains, to take their letters—a precarious and uncertain method.

Calling into council the chief men, the Founder proposed that they should widen and improve the so-called road leading to Goochland, and finding his views favorably received, the project was announced to the people. We can imagine their astonishment at the boldness of his plans; how some of the more timid and indolent would declare the thing impossible; how others would find an excuse, in their private affairs, for not encouraging or wishing to engage in such an enterprise; how it would be argued that the Indian trails through the mountain gaps answered a very good, if not every purpose; how it would be said that by those paths they had arrived in the country and were doing well, and how those who were not satisfied with doing well, ought to be allowed to leave—to go farther and fare better; how it would be reiterated that they could get, and actually did get on pack horses, their salt, iron, steel castings, powder and shot, and whatever they needed, including dress and personal ornaments; how these croakers would dwell upon the time and labor such a work would cost, and finally, when it was constructed, upon the dangers which would menace the community, as by it luxury would be let in in time of peace, and the enemy in time of war. Nothing is too absurd for the discontented to urge on such an occasion. The men, however, who promoted this scheme, were not easily discouraged. Without losing time with malcontents, they explained to the public the advantages to be derived from having a good outlet for the produce of their fields and facilities for procuring the multitude of comforts and conveniences of which they were destitute. Soon the better part of the community was on their side, and the enterprise was begun.

Let us attempt to call up the scene when this work was taken in hand. There comes the venerable "Lord of the hills," as Lewis was called, with Brown, Keer, Pickens, Jones, Preston, Patton, and the leading spirits generally. They are about to go forth with Thomas Lewis, the Surveyor, as Chief Engineer, to locate this highway. A motley crowd assembles in the streets and about the inn door, where horses stand, on whose backs men are packing tents and panniers with provisions. In this crowd stand men in hunting shirts and moccasins, leaning upon their long rifles, and sympathizing, if at all, in the movement, in a listless way. These still hunters, or deer-stalking pioneers, are almost as much opposed as the Red Men to their hunting-grounds being disturbed—opened up by roads. Business is at a stand-still on this morning in the little hamlet, now the city of Staunton, and women and children peer curiously from their doors. It is evident from the stir that a movement of no ordinary importance is on foot. At length the expedition starts, the crowd disperses, and the village relapses into its habitual drowsiness. Weeks pass, and the place is again astir. The venerable fathers reappear on the outskirts of the hamlet at the head of the surveying party and the mass of the people themselves,—all are excited,—some in a lively state of enthusiasm. The road has been located, every preliminary arranged, and the work of its construction is now to begin. The chief men—the elders—are all present and mingle in the crowd; the scene is graced, too, by the presence of ladies—a "store of ladies whose bright eyes rain influence." See the sturdy old pioneer, the venerable Founder, coming to the front, after the blessing of Heaven has been asked upon their undertaking, and casting up the first spadeful of earth, and hear the loud cheers which make the welkin ring! Behold every one now pressing forward to lend a helping hand—even the malcontents, catching the spirit of the hour, hurrying to the front and taking part in the good work. There was a moral grandeur in such a spectacle, in the initiation of such an enterprise,—of turning to practical account, of thus giving a right direction to the industry of the people.

It was no holiday task, but, for that little community, without accumulated capital or mechanical appliances, a prodigious undertaking. The completion of the work,—and it was completed in due time,—ameliorated the condition of the settlers, and it was from time to time followed by other improvements. Thus we see that on the 19th of May, 1749, this order entered of record by the County Court: "That Jas. Montgomerie, and Richard Burton, or any one of them, wait on the Court of Lunenburg and acquaint them that the inhabitants of Augusta have cleared a road to the said county line, and desire that they will clear a road from the court-house of Lunenburg to meet the road already cleared by the inhabitants of Augusta."

A good road, for those days, having been constructed over the mountains to the East, the people used it to market their produce, furs, cattle, etc., obtaining, in return, all necessary articles, and sometimes the luxuries and elegancies of life. The parties which brought in these supplies were so large that they were called Caravans. Soon shops, called "stores," and still so called, were established, and dealers supplied the public wants. About this time a division of labor occurred, and carpenters, wheelwrights, blacksmiths, masons, tailors and shoemakers set up their trades. Work was now done at home, which hitherto, with much delay and expense, was executed at a distance.

In the absence of a system of laws, order was preserved and individual rights protected by virtue of public opinion and what is termed the forest code, – that mysterious power of public opinion, which it is impossible to resist, and than which nothing is more unsteady, more vague or more powerful, and which, capricious though it may be, is nevertheless just and reasonable more frequently than is supposed,—and that backwoodsman's code (a relentless and martial one it is), written in the constitution of their natures and the circumstances of their position. Every State must have its policies, kingdoms have edicts, cities have their charters, and even the wild outlaw, in his forest walks, keeps yet some touch of civil discipline. It is not easy for those never subjected to frontier trials to understand the fierce wrongs which sometimes heat the pioneers' strong passions to the fever point, and the necessity for this martial code. As to the forest code, it is well known that the punishments inflicted by it were well adapted to secure the end in view. Hazing was one of the punishments under it, and intended either to reform or expel an obnoxious character. The term hazing was not then in use, but the practice prevailed, and base conduct on the part of a man led to his being hazed out, or, as the pioneers styled it, "hated out" of the community. The unlucky individual who aroused public indignation was forced to make atonement and to reform, or incur the worse penalty of banishment. This mode of chastisement was common among the Greeks, and is an effectual remedy. Few men have the hardihood to face the general indignation of an outraged community.

Two crimes met with peculiar punishment at the hands of the pioneers,— the first, theft, which was held in such detestation that the culprit was banished, but not before thirty-nine lashes were well laid upon his bare back. The second, seduction, which was punished by death. To extort a confession, they sometimes resorted to the torture of sweating; that is, suspending the accused by the arms pinioned behind his back until he confessed. Thus the stern morality of the leaders became the prop and support of their government. We need not enter further upon the forest code, the spirit and effect of which is clearly seen from the foregoing.

Our sketch would be incomplete without a reference to some of the social customs and rural superstitions of the pioneers. When new comers arrived, or young married people contemplated housekeeping, all united to build them a dwelling. When land was cleared, all aided, as also at harvest, hay-making, and other busy seasons. In times of danger, all men performed military duty, and no case is on record of a pioneer seeking to evade such service. As a rule, the men were brave and the women pretty, seeming to have inherited virtue and valor from their adventurous ancestors. Personal difficulties, when they could not be amicably adjusted by the good offices of friends, were settled by wager of battle—a primitive mode of deciding causes between parties of high antiquity among the rude military people of Europe. This mode of settling disputes made people more conservative and less vulgar in expressing their opinions of others than is common now-a-days. Family pride in Augusta was always great, and family honor was jealously guarded. Such was the chivalric character of our forefathers, that no personal insult or injury to a man or a member of his family was unavenged. Thus it was that crime and license were prevented from distorting humanity in the infantile colony.

People in those days dressed plainly, in half-savage, half-civilized style ; the men generally in a hunting shirt, a kind of loose frock, resembling the Roman tunic, fastened by a belt or girdle about the waist, with loose sleeves and a cape to throw off the rain. In the belt of the tunic the Roman carried his money—in the hunting shirt the pioneer stored away his luncheon. By his side was suspended his knife and tomahawk, both in leathern cases. The hunting-shirt was made of Linsey-Wolsey, or dressed deer skin for Winter, and of tow linen for Summer. The breeches were usually of the same material, and the feet were encased in moccasins.

Previous to the Revolution, the married men usually shaved their heads, and either wore wigs or white linen caps—a custom adopted, no doubt, from the severity of our Summer climate, the heats of which are beyond anything prevailing in Western Europe. The women dressed, ordinarily, in the same plain stuff, woven, during the first twenty years of the colony, by themselves, for they were skilled at the loom and spinning-wheel, thus exemplifying Probs. xxxi.: "She layeth her hands to the spindle, and her hand holdeth the distaff." Their duties were to educate their children, take care of their household, and live retired with their families ; their pleasures, to visit, give feasts, where there was much mirth and enjoyment. They were spiritual and healthful women, and wholly unaffected by that worldliness which so often depraves in fashionable society all the powers and faculties of the soul. From these peerless women sprung the heroic sons whose deeds have since made Virginia famous the world over. We trust the young women of the present day will not be unmindful of their bright example, or despise the duties of ordinary life. There is no position which exonerates a woman from the discharge of female duties, and the higher her talents, the more cultivated her understanding, the better regulated will be her household, the more eminently qualified will she be to perform all the duties of her station, whether it be of high or low degree.

Thus on the frontier grew up a race of vigorous and spirited men, pure and virtuous women, and within a few years the "wilderness ceased to be their habitation, a barren land their dwelling-place." Though remote from the world of *ton* and commerce, they were eminently a happy people—their peace and morals not contaminated with the vices of fashionable life, the rooted depravity of a pretended civilization and a spurious and mock Christianity. The mass of them were poor, it is true, but their poverty might be styled the truest riches, since those who want least approach nearest the gods, who want nothing.

The first settlers of Augusta, as their names indicate, were Scotch and Irish, but soon a few English and many Germans and persons of German lineage, from Pennsylvania, joined the community. Each party brought with them the religion, habits and customs of their ancestors, and this led to the erection of churches of different denominations and to a variety of little social circles, which, however, were never at any time very exclusive. The prevalence of German names evidences that a considerable part of the immigrants were of Teutonic origin. The superior intelligence of the people was due to the fact that the county was populated with adults, and it requires both talent and enterprise to produce voluntary change of country. It may be assumed with confidence as a truth, in our opinion, that there was as much talent, intelligence and spirit in the people of Augusta in 1732-'50, as falls to the lot of any equal number of people in the world.

As the country was, while this influx of immigrants was flowing in, without roads, immigrants made their way into the interior on foot or horseback, following the Indian or buffalo trails, or guided by blazed trees, carrying their worldly goods upon their backs or in packs lashed to horses or mules, crossing water courses on a fallen tree, which served as a bridge, or, in case of rivers or high water, swimming the streams. The men had, for the most part, seen military service in Europe, and became inured, in Pennsylvania, to the hardships of frontier life. The experience of the women must have been terribly severe, though doubtless every possible effort was made to ameliorate their situation. These immigrants are uniformly represented to have been, as a rule, men of staid habits, sterling worth, of high spirit, and untiring energy. And this is no doubt strictly true, for it is only, let us repeat, the courageous and self-reliant who venture on such enterprises. The houses of the pioneers were built of wood and covered with clap-boards; the flooring was split puncheons, smoothed with the broad-axe; the chimneys of stone, or brick dried in the sun. Their furniture was rudely fashioned from the timbers of the forest, oak, walnut, maple; their beds stuffed with feathers from the backs of their geese. It was not until long after 1732, that the pewter plates, dishes and spoons, wooden bowls, treanchers and noggins, strangely mingled on the pioneer's table with family plate brought from Europe by some of the settlers, were replaced by glass, china and silver ware.

Let no one imagine from the rudeness and simplicity of their dwellings and furniture that our conclusions are hastily drawn as to the cultivation and refinement of the early settlers. The people were restrained in improvements by want of labor, the absence of machinery, tools, &c.

Moreover, the industry of the community was specially directed to the fields, where it was certain of an ample reward as a means of supplying not only their own wants, but the heavy demands of incoming parties of strangers. And their immediate wants were for the necessaries, not the luxuries of life.

In front of every house a garden was cultivated in flowers, and hard by in a truck patch, their vegetables. They nourished their bodies by the same earth out of which they were made, and to which all must return. Water was their pure and innocent beverage, though they sometimes indulged in the luxury of blackberry wine or spruce beer.

In the elegant mansions of the present, where one sees displayed the delicacies of every clime, served on plate from the mines of Potosi or Nevada, and which contain accumulated treasures of mahogany, upholstery, pictures, china, glass, etc., one can scarcely realize the brief period within which these transformation scenes have occurred. Our young men no longer disport Linsey-Wolsey hunting-shirts and bear-skin moccasins, but are clothed in fine linen and patent-leather boots. Verily, "Jeroboam has clad himself with new garments."

On arriving in the settlement, the first work which engaged the colonist was the erection of such log huts, or cabins, as we have described. A site having been selected, a hut was erected of round or rifted logs. Each family was supplied by the common labor of all with these rude dwellings, and in a few days after ending their journey the little community of incomers was put under cover of their own roof. The sites of the settlements were always in or alongside of groves, near some spring of pure water. These log huts, which were built around a square, were united by palisades, and thus presented a wooden wall to their enemies. The doors opened into the common square, on the inner side. As an additional protection, around the whole settlement a stockade inclosure was built, with block-houses at the angles, and these rude fortifications formed an impregnable barrier against the red skins. These block-houses were two stories high, the upper story projecting over the lower, that the inmates might discharge their rifles from above upon an enemy. They were of such strength that they afforded perfect security to those within, if the efforts of the Indians to burn them by lighted arrows could be prevented. These cabins, block-houses and stockades were constructed without the aid of a nail or spike.

The two first buildings of a public kind which were erected were the church, or "meeting-house," and the school-house, where religion and the elements of a sound and liberal education were taught, and by the same instructors—the Presbyterian clergymen. Those pious, patient, laborious men, who brought to the wilderness the cultivation and refinement of Europe, became the preceptors of little grammar schools at their own houses, or in the immediate neighborhoods, and gave their pupils a thorough if not extensive course of education. In a word, these good men formed the youth of Augusta, taught them to love their country and to honor their parents, and by their examples and admirable lessons sought to engage them more warmly in the pursuit of virtue. The first of these teachers in Augusta was Rev. John Craig, who did not confine himself to penmanship, history and mathematics, but in his course embraced a classical education. In these schools all received the rudiments of education, and those who wished to pursue a more elaborate course entered the schools of Eastern Virginia—among which may be mentioned that of Rev. James Waddell, where William and Charles Lewis were trained. And in the year 1749, the "Augusta Academy" was established, near the present town of Lexington. In 1782, it was organized, by a charter, as Liberty Hall Academy, and in 1796, Geo. Washington transferred to the institution a gift from the State of Virginia to him for his services in the Revolution, of 100 shares of his James river canal stock, and subsequently the Legislature made this amount $50,000. The name was then changed to Washington Academy, and, in 1813, to Washington College. From these beginnings sprang Washington and Lee University, now one of the principal seats of learning in the South—an institution in which the leading men of Virginia have always manifested a deep interest, and among whose list of trustees the names of such distinguished men appear as Col. Arthur Campbell, Gen. Andrew Moore, Judge Arch'd Stuart, Col. James McDowell, Gen. Sam'l Blackburn, Hon. John Brown, Hon. Allen Taylor, Rev. George Baxter, Hon. James McDowell, Hon. John Howe Peyton, Charles L. Mosby, Esq., Hon. J. W. Brokenborough, Judge Wm. McLaughlin, Rev. Wm. S. White, etc.

In 1865, after the surrender of the Confederate armies, Gen. Lee was appointed President of the University, and on his death, in 1870, the name was changed from Washington College to Washington and Lee University. Since, it has steadily increased in prosperity and usefulness.

Ignorant and illiberal foreigners have, until recently, reproached America with a want of scholars and literary men – thus ungenerously insinuating that our soil is unfavorable to letters, or our people so degraded as to take a pleasure in condemning to obscurity everything formed to diffuse lustre and glory around a state. It is unnecessary to descant on such a fallacy. The local and temporary causes which have retarded our literary development were a virgin soil to be brought under cultivation, roads, canals, bridges, and every kind of public work to be constructed, and this, too, by a sparse and scattered population, inadequately supplied with implements of industry, entirely without capital, and pressed by their own personal necessities. Ours was a country of proprietors, it is true, but every proprietor was a laborer. What opportunity, what leisure, had such a people to devote to letters? "The wisdom of a learned man cometh by opportunity of leisure; and he that hath little business shall become wise. How can he get wisdom that holdeth the plough, and that glorieth in the goad; that driveth oxen, and is occupied in their labors; and whose talk is of bullocks."—[Ecclesiasticus: c. 38, v. 24–25.]

But to return from this digression. When cultivation was going on around these stockade forts, strong places, or infant settlements, pickets were posted to give warning of an enemy's approach. The women and children, when an alarm was raised, retired within the stockade, but the men, seizing their rifles and taking to the trees, contested every inch of ground, rarely seeking the shelter of the fort until every effort to drive off the red skins failed.

Until a supply of domestic animals was reared, one of the most important employments of the men was the taking of game. This was styled hunting, and included the pursuit of both hairy and feathered game. The fur obtained from the wild beast found ready sale east of the mountains, and thus gave them the means of supplying their necessities. The Autumn was devoted to hunting until a Winter's supply of meat was secured. The pioneers soon learned the habits of wild animals, and knew where to find them in all the different stages of the weather. They became guides, hunters, trappers, soldiers, knew every mountain peak and valley, every path and stream. They were fleet and agile as the deer, tireless as the red man, and as indifferent to hunger and cold. The following was one of their devices for taking wild beasts: Wolf pits, fox holes, or bear traps, were excavations thus formed: a hole was dug, say ten feet deep, small at the top and growing wider on all sides as it descended, sloping inwards so much that no beast could climb up. Two sticks were fastened together in the middle at right angles, the longer one confined in the ground, and the shorter—to the inner end of which was attached the bait—swinging across the middle of the pit, so that when the wild beast attempted to seize it, he was precipitated to the bottom.

As the means of support were easily procured, the cost of living moderate, the inhabitants married young, families were large, and the increase of population astonishingly rapid. A brief description of a wedding may not inappropriately, in this connection, be introduced in further illustration of frontier life. The few indoor amusements of the early settlers made a wedding a social event of the highest importance. It attracted the attention of the entire settlement, and was anticipated by old and young with impatient delight. From the house of his father, the groom, attended by his best man and friends, proceeded, on the morning of the happy day, to the home of the bride-elect. Here, the bride and bride's-maids, mounted on fine horses, joined the party, and they made their way to the clergyman's. The ceremony performed, the cavalcade set out on the return to the bride's residence, and now what was called running, or racing, for the bottle occurred. While the wedding party was absent, the father, or next friend of the bride, prepared at the bride's residence a bottle of the best spirits, around the neck of which a white ribbon was tied. When within a mile or two of the house, on their return from the clergyman's, the young men prepared to race for the bottle. Taking an even start, their horses were put at full speed, dashing over mud, rocks, stumps, in total disregard of all impediments. The race was run with as much desire to win as is ever manifested on the turf. The father or next friend of the bride, expecting the racers, stood with the bottle in his hand, ready to deliver it to the successful competitor. On getting it, he forthwith returned to meet the bride, to whom the bottle was presented, and who must at least taste it, then the groom and the attendants. Arrived at the bride's home, instead of the champagne breakfast of the present, with its Bohemian glass and épergnes of silver, its lobster salad, savory jellies, etc., a substantial dinner awaited them. It was generally dinner time when the party returned from the clergyman's. During the dinner, and while the healths were being drunk in blackberry wine or spruce beer, dashed with whiskey, the wedding cake was cut and handed about. The bride's father proposed the health of the bride and groom. They replied themselves, or by friends, and generally with such wit and humor as to bring down the house. After the speechifying, during which there was great hilarity, the gentlemen retired to the shade-trees until the preparations for dancing were completed. Before this, we must not omit to mention, while dinner was progressing, the custom of stealing the bride's shoe was observed. This custom is said to have afforded heart-felt amusement to the guests. To succeed in it the utmost dexterity was required on the part of the younger portion of the company, while equal vigilance was manifested by the attendants to defend her against the theft; and, if they failed, they were in honor bound to pay a penalty, a bottle of wine, for the redemption of the shoe. As a punishment to the bride, she was not allowed to dance until the shoe was restored. The successful robber, on getting possession of the shoe, held it up in triumph to the view of the assemblage.

Dancing having once commenced, it did not stop until the light of the following morning. If any of the dancers showed signs of weariness, there were loud cries to the musicians from the others to strike up with, "Hang out till to-morrow morning."

While the dance was proceeding, the bride made her escape, and the groom, under the guidance of the best man, was soon snugly by her side. If it was a wedding among the Germans, the young people were now admitted to the bed-chamber, and another custom was observed. A stocking rolled into a ball was given to the young females, who, one after the other, would go to the foot of the bed, stand with their backs to it, and throw the stocking over their shoulders at the bride's head, and the first who succeeded in touching her cap or head, was the next to be married. The young men then threw the stocking at the groom's head, in like manner, with the like motive, and hence their eagerness and dexterity in throwing the stocking. These gaieties were kept up for several days at the houses of the parents, until the whole company, completely exhausted by loss of sleep, retired for a long rest, which was necessary before they could return to their ordinary avocations. There was no bridal tour in those days—no traveling dress was to be assumed. Within a few days of the marriage ceremony, on a plot of land given by one of the parents, preparations were made for building the young couple a residence. This rustic edifice having been finished and furnished, the house-warming took place. This consisted of a stout meal similar to the marriage dinner, followed by a night's dancing, after which the happy pair were left to themselves. As far as the means of the respective parents would admit of it, they aided the young couple. In all of their affairs our fathers were prudent and economical, but not mean or niggardly. They knew that extreme avarice is folly, and that to make a proper use of the goods of this world, is to enjoy them. They therefore not only lived well themselves, but assisted the young married of their households to do likewise.

There were no towns of consequence in the early days of Augusta. The churches were all in the country, and around these was the burial-place or grave-yard. Owing to the absence of doctors and the want of medicines, many died who might have been easily cured.

The following were the principal diseases among the pioneers, and their specifics, mode of treatment, &c., in the absence of any disciple of Esculapius:

They gave a solution of common salt, sulphate of iron, or green copperas, to children afflicted with worms.

Roasted onions and garlic, for croup.

Slippery elm bark was applied to burns.

A purging pill was made from the inner bark of the white walnut tree. For snake bite, the snake was killed and cut into pieces, split open and laid on the wound to draw out the poison. The wound was then poulticed with the boiled leaves of the chesnut. After this the snake was burnt to ashes.

Another remedy was a poultice made of the white plantain. As a majority of the settlers were from Ireland, where no poisonous reptiles are found, it is doubtless from the Indians they learned these treatments.

Cupping, sucking the wound, and making deep incisions, which were filled with salt and gunpowder, were among the earliest remedies for snake bites used by the whites, and may be regarded in the light of experiments in the healing art.

Since this work went to press, the efficacy of one of the above modes of treatment has been tested in the writer's family, as will be seen by the following extract from the Staunton (Va.) VALLEY VIRGINIAN of July 20, 1882:

A SERIOUS SNAKE BITE.—On Tuesday last, as Col. Peyton and family were crossing North Mountain, fifteen miles from Staunton, for an outing in the Shenandoah mountains, his bright and intelligent little son, Lawrence, who was walking up the mountain with his mother and a man-servant, stepped upon a moccasin snake coiled under a tuft of grass on the roadside. The venomous reptile instantly struck his fangs deep into the leg of the little fellow, who sprang forward, crying out that he was bitten. The Colonel jumped from his carriage and immediately put his lips to the wound and sucked out the poison, sucking until he had raised a blister. He then steeped the wound in French brandy, and ordered the coachman to return, only delaying a moment to kill the snake, by which time the child's leg was much swollen and very painful. Upon reaching home, Lawrence was placed under the skillful treatment of Dr. Gibson, and is now, we are glad to say, rapidly recovering. We congratulate Colonel and Mrs. Peyton upon what, but for his heroic treatment in extracting the poison, would have proved a fatal calamity.

Wounds were healed with slippery elm bark, flaxseed, &c.

Rheumatism was treated with the oil of rattlesnakes, geese, wolves, bears, raccoons, ground-hogs, polecats, &c.

Coughs and pulmonary consumptions with syrups made with maple sugar and the bark of the wild cherry, etc.

Charms and incantations were also used for the cure of many diseases, and these were practiced by the whites as well as the red men.

Erysipelas was circumscribed by the blood of a black cat. Hence there was scarcely a black cat to be seen whose ears and tail had not been frequently cut off for a contribution of blood.

Blood-letting and draughts of warm water were as popular in all cases of fever as with Dr. Sangrado. Under this system of medicine, the reader will not be surprised to learn that many of the pioneers perished, that the extreme salubrity of the climate and the robust constitutions of the people alone prevented the population from being decimated.

It is by no means certain that their condition would have been improved by the presence of such practitioners as then drove their trade east of the Mountains. In an act passed by the Burgesses for regulating the fees of "the practisers of physic," it recites that "the practice is commonly in the hands of surgeons, apothecaries, or such as have only served apprenticeships to these trades, who often prove very unskillful, and yet demand excessive fees and prices for their medicines, which is a grievance, dangerous and intolerable evil."

It was no more all work and no play with the pioneers, than with Jack of the proverb. Every manly exercise was cultivated. Boys were taught to box and use the cudgel and to draw the bow. At the age of ten or twelve years, they were supplied with firearms, in the use of which they became experts, and aided, not only in supporting the family, but in the public defence. The boys became so skilled in imitating the noise of every bird and beast, that they could decoy any of the tenants of the forests within reach of their rifles. In throwing the tomahawk, another of their sports, they acquired the skill of the savages, and would strike down an enemy with unerring aim at twenty to thirty paces. No athletic sport was neglected, such as running, jumping, pitching (the quoits), wrestling, boxing, but all sports were practiced which tended to make them quick of eye, fertile in expedients, strong of hand, active of foot, and fearless in execution.

To bar out the schoolmaster was one of the customs of the boys, kept up to within the writer's school days, when he has more than once engaged in the sport. About a week before Easter and Christmas, the larger scholars would meet in the night to bar out the master. On his arrival at the school-room, he would take in the situation and endeavor to force his way in, but finding his efforts unavailing, he would proceed to negotiate, and would enter into an agreement to give the scholars holiday at Easter week and between Christmas and New Year's. Sometimes he would agree to give a gallon of some beverage and a lot of gingerbread on Christmas day, and play a game of corner ball with his pupils on the occasion. The terms being understood and agreed upon, the doors would be unbarred, and the duties of the school would be resumed.

It was customary for the ladies to meet at each other's houses usually at three in the afternoon, an hour after dinner, when all the busy occupations of the day were over. These were called " quilting parties," and the ladies presented themselves with their work-bags upon their arms, and work and conversation began together. Gossip, of course, constituted the staple of their conversation. What else was there in these retired societies but the domestic detail of household anecdote and the tattle of the settlement? At five, sassafras tea was brought in, accompanied by a handsome collation, consisting of pastry, fruits, creams and sweetmeats, and often of cold fowl and meats. This substantial kind of refreshment is not found unacceptable after an early dinner, and with the perspective of a solid supper. Pioneers have keen appetites arising from their robust health and the bracing mountain air. Among the heads of families, who had children married, there were regular days—generally once a week—when all the offsprings assembled at the father's or grandfather's house for dinner. There was something respectable, and even affecting, in these patriarchal meetings ; they seemed a means of drawing closer those ties of consanguinity which · are the best refuge against human ills, in which the purest affections of the heart mingle themselves with the wants and weakness of our nature, guiding, with watchful tenderness, the wanderings of youth, and supporting, with unwearied care, the feebleness of age.

The evenings were devoted to amusement, to social pleasure, to friendship, to some object that cheers or soothes the heart. Music and dancing were both practiced, adding much to the general happiness by lessening the laborious monotony of their lives. The round dance of the present, so much praised by poets and denounced by preachers, was not then known. Upon the young the beneficial effects of both music and dancing were apparent, particularly of music which is so well adapted to softening the manners and humanizing the feelings. The young people were introduced in the evenings, and entertained strangers with their songs, the girls often singing the airs of the countries beyond the seas which their parents had left, never to see again, the boys accompanying them on the flute, flageolet or violin. The cultivation of a taste for music and poetry probably led to descanting in the wild style of the rude minstrels of the Middle Ages. The souls of these children of the woods quickly took fire at the beauties of poetry, and the most important benefits of poetry were thus produced, by promoting a repugnance to everything mean and ignoble; by the study of nature in the purity of her poetical forms; by the innocent, and at the same time agreeable, direction which the pursuits of taste impart to the idler propensities of the mind; by the influence of generous and pathetic verse, in keeping open those hearts which are in danger of being choked with the cares of business. The influence of poetry can be seen in the eloquence of such men as Patrick Henry and Rev. Samuel Davies. Music and dancing were, therefore, considered an essential part of their education, and the old field school-houses were the academies where they practiced both. History was in this repeating herself, for, from the earliest ages, music has been much in use. The ancients attached vast importance to it, and ascribed the malignity, brutality and irreligion of some of the peoples of antiquity to their absolute neglect of it. In the days of Laban, music was much used in Mesopotamia, where he resided, since, among other reproaches he makes to his son-in-law, Jacob, he complains that, by his precipitate flight, he had put it out of his power to conduct him and his family "with mirth and with songs, with tabret and with harp."—[Gen., cxxxi, v. 27.]

On both sides of the Blue Ridge mountain, the amusements of the people were such as might be expected in a rural society; and in Eastern Virginia they were those of a people of considerable wealth and comparatively slight education. Horse-racing and racing balls were the events, and fox-hunting, cock-fighting, drinking and card-playing the regular pastimes. In the Virginia Gazette for October, 1737, we read: "We have advice from Hanover county that on St. Andrew's day there are to be horse-races and several other diversions for the entertainment of ladies and gentlemen, at the old field, near Capt. John Brickerton's, in that county, the substance of which is as follows—viz.: It is proposed that 20 horses or mares do run around a three miles' course for a prize of £5.

"That a hat of the value of 20 shillings be cudgelled for, and that after the first challenge made, the drums are to beat every quarter of an hour for three challenges round the ring, and none to play with their left hand.

"That a violin be played for by 20 fiddlers; no person to have the liberty to play unless he bring a fiddle with him. After the prize is won they are all to play together, and each a different tune, and to be treated by the company.

"That 12 boys of 12 years of age do run 112 yards for a hat of the cost of 12 shillings.

"That a flag be flying on said day 30 feet high.

"That a handsome entertainment be provided for the subscribers and their wives; and such of them as are not so happy as to have wives may treat any other lady.

"That Drums, Trumpets, Hautboys, &c., be provided to play at said entertainment.

"That after dinner the Royal health, His Honor, the Governor's, &c., are to be drunk.

"That a Quire of ballads be sung for by a number of Songsters, all of them to have liquor sufficient to clear their wind-pipes.

"That a pair of shoe buckles be wrestled for by a number of brisk young men.

"That a pair of handsome shoes be danced for.

"That a pair of handsome silk stockings, of one Pistole value, be given to the handsomest young country maid that appears in the field; with many other whimsical and comical diversions too numerous to mention.

"And as this mirth is designed to be purely innocent and void of offence, all persons resorting there are desired to behave themselves with decency and sobriety, the subscribers being resolved to discountenance all immorality with the utmost rigor."

These were rough, honest English sports, and prevailed everywhere in Eastern Virginia. At all the county towns, east of the mountains, fairs were held at regular intervals, accompanied by sack and hogshead races, greased poles, and bull-baiting. In fine weather, barbecues in the woods, when oxen, pigs and fish were roasted, were frequent, and were much enjoyed by all, ending usually, among the lower classes, with much intoxication. Another great source of delight was the cock-fight. The small farmers assembled at the taverns to play billiards and drink. The monthly sessions of the courts filled the towns with a miscellaneous crowd. The people were not much given to reading or the sister art of writing. Gov. Spotswood remarked on one occasion, in an official reply to some remonstrance of the House of Burgesses: "I observe that the grand ruling party in your house has not furnished chairmen of two of your standing committees who can spell English or write common sense, as the grievances under their own hand-writing will manifest."

FOLK LORE.

The progress of science has convinced mankind that the material universe is everywhere subject to fixed and immutable laws. In the infancy and less mature state of human knowledge it was otherwise, and man was constantly disposed to refer many of the appearances, with which he was conversant, to the agency of invisible intelligence; sometimes under the influence of good, but oftener of malignant disposition. Omens and portents told these men of good or ill fortune. These superstitions prevailed, to a vast extent, among our English ancestors. Queen Elizabeth consulted Dr. John Dee, an astrologer, respecting a lucky day for her coronation; James I employed much of his time in the study of witchcraft and demology, and in 1664, Sir Matthew Hale caused two old women to be hanged upon a charge of unlawful communion with infernal spirits. A belief in such supernatural agency has existed in all ages and countries—among the Jews, Chaldeans, Egyptians, Greeks and Romans, down to within recent times.

The history of mankind, therefore, will be very imperfect, and our knowledge of the operations and eccentricities of the mind lamentably deficient, unless we take into our view what has occurred under this head. The supernatural appearances, with which our ancestors conceived themselves perpetually surrounded, must have had a strong tendency to cherish and keep alive the powers of the imagination, and to penetrate those who witnessed, or expected such things, with an extraordinary sensitiveness. But whatever were their advantages or disadvantages, at any rate it is good for us to call up in review things which are now passed away, but which once occupied a large share of the thoughts and attention of our ancestors, and in a great degree tended to modify their characters and dictate their resolutions. Vast numbers of persons have been sacrificed as witches in different ages and countries, and stringent laws once existed against dealers in witchcraft in Virginia. As late as 1705, Grace Sherwood was punished in Virginia for witchcraft. An able jury of ancient women was impannelled, and, after search, reported " that she was not like them, nor any other woman."

The witch was, by our ancestors, supposed to be a woman who had formed a contract, signed with her blood, with a mighty and invisible spirit, the great enemy of man, and to have sold herself, body and soul, to everlasting perdition for the sake of gratifying, for a short term of years, her malignant passions against those who had been so unfortunate as to give her offence. They considered such a crime as atrocious above all others, and regarded the witch with inexpressible abhorence. The witch was thought to possess the power of inflicting strange and incurable diseases, particularly on children; of destroying cattle by shooting them with hair balls; of inflicting spells and curses on guns and other things, and of changing human beings into horses, and, after bridling and sadling them, riding them, full speed, over hill and dale, to their places of meeting. The wizard, or man witch, was supposed to possess the same ample powers of mischief, but to exercise his powers, for the most part, to counteract the malevolent influence of the witches. These wizards, or witch-masters, as they were commonly called, went about exercising their art, and many of these impostors were smart enough to make a good living, without work, out of their calling; were pure and unadulterated hypocrites.

All incurable diseases were ascribed to the supernatural agency of a malignant witch, such as epileptic and other fits, dropsy of the brain rickets, &c. For the cure of diseases inflicted by witchcraft, the picture of the supposed witch was drawn on a stump, or piece of board, and shot at with a bullet containing a little bit of silver. This bullet transferred a painful and sometimes mortal spell on that part of the witch corresponding with the part of the portrait struck by the bullet. Another method was to get some of the child's water, which was closely corked up in a vial, and hung up in a chimney. This inflicted the witch with stranguary, which lasted as long as the vial remained in the chimney. The witch could only relieve herself from a spell inflicted on her by borrowing something, no matter what, of the family to which the subject of her witch-craft belonged. Such family was never in a hurry to accommodate her with a loan.

When cattle or dogs were bewitched, they were burnt on the forehead by a branding-iron, or, when dead, burnt to ashes. When disease and pestilence prevailed, fires were lit to ward off both. This was, doubtless, a relic of an older custom. when an animal was offered as a burnt sacrifice to appease the wrath of the gods. If an animal was infected by murrain, the diseased part was cut out while the beast was alive, and solemnly burnt in a bonfire. To the modern scientific mind, these would seem wise precautions to hinder the spread of infection. Any one who knows the rural mind, even at the present day, will be quite sure that the precaution was magical, not sanitary. Witches were often said to milk the cows of their neighbors. This they did by fixing a pin in a new towel for each cow intended to be milked. This towel was hung over her own door, and by means of certain incantations, the milk was extracted from the fringes of the towel after the manner of milking a cow.

The first German glass-blowers, in America, drove witches out of their furnaces by throwing in live puppies.

Bewitched persons sometimes vomited quantities of crooked pins; the palms of their hands were turned outwards, and, if they spoke, it was not in their own voice, but that of the devil, by whom they were possessed—at least, they were said to do so. Such were some of the extravagant fancies of our forefathers, and may afford us a salutary lesson.

At many remote points on the Western frontier, similar settlements to the one we have described on Lewis creek were made by a like class of immigrants. The same virtues of hospitality, of disinterested kindness, prevailed in all these backwoods communities, and were, in some measure, the result of their situation. Unselfish and liberal, these pioneers sought no recompense but the approval of their own consciences, and it has been well said that the greater part of mankind might derive advantage from the contemplation of their virtues. Such were those majestic men of the frontier—the men of 1732–1776–1812—whose souls grew like the shadows of the mountain ridge they walked beneath, "wild, above rule or art, rugged, but sublime !"

The first settlers of Augusta were, for the most part, the descendants, paternally or maternally, of the ancient Caledonians, who boasted that they had never been subjected to the law of any conqueror. They belonged to various Highland clans, and were strongly imbued with the prejudices, feelings, sentiments, &c., of their peculiar clans. One of the circumstances connected with their condition as followers of a chieftain was, that every clan bore the name of their hereditary chief, and were supposed to be allied to him, in different degrees, by the ties of blood. This kindred band, or admitted claim of a common relationship, led to a freedom of intercourse highly flattering to human pride, and communicated to the vassal Highlanders a sentiment of conscious dignity and a sense of natural equality. And every individual sought to show his attachment to his leader as the head of his family. This feeling strongly exhibited itself in the Augusta colony, which, from intermarriages, soon assumed something of the character of a numerous and increasing family. The poorest preserved with pride the facts of this consanguinity, and whatever the distinctions of rank that may have arisen from the unequal acquisition of wealth, they mutually respected themselves and each other. The haughty backwoodsman yielded a cheerful obedience to the head of the clan or colony, whom they regarded somewhat as a father, and who may be supposed to have exercised among them the authority of a judge in peace, and of a leader in time of war.

Such, briefly, was the colony of Augusta from 1732 to 1745, and a more interesting spectacle of undisturbed felicity, quiet progress, notwithstanding the primitive condition of the community, and the roughing incident to their remoteness from commercial centres, it would be difficult to imagine or describe. Of luxury, there was little or none, unless it might be termed a luxury to be without want, without beggars, and without the

enervating diseases which attend on idleness and opulence. There were
no diamonds or pearls, but plenty of bright eyes and rosy cheeks; no
shimmering silks or brilliantly colored velvets and satins, resplendent
with gold and silver lace, but plenty of woollen stuffs, recommended by
their warmth and healthfulness; no theatres, operas, fancy balls, saloons,
or their attendant licentiousness, but plenty of fun and frolic. When we
consider the condition of the people, and their fertile, salubrious and beautiful country; that they married and multiplied, and their virtue, instead of
degenerating, was confirmed by time, and the more they increased the
more examples they furnished to animate succeeding generations, one
feels how impossible it is to describe the happiness of this fortunate people. Could they be other than the favored of Heaven? They who
recognized God in everything, and constantly approached him with gratitude and veneration. Religion coöperated with nature to soften and polish their manners. Nature left but little unfinished; that little, religion
completed.

The brief foregoing account of the manners and customs of the colony
will hold good, generally, up to and long after the Revolution.

EXCERPTS FROM THE RECORDS, ANA, ETC.

The profession of the law seems to have been as popular in Augusta a
hundred and twenty-five years ago as now. Though five attorneys obtained a licence to practice in December, 1745, at the February term, 1746,
less than three months from the organization of the county, five more gentlemen of wig and gown fraternity qualified to practice in the courts,
namely: John Newport, Obediah Merriot, Ben. Pendleton, Jno. Nicholas,
and Wm. Wright.

These professional gentlemen soon began to wrangle in a too characteristic way, and the court, at the same term, was driven to make the following order, viz: "That any attorney interrupting another at the bar, or
speaking when he is not employed, forfeit five shillings."

That the manners of the bar were not over refined may be inferred from
a fine imposed upon the leader of the circuit, Gabriel Jones, at the May
term, 1746, of five shillings, for swearing. His profanity was indulged in
before the court, and doubtless directed to one of his legal rivals.

The fees of lawyers in the county and inferior courts were, as established by act of 1753, for an opinion or advice, ten shillings; in any suit at
common law, or petition, fifteen shillings; in all chancery suits, real, mixt
or personal actions, thirty shillings; on a petition for a small debt, seven
shillings and six pence; and a fine of £50 was levied for any violation of
these prices. A shilling was of the value of sixteen and two-thirds cents.
Attorneys were not likely to grow fat on such moderate fees, but could
live well, if they got plenty of them. For we see the court, March, 1746,
established the following rates for *ordinaries*, and from the scale we infer
that they were very ordinary indeed: "For a hot diet, well dressed, nine
pence; a cold diet, six pence; lodging, with clean sheets, three pence;
stabling and fodder for the night, six pence; rum, the gallon, nine shillings; whiskey, six shillings; claret, the quart, five shillings."

Many of these early colonial lawyers were doubtless lawyers only in name—men not versed in the laws, but picking up a support as commissioners in chancery, conveyancers, paper shavers, or usurers and speculators, who, deriving a knowledge of the troubles of parties from their position, availed themselves of it to make a good turn for themselves.

The early records abound with proofs of the morality of our ancestors, their determination to uphold religion, law and order. At the May term, 1746, the court ordered Edward Boyle to be put in the stocks for two hours and fined twenty shillings for damning the court and swearing four oaths in their presence. All through the records appear cases of persons fined for swearing, fornication. adultery, drunkenness, and other offences, and in August, 1747, the sheriff was ordered to make a duckiug-stool for the use of the county, according to the law of 1705.

The ancient laws of Virginia declared that the court in every county shall cause to be set up near the court-house a pillory, pair of stocks, a whipping-post and a ducking-stool, in such place as they shall think convenient, which, not being set up within six months after the date of this act, the said court shall be fined five thousand pounds of tobacco.

The corporal punishments inflicted upon criminals consisted of the pillory, the stocks, the whipping-post and the ducking-stool. Each of these is described below, for the benefit of those who are unacquainted with those relics of barbarism.

The pillory is one of the most ancient corporeal punishments in England, France, Germany, and other countries. As early as 1275, by a statute of Edward I, it was enacted that every stretch-neck, or pillory, should be made of convenient strength, so that execution might be done upon offenders without peril to their bodies. The pillory consisted of a wooden frame, erected on a stool, with holes and folding boards for the admission of the head and hands. The heroes of the pillory have not been the worst class of men, for we find that a man by the name of Leighton, for printing his Zion's Plea against Prelacy, was fined £10,000, degraded from the ministry, pilloried, branded, and whipped through the city of London, in 1637, besides having an ear cropped and his nostrils slit. The length of time the criminal stood in and upon the pillory was determined by the Judge.

The stocks was a simple arrangement for exposing a culprit on a bench, confined by having his ankles made fast in holes under a movable board. Sometimes the stocks and whipping-post were connected together. The posts which supported the stocks, being made sufficiently high, were furnished near the top with iron clasps to fasten round the wrists of the offender and hold him securely during the infliction of the punishment. Sometimes a single post was made to serve both purposes, clasps being provided near the top for the wrists when used as a whipping-post, and similar clasps below for the ankles, when used as stocks, in which case the culprit sat on a bench behind the post, so that his legs, when fastened to the post, were in a horizontal position.

Women were punished in the ducking-stools. They fasten an armed chair to the end of two strong beams, twelve or fifteen feet long, and parallel to each other. The chair hangs upon a sort of axle, on which it plays freely, so as always to remain in the horizontal position. The scold, being well fastened in her chair, the two beams are then placed as near to the centre as possible, across a post on the water-side, aud being lifted up behind, the chair, of course, drops into the cold element. The ducking is repeated, according to the degree of shrewishness possessed by the patient, and has generally the effect of cooling her immoderate heat, at least for a time.

John Preston, at the May term, 1746, came into court and prayed leave to prove his importation, which was granted him, and thereupon he made oath that at his own charge he had imported himself, Elizabeth, his wife, William, his son, and Lettice and Ann, his daughters, immediately from Ireland into this colony, and that this is the first time of procuring his said right, in order to partake of his Majesty's bounty in taking up land, which is ordered to be certified.

The first court-house of Augusta was no doubt like those common on the frontiers, a log cabin covered, but without daubing, sash or doors. In this hall of justice, a carpenter's bench, with a half-dozen chairs upon it, served as the judgment seat, and though the house was barely sufficient to contain the bench, bar, jurors, and constables, the occasion of the first court must have brought the whole population to the town. The following description of a scene in one of these frontier court-houses will no doubt hold true as to many in that of Augusta. But few spectators could be accommodated on the lower floor, the only one laid; many, therefore, clambered up the walls, and placing their hands and feet in the open interstices between the logs, hung there, suspended like enormous Madagascar bats. Some had taken possession of the joists, and big Jno. McJunkin (who, until now, had ruled at all public gatherings,) had placed a foot on one joist and a foot on another, directly over the heads of their Honors, standing, with outstretched legs, like the Colossus of Rhodes. The Judge's sense of propriety was shocked at this exhibition. The sheriff, John McCandless, was called, and ordered to clear the walls and joists. He went to work with his assistants, and soon pulled down by the legs those who were in no very great haste to obey. Mc'Junkin was the last, and began to growl as he prepared to descend. "What do you say, sir?" said the Judge. "I say I pay my taxes, and has as good a reete here as iny mon." "Sheriff!" Sheriff!" said the Judge, "Bring him before the court!" McJunkin's ire was now up, and as he reached the floor, began to strike his breast, exclaiming, "My name is John McJunkin, d'ye see; here's the brist that niver flinched, if so be it was in a good caase; I'll stan' iny mon in Butler county, if so be he'll clear me o' the la'." "Bring him before the court," said the Judge. He was accordingly pinioned, and if not gagged, at least forced to be silent while his case was under consideration. Some of the lawyers volunteered as *amici curiæ;* some ventured a word of apology for McJunkin. The Judge pronounced sentence of imprisonment for two hours in the jail of the county, and ordered the Sheriff to take him into custody. The Sheriff, with much simplicity, observed: "May it please the court, there is no jail at all to put him in." Here the Judge took a learned distinction, upon which he expatiated for some length for the benefit of the bar. He said "there were two kinds of custody; first, safe custody; second, close custody. The first is, where the body must be forthcoming to answer a demand or an accusation, and in this case, the body may be delivered, for the time being, out of the hands of the law, on bail or mainprize; but where the imprisonment forms a part of the satisfaction or punishment, there can be no bail or mainprize. This is the reason of the common law, in relation to escapes under *capias ad satisfaciendum*, and also why a second *ca. sa.* cannot issue after the defendant has been once arrested and then discharged by the plaintiff. In like manner, a man cannot be twice imprisoned for the same offence, even if he be released before the expiration of the term of imprisonment. This is clearly a case of close custody—*areta custodia*—and the prisoner must be confined, body and limb, without bail or mainprize, in some place of close incarceration." Here he is interrupted by the Sheriff, who seemed to have hit upon a lucky thought: "May it please the court, I am just thinking I can take him to Bowyer's pig-pen; the pigs are killed for the court, and the pen's empty." "You have heard the opinion of the court." said the Judge, "Proceed, Sheriff, and do your duty." The Sheriff accordingly retired with the prisoner, and drew after him three-fourths of the spectators and suitors, while the Judge, thus relieved, proceeded to organize the court. But this was not the end of the affair. Peace and order had scarcely been restored, when the Sheriff came rushing into court with a crowd at his heels, crying out, "Mr. Judge! Mr. Judge! May it please the court!" "What is the matter, Sheriff?" "Mr. Judge! Mr. Judge! John McJunkin's got off, d'ye mind." "What! escaped! Sheriff, summon the *posse comitatus*." "The posse, the posse, what's that, may it please your Honor? Now, I will just tell you how it happened. He was going along quietly enough till we got to the hazle patch, and all at once he pitched off into the bushes, and I after him, but a limb of a tree kitched me first, and I fell back three rods." The Judge could not restrain his gravity; the bar raised a laugh, and there the matter ended, after which the business proceeded quietly enough

Nov. 27, 1751.—The Grand Jury presented Owen Crawford for drinking a health to King James, and refusing to drink a health to King George.

Feb. 19, 1751.—John and Reuben Harrison presented a petition to the court praying to be rewarded for killing two persons, under the command of Ute Perkins, who were endeavoring to rob them.

Feb. 19, 1751.—Catharine Cole being presented for having a bastard child, and refusing to pay her fine or give security for the same, according to law, it is ordered that she receive on her bare back, at the public whipping-post, twenty lashes, well laid on, in lieu of said fine, and that the lashing be done immediately.

May 18, 1749.—Jane Scot, a servant woman, for having a bastard child: Ordered that after the expiration of her servitude by indenture, and serving her master one year for the trouble of his house, the Church Wardens of Augusta Parish sell her for the said offence, according to law.

March 1, 1749.—Robt. Armstrong, in open court, made oath that he saw the Indians kill one, and take away another mare, belonging to Peter Wright, of this county.

Nov. 28, 1750.—The Grand Jury present Jacob Coger, for a breach of the peace, in driving hogs over the Blue Ridge on the Sabbath day; and May 28, 1751, James Frame was presented for a breach of the Sabbath, in unnecessarily traveling ten miles.

May 17, 1754.—Ann, wife of James Brown, having come into court and abused William Wilson, Gent., one of the justices, by calling him a rogue, and that on his coming off the bench she would give it to him like the devil, ordered that she be taken into custody, &c.   •

August 24, 1754.—Joseph Tees, having affronted this court by saying " he got nothing in this court but shuffling," it is ordered that he be fined twenty shillings, &c.

March 17, 1756.—Francis Furgesson, being brought before this court, &c., for damning Robert Dinwiddie, esq., (Governor of the Colony,) " for a Scotch pedling son of a bitch," was found guilty, but was excused on apologising and giving security to keep the peace.

May 21, 1756.—On motion of Thomas Lewis, Gent., setting forth that his negro, Hampton, frequently absconds from his service, and that he has several times attempted to ravish Ann West and other white women, and praying, to prevent the like mischief, he may be dismembered ; it is ordered that the said Lewis employ such skillful person, as he may think proper, to castrate the said slave.

Dec. 8, 1756.—Charles Dever was tried for cursing God and our Sovereign Lord George II, King, &c., but acquitted.

SERVING WRITS.

It was not the easiest thing in the world to bring malefactors to justice in those days, as the following returns, made to executions, will illustrate :

In the case of Johnson vs. Brown, (1751), "not executed by reason there is no road to the place where he (Brown) lives."

Again : " Not executed by reason of excess of weather."

Nov., 1752.—" Not executed by reason of an axe " (the axe being in the hands of defendant, uplifted, no doubt, to cleave the officer's skull.)

" Not executed, because the defendant's horse was faster than mine."

" Not executed, by reason of a gun."

Emlen vs. Miller.—" Kept off from Miller with a club, &c.; Miller not found by Humphrey Marshall."

" Not executed, because the defendant got into deep water—out of my reach."

Nov., 1754.—" Executed on the within, John Warwick, and he is not the man."

" Not executed, by reason of flux being in the house."

August, 1755.—Forty-nine executions returned " not executed, by reason of the disturbance of the Indians."

One of the early vices of the frontier was insobriety among the lower classes, and our ancestors made strenuous efforts, as the records show, to stamp it out. They believed, probably like the ancients, that it was a disease. Five centuries before the Christian era, Herodotus said that " Drunkenness showed that both body and soul were sick." Diogenes and Plutarch assert that " Drink madness is an affection of the body which hath destroyed many kings and noble people." Laws were passed forbidding

/

women to use wine and restricting boys. In the first and second centuries the early Christians urged temperance, and from that time to this it has engaged the attention of the good and wise. Temperance societies have done much to rescue mankind from the horrors of intemperance, and in the early days of Augusta, the County Court was, so to speak, a kind of temperance society. The justices were men of sobriety; the court did not s it idle and see the mighty evil entail untold ruin upon man. They sought, by rigid execution of the laws, to extirpate the evil and to encourage virtuous habits. Thus we see that on Feb. 10th, 1746, the court ordered the sheriff to take William Linwell into custody, and that he be fined five shillings for being drunk. Many similar orders might be cited.

CHAPTER V.

The early settlers were naturally anxious on entering territory which had been held for time immemorial by native inhabitants, to conciliate their good will, and, if possible, to live on friendly terms with them. Policy, no less than humanity and justice, dictated this course. The pioneers had witnessed the good effects of Penn's kind treatment of the simple-hearted children of the forest, and were determined to follow his example. The colonists on Lewis creek did not require advice on this point, but six years after they planted themselves in Augusta, shortly after some acts of injustice had been perpetrated by reckless whites in the Valley, the people were strongly advised to pursue a policy of justice and humanity towards the natives by a venerable and respected member of the Society of Friends, Thomas Chalkley. In a letter dated May 21st, 1738, and addressed to the Friends at Opequon, near Winchester, he urged them "to keep a friendly correspondence with the natives; to recognize their right to the country, and not settle on their lands without their consent or until purchased; to therefore select the most reputable whites to treat with the Indians as to the acquisition, by purchase, of such lands as the whites might wish to possess." He informed them that an opposite course would expose themselves and families to murder by a cruel and merciless enemy. He begged them to consider "that you are in the province of Virginia, holding what rights you have under that government, and the Virginians have made an agreement with the natives to go as far as the mountains and no further, &c.; and you are over and beyond the mountains, therefore out of that agreement, by which you lie open to the insults and incursions of the Southern Indians, who have already destroyed many of the inhabitants of Carolina and Virginia." "The English having gone beyond the bounds of their agreement," says he, "eleven of them were killed by the Indians while we were travelling in Virginia." He informed them that in Pennsylvania no new settlements were made without an agreement with the natives, as was the case in Lancaster, a county far within Penn's grant, and warned them of the danger they would incur from both the Northern and Southern Indians by presuming to squat upon their lands. And, lastly, he assured them that he was moved to give them this advice solely by his love of God and man, and a sincere desire that they might live in peace and happiness.

Lewis and the early settlers recognized, to the fullest extent, the right of the Indians to the country of their nativity. As America, up to the discovery by Columbus, had been unknown to the rest of the world, how could it belong to any foreign prince or State? The native tribes, who possessed it, were free and independent communities, and as such capable of acquiring territorial property. Among the various principles on which a right to the soil has been founded, there is none superior to immemorial occupancy. In this case, no European power could derive a title to the soil from discovery; because, that can give a right only to lands or things which have neither been owned nor possessed, or which, after having been owned or possessed, have been voluntarily deserted. The right of the Indian nations to the soil in their possession was, therefore, founded in nature. It was the free and liberal gift of Heaven to them, and such as no foreigner could rightfully annul. The blinded superstition of the times, however, regarded the Deity as the partial God of Christians, and not as the common father of saints and savages. The pervading influence of philosophy, reason and truth has, since that period, given us better notions of the rights of mankind, and of the obligations of morality. These, unquestionably, are not confined to particular modes of faith, but extend universally to Jews and Gentiles, to Christians and infidels. Unfounded, however, as the claims of European Sovereigns to American territory were, they severally proceeded to act upon them. By tacit consent they adopted, as a new law of nations, that the countries which each explored should be the absolute property of its discoverer. While thus sporting with the rights of unoffending nations, they could not agree in their respective shares of the common spoil, and hence the long and bloody wars between the English, French and Spaniards.

The leaders of the infantile colony in Augusta, not holding the views of their Sovereigns, but the juster sentiments to which allusion has been made, on arriving near Bellefont, sought to acquire lands, by purchase from the aborigines. They soon ascertained that no tribe residing in the

Valley claimed exclusive ownership in the soil, or set up a right to dispose of it by sale. The whites were, therefore, compelled either to withdraw or settle upon the lands and wait for the issue of events. The latter course was adopted. That they afterwards found savages claiming authority to dispose of the country, may be taken for granted from a remark of Jefferson in his "Notes on Virginia" : "That the lands of this country were taken from the Indians by conquest, is not so generally a truth as is supposed. I find, in our historians and records, repeated proofs of purchase, which cover a considerable part of the lower country, and many more would be doubtless found on further search. The upper country (*i. e.*, the Valley,) we know has been acquired altogether by purchase, in the most unexceptionable form." That Lewis and the first settlers of the "Upper Country," did acquire, very soon after their arrival, some such title, may be inferred from the friendly relations which existed between them and the Indians for many years. And from the proofs which are still extant of such purchases in the District of West Augusta—such as the deed quoted in full in the sequel of this chapter, from certain Indian chiefs to George Croghan. A deed acknowledged, by the way, in that N. W. portion of Augusta in which, as will appear later on, justices' courts were frequently held anterior to the Revolution. It is well known that the two races, the whites and Indians, lived in the Valley for above twenty years, from 1732 to 1753, on amicable terms. This could not have been the case had the policy of the whites been one of injustice and inhumanity, and unappreciated by the wild men. For as early as 1712, the Tuscarora Indians, in North Carolina, had massacred one hundred and thirty-seven of the whites in a systematic effort to rid their country of the new-comers. Had the wise course of Penn and of the Augusta settlers been generally followed, there is reason to believe that the continent would have passed into the hands of the superior race without loss of blood or treasure.

In 1732, when Lewis and his associates, if others were associated with him in his adventurous enterprise, entered the present County of Augusta, they had not taken the precaution to secure titles from the Colonial Government to any lands they might wish to locate—a singular omission, if they came from Williamsburg, as has been stated. It was the custom of the times to issue such grants, and in the year 1733, the Governor issued one for 5,000 acres to a German, by the name of Stover, "on the south fork of the Gerando (now Shenandoah) river, on what was called Mesinetto creek," and it is certain that the colonial authorities of Virginia regarded the Valley and country west of the mountains as belonging to the British crown—ignoring, as absurd, any claim to it of natives. This has been the traditional course of Great Britain, and continues her present policy. Hence within the last decade, 1872-'82, she has waged wars with the Zulus in Africa, with the native tribes of India, and other quarters of

the globe, for the possession of their lands, which she had neither purchased nor conquered, but to which she calmly set up a claim.

.Having settled in Augusta, without any other title to their lands than
they may have subsequently acquired from the aborigines, it does not
appear that the whites applied to the colonial authorities for patents. It
is probable, having bought of the red men, they did not consider this
course necessary. If they had given the Indians a satisfactory consideration for the soil they occupied, they no doubt considered an application to
Gov. Gooch unnecessary. The Governor, however, took the European
view of the situation, and commenced sporting with the rights of the Indians in the "Upper Country" by issuing patents for large tracts to his
favorites. Thus we find him issuing a patent to the Augusta section of the
Valley, on the 12th day of August, 1736, to William Beverley and his
associates for 118,491 acres, being a tract known as Beverley Manor. Up
to this date the colonists had, as we have seen, lived upon the demesne
without law, or the authority of English law, and governed by such customs as had grown up among themselves for regulating their intercourse.
Among these were what were termed "corn rights," tomahawk rights, and
cabin rights. The corn right was a title derived from having enclosed and
cultivated a plot of ground. Whoever cultivated one acre in corn acquired
a title to one hundred acres of land. The tomahawk right consisted of
nothing more than the deadening of a few trees, generally round a spring,
and blazing a few trees on the lines of a claim. The cabin right was
derived from building a log hut upon a certain tract of land. Every
escaped trial under the ancient laws of Virginia is, in view of all the facts,
builder of a hut acquired a title to forty acres. The patent to Beverley, the
original of which is in the Circuit Clerk's office, Staunton, is as follows :

PATENT FOR BEVERLEY MANOR.

George II, by the grace of God, of Great Britain, France and Ireland,
King, Defender of the Faith, &c.: To all to whom these presents shall
come, greeting: Know, that for diverse good causes and considerations,
but more especially, for the consideration in an order of our Lieutenant-
Governor, in Council, bearing date 12th of August, 1736, we have given,
granted and confirmed, and by these presents for us, our heirs and successors, do give, grant, and confirm unto William Beverley, of the Co. of
Essex, Gentleman, Sir John Randolph, of the City of Williamsburg,
Knight, Richard Randolph, of the Co. of Henrico, Gentleman, and John
Robinson, of the Co. of King and Queen, Gentleman, one certain tract or
parcel of land, called the Manor of Beverley, containing 118,491 acres,
lying and being in the county of Orange, beyond the great mountains, on
the river Sherando, and bounded as follows, to wit: *Beginning* at five
white oaks, on a narrow point, between a large run, called Thirsty Creek,
and a small run, called Gearer Run, about thirty poles on the east side
through middle (of the) river Sherando, and running thence N. 70°, W.
364 poles, by four linds, with the same river: thence N. 15°, W. 145 poles,
crossing the said river the whole course, being 443 poles, by a large white

oak and two small ones; thence N. 75°, E. 297 poles to four linns and a
red oak on a ridge; thence N. 15°, E. 44 poles to a double walnut and
gum on this ridge of the said Middle River; thence down the same 102
poles to a red oak and hickory by the river side, then from the first mentioned five white oaks S. 364 poles, crossing Gearer Run twice, just below
three small Spanish oaks under a steep hill; thence S. 83°. E. 270, by
five linds; thence S. S. E. 330 poles to three white oaks by the side of a
meadow; thence E. by South 738 poles, across Sherando River, to a
forked white walnut, a black one, a hickory and an ash by the river side;
thence down the same 74 poles to two water oaks, two hickories, a whortle-
berry tree and a walnut; thence E. by South 60 poles to four linds on the
foot of the Blue Ridge, in stony ground; thence South by East 88 poles,
between a white and red oak; thence S. E. 103 poles by four linds and
white oak; thence S. S. W. 492 to three linds; thence South 450 poles
by a red oak, white oak and two linns; thence S. W. 456 poles to five
linns; thence S. 5°, W. 88 poles to a white oak and linn saplins on the
river bank; thence S. S. E. 38 poles by four linns; thence S. W. by West
286 poles to two linns near the river; thence S. 26°, E. 90 poles to three
white oaks; thence S. and by West 134 poles, nigh two red oaks, by a
boiling spring, almost as big as the river in flat grounds; thence S. 60°,
W. 176 poles to three linns nigh the river; thence W. 232 poles by two
red and two white oaks on the river side; thence through several thickets
of the same 1,300 poles, by two Spanish oaks, two red oaks and a white
oak just below three springs, called the Great Springs; thence S. 30 poles
by two linns and a hickory; thence S. W. and by W. 178 poles to three
linds; thence S. 33°, W. 238 poles by four pines; thence West by South
274 poles by two pines and a red oak bush; thence West Northwest 114
poles by three pines; thence North 85°, West 546 poles by four pines;
thence W. 506 poles by a chesnut oak, red oak and pine on the brow of a
hill; thence N. 50°, W. 244 poles to three pines; thence N. 396 poles to
three hickories and a pine by a red oak; thence S. 70°, W. 630 poles by
four hickories near a valley; thence S. 20°, W. 544 poles to three red
oaks on the west side of Hamerk's branch; thence S. W. by West 94
poles by two white oaks and a red oak; thence S W. by South 652 poles
by four red oaks and three hickories just above the head of some of the
Sherando waters; thence N. W. and by West 232 poles to a red oak and
white oak and hickory by the head of a draft that runs into James River;
thence S. W. by West 300 poles, crossing two springs of the James River;
thence N. W. by West 600 poles, crossing the head spring of Sherando
to two hickories, two chesnuts and white oak, with a spring of James
River; thence N. 2,016 poles, crossing four springs of James river to a
white oak by a path; thence N. 75°, W. 106 poles on the side of a very high
hill, (from the foot of which issues a spring about fifty feet broad called
the Black Spring) to a white oak and hickory; thence S. 60°, W. 120
poles to a Spanish oak, hickory and walnut; thence S. 40°, W. 100 poles
by a hickory and white oak; thence N. 50°, W. 92 poles, crossing the
middle river of Sherando, on which we first began to survey the whole
Louisa county, 160 poles, between two white oaks and a hickory at the
foot of a ridge of mountains that lies between this and the north branch of
the same river; thence N. 40°, E. 160 poles by a white oak and hickory;
thence N. 20°, E. 34 poles between two white oak saplings; thence N.
40°, E. 183 poles to a white oak; thence N. by East 47 poles to two
Spanish oaks by a deep valley; thence N. 36°, E. 350 poles along the foot

of the mountains ; thence N. N. E. 270 poles ; thence N. 31°, E. 480 poles thence N. 19°, E. 460 poles ; thence N. 60°, E. 374 poles ; thence S. 34° E. 234 poles to the north of a dry meadow ; and lastly. N. 70°, E. 4,190 poles to the red oak and hickory mentioned at the end of the sixth source by the river side ; with all woods, underwoods, springs, marshes, low grounds, feedings. and their due share of all coal, mines and quarries, as well discovered as not discovered, within the bounds and limits aforesaid, and being part of the said quantity of 118,491 acres of land, and the rivers, waters and water-courses therein mentioned, together with the privileges of hunting, hawking, fishing, fowling, and all other profits, commodities and hereditaments whatsoever to the same or any part thereof belonging or in any wise appertaining : To have and to hold, possess and enjoy the said part or parcel of land, and all other the above granted premises, and every part thereof, with their and every of their appurtenances, unto the said William Beverley, Sir John Randolph, Richard Randolph, and John Robinson, to their heirs and assigns forever, to the only use and behoof them, the said William Beverley, Sir John Randolph, Richard Randolph, and John Robinson, their heirs and assigns forever ; to be held of us, our heirs and successors, as of our Manor of East Greenwich, in the county of Stout, in free and common soccage, and not in villenage, or by Knight's service ; they passing and paying unto us, our heirs and successors, for every fifty acres of land, and so proportionately for a lesser or greater quantity than fifty acres, the fee rent of one shilling yearly, to be paid upon the feast of St. Michael, the archangel ; and also cultivating and improving three acres, part of every fifty of the tract above mentioned, within three years after the date of these presents : Provided always, That if three years of the said free rent shall be in arrear and unpaid, or if the said Wm. Beverley, Sir John Randolph, Richard Randolph and John Robinson, their heirs and assigns, do not, within the space of three years next ensuing after the date of these presents, cultivate and improve three acres, part of every fifty of the tract above mentioned, upon the estate hereby granted, shall cease and be utterly determined, and thereafter it shall and may be lawful to and for us, our heirs and successors, to grant the same lands and premises, with the appurtenances, to such other person or persons as we, our heirs and successors, shall think fit.

In witness whereof, we have caused these, our letters patent, to be made. Witness, our trusty and well-beloved William Gooch, Esq., our Lieutenant Governor, and Commander-in-Chief of our Colony and Dominion of Virginia, at Williamsburg, under the seal of our said colony, the 6th day of September, 1736, in the fourth year of our reign.

WILLIAM GOOCH.

The tract thus conveyed extended across the Shenandoah Valley, and the southern portion included the present site of Staunton. Public attention was attracted by this and similar grants of various tracts of fertile lands at nominal prices, and the basest motives of personal gain were attributed to the parties interested, not excepting the Governor, who, with the grantees, was denounced in unmeasured terms.

The grant for Beverley Manor had no sooner been issued than the grantees sought industriously to attract immigrants from the northern colonies and from Europe. Advertisements, setting forth the advantages of the country, were conspicuously displayed in Alexandria, Philadelphia, and other seaports, and they were sent to Europe by settlers who wished to draw their friends after them.

In this work they were aided by an Englishman by the name of Benjamin Burden, or Borden, who was settled in trade in New Jersey, but who frequently visited Eastern Virginia, and during these visits had ingratiated himself with the Lieutenant-Governor. Burden came to America as the agent of Lord Fairfax, and while in Williamsburg formed the acquaintance of John Lewis, who was on a visit to the city. Lewis was pleased with the social qualities and keen judgment of the enterprising agent, and invited him to Bellefonte. Burden accepted, and spent some months under the hospitable roof of the Founder. He was delighted with the manners and customs of the settlers; with the beauty and fertility of the country, and with the comparative leisure enjoyed by the people—a leisure devoted to hunting, fishing, and rural sports. While at Bellefonte, he shot over the country with the Founder's sons, Thomas, Andrew and William Lewis. During one of their excursions they captured a buffalo calf, which Burden took on his return to Williamsburg and presented to the Governor. The General was so much gratified at this and other civilities on the part of Burden, that he directed a patent to be made out, authorizing Burden to locate 500,000 acres of land on the Sherando (Shenandoah) or James Rivers, west of the Blue Ridge. This large grant extended from the southern line of Beverley Manor, and embraced the whole upper part of Augusta and Rockbridge. It was surveyed by Capt. Jno. McDowell, who, some years later, in December, 1743, fell into an ambush while on this land, near the junction of North and James rivers, and was killed by Shawnee Indians. Burden's grant was upon the sole condition that he would settle, within ten years, one hundred families upon the said land. Burden immediately returned to England, and in 1737, returned with the required number of families, among whom were the McDowells, Crawfords, McClures, Alexanders, Wallaces, Moores, Mathews, and others, who became the founders of some of Virginia's distinguished families.

Neither Burden nor the proprietors of Beverley Manor relaxed their efforts to secure emigrants, and the population increased with such rapidity, as we have seen, that it resulted in the establishment of the county of Augusta the following year. Other causes were at work to hasten the settlement of the country about Staunton. Lord Fairfax held, under patent from James II, all that part of Virginia known as the Northern Neck. Under this grant, Fairfax claimed for the western boundary of his territory a line from the head springs of the Rappahannock, supposed to rise in the Blue Ridge, and the head springs of the Potomac, supposed to rise in the Alleghanies. This claim embraced the lower end of the Shenandoah Valley, now composed of the counties of Jefferson, Berkeley, Morgan, Hampshire, Frederick, Clarke, Warren, Page, Shenandoah and Hardy.

His Lordship's claim was neither admitted in Virginia nor in England, and the colonial government continued to issue warrants to enterprising men, for surveying and appropriating extensive tracts west of the Blue Ridge, on condition of permanent settlements being made. Under these grants, settlements were made on the lands claimed by Fairfax, and extended quickly as far south as Linvel Creek, in Rockingham county, which was in Beverley Manor.

Disputes arose between Fairfax and these settlers, and expensive law suits ensued. This state of things alarmed many immigrants, and in hopes of greater security, they passed south, beyond the limits of Fairfax's claim, and settled in Beverley Manor and to the south of it. The upper Valley was, for these reasons, more rapidly occupied by the Europeans than the lower. Augusta, being thus benefited, made exceptionable progress in both population and wealth, which brought about her organization as a county at the early period of 1745. In the general work of inviting population to the country west of the mountains, the grantees were aided by the whole weight and authority of the government. The Legislature passed an act at the session of 1752 to encourage persons to settle on the waters of the Mississippi, in Augusta, " as well His Majesty's natural born subjects, as foreign Protestants, willing to import themselves and their families and effects, as the settling of that part of the country will add to the strength and security of the colony in general, and be a means of augmenting His Majesty's revenue of quit rents;" and it was enacted that said settlers should be exempt from taxes for the term of ten years.

At this period there existed, as for some time previously in the colony, a regular militia system, rendered necessary by Indian wars, which occurred, more or less, along the entire frontier, from New Hampshire to Georgia, from 1690 to 1794. As from this period, 1752, John Lewis, the Founder, is uniformly styled Colonel, it cannot be doubted that he was about this time commissioned Colonel, or chief officer of the militia. Under this commission, it became the duty of the Colonel to list all free male persons above the age of twenty-one, within the county, under such captains as the Colonel should think fit to appoint. By this act, public officers in the civil service were exempt from duty in the militia, and " any of the people commonly called Quakers." That war was near, and Indian incursions were apprehended, is evident from their acts, requiring the officers and men to be thoroughly armed and accoutred, and every militia man to keep at his house at all times one pound of gunpowder and four of ball. He was also required, when called out, to bring the same into the field with him. These arms, accoutrements, &c., were exempt from seizure and distress. The Colonel was further empowered to require all militia men " to go armed to their respective parish churches." A court-martial was held after every general muster, composed of the field-officers and captains, for trying delinquents, of which the following officers were to be members: the Colonel of the county, the Lieutenant-colonel, and the Major. The militia was regularly trained, and in September of each year was assembled for a general muster or battalion drill. A similar militia system existed in all the colonies, from Massachusetts to Georgia, and by it were trained and formed for service the future Washingtons, Lewises, Lees, Putnams, Waynes, Moultries, Greenes, and Gateses.

As much of our present civilization and progress is due to the pious men who first preached the Gospel in the wilderness, we shall give in the next succeeding chapter a brief account of the Presbyterian Church and other religious sects, which preceded the Established Church in the Valley.

MARY GREENLEE, THE SO-CALLED WITCH—HER DEPOSITION IN THE BURDEN CASE.

Mary McDowell, who married James Greenlee, was the daughter of Ephraim McDowell, one of the early settlers on Burden's grant, and a great aunt of the late Gov. James McDowell, of Rockbridge. She was a woman of more than ordinary brightness and vivacity of intellect, but many aberrations of mind and eccentricities of character and conduct. Early disappointment in a love affair heightened her natural peculiarities, and these, with her superior abilities and her independence, caused her neighbors to regard her as a witch. Nothing in those days was too wild and remote from the reality of things, not to meet with an eager welcome, at least, from many. She was, no doubt, as were all witches, thought to have signed in her own blood a contract with the devil, to abjure the Christian religion and all reverence for the true God; that she would steadily refuse to listen to any one who should desire to convert her or convince her of the error of her ways and lead her to repentance. Many of our ancestors, no doubt, believed this contract was duplicated, to prevent mistakes, and that while the Prince of Darkness retained one copy, the other was in possession of Mrs. Greenlee, and often consulted by her. Such, notoriously, were the supposed conditions and custody of these compacts with Satan. On one occasion, at a "quilting party" at her own house, and when hospitably pressing one of the ladies to eat more, she said gaily, " *The mare that does double work should be best fed.*" The rash ignorance of the party construed this to mean that she herself was a witch, and this woman the mare she rode in her nightly incursions to the consecrated haunts of diabolical intercourse. Her crimes, and many were attributed to her, were said to have proceeded from malignity and resentment, and she was supposed to go forth at night into the open air, and there, amidst darkness and the storm, to curse her victims and pursue her unholy incantations. No wonder the more superstitious of her neighbors shrank from her with holy horror, poured out curses upon her from the bottom of their hearts. In a somewhat mysterious ay, some of the stock of Mr.

Craig, an inhabitant of the Triple Forks, disappeared, and the loss was attributed to Mrs. Greenlee, for witches were understood to have the power of destroying life, without the necessity of approaching the person or beast whose life was to be taken.   One method was by exposing an image of wax to the action of the fire, while in proportion as the image wasted away, the life of the individual, who was the object contrived against, was undermined and destroyed. Another, was by incantations and spells. Either of these was styled " compassing, or imagining the death." Possessed of such subtle and dangerous power, and indulging in such practices, in the opinion of her neighbors, one can readily understand the indignation and abhorrence with which she must have been regarded.

From so much of the story of Mrs. Greenlee as is preserved, it is probable her vanity was flattered at the terror she inspired in her simple neighbors, and that she was greatly amused at the fright she caused these rustics.   Possibly, in the end, she deluded herself, and began to think her imprecations had a real effect; that her curses killed—provided, always, that she indulged in any, which is open to doubt.

Mary Greenlee inherited not only the hard intelligence, but the pluck, of her Covenanter stock ; was the kinswoman of the Founder, surrounded by a powerful family, and indulged few fears of coming to the ordeal of fire and water.   In that superstitious age, however, to pursue, at the expense of her ignorant neighbors, a mysterious conduct might be likened to whetting the knife that was to take her life—digging her own grave.   That she escaped trial under the ancient laws of Virginia is, in view of all the facts, surprising.   Rather would we have expected to hear that she had been seized by the hair of the head, or nape of the neck, and drawn before a judge.   The belief in witchcraft of our ancestors was sincere, and this is the less to be wondered at when we consider that these superstitions are cropping up in the civilized life of the present day in "spirit manifestations."   The belief, however, in these matters is now confined to a class who may be, not inappropriately, styled "cranks."

Let us rejoice that light has broken in upon us, and that amidst the inevitable ills of this life we are no longer harassed, like our forefathers, with imaginary terrors and haunted by frightful images.

In the Burden case, Mrs. Greenlee underwent, in 1806, a long examination, testing her temper and memory.   In the midst of the examination the question was put to her, "How old are you ?"   She tartly replied, " Ninety-five the 17th of this instant; and why do you ask me my age ? Do you think I am in my dotage ?"   Her deposition, which follows, cannot fail to be read with interest.   It casts much light upon our early days, supplies valuable information as to the early settlers, their manners and customs, and has not inaptly been styled the corner-stone of our county history.

DEPOSITION OF MRS. JAMES GREENLEE, TAKEN NOVEMBER 10, 1806, IN
THE SUIT OF JOSEPH BURDEN, PLAINTIFF, VS. ALEX. CUETON AND
OTHERS, DEFENDANTS.

Mrs. Greenlee, being sworn, deposeth and saith:

That she, with her husband, James Greenlee, settled on Burden's large
grant, as near as she could recollect, in the Fall of the year 1737. * * *
That shortly before her settlement on said grant, she, together with her
husband, her father, Ephraim McDowell, then a very aged man, and her
brother, John McDowell, were on their way to Beverley Manor, and were
advanced as far as Lewis'es creek, intending to stop on South river, having, at that time, never heard of Burden's tract. That she remembers of
her brother, James, having, the Spring before, gone into said Manor and
raised a crop of corn on South river, about Turks, near what was called
Wood's Gap. That about the time they were striking up their camp in
the evening, Benj. Burden, the elder, came to their camp and proposed
staying all night. In the course of conversation, said Burden informed
them he had about 10,000 acres of land on the waters of James river, or
the forks, if he could ever find it, and proposed giving 1,000 acres to any
one who would conduct him to it. When a light was made, he produced
two papers, and satisfied the company of his rights. The deponent's
brother, John McDowell, then informed him, said Burden, he would conduct him to the forks of James river for 1,000 acres; showed said Burden
his surveying instruments, &c., and finally it was agreed that said McDowell should conduct him to the grant, and she thinks a memorandum of the
agreement was then made in writing. They went on from thence to the
house of John Lewis, in Beverley Manor, near where Staunton now stands,
who was a relation of deponent's father. They remained with him a few
days, and there, she understood, further writings were entered into, and it
was finally agreed they should all settle in Burden's tract. That said John
McDowell was to have 1,000 acres for conducting them there, agreeable
to the writing entered into, and that the settlers were, moreover, to have
100 acres for every cabin they should build, even if they built forty cabins, and that they might purchase any quantity adjoining at 50 shillings
per hundred acres. The deponent understood that said Burden was interested in these cabin rights, as they were called, for that any cabin
saved him 1,000 acres of land. These cabin rights were afterwards
counted, as deponent understood, and an account returned to the government, then held at Williamsburg, and she has heard, about that time,
many tests of the manner in which one person, by going from cabin to
cabin, was counted, and stood for several settlements.

She recollects, particularly, of hearing of a serving girl of one James
Bell, named Millhollen, who dressed herself in men's cloaths and saved
several cabin rights, perhaps five or six, calling herself Millhollen, but
varying the Christian name. These conversations were current in that
day. She knows nothing of the fact but from information. She understood that it was immaterial where the cabins were built; that they were
to entitle the builder to 100 acres as aforesaid, whenever he chose to lay it
off, and that he had a right to purchase, at 50 shillings as aforesaid, any
larger quantity. One John Patterson was employed to count the cabins
rights, as she understood. He was accustomed to mark the letters on his
hat with chalk, as she has been informed, and afterwards deliver the account to her brother, John McDowell, and remembers to have heard that

her brother had expressed his surprise at so many people by the name of
Millhollen being settled on the land, but which was afterwards explained
by the circumstance of the servant girl above mentioned, and was a subject of general mirth in the settlement. She does not know whether this
plan of saving several cabin rights by one person appearing at different
cabins, was suggested by Burden, the elder, or not. She understood
that every person saving a cabin right got 160 acres for each right so
saved, as he, Burden, was to have a cabin for every 1,000 acres. When
the party with which she travelled, as aforesaid, came, as they supposed,
into the grant, they stopped at a spring, near where David Steele now
lives, and struck their camp, her brother and said Burden having gone
down said branch until they were satisfied it was one of the waters of
James river. The balance of the party remained at that spring until her
brother John and said Borden, as she understood, went down to the forks
formed by the waters of the South and North river, and, having taken a
course through the country, returned to said camp. They then went on
to the place called the Red House, where her brother, John, built a cabin
and settled where James McDowell now lives. The first cabin her husband built was by a spring, near where Andrew Scott now lives, but when
deponent went to see it, she did not like the situation, and they then built
and settled at the place called Browns. They sold this after some short
time, and purchased the land on which her brother, James, had made an improvement, now called Templetons, and where she resided until about the
year 1780, being within sight of where her father, then near a hundred years
of age, resided. This was the first party of white people that ever settled on
the said grant. The said Burden, the elder, remained on the grant from
that time, as well as she can recollect, for perhaps two years and more,
obtaining settlers, and she believes there were more than a hundred settlers before he left them. She believes he was in the grant the whole time
from his first coming up until he left it before his death, but how long before his death he left it, she does not know. He resided some time with
a Mrs. Hunter, whose daughter afterwards married one Greene, and to
whom, she understood, he gave the tract whereon they lived. When the
said Borden left the grant, she understood he left his papers with her
brother, John McDowell, to whose house a great many people resorted, as
she understood, to see about lands, but what authority her brother had to
sell, or whether he made sales or not, she does not know. Her brother,
John, was killed about Xmas before her son, Samuel, her first son of that
name, was born. He was born, as appears by the register of his birth in
the Bible, about April, 1743. The date of this register is partly obliterated,
in the last figure, but from the date of the birth of the preceding and
subsequent child it must have been, as she believes, in 1743, that said
Samuel was born.

Young Benj. Burden came into the grant before her brother's death.
She recollects this from the circumstance of his being then in ordinary
plight, and such that he did not seem much respected by her brother's
wife, and when she afterwards married him she could not but reflect on the
change of circumstances. She understood that he was altogether illiter-
ate. She said Benjamin, junior, lived with her brother, John, whilst in the
grant, but returned to his father's before the death of said John, and after
his father's death returned, fully empowered by his father's will to complete titles and sell lands, and then married the widow of her said brother,
and continued to live at the place where her said brother settled as afore-

said, until his death. This place, now called the Red House place, is about three-quarters of a mile from Templetons, where the deponent resided as above.

Joseph Burden, (a son of old Ben. Burden, the grantee,) had resided at his brother, Benjamin's, some years before his, (Benjamin's) death; had gone to school, and was here at his death; had the small-pox about the time of her brother's death, some time after which (deponent does not recollect precisely, but believes it was not long,) he went away, not being very well liked, as she understood, and not made very welcome; was then but a lad about 18 or 19, as well as she can recollect from his appearance. This deponent recollects John Hart, who had removed to Beverley Manor some short time before the removal of this deponent and her friend, as above stated, but she cannot say whether he surveyed for the said Benjamin or not; she understood he was a surveyor. The people who first settled and purchased did not always have their lands surveyed at the time of the purchase; as she understood, some had their lands surveyed and some had not, but when it was not surveyed, they described it by general boundaries. Beatty was the first surveyor whom she knows that surveyed in the grant. The said Borden had been at Williamsburg, and some one, perhaps the Governor's son-in-law, by name Needler, and his other partners, had in a frolic given him their interest in said grant. She understood there were four of them—the Governor, Gooch, his said son-in-law, and two others whose names she does not recollect, who were interested in the order of Council for said land, and that Burden got it from them, as above; this was his information. She well recollects that her brother, John, assisted one Wood to make the survey of said large grant after they removed to it, as aforesaid, it being at the time of their removal, as aforesaid, held by order of Council, as she understood. The said Woods and her brother made the survey, she believes, after the cabin rights were taken in, as above stated. Many people came up, and many settlements and cabins were made immediately after their settling on the tract, as aforesaid.

Being interrogated as to the value of the lands remaining unsold by Ben. Burden, she stated that one Harden, who, she understood, was an executor, and who was in this country after the death of young Ben. Burden, (which occurred from small-pox in 1753,) and after John Bowyer had married the widow, and who, she understood, was settling Burden's business—but she does not know by what authority—she recollects that said Harden offered to her brother, James, the unsold lands for a bottle of wine, if he would clear him of the quit rents. She also recollects that her said brother consulted with her father about the proposition, who advised him to have nothing to do with it, for it would probably run him into jail. This, she thinks, was shortly after Bowyer's marriage. She does not know whether Benj. Burden, jr., was distressed on account of the quit rents or not, but recollects that shortly before his death, Col. Patton was at her house; a horse of said Burden broke out and came there, which said Patton wished to have caught, that he might take him for some claims against said Burden, but she did not hear what. She had, however, said horse sent home, fearing that as there had been some misunderstanding between deponent's husband and said Burden about this land, he might think they had aided in said seizure. The deponent further states that her husband purchased 1,000 acres of land of old Burden at an early day for fifty shillings per hundred, which she understood he had located on the Turkey Hill, as it is called. After the death of old Burden, his son, Benjamin, disputed giving a deed for the whole quantity there, alleging it was all valuable land, and afterwards, for the sake of peace, it was agreed that a part should be taken there—a part joining Robert Cutton, which was sold to one Buchanan, and a part near John Davidson. This arrangement was made at the time Harden was present, as aforesaid, who seemed willing to give the land, and advised this deponent, whose husband was then abroad, to agree to take it at those places, which she did. All the land purchased by her husband was purchased from old Burden; indeed, he had purchased this 1,000 acres before they came to the tract, at Lewis', as before stated, provided he liked the land when he saw it, which he did.

· The deponent being asked what she knew of the persons named in a mutilated paper purporting to be an account of entries and sales, beginning at " No. 1—McDowell, Jno., to No. 22—Moore, Andrew," on the first side, where the papers appeared to be torn off; beginning on the other side at " No. 42—Martin, Robt., and ending at No. 62, at Brown, Robt.," and whether those persons were settled in the grant at an early day or owned lands in it ?

Answered—That she knew a number of the persons therein named. Many of them lived in Beverley Manor, and others in the Calf Pasture, and elsewhere, but she did not know many of them to have lands in Burden's tract. The McDowells and her husband she had before spoken of. She also knew John Moore, who settled at an early day where Charles Campbell now lives; Andrew Moore, who settled where his grandson, Wm. Moore, now lives. Wm. McCausland also lived in the grant, as did Wm. Sawyers and Robt. Campbell, Sam'l Woods, John Mathews, Richard Woods, John Hays, Chas. Hays, his son, Sam'l Walker, &c., all of whom settled in the grant at an early day.

The deponent being interrogated if she knew Alex. Miller, and if he was an early settler?

Answered—That she did know said Miller. He was the first blacksmith that settled on the tract. She recollects of his shoeing old Burden's horse, and understood he purchased land of said Burden. He lived on land adjoining one John McCroskey's land, who also purchased his land from old Burden. He also joined the plantation, now Stewart's millplace, as she believes, whereon one Taylor, who, she believes, married Elizabeth Paxton, formerly lived. She recollects being at the burial of said Taylor, who was killed by the falling of a tree not long after his marriage. Said Miller's land, she has understood, has been in possession of people of the name of Teeford since the said Millers removed. The deponent recollects one McMullen, who resided some distance above the place where Robt. Stewart's mill now stands, but up the same branch, and near a spring. Said McMullen was living on said land, and had a daughter married there when this deponent's daughter, Mary, was a sucking babe. She recollects this from having gone to the wedding when a daughter of said McMullen was married, and having left her child at home. Her daughter, Mary, was born, as appears from the register of her birth, in May, 1745. Humphrey's Cabins, as they were called, were over the hill, at another spring, not far from where said McMullen lived. She knows not from whom McMullen purchased, but rather thinks her brother, James McDowell, gave him a piece of land there for teaching school. There was no mill where Stewart's mill now is, in the lifetime of Ben. Burden, jr. John Hays' mill was the first mill in the grant, and built very early after the settlement.

The deponent said the people paid no quit rents for two years from the time the grant was first settled. She understood this exemption was granted by the Governor at the instance of one Anderson, a preacher. When they had to pay quit rents, they raised money by sending butter to New Castle, to Williamsburg, and other markets below, and got also in return their salt, iron, &c.

Being asked whether Joseph Burden was frequently in this country after the death of young Ben. Burden, she answered that he was frequently in this country some time after the death of said Benjamin. He called at her house, inquiring for a horse, and she thought she knew his name, and afterwards heard he lodged in the neighborhood, at one Wm. Campbell's. She saw him again at her house about twelve or fifteen years ago. He made some enquiries of her about her husband's estate or something of that kind. She does not recollect the particulars, but she had very little conversation with him. She also heard of his being through this country some little time before this, but does not recollect how long, nor did she see him.

Question by the defendant's agent—Did not many persons, from time to time, in the lifetime of old Burden, settle in the grant, under an expectation of getting the lands at the usual price, and without first contracting with said Burden?

Answer—I believe they did. I think many settled before they had an opportunity of seeing Burden, and Burden would frequently direct them to deponent's husband. to shew them the land, as they said.

Do you not believe that the first deeds were made for the cabin rights?

Answer—I suppose the cabin right, with such land as the settler had purchased, would be deeded together, and perhaps these were the first made.

Did Ben. Burden, jr., appear, when he first entered on the affairs of the estate, to be disposed to do justice to the devisees?

Answer—I thought he did. He appeared to be a good man. She understood he was the heir-at-law, and did not hear of the sisters' claims, except to five thousand acres, which she understood had been assigned to them on Catawba, where the land was good.

Did he ever leave this country and go to Jersey, after he came up and got married?

Answer—No, I believe he did not. I am pretty confident he did not.

Did you know of Archibald Alexander and Magdalen Bowyer selling lands?

Answer—I did not know they were executors, and had a right to sell. I understood John Bowyer sold a great deal and gave away a great deal. Alexander was as respectable a man as any I knew. Bowyer, she understood, claimed what Ben. Burden claimed, though she had no conversation with him about his claim.

Being asked whether Alexander paid Burden any money on account of the estate?

Answered—She never heard that he had, and from her intimacy with the wife of said Bowyer, she believes she would have heard of it, had it taken place.

Question by same—When Burden produced his right to the land, as you have stated. were you not satisfied, and did not the company appear satisfied, that the right was completely in him?

Answer—Yes, the papers appeared perfectly satisfactory.

Did you not understand that your brother, James McDowell, built a cabin and purchased the land where Thos. Taylor, above mentioned, resided?

Answer—My brother, James, purchased a considerable tract, perhaps four or five hundred acres, either at or where Stewart's mill now stands. It run, as she understood, on a large hill, but whether in one or two tracts, she knows not. This tract, she understood, he sold to some person, but does not know who. She does not know whether he had it surveyed or not, but supposes it was merely designated by general boundaries. She thinks if she was on the land, she could point out the tree whereon his name was cut, if it is yet standing. It stood near a deep hole in the creek. Knows not how he acquired it, but understood he had built a cabin on it and saved a cabin right, but never saw the cabin, nor does she know where it stood, but the land was called his very shortly after they went to the grant, and in the lifetime of old Burden.

Sworn before us, 10th November, 1806.

JOSEPH WALKER,
J. GRIGSBY.

Burden succeeded in procuring the erection of ninety-two cabins within two years, and received his patent from the Governor, dated Nov. 8, 1759. He died in 1742, and his will is on record in Frederick county.

ORIGINAL DOCUMENTS, ETC.

Section II.—Deed for 200,000 acres of land from the Chiefs of the Six United Nations to G. Croghan, November 9th, 1768.

To all people to whom these presents shall come—Greeting : Know ye, that we, Abraham, a Mohawk chief; Sennghors, an Oneida chief; Chenaugheata, an Onondaga chief; Tagaaia, a Cayuga chief, and Gaustrax, a Seneca chief, chiefs and sachems of the Six United Nations, and being and effectually representing all the tribes of the Six United Nations, send greeting. Whereas, Johonerissa Scaroyadia, Cosswentanica, chiefs or sachems of the said Six United Nations, did, by their deed duly executed, bearing date the 2nd day of August, 1749, for and in consideration of the following goods and merchandise being paid and delivered to them at a full council of the Six United Nations, Delawares and Shawanese, held at Logstown, on the river Ohio, on the 2nd of August, 1749, that is to say : 240 strouds*, 400 Duffield blankets, 460 pair of half thick stockings, 200 shirts, 20 pieces of calico, 20 pieces of callimancoe, 20 pieces of embossed serge, fifty pounds of vermillion†, 50 gross of gartering, 50 pieces of ribbon, 50 dozen of knives, 500 pounds of gunpowder, 1,000 of bar lead, 3,000 gun flints, 50 pounds of brass kettles, 400 pounds of thread, 1,000 needles, ten dozen jews-harps, 20 dozen tobacco tongs, and 100 pounds of tobacco : Grant and sell unto George Croghan, of the Province of Pennsylvania. Esquire, in fee, a certain tract or parcel of land, situate, lying and being on the southernly side of the river Monongehela : Beginning at the mouth of a run nearly opposite to Turtle creek, and then down

---

*Strouding is a coarse cloth.
†The Indian kept the record of his wounds by shining marks of vermillion on his skin.

the river Monongehela to its junction with the river Ohio, computed to be ten miles; then running down the eastern bank and sides of and unto the said river Ohio to where Raccoon creek empties itself into the said river; thence up the said creek ten miles, and from thence on a straight or direct line to the place of beginning on the aforesaid river Monongehela, containing, by estimation, one hundred thousand acres of land, be the same more or less. And, whereas, the said Johonerissa Scaroyadia and Coswentanica, chiefs or sachems, as aforesaid, for the consideration hereinafter mentioned to them in full council, as aforesaid, paid and delivered, that is to say: 140 strouds, 240 Duffield blankets, 275 pair of half thick stockings, 120 shirts, 12 pieces of calico, 12 pieces of callimancoe, 12 pieces of embossed serge, 30 pounds of vermillion, 12 gross of gartering, 30 pieces of ribbon, 30 dozen knives, 300 pounds of gunpowder, 600 of bar lead, 1,000 gun flints, 30 pounds of brass kettles, 4 pounds of thread, 500 needles, six dozen of jews-harps, six dozen tobacco tongs, and 50 pounds of tobacco, did, by one other deed, bearing date the same day and year last aforesaid, grant, bargain and sell unto the said George Croghan, in fee, one other tract or parcel of land, situate, lying and being on the river Yoxhiogeni, including the Indian village called the Seurchly, old town; the same tract or parcel of land containing 15 miles in length, on the said river, and ten miles in breadth, and including the lands on both sides of the said river Yoxhiogeni, which, 15 miles in length and ten miles in breadth, he, the said George Croghan, has liberty to locate either upon or down the said Yoxhiogeni, but nevertheless in such manner so as to include and locate the said Indian village and land called the Seurchly, old town, which said tract or parcel of land contains, by estimation, 60,000 acres, be the same more or less.

And, whereas, the said Johonerissa Scaroyadia and Cosswentanica did, by one other deed, bearing date the day and year last aforesaid, for the consideration herein mentioned to them in full council, paid and delivered, as aforesaid, that is to say, 96 strouds, 160 Duffield blankets, 184 pair of half thick stockings, 80 shirts, 8 pieces of calico, 8 pieces of embossed serge, 20 pounds of vermillion, 20 gross of gartering, 20 pieces of ribbon, 20 dozen of knives, 200 pounds of gunpowder, 400 of bar lead, 1,000 gun flints, 20 pounds of brass kettle, two pounds of thread, 500 needles, four dozen jews-harps, four dozen tobacco tongs, 50 pounds of tobacco, Grant, bargain and sell unto the said George Croghan, in fee, one other tract or parcel of land, situate, lying and being, and Beginning on the east side of the river Ohio, to the northward of an old Indian village, called Shanopinstown, at the mouth of a run called the two mile run; then up the said two mile run where it interlocks with the heads of the two mile springs, which empties into the river Monongehela; then down the said two mile spring to the several courses thereof unto the sd. Monongehela; then up the said river Monongehela to where Turtle creek empties itself into the same river; then up the said Turtle creek to the first forks thereof; then up the north or northerly branch of the said creek to the head of the same; thence a north or northerly course until it strikes Plum creek; then down said Plum creek until it empties itself into the river Ohio, and then down the said river Ohio to the place of beginning, where, as aforesaid, the two mile run discharges itself into the said river Ohio; containing, by estimation, 40,000 acres, be the same more or less, which said several grants, bargains and sales, duly made and executed, by the last-mentioned chiefs

or sachems, in pursuance of certain powers and authorities delegated to
and vested in them for the purpose aforesaid by the chiefs or sachems of
the Onondaga Council, in full council assembled; and, whereas, the said
first-mentioned chiefs or sachems of the Six United Nations, parties to
these presents, are not only truly and sensible and convinced that the said
George Croghan hath faithfully and justly paid and delivered unto Johonerissa, Scaroyadia and Cosswentanica, chiefs or sachems, as aforesaid, all
and several the goods and merchandize herein particularly recited and
mentioned, but of the great justice and integrity of the said George Croghan, used and reserved by him towards the said Six Nations and their
allies in all his public and private conduct and transactions, wherein they
have been concerned: Now, know ye, therefore, that we, the said chiefs or
sachems of the Six United Nations, in full council assembled, at Fort
Stanwix, for and in consideration of the sum of five shillings to them in
hand paid, by the said George Croghan, the receipt whereof they do
hereby acknowledge, and for and in consideration of the aforesaid goods
and merchandise paid and delivered by him unto Johonerissa, Scaroyadia, Cosswentanica, chiefs as aforesaid, have granted, bargained, sold and
aliened, released, enfeoffed, ratified and fully confirmed, and by these presents do grant, bargain, sell, alien, release, enfeoffe, ratify and fully confirm
as to his Most Sacred Majesty George III, King of Great Britain, France
and Ireland, Defender of the Faith, &c., his heirs and successors, for the
use, benefit and behoof of the said George Croghan, his heirs and assigns,
all those, the above described or mentioned tracts or parcels of land,
granted, or intended to be granted, by the said several recited deeds as
aforesaid, and also all mines, mineral ores, trees, woods, underwoods, waters, and water-courses, profits, commodities, advantages, rights, liberties,
privileges, hereditaments and appurtenances whatsoever the said several
tracts or parcels of land belonging, or any way appertaining; and also the
reversion and reversions, remainder and remainders, rents, issues and
profits thereof, and of every part or parcel thereof, and all the estate right,
title, interest, use, property, possessions, claim and demand of them, the
said Abraham, Sennghors, Sagnarisera, Chenaugheata, Tagaaia, Gaustrax,
chiefs or sachems aforesaid, and of all and every other person and persons
whatsoever, for belonging to said nations of, into and out of the premises,
and every part and parcel thereof, to have and to hold the said several
tracts and parcels of land, and all and singular the said granted or bargained premises, with the appurtenances, unto his said Majesty, his heirs
and successors, to and for the only use, benefit and behoof of the said
George Croghan, his heirs and assigns forever; and the said Abraham,
Sennghors, Sagnarisera, Chenaugheata, Tagaaia and Gaustrax, for themselves and for the Six Nations, and all and every other nation and nations,
tributaries and dependants on the said Six United Nations, and their and
every of their posterity, the said several tracts of land and premises, and
every part thereof, against them, the said Abraham, Sennghors, Sagnarisera, Chenaugheata, Tagaaia and Gaustrax, and against the said Six
United Nations, and their tributaries and dependants, and all and every of
their posteritys, unto his said Majesty, his heirs and successors, to and for
the only use, benefit and behoof of the said George Croghan, his heirs
and assigns, shall and will warrant and forever defend, by these presents;
Provided, always, nevertheless, and it is the true intent and meaning of
these presents, and the said Abraham, Sennghors, Sagnarisera, Chenaugheata, Tagaaia and Gaustrax, do hereby covenant and agree to and with

his said Majesty and his heirs and successors, to and for the only use, benefit and behoof of the said George Croghan his heirs and assigns, that if any or all of the said several tracts of land, or any part thereof, shall hereafter be found to be within the bounds and limits of a certain grant, bearing date the 4th March, 1681, made by Charles II, King of Great Britain, &c., to William Penn, esq., for the tract of country called and known by the name of Pennsylvania, that then, and in such case, his said Majesty, his heirs and successors, to and for the only use, benefit and behoof of the said George Croghan, his heirs and assigns, shall be permitted and shall have and enjoy full right, power and authority to survey and locate the said several quantities of 100,000 acres, 60,000 and 40,000 acres of land, be the same more or less, as contained within the limits and bounds of the said several and respective tracts or parcels of land mentioned and described as aforesaid, in such quantities and in such parts and places of, in and within the lessioner grant of land or territory, which shall be ceded and granted at the conference aforesaid, to the said King of Great Britain by the chiefs or sachems of the said Six United Nations, anything herein contained to the contrary thereof in any wise notwithstanding.

In witness whereof the said chiefs and sachems, in behalf of ourselves, respectively, and in behalf of the whole Six United Nations aforesaid, have hereunto set our hands and seals, in the presence of the persons subscribing as witnesses, hereunto at a Congress held at Fort Stanwix, aforesaid, this, the 4th day of November, in the year 9th of his Majesty's reign, and in the year of our Lord 1768.

ABRAHAM, or TYAHANESERA, a chief of the Mohawks.   The mark [The Steel] (L. s.) of his nation.

WILLIAM, or SENNGHORS, a chief of the Oneidas.   The mark [The Stone] (L. s.) of his nation.

HENDRICK or SAGNARISERA, the chief of the Tuscaroras.   The mark [The Cross] (L. s.) of his nation.

BURT or CHENAUGHEATA, a chief of the Onondagas.   The mark [The Mountain] (L. s.) of his nation.

TAGAAIA, a chief of the Cayugas.   The mark [The Pipe] (L. s.) of his nation.

GAUSTRAX, a chief of the Senecas.   The mark [The High Hill.] (L. s.) of his nation.

Sealed and delivered in the presence of us.

The word "Croghan"* being first written on Rasures eleven times, and the words "and, or down tract," being first interlined.

---

*George Croghan was sub-Commissioner to Sir Wm. Johnson, who was commissioned to treat with the Indians, and met the representatives of more than twenty tribes in a grand council at Niagara, and in August, 1764, concluded a definite treaty at Detroit with them. Croghan accompanied the returning deputies of the Delawares and Shawanese to their homes in the West, and reached Vincennes, Indiana, June 15, 1765, which he describes in his journal as "a village of 80 or 90 French families."

Sealed and delivered in presence of us all, the foregoing interlineations, Rasures and writings on Rasures being first made.

> WM. FRANKLIN, Governor of New Jersey.
> FRE. SMYTH, Chief Justice of New Jersey.
> THOMAS WALKER, Commissioner for Virginia.
> RICHARD PETERS, } of the Council of Pennsylvania.
> JAMES TILGHMAN, }
> JOHN SPINNER, Capt. in the 78th Regiment.
> JOSEPH CHEW, of Connecticut.
> JOHN WEATHERHEAD, of N. Y.
> JOHN WALKER, of Virginia.
> E. FITCH, of Connecticut.
> THOMAS WALKER, JUNIOR, Virginia.
> JOHN BALTER, Interpreter for the Crown.

CHAPTER V.

As the people of the Valley were, considered as a religious community professing Christianity, divided into various sects and denominations, all justifying, explaining, and upholding their respective tenets, however various or contradictory, by an appeal to the same Sacred Writings, we shall, without any remarks as to the propriety or impropriety of any one or the other, give a concise sketch of their external situation, as conducing to general information and a right understanding of the Augusta colony. To observe some order, let us commence with the Presbyterian Church, the first established in Augusta. Brief allusion has been made to its more obvious temporal effects upon the civil characters of its members and the community. Our limits will not admit of an elaborate statement of the causes which led to the emigration of the Scotch-Irish and their settlement in America. Our county was principally settled by these religious refugees who left Ireland after the siege of Londonderry, the entrance of the Prince Orange into London on the escape of James to France, the acceptance of the British throne by William and Mary, and the glorious revolution of 1688. We style this revolution glorious, not only because it aimed at just and worthy ends, but because established without any of those scenes of bloodshed and horror which have so generally been the accompaniments of even beneficial and desirable changes. The highest eulogium that can be pronounced upon the revolution of 1688 is, that it has been England's last; and the last, because, from the midst of servitude, the English people plucked freedom; from anarchy, order; obtained the authority of law, security for property, peace and happiness in their homes, and representative government, as it exists to-day in that country. The Bill of Rights passed by Parliament in 1689, which limits the Royal prerogative, and clearly defines the rights of British subjects, is the only written law respecting the liberties of the British people, except *Magna Charta*.

But we are wandering from our path. These matters cannot be reviewed here, however interesting in themselves, and however intimately connected with the settlement of our Valley. It must suffice to say, that after the siege of Derry, while the Episcopal Church was established in England and the Presbyterian in Scotland, the Irish, by whose bravery and sufferings mainly the Kingdom had been secured to the Prince of Orange, were compelled to pay their tithes to the Established Church, maintain their own ministers, and also suffer other disabilities consequent on an Establishment. And the prospects of the Presbyterians not being improved after Ireland was subdued by William, notwithstanding the passage of the Toleration Act, and favorable reports reaching Ulster from America, many were lured from their homes across the Atlantic. For half a century this emigration continued, and thousands of these poor sufferers found their way to our shores. Early in the eighteenth century they formed congregations in New England, some years previous to 1726 in Pennsylvania, and, as we have seen, came to our Valley in 1732, fixing their residence at Opeckon. Thence Lewis made his way to Bellefonte, and Presbyterian congregations were formed in Augusta by him and his Scotch-Irish neighbors previous to 1740. The Presbyterian Church, thus planted in the Valley, has become almost as much identified with the soil as the deep-rooted trees themselves. From its first seats in Pennsylvania and Western Virginia, it has spread throughout the West and South, becoming the prolific mother of churches in a vast region.

The colonial government, anxious to seat a white population west of the great mountains for the reasons previously mentioned, relaxed its rigor towards the Presbyterians and other Dissenters, and welcomed them, indeed, in 1732, and thereafter, to the upper country of Virginia. From the Scotch and Irish settlements in Pennsylvania emigrants began to pour into the Valley, as soon as the more fertile lands of Pennsylvania and Maryland were located. They were directed and encouraged to do so principally by Vanmeter, of Frederick, Beverley, of Augusta, and Burden, of Rockbridge. For mutual protection, social intercourse, and religious worship, they came in bodies composed of a number of families. If a more adventurous spirit penetrated deeper than usual into the forest, he was soon followed and surrounded by others. Within five years of Lewis' settlement at Bellefonte, so great was his own desire and that of the people for the ordinances of religion, that they sought to secure the services of a Presbyterian minister. On the 2d of September, 1737, a supplication from

the inhabitants of Beverley Manor was laid before the Presbytery of Donegal, Ireland, requesting supplies. The Presbytery "judged it not expedient, for several reasons, to supply them this Winter, but ordered that
Mr. James Anderson should write an encouraging letter to the people, to
signify that the Presbytery resolves, if it be in their power, to grant this
request next Spring."

In 1738, Mr. Anderson visited Virginia, bearing a letter from the Synod
of Philadelphia to Gov. Gooch. His visit was made on the invitation of
John Caldwell and others, who asked protection in the exercise of their
religious preferences. He was kindly received by Gooch, and visited
Augusta with assurances from him that the protection he sought would be
extended to him, Anderson, and the people west of the mountains. Leaving Williamsburg, Mr. Anderson crossed the Blue Ridge, proceeded to
the house of the Founder, where he remained some time, consulting the
leading Presbyterians of the settlement. The Governor was actuated in
his liberal course as well by a desire to place a barrier between the eastern
settlements and the Indians, as by his high opinion of the inhabitants,
whom he well knew to be enterprising, industrious, and spirited—the best
of citizens in times of peace and soldiers in times of war.

The next probationer who visited Augusta was Mr. Dunlap, of the
Presbytery of New York, who spent three months in the neighborhood of
Staunton in the year 1739. In this year, Mr. Jno. Thompson, of the Presbytery of Donegal, also visited the Valley, spent some time in Augusta,
and was active in promoting the Presbyterian cause in Virginia. Through
his instrumentality, Mr. John Craig was sent to Augusta in 1739 by the
Presbytery of Donegal, and ultimately became pastor of Tinkling Spring
and Augusta churches.

Rev. John Craig was ordained in 1740, and immediately commenced his
ministry at Augusta and Tinkling Spring churches. He was thus the first
Presbyterian minister regularly settled in the colony of Virginia. Uniting
the duties of a teacher with those of a preacher and pastor, he was eminently useful in both capacities. Those who may wish to read the story
of his life can find it in an autobiography which he prepared in his old
age, entitled "A Preacher Preaching To Himself, &c.," and embraced in
Foote's Sketches.

Space will henceforward admit of little more than an enumeration of
the churches and their ministers from their organization to the present
time. Those seeking fuller information may obtain it from Foote's excellent sketches of the Presbyterian Church in Virginia.

The OLD STONE, or Church of Augusta, where Mr. Craig's ministry commenced, was built in 1740. It is situated on the Valley turnpike, about
eight miles north of Staunton, and is standing, at the end of one hundred
and forty years, in perfect preservation. It was the second church built

in the Valley. The first church, or "meeting-house," was erected about 1736, at Opeckon. The old Stone Church was erected during that long period of tranquility which followed the settlement of Augusta, but while the Indians were warring among themselves, but friendly to the whites. Doubtless, the apprehension that the savages might turn their arms against the colonists on some future occasion, led to its being built of stone at a vast labor, in order that it might serve, as it subsequently did, the purposes of fort as well as church. The reader can form an idea of the labor spent upon this venerable edifice when he reflects that there were then no roads on which to transport material, no carts or wagons, few trained horses or oxen, and the population rather pastoral than agricultural. The building of the church, was, indeed, an arduous undertaking, and could never have been accomplished in those days but for the persevering labor of all—men, women, and children; for the women and children took part in the good work, carrying in sacks upon their backs the lime and sand necessary for the building, while the men hewed and transported the stone to the spot, night oftener, than otherwise, finding them at their work, and not putting a stop to it. This sacred building, half church, half fortress, was the strong place of the northern part of the county, as Fort Lewis was of the country east, south, and about Staunton, and to its shelter the women and children betook themselves during the Indian forays which occurred so frequently after 1754. The church was surrounded by an earthen embankment, which gave it greater strength, and traces of this rude military work may still be seen.

Mr. Craig was a man of eminent piety and usefulness, and discharged his duties at Augusta Church until his death, in 1774. The church erected at its expense, in 1798, a monument to his memory. His successors have been Revs. Wm. Wilson, until 1805; Conrad Speece, DD., from 1813 to 1836; Wm. Brown, F. M. Brown, I. I. Handy, DD., and the present pastor, Rev. Alex. Sprunt.

TINKLING SPRING.—In the southern part of the settlement, on the triple forks of the Shenandoah, near the present village of Fishersville, the division of the congregation, known as Tinkling Spring, worshipped. Staunton belonged, in its early days, to this congregation, and the Founder, James Patton, John Preston, and the people of Staunton generally, attended its services. The first building used for worship was a log house, belonging to Preston, and Rev. John Craig preached on alternate Sundays. "The members of this congregation were distinguished," says Foote, "for the part they took in the Indian wars, and furnished some of the leading military men in the border wars; the most famous were of the Lewis family."

Shortly after Beverley's grant, a grant of 100,000 acres was made to John Lewis and his associates, under the name of the "Greenbrier Company." Much of this land was located on the Greenbrier river, a name given to the stream by Col. Lewis. James Patton, another member of the congregation, received a grant for 120,000 acres, which he located in the present county of Montgomery, where he was killed by the Indians in 1753. John Preston, who married a sister of Col. Patton, also belonged to this congregation, though his residence was north of Staunton, on Spring farm, which, in 1882, is owned by the city of Staunton.

After Mr. Craig ceased to be the pastor of Tinkling Spring, Rev. John A. VanLear, the son of an emigrant from Holland, became pastor, and, in 1778, was succeeded by Rev. James Waddell, D. D., and he by Rev. John McCue, D. D., whose ministry extended to September 20th, 1818, when he was killed on his way to church by a fall from his horse.

Mr. McCue has been succeeded at Tinkling Spring by the following: Revs. James Wilson, until 1840; B. M. Smith, D. D.; Robert L. Dabney, D. D., the distinguished author and theologian; C. S. M. See, and Givens B. Strickler, the present pastor.

The Rev. John Blair, during his visit to Virginia, in 1746, formed four congregations, embracing the whole width of the Valley, from a little south of Staunton to some distance south of Lexington. The congregations were those of the "Forks of the James."

Timber Ridge, now in Rockbridge, New Providence, and North Mountain.

Timber Ridge and New Providence alone remain.

In the place of North Mountain there are the two congregations of Bethel and Hebron.

BETHEL church was first built about 1772, principally through the exertions of Col. Doake, a few steps from the site of the present brick church, about ten miles south of Staunton, and about midway between the Greenville and Middlebrook roads, leading from Staunton to Lexington. The first minister was Mr. Charles Cummings, who received a call in 1766, and served till 1772. He was followed by Mr. Archibald Scott, who discharged his duties for over twenty years with great zeal and fidelity, and dying in March, 1799, was followed, after a vacancy of some years, by Rev. William McPheeters, D. D., a native of Augusta, who was educated in Staunton and at Liberty Hall, Rockbridge. He took charge of Bethel in 1805. In 1810, Mr. McPheeters removed to Raleigh, N. C., where he died in 1842. His successors have been: Revs. Chapman, D. D., (we believe), Francis McFarland, D. D., who resigned and went to Philadelphia, when Rev. Alex. B. McCorkle took his place. Mr. McC. resigning, Dr. McFarland was recalled, and died, senior member of the church. He was succeeded by Rev. James Murray, the present pastor, who was Dr. McFarland's colleague for many years.

SHEMERIAH was organized about 1832, principally from the congregation of Bethel. The first minister was Rev. Henry Brown. His successors have been: Rev. E. S. Thomas, Luther Emerson, W. G. Campbell, Harvey Gilmer, I. N. Campbell, and the present minister, Rev. I. H. H. Winfree.

HEBRON CHURCH, which was anciently called "Brown's Meeting-House," is situated about four miles west of Staunton, in the midst of much attractive scenery. The original church, under the name of North Mountain, was organized by Dr. John Blair on his visit to Virginia, in 1746, and within the bounds of that congregation there are now Bethel, Shemeriah, and Hebron. In October, 1746, Rev. Charles Cummings received a call from the congregations belonging to Major Brown's meeting-house, in Augusta. He remained pastor until April, 1776, when the services of Rev. Archibald Scott were secured. He was ordained in 1778, preaching from the words, "God is Love." He was a man of great piety, and one of his sons has written an able and instructive work, entitled, "Genius and Faith; or, Poetry and Religion in Their Mutual Relations." N. Y., 1853. After a vacancy of a few days, in May, 1805, Rev. William Calhoun received a call from Staunton and Brown's meeting-house. In 1826, his pastoral relations with Staunton ceased, and for many years thereafter he gave his attention to Hebron church. Mr. Calhoun, whom the writer, as a boy, had the pleasure to know, was one of the strong men of the Presbyterian church. He published a treatise on Christian baptism, which illustrates well his vigorous intellect. He was succeeded by Rev. Isaac Jones, remarkable as a revivalist. The writer remembers some of his terrific discourses and can endorse the general estimate of them—that they excited rather than instructed his listeners. He was succeeded by a native of Ireland, Rev. Solomon I. Love, who continued in charge until 1858, when his place was filled by Rev. John F. Baker. who, from ill-health, gave up his charge in a few months, and was succeeded by Rev. T. L. Preston, D. D.—a descendant of the original John Preston, who settled in Augusta, 1746—who served from 1861-'65, and is now pastor of the First Presbyterian church of Richmond, Va. Mr. Preston was followed by Rev. D. B. Ewing, and he by Rev. F. H. Gaines, the present pastor. Hebron is identified with the fame of Dr. Alexander, the elder, as the place where he was received under care of the Presbytery as a candidate for the ministry.

The Rev. Mr. Paris, missionary to the Sandwich Islands, and Rev. W. W. Trimble, of Missouri, are among the ministers who have gone out from this congregation.

MOSSY CREEK congregation was originally a part of Augusta church, but about the year 1767, became a separate organization upon the request of John Davis and Mr. Makamie. They were stoutly opposed by Rev. John Craig, who said he could "do all the preaching that was needed between the mountains."

In 1768, Mr. Thomas Jackson was received as pastor of Mossy creek, and continued in charge till his death, in 1773. His place was filled by Rev. Samuel Edmondson, in 1773, who soon removed to South Carolina, and was followed by Rev. Benj. Erwin, who was ordained pastor in 1780. His pastorate closed in 1808, when he was dismissed to the Presbytery of Transylvania, Ky. In 1809, Rev. A. B. Davidson was installed at Mossy Creek, over the united congregations of Cooke's Creek, Harrisonburg and Mossy Creek. Mr. Davidson introduced politics into his sermons, thus following the pernicious example of many New England divines, which greatly offended many of his listeners, and probably led to his resignation in 1814. After three years, in 1818, Rev. John Hendren became pastor, and remained many years in charge. In 1835-'36, Rev. Isaac Paul supplied this church a few months, until his death. Rev. John A. VanLear became pastor in 1837, and so continued until his death, in 1850. In 1853, Rev. John Pinkerton was ordained and installed, and served with success until his death, in 1871. He was succeeded by Rev. John W. Rosebro, in 1873. The present church, built during Mr. VanLear's pastorate, is the fourth which has been occupied by this congregation since its organization.

UNION CHURCH was organized February 17th, 1817, Rev. Conrad Speece preaching upon the occasion. The ruling elders were Thomas Hogshead, F. Gilkerson, D. Hogshead and James Irvine. In 1818, Rev. John Hendren was regularly installed as pastor, and his pastorate extended until 1855. He was succeeded by Rev. R. C. Walker, who was installed in 1857, and served until 1877, when he resigned, and for two years Revs. A. S. Moffett and I. N. Campbell preached as supplies. In 1879, Mr. Campbell was installed as pastor, and is at present in charge.

LOCH-WILLOW CHURCH, at Churchville, was organized October 5th, 1866, within the limits of Union church, and the members came from both Union church and Hebron. The first pastor was Rev. P. Fletcher. His successors have been: Revs. McDuff Simpson, A. S. Moffett and J. H. H. Winfree, the present pastor.

MT. CARMEL CHURCH.—South of Staunton 17 miles, near Midway, in the County of Augusta, upon a beautiful eminence, over-shadowed by primitive oaks, stands the neat and tasteful house of worship wherein the Mt. Carmel congregation assembles.

This church was built in 1835, upon an acre of land presented to the congregation for this purpose by David Steele, then living in the village of Midway, but who afterwards removed to Missouri. Prominent among those who exerted themselves to build the church was the late Capt. Jas. Henry. Soon after the house was completed, the ministerial services of the Rev. James Paine, who also preached at Fairfield, were secured for one-third of his time. He commenced his labors in 1836, and continued them until

1856, when he resigned. His successors have been: Revs. John Miller, William Pinkerton, until his death, in 1875, and A. H. Hamilton.

STAUNTON CHURCH.—The Presbyterians of Staunton had no house of worship previous to the Revolution, but were in the habit of attending, as we have mentioned, Tinkling Spring. If a minister preached in Staunton it was in the court-house or some private residence. After the Revolution the Episcopal and Presbyterian congregations occupied the Episcopal church on alternate Sundays.

In 1776, Rev. James Waddell settled in Augusta, as the pastor of Tinkling Spring, and in 1783, received a call by the united congregations of Tinkling Spring and Staunton; on part of the Staunton people the call was signed by Alex. St. Clair and William Bowyer. Dr. W. removed from the county in 1784, and it is not known who, if any one, officiated in Staunton until 1791, when Rev. John McCue became pastor of Tinkling Spring and Staunton. From 1799 to 1804, Rev. John Glendy, from the Root Presbytery, in Ireland, preached occasionally in Staunton. In May, 1804, the church was organized in Staunton, with the following ruling elders: James Bell, Joseph Cowan, Andrew Barry and Samuel Clark. In 1805, Rev. William Calhoun was installed pastor of the united congregations of Brown's meeting-house (Hebron) and Staunton. During his pastorate, a substantial brick church was erected in Staunton, and was used until 1871, when the present commodious and elegant church edifice was commenced and completed in 1873. Mr. Calhoun retired from his connection with the Staunton church in 1826, and devoted himself to Hebron congregation. He was succeeded by Rev. Joseph Smith, D. D., of Pennsylvania, who, while pastor, was also Principal of the Staunton Academy. Mr. Smith retired in 1832, and was succeeded, in 1834, by Rev. John Steele, who removed to Illinois in 1837, and was succeeded by Rev. Paul E. Stevenson, of New York, during whose pastorate the church and congregation made considerable progress in various ways. Amongst the outward improvements was the enlargement of the church grounds and the establishment of the Augusta Female Seminary, under the Rev. R. W. Bailey. In 1844, Mr. Stevenson retired, and was succeeded by Rev. R. R. Howison, the distinguished author of the History of Virginia; at the end of six months he retired, and was succeeded by Rev. B. M. Smith, D. D., who resigned in 1854, when Rev. Joseph R. Wilson accepted a call from the congregation, and remained two years in Staunton. He was succeeded by Rev. William E. Baker, who was installed in 1859, and continues in charge. Under Mr. Baker's pastorate the church and congregation have made marked progress, as well as the Seminary.

SECOND PRESBYTERIAN CHURCH, STAUNTON.—This church was organized in 1875, by many who had previously worshipped in Staunton church. Among the active friends of the movement to establish the

Second church were Major Jed. Hotchkiss, William Jordan, M. H. Effinger, Henry A. Walker, J. W. Morrison, J. S. Lipscomb and J. M. Lickliter. The first elders were Messrs. Morrison and Jordan. The first pastor was Rev. McDuff Simpson, M. A.; the second, the present minister, Rev. J. B. Booker. A beautiful lot was purchased on the northwest corner of Lewis and Frederick streets, and the handsome and substantial brick church, in which the congregation now worships, was erected, and occupied in 1876.

MT. HOREB CHURCH.—This church was formed from the congregation of the Stone church in 1857. The first minister was Rev. David Erwin. His successors have been: Revs. P. M. Custer, H. H. Haws, G. H. Denny, and Thomas M. Boyd.

ROCKY SPRING CHURCH is situated near Deerfield, in the Big Calf Pastures, and the minister is Rev. Mr. Brown.

On the eastern slope of Betsy Bell, about a mile from Staunton, there is a pretty little Presbyterian chapel. It originated in the efforts of Mrs. D. A. Kayser, Miss M. J. Baldwin, and other ladies, who first established a Sunday-school, occupying the public school-house at that place. In 1881, through the zeal and activity of David Doom and other residents of the vicinity, assisted by the ladies of Staunton church, the chapel was erected. Services are regularly conducted in it by Rev. J. B. Booker, and there is also connected with it a flourishing Sunday-school.

SUNDAY–SCHOOLS.

With all of the above-mentioned churches, as, indeed, with those of every denomination of Christians in the County, Sabbath-schools have been for many years organized, and in successful operation. At present they are in a flourishing condition, many of them having excellent circulating libraries for the use of the pupils.

―――

Volumes might be written upon the lives and labors of the noble men whose names have been mentioned, and merely mentioned for want of space in the foregoing account. Our object has been simply to give a proper place in history to those by whose labors and sacrifices the Presbyterian church was established in our county and brought to its present position of usefulness and importance. In our outline we could do no more than place on record names which well deserve to be remembered, and deeply regret our inability to give, at least, sketches of lives so worthy to be studied.

―――

THE METHODIST EPISCOPAL CHURCH IN AUGUSTA.

The Methodists are a comparatively new sect, having sprung up in England about the year 1737, under Rev. John Wesley and George Whitfield, students of the University of Oxford. It was founded in New York in 1766. They received their name from living by a stricter regimen and method than the members of the Church of England, and they are more animated, spirited and zealous than the regular clergy of that church. The Methodists are, however, baptised with the Episcopalians, attend Episcopal services and sacraments, admire the Episcopal liturgy, and only blame the Episcopal church for lukewarmness and want of energy and animation. About the year 1775, John Hagerty and Richard Owens, two Methodist preachers, delivered, at Stephensburg, near Winchester, the first sermons ever preached by any ministers of this sect in the Virginian Valley, making a most favorable impression ; many joined the church, and a place of worship was soon erected in Stephensburg, and the Methodist is now one of the most numerous, wealthy and intelligent denominations in this section of Virginia.

We are under obligations to Rev. J. S. Martin, D. D., for the following account of the church in Augusta :

" The name of Staunton Circuit first appears on the minutes published for the Methodist Episcopal Church in the year 1806. The circuit, then, must have included all of Augusta county, including. under the same name, much of the country beyond the North Mountain ; also the county of Rockbridge. Much of this territory had been served before in con- nection with the Rockingham Circuit. Rockingham Circuit was begun in 1788. William Phœbus was appointed to it as its first preacher. In 1789, Rockingham Circuit had only seventy-nine members, though it then em- braced some four or five counties, from Winchester, beyond Staunton, in the Valley, and west of the North Mountain. In 1806, the membership had increased to seven hundred and sixty. In that year Staunton Circuit, as described above, was formed. In 1807, it embraced two hundred mem- bers, scattered over its extensive territory. Noah Fiddler was the first preacher appointed to Staunton Circuit. In 1833, Staunton Circuit was divided—Rockbridge was taken off under the name of Lexington Cir- cuit. Augusta Circuit, embracing all of Augusta county, was formed, and the town of Staunton was made a distinct station to itself, and which re- ported, in 1834, a few members. In 1838, Staunton had only sixty white members, and unable to support a preacher alone, to whom it had given usually, as a single man, $100 and his board. It was now placed again as one of the appointments on the Augusta Circuit." In 1882, there were twenty Methodist churches in Augusta county, with a membership of 1,511. The value of the church property was $29,100. There were also six parsonages, valued at $11,500. The Wesleyan Female Institute, held by trustees for the Baltimore Conference, Methodist Episcopal Church, South, is located in Staunton, and valued at $60,000. The African portion of the Methodist church is represented in Staunton by two large and flourishing congregations, one of which worships in an imposing brick

edifice, handsomely fitted up, and the other in a substantial and well appointed frame church. Scattered throughout the county are a number of
chapels and churches, in which services are held at regular intervals.

THE BAPTIST CHURCH IN AUGUSTA.

The Baptists differ from other sects chiefly in the mode of administering
baptism, which, they conceive, should always be by immersion, and they
reject the baptism of infants. There were many of this faith in Holland,
Germany, and the north of Europe; in Piedmont and the south. Their
first congregation in England was in 1607. As early as 1754, Mr. Stearns,
a preacher of this sect, and several others, removed from New England to
Opeckon, in the present county of Berkeley, where they formed a Baptist
church, under the care of Rev. John Gerard. This was probably the first
Baptist church founded west of the Blue Ridge in Virginia.

The first effort to plant a church in Staunton was in 1834, and in 1836
Rev. Texas Freeman came into the county and labored as a missionary,
but soon left the work, owing to ill health. In 1849, Rev. T. W. Roberts was sent as a missionary to Nelson and Augusta counties.

In 1853, Dr. S. B. Rice came to Staunton, and a church was organized
in the Town Hall by Revs. L. W. Allen, Samuel Harris and Charles
Wingfield, with about twenty members. Major Wm. H. Peyton and S.
F. Taylor were the principal members. L. W. Allen preached a sermon
from John, ch. xviii, v. 36. Dr. Rice was elected pastor. Funds for erecting a church were raised, principally in Eastern Virginia, and the corner-
stone of the present edifice was laid June 26, 1855, Rev. J. L. Burrows
delivering an address in the Episcopal church. Dr. Rice was succeeded
in 1857 by Rev. Geo. B. Taylor. Under Dr. T., the membership increased
rapidly, the church debt was paid, and the General Association met with
this church, in its first session west of the Blue Ridge, May 31, 1860.
After the Civil War, 1865, most of the colored members were dismissed,
to form a separate organization. In 1870, Dr. Taylor, who had been appointed Chaplain of the University of Virginia, was succeeded by Rev.
W. H. Williams. During his pastorate the Church continued to flourish,
and Prof. Hart's school was removed to Staunton. On Mr. Williams'
resignation, Dr. Taylor was recalled, and was pastor till 1873, when he
resigned, to accept the appointment of missionary to Rome. Rev. Dr. J.
F. Deans was engaged to supply his place, and labored with great acceptance till July, when he removed from Staunton. In the following October,
1873, Dr. Charles Manly became pastor, and served till 1880. He was
an excellent pastor, and did more than any one, during his time, to build
up the Church in the town and county, Rev. Thos. Hume, Jr., followed
Dr. Manly, and served till March 1, 1880, when Rev. J. M. Frost, Jr.,
took charge, and labored with such success that in 1882 more than one
hundred new members have been added to the church. In the county,

Rev. J. H. Taylor and Rev. C. F. Fry have done much toward building up the denomination. The Baptists now have six churches in Augusta and 891 members. Besides these, are two African Baptist churches in Staunton, Mt. Zion and Ebenezer, and a number of small chapels and churches throughout the county.

. THE TUNKER, OR GERMAN BAPTIST CHURCH.

We are indebted to the Rev. Samuel Driver for the following brief account of the Tunker Church in Augusta:

The Tunker, or German Baptist Church, was first organized in Augusta about the year 1790, by Bishop Miller, the father of Bishop John Miller, who now resides near Mount Sidney. Rev. John Miller was the first Bishop permanently settled in the county. After the organization in 1800, the Church received accessions of members, and it was found necessary to district the county, and a Bishop, or Elder, was appointed for each district. The names of the districts are Mt. Vernon, of which the two Elders are Messrs. John Cline and George Wine; 2nd—Barren Ridge— Elder, John Bower; Middle River District—Elder, Levi Garber; 3rd— Valley District—Elders, John Miller and Daniel Miller; Fourth District is Moscow—Elder, Levi A. Wenger. In the above list is included all the Tunker churches in the county, but there are several branches or congregations who worship at different points in the county, notably, one at Union Hall, in the western part of Augusta; one at Jarman's Gap, in the Blue Ridge; and one every fifth Sabbath in the Episcopal Trinity chapel, near Hebron. The Rev. Sam'l Driver preaches thus four times a year in Trinity chapel. There are in Augusta about nine hundred communicants. In the United States the Tunkers have three colleges, the first at Huntington, Penn., the second in Ashland county, Ohio, and the third at Lanarck, Illinois. In connection with all Tunker churches there are Sunday-schools, and the Tunker community is justly celebrated for industry, integrity, and piety.

THE LUTHERAN CHURCH IN AUGUSTA.

Wm. E. Craig, Esq., has kindly furnished the following account of the Lutheran Church:

Among the early emigrants to the Valley of Virginia were many Lutherans, but we have no account of any organized Church in Augusta until about the year 1780, when a congregation was formed, and Coiner's Church built. This church is about five miles southwest of Waynesboro, and we think the first minister was Rev. Adolph Spindle. We have no list of his successors, but the present minister is Rev. Mr. Kuegle, and the number of communicants about 100. The first trustees and organizers of the church were Casper Koiner, Martin Bush, and Jacob Barger. The next church organized was Mt. Tabor, about the year 1785. We have no list of the former ministers, but the present minister is Rev. L. L.

Smith. The number of communicants in this church is about 250. Mt. Zion church, situated about six miles west of Middlebrook, was organized about 1830, with the following trustees: Martin Miller, David C. Arehart, and —— Weaver. Its number of communicants is about 100, with Rev. J. M. Hedrick as its present pastor. Under the charge of Rev. J. M. Hedrick is also Mt. Herman church and congregation, situated at Newport, organized about 1850 by Rev. C. Beard, with A. S. Craig, Wm. Black and David Hull as the first trustees and organizers. The number of communicants is about 75. 4th.—Bethlehem, near Fishersville, was organized about 1845, with the following trustees: Absalom Koiner, Cyrus Koiner, and David W. Coiner. Rev. L. A. Fox, DD., has served this charge for a number of years, and is its present pastor. Number of communicants, 150. 5th.—The second Mt. Zion church, near Waynesboro, was organized about the same time as Bethlehem. Its first pastor was Rev —— Bowman. Rev. C. Beard served this congregation from 1854 to 1881. Rev. J. H. Barb is the present pastor. Communicants, 100. 6th.—The congregation at Staunton was organized and the church built about 1850 by Rev. John B. Davis, DD., and George Shuey, B. F. Points and George Baylor as the first trustees. Col. George Baylor was mainly instrumental in organizing this congregation and building the church. The lot was purchased and the church built by the "Virginia Synod," together with the aid given it by Col. Baylor and other representatives of that Synod, under the charge of Col. Baylor as principal superintendent. Rev. J. B. Davis, DD., was the first pastor, Rev. D. M. Gilbert. DD., the second, Rev. J. I. Miller the third, Rev. M. R. Minnick the fourth, and Rev. J. B. Haskell, the fifth. Number of communicants, about 200. 6th.—Salem church is located near Mt. Sidney, and was built about 1845. It has been served by the pastors in connection with Mt. Zion, No. 2. Its number of communicants is about 100. Its present pastor is Rev. A. C. Gearhart. 7th.—The Churchville church was built also about 1850, under the supervision of Rev. J. B. Davis, DD. Rev. C. Beard is now serving it as a supply. Number of communicants, about 75. 8th.—Bethany, near Waynesboro, and Pleasant View, near Staunton, have been organized within the past five years. The Bethlehem minister serves Bethany, and the Staunton minister Pleasant View. The number of communicants of each church is about 75.

THE CATHOLIC CHURCH, at Staunton, is situated on a beautiful site on the east side of Augusta street, in a fine grove of maples and other native trees. The edifice, a substantial brick structure, was built in 1850, the lot, which embraces half a square, being donated by the late M. Quinlan, Esq. Until about the year 1841, there were but one or two Catholic families in Staunton. The Rev. Daniel Downey made missionary journeys to this section from Lynchburg, and labored with such success that in the year 1850 he was enabled to gather a flock around him sufficiently large to form the nucleus of a congregation. With zeal they undertook the erection of the church, the reverend gentleman's most active helpers being Messrs. M. Quinlan and Patrick McAlear. Having thus secured a handsome house of worship, Rev. Downey became the pastor, and continued to minister to the spiritual wants of the congregation until 1857, when he resigned, and was succeeded by Rev. T. A. Sears, who served until 1859. From 1859 to 1861, the church was supplied from Richmond. Rev. Jos. Bixio, a Jesuit, then became the pastor, and continued in that relation until 1866, when he was succeeded by Rev. J. A. Weed, who died in March, 1871. His successor was the Rev. John McVerry, the present pastor. During his pastorate, the Rev. McVerry has been aided by the following assistant pastors, viz: Rev. J. A. G. Riley, Rev. Peter Fitzsimmons, Rev. H. J McKeefry, and the present assistant, Rev. G. T. O'Ferrall. The church has prospered. Its membership now reaches 700. The church property embraces a handsome brick parsonage. The parochial school was, in 1878, placed under the charge of the Sisters of Charity, and since then a commodious and imposing brick structure has been erected for educational purposes. The school itself has made marked progress, and promises, ere long, to be abreast of Staunton's most flourishing seminaries of learning.

CHAPTER VII.

With the first colonist to Virginia came a clergyman of the Established Church, and from that time onward the Church was protected and fostered in Virginia. Non-conformists were expelled from the colony, and a fine of 5,000 pounds of tobacco was exacted from participants in the meetings of Dissenters. Papists, Presbyterians, and Quakers, were alike persecuted, and those who even entertained a Quaker were liable to a heavy fine. The first sect to make head against this intolerance was the Presbyterian, under Rev. Francis Makemie, and the Scotch-Irish settlers of our Valley. About the year 1698, this intolerant spirit began to decline, and by the year 1776, more than half the people of Virginia were Dissenters, and during the war, the Church went down, apparently unregretted. The course and reason of the change can be readily followed. The reaction which ensued after the intense spiritual excitement of the seventeenth century produced a species of religious lethargy in the eighteenth. Frigid morality, a well-bred abhorrence of anything like zeal, and a worldly indifference, characterized the English clergyman of the latter period and their Virginian brethren. The colonial ministers, as a class, were ruder and narrower than those of the mother country, and their coldness and indifference to great religious principles showed themselves more plainly and coarsely. Religion declined, and "paganism, atheism and sectaries" began to prevail. "Quakers," says Byrd, "prevail in Nansemond county, for the want of ministers to pilot the people a better way to heaven." Advantage was taken of this relaxation by the Presbyterians, who exacted, as we have seen, from Gov. Gooch, promises of toleration to those of their faith. Their eloquent and earnest men, however, soon aroused the latent hostility of the ruling Church, and Gooch himself joined in the resistance to the new doctrines. But the Dissenting sects were full of vitality, and grew apace, while the Established Church, maintained simply as a part of the social system, declined with proportionate rapidity. The success of the Revolution, and the withdrawal of support, caused the Church to fall into ruins.

The Church of England was, as we have said, established by law in Virginia, to the exclusion, and without toleration of any other denomination. The Act of Conformity, passed by the British Parliament, was acknowledged as law, and carried into execution by the magistrates. It must be remembered, however, that while the Church of England was thus recognized, from the settlement at Jamestown down to the Revolution, it was, during this long period of 170 years, kept in a state of bondage to the Government, which never allowed it to organize. For political reasons, it was not permitted to have a bishop, and there were no ordinances or confirmations in Virginia during the whole colonial period. Candidates for orders had to make the voyage to England. The Church was not only denied an executive head, but it had no legislature. It had no authority to pass a law, enact a canon, or inflict a penalty, not even for the discipline of its own ministers and members, and it never performed one of these functions. And this enslavement, no doubt, impaired its spirit, and rendered it less active in the cause of religion than would otherwise have been the case.

In the previous chapter, we have referred to some of the minor reasons which begot a spirit of liberality early in the eighteenth century with the colonial authorities in their policy towards Dissenters west of the Blue Ridge, namely: A desire to erect a barrier against the encroachments of the Indians. Such motives doubtless had their weight with men like Gooch, but there was a deeper and broader motive beginning to influence the people of Virginia, and which showed itself conspicuously at a later period. This was their hostility to the establishment of any religion in America by the British Parliament. This feeling, which existed long before the Revolution, led the sages of 1776 to unite afterwards in destroying all ecclesiastical establishments by the bill for religious freedom, which was passed by the General Assembly of Virginia December 16, 1785.

Though the Episcopal was the established religion, no church existed in Augusta previous to 1746, and Rev. Joseph Doddridge, DD., the first minister of the Episcopal Church who visited the regions of Western Virginia and Eastern Ohio, in his " Notes on the Settlement and Indian Wars of Western Virginia and Pennsylvania, from 1763 to 1783," thus speaks upon the subject of this apathy and neglect :

" The Episcopal Church, which ought to have been foremost in gathering their scattered flocks, had been the last and done the least of any Christian community in the evangelical work. Taking the western country, in its whole extent, at least one-half of its population was originally of Episcopalian parentage, but for want of a ministry of their own, they have associated with other communities. They had no alternative but that of changing their profession, or living and dying without the ordinances of religion. It can be no subject of regret that these ordinances were placed within their reach by other hands, whilst they were withheld by those by whom, as a matter of right and duty, they ought to have been given. One single suffragan bishop, of a faithful spirit, who, twenty years ago, should have ordained these elders in every place where they were needed, would have been the instrument of forming Episcopal congregations over a great extent of country, and which, by this time, would have become large, numerous and respectable ; but the opportunity was neglected, and the consequent loss to this Church is irreparable. So total a neglect of the spiritual interest of so many valuable people, for so great a length of time, by a ministry so near at hand, is a singular and unprecedented fact in ecclesiastical history, the like of which never occurred before. It seems to me that if the twentieth part of their number of Christian people, of any other community had been placed in Siberia, and dependent on any other ecclesiastical authority in this country, that that authority would have reached them many years ago with the ministration of the Gospel. With the earliest and most numerous Episcopacy in America, not one of the Eastern Bishops has yet crossed the Alleghany Mountains, although the dioceses of two of them comprehended large tracts on the western side of the mountains. It is hoped that the future diligence of this community will make up, in some degree, for the negligence of the past. There is still an immense void in this country, which it is their duty to fill up. From their respectability, on the ground of antiquity among the reformed churches, the science of their patriarchs, who have been the lights of the world, from their number and great resources even in America, she ought to hasten to fulfill the just expectations of her own people, as well as those of other communities, in contributing her full share to the science, piety and civilization of our country. From the whole of our ecclesiastical history, it appears that, with the exception of the Episcopal Church, all our religious communities have done well for their country·"

Bishop Meade differs with Dr. Doddridge as to the percentage of Episcopalians in the population, and assigns very reasonable causes for his belief ; but as Dr. Doddridge wrote of a country in which he lived, and with whose people he mingled, he is more likely to be correct than a subsequent writer. We cannot but attribute the tardiness of the church in evangelizing to the character of the Episcopal clergy, of whom the Bishop of London said about this time in a letter to Dr. Doddridge : " Of those who are sent from hence, a great part are the Scotch or Irish, who can get no employment at home, and enter into the service more out of necessity than choice. Some others are willing to go abroad to retrieve lost fortune or lost character. For these reasons, and others of less weight, I did apply to the King, as soon as I was Bishop of London, to have two or three bishops appointed for the plantations, to reside there."

Of the clergy, more particularly the English, as contradistinguished from the Scotch and Irish representatives of the Church in the pulpit, the following is a picture—graphic, and, no doubt, perfectly true:

With some exceptions, the Virginian clergy aped the manners and habits of the laity. Most of them were men who cultivated their glebes like other planters, preaching once a week, and performing the other services of the Church for the sake of an addition to their income. Their morals were loose, and the general tone of the profession was low. Here and there might be found a man of exemplary life and high character; but the average parson was coarse and rough, and his parishioners might be thankful, if he was not also a drunkard and gambler. They hunted the fox and raced horses; they played cards; turned marriages, christenings and funerals alike into revels, and sat out the stoutest planter after dinner to finally accompany him under the table. One reverend gentleman bawled to his church warden during communion, " Here, George, this bread is not fit for a dog." Another commemorated his Church and office by fighting a duel in the grave-yard. Another received a regular stipend for preaching four sermons annually against atheism, gambling, racing, and swearing, although he was notorious as a gambler, swearer, and horse-racer. Still another, of great physical strength, thrashed his vestry soundly, and then added insult to injury by preaching to them next Sunday from the text, " And I contended with them, and cursed them, and smote certain of them, and plucked off their hair."—[Meade, vol. I, pp. 18, 162, 231, 250, 275, 361, 387, 470: Vol. II, 179.] One married a wealthy widow, although he had a wife living in England. Another was brought before a magistrate for drinking and carousing on Christmas Eve, and another, who dined every Sunday with a great planter, was sent home tied in his chaise, under care of a servant. At every race-course and cockpit might be seen reverend divines betting on the contending birds or horses.—[Foote, II : 371.] The petty tradesmen would not trust them beyond their salary, and extorted 150 per cent. for interest.

Among the colonial clergy there was another class, quite the reverse of the rollicking blades described, and less to be admired. These were the self-seeking and ambitious, who, in order to impose upon the world, and secure professional success, kept up a constant appearance of sanctity. There was no defective preaching or evil living on the part of these models of decorum. The sanctity of such, as may be readily imagined, did not proceed from spiritual motives and the sentiments of the heart; it was a certain exterior, which they found themselves compelled to preserve. Their devotion did not spring from devout feelings; it was affected, whether experienced or not. This gave something formal and uncouth to their manners. And it could scarcely have been otherwise. A continual attention to a pious exterior necessarily gives a constrained and artificial bearing to the carriage. The characters of all ministers, under a religion established by law and supported by taxation, are liable to be disadvantageously affected by their situation as legalized guides and teachers of others. They address their audiences at stated periods, and no one is allowed to contradict them. They pronounce the prayers of the congregation, visit the sick, and officiate as oracles to such as are in distress. They seek to govern the thoughts of their parishioners, and to restrain the irregular sallies of their understandings. They warn their flocks against innovation and the intrepidity of thinking. The adversary is silent before them. With other men he may argue, but if he attempt to discuss a subject freely and impartially with them, it is construed into a personal insult. Thus, the circumstances of every day tend to confirm in them a dogmatical, imperious, illiberal and intolerant character. Worthy Bishop Meade, who recounts the doings of our colonial clergy with much sorrow, says there was not only defective preaching, but, as might be supposed, most evil living among the clergy. The natural result followed, and the revival of the eighteenth century broke down the old clergy and their abuses. Then came the ill-advised struggle for salaries, famous as "The Parsons' Cause," the fatuous effort to procure a bishop, and a fatal indecision and lukewarmness in the contest with England. The Revolution was the finishing-stroke, and the old Church of Virginia perished.

But we must return. With such a clergy as above described, no missionaries could be found to cross the Blue Ridge, and there was no Established Church in Augusta until nearly fifteen years after the foundation of the colony, when the ground was already occupied by Presbyterian and other Dissenters. There were doubtless a few Episcopalians in Augusta, though it has been observed, we do not know how truly, that persons of that denomination do not like new countries, or are deficient in zeal, where it is not cherished by parish or tithe. There may have been another reason. Education is in the Episcopal Church a necessary qualification for administering the affairs of both Church and State, and both the education and population of the Valley, to a great extent, belonged to the Scotch-Irish, or Dissenting element. In 1745, steps were taken to introduce the

Established Church in the county, and in 1746 the first election for a vestry of Augusta parish took place and resulted in the choice of the following persons: James Patton, Thomas Gordon, John Buchanan, John Madison, Patrick Hays, John Christian, Robt. Alexander, Jas. Lockhart, Jas. Buchanan, Jr., Jno. Archer, Jno. Mathews, and J. Smith. John Madison was elected clerk, and Robt. Alexander and James Lockhart church wardens, who, before entering upon the discharge of their duties, took the following oaths:

OATH OF ALLEGIANCE.

" I, A. B., do sincerely promise and swear that I will be faithful and bear true allegiance to his Majesty, King George the Second. So help me God."

OATH OF ABJURATION, ENFORCED BY ACT OF 1701, ABOLISHED 1858.

" I, A. B., do swear that I do from my heart abhor, detest, and abjure, as impious and heretical, that damnable doctrine and position that Princes excommunicated or deprived by the Pope, or any authority of the See of Rome, may be deposed or murdered by their subjects, or any other whatsoever. And I do declare that no foreign Prince, Prelate, Person, State or Potentate, hath, or ought to have, any jurisdiction, power, superiority, preëminence, or authority, ecclesiastical or spiritual, within this realm. So help me God."

OATH OF ALLEGIANCE, IMPOSED 1558, CHANGED 1689, MODIFIED 1838.

" I, A. B., do truly and sincerely acknowledge and promise, testify and declare, in my conscience, before God and the world, that our Sovereign Lord, King George the Second, is lawful and rightful King of this realm and all other his Majesty's dominions and countries hereunto belonging; and I do solemnly and sincerely declare that I do believe in my conscience that the person pretended to be Prince of Wales during the life of the late King James, and since his decease pretending to be, and taking upon himself the style and title of the King of England, or by the name of James III, or of Scotland by the name of James VIII, or the style and title of King of Great Britain, hath not any right whatsoever to the crown of this realm, or any other dominion hereunto belonging; and I do renounce, refuse and abjure any allegiance or obedience to him, and I do swear that I will bear faithful and true allegiance to H. M. King George II, and him will defend to the utmost of my power against all traitorous conspiracies and attempts whatsoever which shall be made against his person, crown or dignity; and I will do my utmost to endeavor to disclose and make known to his Majesty and his successors all treasonable and traitorous conspiracies which I shall know to be against him, or any of them: and I do faithfully promise, to the utmost of my power, to support, maintain and defend the successor of the crown against him, the said James, and all other persons whatsoever, which succession, by an act entitled 'An act for the further limitation of the crown and better securing the rights and liberties of the subject,' is and stands limited to the Princess Sophia, late Electress and Duchess, dowager of Hanover, and the heirs of her body, being Protestants; and all other these things I do plainly and severally acknowledge and swear, according to these express words by me spoken, and according to the plain and common sense understanding of the same words, without any equivocation, mental evasion, or secret reservation whatsoever; and I do make this recognition, acknowledgment, abjuration, renunciation, and promise, heartily, willingly, and truly, upon the true faith of a Christian. So help me God."

TEST OATH PASSED 1673, REPEALED 1828.

" I do declare that I do believe that there is not any transsubstantiation in the Sacrament of the Lord's Supper, or in the elements of bread and wine, at or after the consecration thereof by any person whatsoever."

The vestries of that day represented all the local and municipal government there was in Virginia. They had assigned to them, by act of the Burgesses, secular functions, made returns of births, marriages and deaths, presented for crimes, commanded the sheriffs to hold the election for Burgesses and assisted the county courts in building work-houses. They " processioned the lands " every four years, and kept up the roads and ferries.

The first vestry of Augusta parish was doubtless largely composed of Dissenters, men who, so far as religion was concerned, were politically Episcopalians and doctrinally Presbyterians, but willing to submit outwardly to the powers in being, while they held themselves free to have their own private opinions. With the exception of Madison, their names would seem to indicate this. A liberal feeling prevailed for many years after the introduction of the Church of England, and all denominations of Christians attended worship, and now and again dissenting ministers preached from the Episcopal pulpit.

The community still retained strong marks of its Presbyterian leaven; the clergyman abjured gown and surplice; the clerk, a layman, read the lessons; the altar forsook the East windows, and the congregation stood and received the Holy Sacrament. When dissenting ministers increased in numbers, the doctrines of dissent were more widely promulgated; the old spirit of non-conformity awoke; there were many seceders from the church, and almost all the sects extant in England were before the Revolution represented in Augusta.

FIRST RECTOR OF AUGUSTA PARISH.—At the first meeting of the vestry, held in the court-house, 6th of April, 1747, Rev. John Hindman, having produced letters from the Governor and Commissary, directed to Col. John Patton, setting forth his ability as a minister, the vestry agreed to accept of him, conditionally—viz.: That the said Hindman will not insist on the parish purchasing Glebe lands, building a Glebe, and such other necessaries as are prescribed by law for the space of two years, until the parish be more able to bear such charges, and that he agree to preach in this court-house, and in people's houses of the same persuasion, in the different quarters of the parish, as shall be most convenient, and that he administer the Sacrament in the court-house instead of a church, and in different quarters of the parish as aforesaid, unless His Honor, the Governor, thinks proper to reverse the same, which shall not be by complaint of said Hindman or any person for him, and that he bring in his charge at the laying the parish levy for the same.

A GLEBE.—Our English ancestors were particular to make provision for the support of the clergy; to place them above want and the disrespect which too generally attends upon poverty; to place those who were to instruct ignorance, and be the censors of vice, where they would neither incur the contempt nor live upon the alms of the people. The Augusta vestry were ready to comply with the provisions of the law in this matter, but were particular to stipulate, as above, with Mr. Hindman, as a protection against any inconsiderate or rapacious conduct on his part. They looked on his dues as his property, and they intended to protect him in that possession, but they were determined, also, to secure themselves against abuses.

It is not surprising, considering what manner of men many of the Episcopal clergy were in Virginia, that the vestry should have been thus guarded. The sincerity of the Augusta vestry is evident from their action in July, 1747, when a committee was appointed to purchase land for a Glebe, &c., &c., unless a place could be bought with sufficient improvements to answer the purposes. On September 21st, 1747, the vestry proceeded to make the parish levy, when the number of tithables is stated to be 1,670. If we allow five persons to a family, which is a moderate number, the population of the county was, at this time. 8,350, and there were no poor, at least none who had applied for relief, as appears from the order of February 24th, 1747-'48: "That the money levied for fines, &c., be kept in the church wardens' hands until the meeting of the next vestry, the poor not being as yet known." Ordered that the persons appointed to purchase a Glebe meet on Monday next to purchase the same, and that the church wardens advertise and let the public buildings in November next, (September, 1747.) These lands were subsequently purchased of Robert Campbell, for the sum of £60.

The committee appointed for that purpose, having advertised and let out on contract the public buildings, at the meeting of the vestry board, August 22nd, 1748, this order was made:

"John Lewis, gentleman, having undertaken the public buildings of Augusta parish for £140., ordered that he be paid by John Madison, the trustee for the sd. parish, on raising the said buildings, £74, and the remainder on completing the same, unless he want money to carry on the said work, which the said Madison is ordered to supply him with."

These buildings had not been completed in 1750, when, on the 21st of May, it is

"Ordered: That John Lewis, gentleman, do such work as shall be necessary for completing the public buildings on the Glebe, over and above his articles, and that it be valued by workmen, and that he be allowed for the same."

In August, 1750, the vestry, at its meeting on the 6th,

"Ordered that payment be made to Colonel John Lewis of £64.17.1, the balance due him for the Glebe buildings."

At the meeting of the 22d of August, 1748, the vestry proceeded to lay the parish levy as follows:

Augusta Parish.		Dr.
To the Rev. John Hindman 16,000 pounds of tobacco, at three farthings per pound, without any deduction	£50	0 0
To 10 per cent. on ditto for collection	5	0 0
To Mr. Hindman, for board	20	0 0
To Samuel Gay, per agreement with church wardens	1	4 0
To James Portees.	2	5 0
To Robt. McClenachan, per acct	4	15 7
To Daniel Harrison, per acct		10 0
To John Madison, clerk	8	0 0
	£91	14 7

The Parish Dr.		
To the above creditors	£ 91	14 7
To a deposite in the collector's hands	50	6 5
	£142	1 0

Per contra—Creditor.		
To 1,421 tithables, at 2 shilling per pole	£142	1 0

While the church buildings were being constructed, the following provision was made for Mr. Jones (the Rector):

"It appearing to this vestry (22nd November, 1752,) that the Glebe buildings are not yet finished, and the said Jones having acquainted this vestry that John Lewis, gentleman, (the contractor of the same) agrees to allow him at the rate of £20 per annum until the same be finished, for which he declares himself satisfied, and acquits this vestry and parish of any further charge for the same.

"Ordered that a reader to this parish be allowed the sum of £6.5 yearly, and that Rev. Mr. Jones have a liberty to choose the same to officiate at the court-house.

"Ordered that William Preston be allowed the sum of £5 per annum to serve as clerk for this vestry, and that he commence from the 1st September, 1752."

It would seem from the following entry that some difficulty had occurred as to articles supplied the parish:

"Ordered that every particular (thing) to be provided for the parish to be set down in the vestry book."

Accordingly, at the October meeting, we find William Hunter sending in his account for articles furnished Col. James Patton for the parish, which is duly recorded:

3 law books	£4	10	0
3 stitched books		10	6
Wax		3	0
Ink powder		3	9
1 ream post paper	1	8	0
2 8vo. prayer-books	1	1	0
1 folio ditto	2	3	4

$$£9 \quad 19 \quad 7$$

The Glebe buildings seem to have been completed somewhere between 1753–1754, as this order is entered on the 22d of November, 1754 : " That the church-wardens view the Glebe buildings, and make such reparation as they may deem proper, and bring in their charge at the laying of the next levy."

The tradition that the church was built of English-made brick, transported on pack mules across the mountains, is a myth. The community could not have borne such an expense. We have been informed by an aged gentleman that the brick for the Glebe buildings were made on Jos. Ast's farm, near Staunton.

The caution of our ancestors is illustrated by the following entry, made evidently after the death or removal of Mr. Hindman, 21st May, 1750 :

"Col. James Patton having produced a letter, under the hand of Peter Hedgman, gentleman, recommending Mr. Robert McClowseme, and desiring presentation might be made to the Commissary, but the vestry not being acquainted with him, do agree to present none nor receive any minister without a tryal being first had."

The Glebe was sold about this time, and the proceeds invested in the Academy at Staunton.

REV. JOHN JONES, RECTOR.—It does not appear at what precise period Mr. Hindman retired from the rectorship of the parish, but on the 13th of October, 1752, Gov. Dinwiddie recommended the Rev. John Jones to the parish in this note :

" WILLIAMSBURG, 16th October, 1752.

"TO THE VESTRY OF AUGUSTA PARISH :

" Gentlemen,—The Rev. Mr. John Jones has been recommended to me by many persons of good repute and undoubted credit as a worthy and learned divine. As such I recommend him to you, gentlemen, to be your pastor, not doubting but his conduct will be such as will entitle him to your favor by promoting peace and cultivating morality in the parish. Your receiving him to be your pastor will be very agreeable to,

" Worshipful Gentlemen,

" Your very humble serv't,

" ROBERT DINWIDDIE."

A month later Mr. Jones was received as rector, with a salary of £50 a year and £20 for his board. This excellent man continued to hold his position for over twenty-five years, and at the last meeting of the vestry at which he presided, November 19th, 1772, was authorized to employ a

curate.   In this capacity the services of Rev. Adam Smith were secured
but he only remained one year in the parish, and on the 9th of November,
1773, the Rev. Alex. Belmaine was chosen to fill his place.   For more than
four years subsequent to Mr. Belmaine's appointment, Mr. Jones retained
his rectorship, as appears from this entry, made at the meeting of the vestry February 1st, 1777.   Among those present was " Mr. Robert McClenachan, attorney-in-fact of the Rev. John Jones, Rector," &c.   Mr. Jones
was absent, no doubt, from his advanced age and growing infirmities.   It
does not appear how long Mr. Belmaine remained in the parish, but in
1776, he took an active part with the colonists against the mother country,
and became a chaplain in the Revolutionary army.

The financial affairs of the parish still seem to have been in an unsatisfactory condition, and we find this order, passed August 21st, 1753 :

"Whereas, it appears to this vestry that there is no regular account
either in the minute or register books, how the money collected off this
parish, for the use of the same, is laid out,

" I'ts, therefore, ordered that the church wardens and clerk of this vestry wait upon Mr. John Madison, late clerk and treasurer for this parish,
and demand of him a full and perfect account, deb'r and cred'r, with all
the vouchers for all the money collected off this parish, both fines and
levies, since the 6th of April, 1747 ; also a particular account of the persons' names given in the lists of tithable by Mr. Montgomery in the year
1748."

Mr. Madison and his brother officials do not seem to have been rigid
men of business, or ink and paper must have been scarce, for at the next
meeting of the vestry, November 28th, 1753, the following gentlemen,
having apparently neglected to give receipts in writing, were produced
before the vestry, in person—viz.:

" Mr. Robert Campbell, of whom the Glebe land for this parish was
purchased, acknowledged that he received the full sum of £60 of Mr.
James Lockhart, being the price agreed on for the said lands."

"Col. John Lewis came into this vestry and acknowledged that he received of Mr. John Madison the sum of £148, being the full sum agreed
on for building the Glebe work, according to bargain.   He also acknowledged that he will pay this parish £20 per year until the Glebe buildings
be finished, according to agreement, to commence from the first of September last past."

" The Rev. John Jones acknowledged himself satisfied that he receives
of this parish the sum of £20 per year from the 1st September last until
the Glebe buildings are finished, over and above his yearly salary."

To prevent any further irregularities or looseness in business matters,
this order was now made :

"Ordered that the church wardens agree with a collector and take bond
and sufficient security, and that said collector pay the money put into his
hands to the church wardens as he collects it, and discount for the whole
sum with this vestry at the laying of the next levy."

Pursuing a strict business system, the church wardens then took the following among other receipts:

"Received of Mr. James Lockhart the sum of £50, Virginia currency, for salary from the 1st of September, 1752, till the 1st of September, 1753; also £4.6.8 for a visit in July, 1752. I say, received by me.

[Signed]   "JOHN JONES."

"Received of Mr. James Lockhart the sum of £5, which was due from Augusta parish to me for one year's service as clerk to the vestry. I say, received by me.

[Signed]   "WM. PRESTON."

"Received of Mr. James Lockhart the sum of one pound ten, on William Hayne's account, for carrying the vestry books from Williamsburg. I say, received by me.   [Signed]   DAVID STUART."

And so on with all the accounts. That the vestry meant business, is obvious from this order, made Nov. 27, 1754: "It appearing to this vestry that Robt. McClenachan, gent., late Sheriff of Augusta county, and Collector of the parish levy, had collected in the year 1748 eighty-one tithables, at 2s. each, the then parish levy, and had not accounted for the same, and refuseth so to do, it's

Ordered, That the church wardens of this parish employ an attorney, practicing in this court, to prosecute him for the same."

From an act of the General Assembly, passed at the session of 1753, it appears that the salary of £50 a year was not sufficient for the support of the rector. The act provided:

That from and after the passing of this act, the vestries of the parishes of Frederick and Augusta and of Hampshire, when the same shall take place, at the times of laying their respective levies, shall * * * levy and assess upon the tithable persons in their respective parishes an annual salary of £100 for the minister of the said parishes, respectively, with an allowance of 6 per cent. for collecting the said salary, to be collected, levied, distrained for, and paid in the manner directed by the first above mentioned act, instead of, and in full compensation for the said salary of 16,000 pounds of tobacco and cask; and if the vestries of either said parishes shall neglect or refuse to levy said £100, in such case all the vestrymen of the parish neglecting or refusing, shall be liable to the action of the minister injured thereby, his executors or administrators, for all damages which he shall sustain by occasion of such refusal or neglect.

In 1760, it was resolved to build a new brick church in Staunton, 40 feet by 25. The work was undertaken and executed by Francis Smith, gent., of Hanover.

DIVISION OF THE PARISH.

On May 23d, 1774, the House of Burgesses received a petition from sundry inhabitants of the county and parish of Augusta, representing that "the parish is upwards of ninety miles long and near eighty miles wide, and that there are between three and four thousand tithables in it, and but one church; therefore, praying it may be divided." No action seems to have been taken on this subject by the House.

"From the commencement of the Revolution, onward," says Rev. T. T. Castleman, "until the year 1781, the doors of the venerable old church in Staunton remained closed. In that year, however, a portion of the British army, under Tarleton, drove the Legislature from its place of meeting, in Richmond, first to Charlottesville, and thence to Staunton. And here they held their meetings in the old church, and here the proposition was made to create "a dictator." Here they remained in session undisturbed for about sixteen days, and adjourned to meet in Richmond in October following.

"About 1788, the rectorship of the old church was in the hands of a Mr. Chambers. Who he was, or how long he remained in the parish, we are nowhere informed. Tradition says that after a short residence in this place, he removed to Kentucky.

"Years rolled on, in which a long interval occurred in the rectorship of the parish. At length the few friends who had been left from the desolations of the Revolution, and from the withering odium which had fallen on the Church because of its connection with the British crown, began to lift up their heads and to look around with a cautious and timid eye for some one to minister to them in holy things. At length a good old man, moving in the humbler walks of life ; remarkable for nothing but his innocent and inoffensive piety, presented himself as willing to serve them in the capacity of God's minister. He had long been a member of the Methodist church, and had there imbibed that spirit of feeling and ardent religion which seemed so peculiarly to characterize that body of Christians in those dreary days of our Church. Notwithstanding Mr. King's (for that was his name) roughness of manners, his meagre education, his simplicity of intellect, and his humble profession as a steam-doctor, he was taken in hand by a few friends of the Church and pushed forward in his laudable efforts. He was sent off with letters of commendation from Judge Archibald Stuart and the Hon. John H. Peyton to Bishop Madison, who ordained him Deacon, and sent him back to read the services and sermons to the desolate little flock in Staunton. His ministry began in 1811, and closed with his death, in 1819. That was a long and cheerless day for the Church here. No evidence can be found that she had a single communicant, besides the simple-hearted old Deacon, to kneel at her altar. So unpopular was her cause, that none but those whose principles were as true and unbending as steel, would venture openly to avow themselves her friends. An eye-witness told me that on the occasion of the first service after Mr. King's return from Williamsburg, the small congregation, the feeble and disjointed responses, the dampening dreariness of the church, with its old, high-back pews, and the long, sing-song, drawling tones in which the new Deacon attempted to read the service and one of Blair's sermons, presented a solemn ludicrousness he never before or since witnessed. The congregation, numbering not a dozen, left the church, dispirited and ashamed, almost resolved never to repeat the experiment. Mr. King died here, esteemed by all who knew him for his humble zeal and simple-hearted piety.

"On January 1, 1820, Rev. Daniel Stephens, DD., visited the parish and remained till the following Easter. On Easter Monday the congregation assembled and elected Vincent Tapp, Chapman Johnson, John H. Peyton, Briscoe G. Baldwin, Dabney Cosby, Wm. Young, Erasmus Stribling, Jacob Fackler, L. L. Stevenson, Alex. McCausland, A. M. Mosby, and N. C. Kinney. This vestry immediately assembled and passed resolutions highly commendatory of the preaching and living of Dr. Stephens, and unanimously electing him their rector. These were the props and pillars of the Church in its darkest and most trying days. Dr. Stephens labored and preached with a zeal and devotion which secured for him the confidence and love of the great mass of the congregation. Under his ministry, the Church was somewhat revived and the hearts of its friends cheered. At a convocation held in Staunton in May, 1821, the number of communicants reported was fifteen. In 1827, Dr. Stephens removed to the far West, where he died in 1850. His ministry was followed in 1831 by the Rev. Ebenezer Boyden. In the early part of Mr. B.'s ministry, the venerable old church was torn down, and a new one erected near its site. The latter was ready for use on July 23, 1831. Mr. Boyden continued in the parish, with high credit and universal acceptability to his congregation, until Jan. 7, 1833, when he resigned for another field in the West. Next came the Rev. W. G. Jackson, who preached with success and acceptability for several years. He was succeeded by Rev. Fred. D. Goodwin, who continued until 1843, and removed to Nelson county, leaving sixty-two communicants. He was followed by Rev. Thos. T. Castleman, who entered on his duties August, 1843, and continued in them until 1857."

He was succeeded by Rev. J. A. Latane, who served until 1871, when he withdrew from the church, left Staunton, and is now Bishop of the Reformed Episcopal Church of the United States, and a resident of Baltimore. The present rector, Rev. W. Q. Hullihen, was chosen to fill Mr. Latane's place in the year 1871.

Having given, as necessary to faithful history, a brief account of the Established Church in Virginia during the colonial period, when it was a corrupt Church, with an unworthy and hireling clergy—an account we would fain have blotted from the page of history—it is proper to refer, and it gives us no ordinary pleasure to do so, to the wonderful change which has, since the Revolution, taken place in Virginia. It must not be forgotten that while there were defective preaching and evil living among the colonial clergy, many of whom proved faithless shepherds, deserting their flocks during the war, some seeking Canada, others returning to England, and not a few taking to secular pursuits, there was also among them a small number of sincerely pious men, full of zeal and fidelity, whose religion was deeper than a vague, instinctive feeling. Such a man was Alex. Belmaine, who once filled the Staunton pulpit, as we have seen, and who, for this reason, is here specially alluded to. He was a man with enough of the weakness of humanity to have often been led astray by those around him, always warm-hearted, and in his later years, remarkable for his sincere repentance, his fervid piety, and exemplary life. This good, but too frequently erring man, would often, when standing in the chancel on sacramental occasions, refer in eloquent terms, and with tears in his eyes, to his past errors.

When the connection with the Bishop of London, the tie which united the churches in America, was severed by the acknowledgment of our inde-

pendence, steps were taken to form for the United States a future ecclesiastical government. The first move was in 1784, and in 1785 a meeting was held in Philadelphia, in which seven States were represented. At
this meeting the Book of Common Prayer was altered, accommodating it
to the recent changes in the State. Other steps were also taken for a
complete organization. It is unnecessary to go into the details of the
history of the Protestant Episcopal Church, even if our limits and design
admitted of it. Suffice it to say that it has had, since the formation of the
Federal Union, a regular, vigorous growth, and has now a sure footing in
every part of our country; has founded theological seminaries, domestic
and foreign mission societies, Sunday-school unions and book societies,
societies for the promotion of evangelical knowledge, historical societies,
church extension societies, the University of the South and ladies' colleges,
all highly successful, and under control of the General Convention. These
gratifying results have been obtained by reason of the fact that we have
been blessed for nearly a century with a truly pious, humble-minded, and
zealous ministry—men of deep-seated and pervasive piety, many of them
possessing sound, discriminating, well-balanced minds, some gifted with
eloquence, and all preaching diligently and faithfully "unto death." Some
of them have had social dispositions and highly-engaging manners, rendering themselves peculiarly acceptable to and influential with their flocks,
and the whole constituting a body or fraternity every way equal to any
similar body of Christian ministers in the land.

EPISCOPAL CHAPELS.

There are two Episcopal chapels in Augusta, one called Boyden Chapel,
situated near Folly Mills, the other near Hebron church, called Trinity
chapel. No clergyman officiates regularly in either.

ORPHAN CHILDREN.

Previous to the Revolution, the vestries bound out orphan children as
apprentices. They were required to serve until they arrived at the age of
twenty-one, were instructed in some art, were taught to read and write and
arithmetic, given two suits of clothing, etc.

THORNROSE CEMETERY.

To within a comparatively recent period, the grave-yard of the Episcopal church in Staunton was used for the interment of all persons dying in
or near the city. Its overcrowded condition, and the fear that the air
might become tainted, and thus spread disease and death, led to the purchase of twelve acres of land beyond the town limits in 1850, and the laying out of that beautiful City of the Dead, known as Thornrose Cemetery. Since no more bodies are likely to be buried in this cemetery than
the free oxygen contained in the rain and dew carried through the soil
will decompose, the air of Thornrose is not harmful, but fresh and healthy.
In the absence of a park, garden, or other decorative public ground in or

near Staunton, Thornrose is a favorite resort.   In its shady retreats silence
and solemnity reign, diffusing, as it were, a perpetual Sabbath over the
scene.

On the western slope of Betsy Bell, a handsomely improved cemetery
contains the bodies of the Federal soldiers who lost their lives during the
Civil war.

These two lofty and beautiful mounts, which rise above the landscape
near Staunton, piloting the people from every part of the county to the
town, thus derived their names: Some time in the seventeenth century,
during the prevalence of a plague in Scotland, two young girls, Betsy Bell
and Mary Gray, to escape infection, fled from their homes and took refuge
in a solitary booth in the Highlands.   Here they were often visited by an
admirer, who carried them supplies.   During his visits, he unconsciously
communicated the plague to them.   Both became ill, both died, and were
buried near Perth, where their graves, which were carefully sodded over
and attended to by the hands of surviving friends, were long pointed out,
and, for aught we know to the contrary, may still be seen.   Their sad fate
gave rise to a ballad commencing

> " Bessie Bell and Mary Gray, twa bonnie lassies,''

which has been preserved.   This ballad was taken to Ir eland by Scotch
emigrants, and the names it commemorates given to two hills, near Newtown Stewart, in the county of Tyrone.   The early settlers of Augusta no
doubt discovered some resemblance between the Irish mounts and the two
lovely hills which dominate Staunton, and affixed these names to them.

CHAPTER VIII.

From the arrival, in 1752, in Virginia of Gov. Dinwiddie, the history of
the little colony in Augusta becomes more closely connected with that of
the colony of Virginia, as that of Virginia becomes part of the history of
the North American colonies, at the head of which she stood at the opening of the Revolution.   It will have been perceived from the preceding
chapters that the Mississippi Valley was first explored and settled by the
French; that they had a line of forts from New Orleans to Quebec, one of
them being Fort du Quesne, where Pittsburg now stands.   The English
colonies were jealous of these movements, and that jealousy at length
ripened into hostility.   Previous, however, to any open acts of war, the

English sought to gain possession of the western country by throwing a large white population into it by means of land companies. In this way three trading companies came into existence—namely: "The Ohio Company," to which was granted 500,000 acres of land, to be taken on the south side of the Ohio river, between the Monongehela and Kanawha; the "Greenbrier Company," granting to John Lewis, of Augusta, and his associates, 100,000 acres, which he located on the river Greenbrier; the third, the "Loyal Company," incorporated June 12th, 1749, with a grant of 800,000 acres, from the Canadian line north and west. In 1750, the lands of the Ohio Company, and the western country, down to the Miami, were explored by the company's agent, C. Gist. In 1751, Col. John Lewis and his son Andrew, afterwards the distinguished General, surveyed the Greenbrier tract. The movements of the English were closely watched by the French, who, understanding their designs, determined to defeat them. They accordingly crossed Lake Champlain, built Crown Point, and fortified certain positions on the waters of the upper Ohio. A company of French soldiers was sent south as far as the Miami, by whom the English traders among the Indians were ordered to leave the country. The Indians, being unwilling to give them up, and the traders refusing to leave, a fight ensued in 1752, in which fourteen Miamis were killed and four white prisoners were taken. This was the beginning of a contest which resulted in the loss to France of all of her territory east of the Mississippi.

Thus stood affairs in 1752, when Gov. Dinwiddie arrived in Virginia. In 1753, viewing with alarm the French encroachments, he despatched Geo. Washington on a mission to the French commandant. Washington arrived at the French headquarters, near the present city of Pittsburg, November 26, 1773, and delivered his dispatches. The French commandant, who refused to leave, informed Washington that it was his purpose to destroy every English settlement in the West. Having performed his task, Washington left on his return, and reached Williamsburg January, 1774.

Washington's mission did not prevent war, and Virginia, seeing it to be inevitable, proceeded to raise a regiment, under Col. Joshua Fry, with Washington as Lieutenant-Colonel. This force was despatched to the West, and, on 28th of May, reached a place called Redstone, where they encountered a French and Indian force, which they attacked, killing ten and taking the rest prisoners. From the prisoners Washington learned that a French and Indian force of 1,000 men was in his front. Undaunted, he continued his march to the "Great Meadows," where he halted, and built a fort, calling it "Fort Necessity." On the 3d of July, at 11 o'clock, A. M., the whole French and savage force attacked Washington's works, which they attempted to take by assault. The battle raged until 8 in the evening, the air resounding with the sharp report of rifles and the hideous whoops and yells of the savages. The Virginians, animated by their chief, defended the fort with determined pluck. The little fortress was said to resemble a volcano in full blast, roaring and discharging its thick sheets of fire, which carried death to two hundred of the enemy. At the end of nine hours, the French leader, Count de Villiers, sent in a flag of truce, extolled the gallantry of the Virginians, and offered to treat for a surrender of the works on honorable terms. His proposals were accepted, and next morning the Virginians marched out.

The British Cabinet was now satisfied that a war was inevitable, and encouraged the colonies to form a union among themselves. This was done, and a plan, or system, was signed by the agents of the leading northern colonies and Maryland in 1754. Early in the Spring of 1755, the colonies attacked the French at four different points,—Nova Scotia, Crown Point, Niagara, and on the Ohio river. The operations against the French, on the Ohio, were conducted by Gen. Braddock, who arrived from England in February, with two Royal regiments, the 18th, under command of Lieut.-Col. Dunbar, and the 44th, under Sir Peter Halkett. Virginia raised eight hundred men to join Braddock, who arrived at Alexandria, then called Bellhaven, and appointed Washington his aide-de-camp. Braddock now despatched one company of colonial troops, under Capt. Thomas Lewis, of Augusta, to Greenbrier, to build a stockade fort and prevent Indian raids on the white settlements in that region. The captains of the Virginia companies in Braddock's command were Waggener, Cock, Hogg, Stephens, Poulson, Peyronny, Mercer and Stewart. Braddock commenced his march from Alexandria on the 20th April with about 2,200 men, and on the 9th of July, 1755, crossed the Monongehela river. We cannot delay to describe the amazing difficulties he encountered on his march or the disastrous defeat he now sustained. He fell into an ambuscade, was mortally wounded, and the army, after sustaining tremendous losses in killed and wounded, was put to flight. But for the coolness and courage of Washington and the Virginia Blues, as our troops were called, the whole force would have been destroyed. In this battle the British and colonial loss was 777 men killed and wounded.

The alarm and despondency arising from this disaster was soon dispelled by the elastic spirits and indomitable pluck of our people, encouraged by the eloquence of Rev. Samuel Davies and other Presbyterian and dissenting ministers.

Among the Virginians who survived this battle, and were afterwards distinguished in our annals, were Washington, Andrew and William Lewis, Mathews, Field, Grant and others.

It must be mentioned in this connection that Braddock held the provincial troops in contempt, and consequently kept them in the rear. Yet, although equally exposed with the rest, far from being affected by the fears that disordered the regular troops, they stood firm and unbroken, and under Washington, the Lewises, Mathews, Fields and other frontiersmen, covered the retreat of the regulars, and saved them from destruction. The British force retreated one hundred and twenty miles, and had they even stopped here, might have rendered important service by preventing the devastations and inhuman murders perpetrated by the French and Indians during the Summer on the western borders of Virginia and Pennsylvania. Instead of adopting this salutary course, Col. Dunbar, leaving the sick and wounded at Cumberland, marched with his troops to Philadelphia.

The whole frontier of Western Virginia was thus thrown open to the ravages of the Indians. The savages crossed the Alleghanies and pushed into Augusta and the lower Valley, torturing and murdering men, women and children. Some of the settlers fled east of the Blue Ridge, but the vast majority of the inhabitants of Augusta remained at home, prepared for defence, and determined, if necessary, to embrace an honorable death as their refuge against flight. The distresses of the people during this period of war exceed all description. In one of Washington's letters to Gov. Dinwiddie there is a famous passage which brings all this suffering and wretchedness vividly before us. He says: " The supplicating tears of the women, and moving petitions of the men, melt me into such deadly sorrow that I solemnly declare, if I know my own mind, I could offer myself a willing sacrifice to the butchering enemy, provided that would contribute to the people's ease."

The campaign of 1755, closed by the failure of Braddock's expedition and that under Gen. Shirley against Niagara. Although the French and English colonies had been for two years at war, peace was maintained between the two governments at home. An end was put to this unnatural state of affairs by a formal declaration of war by Great Britain against France, May 9th, 1756, and the bloody struggle, known as the French and Indian war, began, wherein most of Europe, North America, the East and West Indies, were engaged. The American colonies were called on to raise a force to coöperate with the royal troops, and Virginia contributed 1,600 men. Washington was commissioned colonel, Adam Stephens, Lieutenant-Colonel, and Andrew Lewis, Major. The force intended to operate in the West was placed under command of Gen. John Forbes, and consisted of 9,000 men. The plan of campaign for 1756-'57, was as extensive as that of the previous year, and resulted in the capture, by the French, of Fort William-Henry, Lake George. The success of the French and Indians brought the colonial affairs of England in America to an alarming situation, and fears were felt that the French would make good their claim to the country from Canada to Louisiana. But the blackest clouds frequently have rays of light in their fleecy folds. There are few days all dark. There are wells in the Sahara, flowers on the edge of the avalanche, and hope in every heart of despair. The fears now felt by a few were not participated in by the many. The mass of the people girded themselves for the contest, and affairs assumed, during the campaign of 1758-'60, a totally different aspect. Victory everywhere crowned British arms, and, in the end, Canada fell into the hands of the English.

During the expedition of 1758, an affair occurred in which Augusta's distinguished son, Gen. Andrew Lewis, was involved, and is so character-istic of the chivalric Virginian that we make room for it. During the march against Fort du Quesne, under Gen. Forbes, Maj. Grant, with 800 men, was sent forward to ascertain the state of affairs at the fort, and on the morning of the 21st of September, was before it. At the first alarm the gates were thrown open, and the French and Indians rushed forth in great numbers. The air was rent with the savage war-whoops as they charged, and before Grant's men had time to bring their guns to bear they were surrounded and captured. Maj. Andrew Lewis, of Augusta, who was at the head of the rear guard, hearing the sound of battle, left the baggage under charge of Capt. Bullitt and fifty men, and hastened to the front. He only arrived in time to see Grant's force prisoners, and be captured himself. The following incident is related of these officers while on parole at Fort du Quesne. Grant, in his dispatches, endeavored to throw all the blame of capture on Lewis, who, in fact, deserved all the credit of saving, by means of Bullitt, the baggage and the few men who escaped to the rear guard. The messenger who had been despatched with the papers by Grant to the British commander, was captured, and the dis-patches fell into the French commandant's hands. Lewis being present when they were opened and read, heard with astonishment and indigna-tion their contents, and, without uttering a word, started in pursuit of Grant, whom he soon found. He instantly charged him with his infamous calumny, drew his sword, and called on Grant to defend himself. Grant declined the combat, when Lewis denounced him as a liar and poltroon, and, in the presence of two French officers, spat in his face.

Hearing of the capture of Grant's force, Gen. Forbes urged forward the main body of his troops, and, on reaching Fort du Quesne, found it aban-doned by the French, who, alarmed at the size of his force, took to their boats and retreated down the Ohio. Before leaving, the French applied a slow match to the magazine and blew up the fort. It was rebuilt by the British and called Pittsburg, in compliment to William Pitt, Earl of Chat-ham, who was very popular in America.

Thus more than a century and a-half after the first permanent settle-ment in America, England completed the conquest of Canada,—an object which had been for seventy years desired by the colony,—effected the expulsion of the French from the Ohio Valley, and, despite the efforts of her rivals, France and Spain, became almost sole possessor of North America. The treaty of Fontainbleau, in 1762, put an end to war.

SANDY CREEK EXPEDITION OF 1756.

Before closing this subject, the leading events of which we have set before the reader in such rapid succession, some allusion must be made to the Sandy Creek expedition. The depredations of the Indians, after Braddock's defeat, led to the fitting out, under Maj. Andrew Lewis, of this force, with orders to attack the Indian towns west of the Ohio. The force consisted of three hundred and forty men, and left Fort Frederick, on New river, in the then County of Augusta, for the mouth of Sandy creek, February, 1756. Among the officers in this command were Capts. Wm. Preston, Peter Hogg, John Smith, Archibald Alexander, R. Breckenridge, —— Woodson and —— Overton, and Capt. David Stewart, commissary. There were also two volunteer companies, under Capts. Montgomery and Dunlap, and a party of friendly Cherokees, commanded by Capt. Paris. The Indian forces against whom they marched were commanded by their celebrated chiefs, Outacité, the Man Killer, Round O, and Yellow Bird. While Lewis' command was at Fort Frederick waiting for supplies, &c., sermons were preached to them by Revs. John Craig, of Augusta, and Mr. Brown. The command crossed the Holstein river February 18th, 1756, and reached Sandy creek on the 28th. Their supplies ran short, and a famine was threatened, men deserted, and but for the wisdom and firmness of Lewis, who possessed the unbounded respect and confidence of his officers and men, the whole expedition would have been destroyed. The sufferings from hunger were so severe that the men cut their buffalo robes into tugs and ate them, and hence the name of the stream, on whose banks it occurred, of Tug river. When within a few miles of the Ohio, Lewis received orders to return, and thus the expedition ended without results of importance. The Indians were much elated at Lewis' retreat, and immediately advanced on the white settlements, carrying death to many a helpless family. Conspicuous among their blood-thirsty chiefs was Killbuck, who, in 1757, drew Capt. Mercer's force of forty Virginians into an ambuscade and killed thirty-four of them. The following year, 1754, the savages reappeared east of the mountains, and one of these parties, consisting of fifty warriors, reached a point nine miles from Woodstock, in Shenandoah. The whites took refuge in the house of one George Painter. Mr. P., attempting to escape, was killed. They then plundered and burnt the house. While the house was burning, they forced from Mrs. P. her four children, hung them in trees, and shot them in savage sport. They then moved off with forty-eight prisoners. On reaching their village, after six days' travel, they tied to a stake Jacob Fisher, a helpless prisoner, who had given them much trouble, and burnt him to death.

After an absence of three years, Mrs. P., her daughters and several others escaped and returned to their homes, but some remained, married Indians, and spent their lives with the savages.

DEATH AND CHARACTER OF THE FOUNDER.

In 1762, the Founder died, thirty years after coming to Augusta, and in his eighty-fourth year. He was a man of superior abilities and virtuous principles, prudent in concerting his plans, and perseveringly vigorous in executing them. The last thirty years of his life were devoted to advancing the interests of the little community he founded. His mind was improved by a liberal education, and few possessed greater knowledge of everything capable of forming and qualifying a man for public employment. Tall, vigorous, and commanding in figure, he was distinguished for the manly beauty of his person, the cordial frankness of his address, the charms of his conversation, and the desperate character of his courage. He was buried at Bellefonte, and an enormous limestone slab, rude and uncut, was placed over his grave, where it still lies half-buried. In 1850, this was replaced by a marble slab, bearing the following inscription:

Here lie the remains of

JOHN LEWIS,

who slew the Irish lord, settled Augusta County,
Located the town of Staunton,
And furnished five sons to fight the battles of the
AMERICAN REVOLUTION.
He was the son of Andrew Lewis, Esq., and Mary Calhoun,
and was born in Donegal Co., Ireland, 1678,
and died in Virginia Feb. 1st, 1762.
He was a brave man, a true patriot and
a firm friend of liberty throughout the world.

Mortalitate relicta, vivit immortalitate inductus.

HANNAH DENNIS, THE QUEEN WITCH OR INVISIBLE PRINCESS.

In 1761, sixty Shawanese warriors penetrated east of the Alleghanies to the James river settlements, committing murders and carrying off prisoners—among them Mrs. Renix and her four children. Mrs. Renix was, under Bouquet's treaty, brought to Staunton, in 1767, and redeemed, as also her son, afterwards Maj. Renix, of Greenbrier, and her other children, except her son Joshua, who became so enamored of savage life that he took an Indian wife, became a chief among the Miamis, amassed a considerable fortune, and died, at Detroit, in 1810.

Among the captives was Hannah Dennis, a clever and spiritual woman, who was sent to reside at an Indian town, near Chillicothe. Instead of giving way to grief at her bondage, she applied herself to learn the Indian language, performed such labor as they required of her with alacrity, professed warm attachment to their ways of life, painted her body like the squaws, and conformed to their manners and customs. She became very popular with the tribe, and in order to enhance her influence, professed a knowledge of medicine, of the properties of plants and herbs, and commenced practice as a doctor among them. She soon discovered the superstitious character of the Indians, and determined to take advantage of it to increase her power and position. Accordingly, she professed witchcraft, and affected to be a prophetess. Unlike most witches, Hannah was exceedingly beautiful, and employed her charms of person and the seducing grace of her manners to enhance her influence. By cunning and craft, by pretending to tame horses and wild beasts by whispering in their ears ; to divine future events from the various indications that manifest themselves in fire, smoke, and in other ways ; by spells and incantations to communicate with the dead ; to foretell earthquakes, allay storms, drive away pestilence, cure disease by virtue of a few words pronounced over the sick person,—a quicker way than with snake-root or ginseng,—this marvelous woman acquired such a reputation among the savages that they not only gave her perfect liberty but looked upon her as a female deity, and honored her as a Queen. Placing little value upon their homage, she determined to escape, and in June, 1763, left Chillicothe, in search, as the Indians supposed, of herbs for medicinal purposes, as was her custom, and did not return, but, crossing the Scioto, set out for Virginia. Alarm spread among the tribe when her disappearance was known; they ran to all parts on foot and on horseback, but she could not be found. The chiefs met ; the utmost consternation prevailed ; scouts were dispatched to scour the country. Finally the pursuing savages caught sight of her beyond the Scioto, forty miles below Chillicothe. They fired upon her but without effect, and probably they did not expect to kill her, as their rifles were loaded with leaden instead of silver bullets. They forded the river and still pursued, but Hannah had disappeared as if the clouds had received her up, or she had been swallowed by the earth. Awed by the mysterious disappearance, they gave up the chase, lit their camp-fires, and passed the night on the spot. Next morning they set out on their return. When they had been gone some time, the invisible princess crept from a hollow log, in which she had concealed herself, and dressed a wound in her foot which had been received during her flight. Knowing enough of the Indian character to feel satisfied they would not return to look after one who had gone, in their opinion, to the spirit land, Hannah spent three days at this point, nursing her wound and recovering her strength, and then resumed her journey for the mouth of the Kanawha. She crossed the Ohio on a log of drift-wood, and after travelling for twenty nights, resting during the day in a cave or under the branches of trees, subsisting on fruits gathered in the forest with difficulty, she finally set down on the banks of a stream which supplied her drink, to die. In this condition, almost expiring from hunger and fatigue, she was discovered by a backwoodsman, relieved by the pioneers, and ministered to until restored, then supplied with a horse, and conducted to Jackson's river, and thence to her home and friends.

HISTORY OF SELIM, AN ALGERINE CONVERT.

Among the curious waifs found astray in Augusta, about the year 1756, was a native of Algiers, by the name of Selim. The particulars of his life are given upon the authority of Rev. Benj. H. Rice. About 1756, Mr. Samuel Givens, of Augusta, when shooting in the forest, near his residence, was startled by seeing in the limbs of a fallen tree a living creature, which he supposed to be a beast of prey, and was in the act of shooting, when he discovered it was a human being. Approaching nearer, he found a man in the most wretched and pitiable condition, his person naked, except his feet, about which a few rags were tied, and covered with scabs and sores, his body emaciated, and the man nearly famished to death. As the man could not speak English, Givens could hold no conversation with him, but acted the part of the good Samaritan by conducting him to his house, supplied his wants, and by tender care, restored him to health and strength. He then accompanied Mr. Givens to the house of Col. Dickerson, near Windy Cave, who entertained him for some months with true backwoodsman's hospitality.

The African, finding it impossible to communicate his history without a knowledge of English, applied himself, with remarkable success, to acquire it. In the course of a few months, being aided by the Colonel and his family, he so far mastered our language as to be able to communicate his ideas, and repaid the kindness of his friends by giving them an affecting narrative of his various unparalleled misfortunes. He said his name was Selim; that he was born of wealthy and respectable parents in Algiers; that when a small boy his parents sent him to Constantinople for education, and that after he had spent some years in that city, he returned to Africa. His visit over, he reëmbarked for Constantinople, to complete his education. The ship was captured by a Spanish man-of-war, and Selim was taken prisoner. Spain was at the time an ally of England and France, and the Spaniards, falling in with a French ship bound for New Orleans, transferred Selim to the vessel, and he was landed in New Orleans (and most probably sold into slavery, though this is not stated). After being some time in that city, he was sent up the Mississippi, to Ohio, to a Shawanese town, and left as a prisoner in their hands. The Indians held a prisoner at this time, a white woman from the frontiers of Virginia, and he, by signs, learned from her whence she came. The woman pointed to the rising sun. Selim was sufficiently acquainted with history and geography to know that there were English settlements on the eastern shore of America, and resolved to escape to them. With no pilot but the sun, no provisions for the journey, and no arms to kill game, he eluded the vigilance of the Indians, and set forth on his journey and traveled through the wilderness, subsisting on nuts and berries and other wild fruit, until his clothes were torn from his body, and, almost famished and' dying, he was found by Mr. Givens near Staunton. The Colonel was so much moved by his tale of woe, that he supplied his every want, made him his companion, and introduced him to his friends and neighbors. Taking him to Staunton on court-day, Selim there saw Rev. Jno. Craig who attracted his particular attention, so much so, that Selim addressed him and asked to accompany him home. Mr. C. consented, and gave him a warm welcome. He afterwards asked Selim the cause of his wish to live with him. Selim replied: " When I was in my distress, I once, in my sleep, dreamed that I was in my own country, and saw the largest assembly of men my eyes ever beheld, collected in a vast plain, dressed in uniform, and drawn up in military order. At the further side of the plain, and at an immense distance, I saw a person, whom I understood to be a person of great distinction; but the distance prevented my discerning what sort of a person he was. I only knew him to be a person of distinction. I saw, every now and again, one or two of this large assembly attempting to cross the plain to this distinguished personage; but when they had got about half over, they suddenly dropped into a hole in the earth, and I saw them no more. I also imagined I saw an old man standing by himself at a distance from this assemblage, and one or two of the multitude applied to him for direction how to cross the plain, and all who received and followed his advice, got safely over." " As soon as I saw you," added Selim, " I knew you to be the man who gave these directions, and this has convinced me that it is in the mind of God that I should apply to you for instruction in religion. It is for this reason I desire to go home with you. When I was among the French, they endeavored to prevail on me to embrace the Christian religion; but as I observed they made use of images, I looked on Christianity with abhorrence, such worship being, in my opinion, idolatrous."

Mr. Craig cheerfully undertook the agreeable work he seemed called to by an extraordinary Providence. He soon found Selim understood the Greek language, which greatly facilitated the business. He gave him a Greek testament. Selim spent his time in reading it, and Mr. C. his leisure hours in explaining to him the Gospel of Jesus Christ. In a fortnight he obtained what Mr. C. considered a competent knowledge of the Christian religion, and was baptized in Mr. C.'s church. Some time after this, Selim expressed a wish to return to his native country. Mr. C. suggested that he might be ill-used by his friends and countrymen, now that he was no longer a Mohammedan, and asked if it would not be better to remain in Virginia, where he might enjoy his religion without disturbance.

To this Selim replied that his father was a man of good estate, and he was his heir; that he had never been brought up to labor, and knew no possible way in which he could obtain a subsistence; that he could not bear the thought of living a life of dependence; that he was sensible of the strong prejudices of his friends against Christianity, yet could not think that, after all the calamities he had undergone, his father's religious prejudices would so far get the better of his humanity as to cause him to ill use his son on that account, and that, at all events, he desired to make the experiment. Mr. Craig urged his temptations to return to Moham- medanism, to which Selim said he would never deny Jesus.

Finding him resolved, Mr. C. and his friends supplied him with money and a letter of recommendation to Hon. Robert Carter, of Williamsburg. Mr. C. gave Selim further aid, and he sailed for England with the flatter- ing prospect of once more seeing his parents and native land. Some years later, Selim reappeared in Virginia, at Mr. Carter's, in a state of insanity. His constant complaint was that he had no friend, and where could he find a friend? From this complaint, and his pitiable condition, it was conjec- tured his father was not his friend. In lucid intervals, Selim gave some account of his life after leaving Virginia. He arrived in England, and proceeded to Africa. He found his parents alive; on learning that he had become a Christian, his father disowned him as a child, and turned him out of doors. Broken-hearted, he returned to England, but finding no way to earn a support there, he set sail for America, and during the voyage such was his grief that he sank into madness. He wandered from Williamsburg to Staunton, and thence to Col. Dickerson's, thence to the Warm Springs, where he met a young clergyman, Rev. Mr. Templeton, who, hearing something of his history, asked him if he was acquainted with the Greek language, to which he modestly replied that he understood a little of it. Mr. T. handed him a Greek testament, and asked him to con- strue some of it. He opened the book, and when he saw what it was, in a transport of joy he pressed it to his heart, and then complied with Mr. T.'s request. He left the Warm Springs, and returned to Mr. Carter's, who was now in Westmoreland, and was finally consigned to the lunatic asylum in Williamsburg. Selim was inoffensive in his behavior, grateful for favors received, always manifested a veneration for religion, and was often seen engaged in prayer. He died with great composure. His por- trait was taken for Gov. Page by Peale, of Philadelphia, and long hung on the walls of Rosewell.

MASSACRE AT SEYBERT'S FORT.

The fatal talent of the Indian for strategy is well illustrated by the cap- ture of Fort Seybert, which stood about twelve miles west of the present town of Franklin, in Pendleton county, and about fifty miles from Staun- ton. This rude fort, composed of log huts enclosing a hollow square, if properly manned, could have resisted any attack of savages. It was the strong place of the surrounding settlements, and into it the people gathered in times of threatened danger. In 1758, a party of Shawanese invested the fort, and demanded a surrender. Finding neither threatening words nor bullets of any avail, the cunning savages, after two days' trial, resorted to strategy, and unhappily, with success. They made various propositions to the besieged to give up, promising to spare their lives; but if not, and the siege continued, and the place was taken, they said every soul would be murdered. The promise of safety lured the unfortunate whites from the line of security, and they surrendered the fort. There were thirty-six persons in the work, and these the savages proceeded to secure. Instantly the whites realized the horror of their situation, and foresaw the fate which awaited them. Of the whole number, all were massacred but eleven. Ten, whom the Indians wished to save, were secured and removed from the fort; the others were tied hand and foot, and seated in a continuous line upon a log. Behind each of the unfortunates stood a stalwart savage, who, at a given signal, sunk his tomahawk through the skull of his quivering victim. The work finished, the fort was destroyed. This horrible scene was witnessed by a boy named Dyer, who was spared, although not of the number removed from the fort. He was led into captivity to the Shawanese towns on the Scioto. After nearly two years captivity, he escaped and returned home. Nothing was ever known of the fate of the ten borne off as prisoners.

BINGAMON AND THE INDIANS.

In 1758, near the present village of Petersburg, Hardy county, lived a giant by the name of Bingamon, whose house was broken open by the Indians at night. Before Bingamon was aware of the danger, the savages were in the house. Bingamon got his parents, wife and children, beneath a bed, and then prepared for action. The hired man was called down, but refused to come. The room was dark, and having discharged his rifle, he clubbed it and beat about at random. He fought with desperation, killing seven men. The eighth rushed from the house, and escaped, telling his tribe he had met a "perfect devil." In the morning, Bingamon could scarcely be prevented from killing his cowardly hired man. Bingamon was greatly distinguished for his firmness and strength.

FURMAN'S FORT, ON THE SOUTH BRANCH OF THE POTOMAC.

In 1764, eighteen Delawares killed Wm. Furman and N. Ashby, who had gone hunting near the fort. They then passed on to Frederick county, and killed D. Jones and his wife and Mrs. Thomas, capturing Miss Thomas. They also killed Mr. and Mrs. Loyd and several of their children, and several others. These are only a few of the murders and captures of this party.

INDIAN FORAYS AND MASSACRES IN SHENANDOAH.

In 1764, a party of eight Delaware Indians, with a white man who had joined their tribe, by the name of Abraham Mitchell, advanced into the present county of Shenandoah, and near Strasburg killed George Miller, his wife and two children. They also, the same day, killed John Dellinreg and took his wife and infant child prisoners. In crossing the mountains the child, who probably retarded the retreat, had its brains beaten out against a tree. A party of white men pursued them, overtook them in the Southbranch Mountains, fired upon them, killing one, when the others fled, leaving everything behind.

In the Autumn of 1765, the savages reappeared in Shenandoah, near Woodstock, and killed George Sigler and some women and children who were with him. Shortly before Sigler's murder two Indians were discovered lurking in the neighborhood of Mill creek. Three whites went in pursuit—M. and John Painter, and Wm. Moore. They had not gone far before they approached a fallen pine tree, with a very bushy top. As they neared it, M. Painter observed, "We'd better look sharp; it is likely the Indians are concealed under the tops of this tree." The words were scarcely spoken before a savage rose up and fired. The ball grazed the temple of J. Painter. Moore and Painter returned the fire. One of their balls passed through the Indian's body, and he fell, as they supposed, dead. The other fled. The whites pursued some distance, but the fugitive was too fleet for them. They gave up the chase and returned to the pine tree; but, to their astonishment, the supposed dead Indian had moved off with both rifles and a large pack of skins. They followed his trail, and when he found they were gaining on him, he got into a sink-hole, and as soon as they approached, commenced firing upon them. He had poured out a quantity of powder on dry leaves, filled his mouth with bullets, and, using a musket which was a self-primer, he was enabled to load and fire with astonishing quickness. He thus fired thirty times before they got a chance to dispatch him. At last Moore got an opportunity, and shot him through the head, and Moore received the premium allowed by law for Indian scalps. The fugitive who made his escape met a young white woman, Miss Sethorne, near the present town of Newmarket, whom he pulled from her horse, and forced off with him. After travelling twenty miles, it is supposed the young captive broke down from fatigue, when the savage beat her to death with a pine knot. Her screams were heard by some whites living two miles from the scene of horror. On going, next day, to ascertain the cause, they found her dead body, naked, and covered with blood and bruises.

RAID ON JACKSON'S RIVER AND CATAWBA.

In 1764, a party of forty or fifty Mingos and Delawares came up Sandy to New river, where they separated, one party going towards Roanoke and Catawba, the other in the direction of the Jackson's river settlement. The party for Jackson's river traveled down Dunlap's creek and crossed the river, and killed a Mr. Carpenter, took his son, two young Browns and a woman, all of whom were working in the fields, prisoners. They then robbed the house and fled. Capt. Paul and twenty men went in pursuit and accidentally fell upon the first party, who had gone towards Roanoke. The savages were discovered about midnight, and were all lying round a small fire wrapped in their skins and blankets. Paul's men fired upon them, killing three and wounding others. The rest fled and escaped. Several captives, taken on the Roanoke, were liberated, and considerable plunder recovered. The deadening effects of these terrible scenes may be derived from the reply of a prisoner rescued at this time, a Mrs. Glass, of English birth. She had known Capt. Paul, and recognized his voice. She called his name just as one of his men, supposing her to be a squaw, was about tomahawking her. She made no resistance, and, when asked the reason, replied: " I would as soon die as not; my husband is murdered, my children slain, my parents are dead. I have not a relative in America; everything dear to me is gone. I have no wishes, no hopes, no fears; I would not rise to my feet to save my life." Such were some of the horrors experienced on the frontier.

The British Government, anxious to secure peace on any honorable terms, directed Col. Bouquet to issue a proclamation forbidding the whites to settle or hunt west of the Alleghanies. In accordance with these instructions, Col. B. issued the following proclamation, which was posted against the trees, on the booths at the trading points, and on the trails or road sides leading to the west:

" Whereas, by a treaty at Easton, in the year 1758, and afterwards ratified by his Majesty's ministers, the country to the west of the Alleghany mountain is allowed to the Indians for their hunting ground; And as it is of the highest importance to H. M.'s service, and the preservation of the peace and good understanding with the Indians, to avoid giving them any just cause of complaint: This is, therefore, to forbid any of H. M.'s subjects to settle or hunt west of the Alleghany Mountains, on any pretense whatever, unless such have obtained leave in writing from the general or governors of their respective provinces, and produce the same to the commanding officer at Fort Pitt. And all the officers and non-commissioned officers, commanding at the several posts erected in that part of the country for the protection of the trade, are hereby ordered to seize, or cause to be seized, any of H. M.'s subjects who, without the above authority, should pretend, after the publication hereof, to settle or hunt upon the said lands, and send them, with their horses and effects, to Fort Pitt, there to be tried and punished, according to the nature of their offence, by the sentence of a court martial."

In October, 1764, a similar proclamation was issued by the government, and in 1765, to accomplish the object in view, two movements were made into the Indian territory. The first, under Gen. Bradstreet, who proceeded

to Lake Erie, and the second, under Col. Bouquet, who marched to the
Muskingum. Bradstreet had a grand council, at Niagara, with twenty
tribes, in June, who had sued for peace, and concluded a treaty. Bouquet
proceeded, at the head of a force, from Fort Pitt, in the Autumn, and,
reaching the Muskingum, convened in council the Delaware and Shawanese, negotiated and signed a peace with them, and received from them
two hundred and six prisoners, ninety of whom were Virginians, or West
Augusta people, and one hundred and sixteen Pennsylvanians. · He also
received from the Shawanese hostages for the delivery of other captives,
who could not be brought in at that time. A number of distinguished
chiefs united in forming this treaty, among them Kyashuta, Red Hawk,
Custaloga and Captain John.

THE HORSE'S SAGACITY AND HATRED OF THE SAVAGE.

Not only the people but their domestic animals, at least the horse, detested the savages, and many a pioneer owed his life to his sagacity. The
animal snuffed the presence of the Indian in the tainted air, and neither
whip nor spur could urge him to the dreaded spot. Many instances could
be cited to prove the intelligence and fidelity of the horse. The following
will suffice: A gentleman, riding home through a wood at night, struck
his head against the branch of a tree and fell stunned from his horse. The
steed immediately returned to the house which they had lately left, and
which was now closed and the family in bed, but he pawed at the door
until some one arose and opened it. He turned about, and the man, wondering at the affair, followed him, and the faithful animal led him to the
place where his master lay senseless on the ground.

CHAPTER IX.

The affairs of the people of Augusta, and more particularly of the district
of West Augusta, were further complicated for over twenty years previous
to the Revolution. This was caused by a disagreement between the colonies of Virginia and Pennsylvania as to their boundary line, a question in
which the Indians were also deeply interested, and which intensified their
hostility to the Augusta or Virginian people, who were settling on their
lands without purchase. We purpose now giving a brief history, derived
from Dr. Creigh's interesting and valuable work, of this controversy, and
of Mason & Dixon's line, by which, in 1784, the matter was forever
settled.

As far back as 1752, a controversy existed as to the boundary line between Virginia and Pennsylvania—Virginia relying upon the charter of James I, and Pennsylvania claiming under her charter from Charles II, in 1581. The Pennsylvanians contended that their line extended several miles beyond Pittsburg or Fort du Quesne, while Virginia claimed all the territory between the parallels of 36° 30′ and 39° 40′ North latitude, from the margin of the Atlantic due west to the Mississippi. Settlements had occurred on the Monongehela, the Youghiogheny and on other tributaries of the Ohio for one hundred and twenty miles south of Fort du Quesne, as well as on the Greenbrier, the Elk and the Little Kanawha, or in the whole region of Northwestern Virginia and Southwestern Pennsylvania, and were claimed by Virginia as part of Augusta County, including Pittsburg, a frontier town, where, as will appear later on in this chapter, the County Court of Augusta was often held before the Revolution. The Pennsylvanians appealed to history in support of their rights, and quoted the instructions from George II to Penn, Lieutenant-Governor of Pennsylvania in 1765, in which H. M. said : "Whereas, it hath been represented unto us that several persons from Pennsylvania and the back settlements of Virginia have emigrated to the westward of the Alleghany Mountains, and there have seated themselves on lands contiguous to the river Ohio, in express disobedience of our royal proclamation of October 7, 1763, it is, therefore, our will and pleasure, and you are enjoined and required, to put a stop to all these and all other the like encroachments for the future."

On December 11, 1766, the Governor of Virginia wrote the Governor of Pennsylvania : " No regard is paid to the proclamation of October 7th and April, 1766, by you. But the commander-in-chief has taken a more effectual method to remove these settlers by giving orders to our officer and party to summon the settlers on Redstone creek to warn them to quit these illegal settlements, and, in case of refusal, to threaten military execution."

And in July, 1766, Gen. Gage wrote to Gov. Penn : "The garrison of Fort Pitt shall assist to drive away the settlers," (the settlers on Redstone creek, near Brownsville.)

In May, 1766, the chiefs of the Six Nations held a council at Fort Pitt, and said, as soon as peace was made, in 1765, contrary to their engagements, many white people came over the great mountains and settled at Redstone creek and on the Monongehela. George Croghan, the Indian agent, wrote to Gen. Gage: " If some effectual measures are not speedily taken to remove these people, till a boundary line can be settled, and the governors pursue vigorous measures, the consequences may be dreadful, and we be involved in all the calamities of another general war."

In consequence of this state of affairs, Gov. Penn issued a proclamation warning the settlers of the Indian complaints that they had settled on their lands without purchase and contrary to the King's proclamation; ordering them to assemble to be told of their lawlessness, and, in case they refused to collect or leave, directed the commander-in-chief to seize and make prize of their goods; after which they would be driven from "the lands to the westward of the Alleghanies, the property of the Indians."

Gov. Fauquier at the same time, July, 1766, ordered the same people to evacuate the lands, and if they failed to do so, "they must expect no protection or mercy from the government, and be exposed to the revenge of the exasperated Indians."

In September, 1766, the Speaker of the House of Delegates of Pennsylvania acknowledged that "the boundary has not been exactly ascertained." In October, Gov. Penn asked the aid of Virginia in removing the settlers, and the Governor of Virginia replied that he had already issued three proclamations to these settlers, and had given orders on the subject to the military, but that a large majority of the families remained. Gov. Penn now acknowledged that the boundary line between the two colonies, near their western limits, had not been made, and that the settlers would shelter themselves under a disputed jurisdiction, which subsequent events fairly demonstrated. Gov. Penn, in 1768, issued a proclamation denouncing death without the benefit of clergy against the settlers who remained on the lands thirty days after the 1st of May, 1768. In addition, he sent commissioners to read the proclamation to the people, and to expostulate with them on the folly and injustice of their settling on the Indian lands, etc. The commissioners reached Redstone March 23d, 1768, read the proclamation, etc. A meeting of the people took place, and while in progress a number of Indians arrived. The business was explained to all parties, and they agreed, both whites and reds, that nothing should be done as to the removal of the whites until after the conclusion of a treaty then in progress between Geo. Croghan and the Indians. In these settlements there were only about one hundred and fifty families, or, say, seven hundred and fifty persons.

George Croghan, J. Allen and J. Shippen were appointed commissioners to meet the chiefs of the Six Nations and form a treaty, and they accordingly met in conference at Pittsburg, May 9, 1768. The result of the conference was that two messengers were sent to the settlers to signify to them the great displeasure of the Six Nations, and that the Indians expected them to remove without further notice. These two deputies were to be accompanied by the White Mingo and the three deputies sent from the Six Nations' country; but, when the time of their departure arrived, they refused to go, saying that their instructions were only to attend to making a treaty, and that driving the white people away from these settlements was a matter which no Indian could with any satisfaction be concerned in, and they thought it most proper for the English themselves to compel their own people to remove from the Indian lands.

The commissioners, finding all efforts fruitless to gain over the Indian deputies, determined to return to Philadelphia, and, while making their arrangements, they were visited at their lodgings by one of the principal warriors of the Six Nations, who stated that he regretted the state of affairs, fearing the ill-will of the white people, yet pledging his Indian faith and Indian honor, that the Six Nations had good hearts to all their English brethren. Thus ended the treaty at Fort Pitt, and the white settlers were left on the lands.

From this period the country west of the Alleghanies began to fill up with a further white immigration, but the boundary question was still a source of trouble, involving not only the extent of Pennsylvania, but the title to lands. The difficulties, too, were aggravated by one Michael Cresap, who sought to create disturbances on the boundary question, declaring that the province of Pennsylvania did not extend west of the Alleghanies, but that all "westward of them was the King's land."

In the midst of the trouble, Dr. John Connolly, a citizen of Virginia, appeared, and posted up the following significant notice, taking up the controversy on behalf of Virginia:

"Whereas, his Excellency, John, Earl of Dunmore, Governor of the colony of Virginia, has been pleased to nominate and appoint me Captain-Commandant of the militia of Pittsburg and its dependencies, with instructions to assure his Majesty's subjects, settled on the western waters, that having the greatest regard to their prosperity and interest, and convinced, from the reported memorials of the grievances of which they complain, that he purposes recommending to the House of Burgesses the necessity of erecting a new county, to include Pittsburg, for the redress of your grievances, and to take every other step that may tend to afford you that justice which you solicit. In order to facilitate this desirable circumstance, I (John Connolly) hereby require and command all persons in the dependency of Pittsburg to assemble themselves there, as militia, on the 25th inst., at which time I shall communicate other matters for the promotion of public utility."

The Pennsylvanians immediately arrested Connolly, and on his refusal to find security for his good behavior, committed him to gaol. Connolly induced the Sheriff to give him leave of absence for a few days. during which, guarded by the settlers of Redstone, with Virginian predilections, he returned to Virginia. Penn wrote to Dunmore demanding an explanation of his sending Connolly to the State, and calling on and requiring the law officers of Pennsylvania to assert her rights and protect her people "within her own limits."

The correspondence between Penn and Dunmore was spicy, and in it Dunmore supported Connolly, who returned to Pittsburg, and kept around him an armed body of men, to execute his orders in defence of Virginia's laws. The magistrates of Westmoreland county, Pennsylvania, refusing to acknowledge any authority but that of Pennsylvania, were arrested when returning from court, April 9, 1774, by order of Connolly, and refusing to give bail under the laws of Virginia, arrangements were made, and they were sent to Staunton for trial. The magistrates sent to Staunton were Smith, Mackay, and McFarland. On their way to Staunton, Mackay called at Williamsburg to visit Lord Dunmore, who informed him that Connolly was authorized by him to prosecute the claim of Virginia to Pittsburg and its dependencies. On arriving in Staunton, the three justices gave security and returned to their homes.

Col. Wm. Crawford, President of the Court, immediately sent an express to Gov. Penn, detailing the facts, and at the same time stating that Capt. Connolly, a few weeks before, went to Staunton, and was sworn in as a Justice of the Peace for Augusta county, in which " it is pretended that the country about Pittsburg is included, and he is constantly surrounded by about 180 militia, and obstructs the execution of every legal process."

The Provincial Council ordered the arrest of Connolly, and sent commissioners to Lord Dunmore. At the same time, they deprecated the alarming situation of affairs, and advised Col. Crawford, as " Virginia had the power to raise a much larger military force than Pennsylvania, prudence would dictate the propriety of not attempting to contend with them by way of force."

The commissioners sent to Dunmore were Jas. Tilghman and A. Allen, and arrived in Williamsburg in May, 1774. Dunmore informed them that "the jurisdiction of Fort Pitt would not be relinquished by Virginia without His Majesty's order." This put an end to their mission. On the departure of the commissioners, Dunmore issued the following proclamation :

"Whereas, I have reason to apprehend that the government of Pennsylvania, in prosecution of their claim to Pittsburg and its dependencies, will endeavor to obstruct His Majesty's government thereof, under my administration, by illegal and unwarrantable commitment of the officers I have appointed for that purpose, and that that settlement is in some danger of annoyance from the Indians, also, and it being necessary to support the dignity of His Majesty's government and protect his subjects in the quiet and peaceable enjoyment of their rights, I have therefore thought proper, by and with the consent of His Majesty's Council, by this proclamation, in His Majesty's name, to order and require the officers of the militia in that district to embody a sufficient number of men to repel any insult whatever, and all His Majesty's liege subjects within this colony are hereby strictly required to be aiding and assisting therein, as they shall answer the contrary at their peril. And I do further enjoin and require the several inhabitants of the territory aforesaid to pay His Majesty's quit rent, and all public dues, to such officers as are or shall be appointed to collect the same, within this Dominion, until His Majesty's pleasure shall be known."

Events were hastening to a crisis between Virginia and Pennsylvania, and the Indians, who considered themselves as injured parties, determined to avail themselves of a conflict, to join the Pennsylvanians, and be avenged on the Virginians. Pennsylvania, too, took immediate steps to meet the emergency, though Gov. Penn sent word to the Shawanese that if any wicked Virginians had murdered any of their tribe, he would make complaint to the Governor of Virginia, have the guilty parties punished, and that they should not seek to take revenge upon innocent people. Similar messages were sent to the Delawares, and the Indians met in council at Pittsburg, June, 1774, and all unhappy differences were satisfactorily settled, and the red men determined, in their own language, "to hold fast the chain of friendship, and make their young men sit quiet."

Capt. Connolly was not satisfied with this friendly alliance between the Indians and the Pennsylvanians, and thus spoke in a letter to Gen. A. St. Clair in July: "I am determined no longer to be a dupe to their amiable professions, but, on the contrary, shall pursue every measure to offend them, the Indians, whether I may have the friendly assistance or not of the neighboring country."

Connolly's course hastened on the war of 1774, and its outbreak was so immediately due to the conduct of Capt. Michael Cresap, that it was by some styled "Cresap's war." Space does not admit of our entering into explanatory details.

In 1775, the conflicting jurisdiction of the provinces gave rise to further troubles, and magistrates, acting under Pennsylvanian authority, were threatened with imprisonment. Virginians, who were in prison under Pennsylvania laws, were turned loose by an armed mob, claiming to act under the laws of Virginia. Confusion reigned; lands, already occupied, were given to friends and favorites by Virginia officers: the courts of justice, under Pennsylvania laws, were obstructed, and land offices were opened by the direction of the Government of Virginia.

The court of the District of West Virginia also engaged in promoting the interest of Virginia, as is obvious from the following facts:

"At a justice's court held at Fort Dunmore (Pittsburg), February 22, 1775, (this was a court of Augusta), James Caveat was arraigned before the court for malevolently upbraiding the authority of His Majesty's officers of the government of Virginia at sundry times, and for riotously opposing the legal establishment of His Majesty's laws. He offered as a plea the want of jurisdiction of the court, which was overruled, and he was required to give security for one year and a day, and desist from acknowledging, as a magistrate, within the colony of Virginia, any authority derived from the province of Pennsylvania.

"May 1, 1775, Thomas Scott was also bound over for acting and doing business as a Justice of the Peace under Pennsylvania laws, in contempt of the Earl of Dunmore's proclamation, and also other misdemeanors, and was required to desist from acting as a magistrate within the colony of Virginia.

"September 20, 1775, George Wilson, gentleman, was bound over for aiding, advising, and abetting certain disorderly persons, who, on the morning of the 22d of June last, violently seized and carried away Capt. John Connolly from Fort Dunmore, and also advising others not to aid the officers of justice, when called upon, to apprehend the aforesaid disturbers of the peace. He, not appearing, his recognizance was forfeited."

These acts aroused the Pennsylvanians, and they seized Capt. Connolly and took him to Philadelphia, whereupon the county court of Augusta directed that Geo. Wilson, D. Smith and I. Spear should be kept as hostages for his safe return, and, to prevent their rescue, they were sent in a flat-boat to Wheeling. These matters must have led to open hostilities between the provinces, but for the merging of all local affairs in the all-absorbing question of the freedom of America, and nothing more is heard of the boundary until the second year of the Revolutionary war, when, in 1777, Pennsylvania proposed to Virginia a final settlement of the disputed boundary. The correspondence on the subject led to the appointment on part of both States of Commissioners to settle the matter.

Virginia appointed Bishop Madison and Robt. Andrews, to settle the matter, and Pennsylvania, Geo. Bryan, Rev. John Ewing, DD., and David Rittenhouse. They met in Baltimore, Aug. 31, 1779, and after four days' negotions, came to this agreement: "That Mason and Dixon's line be extended due West 5°, to be computed from the river Delaware for the southern boundary of Pennsylvania, and that a meridian, drawn from the western extremity thereof to the northern limits of the said States, respectively, be the western boundary forever," &c. This agreement, with the conditions annexed for the protection of individual rights, was adopted by the Legislature of Pennsylvania, September, 1780, and transmitted to Virginia for confirmation. While the negotiations were pending, Congress passed the following preamble and resolution, December 27, 1779:

"Whereas, It appears to Congress, from the representation of the delegates from the State of Pennsylvania, that disputes had arisen between the States of Pennsylvania and Virginia relative to the extent of their boundaries, which may probably be productive of serious evils to both States, and tend to lessen their exertions in the common defence; therefore

Resolved, That it be recommended to the contending parties not to grant any part of the disputed lands, or to disturb the possession of any person living thereon, and to avoid every appearance of force, until the dispute can be amicably adjusted by both States, or brought to a just decision by the intervention of Congress; that possessions forcibly taken be restored to the original possessors, and things be placed in the situation in which they were at the commencement of the present war, without prejudice to the claims of either party."

In 1784, Virginia confirmed the line agreed upon by the Commissioners in August, 1779, and the boundary was temporarily settled; but it was not finally disposed of until the adoption, extension, and approval of the Mason & Dixon line.

THE MASON & DIXON LINE.

As this line forever put to rest all questions as to boundary between the two States, a brief history of it will not be here out of place. It was fixed in the years 1763-4-5-6-7 by two distinguished mathematicians and astronomers, Chas. Mason and Jer. Dixon, of London, afterwards extended by authority and consent of Virginia and Pennsylvania temporarily, and finally adjusted in 1784. The line properly begins at the northeast corner of Maryland, and runs due west. The Indians, as we shall see, were troublesome to the surveyors, but, by treaties, they permitted them to proceed as far west as the old war-path, within thirty-six miles of the whole distance to be run, when the Indian escort informed them that it was the will of the Six Nations the surveyors should cease their labors. There was no alternative. The surveyors stopped, and hence arose the difficulties which we have narrated in the preceding part of this chapter as to the boundary.

By reference to the charter granted by King Charles II to William Penn, his heirs and assigns, on the 4th of March, 1681, we find the following described land:

"All that tract or part of land in America, with all the islands therein contained, as the same is bounded on the east by Delaware river, from twelve miles distant northwards of New Castletown unto the three and fortieth degree of northern latitude, if the said river doth extend so far northward; but if the said river shall not extend so far northward, then by the said river so far as it doth extend; and from the head of the said river, the eastern bounds are to be determined by a meridian line, to be drawn from the head of the said river unto the said three and fortieth degree. The said land to extend westward five degrees in longitude, to be computed from the said eastern bounds, and the said lands to be bounded on the north by the beginning of the three and fortieth degree of northern latitude, and on the south by a circle drawn at twelve miles distance from New Castle northwards, and westwards unto the beginning of the fortieth degree of northern latitude, and then by a straight line westwards to the limits of longitude above mentioned."

It is evident that Penn's grant of land from King Charles was to lie west of the Delaware river, and north of Maryland, because the charter by Lord Baltimore for Maryland included all the land to the Delaware Bay, "which lieth under the 40° of north latitude, where New England terminates"; hence the only mode by which the form and extent of Pennsylvania could be determined was by the two natural landmarks—viz.: New Castletown and the river Delaware. This river being her eastern boundary, New Castletown was to be used as the centre of a circle of twelve miles radius, whose northwestern segment was to connect the river with the beginning of the 40°, while the province was to extend westward 5° in longitude, to be computed from said eastern bounds.

The Penns claimed, for the western boundary, a line beginning at 39°, at the distance of 5° of longitude, from the Delaware; thence at the same distance from that river in every point to north latitude 42°, which would take into the province of Pennsylvania some fifty miles square of northwestern Virginia, west of the west line of Maryland. Lord Dunmore, however, rejected this claim, and insisted it would be difficult to ascertain such a line with mathematical exactness, and that the western boundary of Pennsylvania should be a meridian line run south from the end of 5° of longitude from the Delaware, on the line of 42°. This claim, on the other hand, would have thrown the western line of Pennsylvania fifty miles east of Pittsburg.

The foundation of the Mason & Dixon's line was based upon an agreement entered into July 4th, 1760, between Lord Baltimore and Thomas Penn, and the three lower counties of New Castle, Kent and Sussex, on the Delaware, on account of the very long litigations and contests which had subsisted between these provinces from the year 1683. These parties mutually agreed, among other things, to appoint a sufficient number of discreet persons, not more than seven on each side, to be their respective commissioners, with full power to the said seven persons, or any three or more of them, for the actual running, marking, and laying out of the said part of the circle, (as mentioned in the charter from Charles II to William Penn,) and the said before mentioned lines. The commissioners were to fix upon their time of commencing said lines not later than the following October, and proceed with all fairness, candor and dispatch, marking said line with stones and posts on both sides, and complete the same before the 25th December, 1763, so that no disputes may hereafter arise concerning the same.

James Hamilton, (Governor), Richard Peters, Rev. Dr. John Ewing, William Allen, (Chief Justice), William Coleman, Thomas Willing, and Benjamin Chew were appointed commissioners on the part of the Penns.

Horatio Sharpe, (Governor), J. Ridout, John Leeds, John Barclay, George Stewart, Daniel St. Thomas Jenefer, and J. Beale Boardley, on behalf of Lord Baltimore.

The Board of Commissioners met at New Castle in November, 1760, and each province selected its own surveyors. The Pennsylvania surveyors were John Lukens and Archibald McClain ; those of Maryland were John F. A. Priggs and Jonathan Hall.

The commissioners and surveyors agreed that the peninsula lines from Henlopen to the Chesapeake, made under a decree of Lord Hardwicke, in 1750, were correct, hence they fixed the court-house at New Castle as the centre of the circle, and the surveyors proceeded on this data to measure and mark the lines. James Veech, in his history of Mason & Dixon's line, quoted by Dr. Creigh, says:

"Three years were diligently devoted to finding the bearing of the western line of Delaware, so as to make it a tangent to the circle, at the end of a twelve mile radius. The instruments and appliances employed seem to have been those commonly used by surveyors. The proprietors residing in or near London, grew weary of this slow progress, which, perhaps, they set down to the incompetency of the artists. To this groundless suspicion we owe their supersedure and the introduction of the men, Mason & Dixon, who have immortalized their memory in the name of the principal line which had yet to be run."

In August, 1763, Mason & Dixon were selected by Lord Baltimore and the Penns to complete their lines, and arrived in Philadelphia in November, bringing the most approved instruments, among them a four-foot zenith sector. An observatory is erected in Cedar street, Philadelphia, to facilitate the ascertainment of its latitude, which they use until January, 1764. They then go to New Castle, adopt the radius as measured by their predecessors, and, after numerous tracings of the tangent line, adopt also their tangent point, from which they say they could not make the tangent line pass one inch to the eastward or westward. They, therefore, cause that line and point to be marked, and adjourn to Philadelphia to find its southern limit in Cedar or South street. This they make to be 39° 56' 20", while the latitude of the State has been marked as 39° 56' 20". They then extend that latitude sufficiently far to the west to be due north of the tangent point. Thence they measure down south fifteen miles to the latitude of the great due west line, and run its parallel for a short distance. Then they go to the tangent point and run due north to that latitude, and at the point of intersection, in a deep ravine, near a spring, they planted the corner-stone, at which point begins the celebrated Mason & Dixon's line.

Mr. Veech continues : " Having ascertained the latitude of this line to be 39° 43' 32" (although more accurate observations, make it 39° 43' 26" .8, or a little over nineteen miles south of 40° as now located), they, under instructions, run its parallel to the Susquehanna, twenty-three miles ; and, having verified the latitude there, they return to the tangent point, from which they run the due north line to the fifteen mile corner and that part of the circle which it cuts off to the west, and which, by agreement, was to go to New Castle county. (This little bow or arc is about a mile and a-half long, and its middle width one hundred and sixteen feet. From its upper end, where the three States join, to the fifteen mile point, where the great Mason & Dixon line begins, is a little over three and a-half miles, and from the fifteen mile corner, due east to the circle, is a little over three-quarters of a mile. This was the only part of the circle which Mason & Dixon run, Lord Baltimore having no concern in the residue. Penn, however, had it run, and marked with 'four good notches,' by Isaac Taylor and Thomas Pierson, in 1700-'1.) Where it cuts the circle is the corner of three dominions, an important point, and, therefore, they caused it to be well ascertained and well marked. This brings them to the end of 1764."

They resumed their labors in June, 1765. If to extend this parallel did not require so great skill as did the nice adjustment of the other lines and intersections, it summoned its performers to greater endurance. A tented army penetrates the forest, but their purposes are peaceful, and they move merrily. Besides the surveyors and their assistants, there were chain-bearers, rod men, axe men, commissioners, cooks and baggage carriers, with numerous servants and laborers. By the 27th of October, they come to the North (Cove or Kittatiny) mountain, ninety-five miles from the Susquehanna, and where the temporary line of 1739, terminated. After taking Captain Shelby with them to its summit to show them the course of the Potomac, and point out the Alleghany mountains, the surveyors and their attendants return to the settlements to pass the Winter and get their appointment renewed.

Early in 1766, they are again at their posts, and by the 4th of June they are on the top of the Little Alleghany mountain, the first west of Wills' creek. They have now carried the line about one hundred and sixty miles from its beginning. The Indians, into whose ungranted territory they had deeply penetrated, grow restless and threatening. They forbid any further advance, and they had to be obeyed. The agents of the pro-prietors now find that there are other lords of the soil whose favor must be propitiated. The Six Indian Nations were the lords paramount of the territory yet to be traversed. To obtain their consent to the consumma-tion of the line, the Governors of Pennsylvania and Maryland, in the Winter of 1766-'7, at an expense of more than £500, procured, under the agency of Sir William Johnston, a grand convocation of the tribes of that powerful confederacy. The application was successful, and early in June, 1767, an escort of fourteen warriors, with an interpreter and chief, deputed by the Iroquois council, met the surveyors and their camp at the summit of the Great Alleghany to escort them down into the Valley of the Ohio, whose tributaries they were soon to cross.

Safety being thus secured, the extension of the line was pushed on vigorously in the Summer of 1767. Soon the host of red and white men, led by the London surveyors, came to the western limit of Maryland, "the meridian of the first fountain of the Potomac," and why they did not stop there is a mystery, for there their functions terminated. But they pass by it unheeded, because unknown, resolved to reach the utmost limit of Pennsylvania, "five degrees of longitude" from the Delaware, for so were they instructed. By the 24th of August they came to the crossing of Braddock's road. The escort now became restless. The Mohawk chief and his nephew leave. The Shawanese and Delaware tenants of the hunting-grounds begin to grow terrific. On the 27th of September, when encamped on the Monongehela river, two hundred and thirty-three miles from the Delaware river, twenty-six of the laborers desert, and but fifteen axe-men are left. Being so near the goal, the surveyors (for none of the commissioners were with them,) evince their courage by coolly sending back to Fort Cumberland for aid, and in the meantime they push on. At length they came to where the line crosses the Warrior branch of the old Catawba war path, at the second crossing of Dunkard creek, a little west of Mount Morris, in Greene county, and there the Indian escort say to them, "that they were instructed by their chiefs in council not to let the line be run westward of that path." Their commands are peremptory, and there, for fifteen years, Mason & Dixon's line is stayed.

Mason and Dixon, with their pack-horse train and attendants, return to the East without molestation, and report to the commissioners, who approved their conduct, and on the 27th of December, 1767, grant to them an honorable discharge, and agreed to pay them an additional price for a map or plan of their work

The commissioners caused stones to be erected upon the lines and at the corners and intersections around and near the three counties of Delaware. On the 9th day of November, 1768, they made their final report to the proprietors.

It would be well to remark that along the line and at the end of every fifth mile a stone was planted on which were graven the arms of the proprietors on the side facing their possessions, respectively, while the intermediate miles were noted by a stone bearing the initials of the respective States thereon. The line opened was of the breadth of twenty-four feet, made by felling all the large trees, which were left to rot upon the ground; the stones were erected along the middle of this pathway.

The instruments used by Mason & Dixon were an ordinary surveyor's compass, to find their bearings generally, a quadrant, and the four-feet zenith sector, for absolute accuracy, and which enabled them to be guided by the unerring luminaries of the heavens.

The measurements were made with a four-pole chain of one hundred links each, except that on hills and mountains one of two poles, and some times a one-pole measure, was used. These were frequently tested by a statute chain carried along for the purpose. Great care was enjoined as to the plumblings on uneven ground, and, so far as they have been since tested, the measurements seem to have been very true.

The width of a degree of longitude varies according to the latitude it traverses, expanding towards the equator and contracting towards the pole. In the latitude of our line, Mason & Dixon computed it at fifty-three miles and one hundred and sixty-seven and one-tenth perches. They subsequently made Penns' five degrees of longitude from the Delaware, to be two hundred and sixty-seven miles and one hundred and ninety-five and one-sixteenth perches. To their stopping-place, at the war-path on Dunkard, they say was two hundred and forty-four miles, one hundred and thirteen perches and seven and one-fourth feet. Hence they left, as they computed it, twenty-three miles and eighty-three perches to be run. It was subsequently ascertained that this was about a mile and a-half too much, as the surveyors of 1784, made it two hundred and sixty-six miles, ninety-nine and one-fifth perches.

The boundary between Virginia and Pennsylvania, after a long controversy, was finally settled, as we have seen, by the commissioners of the respective States in 1784. From the accounts of the commissary to the commissioners, it is evident that while discharging their trust they lived well. The bill calls for 120 gallons of spirits, 40 gallons of brandy, 80 gallons of Madeira wine, 200 pounds of loaf sugar, a small keg of lemon juice, 6 pounds of tea, 106 pounds of coffee, 60 pounds of chocolate, 40 pounds of Scotch barley pepper, 6 bushels of salt, 4 tin mugs, 1 coffee mill, 1 pewter tea-pot, 1 tin coffee pot, 1 frying-pan, 1 gridiron, 6 boiling kettles, 1 Dutch oven, 1 tea kettle, 2 pair snuffers, 4 candle-sticks, 2 funnels, 100 pounds candles, 2 hand-saws, 1 cross-cut saw, 6 files, 2 hammers, 12 gimlets, 50 pounds nails, 1 set knives and forks, tea-cups, glasses, tumblers, bowls, dishes, plates, spoons and basins, 6 large camp stools, 6 small ditto, 2 marquees, or 4 horsemen's tents, 60 felling axes, 100 pounds steel, 6 shovels, 6 pickaxes, 6 spades, 12 pair of H. L. hinges, 3 four-horse wagons and one light wagon, with 4 horses, 20 fathom ½ inch rope, 2 crow bars, 2 planes, 2 augurs, 4 broad-axes, 2 drawing-knives, ½ box window-glass, 1 ream of paper, 100 quills, 6 sticks of wax, 2 dozen pencils, 1 box of wafers, 2 ink stands, 2 large camp tables, 1 dozen memorandum books, cheese, 2 dozen hams, 1 dozen kegs of white biscuit.

The commissioners for whom such excellent provision was made were, on behalf of Virginia, Bishop Madison, Robert Andrews, John Page, and Andrew Elliott; and for Pennsylvania, John Ewing, D. Rittenhouse, John Lukens and Thomas Hutchins.

As public documents are difficult of access, owing to our distance from any great public library, the original reports of the commissioners are inserted below for future reference:

JOINT REPORT OF THE COMMISSIONERS ON THE BOUNDARY LINE BE-
TWEEN VIRGINIA AND PENNSYLVANIA.

Agreeably to the commission given by the State of Virginia to James Madison, Robert Andrews, John Page, and Andrew Elliott, and by the State of Pennsylvania to John Ewing, David Rittenhouse, John Lukens, and Thomas Hutchins, to determine, by astronomical observations, the extent of five degrees of longitude west from the river Delaware, in the latitude of Mason & Dixon's line, and to run and mark the boundaries which are common to both States, according to an agreement entered into by commissioners from the said two States, at Baltimore, in 1779, and afterwards ratified by their respective Assemblies, we, the underwritten commissioners, together with the gentlemen with whom we are joined in commission, have, by corresponding astronomical observations, made near the Delaware and in the western country, ascertained the extent of the said five degrees of longitude; and the underwritten commissioners have continued Mason & Dixon's line to the termination of the said five degrees of longitude, by which work the southern boundary of Pennsylvania is completed. The continuation we have marked by opening vistas over the most remarkable heights which lie in its course, and by planting on many of these heights, in the parallel of latitude, the true boundary, posts marked with the letters P. and V., each letter facing the State of which it is the initial. At the extremity of this line, which is the southwest corner of the State of Pennsylvania, we have planted a squared unlettered white oak post, around whose base we have raised a pile of stones. The corner in the last vista we cut on the east side of a hill, one hundred and thirty-four chains and nine links east of the meridian of the western observatory, and two chains and fifty-four links west of a deep narrow valley, through which the said last vista is cut. At the distance of fifty-one links, and bearing from it north twenty-three degrees east, stands a white oak marked on the south side with three notches, or bearing south twelve degrees west, and at the distance of twenty-nine links, stands a black oak on the north side with four notches. The advanced season of the year, and the inclemency of the weather, have obliged us to suspend our operations, but we have agreed to meet again at the southwest corner of Pennsylvania on the 16th day of May next, to complete the object of our commission.

Given under our hands and seals, in the county of Washington, in Pennsylvania, this 18th day of November, 1784.

> ROBERT ANDREWS, [Seal.]
> JOHN EWING, [Seal.]
> ANDREW ELLIOTT, [Seal.]
> DAVID RITTENHOUSE, [Seal.]
> THO. HUTCHINS, [Seal.]

The report of the Virginia commissioners, which we have not been able to procure in time for this volume, is no doubt identical with the following report of the Pennsylvania commissioners, which was received by the Executive Council, December 23, 1784:

To His Excellency, John Dickerson, President of the Senate, and to the Hon. the Supreme Executive Council of the Commonwealth of Pennsylvania :

The commissioners appointed for ascertaining the length of five degrees of longitude, and for determining and fixing the boundary line between this State and Virginia, by astronomical observations, beg leave to report :

That after procuring the necessary instruments, according to the directions of council in the preceding Spring, we set off for our respective places of observation about the middle of June, Messrs. Rittenhouse and Lukens to Wilmington and Ewing and Hutchins to the southwest corner of the State.

The observers at Wilmington completed their observatory and furnished it with the necessary instruments, so as to begin their astronomical operations in conjunction with Messrs. Page and Andrews, commissioners from Virginia, about the beginning of July, where they continued observing the eclipses of Jupiter's satellites till the 20th September, that they might have a sufficient number of them, both before and after his opposition to the sun ; and although the Summer proved very unfavorable for astronomical purposes, they were fortunate enough to make amongst them near sixty observations of these eclipses, besides many other observations of the other heavenly bodies for the regulation of their clock and fixing their meridian line, so that they were well ascertained of their time to a single second.

In the meantime the other observers, setting out for Philadelphia, pursued their route to the southwest extremity of the State, where they arrived about the middle of July, having been greatly retarded by the badness of the roads through that mountainous country. There they met with Messrs. Madison and Elliott, the commissioners from the State of Virginia, who had arrived about the same time. With all possible dispatch they erected their observatory on a high hill, at the place where the continuation of Messrs. Mason & Dixon's line by Messrs. Neville & McClean ended, supposing this place would prove to be near to the western extremity of five degrees of longitude from the river Delaware. After erecting their instruments, which had not sustained the least damage from the journey over bad roads, they began their astronomical observations about the middle of July, and they continued them night and day till 20th September. Although they were frequently interrupted and disappointed by an uncommon quantity of rain and foggy weather, which seems peculiar to that hilly country, yet by their attention to the business of their mission, they made between forty and fifty observations of the eclipses of Jupiter's satellites, many of which were correspondent with those made by the other astronomers at Wilmington, besides innumerable observations of the sun and stars for the regulation of their time-pieces and the marking of their meridian with the greatest precision.

In this part of their work, situated thirty miles beyond any of the inhabitants, the Commissioners were greatly assisted by the diligence and indefatigable activity of Col. Porter, their commissary, to whose industry, in providing everything necessary, and prudence in managing the business in his department with the utmost economy, the State is greatly indebted.

The astronomical observations being completed on 20th September, the eastern astronomers set out to meet the other Commissioners in the West, in order to compare them together. Messrs. Rittenhouse and Andrews carried with them the observations made at Wilmington, while Messrs. Lukens and Page returned home, not being able to endure the fatigues of so long a journey, nor the subsequent labor of running and marking the boundary line. Mr. Madison continued with the western astronomers till the arrival of Messrs. Rittenhouse and Andrews, when the affairs of his family and public station obliged him to relinquish the business at this stage and return home, after concurring with the other Commissioners as to the principles on which the matter was fully determined.

Upon comparison of the observations made at both extremities of our southern boundary, your commissioners have the pleasure of assuring you that no discouragements, arising from the unfavorable state of the weather, or the unavoidable fatigues of constant application by day and frequent watchings by night, have prevented them from embracing every opportunity, and making a sufficient number of astronomical observations, to determine the length of five degrees of longitude with greater precision than could be attained by terrestrial measures of a degree of latitude in different places of the earth; and further, that they have completed their observations with so much accuracy and certainty as to remove from their minds every degree of doubt concerning their final determination of the southwestern corner of the State.

In the result of the calculations, they found that their observatories were distant from each other twenty minutes and one second and an eighth part of a second of time. But, as the observatory at Wilmington was fixed at one hundred and fourteen chains and thirteen links west of the intersection of the boundary line of this State with the river Delaware, and as twenty minutes of time are equivalent to five degrees of longitude, they made the necessary correction for the said one hundred and fourteen chains and thirteen links, and also for the said second and one-eighth part of a second, which is equal to nineteen chains and ninety-six links, and accordingly fixed and marked the southwestern corner of State in the manner mentioned in the joint agreement and report of the Commissioners of both States, under their hands and seals, which we have the honor of laying before the Council.

After these calculations were made, the Commissioners proceeded with all convenient dispatch to the place where Mason & Dixon formerly were interrupted by the Indian nation in running the Southern boundary of this State, in order to extend the said boundary westward to the length of five degrees from the river Delaware. Being prevented by rainy weather for near a week from making any astronomical observations, in order to ascertain the direction of the parallel of latitude which we were to extend, we concluded, to save time and expense, that it would be eligible to take the last direction of Mason & Dixon's line and correct it, if necessary, when we should have an opportunity of a serene sky. Upon extending the line in this manner one hundred and ninety-five chains from the place where they ended their work, we found, by astronomical observations, that we were thirty-two feet and five inches north of the true parallel, and we accordingly made the necessary correction here, and marked a tree with the letters P on the north side and V on the South. From thence we assumed a new direction, which we again corrected in like manner at the distance of five hundred and seventy-five chains, where we found our line to be seventy-three feet and six inches north of the parallel of latitude. We made the offset accordingly, and planted a large post in the true parallel, marked as above. From thence we found another direction, by calculation, which, beginning at the said post, should, at the distance of eight miles from it, intersect the said parallel, making offsets at convenient distances, and planting posts in the true parallel. This direction being continued thirty-three chains further than the eight miles above mentioned, fell twenty-three inches south of the parallel, where we also planted a post in the true boundary, marked as before, and from thence, to the southwest corner of the State, we assumed a new direction, which, being continued, fell two feet and eight inches south of the said corner. This correction, therefore, being made, we planted a squared white oak post in the said point, and marked its bearing from different objects, as mentioned in our joint report. Besides the marking of this boundary line by the posts and stones above mentioned, your Commissioners took good care to have a vista of twenty or thirty feet wide cut over all the most remarkable ridges which were in the direction of the parallels.

For a more full description of this part of our work, we beg leave to refer to the annexed plan (this plan has never yet been found among the State papers) and sketch of the country through which the line passes. The season being now far advanced, we were obliged to desist from any further prosecution of the work, and agreed with the Virginia Commissioners to meet them at the southwestern corner of our State on the 17th of May next, to proceed in running and marking the western boundary of this State.

Agreeably to our commission, we were required to report the situation of the country, and the best means of preserving the communication between the eastern and western parts of the State. We beg leave to observe that the natural obstructions to so desirable a purpose may be in a great measure removed by a few easy instances of attention paid by the Legislature of this State to the situation and exhausted condition of the western citizens. Their public roads are numerous, extensive, and in bad order, while the citizens being few in number, scattered at a distance from each other, and being harassed and exhausted by an Indian war, are unable to repair their roads or to open them through more easy and convenient passes over the hills and mountains. A few hundred pounds, not exceeding one thousand, judiciously and frugally applied, would, in our opinion, make a tolerable good wagon road from York county to the Monongehela, and thereby facilitate the exportation of goods from this city to that western country, and secure their trade with us, especially if the ferry over the Susquehanna was made free to all the citizens of the State. It appears probable to us, that otherwise, the exertions of Maryland and Virginia to repair their roads to that country, will frustrate the expectation which we are entitled to entertain of enjoying the advantages of the trade with the western parts of our own State. We beg leave further to observe that the natural attachment of the western citizens to this State might be increased and fixed by an indulgence to their distressed situation, in the price of their lands and the terms of payment, and particularly in the remission of the interest due on the purchase money during the time they have been obliged to evacuate their possessions by the savages and fly to forts for the security of their lives and families.

> JOHN EWING,
> JOHN LUKENS,
> DAVID RITTENHOUSE,
> THOMAS HUTCHINS.

CHAPTER X.

Five years after Francis Fauquier* became Governor of Virginia, a treaty of peace was signed, February 10, 1763, at Fontainbleau, between England and France. As, however, all questions as to boundary between their American colonies were left unsettled, it did not bring peace to our frontier. On the contrary, the year 1764-65 is memorable for the great extent and destructive character of a war waged by the united Indian tribes of the western country—from the northern lakes to the mountains of North Carolina—with a view to the extermination of the whites. We shall only

---

*Fauquier was ruined at the gaming-table, but fascinating and high-bred, a gentleman and scholar, a charming companion and a popular Governor, he came to Virginia the friend of William Pitt and fully imbued with the spirit of the Great Commoner.

refer to the events of this war so far as to give a connected view of the military operations of this disastrous season. The savages were exasperated at the cession of Canada to the English, especially as they knew that the English government claimed the jurisdiction of the western country generally. They saw forts being built far and near, on the Susquehanna, at Pittsburg, Bedford, Ligonier, Niagara, Detroit, Mackinac, and all manned by British troops. The various tribes decided, therefore, with great unanimity, upon war, and war to the knife. It was evident to them that the time had come when they must either defend or renounce their country. Their resolution once taken, they were not slow in carrying out their plans of slaughter. They no longer considered the smallness of their numbers and their want of resources, but entered the unequal contest with the impetuosity of passion, determined, if they could not rescue their lands from a detested foe, to die like men. Their plan of campaign was that of a general massacre of all the English settlers in the western country, as well as of those occupying lands which they claimed on the Susquehanna.

  "Never," says an old historian, "did the commanders of any nation display more skill, or their troops more steady and determined bravery, than did those red men in the prosecution of their gigantic plan for the recovery of their country. It was a conflict which exhibited human nature in its native state, in which the cunning of the fox is associated with the cruelty of the tiger. We read the history of this war with feelings of the deepest horror, but why? On the part of the savages, theirs was the ancient mode of warfare, in which there was nothing of mercy. If science, associated with the benign influence of the Christian system, has limited the carnage of war to those in arms, may not a farther extension of the influence of those powerful, but salutary agents, put an end to war altogether?"

  The English traders among the Indians were the first victims of the contest, and out of one hundred and twenty of them, only two escaped being murdered. The forts of Presque Isle, St. Joseph, and Mackinac, were taken, with a general slaughter of their garrisons. They invested Fort Pitt, but the garrison had resolved to resist to the last extremity, and even perish by famine rather than surrender. In this situation, Col. Bouquet sent Gen. Amherst to its relief. This escort was attacked by a large body of Indians in a narrow defile on Turtle creek, and would have been destroyed but for a successful stratagem employed by Gen. Amherst for extricating his force. After sustaining a furious contest from one o'clock till night, and for several hours the next morning, a retreat was feigned, with a view to drawing the Indians into a close engagement. Previous to this movement, four companies of infantry and grenadiers were placed in ambuscade. The plan succeeded. When the retreat commenced, the Indians thought themselves victorious, and, pressing forward with great vigor, fell into the ambuscade, and were dispersed with great slaughter. The loss on the English side was one hundred killed and wounded; that of the savages was never known. The reduction of Fort Pitt, which they had so much at heart, was now placed out of their reach. It was during this war that the dreadful massacre took place at Wyoming, and desolated the settlements of the New England people along the Susquehanna. The extensive and indiscriminate slaughter of both sexes and all ages by the Indians, at Wyoming and other places, so exasperated a large number of men, denominated the "Paxton boys," that they rivaled the most fero- cious of the Indians themselves in deeds of cruelty. The Conestoga In- dians had lived in peace more than a century near Lancaster, Pennsyl- vania. Their number did not exceed forty. Against the unoffending descendants of the first friends of Penn, the Paxton boys first directed their more than savage vengeance. Fifty-seven of them, in military array, entered the village and instantly murdered all whom they found at home, to the number of fourteen men, women, and children. Those who did not happen to be at home at the massacre, were lodged in the jail of Lan- caster for safety. This precaution was unavailing. The Paxton boys broke open the jail door, and murdered the whole of them, between fifteen and twenty. It was in vain that these poor, defenceless people protested their innocence, and on their knees begged for mercy. Blood was the order of the day with these ferocious "boys." The death of their victims did not satisfy their rage. They mangled the dead bodies with their scalping-knives and tomahawks, scalping even the children, and chopping off the hands and feet of most of them.

While we read, with feelings of the deepest horror, the record of the murders which have at different times been inflicted on the unoffending Christian Indians, it is some consolation to reflect that our Government has had no participation in these murders, but, on the contrary, has at all times afforded the peaceable Indians the protection which circumstances allowed.

We now come to events which transpired nearer home—the massacres of Big Levels and Muddy Creek, in Greenbrier, when Cornstalk, who after- wards became so distinguished in the border wars, for the first time attracted public attention. Those two were the principal settlements in the Green- brier region, and were about fifteen miles apart. The destruction of these settlements was determined on, and they were visited, in 1763, by the In- dians, before the whites were aware of the existence of war. The party of Indians who went to the settlement on Muddy creek, apparently on a friendly visit, consisted of sixty men, and were kindly received and hospi- tably entertained. After feasting, they suddenly fell upon the unsuspect- ing and unarmed whites, murdering all the men, and making prisoners of the women and children. Having thus repaid the hospitality of the whites, they proceeded to the Big Levels, and on the next day, after having been as hospitably entertained as at Muddy creek, they reënacted the revolting scenes of the previous day. Every white man in the settlement, but Conrad Yolkom, who was some distance from his house, was slain, and every woman but Mrs. Glendinin. Yolkom, when alarmed by the outcries of the women, took in the situation and fled to Jackson's river, telling the story. The people were unwilling to believe him, till convinced by the approach of the Indians. All fled before them, and they pursued on to Carr's creek, in Rockbridge, where many families were murdered and others captured.

The following graphic, life-like, and, no doubt, perfectly veracious account of the raids on Carr's creek, is derived from the venerable Samuel Brown's narrative, published in the " Rockbridge Citizen :"

" There were two raids on Carr's, or Kerr's creek, but the accounts are so mixed that it is not known certainly whether the incidents related as to them occurred at the first or second. This settlement dates back to 1737-38, when Burden was exerting himself to settle his lands, and was composed mostly of Scotch-Irish. The first invasion by Indians was early in 1763, and the second in October, 1764. The number of Shawanese warriors in the first invasion was twenty-seven, and was part of a larger force who had been on a hostile expedition against the Cherokees or Catawbas, and were on their return to their villages north of the Ohio. Some knowledge of their approach led to a hastily organized company under Capt. Moffett, who, marching to the mouth of the Falling Spring Valley, on Jackson's river, on the estate long owned by the late Hon. John H. Peyton, halted there to await the Indians. The Indians, who were hid behind a ridge on the right bank of the river, watched the movements of the whites, and at a favorable moment opened a destructive fire upon them from their concealed position. A number of whites were killed, among them, Jas. Sitlington, of Bath, and the force so demoralized by the terrific fire from the unseen foes that it took to flight. The Indians pursued on to the Cow Pasture river, where they burned the smithy of —— Dougherty, who, with his wife and two children, escaped to the mountain, west of Peyton Falls, and thus saved their lives. The Indians continued their eastern progress, and arrived at Millboro', where the force divided, the larger part setting out for the Ohio, and the smaller party, of twenty-seven warriors, for Kerr's creek. The larger party killed a man at the Blowing Cave, in Panther's Gap, crossed the Warm Spring Mountain, and encamped on the lands now owned by the Heckman family. A company of whites was quickly formed, and pursued the savages. On reaching Heckman's, they found a rude bier, on which a wounded Indian had been carried, and afterwards his grave. The whites hastened on, and overtook the Indians in their encampment, near the head of Back creek. The whites rushed upon the camp, routed the savages, killing many of them, and capturing all their camp equipage. Among the whites killed was Capt. Dickinson, of Bath ; John Young, grandfather of Col. D. S. Young, of Staunton, who resided near Hebron church, in Augusta, and others. * * * * * * The whites returned, bringing back as trophies of their victory a number of scalps, which were recognized by their friends. Among them was the scalp of Jas. Sitlington, known by his long, red hair.

We shall now return to follow the trail of the smaller party, which set out for Kerr's creek. This party crossed Mill mountain at a point still called "Indian trail," and the North mountain, where the road now crosses leading from the Rockbridge Alum to Lexington. At the base of the mountain they were on the head waters of Kerr's creek, and proceeding on came to the house of Chas. Dougherty, where they murdered the whole family. They next came to the house of Jacob Cunningham, who was from home. His wife was killed, and his daughter, ten years of age, struck down with the tomahawk and scalped. After the Indians left, she revived and lived, but fell into their hands on their second invasion in 1765, was taken north of the Ohio, where the Indians placed on her head what they said was her scalp, and, with great demonstrations of mirth and joy, danced around her. She was afterwards ransomed, rejoined her friends, and lived many years, but ultimately died from the effects of the scalping, her head never having properly healed. The Indians next came to the house of Thomas Gilmore, which they burned, killing and scalping him and his wife. The rest of the family saved themselves by flight. The alarm now spread, and the inhabitants were flying in every direction. The next house they attacked was Robert Hamilton's, where they killed five of the ten members composing the family. The Indians went no further on this occasion, but retreated, not so much, it is supposed, because their thirst for blood was satiated, as because they feared to encounter a white force which must have been now collecting. One savage, however, pushed on to the house of John McKee, who had sent his six children to the house of a friend on Timber Ridge, intending soon to follow with his wife. When the alarm reached him, he and his wife fled down the creek about a mile to a thicket, followed by the savage. Seeing they would be overtaken, Mrs. McKee implored her husband to leave her to her fate and make his escape. This he refused to do. She appealed to him again and again to leave her for the sake of their children. If he remained, being unarmed, both would be slain, but, if he escaped, their young children would still have a protector. He yielded to her entreaties, and they parted, to meet no more on earth. After running a short distance, he saw the tomahawk descend on his wife's head. The Indian, without halting, followed McKee, but was unable to find him in the bush, and, with a loud whoop, gave up the search. At night, McKee returned to the spot where he had left his wife, and found her dead. Loaded with scalps and plunder, the savages left the settlement, and the whites, returning, buried their dead. The number of persons killed on this occasion was less than would otherwise have been the case, from the fact that many were at church, at the old Timber Ridge Church, to hear Rev. John Brown, the pastor.

The second invasion of Kerr's creek was 10th October, 1765, and was composed of about forty Shawanese. The Indians came over North mountain and encamped in a secluded spot, from whence their spies went out. They remained concealed two days, but their presence was detected by their foot-prints in a corn field. The alarm was given about the time they set forth to make an attack. The whites rallied at the "Big Spring," in the house of Jonathan Cunningham, to the number of a hundred—men, women and children. Mr. Gilmore and another settler went up the creek to watch the barbarians. The savages shot both from their place of concealment, and then rushed on the promiscuous crowd of whites. Some young men advanced to meet them, and were killed. Then commenced a scene which beggars description; the screaming of women and children, and the utter dismay which seized upon all. Many concealed themselves in a thick growth of weeds and brush—among them a Mrs. Dull, who witnessed the awful tragedy. She said the terror-stricken whites ran in every direction trying to hide, and the swift savages, each singling out his prey, pursued them round and round with yells. Some threw up their hands for mercy. Some were spared their lives, but the most fell under the tomahawk. All the men who attempted resistance were shot down. The whites had few arms, and, under the circumstances, any resistance was vain. The wife of Thomas Gilmore, standing with her three children over the body of her husband, fought the Indian who sought to scalp him with desperation. A second Indian came forward to aid his brother, but the first warded off the blow of his tomahawk and saved her life, saying, " She is a brave squaw "—such was their admiration of courage. Mrs. Gilmore, her son and two daughters were made prisoners. Cunningham was killed and his house burned, and the bloody work did not cease until all who could be found were killed or captured. Gathering their prisoners in a group, the Indians prepared to leave. Among their captives were James and Margaret Cunningham, Archibald Marion and Mary Hamilton, Mrs. Gilmore and her three children, and Betsy Henry. Among the killed in the two invasions were the entire Dougherty family, Mrs. Cunningham, five of the Hamiltons, Thomas Gilmore, Mrs. Gilmore and their son, and James McKee. The names of others killed and captured are not known to the writer, but the whole number slain was not less than sixty to eighty, and twenty-five to thirty were led into captivity.

The following incidents were related by some of these captives, who were redeemed by their friends and returned from the Shawanese towns north of the Ohio. On the evening of their first day's march, the savages opened their kegs of whiskey, made and captured at Cunningham's distillery, and spent the night and until the afternoon of the next day in a drunken revel. The prisoners were hoping all night that a company of whites would come to their rescue, but none came. While here, two warriors returned to " Big Spring," no doubt to get more whiskey. On their way to Ohio the savages made other prisoners on the Cow Pasture. One of the white children taking sick, and becoming fretful, a savage seized it and dashed its brains out against a tree, and threw the bloody corpse over the neck and shoulders of a young girl sitting at the root of a tree. The prisoners construed this as a signal that she should soon die, which proved true, for she was killed the next day. Another mother caused delay by being exhausted carrying her babe. This exasperated the savages, who took the child, laid it on the ground, and, running a sharpened pole through its body, elevated it in the air. On one occasion some of the prisoners were drying some leaves of the New Testament by the fire; a savage snatched them away and threw them into the fire.

After crossing the Ohio the prisoners were divided, the Indians separating into several parties. Mrs. Gilmore and her son fell to one party and her daughters to another. The last she heard of them was their heart-rending cries as they were torn from her. Soon mother and son were parted. She was sold to a French trader and taken to Fort Pitt; her son remained with the Shawanese. He was afterwards redeemed, taken back to Jackson's river by Jacob Warwick, where his mother, at the end of three years, joined him, after being ransomed. The son married and left a family. A number of others, among them Mary Hamilton, were ransomed and brought back."

During one of these raids some of the savages continued their pursuit until within a few miles of Staunton, where they were met by hastily organized bodies of men, who drove them back.

In the wars of 1763-'64, the Indians, no longer controlled by their former allies, the French, indulged their native ferocity of disposition, and perpetrated every species of perfidy and cruelty. This led to retaliation on the part of the whites, and occasioned the revolting and sanguinary scenes which characterized all future wars with the barbarians.

The scenes which were occurring on the frontier aroused the people of Augusta to the necessity of preparation. and as early as 1763, they took steps towards a military organization. This appears from the following entry:

"At the Court of Augusta, held in Staunton, August 16th, 1763,

"Andrew Lewis, gentleman, took the usual oaths to H. M. person and government and subscribed the abjuration oath and test, which is, on his motion, ordered to be certified on his commission of Lieutenant of the County."

The Lieutenant of the County was the commander-in-chief of the military forces of the county, and Lewis, the leader of greatest experience and ability west of the mountains, was thus commissioned, in view of the threatening aspect of affairs. At the same court William Preston qualified as Colonel of the County, and the following as Captains: Walter Cunningham, Alexander McClenehan, William Crow, and John Bowyer; as Lieutenants: John McClenahan, Michael Bowyer and David Long, and as Ensign, James Ward.

At the opening of the Indian war upon the frontier, in 1764, the Six Nations were conspicuous. These Indians had previously been known as the Five Nations, and called by the French, Iroquois. These five tribes, the Mohawks, Oneidas, Senegas, Onandagos and Cayugas had, in 1712, been joined by the Tuscaroras, who had resided in North Carolina and had been driven from their hunting-grounds, and became the sixth of this powerful confederacy. They were called the Six Nations because they all spoke the same language. These Six Nations united, in 1763-'64, with the Shawanese and all the other tribes of the western country in the war against Virginia, Pennsylvania and the other colonies. Both Virginia and Pennsylvania had attempted to restrain their people from settling west of the Alleghanies, because the lands had not been purchased of the Indians. The people, however, defied the authorities, and, undaunted by fear of the red men, crossed the mountains. Unable to look to their governments for protection, they erected forts and block-houses in the west for their security. The savages, finding the colonial authorities unable or unwilling to prevent this invasion of their country, and believing them insincere in their professions, resolved to take up the hatchet, and either to expel or exterminate the whites. The following extracts from letters written about this time, and subsequently, will show that the Indians had reason to be exasperated; that all the blame for these massacres and wars does not attach to them. In a letter dated Winchester, April 30th, 1765, the following passage occurs:

"The frontier inhabitants of this colony and Maryland are removing fast over the Alleghanies in order to settle and live there. The two hunters who killed the two Indians near Pittsburg, some time ago, are so audacious as to boast of the fact and show the scalps publicly. What may such proceedings not produce? One of these hunters, named Walker, lives in Augusta County, Va."

EXTRACT OF A LETTER FROM CARLISLE.

"A number of men from this settlement went up to Shamokin (Fort Augusta) to kill the Indians there, which caused them all to fly from that place."

EXTRACT OF A LETTER FROM FORT LOUDOUN, 1768.

"The last news we have had here is the killing of nine Shawanese Indians in Augusta County, Va., who were passing this way to the Cherokee Nation, to war against them, and had obtained a pass from Col. Lewis, of that county. Yet, notwithstanding, a number of county people met them a few miles from Col. Lewis' and killed nine, there being but ten in the Company."

FROM LORD BOTETOURT, 1770.

"I send the body of John Ingman, he having confessed himself concerned in the murder of Indian Stephen. You will find there never was an act of villainy more unprovoked and more deliberately undertaken."

FROM FORT PITT, 1771.

"I take the liberty to enclose for your perusal the copy of an affidavit relative to the murder of two Senecas Indians. I have had several meetings with the chiefs, who seem well pleased with the steps taken in the affair."

This bloody war, after a course of twelve months, was ended by a treaty negotiated in the Autumn of 1764, by Col. Bouquet, near Muskingum, and another, concluded by Sir William Johnson, at German Flats, when, as we have seen, the Indians surrendered two hundred and six prisoners. The most conspicuous negotiator on behalf of the barbarians was the celebrated chief, Captain John—than whom no warrior among the Shawanese or Delawares was more brutal or ferocious. He possessed great courage, energy and sagacity, and wielded a vast influence. This desperate and blood-thirsty savage was over six feet high, and celebrated for his strength, activity and dexterity with the tomahawk. On one occasion he encountered, in single combat, an Indian chief by the name of Cushion, almost as noted as himself for physical power and bull-dog courage. They fought with tomahawks, and the fight resulted in the death of Cushion, whose skull was cloven in twain. Captain John quarreled with his squaw,

They agreed to divide their worldly goods and separate. The mother held fast to their only child. The Captain jerked it from her arms, and, dividing the body with his tomahawk and scalping-knive into two parts, threw her one half, saying, "Be off, or I'll serve you in the same way."

It will not be uninteresting, and will conduce to an understanding of western affairs, if we pause at this point to give a brief account of western land titles. At the close of the war of 1763-'4, the country, from the Alleghanies to the Wabash, was an almost unbroken wilderness; a few military posts and an occasional pioneer settler were all there was of civilization in that vast region. But the tide of emigration to the west was about to set in with force. Already, in 1762, some families had settled in Greenbrier, and had refused to leave on the King's proclamation, "enjoining and requiring all persons whatsoever, who have either willfully or inadvertently seated themselves upon any lands within the countries above described, or upon any other lands which, not having been ceded to or purchased by us, are still reserved to the said Indians as aforesaid, forthwith to remove themselves from such settlements." From Greenbrier, the whites penetrated to and settled on the New river previous to 1776, and at various points were, in contravention of treaties, entering upon and cultivating the lands of different tribes. The Indians witnessed these encroachments with bitter feelings; lost faith in such proclamations as that of Bouquet, given in the preceding chapter, and in all treaties, and though Col. Johnson had ordered the whites, by proclamation, to leave, they learned that he contemplated, himself, founding a colony south of the Ohio river. This is true, but it was Johnson's intention to purchase lands before commencing operations. From Franklin's letters, we learn that this plan was in contemplation as early as the Spring of 1766. At this time Franklin was in London, and was written to by his son, Governor Franklin, of New Jersey, with regard to the proposed colony. The plan seems to have been to buy of the Six Nations the lands south of the Ohio, a purchase which, it was not doubted, Sir William might make, and then to procure from the King a grant of as much territory as the company, which it was intended to form, would require. Governor Franklin, accordingly, forwarded to his father an application for a grant, together with a letter from Sir William, recommending the plan to the ministry, all of which was duly communicated to the proper department. But at that time there were various interests bearing upon this plan of Franklin. The old Ohio Company was still suing, through its agent, Col. Mercer, for a perfection of the original grant. The soldiers, claiming under Dinwiddie's proclamation, had their tales of rights and grievances. Individuals, to whom grants had been made by Virginia, wished them completed. Gen. Lyman, from Connecticut, we believe, was soliciting a new grant similar to that now asked by Franklin, and the ministers themselves were divided as to the policy and propriety of establishing settlements so far in the interior, Shelburne being in favor of the new colony, Hillsborough opposed to it.

The company was organized, however, and the nominally leading man therein being Thomas Walpole, a London banker of eminence, it was known as the Walpole Company. Franklin continued, privately, to make friends among the ministry, and to press upon them the policy of making large settlements in the west; and as the old way of managing the Indians by superintendents was just then in bad odour, in consequence of the expense attending it, the Cabinet Council so far approved the new plan as to present it for examination to the Board of Trade, with members of which Franklin had been privately conversing.

This was in the Autumn of 1767. But, before any conclusion was come to, it was necessary to arrange definitely that boundary line which had been vaguely talked of in 1765, and with respect to which Sir William Johnson had written to the ministry, who had mislaid his letters, and given him no instructions. The necessity of arranging this boundary was also kept in mind by the continued and growing irritation of the Indians, who found themselves invaded from every side. This irritation became so great, during the Autumn of 1767, that Gage wrote to the Governor of Pennsylvania on the subject. The Governor communicated his letter to the Assembly on the 5th of January, 1768, and representations were at once sent to England expressing the necessity of having the Indian line fixed. Dr. Franklin, all this time, was urging the same necessity upon the ministers in England, and about Christmas of 1767, Sir William's letters on the subject having been found, orders were sent him to complete the proposed purchase from the Six Nations and settle all differences. But the project for a colony was, for the time, dropped—a new administration coming in which was not that way disposed.

Sir William Johnson having received, early in the Spring, the orders from England relative to a new treaty with the Indians, at once took steps to secure a full attendance. Notice was given to the various colonial governments, to the Six Nations, the Delawares and the Shawanese, and a congress was appointed to meet at Fort Stanwix during the following October (1768.) It met upon the 24th of that month, and was attended by representatives from New Jersey, Virginia and Pennsylvania, by Sir William and his deputies, by the agents of those traders who had suffered in the war of 1763, and by deputies from all the Six Nations, the Delawares and the Shawanese.

The first point to be settled was the boundary line, which was to determine the Indian lands of the west from that time forward, and this line the Indians, upon the 1st of November, stated should begin on the Ohio, at the mouth of the Cherokee (or Tennessee) river; thence go up the Ohio and Alleghany to Kittatinny; thence across to the Susquehanna, &c., whereby the whole country south of the Ohio and Alleghany, to which the Six Nations had any claim, was transferred to the British. One deed, for a part of this land, was made on the 3d of November to William Trent, attorney for twenty-two traders, whose goods had been destroyed by the Indians in 1763. The tract conveyed by this was between the Kanawha and Monongehela, and was, by the traders, named Indiana. Two days afterwards a deed for the remaining western lands was made to the King, and the price agreed on paid down. These deeds were made upon the express agreement that no claim should ever be based upon previous treaties, those of Lancaster, Logstown, &c.; and they were signed by the chiefs of the Six Nations for themselves, their allies and dependants, the Shawanese, Delawares, Mingos of Ohio, and others; but the Shawanese and Delaware deputies present did not sign them.

Such was the treaty of Stanwix, whereon, in a great measure, rests the title by purchase to Western Virginia, Pennsylvania and Kentucky. It was a better foundation, perhaps, than that given by previous treaties, but was essentially worthless, for the lands conveyed were not occupied or hunted on by those conveying them. In truth, we cannot doubt that this immense grant was obtained by the influence of Sir William Johnson, in order that the new colony, of which he was to be the Governor, might be founded there. The fact that such a country was ceded voluntarily—not after a war, not by hard persuasion, but at once and willingly—satisfies us that the whole affair had been previously settled with the New York savages, and that the Ohio Indians had no voice in the matter.

But besides the claim of the Iroquois and the northwest Indians to Kentucky, it was also claimed by the Cherokees; and it is worthy of remembrance that after the treaty of Lochabar, made in October, 1770, two years after the Stanwix treaty recognized a title in the Southern Indians to all the country west from a line drawn from a point six miles east of Big or Long Island, in Holsten river, to the mouth of the Great Kanawha; although, as we have just stated, their right to all the lands north and east of the Kentucky river was purchased by Col. Donaldson, either for the King, Virginia, or himself, it is impossible to say which.

But the grant of the great northern confederacy was made. The white man could now quiet his conscience when driving the native from his forest home, and feel sure that an army would back his pretensions. A new company was at once organized in Virginia, called the "Mississippi Company," and a petition sent to the King for two millions and a-half of acres in the west. Among the signers of this were Francis Lightfoot Lee, Richard Henry Lee, George Washington and Arthur Lee. The gentleman last named was the agent for the petitioners in England. This application was referred to the Board of Trade on the 9th of March, 1769, and after that we hear nothing of it.

The Board of Trade was, however, again called on to report upon the application of the Walpole Company, and Lord Hillsborough, the president, reported against it. This called out Franklin's celebrated "Ohio Settlement," a paper written with so much ability that the King's Council put by the official report and granted the petition, a step which mortified the noble Lord so much that he resigned his official station. The petition now needed only the royal sanction, which was not given until August 14th, 1772; but, in 1770, the Ohio Company was merged into Walpole's, and the claims of the soldiers of 1756, being acknowledged both by the new company and by government, all claims were quieted. Nothing was ever done, however, under the grant to Walpole, the Revolution soon coming upon America. After the Revolution, Walpole and his associates petitioned Congress respecting their lands, called by them "Vandalia," but could get no help from that body. What was finally done by Virginia with the claims of this and other companies we do not find written, but presume their lands were all looked on as forfeited.

During the ten years in which Franklin, Pownall and their friends were trying to get the great western land company into operation, actual settlers were crossing the mountains all too rapidly, for the Ohio Indians "viewed the settlements with an uneasy and jealous eye," and " did not scruple to say that they must be compensated for their right if people settled thereon, notwithstanding the cession by the Six Nations." It has been said, also, that Lord Dunmore, then Governor of Virginia, authorized surveys and settlements on the western lands, notwithstanding the proclamation of 1763, but Sparks gives us a letter from him in which this is expressly denied. However, surveyors did go down even to the Falls of the Ohio, and the whole region south of the Ohio was filling up with white men. The futility of the Fort Stanwix treaty, and the ignorance or contempt of it by the fierce Shawanese, are well seen in the meeting between them and Bullitt, one of the early emigrants, in 1733. Bullitt, on his way down the Ohio, stopped, and singly sought the savages at one of their towns. He then told them of his proposed settlement, and his wish to live at peace with them, and said that, as they had received nothing under the treaty of 1768, it was intended to make them presents the next year. The Indians considered the talk of the Long Knife, and the next day agreed to his proposed settlement, provided he did not disturb them in their hunting south of the Ohio—a provision wholly inconsistent with the Stanwix deed.

Among the earlier operators in western lands was Washington. He had always regarded the proclamation of 1763, as a mere temporary expedient to quiet the savages, and being better acquainted with the value of western lands than most of those who could command means, he early began to buy beyond the mountains. His agent in selecting lands was the unfortunate Colonel Crawford. In 1767, we find Washington writing to Crawford on this subject, and looking forward to the occupation of the western territory; in 1770, he crossed the mountains, going down the Ohio to the mouth of the Great Kanawha; and in 1773, being entitled, under the King's proclamation of 1763, (which gave a bounty to the officers and soldiers who had served in the French war,) to ten thousand acres of land, he became deeply interested in the country beyond the mountains, and had some correspondence respecting the importation of settlers from Europe. Indeed, had not the Revolutionary war been just then on the eve of breaking out, Washington would, in all probability, have become the leading settler of the west, and all our history have been changed.

But while in England and along the Atlantic men were talking of peopling the west south of the river Ohio, a few obscure individuals, unknown to Walpole, to Franklin, and to Washington, were taking those steps which actually resulted in its settlement.

These deeds were made upon the express agreement that no claim should ever be based upon previous treaties—those of Lancaster, Logstown, &c. The deeds were signed by the chiefs of the Six Nations, for themselves, their allies and dependents. The Shawanese and Delaware deputies present refused to sanction the treaty by their signatures. Such was the treaty of Stanwix, whereon, in a great measure, rests the title, by purchase, of Western Virginia, Pennsylvania, and Kentucky.

In 1769, a new company was formed in Virginia called the "Mississippi Company," and asking of the King a grant of 2,500,000 acres.

Lord Botetourt encouraged these companies, as did also his successor. Botetourt died in 1771, and the Earl of Dunmore, who was appointed to the Governorship, arrived in Virginia in 1772. Under the favor of both Governors, settlers were crossing the mountains in considerable number, and to the very great annoyance of the natives. In order to protect these settlers, a small force was sent, in 1773, under Gen. McIntosh, for the defence of the frontier, and to attack the Indian towns on the Sandusky. McIntosh's operations were unsuccessful, and his campaign ended after severe losses in killed and wounded. That both sides of the question may be seen, we give the following extracts from letters written in 1774 by Gen. Arthur St. Clair and others:

FROM ARTHUR ST. CLAIR, 1774.

"The murder of a Delaware Indian chief was perpetrated eighteen miles from this place (Ligonier). It is the most astonishing thing in the world—the disposition of the common people of this country. Actuated by the most savage cruelty, they wantonly perpetrate crimes that are a disgrace to humanity, and seem, at the same time, to be under a kind of religious enthusiasm. The Delawares are still friendly, and it may, perhaps, prevent a general war, if they can be kept in temper."

FROM ALEX. M'KEE, FORT PITT, 1774.

"You must, ere this, be acquainted with the critical situation of this country, and the unhappy circumstances which have lately arisen between the Virginians and the Indians, the event of which still continues doubtful —whether matters will be brought to a general rupture or an accommodation. Hostilities have been commenced on both sides. * * Some wise interposition of Government is truly necessary, or thousands of inhabitants must be involved in misery and distress. But, to do the Indians justice, they have given more proof of their pacific disposition, and have acted with more moderation, than those who ought to have been more rational, a few Mingos and Shawanese excepted, who have long been refractory. There are more effective means of chastising them for their insolence and perjury than by involving the defenceless country in a war."

FROM D. SMITH, PITTSBURG, 1774.

"The Indians were surprised to see a number of armed men at this place, with their colors, at different times, making a warlike appearance, and said some of the militia fired on them at their camps near the mouth of Saw-mill Run."·

FROM A. MACKAY, PITTSBURG, 1774.

"We do not know what day or hour we will be attacked by our savage and provoked enemy, the Indians, who have already massacred sixteen persons, to our certain knowledge, about Ten-mile creek. A party of militia, consisting of Capt. McClure, Lieut. Kincaid, and forty privates, were on their march to join Connelly, at the mouth of Wheeling, where he intended to erect a fort, when they were attacked by four Indians, who killed the Captain on the spot, wounded the Lieutenant, and made their escape."

FROM JNO. MONTGOMERY, 1774.

"The Shawanese seem well disposed and inclinable to peace, and will continue so, unless provoked by the Virginians. The Delawares are all for peace. Logan's party had returned, and had thirteen scalps and one prisoner. Logan says he is now satisfied for the loss of his relatives, and will sit still until he hears what the Long-knives (Virginians) will say. I am in hopes the storm will blow over."

In June, 1774, Col. McDonald, with four hundred men, was ordered to Wheeling. After capturing the Indian village of Wappatomi, the savages sued for peace, and while negotiations were pending, removed their women and children, burnt their towns, destroyed their crops, and reduced the whites to the verge of starvation.

But we are anticipating events. At the close of the war in 1764, the English colonies in America were thirteen in number, with a population of 2,500,000. In the French and Indian war, to which we have briefly referred, they all took part, and while England contributed some men and money, on the colonies fell the heaviest share of the burden, and to them belongs the merit of success. By their union, in this war, they laid the foundation of that union in the Revolution which resulted in the establishment of the United States. The year 1765 is memorable for the stand taken by Virginia as to those questions which were causing a state of hostility between the colonies and the mother country, which resulted in a long and bloody war, and ended in a final separation.

BATTLE OF BACK CREEK.

From D. S. Young, Esq., we have obtained the following account of his ancestors' participation in this affair: "About the year 1764, a party of Indians, passing through the country, made a raid upon the settlers on Kerr's creek, in Rockbridge, murdering men, women and children. The whole country was aroused, and a number of brave Augustians armed themselves hastily and went in pursuit. Crossing the Warm Spring mountain—following the Indian trail, they overtook the savages on Back Creek, in the present county of Bath. A hand-to-hand fight instantly commenced, the whites making an attack with such fury that the guilty barbarians had no time to fly. The engagement, which resulted in the defeat and death of almost every blood-stained savage, was deplored by the Young family for the loss of Thomas Young, one of the two sons of the original founder of the family in our county. This occurred in the following manner: In the heat of the contest, Thomas Young became engaged in mortal combat with two of the savages. While thus contending, a third savage approached him from the rear, and with one blow buried his tomahawk deep into the skull of the brave white. Death ensued instantly, and, in the twinkling of an eye, the savage scalped his victim. John Young, although fighting desperately, saw the whole proceeding, and marked the murderer. Having disposed of his assailants, he fired upon the slayer of his brother. The shot took effect in the Indian's hip, who sank upon his knees. Young rushed upon him with his sword. His first blow was parried by the savage, who threw up his gun, on the barrel of which the sword was broken. With the remaining portion of the rapier, Young hacked and hewed the savage to pieces. Thomas Young's body was buried on the battle-field. His scalp was brought home and interred in the grave of his father—in the Glebe burying-ground, near the North Mountain, in Augusta."

CHAPTER XI.

The year 1764, which witnessed the close of the Indian war, is memorable for the commencement of the narrow policy of Colonial oppression, which, after disturbing the ancient harmony of the two countries for twelve years, terminated in a dismemberment of the British Empire. Space does not admit of our entering upon the origin and history of the disputes between the colonies and mother country; upon the reciprocal insults, which soured the tempers; the mutual injuries, which embittered the passions of the opposite parties, made reconciliation impossible, and finally led to the establishment of the Federal Government. We must confine ourselves to matters nearer home. During the Spring of 1774, it was evident that an Indian war was impending on our frontier. Such was the general belief in its imminency, that the traders and other adventurers who had penetrated into the territory of the red men, left the wilderness, and collected at Wheeling. That post was then commanded by Capt. M. Cresap, and was called the "Key of the West." It must be remembered that Pennsylvania and Virginia laid equal claim, in 1752-54, to Pittsburg and the surrounding country, and doubt still existed as to which colony it belonged. This led to the controversy treated of in the ninth chapter, and caused further irritation and trouble in 1774. Early in the Spring of this year, Dunmore, prompted by Col. Croghan, and his nephew, Dr. Jno. Connolly, an intriguing and ambitious man, determined, as we have seen, to assert the claims of Virginia upon Pittsburg and its vicinity. Then commenced a series of contests, complaints and outrages which are too extensive and complicated to be described within our limited space. The upshot of the matter was this: Connolly took possession of Fort Pitt, dismantled and nearly destroyed it, and then rebuilt and named it Fort Dunmore. He also wrote to the settlers along the Ohio that the Shawanese were not to be trusted, and he desired all to be in readiness to redress any wrongs these savages might perpetrate. One of these circulars he addressed to Capt. Michael Cresap, at Wheeling. A few days previous to the date of Connolly's letter, April 16, 1774, a canoe loaded with goods for the Shawanese towns, the property of Mr. Butler, a Pittsburg merchant, had been attacked by three Cherokee Indians about sixty miles above Wheeling, and one of the whites killed. This greatly excited the Virginians at Wheeling, and when, a few days later, it was reported that a canoe containing Indians was coming down the river, a resolution was at once taken to attack it. Connolly was endeavoring to foment a war, and the whites, largely participating in his views, exhibited at this time the blind impetuosity of barbarians. Cresap, one of the leaders of the war party, went up the river with several men, and, firing into the boat, killed two Indians, whom they scalped. Next day, several boats containing Indians were discovered a few miles up the river. Pursuit was given, and that night, while the Indians were encamped near the mouth of Captina creek, twenty miles below Wheeling, the Virginians attacked them, killing and wounding several. Shortly afterwards, April, 1774, Daniel Greathouse massacred twelve Indians at Baker's house, on the Big Yellow creek, where a considerable number of red men were encamped. By a disgraceful device, many of them were made drunk on rum, then murdered and scalped. Among the slain was the entire family of the famous chief, Logan, though Logan had hitherto been friendly to the whites, and warmly espoused a peace policy. These were the exciting causes of the war of 1774, though, as already premised, the magazine was charged, and needed only the application of the match to cause an explosion.

The settlers, well knowing what would follow such brutalities, left the frontier and retired into stockade forts. As they anticipated, the Indians were soon on the war path. It was not a single tribe, but a combination, or confederacy of all the tribes of the northwest, conspicuous among them the Shawanese, Mingos, and Delawares. Having, by their own conduct brought affairs to this point, with the hope that, during a general war, the Indians would be "polished off the earth," to use the slang phraseology of the frontier, Connolly and Cresap despatched a scout to Williamsburg, where the Legislature was at the time in session, to inform the Governor.

Gen. Lewis, a member of the House of Burgesses for the county of Botetourt, was then in Williamsburg, attending its deliberations. He was widely distinguished for his great actions and the important services he had rendered his country. He was now in his fifty-sixth year, and his strong understanding fortified by large experience. The Governor immediately sent for him, and, after a conference, decided on raising an army and appointing Lewis to its command. He asked the General his views as to a campaign. Lewis soon explained to him a plan of campaign that was simple, bold, and judicious. The General knew that no such formidable union of savage tribes as now existed had ever taken place on the continent; that no such able and astute leaders as Logan, chief of the Mingos; Cornstalk, sachem of the Shawanese, and King of the Northern Confederacy; Outacité, the Man-killer, King of the Cherokees; and Blue Jacket, had ever been formed against the whites, or occupied such a geographical advantage over their enemy. He informed Lord Dunmore that the savages must not only be attacked in front, but on the flank; that he should advance by the Kanawha, or the River of the Woods, to the Ohio, while a coöperating force from Fort Pitt, coming down the river, would be prepared to strike the left of the Indian army, advancing from the west. He explained his campaign in detail, and the Governor heartily approved the prospective acuteness of his plans, and said he would take command in person of the force to move from Fort Pitt. Gen. Lewis immediately left the capital for Staunton, and applied himself, with unexampled energy, to raising from the southern counties his force, and performed such wonders of labor as could hardly have been expected from a human body and a human mind. He selected and appointed his own officers, and, under them, volunteers came in with such alacrity that there was no occasion to resort to a draft, which he was empowered to do, if necessary. As the companies were completed in Staunton, they were sent off to Camp Union, on the Greenbrier, and, when completed, the force there consisted of the following:

GEN. LEWIS' FORCE.

I. Regiment of Augusta troops, under Col. Charles Lewis. The captains in this regiment were: Geo. Mathews, (afterwards Governor of Georgia); Alex. McClenachan; John Dickinson; John Lewis, (son of Col. Wm. Lewis, afterwards of the Sweet Springs,) then only sixteen years of age, but celebrated for his martial spirit and herculean strength; Benj. Harrison; Wm. Paul; Jos. Haynes; Sam'l Wilson.

II. The Botetourt regiment, under Col. Wm. Fleming. The captains in this regiment were: Mathew Arbuckle; John Murray; John Lewis, (son of the General in command); James Robertson; Robt. McClenachan; James Ward; John Stuart, (author of a Memoir of this campaign).

III. The regiment from Culpeper, under Col. John Field.

Three Independent companies from Washington county, Va., under command of Col. Wm. Christian. Their captains were: Evan Shelby, Wm. Russell, —— Harbert.

An Independent company from Bedford county, Va., under command of Capt. Thos. Buford.

These citizen-soldiers were men hardened by exercise and toil. Their bodies seemed inaccessible to disease or pain. War was their element. They sported with danger, and met death with composure. To such men the colony of Augusta, the State of Virginia, and the Republic of the United States, owe their present greatness. They remind us of the founders of Rome, of whom Cato, the elder, said to the Roman Senate: "Think not it was merely by force of arms that our forefathers raised this republic from a low condition to its present greatness. No! By things of a very different nature—industry and discipline at home, abstinence and justice abroad, a disinterested spirit in council, unblinded by passion and unbiassed by pleasure."

Gen. Lewis' last preparations completed, he left Staunton, arrived at Camp Union early in September, and assumed command. On the 11th of September, 1774, unsheathing the old sword he had carried twenty years before at the defeat of Braddock, and in the war of '63-'64, he pointed to the West and commenced his march into the friendless wilderness. Never had the Virginians taken the field with so numerous and formidable a force, but Lewis knew he was marching against a powerful Confederacy. He therefore sought to impress upon his men that they should not show themselves inferior in valor to the heroes of 1755, nor sink below public expectation. He maintained a rigid discipline, and, as far as practicable, the regularity of his march, as if in constant expectation of an attack, and illustrated the necessity of this course by a reference to the defeat of Braddock, and the well-known fact that an inferior number, well posted and handled with ability, has often proved too much for a more numerous body, whom contempt for their enemy exposes to attacks for which they are unprepared. They were on hostile ground from the day of their march, and the wisdom of his precautions cannot be doubted.

There was no road, or even pathway, from Camp Union to the Ohio, a distance of one hundred and sixty miles. The whole country was an unbroken forest or trackless desert. Through this gloomy region the army was to be piloted by Capt. Arbuckle, a skillful backwoodsman. Their supplies of flour, salt and ammunition were to be transported on the backs of unshod horses, and their cattle driven in rear of the army. After a painful march of nineteen days, the army arrived on the 1st of October, 1774, at the mouth of the Kanawha. The troops had thus marched, on an average, eight-and-a-half miles a day—an astonishingly good progress under all the circumstances. This result could not have been attained but for the good health and vigorous character of the men. They had neither spirits, wine, nor malt liquor, and drunkenness, disease, crime, and insubordination were unknown. When the army reached Point Pleasant, the soldiers were almost naked. Their rations consisted of a small quantity of meal or flour, a little beef, and such game as they could kill—no tea or coffee. No men were ever called on to perform harder or more continuous labor, and yet they were always cheery, and worked with a will that could not be surpassed. We conclude from this, that water is better than grog, and that the theory of old army officers—especially those of the British army—that rum is essential to the good health and good humor of the soldier, is erroneous.

The privations, the waste of strength and health, on such a march, are enormous, but owing to the temperance of the men, the high morale of the force, the troops were, notwithstanding some loss of physical condition, ready for action on reaching the Ohio. The General, who was then nearly sixty years of age, and was always worse lodged, worse served, and more plainly dressed than the youngest of his officers, was full of strength and vivacity, and elated at his success in crossing the wilderness. Owing to his failure to hear from Dunmore, and the fatigue of some of the less vigorous of his men, Gen. Lewis now, as he had previously resolved on doing, formed and fortified a camp at this point,—selecting an elevated spot of land, where there was plenty of fresh air, good water, and excellent drainage. Here the General remained nine days, until rest and a supply of wholesome food fully restored the bodies and spirits of his surviving soldiers, and made them, if not more ready, better prepared for action.

While the events we have related, commencing with April, 1774—the recruiting of Lewis' force, the march to Point Pleasant, &c.—were transpiring east of the Ohio, the barbarians, fully advised by their spies and scouts, began to collect northwest of the Ohio in force. They were animated by their ancient hatred of the Virginians, whom they styled " Long Knives ;"* by a desire for revenge; by a wish to rid the country forever of the pale faces; and by a natural fondness for war. They mustered with such celerity, and in such force, that, greatly outnumbering the Virginians, they believed Lewis would not dare to meet them, or, if rash enough to do so, he would be ignominiously defeated. Their commander-in-chief, the famous Cornstalk, exerted himself to bring this force together with incredible zeal and activity, and planned to take the two divisions of Lewis and Dunmore in detail. Accordingly, he advanced to meet Lewis, and was in the neighborhood of Point Pleasant, watching the progress of affairs, when Lewis arrived. From his lair, he witnessed the arrival of Lewis' force and the disposition made of them.

On the 9th of October, three white couriers, who had previously lived among the Indians as traders, arrived in Lewis' camp, bearing dispatches from Dunmore, to inform Lewis that he, Dunmore, had changed the plan of campaign, and would not attempt to join Lewis at Point Pleasant, and ordering Lewis to march directly to the Indian towns on the Scioto, where Dunmore would join him. It is believed that this order was given with the base hope that Lewis' command would encounter an overwhelming savage force and be destroyed. In such cases, it is the duty of the historian to give matters of fact, without reserve, without endeavoring to dive into the motives.

It is charged by historians that Dunmore was now, and had long been, engaged in fomenting jealousies and feuds between the colonies, hoping thus to draw off their attention from the encroachments of the British Government upon their constitutional rights. He is also accused of encouraging and inciting the savages to hostilities by his intrigues. And his purpose to take command of the force to rendezvous at Fort Pitt, is believed by them to have proceeded from a desire to allow, in his absence, the whole confederated Indian force to fall upon and annihilate Lewis. If

---

*The origin of that term was as follows: Little Eagle, a noted Mingo chief, in a rencontre, in the war of 1755, with some whites, under Col. Gibson, attempted to shoot the Colonel, but the ball missed the target. With the quickness and ferocity of a tiger, Gibson sprang upon his foe, and with one sweep of his sword, severed Little Eagle's head from his body. The Indians fled, and reported that the white captain had cut off their chief's head with a "long knife"—hence the term.

such was his object, he was signally defeated through the gallantry of
Lewis' forces. Thus strangely do events confound all the plans of man.

One of the scouts who came to Lewis from Dunmore was McCulloch,
and, no doubt, the Major Samuel McCulloch afterwards so famous as a
scout, hunter and warrior. McCulloch informed Lewis that he had recently left the Shawanese towns, on the Ohio, and gone to Dunmore's
camp; that the combination against the whites was formidable—composed
of a larger number of men than under command of either Lewis or Dunmore, and all of them eager for the fray. "They will give you grinders,
and that before long," said McCulloch, and repeating it, he swore "the
whites would get grinders very soon." The express returned immediately
to Dunmore, and the day after they left, the battle of the Point was fought.

On the night of the 9th, Gen. Lewis' scouts reported no Indians within
fifteen miles, and preparations were made to break camp and commence
the march westward on the next morning. The morning of October 10,
1774, had hardly dawned, however, before Lewis' force was startled by
the report of rifles. The alarm was beaten, the enlivening strains reverberating over the surrounding solitudes. Lewis' pickets came in rapidly,
and reported the enemy advancing in force, one of them declaring that he
had seen " a body of Indians covering four acres of ground."

Another scout declared the whole woods was swarming with painted
warriors, armed with rifles, tomahawks, war clubs and battle axes. The
rapidity with which Gen. Lewis formed his troops for battle alone saved
the command from destruction. In this unexpected emergency, the excitement, the noise and confusion, Gen. Lewis was perfectly composed and,
with the utmost coolness and presence of mind, took the necessary measures to meet and repel the attack. He ordered to the front the Augusta
troops, under his brother, Col. Charles Lewis. He personally knew every
man in this regiment—had known them from boyhood, and knew they
could be depended on in the hour of danger. The Augusta regiment had
hardly passed the outposts of the camp, when a furious onset was made
upon them by an overwhelming force of Indians. Col. Charles Lewis fell
mortally wounded at an early hour, but his brave troops kept up a stub-
born resistance, until, overborne by superior numbers, they showed signs
of being pressed back. At this moment, Gen. Lewis ordered forward Col.
Fleming's regiment, which gallantly maintained the fortunes of the day
until he, too, was struck down by a fatal shot, and was borne, dying, as his
men believed, from the field. At this hour the aspect of affairs was terribly gloomy, and less determined men would have been overborne and
swept from the field. Gen. Lewis, who comprehended the critical situation, (he was not more distinguished for the even tenor of his mind in excitement than for his intrepidity in action) determined to make a supreme
effort. He immediately brought into action the entire reserve—men who

rushed into the fray like bloodhounds cut loose from their leashes, and the fight raged from one end of the line to the other, both parties exhibiting the "stern joy which warriors feel in meeting foemen worthy of their steel." The barbarians, who thought their victory sure when they saw the whites waver after the fall of Cols. Lewis and Fleming, became frantic with rage as Fields' long-knives were seen advancing. "With convulsive grasp they seized their weapons, and would have rushed headlong upon the whites, had the latter not kept up a most galling fire, which had the double effect of thinning their ranks and cooling their rage." "The battle scene was now," says de Hass, "terribly grand. There stood the combatants; terror, rage, disappointment and despair riveted upon the painted faces of one, while calm resolution and the unbending will to do or die, were marked upon the other. Neither party would retreat, neither could advance. The noise of the firing was tremendous. No single gun could be distinguished—it was one constant roar. The rifle and tomahawk now did their work with dreadful certainty. The confusion and perturbation of the camp had now arrived at its greatest height. The confused sounds and wild uproar of the battle added greatly to the terror of the scene. The shouting of the whites, the continual roar of firearms, the war whoop and dismal yelling of the Indians, were discordant and terrific." About twelve o'clock the enemy's fire slackened, and Gen. Lewis detached the companies of Capts. Stuart, Mathews and Shelby to turn their flank. This manœuvre was handsomely executed, and by four o'clock the barbarians commenced a good-ordered retreat under Cornstalk, and effected their escape across the Ohio.

It was throughout a terrible scene—the ring of rifles and roar of muskets, the clubbed guns, the flashing knives—the fight hand-to-hand—the scream for mercy, smothered in the death-groan—the crashing through the brush—the advance—the retreat—the pursuit, every man for himself, with his enemy in view—the scattering on every side—the sounds of battle, dying away into a pistol shot here and there through the wood, and a shriek—the collecting again of the whites, covered with gore and sweat, bearing trophies of the slain, their dripping knives in one hand, and rifle-barrel bent and smeared with brains and hair in the other;—no language can adequately describe it.

The calamity of our loss on that day was heightened by the death of Col. Charles Lewis, who abandoned himself too much to his passion for glory, and forgot that there is a wide difference between an officer and a private. Instead of confining himself to giving orders, he sought to execute them also. Rushing headlong into the fray, a more than ordinarily conspicuous object by reason of a scarlet waistcoat which he wore, against the remonstrances of his friends, he fell early under the enemy's fire. Not inferior to his brother, the General, in courage, intrepidity and military

genius, he surpassed him in some respects.   He knew how to oblige with
a better grace, how to win the hearts of those about him with a more engaging behavior.   He, consequently, acquired the esteem and affection of
his men in a remarkable manner.   To perpetuate the memory of his public
and private virtues, his eminent services in the field, and his heroic fate, the
General Assembly of Virginia, in 1816, named Lewis county in his honor.

The following is a list of our killed on this occasion—a very incomplete
list it is—as many subalterns and privates were slain whose names could
not be obtained;

Colonels—Lewis and Field.

Captains—Morrow, Buford, Wood, Murray, Cardiff, Wilson, and Robt.
McClenachan.

Lieutenants—Allen, Goldsby, and Dillon.

The historian can scarcely do adequate justice to these heroes.   According to some accounts, Col. Christian's force did not reach the Point until
the day after the battle.   Others are to the effect that he came upon the
ground about mid-day, and aided in routing the barbarians.

Among the men in this battle who subsequently became distinguished
were; Gen. Isaac Shelby, first Governor of Kentucky; Gen. Wm. and Col.
John Campbell, heroes of "King's Mountain;" Gen. Evan Shelby, of
Tennessee; Col. Wm. Fleming, acting Governor of Virginia during the
Revolution; Gen. Andrew Moore, U. S. Senator; Col. John Stuart, of
Greenbrier; Gen. Tate, of Washington county; Col. Wm. McKee, of
Kentucky; Col. John Steele, Governor of Miss.; Col. Chas. Cameron, of
Bath; Major John Lewis, of Monroe; Gen. Wells, of Ohio; Gen. George
Mathews, Governor of Georgia.

At the commencement of the Revolution, Washington considered Lewis
the foremost military man in America.   His energies were in 1776, however,
much impaired by disease and age—premature old age from illness and
sufferings.

The Indian army comprised the pick of the northern and western confederated tribes.   Cornstalk, King of the Northern Confederacy, was
commander-in-chief, supported by Blue Jacket, Red Hawk, a Delaware
chief, Scoppothus, a Mingo sachem, Elinipsico, son of Cornstalk, Chiyawee,
chief of the Wayandottes, and the celebrated chief of the Cayugas, Logan.
All of these warriors performed prodigies of valor during the battle, and
above the din, the loud voice of Cornstalk was heard encouraging his
men.   In the heat of battle, seeing one of his men retreating, he slew him
him with a stroke from his tomahawk.

No witness of this battle, no one acquainted with the conduct of the red
men in war, could doubt of their Asiatic origin.   In all their habits they
resemble the wandering Tartars; support, with astonishing fortitude, hunger, cold, fatigue, and all the hardships of war.   In battle, they exhibit

the same want of discipline, the same fury to attack, the same readiness to fly from and return to the attack, and the same disposition to slaughter when they are conquerors.

The battle was no sooner won, and the Indians in flight, than General Lewis, with that enthusiasm which is peculiar to great minds, took steps to reap the fruits of victory. He ordered preparations for pursuit, and, while these were progressing, had the wounded cared for, the dead buried, and himself laid off a rectangular stockade fort, eighty feet long, with block-houses at two of the corners. It was built for the protection of the sick and wounded. The next morning he crossed the Ohio with his fighting men, and proceeded, though deep ravines and impenetrable thickets impeded his progress, by forced marches for the Pickaway Plains. The savages, who fled before him or hung upon his flanks, now regarded with admiration and terror his spirit and energy; and, notwithstanding the losses of Lewis at the battle of the Point, he appeared to them as more formidable and more powerful than ever. They saw the folly of opposing such a man, and made up their minds to sue for peace. Thus this great soldier and wise man not only shaped the opinions and directed the conduct of his own men, but those of his enemies. At the Plains, Lewis was met by a courier from Dunmore, ordering him to halt, as he, Dunmore, was negotiating a peace with the barbarians. Lewis indignantly disregarded this order, and pushed on. He received a second order from Dunmore, which he equally scouted, and continued his march until within three miles of Dunmore's detachment. Dunmore, alarmed, proceeded, with a barbarian chief called White Eyes, to visit Gen. Lewis, whom he peremptorily ordered to halt. The fury of Lewis' men, at what they considered the treachery of Dunmore, was such that Lewis only, with great difficulty, preserved his life.

Gen. Lewis' orders were to return to Point Pleasant, and thence to Greenbrier, where his forces were to be disbanded. Dunmore retired to his camp, concluded a treaty of peace with the barbarians,—the treaty of Camp Charlotte,—and returned to Williamsburg. It was on this occasion that the famous Mingo chief, Logan, made his celebrated speech. He would not oppose the treaty negotiated by Dunmore, and yet would not meet the whites in council. Dunmore, feeling the importance of securing his assent to the treaty, sent Col. Gibson to Logan, who was in his tent brooding in melancholy silence over his accumulated wrongs. Col. Gibson returned without Logan, but with the following speech, which has given its author an imperishable immortality, though not a few doubt its authenticity. Jefferson regarded the speech as one of the most eloquent passages in the English language, and said of it, " I may challenge the whole orations of Demosthenes and Cicero, and of any more eminent orators, if Europe has furnished more eminent, to produce a single passage superior to it." It was in these words :

"I appeal to any white man to say if he ever entered Logan's cabin hungry, and he gave him not meat; if ever he came cold and naked, and he clothed him not. During the course of the last long and bloody war, Logan remained idle in his cabin, an advocate of peace. Such was my love for the whites, that my countrymen pointed as they passed and said, 'Logan is the friend of the white men.' I had even thought to live with you, but for the injuries of one man. Colonel Cresap, the last Spring, in cold blood and unprovoked, murdered all the relations of Logan, not even sparing my women and children. There runs not a drop of my blood in the veins of any living creature. This called on me for revenge. I have sought it; I have killed many; I have glutted my vengeance. For my country, I rejoice at the beams of peace; but do not harbor a thought that mine is the joy of fear. Logan never felt fear. He will not turn on his heel to save his life. Who is there to mourn for Logan? Not one."

Though the peace thus secured continued through the year 1775, there were occasional symptoms of awakening hostility on the part of the Shawanese and other confederated tribes, which were instigated by the British, who saw that a contest between the mother country and her colonies was impending. With a view to coming events, the English sought, in May, 1774, and with too much success, to bring over to their side the Six Nations. Consequently, during the Revolution, no one outside of a fort was safe on the frontiers of Virginia and Kentucky..

The following letter, fortunately found by the author some years since, and communicated to the public through a Richmond paper, is thought worthy of insertion at this point:

THE BATTLE OF POINT PLEASANT.

TO THE EDITORS OF THE STANDARD:

Gentlemen,—Many years since, when making some researches in the British Museum, I came across the following letter (without the writer's signature), dated at Williamsburg, Va., November 10, 1774. It gives, obviously from hearsay, a brief and incomplete, but, I imagine, a generally accurate account of the battle of Point Pleasant. You will probably consider it of sufficient interest to justify publication in "The Standard." Some of the names of the killed and wounded are inaccurate. Captain Blueford is doubtless intended for Buford. The letter appears in Vol. XLV of the "Gentleman's Magazine," page 42—that is to say, in the January number for the year 1775. Yours truly, J. L. PEYTON.

Staunton, February 10, 1882.

———

"WILLIAMSBURG, November 10, 1774.

"On the 10th of October last a battle was fought on the Ohio, of which the following are the particulars; On Monday morning, an hour before sunrise, two of Captain Russell's company discovered a large party of Indians about a mile from the camp, one of which men was shot down by the Indians, the other made his escape and brought in the intelligence; in two or three minutes after, two of Captain Shelvey's men came in and confirmed the account.

"Colonel Andrew Lewis being informed thereof, immediately ordered out Colonel Charles Lewis to take command of 140 of the Augusta troops, and with him went Captain Dickenson, Captain Harrison, Captain John Lewis, of Augusta, and Captain Lockridge, which made the First division; Colonel Fleming was ordered to take the command of 150 more of the Botetourt, Bedford and Fincastle troops, which made the Second division.

"Colonel Charles Lewis' division marched to the right, some distance from the Ohio, and Colonel Fleming, with his division, on the bank of the Ohio, to the left.

"Colonel Charles Lewis' division had not marched quite half a mile from the camp, when, about sunrise, a vigorous attack was made on the front of his division by the united tribes of Shawanese, Delawares, Mingos, Tawas, and of several other nations, in number not less than 800. In this heavy attack, Colonel Charles and several of his men fell, and the Augusta division was obliged to give way to the heavy fire of the enemy. The enemy instantly engaged the front of Colonel Fleming's division, and in a short time the Colonel received two balls through his left arm and one through his breast, and, after animating the officers and soldiers, retired to the camp.

" His loss in the field was sensibly felt, but the Augusta troops being shortly after reinforced from the camp by Colonel Field with his company, together with Captain McDowell's, &c., the enemy, no longer able to maintain their ground, was forced to give way. In their precipitate retreat Colonel Field was killed. During this time, which was till after 12 o'clock, the action continued extremely hot. The close underwood, many steep banks, and logs, greatly favoured the retreat of the Indians; and the bravest of their men made the best use of them, whilst others were throwing their dead into the Ohio, and carrying off their wounded.

" Soon after 12 the action abated, but continued, except at short intervals, sharp enough until sunset, when they found a safe retreat.

" They had not the satisfaction of carrying off any of our men's scalps, save one or two stragglers, whom they killed before the engagement. Many of their dead they scalped, rather than we should have them; but our troops scalped upwards of twenty men that were first killed. It is beyond doubt their loss in number far exceeded ours, which is considerable.

" The following is a return of the killed and wounded in the above battle : Killed, Colonels Charles Lewis and John Field, Captains John Murray, R. M'Chenechan, Samuel Wilson, James Ward, Lieutenant Hugh Allen, Ensigns Cantiff, Bracken, forty-four privates—total killed, fifty-three.

" Wounded, Colonel William Fleming, Captains Joe Dickenson, Thomas Blufford, J. Skidman, Lieutenants Goldman, Robinson, Lard, Vance, seventy-nine privates—total wounded, eighty-seven; killed and wounded, 146.

" The account further says that Colonel Fleming and several others are since dead of their wounds."

CORNSTALK.

It is to be regretted that those early writers who treated of the discovery and settlement of our country have not given us more frequent and candid accounts of the remarkable characters that flourished in savage life.

The scanty anecdotes that have reached us are full of peculiarity and interest; they furnish us with nearer glimpses of human nature, and show what man is in a comparatively primitive state, and what he owes to civilization.   There is something of the charm of discovery, in happening upon those wild, unexpected tracts of human nature; in witnessing, as it were, the native growth of moral sentiment, and perceiving those generous and romantic qualities which have been artificially wrought up by society, vegetating in spontaneous hardihood and rude magnificence.   In civilized life, where the happiness and almost existence of man depends so much upon public opinion, he is forever acting a part.   The bold and peculiar traits of native character are refined away or softened down by the leveling influence of what is termed good breeding, and he practices so many amiable deceptions, and assumes so many generous sentiments for the purposes of popularity, that it is difficult to distinguish his real character from that which is acquired or affected.   The Indian, on the contrary, free from the restraints and refinements of polished life, and living, in a great degree, solitary and independent, obeys the impulses of his inclination or the dictates of his individual judgment, and thus the attributes of his nature, being freely indulged, grow singly great and striking.   Society is like an artificial lawn, where every roughness is smoothed, every bramble eradicated, and the eye is delighted by the smiling verdure of a velvet surface.   He, however, who would study nature in its wildness and variety, must plunge into the forest, must explore the glen, must stem the torrent, and dare the precipice.   Such reflections arise on reading the accounts of the outrages of the savages upon the early settlers; how the footsteps of civilization in our country may be traced in the blood of the aborigines; how easily the colonists were moved to hostility by the lust of conquest; how merciless and exterminating was their warfare.   The imagination shrinks at the idea of how many intellectual beings were hunted from the earth; how many brave and noble hearts, of nature's sterling coinage, were broken down and trampled in the dust.

Such was the fate of Cornstalk, an Indian warrior, whose name was once a terror throughout Virginia and the west.   He was the most distinguished of a number of cotemporary sachems, who ruled over the Shawanese and other northwestern tribes the latter part of the eighteenth century—a band of native, untaught heroes, who made the most generous struggle of which human nature is capable; fighting to the last gasp for the deliverance of their country, without a hope of victory or a thought of renown; worthy of the age of poetry, and fit subjects for local story and romantic fiction, they have left scarcely any authentic traces on the page of history, but stalk, like gigantic shadows, in the dim twilight of tradition.

This Shawanese chief was king of the northern confederacy, and was born in that portion of the County of Augusta now comprehended within the limits of the county of Greenbrier, about the year 1747. He was first heard of when about sixteen years of age, when, in 1763-'64, he took an active part in the massacres of Muddy Creek and Big Levels, in Greenbrier. The savages were received as friends, and provisions given them with confidence. Unprovoked, as we have seen, they suddenly massacred the men and took the women and children prisoners. Cornstalk accompanied the party to the mouth of the Falling Spring, on Jackson's river, thence to Kerr's creek, and, in the same year, crossed the North mountain and committed some depredations near Staunton. The massacre on Kerr's creek was, says Foote, terribly visited on Cornstalk, when a defenceless hostage, after the lapse of more than twenty years. All savages seem alike, as the trees in the distant forest. Here and there one unites in his person the excellence of the whole race, and becomes the image of savage greatness. Cornstalk was gifted with eloquence, statesmanship, heroism, beauty of person, and strength of frame. In his movements, he was majestic; in his manners, easy and winning. Of his oratory, Col. Wilson, an officer in Dunmore's army, says: " I have heard the first orators in Virginia, Patrick Henry and R. H. Lee, but never have I heard one whose power of delivery surpassed that of Cornstalk."

The whole savage race was alarmed at the attempts of the whites to occupy Kentucky, and the preparations to lay off the bounty lands for the soldiers of Braddock's war, near Louisville, at the falls of the Ohio, drove them to exasperation. A confederacy was formed, at the head of which Cornstalk was placed. Mutual aggravations on the frontiers, followed by plunderings and murders, of which the whites would no more say they were innocent than the savages, brought on the war. In April, 1774, Col. Angus McDonald, of the Valley of the Shenandoah, led a regiment against the Indians on the Muskingum. He destroyed their towns and secured some hostages; and the hope was indulged that the frontier would be safe. The Indians, fully convinced that acting by tribes, or small companies, they would all share the fate of the Muskingums, made the last effort of savages, and acted in concert. Virginia had now no alternative but to meet the Indians with an adequate force. When he learned of the preparations of the Virginians, in 1774, to invade the Indian territory, under Gen. Lewis and Lord Dunmore, and he had, through his spies, early intelligence of the proposed campaign, Cornstalk organized his forces, and planned an attack upon the whites with great skill and ability. He saw the advantage which would result from defeating the separate columns before their junction at Point Pleasant, and accordingly advanced, by forced marches, against Gen. Lewis, and reached the Point about the same time with him. He lost no time in ascertaining the position of the Virginians, but, crossing the Ohio in the night, attacked the whites, who were taken by surprise, and with the disastrous result to himself as related.

After the battle, Cornstalk opposed the treaty of peace concluded with the Indians by Dunmore, and in his speech in reply to Dunmore's charges against the red men for their infraction of former treaties, and their many unprovoked murders, he proved himself an orator as well as soldier. He rose to make his speech in no way confused or daunted, and spoke in a distinct and audible voice, without stammering or repetition, and with peculiar emphasis. His appearance is said to have been truly grand, yet graceful and attractive. He sketched in his remarks, in lively colors, the once prosperous and happy condition of his tribe, inveighed against the perfidy of the whites and the dishonesty of the traders; and proposed that no one should be permitted to trade with the Indians on private account; that fair wages should be agreed upon and the traffic be committed to honest men, and, finally, that no "fire-water," which brought evil to the Indians, should be sent amongst them.

It is not known how Cornstalk spent the next three years, but, in the Spring of 1777, he visited Point Pleasant with Red Hawk and a few attendants. He informed Captain Arbuckle, who commanded the post at the time, that, with the exception of himself and the Shawanese, all the nations had joined the English, and that, unless protected by the whites, "they would have to swim with the stream." Capt. A. thought proper to detain Cornstalk and his companions as hostages for the good conduct of the tribe to which they belonged. They had not been long in this situation before a son of Cornstalk, concerned for the safety of his father, came to the opposite side of the river and hallooed; his father, knowing his voice, answered him. He was brought over the river. The father and son mutually embraced each other with the greatest tenderness.

On the day following, two Indians, who had concealed themselves in the weeds on the bank of the Kanawha, opposite the fort, killed a man of the name of Gilmore, as he was returning from hunting. As soon as the dead body was brought over the river, there was a general cry amongst the men who were present, "Let us kill the Indians in the fort." They immediately ascended the bank of the river, with Capt. Hall at their head, to execute their hasty resolution. On their way they were met by Capt. Stuart and Capt. Arbuckle, who endeavored to dissuade them from killing the Indian hostages, saying that they certainly had no concern in the murder of Gilmore; but remonstrance was in vain. Pale as death with rage, they cocked their guns and threatened the captains with instant death if they should attempt to hinder them from executing their purpose.

When the murderers arrived at the house where the hostages were confined, Cornstalk rose up to meet them at the door, but instantly received seven bullets through his body; his son and his other two fellow-hostages were instantly despatched with bullets and tomahawks.

Thus fell the Shawanese war chief Cornstalk, who, like Logan, his com-

panion in arms, was conspicuous for intellectual talent, bravery and misfortune. _

The biography of Cornstalk, as far as it is now known, goes to show
that he was no way deficient in those mental endowments which constitute
true greatness. On the evening preceding the battle of Point Pleasant he
proposed going over the river, to the camp of Gen. Lewis, for the purpose
of making peace. The majority in the council of warriors voted against
the measure. "Well," said Cornstalk, "since you have resolved on
fighting, you shall fight, although it is likely we shall have hard work to-
morrow; but if any man shall attempt to run away from the battle I will
kill him with my own hand," and accordingly he fulfilled his threat with
regard to one cowardly fellow.

After the Indians had returned from the battle, Cornstalk called a council at the Chillicothe town, to consult what was to be done next. In this
council he reminded the war chiefs of their folly in preventing him from
making peace before the fatal battle of Point Pleasant, and asked, "What
shall we do now? The Long-knives are coming upon us by two routes.
Shall we turn out and fight them?" All were silent. He then asked,
"Shall we kill our squaws and children, and then fight until we shall all be
killed ourselves?" To this no reply was made. He then rose up and
struck his tomahawk in the war post in the middle of the council house,
saying, "Since you are not inclined to fight, I will go and make peace,"
and accordingly did so.

On the morning of the day of his death, a council was held in the fort
at the Point in which he was present. During the sitting of the council,
it is said that he seemed to have a presentiment of his approaching fate.
In one of his speeches, he remarked to the council, "When I was young,
(he was at this time only thirty years of age,) every time I went to war I
thought it likely I might return no more; but I still lived. I am now in
your hands, and you may kill me if you choose. I can die but once, and
it is alike to me whether I die now or at another time." When the men
presented themselves before the door for the purpose of killing the Indians,
Cornstalk's son manifested signs of fear, on observing which his father
said, "Don't be afraid, my son; the Great Spirit sent you here to die
with me, and we must submit to his will. It is all for the best." He then
turned to meet the enemy at the door of his cell. In a moment he fell
dead, pierced by seven bullets. His son was killed in the same way. Red
Hawk was also shot dead while trying to escape. Thus perished one of
the greatest heroes among the red men of the frontier—a brave and noble
man, for whose death the Shawanese afterwards took ample vengeance on
the whites;—a chief remarkable for many great and good qualities, he was
disposed at all times to be the friend of white men, as he ever was the advocate of honorable peace. Dr. de Hass, from whose valuable work we

have derived much aid, says, p. 173: "The Governor of Virginia offered a reward for the apprehension of the murderers, but without avail. Congress, too, made every suitable concession to the Shawanese, through Col. Morgan, but the savages would not be appeased, and bitterly did the frontier suffer for this imprudent act of a few lawless men."

MRS. JAMES HAGERTY, THE SO-CALLED WITCH.

The laws of nature, and the ever-lasting chain of antecedents and consequences, were little recognized in the early days of Augusta. Our forefathers, though many of them were highly enlightened men, belonged to a community in which were still traces of the ignorance and barbarism of the Middle Ages. They understood few of the laws of nature, and every unusual event was contemplated with more or less of awe and alarm. They saw perpetually in events the supernatural and miraculous, and imagined that there existed among their fellow-creatures a gifted race that had command over the elements, held commerce with the invisible world, and could produce the most stupendous and terrific effects, and a race of perverse and badly disposed, who delighted in mischief, and were thought able to bring on those to whom they were hostile the direst calamities. Science was already making advances, Dr. Franklin having discovered the identity of electricity and lightning, but there was still enough of credulity remaining to display in glaring colors the aberrations of the human mind, and to furnish forth many curious tales. The greater part of these strange stories and marvellous adventures are swallowed up in oblivion, but the following survives as to one of Staunton's so-called witches.

One of the singular personages of early days in Staunton, of whom the writer has heard much from several venerable gentlemen still living, was Mrs. James Hagerty—a supposed witch. She lived in great poverty in a villainous little alley running by the Episcopal burying-ground. Witches are said to meet their master, the devil, frequently in churches and church yards, and one cannot help wondering at the boldness of Satan in thus invading consecrated ground. The alley was, in those days, called Spring Lane, but is at present better known as Irish Alley. Mrs. Hagerty was a poor, decrepit old woman, bending under the weight of years and infirmities. The lingerings of decent pride were visible in her appearance; her dress, though humble in the extreme, was scrupulously clean. Years before, she was the victim of an accident, by which the lower part of her face was horribly burnt and scared. To conceal the disfigurement, she wore a scarlet handkerchief across her face, above which two bright, twinkling eyes shot forth penetrating glances. Born in Ireland, she came, at an early day, with her husband, to Staunton. After his death she was left with three children in such abject poverty that they were compelled to engage in the meanest offices for bread. The eldest child, James Hagerty, was kept for some time from starvation by tramping up clay, the ordinary task of a horse, for brick making. Though unable to more than half nourish themselves, Mrs. Hagerty was always attended by a fat black cat—the most faithful of companions. The cat was supposed to be a distinguished demon, a confederate in works of darkness. She and the cat were thought now and again to change shape, to make journeys together on a broom stick, and to be always plotting mischief. Mrs. Hagerty's body was lean and bony, only an excuse for a body on which material life had little hold, but her mind was transcendently bright and vigorous. These circumstances were sufficient to gain for her the reputation of being a witch, of living in a sulphureous atmosphere with the damned everywhere around her. Beelzebub was thought, by the juvenile community, at least, to make a daily visit to her humble abode, and this prince of demons, not even excelled by the black cat in fidelity, was reported to have once taken her on the grand tour of Tartarus. Thus this old, decrepit, poverty-stricken, harmless and miserable woman was believed to be the incarnation of malice—able and delighted to blight the harvest, to cover the heavens with clouds, to destroy the health of an enemy,—in a word, to do everything that was wrong, and hence everything that went wrong was attributed to her. The young people carried their superstition so far as to have conceived a terror of passing her house. This, no doubt, accounts for the rural aspect of Spring Lane in the writer's boyhood. He well remembers to have seen grass growing in the lane, and sleek cows grazing in what now is one of Staunton's busiest thoroughfares.

Her eldest child, James Hagerty, the mud-mixer, attracted the attention of Robert Gamble, one of the leading merchants, of that day, in Staunton. Gamble was struck with the quickness of the boy's answers to such questions as were propounded to him, and took him into his employment and put him to school. Here his exemplary conduct and rapid acquisition of learning soon procured him many patrons, whose assistance enabled him to prosecute his studies and ameliorate the last days of his mother. Some years after, 1783, Gamble removed to Richmond, Va., and there resumed business, with Hagerty as one of his assistants. Hagerty remained with him till about 1805, frequently, during this period, making voyages to Liverpool in the interest of Gamble, and forming the acquaintance of her principal men of business. About 1805-1806, Hagerty removed to Liverpool, and there opened, on his own behalf, a business house in the cotton and tobacco trade, was successful, and became one of Liverpool's merchant princes. In 1841, he was appointed United States Consul for that port, and a few years later died, without issue.

We may add that Robert Gamble, who acquired large fortune, married Letitia, a daughter of Gen. James Breckenridge,—a cousin of the writer,— and left two sons, one of whom became Governor of Florida and the other of Missouri. One of his three daughters married William Wirt, another

Chancellor Harper, of South Carolina, and the third W. H. Cabell, Governor of Virginia.

EXCERPTS, ANA, ETC.

Previous to 1772, there was only a pathway, or Indian trail, between Staunton and the Warm Springs. This year the Governor, Council and Burgesses enacted that John Wilson, Thomas Lewis, Andrew Lewis, Samuel McDowell, Charles Lewis, William Preston, John McClenechan, George Moffett, and James Loving, gentlemen, be and they are hereby appointed trustees for carrying into execution the laying out and clearing a road from the Warm Springs to Jenning's Gap.

Among the successful natives of Ireland in Staunton, in 1770-'80, were George and Sampson Mathews—the first of whom became Governor of Georgia. The latter left descendants in Staunton, one of his daughters marrying Samuel Clark, Mayor in 1820, and the other Gen. Blackburn, who died s. p.

While recruiting his force previous to the campaign of 1774, Staunton was a general rendezvous for Gen. Lewis' men. Sampson Mathews kept an ordinary in the long frame building, afterwards occupied by Lawrence Tremper, on Augusta street, and now replaced by the brick building occupied by O'Rork and Alexander. Tradition relates that the height of the men composing one of the companies was marked on the bar-room wall, and not a man, in his stocking feet, was under six feet, and most of them were six feet two inches high.

From a cabin in Western Virginia a song emanated after the battle of the Point, in which these lines occur:

> "Col. Lewis and some noble Captains,
> Did down to death like Uriah go;
> Alas! their heads wound up in napkins,
> Upon the banks of the Ohio."

Another poetaster, evidently an old European soldier, thus closes some hot-blooded poetry, which is still sung by the mountaineers:

> " I have been where cannons roared and bullets rapidly did fly,
> Yet I would venture once more the Shawanee to conquer or die."

The following letter from Washington to Lord Dunmore has never been published. It was found by the author in the Clerk's Office of the Superior Court of Augusta. It possesses little interest, beyond being the production of the illustrious Father of his Country, being from his pen, and referring to the compensation received by many engaged in the campaign of 1754, of whom numbers were from Augusta, including our colonial hero, Gen. Andrew Lewis. It will be read not without interest:

To the Right Hon'ble John, Earl of Dunmore, his Majesty's Lieut.-Gov.
General of the Colony and Dominion of Virginia, and to the Hon' ble,
the Council:

MY LORD, AND GENTLEMEN: The whole quantity of 200,000 acres of
land granted by the Hon. Robert Dinwiddie's proclamation of the 19th of
Feb., 1754, being now fully obtained, (within the number of surveys limited) and the last certificates thereof lodged in the Secretary's office, I
take the liberty humbly to inform your Excellency and Hon'rs that the
surveys formerly made are already patented, agreeably to an order of
Council of the 6th of Nov., 1772, and that the certificates lately returned
and unappropriated, are for 28,400, 21,941, 7,276, 7,894, and 6,788 acres,
in all, 72,299 acres. It is also necessary to inform the Board that the following claims, including not only those which were given on the —— day
of Oct. 1771, but such as have been entered here, are yet to be acknowledged and satisfied accordingly:

Col. Joshua Fry's heir, being short of his full ninth at the last distribution					7,242	acres.
George Washington, also short of his ninth at that distribution					453	"
Col. Muse & others,	do.	do.	do.	do.	199	"
And'w Wagener,	do.	do.	do.	do.	2,672	"
John Savage,	do.	do.	do.	do.	2,672	"
Dr. James Craik,	do.	do.	do.	do.	394	"
Robt. Stobos' heir, for his full proportion of the 200,000 acres					9,000	"
Jacob Vanbraam,	do.	do.	do.	do.	9,000	"
William Bronaugh,	do.	do.	do.	do.	6,000	"
James Forest's heir,	do.	do.	do.	do.	6,000	"
Thomas Bullet.	do.	do.	do.	do.	2,500	"
John Wright's heir,	do.	do.	do.	do.	2,500	"
Jno. David Welfer,	do.	do.	do.	do.	600	"
And'w Tonler,	do.	do.	do.	do.	400	"
Francis Self,	do.	do.	do·	do.	400	"
Arthur Watts, dec'd,	do.	do.	do.	do.	400	"
Robert Stewart,	do.	do.	do.	do.	400	"
Alex'r Bonny,	do.	do.	do.	do.	400	"
Wm. McAnulty,	do.	do.	do.	do.	200	"
Thos. Napp,	do.	do.	do.	do.	400	"
Jesse May,	do.	do.	do.	do.	400	"
Robt. Murphey,	do.	do.	do.	do.	400	"
Jno. Smith,	do.	do.	do.	do.	400	"
Wm. Horn, dec'd,	do.	do.	do.	do.	400	"

53,432 acres.

This ninth of 53,432 acres of land, taken from the amount of the survey
on the other side, leaves, of the 30,000 acres, (set apart in Oct., 1771, for
satisfying any claims which might thereafter come in, and for the further
purpose of reimbursing the few who had been at the trouble and whole
risque,) 18,867 acres, which, if appropriated to those who were full in advance at that time, and distributed according to the former proportions,
will go thus: To George Washington, 3,500; to Geo. Muse, 3,500; to
Geo. Mercer, 2,800; Adam Stephen, 2,100; Andrew Lewis, 2,100; Peter
Hog, 2,100; John West, 1,400; and James Craik, 1,400 acres. And if this
method of proportioning the 18,867 acres of land is approved of by Y'r

Exc'll'y and Hon'rs, and you are pleased to order, as before, an association of names into each Patent, so as to bring the amount of their several claims as near to the quantity of land in the survey as may be, the following method of doing it probably will be found to answer as well as any other, as it cost some hours in shifting and changing the claims from one survey to another, to bring them so near; but if any other method, better approved of, it cannot but be equally agreeable to the parties concerned, as chance, at all events, must have the government of this matter.

TRACT OF 7,276 ACRES.

To Geo. Washington, for his div. of the last distribution . . .   453
And for his div. of the 18,867 acres   3,500
                                                              ―――――
                                                               3,953
To Geo. Muse, the residue   3,323
                                                         ―――― 7,276

THE TRACT OF 28,400 ACRES.

To Capt. Stobos' heir in full   9,000
To Capt. Vanbraam   9,000
To representative of James Towners, dec'd   6,000
To Andrew Fowler   400
To Thomas Napp.   400
To Arthur Watts, dec'd   400
To Jesse May, (assigned to M. Fox)   400
To Frank Self   400
To Jno. Smith   400
To Alex. Bonny   400
To Wm. Horn, dec'd   400
To Wm. McAnulty   400
                                                         ―――― 28,400

THE TRACT OF 7,894 ACRES.

To Wm. Bronaugh, in full   6,000
Dr. Craik, for his div. at the last distribution   394
    do.   for his div. of the 18,867 acres   1,400
Col. Muse, for residue   100
                                                         ―――― 7,894

THE TRACT OF 6,788 ACRES.

To And'w Wagener, for his div. at the last distribution . . .   2,572
Jno. West, his div. to the 18,867 acres   1,400
Col. Mercer, for the remainder of the tract—with what he received over his proportion at the last distribution, it more than pays him   2,816
                                                         ―――― 6,788

THE TRACT OF 21,944 ACRES.

To the heirs of Col. Fry, for his div. at the last distribution . .   7,242
John Savage,   do.   do.   do.   do.   . .   2,572
Thos. Bullet, in full of the grant   2,500
Wm. Wright, dec'd,   do.   2,500
John David Welfer   600
Adam Shepherd, for his div. of 18,867 acres   2,100
Andrew Lewis . . . . ·   2,100
Peter Hog   2,100
                                                         ―――― 21,944

As the opening of the patents for these lands will put an end to the business of this tract of 1754, so far as depends upon Y'r Excellency and Hon'rs, I would beg leave to offer two points of material interest to some of the trustees to the serious consideration and determination of the Board. The first is, as none of the patentees, under the mode adopted of granting land to numbers in the same patent, can be ascertained of their particular property therein till a legal division is established, which, (as in the case of a late grant of 28,667 acres to sixty odd patentees, is scarcely practicable to accomplish, and, of consequence, the saving of the land by cultivation and improvement, next to impossible; by this means the intended bounty offered for a valuable consideration is not only rendered void, but to those who have contributed to the expense, evidently injurious, inasmuch as they have paid for that which it is not in their power to come at,) I say, under these circumstances, whether some expedient cannot be hit upon to serve those who are willing and desirous of complying with the theory of the grant, either by prolonging the time of cultivation, if this can be done, or by directing each man's share in any patent to be laid off (if the division is not effected by consent of parties) within a certain limited period, of which public notice to be given, as each patentee thereafter that respectively apply to the Surveyor, who may be entrusted, to lay the same in one body and in a good figure, to prevent injustice.

The second matter to be offered is: whether something cannot, and if it can, ought not to be done, recompensing those who have never paid one farthing, or taken one single step towards obtaining their lands, (not even the fees of office on their own particular tracts,) to contribute in proportion to the quantity of land they have and are to receive? Without something of this sort can be done previous to the patenting, or in the patenting of these lands, nothing is to be expected from them afterwards; for where men (I am speaking of those who hold principal shares in this grant, for, as to common soldiery, little ever was expected from them,) are found so remiss, after repeated exhortation, as neither to afford time nor money for the purpose of conducting a work which could not possibly have gone without both, little of the latter is to be expected after the business is at an end and their patents delivered to them, unless litigious law-suits are commenced, some of which against infants, and some against persons beyond sea, and, without this, I must, after having been already saddled with almost the whole trouble and many expenses peculiar to myself, submit to considerable loss, as I have been obliged to advance all the fees of office, and many drafts of the Surveyor, and considered, I dare say, by him, as liable for his whole fees, assured by having one, in that case, for the before-mentioned tract of 28,600 acres patented to the common soldiery to pay for account. (I fear their being a penny the better of it.) [A line illegible here.] One year of the three gone, and one-half of them may never more be heard of.

I have thus, may it please Y'r Excellency and Hon'rs, endeavored to draw the whole of this matter into one short view, to save you the trouble of referring from one order of Council to another. I have now to beg pardon for the trouble I have had occasion from time to time to give in prosecuting this matter, and have the honor to be,

Your Lordship's and Hon'rs
Most obed't and most humble serv't,
GO: WASHINGTON.

CHAPTER XII.

The right claimed by Great Britain to tax the colonies caused dissensions between the mother country and her American dependencies, soon after the peace of 1763. Previous to 1763, the colonies had been permitted to tax themselves without the interference of Parliament. The first act for the avowed purpose of raising a revenue from the Colonies was passed by the British Parliament in 1764, laying a duty on sundry articles of American consumption. Of this act the Colonies highly disapproved, because it proceeded on the right to tax them without their consent. In pursuance of the same policy, the notorious stamp act was passed the following year, and excited general indignation throughout America. Virginia led the way in opposition to this act by the adoption of Patrick Henry's resolutions, May 29, 1765. These resolutions were warmly supported in the House by our distinguished delegate at that time, Hon. Thos. Lewis. The controversy thus introduced continued for ten years, increasing in animosity, and had gathered strength and maturity from various circumstances of aggression and violence. The Ameriaans had no desire for independence, and neither party seems to have anticipated a civil war. Matters were, however, obviously tending towards that point at which all hope of reconciliation must be banished forever, and in 1776, America made a formal declaration of independence. From this time, local and colonial contests were swallowed up by the novelty, the grandeur, and the importance of the struggle which then opened between Great Britain and America. Within four months of the day on which the Boston port bill reached America, the deputies in the first Continental Congress convened in Philadelphia. On the meeting of Congress, Hon. Peyton Randolph was chosen President, and Charles Thomson, Secretary. Congress, soon after their meeting, agreed upon a declaration of their rights, by which it was, among other things, declared that the inhabitants of the English colonies in North America, by the immutable laws of nature, the principles of the British Constitution, and the several charters, were entitled to life, liberty, and property, and that they had never ceded to any sovereign power whatever a right to dispose of either, without their consent, &c. Congress also resolved that the colonists were entitled to the common law of England, and, more especially, to the privilege of being tried by their peers of the vicinage, &c., and that sundry acts, which had been passed in the reign of George III, were infringements and violations of the rights of the colonists, and Congress declared that they could not submit to these grievous acts and measures. In hopes that Great Britain would restore the colonists to happiness and prosperity by a repeal of the obnoxious laws, they resolved, for the present, only to pursue peaceable measures, such as a loyal address to his Majesty, an address to the people of Great Britain, and non-intercourse. Congress having finished this important business in less than eight weeks, dissolved themselves on the 26th of October, after giving their opinion that another Congress should be held at Philadelphia on the 10th of May next. Accordingly, on the 10th of May, 1775, the second Congress met in Philadelphia, of which that distinguished Virginian, Hon. Peyton Randolph, was President.

Previous to the meeting of this Congress, the threatening aspect of affairs led the Royal Governor of Virginia secretly (April, 1755,) to remove the gunpowder from the magazine at Williamsburg to a British man-of-war anchored off Yorktown. Exasperated at the Governor's conduct, the people of Virginia were only restrained from taking up arms to "defend the laws, the liberties, and the rights of this or any sister colony,'' by the advice of Peyton Randolph and Edmund Pendleton. Every county in Virginia was now aroused to the dangers that beset them, and committees were appointed to take measures of defence.

Foremost among the counties to act was Augusta, and the spirit which animated her people is derived from the proceedings of a public meeting held in Staunton on the 22d of February, 1775. This meeting occurred two months prior to the removal of the gunpowder from Williamsburg, and the resolutions adopted amounted to a declaration of independence on the part of Augusta—a declaration of a determination on the part of her citizens to be a free people.

MEETING OF THE FREEHOLDERS OF AUGUSTA.

"After due notice given to the freeholders of the county of Augusta to meet in Staunton, for the purpose of electing delegates to represent them in colony convention at the town of Richmond on the 20th of March, 1775, the freeholders of said county thought proper to refer the choice of their delegates to the judgment of the committee, who, thus authorized by the general voice of the people, met at the court-house on the 22d of February, and unanimously chose Capt. Thos. Lewis and Capt. Sam'l McDowell to represent them in the ensuing convention.

Instructions were then ordered to be drawn up by Rev. Alex. Belmaine, Mr. Samson Mathews, Capt. Alex. McClanechan, Mr. Michael Bowyer, Mr. William Lewis, and Capt. Geo. Mathews, or any three of them, to be delivered to the delegates thus chosen, which are as follows:

To Mr. Thomas Lewis and Capt. Sam'l McDowell: The committee of Augusta county, pursuant to trust reposed in them by the freeholders of the same, have chosen you to represent them in Colony Convention, proposed to be held in Richmond on 2d of March instant. They desire that you may consider the people of Augusta county as impressed with just sentiments of loyalty and allegiance to His Majesty, King George, whose title to the imperial crown of Great Britain rests on no other foundation than the liberty, and whose glory is inseparable from the happiness of all his subjects. We have also respect for the parent State, which respect is founded on religion, on law, and on the genuine principles of the Constitution. On these principles do we earnestly desire to see harmony and good understanding restored between Great Britain and America.

Many of us and our forefathers left our native land and explored this once savage wilderness, to enjoy the free exercise of the rights of conscience and of human nature. These rights, we are fully resolved, with our lives and fortunes, inviolably to preserve; nor will we surrender such inestimable blessings, the purchase of toil and danger, to any ministry, to any Parliament, or any body of men on earth, by whom we are not represented, and in whose decisions, therefore, we have no voice.

We desire you to tender, in the most respectful terms, our grateful acknowledgments to the late worthy delegates from this colony for their wise, spirited, and patriotic exertions in the General Congress, and to assure them that we will uniformly and religiously adhere to their resolutions, providentially and graciously formed for their country's good.

Fully convinced that the safety and happiness of America depend, next to the blessing of Almighty God, on the unanimity and wisdom of her people, we doubt not you will, on your parts, comply with the recommendations of the late Continental Congress, by appointing delegates from this colony to meet in Philadelphia the 10th of next May, unless American grievances be redressed before that time. And so we are determined to maintain unimpaired that liberty, which is the gift of Heaven to the subjects of Britain's empire, and will most cordially join our countrymen in such measures as may be deemed wise and necessary to secure and perpetuate the ancient, just and legal rights of this colony and all British America.

Placing our ultimate trust in the Supreme Disposer of every event, without whose interposition the wisest schemes may fail of success, we desire you to move the Convention that some day, which may appear to them most convenient, be set apart for imploring the blessing of Almighty God on such plans as human wisdom and integrity may think necessary to adopt for preserving America happy, virtuous and free.*

In obedience to these instructions, the following letter was addressed:

To the Hon. Peyton Randolph, President, and the other Delegates from this Colony to the General Congress:

Gentlemen,—We have it in command from the freeholders of Augusta County, by their committee, held on the 22d of February, to present you with the grateful acknowledgements of thanks for the prudent, virtuous and noble exertions of the faculties with which Heaven has endowed you in the cause of liberty, and of everything that man ought to hold sacred, at the late General Congress,—a conduct so nobly interesting that it must command the applause not only from this but succeeding ages. May that sacred flame that has illumined your minds and influenced your conduct in projecting and concurring in so many salutary determinations for the preservation of American liberty ever continue to direct your conduct to the latest period of your lives! May the bright example be fairly transcribed on the hearts and reduced into practice by every Virginian, by every American! May our hearts be open to receive, and our arms

---

*These resolutions, printed on white satin, were distributed throughout the colonies.

strong to defend, that liberty and freedom, the gift of Heaven, now being banished from its latest retreat in Europe! Here let it be hospitably entertained in every breast, here let it take deep root and flourish in everlasting bloom, that under its benign influence the virtuously free may enjoy secure repose and stand forth the scourge and terror of tyranny and tyrants of every order and denomination till time shall be no more.

Be pleased, gentlemen, to accept of their grateful sense of your important services, and of their ardent prayers for the best interest of this once happy country; and vouchsafe, gentlemen, to accept of the same from your most humble servants,

THOMAS LEWIS,
SAMUEL McDOWELL, } Delegates.

To Thomas Lewis and Samuel McDowell, Esqs.:

Gentlemen,—Be pleased to transmit to the respectable freeholders of Augusta County our sincere thanks for their affectionate address approving our conduct in the late Continental Congress. It gives us the greatest pleasure to find that our honest endeavors to serve our country on this arduous and important occasion have met their approbation,—a reward fully adequate to our warmest wishes;—and the assurances from the brave-spirited people of Augusta that their hearts and hands shall be devoted to the support of the measures adopted, or hereafter to be taken, by the Congress for the preservation of American liberty, give us the highest satisfaction, and must afford pleasure to every friend of the just rights of mankind. We cannot conclude without acknowledgments to you, gentlemen, for the polite manner in which you have communicated to us the sentiments of your worthy constituents, and are their and your obedient and humble servants, PEYTON RANDOLPH,
and the other delegates from Virginia.

The Augusta resolutions are attributed to Rev. A. Belmaine by Bishop Meade. But for this, posterity would, doubtless, have credited them to Col. William Lewis, from whom they would have come more naturally. It must be remembered that the Episcopal clergy were pensioners on the bounty of the British Government, and were not likely to engage in efforts for its overthrow. In the southern colonies, it is true, there were some warm Whigs among the clergy, who, foreseeing the downfall of the religious establishment from the success of the Americans, zealously espoused the patriotic cause. Mr. Belmaine was evidently a southern Whig, as his course now and later demonstrates. It is a small matter by whom they were penned. They but embody the sentiments of the people of Augusta —sentiments which prevailed with the entire population west of the mountains. This is evident from a meeting, held about this time, at Pittsburg, to give public expression to the views and opinions of the inhabitants of that remote district. Dr. Joseph Smith, in his "Old Redstone, or Sketches of Western Presbyterianism," thus refers to this matter: "This difficulty (the boundary line between Virginia and Pennsylvania) had brought the western people, at one time, almost to the verge of civil war. And yet, though they were also involved in hostilities with Indian tribes, when the United States began their Revolutionary struggle, there was but one common feeling among both parties on that subject. They held two meetings on the 16th of May, 1775, only four weeks after the battle of Lexington, the Virginia party mainly, not exclusively, at Pittsburg, calling it a meeting of the inhabitants of that part of Augusta County west of Laurel Hill; the Pennsylvania party at Hannastown; both adopting unanimously strong Whig resolutions, in consonance with the public feeling of the land." Among the proceedings of the Virginia meeting, it was determined that the "landholders of the district of West Augusta shall be considered a distinct county, and have the liberty of sending two delegates to represent them in a convention for devising a plan to resist the oppressions of the mother country."

THE DISTRICT OF WEST AUGUSTA.

The first mention in the Statute Book of West Augusta occurs in an Act of the General Assembly, passed October, 1776, for ascertaining the boundary between the County of Augusta and the District of West Augusta. The preamble to this Act is in these words: Whereas, it is expedient to ascertain the boundary between the County of Augusta and the District of West Augusta: Be it, therefore, enacted, That the boundary between the said district and county shall be as follows: Beginning on the Alleghany mountains, between the heads of the Potomac, Cheat and Greenbrier rivers, (Haystack Knob, or north end of Pocahontas county,) thence along the ridge of mountains which divides the waters of Cheat river from those of Greenbrier, and that branch of the Monongehela river called Tyger's Valley river, to the Monongehela river; thence up the said river and the west fork thereof to Bingerman's creek, on the northwest side of the said west fork; thence up the said creek to the head thereof; thence in a direct course to the head of Middle Island creek, a branch of the Ohio, and thence to the Ohio, including all the waters of said creek in the aforesaid District of West Augusta, all that territory lying to the northward of the aforesaid boundary, and to the westward of the States of Pennsylvania and Maryland, shall be deemed and is hereby declared to be within the District of West Augusta.

At a court of the District of West Augusta, held at Fort du Quesne, (Pittsburg), September 18, 1776, the court decided that on the passage of the ordinance they became a separate and distinct jurisdiction from that of East Augusta, and, as such, West Augusta assumed and exercised independent jurisdiction over its entire territory.

After the Declaration of Independence, the Legislature of Virginia passed an Act, 20th August, 1776, enabling the present magistrates of West Augusta to continue the administration of justice until the same can be more amply provided for.

JUSTICES' COURTS.

Lord Dunmore, Lieutenant-Governor of Virginia, organized justices' courts as early as 1774, and issued a commission adjourning the County Court of Augusta from Staunton to Fort Dunmore. This fort was originally called Fort Pitt, but in 1773, the British Government abandoned it, and Dr. John Connelly took possession of it in the name of Virginia, and named it Fort du Quesne. It is evident, therefore, that three years before the Declaration of Independence, Pittsburg and the surrounding country was claimed as belonging to the District of West Augusta.

The District of West Augusta was, by Act of the Legislature of Virginia, November 8, 1776, divided into three counties—viz.: Youghiogheny, Ohio and Monongalia.

Previous to the ratification of the report of the surveyors by the Legislature of Virginia, October 8, 1785, Ohio county had been formed from Youghiogheny by the line of Cross Creek. On the settlement of the boundary question, that portion of Youghiogheny county lying north of Cross Creek was added to Ohio county, being too small for a separate county, and the county of Youghiogheny became extinct.

The courts of each district were required to administer and dispense justice, establish ferries, confirm roads when reported as necessary, bind out orphan children, grant letters of administration, probate wills, appoint subordinate officers, grant tavern licenses, try for crimes and misdemeanors, and perform such duties as would advance the interests of the community. Many of these duties had been performed, before the Revolution, by the vestry boards.

NATURALIZATION.

Previous to the Revolution, naturalization partook of a religious rite or ceremony. The certificate ran as follows. Let us preserve it as a relic of the past:

"I do hereby certify that at a court held at ———, before ——— judges of the court, the following foreigner, having inhabited and resided for the space of seven years in his Majesty's colonies in America, and not having been absent out of the said colonies for a longer space than two months at one time during the said seven years, and having produced to the said court a certificate of having taken the Sacrament of the Lord's Supper within three months before the said court, took and subscribed the oaths, and did make and repeat the declaration, according to the directions of an act of Parliament, made 13th year of George II, entitled, 'An act for naturalizing such foreign Protestants and others therein mentioned, as are settled or shall settle in any of his Majesty's colonies in America'; therefore was admitted to be H. M.'s natural-born subject of the Kingdom of Great Britain.   A.— B.—, Clerk."

During the troublous times of the Revolution, the courts granted passports indorsing the character of good and true citizens. The following was the form:

WAR OFFICE, YORKTOWN, October 15, 1777.
"To all Continental Officers, and others whom it may concern:

"Tacitus Gilliard, esq., late an inhabitant of the State of South Carolina, being on his way to Florida, or some of the countries or places on this side thereof, or adjacent thereto, where he purposes to form a settlement; and having applied for a passport to enable him to go and travel through the parts of the country in allegiance to and in amity with the United States of America, and having produced the testimony of his having taken the oaths of allegiance and fidelity to the said States: these are to permit the said T. G., esq., freely to pass with his family, servants, attendants and effects down the Ohio river, and all persons are desired not to molest the said T. G., esq., and his family, servants and effects on any account or pretence whatever.

"By order of the Board of War.

"RICHARD PETERS, Sec'y."

All classes of the people, more especially the Dissenters, were attached to the cause of independence, feeling that the final success of Great Britain would result in the establishment of a church hierarchy.

From these events, affairs moved on to a formal declaration of independence, July 4th, 1776, and the war of the Revolution began. The colonies were poor, and had placed themselves in open hostility to the most powerful empire in the world. They were confident, nevertheless, for it is not scarcity of money that debilitates a State; it is the want of men, and men of spirit and ability; and this want America did not suffer.

A regular system of military opposition having been decided upon by Congress, Washington was appointed Commander-in-Chief of the Army, and among the Augustians now and shortly afterwards commissioned were Andrew· Lewis as a Brigadier-General; as Colonels, William Lewis George Mathews, Alexander McClenechan and Thomas Fleming; Majors, M. Donovan, John Lewis. Gen. Lewis took command of that portion of the American army stationed at and near Williamsburg, Va., and his orderly book from March 18th to August 28th, 1776, has been preserved and published. The circumstances connected with the preservation of the MS. are not known. From it we republish the following orders, which illustrate his character as a disciplinarian:

"WILLIAMSBURG, May 14th, 1776.

PAROLE—LIBERTY.

"The many applications for furlough make it necessary for Brigadier-General Lewis to mention it in orders as improper in our critical situation, and he hopes that no request of this kind for the future (until circumstances will admit) will be made.

"Officer of the day to-morrow, Lieut.-Col. McClenechan; officers for guard, Lieutenant Garland, Ensign Barksdale. For guard, 8 p. l s. l c."

"WILLIAMSBURG, May 17th, 1776.

PAROLE—CONVENTION.

"Let it not be forgot that this day is set apart for humiliation, fasting and prayer; the troops to attend divine service."

On the next day he issued the following order : .

"WILLIAMSBURG, HEADQUARTERS, March 19th, 1776.

PAROLE—MARYLAND.

"All officers, upon their coming into camp, are to consider it their indispensable duty to wait on the commanding officer to make him acquainted with their arrival. The Brigadier-General leaves the camp to-day ; he expects the soldiers will pay the strictest attention to their duty and exert themselves to learn the discipline, so necessary to their own honour and safety ; that they will behave themselves with decency to their fellow-citizens, whose persons and property they were ordained to protect and defend, and that they will not by any unworthy conduct disgrace the profession of a soldier. It is recommended and expected of all officers that they will, to the utmost of their power, keep order and decorum in camp, be diligent in learning their own duty and instructing the soldiers in theirs, that they will spare no pains nor think much of any labor or difficulty to make themselves fit for that important end they were intended to answer— that of defending the darling Rights of Liberty and property of their country."

"WILLIAMSBURG, April 21st, 1776.

PAROLE—LEE.

" Brigadier-General Lewis is happy to find himself with part of the army from whom he has all the inclination imaginable to believe that their country will have reason to be satisfied with their service, and more so under conduct of Major-Gen. Lee, whose experience and confessed abilities have deservedly led him to the command. The army, which has the happiness to serve under him, may with great confidence rest assured that the strictest justice to every officer and soldier will be observed, and he flatters himself they will distinguish themselves by their regularity and compliance with good order and discipline ; and that none will be so regardless of their character and the duty they owe their country as to commit such improper and immoral actions as will bring them to disgrace and punishment. That none may plead ignorance, the articles of war are to be read frequently at the head of each company ; the captains to examine the men's arms daily, and their ammunition, of which they are to be very careful, and be answerable," &c.

"SPRINGFIELD, June 16th, 1776.

PAROLE—STAUNTON.*

"As the centinals have of late made a practice of firing in the night at nothing, the officers on guard will, for the future, give them a caution about discharging their muskets, which they are by no means to do unless at an enemy."

"SPRINGFIELD, July 17th, 1776.

"General Lewis hopes that the reports of some of the officers gaming to excess is without foundation. He begs that the field officers will make diligent enquiry into it, and, if true, to arrest such officers, that a total stop may be put to such infamous practices.

"Officer of the day, Lieut.-Colonel Weedon."

---

*Staunton was founded by John Lewis, the father of Gen. Lewis, which no doubt caused the selection of this parole.

"SPRINGFIELD, July 24th, 1776.

"The Declaration of Independence is to be proclaimed to-morrow in the city of Williamsburg, by order of the council, when all the troops off duty are to attend."

"WILLIAMSBURG, July 26th, 1776.

PAROLE—STEPHEN.

"A fatigue of one captain, two subalterns, two sergeants, and sixty rank and file, to be warned from the college camp, to carry on the work intended to be thrown up on the road to Jamestown."

War was no sooner seen to be inevitable between England and her colonies than both parties made extensive preparations for the contest. England not only directed her vast resources against the colonies, transporting to our shores large armies recruited from her own population, but the mercenaries of a foreign prince. Still dubious of success in a bad cause, she sought, in order to complete the works of death, desolation and tyranny in America, to bring on the "inhabitants of our frontiers the merciless Indian savages, whose known mode of warfare is an undistinguished destruction of all ages, sexes and conditions." The savages, burning with grief and indignation at their wrongs, were easily won over by British diplomacy, and inflicted terrible sufferings on the colonists during the Revolution, making the year 1777 memorable in the annals of the frontier as the "bloody year," though all of them were bloody enough. Directed by the superior intelligence of their European allies, supplied with arms, ammunition, food and clothing, the red men were more efficient tools in the hands of George III than his own troops or his Hessian hirelings. In the language of the late Earl of Beaconsfield, the savages were "educated" for their diabolical work ; were informed that they should rely upon their superior craft and sagacity to get the better of an enemy, and not venture to meet the settlers in pitched battles. To satisfy any scruples these barbarians might have,—and the Indian is punctilious on the point of honor as he understands it,—it was impressed upon them that man is naturally prone to subtlety rather than open valor, because of his physical weakness in comparison with other animals, and, therefore, it was his right and duty to resort to craft and cunning to gain an advantage over an enemy. Even the untutored Indian could understand this logic. He had long practised on it without analyzing his motives. It was explained to him that the lower animals are endowed with weapons of defence, with horns, with tusks, with hoofs and talons—that man, alone, was born weak and helpless, and had to depend upon his superior sagacity. In all his encounters with the beasts, his proper enemies, he had a right to resort to stratagem, and when warring with his fellow man, the British now told him, that he should continue the same subtle mode of warfare. Thus prepared in mind and body for the fray, the red men were soon on the warpath, and separating into small detachments, or "scalping parties," they penetrated at various points into the settlements.

How different might have been the fate of the red men and the lives of the settlers had the policy of Penn towards the Indians been generally adopted; how futile would have been England's diplomacy, her efforts to array them against the settlers. Lest a better opportunity should not occur, we may here say, for the information of the reader, that Penn enacted, with regard to the native inhabitants, that "whoever should hurt, wrong or offend any Indian should incur the same penalty as if he had offended, in like manner, against his fellow-planter"; also, that the planters should not be their own judges in case of any difference with the Indians, but that all such differences should be settled by (12) referees, (6) Indians and (6) planters under the direction, if need be, of the governor of the province and the chief of the Indians concerned. Penn's letter to the natives, sent with the first passengers to settle on his grant, is worthy of a place here for its singular plainness and the engaging honesty of its manner. It is as follows:

"There is a great God and Power, which hath made the world and all things therein, to whom you, and I, and all people, owe their being and well-being, and to whom you and I must one day give an account for all that we have done in the world.

"This great God has written his law in our hearts; by which we are taught and commanded to love, and to help, and to do good to one another. Now this great God hath been pleased to make me concerned in your part of the world; and the king of the country where I live hath given me a great province* therein; but I desire to enjoy it with your love and consent, that we may always live together as neighbours and friends; else what would the great God do to us, who hath made us (not to devour and destroy one another,) but to live soberly and kindly together in the world? Now, I would have you well observe, that I am very sensible of the unkindness and injustice which have been too much exercised towards you by the people of these parts of the world, who have sought themselves to make great advantages by you, rather than to be examples of goodness and patience unto you. This I hear hath been a matter of trouble to you, and caused great grudging and animosities, sometimes to the shedding of blood; which hath made the great God angry. But I am not such a man, as is well known in my own country. I have great love and regard towards you, and desire to win and gain your love and friendship by a kind, just and peaceable life; and the people I send are of the same mind, and shall in all things behave themselves accordingly; and if in any thing any shall offend you or your people, you shall have a full and speedy satisfaction for the same, by an equal number of just men on both sides, that by no means you may have just occasion of being offended against them.

"I shall shortly come to see you myself, at which time we may more largely and freely concur and discourse of these matters. In the mean time I have sent my commissioners to treat with you about land and a firm

*Penn, on receiving his charter from Charles II, in 1681, intended to call the country New Wales, but the Under Secretary of State at the time was a Welshman, and thought that this was using too much liberty with the ancient principality, and objected to it. He then suggested Sylvania, and the King insisted on adding Penn to it. After some struggles of modesty, Penn submitted to the King's desire, and hence the name of Pennsylvania.

league of peace. Let me desire you to be kind to them and to the people, and receive the presents and tokens which I have sent you as a testimony of my good will to you, and of my resolution to live justly, peaceably and friendly with you.

     " I am your loving friend,

            "WILLIAM PENN."

Turning from the inviting field of general history, we shall now briefly glance at some of the bolder acts in the bloody drama performed on the frontier of Virginia, or of that ancient County of Angusta, from which we emerged, in 1790, with our present confines.

One of the first acts of the scalping parties on our borders was to seize and carry into captivity Mrs. Grisly and her two children. Mr. G. was absent at the time, but, returning soon after, and missing his family, suspected the true cause. Rallying some of his neighbors, pursuit was given. Keeping the Indian trail for six miles, the horror-stricken husband came suddenly upon the ghastly form of his murdered wife and child. The savages, finding Mrs. G. unable to travel on account of her delicate situation, most inhumanly tomahawked her, together with her younger child.

SIEGE OF FORT HENRY, IN NORTHWEST VIRGINIA, BY SIMON GIRTY.

The autumn of 1777 was memorable in the annals of the West for the united and determined attack by British and Indian troops against the stockade fort, Henry, near Wheeling. Early in August, flying reports reached the settlers that the Indians were gathering in great numbers, with a view to attacking the settlement. Every precaution was taken to guard against an insidious foe. Scouting parties were kept out, who, with sleepless vigilance watched all the movements of the enemy. Information had been conveyed to Gen. Hand, commanding at Fort Pitt, by some friendly Moravian Indians, that a large party of Indians, composed of warriors from the Northwestern Confederacy, were making extensive preparations to strike a terrible blow upon the settlements on the Ohio. It was further stated that this chosen body of savages would be under command of Simon Girty, a man whose known relentless ferocity toward his foresworn countrymen could not but add to the fearful prospect before them. Gen. Hand lost no time in widely disseminating the information thus obtained. As it was uncertain where the expected blow would fall, all was activity, fear and alarm at the several little half-finished stockades stretching at distances from one to two hundred miles, between Fort Pitt and the Great Kanawha. But it soon became manifest at what point the enemy intended to strike. The settlers at Wheeling, about thirty families, betook themselves to their fort, to await the issue.

Early in the evening of August 31st, Capt. Ogle, who had been sent out some days before at the head of ten or fifteen men to scout along the different routes usually followed by the barbarians, returned and reported no immediate cause of danger. The barbarians, with their usual sagacity, suspecting that their movements might be watched, abandoned all the trails commonly trodden, and, dividing, as they approached the river, into small parties, struck out for Wheeling along new lines. Without discovery, they reached Bogg's Island, two miles below Fort Henry, and there, consolidating their force, crossed the river and proceeded directly, under cover of night, to the vicinity of the Fort, and made their final dispositions for an attack next morning.

The Indian army consisted of 350 well-armed Mingos, Shawanese and Wyandottes, commanded by the renegade, Girty. Girty disposed his men in two lines across the bottom, opposite the Fort, and concealed them in the high weeds and maize. Posted near the centre of these lines, and close to a path leading from the Fort (which they supposed some of the whites would pass along in the morning), were six Indians. Shortly after daybreak of the 1st of September, Dr. McMechon, who was about to return east of the mountains, sent out a white man named Boyd and a negro to catch the horses. The two men had not proceeded far before they discovered the six Indians already referred to. They turned to fly, but Boyd was killed. The negro was permitted to return, doubtless to mislead the whites as to the number of their foe. The commandant immediately ordered Capt. Mason to dislodge the enemy. With fourteen men he sallied forth, and discovering the six Indians, fired upon them. Almost simultaneously with this discharge, the whole barbarian army arose, and, with horrid yells, rushed upon the little band of whites. Mason ordered a retreat, and in person commenced cutting his way through the Indian line which surrounded them. This he succeeded in doing, but twelve out of his little band perished.

Soon as the disaster to Mason was known at the Fort, Capt. Ogle, with his twelve scouts, advanced to his relief, guided by the yells of the savages and the shrieks of the whites. The barbarians, seeing Ogle's approach, rushed upon him with the fury of demons, and all but three,—Ogle, his sergeant, and Wetzel,—shared the fate of Mason's party. The loss of so many brave men at such a time was a sad blow to that part of the country. Those who fell were the pride of the little fortress. They were heroes in every sense of the word; men of iron nerve, indomitable courage, and devoted patriotism. Scarcely had the shrieks of the wounded and dying been quieted, than the barbarian army presented themselves in front of the Fort and demanded a surrender. The appearance of the enemy, as they advanced, was most formidable. They advanced in two lines with drum, fife, and British colors, many of the savages holding up the reeking scalps just torn from the heads of Mason's and Ogle's ill-fated parties. The morning was calm and bright. As the savages advanced, a few shots were fired at them from the Fort, without, however, doing much

execution. Girty, having brought up his forces, disposed of them as follows: The right flank was brought around the base of the hill, and distributed among the several cabins convenient to the Fort; the left defiled
beneath the river bank, close under the Fort, but well sheltered. Thus
disposed, Girty presented himself at the window of a hut, holding forth a
white flag and offering terms of peace. He read the proclamation of
Hamilton, Governor of Canada, and in a stentorian voice demanded the
surrender of the Fort, offering, in case they complied, protection, but if
they refused, immediate and indiscriminate massacre. He referred, in a
boastful manner, to the great force at his command, and called upon them,
as loyal subjects of George III, to give up, in obedience to the demand of
His Majesty's agent. Although there were only twelve men in the Fort,
they refused to surrender, and defied the renegade and all the power of
King George. The commandant of the Fort, Col. Shepherd, thus responded to Girty: "Sir, we have consulted our wives and children, and all
have resolved, men, women and children, to perish at their posts, rather
than place themselves under the protection of a savage army, with you at
its head, or abjure the cause of liberty and the American colonies." The
outlaw attempted to reply, but a shot from the Fort put a stop to any
further harangue.

A darker hour had scarcely ever obscured the hopes of the West.
Death was all round the little fort, and hopeless despair seemed to press
upon its inmates; but still they preferred death to surrender. Unable to
intimidate them, and finding the besieged proof against his vile promises,
Girty disappeared from the hut window, and was seen in a few minutes
advancing with a large force of savages, who made a dash at the fort.
They attempted to force the gates, and test the strength of the pickets by
muscular effort. Failing to make any impression, Girty drew off his men
a few yards and commenced a general fire upon the port-holes. Thus
continued the attack during most of the day and part of the night, but
without any sensible effect. About noon, a temporary withdrawal of the
enemy took place. During the cessation, active preparations were carried
on within the fort to resist further attack. Each person was assigned some
particular duty. Of the women, some were required to run bullets, while
others were to cool the guns, load and hand them to the men, &c. Some
of them, indeed, insisted upon doing duty by the side of the men, and two
actually took their position at the port-holes, dealing death to many a
dusky warrior.

About three o'clock the Indians returned to the attack with redoubled
fury. They distributed themselves among the cabins, behind fallen trees,
&c. The number thus disposed of amounted to perhaps one-half of the
actual force of the enemy. The remainder advanced along the base of
the hill south of the fort, and commenced a vigorous fire upon that part of

the stockade. This was a cunningly devised scheme, as it drew most of the inmates to that quarter. Immediately a rush was made for the cabins, led on by Girty in person, and a most determined effort made to force the entrance. The attempt was made with heavy timber, but failed, with the loss of many of their boldest warriors.

Several similar attempts were made during the afternoon, but all alike failed. Maddened and chagrined by repeated disappointment and ill-success, the savages withdrew to their covert until night-fall. Day at length closed, darkness deepened over the waters, and almost the stillness of death reigned around. About nine o'clock the savages reappeared, making night hideous with their yells, and the heavens lurid with their discharge of musketry. The lights in the fort having been extinguished, the inmates had the advantage of those without, and many a stalwart savage fell before the steady aim of experienced frontiersmen. Repeated attempts were made during the night to storm the fort and to fire it, but all failed, through the vigilance and activity of those within.

At length that night of horror passed, and day dawned upon the scene but to bring a renewal of the attack. This, however, did not last long, and despairing of success, the savages prepared to leave. They fired most of the buildings, killed the cattle, and were about departing, when a relief party of fourteen men, under Col. Andrew Swearengen, from Holli-day's Fort, twenty-four miles above, landed in a pirogue, and, undiscov-ered by the Indians, gained entrance to the fort. Shortly afterwards, Maj. Samuel McColloch, at the head of forty mounted men, from Short Creek, made his appearance in front of the fort, the gates of which were joy-fully thrown open. Simultaneously with the appearance of McColloch's men, reappeared the enemy, and a rush was made to cut off the entrance of some of the party. All, however, succeeded in getting in, except the gallant Major, who, anxious for the safety of his men, held back until his own chance was entirely cut off. Finding himself surrounded by savages, he rode at full speed in the direction of the hill. The enemy, with exult-ing yells, followed close in pursuit, not doubting they would capture one whom, of all other men, they preferred to wreak their vengeance upon. Greatly disappointed at the escape of the gallant Major, and knowing the hopelessness of attempting to maintain a siege against such increased numbers, the Indians fired a few additional shots at the fort, and then moved rapidly off in a body for their own country. It has been conjec-tured that the enemy lost on this occasion from forty to fifty in killed and wounded. The loss of the whites has been already stated. Not a single person was killed within the fort, and but one slightly wounded.

GRAVE CREEK AMBUSCADE.

In 1777, Capt. W. Foreman organized a volunteer company in Hamp-shire county and marched to the frontier, at Wheeling, to aid in defence of the settlements. He was a gallant soldier, but unfamiliar with Indian warfare. The Indians had left Wheeling, and nothing had been seen or heard of them for some time. On September 26th, 1777, a smoke was noticed at Wheeling, in the direction of Grave creek, which caused apprehensions that the savages might be burning the stockade and house of Mr. Tomlinson. Col. Shepherd despatched Capt Foreman's company and a few scouts to ascertain the cause. The party reached Grave creek and found all safe. They camped there for the night, and on the following morning started on their return. When they reached the lower end of Grave creek narrows, some of the scouts suggested the expediency of leaving the river bottom, and returning by way of the ridge. The captain hooted at the idea of so much caution, and continued on. Some declined to follow, among them a man named Lynn, of great experience as a scout and spy. During the interchange of views between the captain and Lynn, a man named Harkness said that the controvery ran high at times. Foreman, who prided himself on being a thoroughly disciplined officer, was not disposed to yield to the suggestions of a rough backwoodsman. Lynn, on the other hand, convinced of the fatal error which the other seemed determined to commit, could not but remonstrate, with all the powers of persuasion at his command. Finally, when the order to march was given, Lynn, with some six or eight others, struck up the hill-side, while Foreman, with his company, pursued the path along the base. Nothing of importance occurred until the party reached the extreme upper end of the narrows. Just where the bottom begins to widen, those in front had their attention drawn to a display of Indian trinkets, beads, bands, &c., strewn in profusion along the path. With a natural curiosity, but a great lack of perception, the entire party gathered about those who picked up the articles of decoy, and whilst thus standing in a compact group, looking at the beads, &c., two lines of Indians stretched across the path, one above, the other below, and a large body of them simultaneously arose from beneath the bank, and opened upon the devoted party a destructive fire. The river hill rises at this point with great boldness, presenting an almost insurmountable barrier. Still, those of the party who escaped the first discharge, attempted to rush up the acclivity, and some with success. But the savages pursued and killed several. At the first fire, Foreman and his two sons fell dead, and about twenty others. When Lynn and his party heard the firing, they rushed down the hill, hallooing. This had the effect of restraining the Indians in pursuit, and doubtless saved the lives of many. Among those who escaped were Harkness and Collins. The former, pulling himself up by a sapling, had the bark driven into his face by a ball from an Indian's gun. Collins was disabled by a ball through his thigh, but recovered and lived many years. Those who escaped this terrible affair made their way to Wheeling. On the second day, a party went down and buried the dead in a common grave.

In 1835, a few gentlemen caused a stone to be erected on the spot of their interment, with this inscription:

" This humble stone is erected to the memory of Captain Foreman and twenty-one of his men, who were slain by a band of ruthless savages,—the allies of a civilized nation of Europe—on the 26th of September, 1777.

" So sleep the brave, who sink to rest,
By all their country's wishes blest."

The inhabitants continued to observe their usual watchfulness until towards the close of November, when a fall of snow occurring, they relaxed their vigilance. As a rule, the savages withdrew on the commencement of Winter, and did not reappear until the coming Spring. Instances were very rare in which they disturbed the settlements during Winter. The readiness by which they could be tracked, together with the severity of the weather, compelled them to such a course.

This snow to which we have referred, lulled the inhabitants into false security. About twenty Indians had penetrated the settlement in Tygart Valley, and were waiting to make an attack, when the snow fell. Not liking to return without some trophy of their valor, the savages concealed themselves until the snow disappeared. On the 15th day of December, they came to the house of Darby Connoly, at the upper extremity of the Valley, and killed his wife, himself, and several of their children, taking three other prisoners. Proceeding to the next house, they killed Jno. Stewart, his wife and child, and took Miss Hamilton, his wife's sister, captive. They then set out for home with their captives and plunder. During the afternoon of the day on which these outrages occurred, John Hadden, passing by the house of Connoly, saw an elk which the family brought up, lying dead in the yard, and suspecting all was not right, entered the house and saw the corpses. He alarmed the neighborhood, and Capt. Wilson, on the next day, with thirty volunteers, went in pursuit. For five days they followed the trail through cold, rain and snow, often wading and swimming streams, and then traveling miles before they could make a fire to thaw off the icicles. Still they could not overtake the savages, and at length the men refused to go further, and so the Indians escaped with their prisoners and booty.

In view of the defenceless condition of the frontier and the sufferings of the people, Congress lost no time in despatching a force across the Alleghanies, in 1778, under Gen. McIntosh; but before an invasion of the Indian territory was made, it was thought advisable to convene the Delaware Indians, at Fort Pitt, and obtain their consent to march through their country. The United States Government therefore dispatched two Commissioners, namely, Gen. Andrew Lewis, and his brother, Hon. Thos. Lewis, to treat with the Indians. They negotiated a treaty on September 17th, 1778, which was signed by the U. S. Commissioners and the Indian chiefs in presence of Cols. L. McIntosh, D. Broadhead, Wm. Crawford, John Gibson, and others.

Gen. McIntosh now advanced into the enemy's country, and erected a fort called Laurens, in honor of the President of Congress. The demand for men in the East and North, to meet the British army, interfered with these operations, and McIntosh, likely to be overpowered, retreated. Fort Laurens was subsequently invested by Indians, and the garrison reduced almost to starvation. A second advance of McIntosh relieved them, and the fort was then abandoned, thus bringing McIntosh's operations to an end without any good result, and after great sufferings endured by the whites.

Col. Broadhead succeeded McIntosh, and conducted a campaign in 1781 against the Indians west of the Ohio, and took many prisoners, among them sixteen warriors, who were bound and then killed with toma-hawks and spears. During Broadhead's return march, twenty Indian prisoners were murdered.

WILLIAMSON'S CAMPAIGN,

in 1782, must not be passed over, though we would gladly do so. It re-sulted in the diabolical murder of the Christian or Moravian Indians, who consisted mainly of Delawares and a few Mohicans. They were con-verted to Christianity by Moravian missionaries, and had lived, from 1772 to 1782, in peace and quietness. They were suspected by both parties; by the whites, they were thought to harbor hostile Indians, and by the In-dians, because they had abandoned the customs of their race. Their four towns were on the direct route from Sandusky to the Ohio, and they were compelled to furnish supplies to both parties as they passed. They were neutral during the Revolution, but were suspected by the border settlers. In the Spring of 1782, a party of Indians entered the white settlements and killed eight whites. It was thought that this party had wintered with the Moravians, and in March eighty-nine men set out for the Moravian villages to seek vengeance. They reached the peaceful settlements, pro-fessed friendship, telling the Indians they were to be taken for safety to Pittsburg. They thus secured whatever arms these dusky Christians pos-sessed, and then made them prisoners. A vote was then taken as to what course should be pursued, and it was decided to murder them, and they were told to prepare for their fate. After the first burst of horror was over, they patiently suffered themselves to be led into buildings, in one of which the men, and in the other the women and children were confined, like sheep for slaughter. They passed the night in praying, exhorting each other to remain faithful to our Saviour, asking pardon of each other for any offences they had committed, and singing hymns of praise to God. In the morning they were all scalped and murdered, namely, ninety-six, one-third of whom were women, and thirty-four children. The town was then plundered and burnt. We need not dwell upon the atrocity of this massacre—a stain upon the country and a stigma upon the memory of every man engaged in it.

CRAWFORD'S EXPEDITION.

We now come to Col. Crawford's unfortunate expedition and his tragic fate. It is easy to trace it back to the Moravian massacre.

During the Spring of 1782, efforts were made to fit out another expedition against the Indian settlements at Sandusky. The success with which the Moravians had been destroyed induced many who had been with Williamson to join it. Placards were posted at Wheeling, Catfish, and other places, stating that a new State was to be organized on the Muskingum, and inviting the people to enlist in the campaign. No effort was left untried that could excite either the cupidity or revenge of the frontier people. A force was soon raised in Pennsylvania and Virginia of 480 men, well mounted and armed. Each man furnished his own horse and equipments. The place of rendezvous was Mingo Bottom, where, on the 25th of May, 1782, nearly 500 men mustered and proceeded to elect their commander. The choice fell on Col. Wm. Crawford, an old friend and agent of Washington. Col. C. was a native of Berkeley county, in the Valley of Virginia, and was born in 1732, ever memorable for the births of Washington and Marion.

The army pursued "Williamson's trail" until they arrived at the Moravian ruins, where some Indians were lurking. From the time of the Moravian massacre, the Indians, the savages, had kept out spies to guard against surprise. They therefore well knew of the organization and march of Col. Crawford's force, its size, &c. They visited every encampment immediately after the whites left it, on their march, and saw from writings on the trees and scraps of paper that "no quarter was to be given to any Indian, man, woman or child." Nothing of importance occurred until the 6th of June, when they reached the site of a Moravian settlement on the upper waters of the Sandusky from which the Moravians had been driven by the Wyandottes. The place was covered with grass, and there were neither Indians nor plunder, but only vestiges of desolation. Finding the Moravians, whom they had hoped to murder and plunder, gone, and seeing indications that a hostile force was in their neighborhood, they held a council, and it was decided to march one day longer in the direction of the upper Sandusky, and if they should not reach a Moravian or Wyandotte town which they could plunder by "a dash," they would retreat. They hoped, by a rapid retreat, to reach a secure place before the savages could muster in formidable force. Accordingly, the march commenced on the morning of the 7th of June, and about two o'clock the advance guard was attacked and driven in by the Indians, who were soon discovered in large numbers in the high grass, lying by the side of a forest. The battle commenced at once, and became general, the Indians soon being dislodged from the shelter of the trees. The fight continued with unabated fierceness until night, during which both armies lay on their arms. Both adopted the policy of kindling large fires along the line of battle, and then retiring some distance in rear of them, to prevent being surprised by a night attack. In the morning Crawford's force occupied the battle-ground of the preceding day. The Indians did not renew the attack until late in the afternoon, but were seen traversing the plains in large numbers in various directions. Some seemed employed in carrying off their dead and wounded.

During the forenoon a council of officers was held, in which a retreat was resolved on, as the only means of saving the army, the Indians appearing to increase in numbers every hour. During the sitting of the Council, Col. Williamson, the leader of the former expedition, proposed to take 150 volunteers and march against whatever odds directly to the Upper Sandusky. To this Col. Crawford objected.

During the day the Indians discovered Crawford's preparation for a retreat, and about sundown attacked him with great force and fury, in every direction but that of Sandusky. By this, the only opening, the army began its retreat, and, by a circuitous route, reached the trail by which they had come. The retreat was continued during the day and that following, the pursuit being retarded by a rear-guard of sharpshooters.

Unfortunately, when a retreat was resolved on, a difference of opinion prevailed concerning the best mode of effecting it. The majority thought it best to keep in a body, while a considerable number thought it best to break off in small parties and make their way home in different directions. Many attempted to do so, thinking the Indians would follow the main body. In this they were mistaken. The Indians paid little attention to the main body of the army, but pursued the detached parties with such activity that but few escaped. The only successful detached party was that of about forty men, under Col. Williamson. It broke through the Indian lines late at night, under a galling fire, and made good its retreat.

At the commencement of the retreat, Col. Crawford placed himself at the head of the army, and continued there until they had gone about a quarter of a mile, when, missing his son, son-in-law, and two nephews, he halted and called for them as the line passed him, but in vain, After the army had passed him, he was unable to overtake it, owing to the weariness of his horse. Falling in company with Dr. Knight and two others, they traveled all night, first north, then east, to avoid pursuit. On the next day they fell in with Capt. Biggs and Lieut. Ashley, and encamped together the succeeding night. On the next day, while on their march, they were attacked by a party of Indians, who made prisoners of Crawford and Knight, while the others escaped. The prisoners were taken to an Indian encampment near by, where they found nine fellow prisoners and seventeen savages. On the next day they were marched to the old Wyandotte town, and the following morning four of the prisoners were scalped and tomahawked.

Preparations were now made for the execution of Col. Crawford.

It was on the 11th day of June, and the afternoon was well spent, when Crawford, under escort of his tormentors, arrived at this ever-memorable spot of ground. They here met many Wyandottes from the Half King's town, and men, squaws and children from Capt. Pipe's village just below. A fire was brightly burning. Crawford was stripped naked and ordered to sit down near the fire. The Indians now beat him with their fists and sticks. The fatal stake—a post about fifteen feet high—had been set firmly in the ground, and piles of hickory poles rather thicker than a man's thumb, and from eight to twelve feet long, lay at the distance of four or five yards from the stake. Crawford's hands were tied behind his back. A strong rope was produced, one end of which was fastened to the ligature between his wrists, and the other tied to the post near the ground. The rope was long enough to permit him to walk around the stakes several times and then return.

Crawford, observing these terrible preparations, called to Simon Girty, who sat on horseback at the distance of a few yards from the fire, and asked if the Indians were going to burn him. Girty very coolly replied in the affirmative. Crawford heard the reply with firmness, merely observing that he would bear it with fortitude.

When the poles had been burnt asunder in the middle, Captain Pipe arose and addressed the crowd in a tone of great energy, and with animated gestures, pointing frequently to Crawford, who regarded him with an appearance of unruffled composure. As soon as he had ended his harangue, a loud whoop burst forth from the assembled throng, and all made a rush for the unfortunate prisoner. For several seconds the crowd was so great around Crawford that Knight, who was seated a little distance away, could not see what they were doing, but in a short time they sufficiently dispersed to give him a view of the Colonel. His ears had been cut off, and the blood was streaming down each side of his face.

A terrible scene of torture now commenced. The warriors shot charges of powder into his naked body, commencing with the calves of his legs, and continuing to his neck. It was the opinion of Knight that no less than seventy loads were discharged upon him. Three or four Indians by turns would take up one of the burning pieces of poles and apply the burning end to his naked body, already burnt black with powder. These tormentors presented themselves on every side of him, so that whichever way he ran round the post they met him with the burning brands. Some of the squaws took broad pieces of bark, upon which they could carry a quantity of burning coals and hot embers, and threw them on him, so that in a short time he had nothing but coals of fire and hot ashes to walk upon!

In the midst of these extreme tortures, Crawford called Girty, and begged of him to shoot him through the heart. "Don't you see I have no gun, Colonel?" replied the white savage monster, bursting into a loud laugh, and then, turning to an Indian by his side, he uttered some brutal jest upon the naked and miserable appearance of the suffering prisoner, and seemed delighted at the horrid scene. The terrible ordeal had lasted more than two hours, and Crawford had become much exhausted. He walked slowly around the stake upon his fiery pathway, and in a low tone of voice earnestly besought God to pardon all his sins and have mercy on his soul. His nerves had lost much of their sensibility, and he no longer shrank from the firebrands with which his tormentors incessantly touched him. At length he sank in a fainting fit upon his face, and lay motionless. Instantly an Indian sprang upon his back, knelt lightly upon one knee, made a circular incision with his knife upon the crown of his head, and, clapping his knife between his teeth, tore the scalp off with both hands. Scarcely had this been done when a withered old hag approached with a piece of bark full of coals and burning embers, and poured them upon the crown of his head, now laid bare to the bone. The Colonel groaned deeply, arose and again walked slowly around the stake. Nature, at length, could endure no more, and at a late hour in the evening he fell for the last time, and sweetly welcomed death, which at one stroke bore Col. Wm. Crawford beyond the reach of his tormentors, and gave Wyandotte county a martyr hero of whom she is justly proud. Crawford's disastrous campaign was the last which occurred during the Revolution in the Sandusky settlements.

By the treaties of Fort Stanwix, 1784, and that of 1785, between the United States and the Wyandottes, Delawares, Chippeways and Ottoways, the United States acquired all the lands lying west of Pennsylvania—the vast western domains of those tribes. These treaties did not bring peace ; the barbarians were constantly on the war-path, and the government, in 1794, dispatched Gen. Wayne to the west with a large force. He met the Indians in battle at the rapids of the Great Maumee, August, 1794, and totally routed them, inflicting on them terrible losses in killed and wounded. And thus was terminated the long and sanguinary wars on the western frontier.

SECOND SIEGE OF FORT HENRY.

In September, 1782, a body of three hundred and fifty Indians and British, under command of George Girty, a brother of the notorious Simon Girty, and said to be a more ruthless man, and a company of Queen's Rangers, commanded by Capt. Pratt, made their appearance in front of the fort and summoned it to surrender. The besiegers marched up, headed by a fife and drum, and with the British flag flying. To the demand for a surrender of the fort, the inmates returned a contemptuous refusal, and defied the white and red savages to do their worst. Girty deemed it imprudent to make the attack until nightfall, and continued to palaver, during which the besieged loaded the renegade with abuse, and occasionally fired a shot at him, but the distance was too great for effect.

Fortunately for the inmates that the attack had not commenced half an hour earlier, for some days previous to the appearance of the savages scouts had been across the Ohio, but discovering no traces of the enemy, returned on the afternoon of Saturday and reported accordingly. This news had the effect of lulling the inmates into a feeling of security, so that it was scarcely deemed necessary to fasten the gates at night.

A day or two previous to the time of which we write, Andrew Zane had gone to Catfish for a supply of liquor. Returning with two kegs (one in each end of a bag) he discovered, as he supposed, when near the present site of Mount Wood Cemetery, indications of Indians. Concealing his kegs, he hurried to the fort with all haste, and gave the alarm. Those who had just returned from the Indian country laughed at his fears, but most of the men said they would go along and have a "spree."

Nearly the whole efficient force of the garrison accompanied Zane, and finding no Indians, repaired to the spring already alluded to, and there treated themselves to a glorious "blow out." Before starting with Zane, it was deemed advisable, with the characteristic caution of experienced frontiersmen, to send across the river two spies, who might give the alarm in case of danger. As the party at the spring were busy with their "grog," the alarm guns of the scouts were fired on the island, and at the same moment a large body of Indians were crossing the creek just above back-water. A simultaneous rush was made for the fort, and scarcely had the last man entered when the Indians appeared in large numbers crossing the bottom.

All at once became activity and bustle in the fort. The men prepared for an energetic defence, each arming himself with a rifle, tomahawk, scalping-knife and spear. The women were busy in running bullets, securing the children, etc. The whole number of fighting men within the stockade did not exceed eighteen, while the number of women and children was about forty.

Shortly before the enemy appeared, a canoe loaded with cannon balls, designed for Gen. Clark, at Louisville, in charge of a man named Sullivan and two others, landed at Wheeling, to remain over night. Sullivan was a shrewd and experienced soldier, well versed in Indian cunning, and on this account was selected to manage the affairs of the fort during the seige, as the commandant, Capt. Boggs, had gone for succor immediately

25 ‡

on the alarm of the enemy's approach. Sullivan was a man of discrimination and courage, and well qualified for the post of commander. His shrill voice could be heard at all hours, urging on the men and consoling the women. But at length he was wounded, and for a time had to give way.

About sundown, Girty made a second demand for surrender, declaring that should be his last summons, and swearing, if they refused, that the fort would be stormed and every soul massacred. He was answered by taunts of defiance. The besieged said they remembered too well the fate of Col. Crawford to give up and be butchered like dogs. Girty replied that their doom was sealed; he had taken their express, and all hope of safety might be given up. Sullivan inquired what kind of looking man the messenger was. "A fine, smart, active young fellow," answered the outlaw chief. "That's a d——d lie," said Sullivan; "he is an old, gray-headed man."

Finding all attempts to intimidate in vain, Girty led on his white and red army of savages, and attempted to carry out his threats of storming the fort. Near the centre of the stockade, and at a point sufficiently elevated to clear the pickets, was a small French cannon, which the enemy could at times see, but which they tauntingly said was "wood," and dared them to shoot. Having approached within a convenient distance, and just as the whole party was pressing up in deep columns, the "bull-dog" was let off, cutting a passage through the ranks of wondering and affrighted savages. Captain Pratt, who had heard guns and knew how they sounded, cried out to his swarthy comrades, "Stand back! By G—, there's no wood about that!" The Indians and the "Rangers" gave way at the first discharge, but soon rallied and returned. Girty divided his force into small parties, and attacked the fort at different points; now attempting to storm it, and again to fire it. In this manner the seige was kept up during the whole night, and but few such nights were ever passed upon the frontier.

One of the bastions having given way, but two were of use, and these the men occupied in turn. The women, during that long and perilous night, proved themselves heroines of no ordinary type. They stood at their posts like soldiers of a dozen campaigns, cooling and loading the rifles of their husbands, brothers and lovers. Such women were worthy the love and devotion of men like these. No timid shrieks escaped them; no maidenly fears caused them to shrink from their self-imposed and most onerous task. Such were the pioneer mothers of the west—women whose souls and bodies were so sorely tried in the fierce fire of our Indian wars. Through the whole of that long and terrible night, without food and without rest, did these brave and noble women stand to their duty, regardless of fatigue, but nerving their hearts to the contest and animating the men with hope and courage. The Greek matron who urged her son to the conflict, charging him to return with his shield or upon it, displayed no more zeal, devotion and true courage than these hero-women of the west. History is full of examples of female heroism. Israel had her Judith and Deborah; France glories in her Joan and Lavalette; two of them unsexed themselves in the excitement of battle; one ingloriously stained her hands in human gore, and the other had nothing to lose by her successful efforts; but the western heroines, without the eclat of female warriors, displayed more true courage throughout the long and stormy days of our Indian warfare, and exhibited more of the true spirit of heroism, than any examples in ancient or modern history.

At an early hour of the evening, the Indians descried the canoe already referred to, and at once resolved to try the sport of cannonading. Procuring a stout log of sufficient size and length, these simple-minded men split it open, and having cut out the centre with their tomahawks, fastened the parts together with iron bands and chains, found in a smith's shop belonging to a man named Reikart. They then charged it heavily with powder and ball, and first announcing that their artillery had arrived, applied the torch, when instantaneously a half-dozen of the gaping savages, who had clustered around to witness the discharge, were blown into eternity. Their frail gun had bursted, scattering death and consternation all around.

During the night, a large number of Indians posted themselves in the loft of a house, which stood thirty or forty yards north of the fort. These amused themselves by dancing, shouting and yelling, making night hideous with their horrid noise. Thinking to dislodge them, several ineffectual attempts were made to do so with grape-shot; but, failing, a full-sized ball was fired, which cut off a sleeper, and let the whole mass down together. This disaster frightened the assailants off for a time.

The cannon was fired sixteen times during the first night, doing more or less execution at each discharge. It was managed by a man named John Tait, shortly afterwards killed, and partly eaten, by the savages, on Dillie's bottom, opposite Grave creek.

At the time of the Indian visitation in 1777, it will be remembered, they burned all the houses, killed the cattle, etc. Similar outrages were again attempted in 1781, and then Col. Ebenezer Zane resolved that should the savages again visit the settlement he would remain in his house and perish, sooner than abandon it to the torch of the enemy. On the reappearance of the Indians, Col. Zane continued at his house, and declared his fixed determination to defend it to the last. In the house with him were several members of his family, including his brother, Silas. There were also two brothers by the name of Green; and a black servant by the name of Sam. So constantly did these four keep up the fire against the enemy that they were slow to approach within range of the guns.

The fortunes of the night were often variable; the enemy at one time appeared to have the vantage, but again their schemes were frustrated by the energy and skill of those within the fort.   More than twenty times did they attempt to fire the stockade, by heaping bundles of hemp against the walls, and kindling them at different points.   Most fortunately, however, the hemp was wet, and could not be made to burn.   Dry wood and other combustibles were tried, but all in vain.   Day at length dawned upon the hopes of that almost despairing people, and never did Aurora display her beauties to a more admiring or a more rejoicing group.   The night had been long, and full of gloomy terror.   They knew not at what moment the formidable enemy would crush the walls of their frail enclosure; but, come what might, they resolved to stand firm to the last.

Immediately after daybreak the Indians and British withdrew to the spring, and a cessation of hostilities for several hours ensued.

It was about noon of this day that an incident occurred which has been the theme of history, poetry and romance.   We allude to the "gunpowder exploit," as it is familiarly known in border story.

As we have already stated, Colonel Zane remained in his cabin, near the fort, during the whole seige.   Finding that his supply of powder was likely to run out, he proposed to those present that some one of them would have to visit the fort and renew the stock.   It was known to be a hazardous undertaking, and, unwilling to order either of the white men to so perilous an enterprise, Col. Zane submitted the matter to their own devotion and courage.   One of them instantly proffered his services, but a female member of Col. Zane's family came forward and said: " No, I will go; should I be killed, I can be better spared than one of these men." That woman, according to the traditionary accounts of the country, was Elizabeth Zane, sister to Col. Zane.   She is represented to have been a young woman of great resolution and much energy of character, and those who knew her intimately say, unhesitatingly, that she was just the person for such an exploit.   Preparing herself for the feat, the intrepid girl stepped from the cabin and bounded to the fort with the speed of a deer. A number of Indians, concealed in the neighborhood, saw her emerge from the cabin, but did not attempt to shoot, only exclaiming, with contemptuous epithets, "Squaw! Squaw!"   She reached the fort, and tying about her person eight or ten pounds of powder, again ventured forth and moved rapidly towards the cabin of Col. Zane.   Suspecting all was not right, the savages opened upon her a volley of rifle balls, but unscathed the courageous girl bounded into the arms of those who stood ready to receive her.   That act of the heroic and single-hearted female saved the inmates of Col. Zane's house from certain destruction.   Their ammunition had been exhausted, and every soul would have fallen a sure prey to the fury of the savages had not a supply been obtained.

Night closing in, the enemy renewed the attack, and maintained it without intermission until daybreak. Shortly after sunrise the enemy, despairing of success, commenced killing the cattle, burning the vacant cabins, &c. About 10 o'clock, A. M., an Indian spy returned, and when within sight of the fort, gave a long, deep, peculiar whoop, which the well-trained Indian hunters fully understood as a signal to be off. Scarcely had the echoes of his shout ceased reverberating along the valley than the entire hostile army moved rapidly toward the river, which they crossed near where the Northwestern Bank now stands. In less than half an hour after their retreat, Captain Williamson, with seventy mounted men, rode up to the fort, and great was the rejoicing at the appearance of his gallant band.

Thus ended the final investment of Fort Henry. The Indians never again attempted to molest it, but gave the place as wide a latitude as convenient in their expeditions against the back settlements.

ATTACK ON FORT RICE.

Previous to the Indian attack on Fort Rice, in September, 1782, several of the men belonging to it had gone to Hagerstown to exchange peltry and furs for salt and ammunition. A few days before attacking Fort Rice, the Indians made their last attack on Fort Henry, and being defeated, they held a council, and decided that two hundred warriors should return home and one hundred picked men make a dash into the country and strike a heavy blow somewhere before their return. It was their determination to take a fort and massacre all its people, in revenge for their defeat at Fort Henry. Two white men, who had been long prisoners among the Indians, deserted, fled to Fort Rice, and gave notice of the Indian plan. They only reached the fort thirty minutes before the hostile savages themselves. On receiving the news, the people of the fort prepared for defence. The Indians soon surrounded the fort, commenced firing, and ran from all directions towards the fort, which they hoped to take by assault, rending the air with their horrid war-whoops. There were only six men in the fort, but they were fearless, and the best of marksmen. They fired with deliberate aim on the enemy, brought down six at the first fire, scattering the assaulting party, which broke, every Indian hiding behind a tree, log or stump. The firing was kept up for four hours. In the intervals of the firing, the savages called out to the people in the fort: "Give up, give up; too many Indian; Indian too big; no kill you." They were answered by the brave whites: "Come on, you cowards; we are ready for you; show your yellow hides, and we'll make holes in them for you." During the evening the Indians amused themselves, out of musket range, shooting horses, cattle, pigs and sheep, until the ground was strewed with dead bodies. About 10 o'clock at night they fired a barn, about thirty yards from the fort. It was large, and full of grain and hay. The flame was frightful, and at first the fort seemed in danger, but as the night was calm, it was saved. The light of the burning barn prevented the near approach of the savages, which prevented their burning the dwellings. After the barn was set on fire, the Indians collected on the side of the fort opposite the barn, so as to have the advantage of the light, and kept up a pretty constant fire, which was as steadily answered by that of the fort, until about two o'clock, when the Indians left the place and made a hasty retreat.

Thus was this little place defended by a Spartan band of six men against one hundred chosen warriors, exasperated to madness by their failure at Wheeling fort. Their names shall be inscribed in the list of heroes of our early times. They were Jacob Miller, George Lefler, Peter Fullenweider, Daniel Rice, George Felebaum and Jacob Lefler, jun. George Felebaum was shot in the forehead, through a port-hole, at the second fire of the Indians, and instantly expired, so that in reality the defense of this place was made by only five men.

The loss of the Indians was four, three of whom were killed at the first fire from the fort, and the other was killed about sundown. There can be no doubt but that a number more were killed and wounded in the engagement, but were concealed or carried off.

A large division of these Indians, on their retreat, passed within a little distance of another fort. In following their trail, a few days afterwards, a large poultice of chewed sassafras leaves was found. This is the dressing which the Indians usually apply to recent gunshot wounds. The poultice, having become too old and dry, was removed and replaced with a new one.

Examples of personal bravery and hair-breadth escapes are always acceptable to readers of history. An instance of both of these happened during the attack on this fort, which may be worth recording.

Abraham Rice, one of the principal men belonging to the fort of that name, on hearing the report of the deserters from the Indians, mounted a very strong, active mare and rode in all haste to another fort, about three and a-half miles distant from his own, for further news, if any could be had, concerning the presence of a body of Indians in the neighborhood. Just as he reached the place, he heard the report of the guns at his own fort. He instantly returned, as fast as possible, until he arrived within sight of the fort. Finding that it still held out, he determined to reach it and assist in its defense, or perish in the attempt. In doing this, he had to cross the creek, the fort being some distance from it on the opposite bank. He saw no Indians until his mare sprang down the bank of the creek, at which instant about fourteen of them jumped up from among the weeds and bushes and discharged their guns at him. One bullet wounded him in the fleshy part of the right arm above the elbow. By this time several more of the Indians came up and shot at him. A second

ball wounded him in the thigh, a little above the knee, but without breaking the bone, and the ball passed transversely through the neck of the
mare. She, however, sprang up the bank of the creek, fell to her knees,
and stumbled along about a rod before she recovered. During this time
several Indians came running up to tomahawk him. Yet he made his
escape, after having about thirty shots fired at him from a short distance.
After riding about four miles he reached Lamb's fort, much exhausted
with the loss of blood. After getting his wounds dressed and resting
awhile, he sat off late in the evening with twelve men, determined, if possible, to reach the fort under cover of the night. When they got within
about two hundred yards of it, they halted. The firing still continued;
ten of the men, thinking the enterprise too hazardous, refused to go any
further, and retreated. Rice and two other men crept silently along towards the fort, but had not proceeded far before they came close upon an
Indian in concealment. He gave the alarm yell, which was instantly
passed round the lines with the utmost regularity. This caused the savages
to make their last effort to take the place, and make their retreat under
cover of the night. Rice and his companions returned in safety to Lamb's
fort. About 10 o'clock next day, sixty white men collected at Rice's fort
for its relief. They pursued the savages, who kept in a body for two
miles. The Indians then dispersed in small parties, and the pursuit was
given up. A small division of the Indians had not proceeded far after
their separation when they discovered four men coming from a neighboring fort. The savages hid near the path and shot two, and the others
fled. One of them made good his escape; the other was overtaken by a
savage. The white turned and snapped his gun at the red skin. The
Indian threw his tomahawk at the white's head, but missed him. They
then closed, and during the fight the Indian was killed.

AN EXPECTED ATTACK.

The following interesting account of affairs in a fort anticipating an attack is given by Kercheval, who was an inmate of Fort Dodderidge at
the time. When advices reached the fort, in 1782, that the Indians were
but a few miles distant encamped, it was believed that they would assault
the place early next morning:

"In order to give the reader a correct idea of the military tactics of our
early times, I will give, in detail, the whole progress of the preparations
which were made for the expected attack, and, as nearly as I can, I will
give the commands of Capt. Teter, our officer, in his own words.

"In the first place he collected all our men together, and related the
battles and skirmishes he had been in, and really they were not few in
number. He was in Braddock's defeat, Grant's defeat, the taking of Fort
Pitt, and nearly all the battles which took place between the English, and
the French and Indians, from Braddock's defeat to the capture of that
place by Gen. Forbes. He reminded us, ' that in case the Indians should
succeed, we need expect no mercy; that every man, woman and child

would be killed on the spot. They have been defeated at one fort, and now they are mad enough. If they should succeed in taking ours, all their vengeance would fall on our heads. We must fight for ourselves and one another, and for our wives and children, brothers and sisters. We must make the best preparations we can ; a little after daybreak we shall hear the crack of their guns.'

" He then made a requisition of all the powder and lead in the fort. The ammunition was accurately divided amongst all the men, and the amount supposed to be fully sufficient. When this was done, 'Now,' says the captain, 'when you run your bullets, cut off the necks very close, and scrape them, so as to make them a little less, and get patches one hundred finer than those you commonly use, and have them well oiled, for if a rifle happens to be choked in the time of battle, there is one gun and one man lost for the rest of the battle. You will have no time to unbritch a gun and get a plug to drive out a bullet. Have the locks well oiled and the flints sharp, so as not to miss fire.'

" Such were his orders to his men. He then said to the women, 'These yellow fellows are very handy at setting fire to houses, and water is a very good thing to put out fire. You must fill every vessel with water. Our fort is not well stockaded, and these ugly fellows may rush into the middle of it, and attempt to set fire to our cabins in twenty places at once.' They fell to work, and did as he had ordered.

" The men having put their rifles in order, 'Now,' says he 'let every man gather in his axes, mattocks and hoes, and place them inside of his door ; for the Indians may make a dash at them with their tomahawks to cut them down, and an axe in that case might hit, when a gun would miss fire.'

" Like a good commander, our captain, not content with giving orders, went from house to house to see that every thing was right.

" The ladies of the present day will suppose that our women were frightened half to death with the near prospect of such an attack of the Indians. On the contrary, I do not know that I ever saw a merrier set of women in my life. They went on with their work of carrying water and cutting bullet patches for the men, apparently without the least emotion of fear ; and I have every reason to believe that they would have been pleased with the crack of the guns in the morning.

" During all this time we had no sentinels placed around the fort, so confident was our captain that the attack would be made before daybreak. I was at that time fourteen years of age, but ranked as a fort soldier. After getting my gun and all things else in order, I went into the garret of the house, and laid down on the floor, with my shot-pouch on and my gun by my side. I did not awake till sunrise, when the alarm was over. The family we supposed had been killed came into the fort about daybreak. Instead of their house being burnt, it was an old log on fire near the house, which had been seen by our expresses."

INDIAN SUMMER.

The derivation of the term, " Indian Summer," has given rise to much speculation. The best theory as to its origin is this : The term originated in the Valley among the early settlers, and the backwoodsman seldom heard it without a chill of horror, as it recalled painful recollections of its original application. The Indians were accustomed to make their predatory incursions into the settlements of the whites during the Summer. They seldom or ever visited the territory of the whites after the frosts and snows set in. The commencement of Winter was therefore hailed by the inhabitants with delight. During that inhospitable season they would enjoy peace and freedom from the confinement of forts. At the approach of Winter, therefore, the planters would remove to their farms with the joyful feelings of a prisoner set free. All was bustle and hilarity preparing for Winter—the gathering of corn, digging of potatoes, fattening pigs, beef and turkeys, and repairing their dwellings. It sometimes happened, however, after the apparent commencement of Winter, the weather became warm ; the smoky time commenced, and lasted for a considerable number of days. This was the Indian Summer, because it afforded the Indians another opportunity of visiting the settlements with their destructive warfare. The melting of the snow saddened every countenance, and the genial warmth of the sun chilled every heart with horror. Hence this season of calm, during which the settlers were distressed by apprehensions when not driven by actual attack into the detested forts for safety, was called the Indian Summer. It corresponds to "the halycon days" of the Greeks, a name given to the seven or eight days which preceded and followed the Winter solstice when the weather was very calm and the air genial. Towards the latter part of February there was a fine spell of weather, during which the snow melted away. This was denominated the "palavering," or "paw-wawing season," as the Indians now held their War Councils, and planned their Spring campaigns against the settlements. Sometimes it happened that the savages ventured to make their excursions too late in the Autumn or too early in the Spring for their own convenience. A man by the name of Carpenter was taken early in the month of March, 1782, near the present town of Wellsburg. There had been several warm days, but on the night preceding his capture, there was a heavy fall of snow. His two horses, which the Indians took with him, nearly perished in swimming the Ohio. The savages, as well as himself, suffered severely with the cold before they reached the Moravian towns on the Muskingum. The morning after the first day's journey beyond the Moravian towns, the barbarians sent out Carpenter to bring in the horses, which, after being hobbled the evening before, were turned out to graze. The horses had made a circuit of the towns, fallen into the trail, and were making their way homewards. When Carpenter overtook them, and had taken off their fetters, he had to make an awful decision. He had a chance—barely a chance—to make his escape, with a certainty of death, if recaptured. On the other hand, there was the horrible prospect of being tortured to death by fire at the stake. He was the first prisoner taken that Spring, and it was the Indian custom to burn the first prisoner every Spring. After spending a few minutes making his decision, he resolved on making an attempt to escape, and effected it by way of Forts Laurens, McIntosh,

26 ‡

and Pittsburg. The capture of Carpenter and the murder of two families, about the same time, contributed materially to the Moravian campaign and the murder of that unfortunate people.

THE VIRGINIA LEGISLATURE IN STAUNTON.

On the 5th of January, 1781, Benedict Arnold entered Richmond, which had recently become the capital of Virginia, and ravaged the place. The Legislature had previously taken refuge at Charlottesville, where they were pursued and dispersed by Tarlton. On June 3, the committee previously appointed to prepare a bill to " establish martial law within —— miles of our camp and that of the enemy," was enlarged by Messrs. Jno. Taylor, Nicholas, Francis Peyton, of Loudoun; Talbot, Campbell, of Washington; and Triplett.

On June 4th, the House adjourned (so near were the British), to meet in Staunton on June 7th, where it met on that day, in the Episcopal church, according to adjournment. On Sunday, June 10th, 1781, the House met and resolved, That this House do adjourn until to-morrow morning, at ten o'clock, then to meet in this place; but if there shall appear danger in so doing, from the enemy, then that this House be adjourned until Thursday next, then to meet at the Warm Springs, in this county, at which time and place, if a sufficient number of members to adjourn the House should fail to appear, the Speaker is invested with power, as well to adjourn the House from day to day, as to appoint, in case of necessity, any other time and place for the meeting of this House, as to him shall seem advisable.

On June 12th, Thomas Nelson, Jr., Esq., was elected Governor of the Commonwealth, and Wm. Cabell, Sam'l Hardy, and Sam'l McDowell members of the Council of State.

On June 13th, James Madison, Ed. Randolph, Jos. Jones, Theodorick Bland and John Blair were appointed delegates in Congress to represent Virginia for one year.

On June 14th, Mr. Henry reported from the Committee of Privileges and Elections that the committee had, according to order, inquired into the conduct of Zachariah Johnston (delegate from Augusta), upon the information of Thos. Hughes against him, for being the principal instigator of an opposition which has been made by some of the people of Augusta in arms to a law passed by a former Assembly; and had agreed upon a report, and come to a resolution thereupon, which he read in his place, and were agreed to by the House, as followeth:

" It appears to your committee, from the testimony of various witnesses, that Zachariah Johnston hath uniformly recommended to the people of the county of Augusta an obedience to the law " for recruiting this State's quota of troops to serve in the Continental army," and did by no means instigate them to an opposition to the said law,

Resolved, therefore, That the said information is groundless."

On the same day, William Campbell, Esq., was appointed a Major-General in the militia.

On Saturday, June 16th, Mr. Henry reported from the committee to whom the petition of John Poage was referred, that the committee had agreed upon a report, as follows:

"It appears to your committee that James Graham, deputy sheriff for the county of Augusta, was robbed of the sum of £35,000 ($175,000), being the tax money of the said county, on his way to the treasury, and that a judgment has been obtained against John Poage, the sheriff of said county, for the sum of £35,345.05, on account of said money so stolen, and not paid into the Treasury,

Resolved, therefore, That the said petition is reasonable; but that the final determination thereon ought to be postponed to the next meeting of Assembly, and, in the meantime, that the Public Solicitor be directed not to take out an execution on the said judgment."

On June 18th, the Speaker laid before the House a letter from the Hon. Major-General Marquis La Fayette, respecting the present state and movements of the army under his command, which was read and ordered to lie upon the table.

This resolution was agreed to by the House: That all horses impressed for the use of the army, by order of the Marquis La Fayette, Major-General Baron Steuben, or Gen. Nelson, ought to be paid for by the Treasurer of this Commonwealth, by warrant from the Auditors of Public Accounts.

On June 21st, this resolution was passed: That the Treasurer do receive on account any money which may be offered him by Henry Peyton, Esq., late Sheriff of Prince William county, so that if the said sales be confirmed, he may be saved harmless from all penalties for the non-payment thereof, and if not, that the value thereof may be returned, according to the present state of depreciation, to the purchaser.

On June 22d, the Speaker laid before the House a letter from George Mathews, Esq., late Colonel of the Ninth Virginia regiment, containing a representation of sundry matters on behalf of himself and the officers of the said regiment, which was read and referred.

This resolution was adopted: That the Governor be empowered to appoint a Secretary, who shall be allowed at the rate of 30,000 pounds of tobacco per annum.

On June 23d, the House came to the following resolution:

It appearing to the General Assembly that Col. Wm. Fleming (one of the gallant survivors of the battle of Point Pleasant), being the only acting member of Council for some time before the appointment of a Chief Magistrate, did give orders for the calling out the militia, and also pursued such other measures as were essential to good government, and it is just and reasonable that he should be indemnified therein,

Resolved, therefore, That the said Wm. Fleming, Esq., be indemnified for his conduct, as before mentioned, and the Assembly do approve of the same.

And then the House adjourned to meet on the first Monday of October, 1781, at Richmond, and " if the movements of the enemy make it improper to hold the Assembly in said town, then the Governor, with the advice of Council, appoint it to meet at Fredericksburg, or at Winchester, in Frederick county, or at such other place as they shall deem expedient "

During this dark period in our history, considerable gloom filled the minds of members. Washington, who had been struggling against the British, in Long Island, was retreating through New Jersey and Delaware, the pursuing enemy wasting fields, destroying cattle, and committing every kind of violence upon the defenceless inhabitants. In this bitter hour of defeat, one of the members, recalling the history of Rome, who, when torn with intestine strife and deluged with blood, put a dictator at her head, suggested the idea of appointing Patrick Henry, Dictator. It found no countenance with Henry or the members, and one of them, Archibald Cary, meeting Henry's brother-in-law, addressed him with heat in these terms : "Sir, I am told that your brother wishes to be Dictator: tell him, from me, that the day of his appointment shall be the day of his death, for he shall feel my dagger in his heart before the sunset of that day."

To all the numerous calls made for volunteers to fight the Indians and the British during the Revolution, the people of Augusta responded with an alacrity which evinced their spirit and patriotism. The writer much regrets his inability to supply a list of the officers and men furnished by the county to these wars. The following extract from a letter of Adjutant-General James McDonald, of date Richmond, July 23, 1881, will explain the cause :

To COL. J. LEWIS PEYTON, Steep-hill :

MY DEAR COLONEL : I duly received your letter, and regret to say that the office of the Adjutant-General, together with its contents, was destroyed by fire at the evacuation of this city by the Confederate forces in 1865. Consequently, nothing relating to the wars of the Revolution, of 1812, and with Mexico, can now be found in it. But I was anxious, if possible, to serve you, and accordingly set my friend, Col. Sherwin McRae, acting State Librarian, to rummage the State Library for information. He reports, after search, that while there are printed rolls of Virginia troops in all those wars, the counties, &c., from which they come are not designated.

On the 26th of December, 1776, Washington defeated the British and Hessians at Trenton, N. J., taking many Hessian prisoners, and several hundred of them were sent to Staunton, where they remained for some years in custody. During this time, they built of bricks, dried in the sun, the house still standing on Spring farm, and occupied, in 1882, by the Superintendent of the Staunton Water-works.

The Revolutionary war closed in 1783, the British Government having, after the surrender of Lord Cornwallis at Yorktown, in 1781, abandoned all hope of conquering America. Provisional articles of peace between the two governments were signed at Paris, November 30th, 1782, a formal proclamation of a cessation of hostilities was made throughout the British army 19th of April, 1783, and the definite treaty, acknowledging the colonies to be free and independent States, was signed September 30th, 1783.

For eight years the Americans had been subjected to the miseries of a devastating war. In a short time, they found the Confederative system defective, and incapable of subserving the great ends for which it was instituted, and in 1787 Commissioners from all the States, excepting Rhode Island, assembled at Philadelphia, and their labors resulted in the formation of the Federal Constitution. The fundamental distinction between the articles of Confederation and the new Constitution, consisted in this : The former acted only on States, the latter on individuals ; the former could neither raise men nor money by its own authority, but was dependent on the discretion of thirteen different legislatures, and without their unanimous concurrence, could not provide for the public safety or for the payment of the national debt. The more perfect organization effected by the Federal Constitution in our system of government gave a new aspect to the political affairs of the country. A Constitution of more ample powers gave new vigor and efficacy to the measures of the General Government, and prepared the way for the wonderful prosperity which has since characterized our national annals.

Under the Constitution, religious liberty was guaranteed,—the liberty of conscience, or freedom of a man to worship God according to his belief and the dictates of his conscience, provided he does not thereby disturb the peace of the Commonwealth. The Constitution makes no provision for the support of any religion, but the clergy are maintained by the voluntary contributions of the people, and are excluded from holding offices under the Government.

Our English ancestors, in sustaining a religious establishment, acted on the experience of antiquity, for they regarded their clergy as the preservers, not only of a ritual, but of the truths which it symbolized, and saw united in them the spirit of the priest and the wisdom of the sage. While this clergy defended the faith, they advanced continually in a better knowledge of it, subjecting all dogmas to the discipline of reason. Under the churches of England and Scotland, religious and civil liberty reached maturity together. But even with these, the doctrines of blind obedience prevailed so far, by an old corruption of the blood, as to multiply sects and breed incurable miseries in the State. As far as possible to escape these miseries, the framers of our Constitution refused any longer to sustain a Church, and extended liberty of belief to all, trusting that each community would provide for its own instruction in morality, and choose its own ministers of religion. We are not, therefore, to suppose in them an ignorant carelessness, or a contempt for the office of religion; but only that they held it to be unjust that one man should be taxed for the religion of another; and there is little doubt that public instruction in the principles of virtue and religion would have seemed to them an object of the first importance, and to be sustained by legislation, had it been possible to establish a religion or a system of morals in which all dogmas and superstitions might be reconciled and dissolved.

The following are the proceedings of the meeting referred to (ante p. 176), and may be found in 3d Vol. Am. Archives, 4th series:

" At a meeting of the inhabitants of that part of Augusta county that lies on the west side of Laurel Hill, at Pittsburg, the 16th of May, 1775, the following gentlemen were chosen a committee for the said district, viz: George Croghan, John Campbell, Edward Ward, Thos. Smallman, Jno. Cannon, John McCullough, Wm. Gee, Geo. Vallandingham, John Gibson, Dorsey Penticost, Edward Cook, Wm. Crawford, Devereux Smith, Jno. Anderson, David Rodgers, Jacob Vanmetre, Hy. Enoch, Jas. Ennis, Geo. Wilson, W. Vance, David Shepherd, Wm. Elliott, Richmond Willis, Sam. Sample, John Ormsbey, Richard McMaher, Jno. Nevill and Jno. Sweringer.

The foregoing gentlemen met in committee, and resolved that Jno. Campbell, Jno. Ormsbey, Ed. Ward, Thos. Smallman, Sam'l Sample, Jno. Anderson, and D. Smith, or any four of them, be a standing committee, and shall have full power to meet at such times as they shall judge necessary, and, in case of any emergency, to call the committee of this district together, and shall be vested with the power and authority as the other standing committees and committees of correspondence are in the other counties within this colony.

Resolved, unanimously, That the cordial and most grateful thanks of this committee are a tribute due to John Harvie, Esq., our worthy representative in the late Colonial Convention held at Richmond, for his faithful discharge of that important trust reposed in him; and to John Nevill, Esq., our other worthy delegate, whom nothing but sickness prevented from representing us in that respectable assembly.

Resolved, unanimously, That this committee have the highest sense of the spirited behavior of their brethren in New England, and do most cordially approve of their opposing the invaders of American rights and privileges to the utmost extreme, and that each member of this committee, respectively, will animate and encourage their neighborhood to follow the brave example.

This committee, therefore, out of the deepest sense of the expediency of this measure, most earnestly entreat that every member of this committee do collect from each tithable person in their several districts the sum of 2s. 6 pence, which we deem no more than sufficient for the above purpose, and give proper receipts to all such as pay the same into their hands; and the sum so collected to be paid into the hands of John Campbell, Esq , who is to give proper security to this committee, or their successors, for the due and faithful application of the money so deposited with him; and this committee, as your representatives, and who are most ardently laboring for your preservation, call on you, our constituents. our friends, brethren, and fellow-sufferers, in the name of God, of everything you hold sacred or valuable, for the sake of your wives, children, and unborn generations, that you will, every one of you, in your several stations, to the utmost of your power, assist in levying such sum, by not only paying yourselves, but by assisting those who are not at present in a condition to do so. We heartily lament the case of all such as have not this small sum at command in this day of necessity; to all such we recommend to tender security to such as Providence has enabled, to lend them so much; and this committee do pledge their faith and fortunes to you, their constituents, that we shall, without fee or reward, use our best endeavors to procure, with the money so collected, the ammunition our present exigencies have made so exceedingly necessary.

"As this committee has reason to believe, there is a quantity of ammunition destined for this place for the purpose of government; and as this country on the west side of Laurel Hill is greatly distressed for want of ammunition, and deprived of the means of procuring it by reason of its situation, as easy as the lower counties of this colony, they do earnestly request the committees of Frederick and Augusta and Hampshire that they will not suffer the ammunition to pass through their counties for the purposes of government, but will secure it for the use of this destitute country, and immediately inform this committee of their having done so."

The committee adopt another resolution, approving of "a resolution of the committee of the other part of this county," cultivating a friendly intercourse with the Indians.

They direct, also, the "Standing Committee" to secure arms and ammunition not employed in actual service, or private property, and to have them repaired and put into the hands of such captains of independent companies as may make application for them. They also raised £15 to transmit to Robert C. Nicholas for the use of the deputies sent to the general congress from "this colony." They also adopted "instructions to the delegates." These were reported by Mr. John Campbell, of the Select Committee, the first part of which is in these words:

To JOHN HARVIE AND GEORGE RODES, ESQS.: GENTLEMEN;

You being chosen to represent the people on the west side of Laurel Hill, in Colonial Congress, for the ensuing year, we, the committee for the people aforesaid, desire you will lay the grievances hereafter mentioned before the Congress at their first meeting, as we conceive it highly necessary they should be redressed, to put us on a footing with the rest of our brethren in the colony." They complain, first, of having had to supply the soldiers in the last Indian war with their provisions, and thereby having brought themselves well-nigh to suffering; second, that the garrison maintained there had to be supported by the inhabitants; third, "that this country, adjoining the Indian territory and Province of Quebeck," is exposed to the inroads of the savages and the militia of that province, and consequently their civil and religious liberties were in danger; fourth, that for want of freeholders, they could not get grand juries; fifth, "that the unsettled boundary between this colony and Pennsylvania is the occasion of many disputes"; sixth, that the collecting the duty on skins and furs will banish the Indian trade from this place and colony," which report being agreed to: Resolved, unanimously, That a fair copy be drawn off and delivered to our delegates as their instructions. Ordered that the foregoing proceedings be certified by the clerk of this committee, and published in the "Virginia Gazette." By order of the committee.

JAMES BERWICK, Clerk.

The delegates from Augusta to the Virginia Convention, which met in Richmond, March 20th, 1765, were Thomas Lewis, Samuel McDowell and John Harvie.

On March 21st, 1775, a letter from the inhabitants of that part of Augusta county, which lies to the westward of the Alleghany mountains, desiring that John Nevill and John Harvie, Esqs., may be admitted into this convention as their delegates, being read; upon a motion,

Resolved, that the said John Nevill and John Harvie be admitted as delegates for the County of Augusta.

Peyton Randolph was the president and John Tazewell clerk of the Convention

ANA, EXCERPTS, ETC.

All people abhor the character of a spy, moving in friendly garb, however useful his treachery may be to his employers, and will not regret the fate of Tarlton's. One of Tarlton's men crossed the Blue Ridge as a spy in 1781. He was captured near Fishersville on Sunday morning, and taken to Tinkling Spring. The people were plunged into great excitement, thinking Tarlton was following on the heels of his scout. The congregation was immediately dismissed by the pastor, Mr. Waddell, who exhorted the people to repair to the mountain and oppose the enemy, offering to lead them himself. The spy was placed in custody of a young man named Long, who volunteered to deliver him to the jailor in Staunton. Cocking his rifle, Long ordered the spy to march before him. When they reached Christian's Creek, Long, who wore moccasins, and who did not wish to wet them, ordered the spy to halt till he could take them off. The prisoner paid no attention to his order, but doggedly kept on. Finding he would escape, Long, after warning him in vain, discharged his rifle at and mortally wounded the captive. The wounded man lingered several days, during which he acknowledged that he belonged to Tarlton's command, and was a spy in search of information.

BURGESS WILSON.

The old Glebe burying-ground (mentioned ante, p. 150,) near to the once Glebe parsonage of Augusta county, is about five miles north of Middlebrook, near the Middle River, and occupies a beautiful site. Among the tablets there is the following:

"Here lys the interred body of Col. Jno. Willson, who departed this life, in the year of our Lord, 1773, in the 72d year of his age, having served his country 27 y'rs a representative in the honorable house of burgesses in Va., &c."

On the same, below:

"Likewise, the interred body of Martha, his well-beloved wife, who departed this life July 10th, 1755, in the LX year of her age."

Col. Willson, who so long served the county, was a member of great weight and influence. He was one of the early Scotch-Irish settlers, and resided on his estate, on Middle River, at the place occupied by his descendant, Mathew Willson, Sr., an elder in Bethel church thirty years ago. He was commonly called "Old Burgess Willson," from his long service in the House, and has left many highly respectable descendants in Augusta.

THE CAPTIVE BELLE.

In 1774, the Shawanese commenced their outrages on New River, in Giles, killing and scalping five children of Jno. Lybrook, who were playing near the stream. Among the prisoners they made was Mrs. Margaret Hall, who remained in captivity in Ohio until 1794, or eighteen years, until Wayne's victory. She was transferred to the Delawares, where she was adopted into the family of a chief. The Indians were somewhat civilized—had a few cattle, and made butter, fritters and pancakes. Shortly before Mrs. Hall's return home, a young chief fell violently in love with her, and urged his suit, and upon her refusal to marry him, threatened to take her life. Her foster mother used her persuasion in his behalf, and the young squaws congratulated her on the offer. Annoyed, she fled on horseback seventy miles distant, where her foster sister and brother had removed. She was pursued by the young chief, who again told her she must marry him or die. She persisted in her refusal. He made a lunge at her with a knife, when the foster sister threw herself between them, and received a slight wound in the side, the point of the knife striking a rib. The Indian girl seized the knife by the blade, wrenched it from his hand, broke it, and threw the pieces away. A fight ensued, in which the girl proved the conqueror, and drove the savage lover from the field. Her foster brother, who was absent, on his return told her not to be uneasy, denounced the lover, and threatened to kill him if he gave her further annoyance. The disappointed lover went off and was soon killed in battle.

————

The following lines, by a native of West Augusta, on Wayne, whose victory, in 1794, resulted in the peace of Greenville, are inserted as a specimen of our early poetry:

"The birth of some great men, or death,
    Gives a celebrity to spots of earth;
    We say that Montcalm fell on Abraham's plain;
    That Butler presses the Miami bank;
    And that the promontory of Sigeum
    Has Achilles' tomb.
    Presqu' Isle saw Wayne expire;
    There the traveller shall see his monument;
    At least his grave. For this,

27 ‡

> Corroding jealousy will not detract;
> But allow a mound—
> Some little dwelling of the earth,
> To mark the interment of his bones.
> Brave, honest soldier, sleep—
> And let the dews weep over thee,
> While gales shall sigh across the lakes;
> Till man shall recognize thy worth,
> And coming to the place will ask,
> ' Is this where Wayne is buried?' "

CONTINENTAL MONEY.

During the Revolutionary war, Congress issued paper money, called continental money, to carry on the war, for the redemption of which the faith of the colonies was pledged. The dates and amounts of issue are as follows, and its value at certain periods:

1775.—June 22, issued $2,000,000, and between this time and 1780, $200,000,000 were issued, and none redeemed.

1777.—January, paper currency 5 per cent. discount; in July, 25 per cent., and before the end of the year, $3 in paper would not command a silver dollar.

1778.—April, $4 in paper to one dollar in coin; September, $5 to one in coin, and December, $6.50 to one in coin.

1779.—February, $8.50; May, $12; September, $18 to one in coin, and before the close of the year a paper dollar was worth only four cents.

1780.—March, $1 in paper worth three cents; May, two cents, and in December, $74 in paper was worth one dollar in silver.

A VIRGINIA MATRON.

The patriotic women of the Revolution assisted our heroic men in every possible way, and displayed that enthusiastic courage which great occasions will generally find lodged in those bosoms which are the seat of every gentle, every tender feeling, and which ought only to heave with the tenderest emotions. When the Legislature fled to Staunton, the Governor was the guest of Col. William Lewis, at Fort Lewis. During his first dinner, His Excellency expressed some uneasiness lest Col. Tarleton might swoop down upon and take them captive. Mrs. Lewis, who was at the head of the table, said, with some animation: " Do not allow yourself, Mr. Governor, to be disturbed by such apprehensions. I have sent my three sons to Rockfish Gap, and Col. Tarleton will never cross the mountains except as a prisoner or corpse."

"At the time Tarleton drove the Legislature from Charlottesville," says Howe, p. 183, "the stillness of the Sabbath eve was broken in the latter town by the beat of the drum, and volunteers were called for to prevent the passage of the British through the mountains. The elder sons of Col. William Lewis, who resided at Fort Lewis, were absent with the northern army. Three sons, however, were at home, whose ages were seventeen.

fifteen and thirteen years. Col. Lewis was confined to his bed by illness, but his wife, with the firmness of a Roman matron, called them to her and bade them fly to the defence of their native land. "Go, my children," said she; " I spare not my youngest, my fair-haired boy, the comfort of my declining years. I devote you all to my country. Keep back the foot of the invader from the soil of Augusta, or see my face no more." When this incident was related to Washington, shortly after its occurrence, he enthusiastically exclaimed: " Leave me but a banner to plant upon the mountains of Augusta, and I will rally around me the men who will raise our bleeding country from the dust and set her free."

PATRICK HENRY CARRIES THE NEWS OF TARLETON'S RAID TO STAUNTON.

Among the stories told for a long time after the dispersion of the Virginia Legislature by Tarleton, says Gov. Gilmer, was one that Mr. Jefferson concealed himself in Carter's mountain, and another that Patrick Henry, flying to Staunton in the greatest haste, met Col. William Lewis in one of the streets, to whom he immediately related the adjournment and flight of the Legislature, then making their way to Staunton. Col. Lewis, not knowing who Henry was, said to him: " If Patrick Henry had been in Albemarle, the British dragoons never would have passed over the Rivanna river."

A number of gentlemen, fearing Tarleton would capture them, left Staunton, and went, during the night, to the estate of Col. George Moffett, near which they heard there was a cave in which they might conceal themselves. Breakfast was announced shortly after their arrival, and whilst discharging the duty of hostess, Mrs. Moffett, who was an enthusiastic Whig, remarked there was one member of that legislating body she knew would not run. The question was asked by one of the party, " Who is he?" Her reply was, Patrick Henry. At that moment a gentleman with one boot colored considerably. The party soon left, in search, no doubt, of the caverns. Very soon after their departure, a servant rode up with the lost boot, and inquired for Mr. Henry, stating that Patrick Henry had left Staunton in such haste that he had forgotten the boot. Mrs. Moffett ascertained who it was the boot fit. What her emotions and feelings then were, I know not, but I suppose Patrick's were, about that time,

"Give me liberty—not death."

MRS. INGLIS' CAPTIVITY AND ESCAPE.

One of the most remarkable incidents in the early wars was the capture of the Draper family. Geo. Draper, with his son, John, and wife, and his daughter, Mary, and her husband, Mr. Inglis, removed about 1750 from Pennsylvania to Southwestern Virginia, and settled where Smithfield, long the seat of the Prestons, now stands, in the present county of Montgomery. Here they resided in peace and quietness for six years, during which time many families were drawn to the settlement, and George Draper died. The Shawanese frequently passed the settlement on their expeditions against the Catawbas, but without molesting the inhabitants, till the year 1756. In the summer of this year, they made a descent upon the inhabitants while the men were all in the harvest-field. The savages surrounded the dwellings in which were the women and children and arms of the families, murdered the widow of George Draper, and also Col. James Patton, of Augusta, who was on an exploring expedition, and sojourning a few days in the settlement. They took captive Mrs. John Draper, Mrs. Inglis, and her two sons, Thomas and George. The men, believing resistance ineffectual, concealed themselves until the departure of the Indians, who moved off towards New River. Reaching the river, they proceeded down the stream, on their way to their towns in Ohio. They were partial to Mrs. Inglis, whom they allowed to ride on horseback, carrying her two children. Mrs. Draper, who was wounded, and had her arm broken in the attack on the settlement, was less kindly cared for. Mrs. Inglis was permitted to search in the woods for herbs and roots to poultice the wounds of Mrs. Draper, the Indians trusting to her love for her children for her speedy return. She thus had opportunities of escaping, but would never avail herself of them, and leave her children behind. On reaching the Kanawha salines, the Indians halted several days to make salt. About thirty days after leaving Montgomery, the party reached the Shawanese town at the mouth of the Big Scioto. Here the kindness of the Indians for Mrs. Inglis continued. She was not required to run the gauntlet, as was Mrs. Draper, though her wound was unhealed. When the captives were divided, Mrs. Inglis was separated from her sons. About this time, some French traders from Detroit came to the village, and Mrs. Inglis exercised her skill in making shirts of gaudy-colored calico for the savages, which greatly delighted them, and increased their admiration for her. After some time, probably six weeks, Mrs. Inglis was separated from Mrs. Draper, and taken, with an elderly Dutch woman, one hundred miles south of the Ohio to Big Bone Lick, to make salt. The cruelty of the savages, in thus separating her from her children, determined her to escape. She prevailed upon the Dutch woman to accompany her. Obtaining permission from the Indians to go in the woods to gather grapes, they left the camp in the afternoon, provided with a blanket each, a tomahawk and knife. They hastened to the Ohio, and proceeded up the left bank of the stream for five days to the mouth of the Scioto, opposite the site of an Indian village. Here they captured a horse, and both mounting, continued up the river unperceived. Being on the south side of the river, they were less exposed to observation by the Indians. The barbarians, missing them, made diligent search, but finding no trail, and never dreaming of such a thing as an attempt of the women to return to Virginia, gave up the pursuit, under an impression that they had become lost and been devoured by wild beasts. The fugitives continued up the river, subsisting on maize and wild fruit, and reached the Big Sandy river. In crossing the stream, they lost their horse. Their sufferings were so great before reaching the Kanawha, that the Dutch woman, frantic with hunger and pain, threatened to take Mrs. Inglis' life for persuading her to the journey. On reaching the Kanawha, their spirits revived, and they continued up the river until within fifty miles of Mrs. I.'s home. Here the Dutch woman attempted to kill Mrs. I. Mrs. Inglis escaped from her grasp, and outran her, and hid under the river bank. After a while, she left her concealment, and finding a canoe, crossed the stream. The following morning the old woman saw her, and begged her to recross and join company, promising future good behavior. Mrs. I. declined the invitation, and proceeded on her journey. Her clothes were worn and torn into fragments and her limbs swollen from the increasing cold (a slight fall of snow having taken place) and her exposure in wading streams, &c. After traveling forty-and-a-half days, she reached the cabin of Adam Harmon, on New River, and was treated in the kindest manner. After a few days rest, Mr. H. took her on horseback to the fort in Dunkard's bottom, where, the next day, her husband and her brother, John Draper, came unexpectedly. The surprise of the meeting was mutual and happy. Thus ended the captivity and escape, embracing five months. While at Harmon's, Mrs. Inglis entreated him to go or send for the old Dutch woman. He positively refused, on account of her bad conduct, but in a short time the wanderer found her way into the settlement.

In the Spring, Mr. Inglis, his wife being unwilling to live longer on the frontier, removed to Vause's fort, on the Roanoke, and thence to Botetourt county. This was providential, for in the following Autumn a French and Indian force took the fort and murdered or made prisoners of all the inmates. Among the killed and captured were John and Mathew Inglis and their families. John Inglis was killed, and Mathew taken prisoner. Mary and William Inglis had six children,—Thomas and George, born before the captivity, Susan, Rhoda, Polly and John afterwards. George died in captivity. The other five married and left large families. Thomas escaped from the Indians after thirteen years' residence among them. He was, in 1774, at the battle of Point Pleasant, and after the victory and Lewis' advance into Ohio, met many of his old savage comrades. On his return he married Miss Ellen Grills, and settled on Wolf creek, a water of New river. Here he lived a short time, and then removed to Burke's Garden, where he was unmolested till 1782. In this year, the Indians attacked his house and burnt it, and took his family prisoners. They were soon pursued by the whites, who on the seventh day overtook the savages. As soon as the Indians saw Mr. Inglis and the whites they commenced, as was their custom, tomahawking their prisoners. Mr. Inglis rushed forward to rescue his wife and children, but was too late. All were tomahawked and all died but his wife. In the affair, Capt. Maxwell was killed. William Inglis removed to Tennessee, and thence to Mississippi. Susan, the eldest daughter of William and Mary Inglis, married General Trigg; another daughter, Mr. Charles Taylor; and a third, Judge Allan Taylor, whose daughter, Sallie A. E. Taylor, married, in 1826, the late Col. William Madison Peyton, of Roanoke. Polly Inglis married a brother of John's wife. The youngest son left eight children. Mrs. Inglis died in 1813, aged eighty-four. Her descendants are numerous, highly respectable, and contemplate with wonder and admiration her energy, boldness and endurance.

CHAPTER XIII.

On the 14th of December, 1790, the counties of Bath and Pendleton were formed from Augusta, and the latter was left with her present boundaries. Here, probably, it might be thought our work should close—that of a county so limited in extent and population as Augusta now is nothing remained to be said. This is not the case. The county has not been barren of historical interest the past ninety years. In point of size, too, Augusta, as she now stands, exceeds the celebrated island of Ithaca, which was part of the Kingdom of Greece, and long the residence of Ulysses, whose adventures, on his return to it from the Trojan war, form the subject of Homer's Odyssey.

The officers of the county, in 1790, were gentlemen justices William Bowyer, Thomas Hughart, Joseph Bell, John Wilson, J. Bell, jun., Robert Gamble, David Stephenson, William Moffett, Alexander Nelson, James Berry, John Tate, Alexander St. Clair, Robert Douthat, Charles Cameron, James Searight, James Ramsey and William McPheeters. Clerk, A. McClenechan. The county court system, which originated in Virginia as early as 1623-'4, was not materially changed by the Revolution as to its jurisdiction or general powers and duties.

Under this system, John Coalter was Attorney for the Commonwealth until 1809, when he resigned the office in order to accept the position of judge of the general court of Virginia, to which he was elected. Chapman Johnson was his successor, and served until 1812, when John H. Peyton was elected, and discharged the duties of the office until 1844, when he resigned from ill-health. Thomas J. Michie was then elected, and served until 1851, when William H. Harman was appointed and served until 1861, when James Bumgardner received the appointment and continues in office. In 1809, the clerk of the county was Jacob Kinney, who was succeeded by Erasmus Stribling, who, in 1828, was succeeded by Jefferson Kinney, who was succeeded, in 1858, by J. D. Imboden, and he, in 1864, by William A. Burnett, who has been reëlected every six years to the present time.

From the foundation of the Commonwealth, June 20th, 1776, down to 1831, the administration of law and equity was wholly separate in Virginia, except in the county and corporation courts. The two jurisdictions of law and equity were lodged in the hands of two different judges. In 1802, the Commonwealth was divided into three districts, and a chancery court provided for each. Staunton was the seat of the chancery court for a district extending to the Ohio, and the first chancellor was John Brown, who served till 1814, and was succeeded by Allan Taylor, who served till the adoption of the new constitution in 1831. Henry J. Peyton was clerk of the chancery court until he removed from Staunton in 1814, and was succeeded by William S. Eskridge, who served till 1831.

At the same time, Staunton was the seat of a common law court, of which Archibald Stuart was elected judge.

In 1809, that arrangement was superceded by "Superior Courts of Law," held by a single judge twice a year in every county and corporation. Judge Stuart continued to preside, and in 1809, appointed John Howe Peyton Attorney for the Commonwealth, and Chesley Kinney clerk. Mr. Peyton was not at the time, nor had he ever been, a resident of Augusta, but was practicing in the Fredericksburg circuit, and was the distinguished representative of the people of Stafford in the House of Delegates of Virginia. After his removal to Staunton, and while discharging the duties of Commonwealth's Attorney for this district, he served the session of 1808-1809, in the Legislature for the county of Stafford. He discharged the duties of Commonwealth's Attorney, under the old constitution, until 1831, when the new constitution was adopted ; was reappointed under it, and served until 1838, when he was elected Senator for the Augusta and Rockbridge district, and resigned.

In 1831, the law and equity courts were united, and L. P. Thompson, of Nelson county, was elected judge, and appointed N. C. Kinney clerk, who served till his death, in 1859, when his son, Alexander F. Kinney, was appointed, and served until 1864, when Joseph N. Ryan was elected, and has been reëlected at each successive election to the present time.

After the year 1790, little of interest occurred in the county for some years. The population, wealth and resources of the community continued to increase steadily and rapidly, but the public prosperity was impaired from this time forward by a considerable exodus or migration from the county to the west and southwest. Among the old families who have left the county are the Lewises, who removed to Bath, Monroe, Greenbrier and the Valley of the Kanawha, and have thence branched off into the south, the west and southwestern States; the Prestons, who removed to Montgomery, and have since followed the path of the Lewises; the Breckenridges, who settled in Kentucky; the Gambles in Florida, and the Pattons and others in different quarters of the new States. Those who remained after 1790, continued to prosper, and the population increased steadily if not rapidly in spite of these migrations. Owing to the equality of fortune and simplicity of manners which still prevailed among the people, and the ease and comfort in which all lived, the inhabitants multiplied beyond the proportion of older communities corrupted by the vices of wealth and vanity.

In 1811, the Augusta Agricultural Society was formed,—one of the first ever established in Virginia, and a more particular notice of which will be given subsequently.

The encroachments of Great Britain upon the maratime rights of the United States had, for some years previous to 1812, been a subject of controversy between the two countries. No satisfactory concession had been made by the British Government after repeated negotiations. On the contrary, their depredations upon American commerce still continued. President Madison, as a last resort, recommended an appeal to arms, and war was declared June 18th, 1812, by the United States against Great Britain. The grounds of the war are set forth in the President's message to Congress, and need not be recited nor can the history of the war find a place here.

The people of Augusta immediately prepared for the contest, and on the 20th of June, 1812, formed a Military Association in Staunton to devise plans for military schools in which the recruits might be instructed. The following officers were elected at the first meeting: Robert Porterfield, president; Alexander Nelson, vice-president; James Bell, treasurer; C. Johnson, secretary, and the following committee of correspondence appointed: Gen. John Brown, John H. Peyton, William Boys, Thomas Jackson and James McNutt. The meeting also appointed a committee to prepare a plan of action, which said committee subsequently reported the following preamble and resolutions:

The committee to whom was referred a resolution of the Staunton Military Association, which has for its object the establishment of military schools in the counties of Augusta, Rockingham and Rockbridge, having had that object under consideration, beg leave to report the result of their deliberations and enquiries :

The committee deem it unnecessary to refer to any other authority than the good sense and honest feelings of every man to prove the great utility at all times, but more especially at this time, of military instruction to the people of this county. The subject, here at least, is a new and difficult one, and the committee are very sensible that any plan which they can suggest will have many palpable obstacles to encounter, and may be exposed to various others which they cannot foresee. They rely for every hope of success upon the acknowledged value of the object in view ; upon the patriotism of the people ; upon the order of the present times, and upon the success of the experiment which this Society has made.

A military school, in which would be taught the complete discipline of a regiment, the different exercises of the rifle corps, the artillery and the infantry, together with the cavalry exercise of the sword, though it could not promise to teach the whole principles of war as a science, would certainly promise much that would be eminently useful to every soldier and officer in the militia. And your committee cannot refrain from suggesting that a school for these purposes, successfully conducted, might serve as an introduction to some more extensive and some more perfect system of military education.

To obtain a person capable of conducting such a school would not always be easy ; such a person is not very readily met with, and what is yet more difficult, funds to remunerate his services are to be raised by voluntary contribution. But at present, judging from their own experience in this Society, your committee think that a person whose skill, information and zeal in military affairs would enable him to conduct such a school, may be found in your own commandant, and they hope that funds to compensate his services are within the reach of an active and spirited exertion. They hope that the neighbouring counties of Rockbridge and Rockingham would consider the subject as worthy of their attention, and might be induced to unite with the people of Augusta in their endeavors to attain it. A sufficient number of subscribers in the County of Augusta alone would probably not be obtained to induce any one properly qualified to devote his time to their service. But by the union of Rockingham and Rockbridge this might be effected.

Your committee would therefore recommend to the Society the adoption of the following resolution :

Resolved, That subscriptions be opened in the County of Augusta under the immediate superintendence of a committee of seven persons, appointed by this society, for establishing a military school in the town of Staunton, to be denominated the Staunton Military School, to commence on the 15th day of July next, and continue for one year thereafter, and be under the direction of Capt. George Turner, the present commandant of this Society ; that the times of teaching and price to subscribers be regulated by said committee and the commandant in conjunction, so that the days of teaching be not less than one day in each fortnight, and the price to subscribers be not more than ten dollars per annum, payable quarterly in advance.

Resolved, That it be recommended to the commandant to endeavor to establish similar schools in the neighbouring counties of Rockingham and

28 ‡

Rockbridge, and that the committee aforesaid be instructed to invite, respectfully, the coöperation of those counties.

JOHN H. PEYTON,   C. JOHNSON,
WILLIAM TAYLOR,   WILLIAM YOUNG,
E. STRIBLING,   M. McCUE,
            JAMES CRAWFORD.

The opening of the war was, unfortunately, signalized by the surrender of Detroit, with 2,500 men, by Gen. Hull. Hull was charged with treason, cowardice, and unofficer-like conduct, was tried by court-martial and sentenced to death, but the sentence,—in consideration of Gen. Hull's great age and consequent mental incapacity,—was remitted by the President. The event, however, inspired the British with great enthusiasm and confidence. We cannot enter into the particulars of the war, the scenes of the conflict being, for the most part, far removed from Virginia. Virginia, however, did not entirely escape invasion. A British fleet, under Admiral Cockburn, in May, 1812, entered Chesapeake Bay and ravaged the coasts of Maryland and Virginia. He sought to capture Norfolk, but was defeated by a flotilla of American gun-boats off Craney island, which stands at the entrance of Norfolk harbor. Cockburn withdrew, and took possession of the unfortified and unprotected village of Hampton, where he committed every species of outrage. The most uncontrolable excitement now burst over Virginia. A call was made for volunteers, and the people of Augusta responded with enthusiasm. Robert Porterfield, an old Revolutionary officer of skill and ability, then in the sixty-second year of his age, was commissioned Brigadier-General, and appointed John H. Peyton his chief-of-staff, and Dr. Williams, of Waynesboro, surgeon.

The companies marched to Camp Holly, near Richmond, and thence to Craney island, and as near as we have been able to ascertain, were officered as follows: Captains: B. G. Baldwin, C. Johnson, J. C. Sowers, (artillery); John Mathews, Hugh Young, (riflemen); Abraham Large, from the Cowpastures; Christian Morris, Joseph Larew, Greenville; Samuel Doake, cavalry from neighborhood of Tinkling Spring; Samuel Steele, (Waynesborough); Alexander Givens, (Mt. Meridian); George C. Robertson, (New Hope); W. G. Dudley, (Middle River); James Kirke, (Jenning's Gap); John Sperry and John H. Peck, commissaries.

These troops were quartered in barracks on the eastern slope of Betsy Bell, on Glendale, the estate owned, in 1882, by Col. George Lyttleton Peyton. There was plenty of pure water and good firewood at this point, and the land well adapted for military manœuvres. From this camp they were dispatched, as soon as trained and uniformed, to Camp Holly, near Richmond. We cannot follow the fortunes of this force. The war to which they so gallantly contributed their services, was terminated by the treaty of Ghent, which was signed by the commissioners of the two coun-

tries on the 24th of December, 1814, and ratified by the President and
Senate on the 17th of the following February. This was one of the most
singular treaties ever signed. It made no provision in regard to the subject for which the war was avowedly undertaken. It was, however, contended by the friends of the administration that, as the orders in council
had been repealed, and the motives for impressment ceased with the wars
in Europe, the grounds of the controversy no longer existed.

The termination of hostilities presented an opportunity for resuming the
pursuits of private business and the great plans of improvement in Virginia. Real estate rose rapidly in value, especially in the town of Staunton and its vicinity, and there was a rapid revival of prosperity in every
portion of our county.

During the war thus closed, we have seen that Augusta contributed
liberally in treasure and the services of her sons to the defence of the
country, and her sons submitted to the toils and perils of the camp and
field without a murmur. Hundreds paid the forfeit of their lives in a climate fatal to their constitutions. Laying down the sword at the end of
the war, the soldiers returned to their peaceful employments, and nothing
of sufficient importance to be noticed by the annalist or historian occurred
in her history, or, indeed, in that of the State, for many years.

In October, 1829, a general convention assembled in Rich mond to revise
the State Constitution, which had existed from a period prior to the Revolution, and was therefore consecrated in the affections of a large portion of
the people. Many of our leading citizens were in favor of the mixed basis
of representation, and opposed a convention. The advocates of the white
basis of representation were, however, in the ascendancy, and the delegates
from this county were C. Johnson and B. G. Baldwin. The labors of the
convention, though it was composed of men of wisdom, varied talents and
ripe experience, resulted in no essential good, but in much practical mischief.

In 1835, Texas declared her independence of Mexico, and in 1836,
adopted a constitution and elected a president. Her independence was
acknowledged by the United States in 1837, and by England, France and
Belgium in 1840. The question of her annexation to the United States
was discussed in both countries, and she was finally admitted into the
Union the 27th December, 1845, which resulted in a war between Mexico
and the United States. To this war, Augusta contributed a volunteer
company, under command of Capt. Harper and the following officers: R.
H. Kinney, V. E. Geiger, William H. Harman, Lieutenants; George W.
Allen, C. H. Ball, William Blackburn, C. G. Merritt, Sergeants; William
O. Bickle, L. Clarke, O. C. Lavelle and B. F. Imboden, Corporals. The
company marched to Norfolk, where it took shipping for Corpus Christi,
Texas, and landing, proceeded, under command of Col. Hamtramck, to

whose regiment it was attached, up the Rio Grande. Col. Hamtramck served under Gen. Taylor in northern Mexico until the close of the war, but the regiment was never so lucky as to be in any engagement.

For many years previous to 1847, the people of Augusta had been anxious to secure more ample means of intercommunication, and a fresh impetus was given to the subject by the reviving prosperity resulting from the tariff of 1842. This led to meetings on the subject in different parts of the State. Among them one took place in Augusta, the proceedings of which we publish below:

At a meeting of the friends of internal improvement, held at the court-house, October 3rd, 1846, William Kinney, Esq., was called to the chair and Chapman Johnson, jr., appointed secretary.

John L. Peyton, Esq., now addressed the meeting in a pertinent and forcible speech upon the great importance of internal improvements, and the advantages that would accrue to the county and State from an extension of the Louisa railroad. At the conclusion of his address, he offered the following preamble and resolutions, which were unanimously adopted:

"Whereas, the citizens of Augusta have witnessed with much pleasure the recent manifestations in both sections of the State of a disposition to improve the means of communication between the east and west. Regarding a judicious system of internal improvements as indispensable to the prosperity of the Commonwealth, they trust the spirit now spreading throughout the land is the harbinger of a brighter destiny for the Old Dominion. Should the great lines of communication between the east and the west be completed, they feel assured that there will be a rapid improvement in the agriculture, manufactures, trade and commerce of Virginia, and a consequent increase in her wealth and population. Entertaining these views, a portion of the people of Augusta have met together in response to a call from their fellow-citizens of Bath and other counties, to give expression to their sentiments. Be it, therefore,

Resolved, 1st. That we cordially approve the proposition for the holding of a convention from those counties friendly to an extension of the Louisa railroad and the James river and Kanawha canal.

Resolved, 2d. That it is the opinion of this meeting that the convention should also consider and report upon such other schemes of improvement as may, in their opinion, be calculated to advance the great interests of the State.

Resolved, 3d. That twenty-five delegates be appointed by the chairman to represent the county in said convention.

The chairman, at his leisure, appointed the following delegates: John B. Baldwin, James Crawford, J. A. Cochran, J. A. Davidson, A. R. Givens, J. G. Fulton, K. Harper, Samuel Harnsbarger, T. J. Michie, I. Newton, John McCue, C. Johnson, jr., P. A. Heiskell, John L. Peyton, James Lilley, Joseph Smith, A. H. H. Stuart, H. W. Sheffey, James Points, J. B. Trimble, William Young, George Searight, L. Waddell.

The convention, as suggested, assembled in Staunton on the day recommended, October 30, 1846, and was attended by delegates from Albemarle, Augusta, Bath, Greenbrier, Hanover, Louisa, Rockbridge and Richmond city, and was presided over by Dr. John Brokenborough, of

Bath, with A. H. H. Stuart and T. J. Randolph as vice-presidents. The convention adopted resolutions in accordance with the recommendations of the Bath and Augusta meetings.

Another convention on the subject of internal improvements was held in Staunton, October 2, 1848, with delegates from Augusta, Alexandria, Alleghany, Bath, Botetourt, Fayette, Greenbrier, Jefferson, Frederick, Highland, Hampshire, Hanover, Kanawha, Mason, Monroe, Pocahontas, Rockbridge, Richmond city and Randolph. It was presided over by John S. Gallaher, of Frederick, and the secretaries were N. C. Kinney, D. A. Stofer and J. L. Peyton. The following resolutions were adopted:

Resolved, 1. As the opinion of this convention, that the General Assembly should extend such liberal support to those great lines of improvement now being constructed, as would bring into market the abundant natural resources of the Commonwealth.

2. That the General Assembly should commence, without delay, making appropriations for the construction of a railroad on State account, suitable for the transportation of heavy burthens from some point near the head of steamboat navigation, on the Kanawha river, to some point at or near Covington, having in view the ultimate extension to the most suitable point on the Ohio river.

3. That the Blue Ridge of mountains constitute a barrier to the communication between the eastern and western parts of the State, the removal of which barrier is an object of great interest to the whole Commonwealth, and therefore the General Assembly ought to appropriate a sum adequate to the construction of the Louisa railroad from the eastern to the western base, requiring of the Louisa Railroad Company to pay into the treasury of the Commonwealth a reasonable sum on the staple productions of the country, and a capitation tax on all passengers transported over that part of the road.

4. That the capital of the Louisa Railroad Company ought to be increased, so as to enable them to extend the road to a point at or near Covington.

5. That the extension of the Louisa railroad from the junction to the dock, in the city of Richmond, as an independent improvement, is a measure of very great interest to a large portion of the people of Virginia, now looking to that road as a medium of transportation to market.

6. That a committee be appointed to memoralize the Legislature on these subjects, &c.

An impulse was thus given to the cause which has resulted in Virginia's having, at this day, improvements penetrating into every quarter of the State.

———

As a means of encouraging thrift and economy among a people too prone to lavish expenditure and generous living, a financial institution was established in the county in 1848,—the first which had ever existed in the community,—called the Augusta Savings Bank. It went into operation with the following officers, elected by the stockholders: Benj. Crawford, president; Robert Cowan, treasurer; J. Lewis Peyton, secretary. Directors: J. A. Cochran, H. W. Sheffey, Thomas J. Michie, L. L. Stevenson and George K. Snapp. It was·highly prosperous and accomplished much good, but went out of existence during the war.

———

There were other questions, in 1845-50, occupying the public mind, or, at least, the thoughts of the more prominent of our citizens. These had reference to the universal improvement of the human race, and give evidence that our community was advancing, had always been advancing, and will continue to advance, by a law of their nature, of the existence of which their early history and their present condition leaves no room to doubt. Unlike those stationary nations of Asia and Africa, Augusta was moving forward from her settlement, and was every day the wiser from her past experience. She recognized the benefits and blessings of having had at the opening of her career those earnest, pious, learned teachers among her—the Presbyterian ministers—and after the lapse of a hundred years, she perceived that further efforts were necessary to keep pace with modern progress. Thus she sought, as we have seen, to perfect her communications with every part of the country and the world, by an extensive system of public improvements. Deeper than was even the case with their forefathers, was their conviction now that liberty and morality are both dependent on intelligence ; that the only sure and ultimate guardian of either freedom or virtue is enlightened public opinion ; that such a general illumination of the intellect should take place as would make every man fully aware of the consequences of his actions, and not become, through ignorance, the innocent cause of misery to himself and others. They proposed thus to banish from the face of society the misery that arises from vice and ignorance, which causes war and poverty and other untold evils, and that the empire of justice and benevolence should be extended, so as to open up those true sources of enjoyment when a people seek their own· happiness in a constant endeavor to promote that of their neighbors. These convictions led in 1846 to active movements on the subject of a general system of primary education. Meetings were held in Staunton, at Mt. Carmel, and in other localities, strongly condemning the inefficient plan then in existence as defective and altogether inadequate, and declaring it to be the duty of the Legislature to devise and adopt a general scheme for the education of the indigent children of the Commonwealth.

On the 11th of September, a meeting was held in Staunton to form an Educational Association for the town, auxiliary to a similar Association of the county recently established. At this meeting the late Charles H. Lewis was elected President, in recognition of his earnest efforts in the cause of popular education and of his literary abilities. Mr. Lewis was a poet by no means unworthy of mention. Though his fugitive pieces abounded in defects of execution, and exhibited evident marks of haste, they also exhibited beauties of no ordinary kind. Lyttleton Waddell was chosen Vice-President, having been long successfully associated with the cause of education as Principal of the Staunton Academy, a venerable institution which has turned out some of the first men in Virginia. J. L, Peyton was made Secretary, and Judson McCoy, Treasurer.

A meeting was also held at Greenville, and an Association formed, of which Dr. J. K. Moore was elected President, Dr. Isaac Hall and John Merritt, Vice-Presidents, and Mathew Pilson, Secretary. The many resolutions and addresses adopted and put forth by these and other meetings cannot, however interesting in themselves, for want of room, be here introduced.

RETURN OF THE AUGUSTA VOLUNTEERS.

In August, 1848, this company of Augusta volunteers, after a long and arduous campaign—none the less arduous to the gallant soldiers because confined to guarding fields already won by the valor of others more fortunate than themselves, because earlier on the theatre of operations—returned to Staunton. As soon as the landing of the company at Fortress Monroe was known, our citizens met in public meeting and took measures for giving them a proper reception, as the following correspondence will explain:

"STAUNTON, August 7, 1848.

DEAR SIR : At a public meeting of the citizens of the town of Staunton, and county of Augusta, held in this place on the 4th inst., it was unanimously resolved to tender to you and the officers and men lately under your command in Mexico, a public dinner, and a committee was appointed to make every arrangement for the same.

On behalf of that committee, and the community represented by them, it gives me much pleasure to convey to you, and through you to the officers and men composing your command, their earnest desire that you should partake with them of a public dinner, to be given at this place on Friday next.

The people are grateful to the Mexican volunteers for the sacrifices they have made in defence of the interests and honor of the country, and are anxious to testify in a becoming manner their appreciation of such gallant and patriotic conduct.

They know that while it was not your good fortune to meet the enemy in the field, you endured all the hardships and privations of a soldier's life, and that you enlisted, not for a limited period, but with a determination to remain in the service till the war should be successfully and honorably terminated; and they cannot consent that a favorable opportunity, when you are still together, should pass, without paying a tribute to such distinguished patriotism.

Let me express the hope that you may find it convenient and agreeable to meet your friends and fellow-citizens on the occasion mentioned for showing you this evidence of respect and esteem.

With sentiments of high regard,

Your friend and ob't serv't,

JOHN L. PEYTON."

REPLY.

"STAUNTON, August 7, 1848.

SIR : I have the honor to acknowledge the receipt of your letter of this

date, inviting me and the officers and men of my late command to partake
of a public dinner proposed to be given by the citizens of Staunton and
the county of Augusta on Friday next.

Although I have not the means of conferring generally with those, my
late associates in arms, who are intended to be the objects of this public
manifestation of esteem and regard, I do not doubt that it would be highly
gratifying to them all to have the opportunity of meeting their friends and
fellow-citizens and mingling their gratulations and sympathies around the
festive board, after their long separation.   The invitation therefore is most
cordially accepted.   With high respect,

Your friend and fellow-citizen,

To JOHN L. PEYTON, ESQ.   KENTON HARPER."

In pursuance of these arrangements, large numbers of our town and
county people assembled in Staunton on August 11th, including many
ladies, and, escorted by the Middlebrook Rifles, Capt. Shuey, proceeded
to Ast's Grove, near Staunton.   Here L. Waddell made an appropriate
address of welcome to the officers and men, to which the Captain replied
in befitting terms.   After this a sumptuous dinner was served up, and the
day closed with these festivities.

The Mexican war was concluded February, 1848, by the loss to Mexico
of Texas, California, Utah, and New Mexico.   Previous to this time, there
had been an agitation for a change in the State Constitution.   This movement was now renewed, and resulted in the Convention of 1850.   The
calling of this Convention was opposed, as had been that of 1830, by some
of our wisest and best men.   The party of innovation, or progress, as it
was styled, proved in a majority, and the following delegates were elected
from the county : Col. Geo. Baylor, and Messrs. D. Fultz and H. W. Sheffey.   A new Constitution was framed, submitted to a popular vote, and ratified in 1851.

ANA.

It may not be uninteresting to mention that after the signing of the
treaty of peace in December, 1814, the British fleet, consisting of sixty
sail, appeared off the coast of the Mississippi.   A detachment of 15,000
men were landed, under command of Major-Gen. Sir Edward Packenham,
and on the 8th of January, 1815, attacked the Americans, consisting of
6,000 militia, under Gen Andrew Jackson, before New Orleans.   After an
obstinate engagement, the British were put to flight, with the loss of their
commander, and near 3,000 men killed, wounded and prisoners.   The late
Major-Gen. C. Rochforth Scott, R. A., C. B., Lieut.-Gov. of Guernsey in
1867-1872, author of " Excursions in Egypt and Candia, " The Life of the
Duke of Wellington," &c,, who, when an ensign in the army, was engaged in the battle of New Orleans, informed the writer that the British
officers, who had gone through the wars of Napoleon, declared they had
never faced such a destructive and well-directed fire as that from Jackson's

militia. He also said that after their retreat, the supply of provisions in
the fleet was so small they must all have starved; but for the news of the
treaty of Ghent, received a few days after the battle, which enabled them
to go into the harbor of Mobile, Alabama. In numerous conversations
held by the author with another English friend, Col. Thos. Faunce, of H.
M. 4th foot, whose father commanded that regiment in the battle of New
Orleans, Col. Faunce confirmed Gen. Scott's account, and said it was
almost a miracle the overweening confidence of Gen. Packenham had not
led to the destruction of the entire British force.

CHAPTER XIV.

From the adoption of the new Constitution in 1851, for nearly ten years
little of interest, nothing of importance, occurred in the State or county.
Meanwhile, events taking place in the nation were hastening to a crisis
between the two great sections of the Federal Union. While these events
and disputes were going on, the sudden raid of John Brown aroused an
excitement and created a tumult which startled the Southern people like
" a fire-bell in the night." This raid, which contributed so much to kindle
the flame of civil war, occurred on the night of the 10th of October, 1859,
when Brown and a party of armed men made a sudden descent upon
Harper's Ferry and seized the U. S. Arsenal. On the 18th the arsenal
was recaptured, Brown was taken prisoner, tried for treason, found guilty
and hanged December 2d, 1859. His fate made an extraordinary impression upon the minds of the Northern people, and there was practically
thenceforward only two parties in the country—one, the slavery, and the
other, the anti-slavery party. On the 6th of November, 1860, Abraham
Lincoln was chosen President of the United States, and on the following
4th of March was inaugurated amid a grand display of military. The assemblage of large forces of all arms at Washington was deemed necessary
in view of events transpiring in the South.

On the 4th of February, 1861, the Confederate Government, composed
of the Southern Cotton States which had seceded from the Federal Union,
was formed at Montgomery, Alabama, and Jefferson Davis was on the
same day elected President, and on the 12th-13th of April, Fort Sumter,

S. C., was bombarded, when President Lincoln (15th of April) took the first material step for reducing the rebellious States to obedience by issuing a proclamation calling forth 75,000 militia, in which he "appealed to all loyal citizens to favor, facilitate and aid this effort to maintain the honor, the integrity, and the existence of our National Union." Thus, from a state of perfect tranquility, the country passed into one of war, and the whole land resounded with the noise of armaments, and the treasure of the people was exhausted in vast preparations for hostilities.

In all the Southern border States there was a large Union party, and on this party President Lincoln relied for support—too confidently, as the sequel will show. In the county of Augusta, a great majority of the people opposed secession, and were also opposed to coercion.

The people of Augusta had contributed their all in men and treasure to the formation of the Union, and they believed it still capable of protecting every interest of themselves and the entire country. At this crisis they wished to act in the spirit of moderation and compromise which characterized the framers of the Constitution, and as if the venerable forms of those who bequeathed it to us were "bending down to behold us, from the abodes above, and as if that long line of posterity were also viewing us, whose eye is hereafter to scrutinize our conduct." They felt that no local policy or feeling, no temporary impulse, should cause them to abandon their foothold on the Constitution and the Union, but that, so far as honor would permit, they should exert themselves to the end that these States should continue united—" united in interest and affection, united in war, for the common defence, the common renown, and the common glory, and united, compacted, knit together in peace, for the common prosperity and happiness of themselves and their posterity."

Entertaining these sentiments, and viewing the progress of affairs with painful distrust of the future, the people of the county, after due notice—the sober and solid men—met in Staunton and appointed a committee to consider of the state of affairs, and at a future meeting to report the result of their deliberations. This committee was composed of men to whom the people were in the habit of looking in times of trouble for direction. They were all natives of the county, having a deep property stake in the community, and were of liberal education and of dispassionate minds and conservative characters. The result of their deliberations is contained in the following proceedings:

AUGUSTA COUNTY UNION MEETING.

Pursuant to adjournment, a large meeting of the friends of the Union in the County of Augusta, irrespective of parties, was held in the court-house, at Staunton, on Monday, November 26. 1860, Hon. Alex. H. H. Stuart in the chair, and John L. Peyton acting as secretary.

The committee, composed of the following gentlemen: Hon. A. H. H.

Stuart, H. W. Sheffey, G. K. Harper, J. B. Baldwin, G. B. Stuart, John L. Peyton, John McCue, J. A. Waddell, Robert Guy, J. D. Imboden, Benj. Crawford, G. M. Cochran, jr., and George Baylor, who were appointed at the previous meeting to prepare them, presented the following preamble and resolutions:

The people of Augusta, in general meeting assembled, solemnly impressed with a sense of the danger which instantly threatens the existence of the Government and the Union of the States; cherishing a hereditary loyalty to the Constitution of the United States; citizens of a Commonwealth allied to the south in its domestic institutions, affections and sympathies, but bordering on the north, and, therefore, in immediate contiguity to the perils which may follow a dissolution of the Union; far more vitally concerned in the issues of the conflict between the contending sections of the country than our more southern brethren can possibly be; as deeply aggrieved as they by the recent election of a sectional President; as keenly alive as they to the aggressive tendency of the step just taken. by the north, and as firmly resolved as they to resist infractions of their constitutional rights, yet unwilling to believe the experiment of republican government a failure, deem it to be their privilege, and in view of the important interests at stake, their duty, speaking to the north as well as the south, calmly but firmly, to declare—

1. That the Constitution of the United States, under the protecting power of which the country has become so strong at home and so respected abroad, with checks and balances so wisely adjusted, by which abuses are controlled and grievances are redressed; imperfect it may be in some respects, working badly it may be on some occasions, is nevertheless the easiest yoke of government a free people ever bore, and yet the strongest protector of rights the wisdom of man ever contrived; and so long as it continues to secure our equality and rights as citizens of a common country " in the fullness of its spirit and to the highest extent of its honest interpretation," we will stand by and maintain it.

2. That the Union of these States, still esteemed by them as it was sixty-four years ago by the " Father of his Country," as the " palladium of their political safety and prosperity—as the main pillar in the edifice of their real independence—the support of their tranquility at home, their peace abroad—and of that very liberty which they so highly prize," is, as it has ever been, the object of the unwavering attachment of the people of Augusta; and as for them and their households they will cling to it until the stern command of honor and the conviction that their rights can no longer be preserved under it, shall compel them, in sorrow, to let it go !

3. That the right of each State to form and regulate its own domestic institutions is perfect and complete under the Constitution, and that any organizations or discussions in other States intended to impair that right, or incite forays upon our borders for the purpose of disturbing our peace or robbing us of our property, are flagrant wrongs and breaches of faith inconsistent with the tranquility of the Union.

4. That, apart from the consideration of the question whether, as Virginia declared, in 1798, should be the case, to justify HER in " interposing to arrest the evil " of Federal power, there has yet been, on the part of the General Government, " a deliberate, palpable and dangerous exercise of other powers not granted by the Federal compact," and apart also from the consideration of the right in itself, and the expediency in other

respects of State secession from the Union, it is the opinion of this meet-gin that, bordering, as Virginia does, on that portion of the Confederacy from which danger to the institution of slavery is threatened, so far as her interests in that institution are concerned, secession is no remedy.

5. That sympathizing deeply with their brethren in the extreme south-ern states in their sense of the outrage inflicted on the sentiments of the south by the election of Lincoln; but having still an abiding faith, if not in the sense of justice, in the intelligent self-interest of the American peo-ple; and confiding in the efficacy of constitutional means to protect their rights within the Union, the people of Augusta, as brothers speaking to brothers, bound together by the most sacred ties, beseech the gallant and patriotic people of the cotton states to pause and calmly consider the yet unimagined evils which must result from the dissolution of the Union, and before taking the step, from which there will be no receding, to unite with Virginia in testing the efficiency of remedies provided by the Constitution and within the Union!

6. That not regarding the mere election of any citizen to the Presidency in accordance with the Constitution and the laws as sufficient cause for breaking up the government, and therefore in the spirit of patriotic for-bearance, being willing to yield obedience to the Constitution and to ac-quiesce in the recent decision of the northern people, with no purpose to threaten or intimidate, but speaking as brave men to brave men, appealing to their loyalty to the Constitution and ' the Union, and to their regard for the peace, concord and continued happiness of a united country, the peo-ple of Augusta, who have been wont in times past, as Washington taught them, " indignantly to frown upon the first dawning of every attempt to alienate any portion of our country from the rest, or to enfeeble the sacred ties which bind together the various parts," solemnly declare to the peo-ple of the nonslaveholding states that the vexatious agitation of the sub-ject of slavery in Congress and in the northern communities, the distur-bance of our peace by the dissemination of incendiary documents in the south, the invasions of our rights of property in slaves by emissaries sent into our midst to decoy our slaves from our homes, the disregard by the governors and the people of the nonslaveholding states of their constitu-tional obligations in respect to the rendition of fugitives from service and from justice, the practical nullification by many of their state legislatures of the " Fugitive Slave Law," and the organization and triumph of a sec-tional party, united together by sentiments deemed to be hostile to the south, whose recent victory has been heralded by one high in its ranks as "the death-blow to slavery," constitute such grievances and outrages to the feelings and rights of the people of the south as will, if persisted in, extend over the whole south the fatal sentiment of disunion now so fear-fully on the increase. And the people of Augusta, convinced that there can be no permanent union without a strict adherence to the Constitution and a just enforcement of federative obligations upon the authority and people of the states, think they have a right to ask, nay, respectfully to urge, as essential to continued brotherhood between the north and the south that the people of the nonslaveholding states require their public servants to observe their constitutional obligations to the south, to remove from their statute books the acts intended to thwart, if not to nullify, the act of Congress concerning fugitive slaves, and that they instruct their representatives, as we shall instruct ours, to keep from the halls of Con-gress that bitter apple of national discord—the agitating discussion of slavery.

7. That we cherish the sincerest sympathy and most fraternal regard for those noble and true men in the non-slaveholding states who have battled so gallantly against faction and fanaticism in defence of the Constitution of the country and the rights of the south, and that we are unwilling to desert them, and that we yet hope, with their aid, to beat back the enemies of our peace and bear aloft in triumph, "not a stripe obliterated nor a star obscured," the glorious flag of the Union.

8. That our Senator and delegates be requested, in discharge of the responsible duties which will soon devolve upon them, in the spirit of harmony and conciliation attempted to be expressed in these resolves, to bend all their energies to keep Virginia to her moorings as "the flag-ship of the Union," and to induce her, placed as she is between the north and the extreme south, with moderation, forbearance and wisdom worthy of her ancient renown, to exert her power and influence to preserve on the one hand the known and equal rights of her own people as citizens of a common country, and on the other the harmony of the Union and the integrity of the Constitution; and to this end they are authorized at whatever cost to adopt such measures as their judgments shall approve, to carry out the great work of mediation and pacification, which the people of Augusta invoke the General Assembly of Virginia to undertake.

Mr. J. H. Skinner moved as a substitute the following resolution, which was rejected:

Resolved, In view of the wrongs which have been done to Virginia and her sister southern states by the unconstitutional and unfriendly action of the northern states of the confederacy, growing out of the hostility entertained by them to the institution of domestic slavery, and in consideration of the dangers with which we are threatened by the inauguration of a sectional Republican Administration, elected upon principles which, if carried into action, would be destructive of our equality, our interests and our safety, and injurious to our honor, it is proper and all important, in our judgment, that a convention of delegates of the people of Virginia should be held, at an early day, to consider of the state of the Federal Union, to preserve said Union, if it can be done consistently with our rights under the Constitution, and at all events to protect the State of Virginia from any detriment.

A lengthy discussion took place upon the resolutions, in which the following gentlemen participated: Gen. William H. Harman, Col. John B. Baldwin, R. D. Hill, J. A. Harman, J. H. Skinner, T. J. Michie, Gen. K. Harper, and Dr. E. G. Moorman.

The vote upon the preamble and resolutions was taken seriatim, and they were each and all passed by very large majorities.

On motion, they were ordered to be signed by the president and secretary, and published in the papers of Virginia.

A. H. H. STUART, President.

JOHN L. PEYTON, Secretary.

Though the people of Augusta were warmly attached to the Union, they sympathized deeply with their southern brethren. Standing between the north and south, they considered the occasion one presenting to them the opportunity to reconcile, if possible, all political differences between the two,—differences which they believed subordinate to the public good, and capable of adjustment within the Union and under the Constitution. Accordingly they convened in mass-meeting, as their forefathers had done in May, 1775, under the lead of their wisest and best men—men of temper and judgment, of virtue and prudence, and alike inaccessible to the seductions or menaces of power. The meeting appointed the committee above mentioned ; this committee deliberated, and then came forward to the adjourned meeting, whose proceedings have been above reported with the resolutions adopted, in which the truth was declared without diffidence and without acrimony, but in earnest and energetic terms, which left no mistake as to their position. This was the cool, dispassionate action of the people of Augusta at a period of great excitement, and taken in order if at last driven to extremities they might assume with more decency that attitude of hostility to the government of our fathers which events might render necessary in the interest of their security and happiness.

While our delegates were striving in Richmond and Washington to secure peace and preserve the Union, the President's proclamation, calling forth 75,000 men, brought the people of Augusta to almost entire unanimity. Though they did not believe in secession, they all maintained the right of Revolution, and were now of the opinion that the time for exercising it had come. They indignantly resented the proclamation, coming at the time it did, considered war as rudely and recklessly forced upon them, and they not only accepted the issue, but, inflamed with rage at the insult, they flew to arms. From this time forward there were no Union men in Augusta, and few in Virginia.

The Staunton Artillery, commanded by Capt. J. D. Imboden. and the following officers: Lieuts. T. L. Harman, A. W. Garber, W. L. Balthis and G. W. Imboden ; Sergeants M. C. Garber, J. S. Shumate, U. V. Dabney, P. H. Prostor, W. T. Jewell, Powell Harrison ; Q. M. Sergeant A. H. Fultz ; Corporals P. Hounihan, M. Carmody, A. Weaver, C. Berkeley, W. J. Nelson, T. J. Galt ; Color Sergeant, T. Shumate ; Artificers G. M. Stanton, J. Rohr, J. W. Heiser, G. H. Hudson and C. C. Toothacre proceeded to Harper's Ferry and was attached to Stonewall Jackson's command.

The West Augusta Guard, of Staunton. also marched to that point, with the following officers: Capt. W. S. H. Baylor ; Lieuts. H. K. Cochran, J. H. Waters, J. Bumgardner, W. Blackburn ; Sergeants C. T. Arnall, J. B. Engleman, J. C. Marquis, P. Scherer ; Corporals R. Bucher, P. Maphis, B. Wilson and R. Wilson.

Two companies of cavalry were immediately formed, the first under Capt. Wm. Patrick, which also proceeded to Harper's Ferry, and was attached to the First Regiment of Virginia cavalry. Subsequently, Capt. P. was promoted to be Major of the 11th battalion, and was killed at the second battle of Manassas. The second company was commanded by Capt. F. F. Sterrett, and marched from Churchville to Rich Mountain, and was attached to the 14th regiment, under command of Col. James W. Cochran, of Augusta, (a descendant of the founder.)

Two regiments of volunteer infantry were also raised, the first called the 5th Virginia, the second the 52d Virginia. The 5th regiment was composed mainly of troops from Augusta, and was organized in May, 1861, at Harper's Ferry. The field officers were: K. Harper, Colonel; Wm. H. Harman, Lieut.-Colonel; Wm. S. H. Baylor, Major; and Capt. James Bumgardner, Adjutant. The 5th, with the 2d, 4th, 27th, and 33d regiments formed the First Brigade of Virginia infantry, and was under the command of Col. T. J. Jackson, afterwards the celebrated "Stonewall" Jackson, and acquired the distinction of "Stonewall Brigade" by the gallant fight they made at the first battle of Manassas. Company A. commanded by Capt. J. H. S. Funk, and Company K, commanded by Capt. John Avis, were from Winchester. In the autumn of 1861, Col. Harper resigned; Harman was promoted to be Colonel; Baylor, Lieut.-Colonel; and A. Koiner was assigned to the regiment as Major. At the reorganization, in March, 1862, Maj. Baylor was elected Colonel; Capt. Funk, Lieut.-Colonel; Capt. H. J. Williams, Major; and C. S. Arnall was commissioned Adjutant. After the death of Col. Baylor at the second Manassas, Lieut.-Col. Funk was promoted to Colonel; Maj. Williams to Lieut.-Colonel; and Capt. Jas. W. Newton to be Major. Col. Funk fell at the battle of Winchester, Sept. 19th, 1864. The commandants of companies were: Company B—Rockbridge Rifles—Capt. S. H. Letcher, and was transferred in July, 1861, to the 27th regiment in the same brigade; Company C, Capt. Robert Doyle—after reorganization, Capt. Jacob Trevy; Company D, Capt. H. J. Williams—after reorganization, Capt. McHenry; Company E, Capt. James Newton—after reorganization, Capt. Lycurgus Grills; Company F, Capt. St. Francis Roberts—after reorganization, Capt. Peter Wilson; Company G, Capt. Geo. T. Antrim—after reorganization, Capt. James Gibson: Company H, Capt. Asher W. Harman—after reorganization, Capt. Richard Simms; Company I, Capt. O. F. Grinnan—after reorganization—Capt. E. L. Curtis; Company L, Capt. Jas. H. Waters—after reorganization, Capt. Thos. J. Burke. Capt. Milton Bucher, A. Q. M. and A. C. S.

The second regiment,—the 52d Virginia infantry. This regiment, like the 5th, consisted mainly of Augustians. Two companies, however, were made up of men from Rockbridge. It was officered as follows: Colonel, Jno. B. Baldwin; Lieut.-Colonel, M. G. Harman; Major, J. D. H. Ross; Adjutant, John W. Lewis, of Bath (a descendant of the Founder); Surgeon, Livingston Waddell, M. D.; Assistant Surgeon, John Lewis, M. D., of Albemarle (a descendant of the Founder); Quartermaster, Geo. M. Cochran, jr.; Commissary, B. Christian; Captains of Companies—Wm. Long, E. M. Dabney, J. F. Hottle. J. H. Skinner, Thos. Watkins (Rockbridge),

Samuel McCune, J. C. Lilley, John H. Humphreys, John Miller (Rock-bridge).

In addition to these, there was another company raised in Augusta, called the Augusta Lee Rifles, of which Robt. D. Lilley was captain. The following were the officers; Lieutenants, C. G. Merritt, J. B. Smith, C. Davis; Sergeants, C. D. McCoy, D. B. Wilson, H. Marshall, Jno. Hawpe and Wm. Burns; Corporals, J. B. Wright, J. S. Hawpe, Th. Opie, Jas. Larew; Color-bearer, Jas. Van Lear. It was attached to the 25th regiment. Capt. Lilley lost an arm at Ramseur's stampede, near Winchester, in the autumn of 1864, having previously been raised to the rank of Brigadier-General. He was at the time commanding Pegram's brigade.

Altogether there were sixteen field officers, natives of Augusta, in the Confederate army.

The writer was engaged, in May, in raising a company to form part of a regiment to be styled the West Augusta Rifles. The following notice, published in the "Staunton Vindicator," in May, 1861, shows when the first drill occurred:

"Col. John L. Peyton is now raising a volunteer company to be called the West Augusta Rifles, to be drilled *a la Zouve*. He now has some fifty names enrolled, and will soon have sufficient to organize. Those enrolled received their first drill on Wednesday night last. This promises to be an efficient and useful company, and something new with the military of Virginia."

While thus occupied, he was called to Raleigh, and during a sojourn of a few days there, was not only tendered by the authorities of North Carolina a foreign mission, but was urged to accept it by Gov. Clarke, Hon. D, M. Barringer, and the entire privy council. To this was added the solicitations of ex-Gov. Wm. A. Graham, Gen. Branch and other friends, who pressed his acceptance on the grounds of duty and patriotism. This appointment was accordingly accepted. The Confederate Government placed at his service the man-of-war Nashville, then lying at Charleston, S. C. In this vessel he broke the blockade of Charleston, S. C., in October, 1861, and arrived in England the latter part of the following November.* Meanwhile the men recruited for the Rifles joined other companies.

We cannot follow these Augusta companies and regiments through the war, nor enter into the history of that great strife, which forms one of the most memorable epochs in the history of the world. The circumstances of the times, the character of the people, the issues involved, all conspire

*The incidents of the voyage from Charleston to Bermuda, thence over the stormy deep in Winter to the Azores, the capture and burning of the American packet ship "Harvey Birch," the arrival in Southampton, and some of Colonel Peyton's European experiences and impressions are given in his highly interesting and valuable work entitled, "The American Crisis; or, Pages from the Note-Book of a State Agent During the Civil War in America;" published in two vols 8vo in London in 1865.
                                                                    THE PUBLISHERS.

to render it interesting. The majority of the southern people enlisted in it under a belief that all that was dear to them,—liberty, honor and property,—was involved by an abuse of power and a breach of plighted faith on the part of the north, and by the Federalists for the maintenance at every hazard of the Union and common government founded by our ancestors, and the existence of which they believed they had the constitutional and moral right to preserve at whatever sacrifice of life and treasure. We must however, confine ourselves to events immediately connected with the county—one of the most striking being the battle of Piedmont.

BATTLES OF MT. CRAWFORD AND PIEDMONT.

The first movement made against Lynchburg, in May, 1864, miscarried. The second move by the Federal troops against the Virginia and Tennessee railroad, and for the occupation of Lynchburg, thereby to coöperate with Gen. Grant against Richmond, commenced 31st of May, 1864. Gen. Hunter was placed in command of the Department of West Virginia, and the commands of Gens. Crook and Averill were reorganized for a simultaneous advance on Lynchburg, while Gen. Burbridge, in Kentucky, advanced upon extreme Southwest Virginia. The Confederates were unfavorably situated to oppose their advances. Gen. Breckenridge, with the only Confederate force of importance west of the Blue Ridge, had been withdrawn to the army of Gen. Lee, leaving nothing but a few small brigades of cavalry, about two regiments of infantry, and a small brigade made up of dismounted troops, acting as infantry. To supply the place of Gen. Breckenridge, the little force of Gen. McCausland was sent from Dublin Station to the front of Staunton, and Gen. W. E. Jones was ordered to take all the troops which he could gather in Southwestern Virginia to the same point. Gen. J. accordingly got together all the Confederate troops west of New river, dismounted the cavalry, and moved to Staunton. His force was greatly inferior to that of the enemy, but what was wanting in numbers was made up in valor. Meanwhile the Federals were proceeding with their general plan, and Hunter moved from Cedar creek, near Woodstock, early in June, against Staunton. Confederate sharpshooters harassed his march, and frequently destroyed his communications. He advanced, however, to Harrisonburg, and on leaving that place divided his force into two columns—one of which took the road to Port Republic and the other direct to Staunton. The movement to Port Republic was a demonstration against the Confederate right, and it encountered a movement of Gen. Jones against the Federal left. At the same time the main body of Federals advanced to the North river, twelve miles from Staunton. A hot engagement ensued at this point, called the battle of Mount Crawford, but the Confederates were forced, by superior numbers, to fall back and, to avoid Gen. Crook's Federal force, advancing from the west, continued their retreat to Waynesborough. A conflict

30 ‡

also occurred at Piedmont, near New Hope, between the Federal left and the Confederate right, in which the Confederates were overpowered and driven back with severe loss. The following account of this affair was derived from conversations held with several who participated in the engagement. The Confederate cavalry, under Imboden, but a handful of veteran troopers, had been falling back before an overwhelming Federal force until the 4th of June. On that day they reached the North river, where they halted, and the ground being favorable, prepared to give battle. Gen. Jones, the Confederate general in command, came up from the south during the night with reinforcements, consisting, principally, of the reserves of Augusta and the adjoining counties—these reserves being, mainly, boys and convalescent soldiers. On the morning of the 5th of June the Federal force advanced upon the Confederate position near Mt. Crawford, and a hot engagement occurred, during which the boys and cripples held their ground and kept back the enemy. Unable to drive the Confederates from the field, the Federal General ordered a flank movement. Their long anaconda line was soon seen stretching out to the right and left with a view to envelope the Spartan band in its deadly embrace. Gen. Jones saw no alternative but a retrograde movement, and commenced falling back. When the Confederates reached Piedmont, a hamlet two miles north of New Hope, Gen. Jones halted, and formed his troops in line of battle. The Augusta officers in the force, knowing the country better than the General, urged a further retreat to Mowry's Hill. This was a short distance south of New Hope, and a very strong position, where it was believed a successful defence might be made. The General, however, declined this advice, and kept his ground. The Federal force was soon in the Confederate front, advancing in that cool, dogged and deliberate manner so characteristic of the Yankee, and this force was composed almost entirely of native troops. The Confederate cavalry was drawn up ready for battle by Capt. Frank B. Berkeley, of Staunton, acting brigade adjutant. It was ordered to advance, and did so at a gallop, the blooded horses bounding lightly over ditches, fences and every obstruction. They rushed upon the Federal cavalry like an avalanche, sabering the officers and men and driving them from the field like chaff before the angry winds. As the enemy's cavalry broke and fled the Confederate troopers found themselves confronted by long unbroken lines of Federal infantry, and retired. The Federals continued their dogged advance in line of battle. When a short distance from the Confederate lines, they halted to gather breath, and after a little rest, during which many were shot down, they advanced in the face of a destructive fire, and made a fierce attack on our lines. The Confederates behaved like veterans—the boys emulating the example of their sires, those old heroes who had been so hewed and hacked to pieces during the war that there was now nothing whole about

them but their hearts. Incredible as it may seem, this force repelled the
enemy's attack, driving them back broken and confused, like the waves
which dash impotently against the rocks. The Yankees halted at the
point from which they made their last advance, stunned and astounded.
Not dispirited, however, they closed up their ranks and moved forward a
second time—not with Confederate impetuosity, but with the same deliberate, sullen determination which belongs to that eminently bull-dog race.
They were again driven back with much slaughter. Once more the Yankees formed in close order, and a third time advanced to the attack. This
time they brought up their reserves. These fresh troops were directed to
the weak point in the Confederate lines,—the left wing,—which was decimated by a withering fire kept up by these cold-blooded Federals, whose
guns seemed never empty, however frequently fired.* The Confederates
finding longer resistance impossible, began a retreat—gray-headed cripples, one-armed convalescents and young boys retiring slowly, loading and
firing as they fell back, and thus preventing a panic and rout. The retreat
was continued to Fishersville. The infantry was aided in getting off by
the gallant conduct of two young artillery officers, both natives of Augusta,
who deserve special mention. These young officers were Lieutenants
Carter Berkeley and H. H. Fultz, both in command of sections of Mc-
Clenechan's horse artillery of two guns each. When they saw the left
wing of Jones' force fall back, heard of the death of Jones himself, and
saw the right give way in confusion, they advanced without orders to the
front. Here they took up a position with their guns on either side of the
highway, opposite the centre of that imperturbable mass of phlegmatic
Yankees, which was still advancing with a slow pace and determined air.
Acting on their own impulses, Berkeley and Fultz now opened fire on the
host in their front, cutting wide gaps in the Federal lines and retarding
their advance. The enemy, seeing the desperate conduct of these batteries unsupported by infantry, ordered the First New York Cavalry to spike
the rebel guns. This fine regiment of Knickerbockers advanced at full
speed. As they galloped up the guns plowed wide gaps in their ranks,
hurling horses and riders to the ground. This did not stop them. On the
troopers came, sabreing men right and left. Reaching the batteries, a free
fight occurred over the cannon, but some Confederate sharp-shooters, who
lay in ambush, brought down such numbers of horsemen that the regiment retreated, or rather those who survived, without carrying out their
orders to spike the guns. These well-directed guns continued to scatter
death in the Federal ranks, and Imboden coming up with more sharp-
shooters, the Federal advance was further delayed. During the time these
two batteries, supported by a few hundred Augusta riflemen, kept back
the northern host, the Confederate fragments of an army made good its

*Many were armed with Winchester rifles, which fire thirty times before it is necessary to reload.

retreat without confusion or panic. This object secured, Berkeley and Fultz also retired with the sharp-shooters. The Federals, on reaching the ground so recently occupied by the Confederates, called a halt, buried their dead, lit their camp-fires, and gave up the pursuit until the following morning.

The Confederates from the county of Augusta engaged in this action were Imboden's cavalry; G. W. Imboden's regiment of infantry—the 18th Virginia; Harper's Reserves—one company commanded by Jas. C. Marquis, composed of boys from sixteen to eighteen years of age; one company commanded by John N. Opie, also composed of boys and old men; one battery of flying artillery commanded by John H. McClenechan; one battery of two guns, commanded by Lieut. Carter Berkley; and one of two guns, commanded by H. H. Fultz.

The distinguished Confederate officers killed were: Wm. E. Jones, General in command; Col. Brown, commanding 60th Virginia regiment; Lieut.-Col. Robt. L. Doyle, Capt. J. M. Templeton.

The list of the killed and wounded in Harper's regiment at the battle was as follows:

Company A—Capt. Hardy—wounded, Lieut. Steinbuck, Lieut. Wright, and D. H. Snyder.

Company B—Killed, Capt. R. L. Doyle, Jno. Meredith; wounded, Sergeant Helms, G. F. Myerley, Wm. Cason.

Company C—Killed, Capt. J. M. Templeton; wounded, Corporal A. H. Lackey, Jas. Welch, A. H. Hanger, Jas. Mitchell.

Company D—Capt. Peck, commanding—none killed; wounded, Wm. J. Rush; captured, Sam'l Hunter.

Company E—Capt. J. N. Opie; killed, —— McKamy; wounded, —— McCormick.

Company F—Capt. Rippetoe—none killed; wounded, Capt. Rippetoe, A. Staubus, J. Brown.

Company G—Capt. Byrd—none killed; wounded, Lieut. J. A. Syms, Chas. Ridgway, Wm. L. Kyser.

Company H—Capt. Hilbert—killed, Jos. Granitto; wounded, Robt. Birtreit, mortally; Jas. Locker, W. Kerford, W. Reswick, Harmon J. Lohr.

Company I—Capt. Bacon—killed, First Serg't W. W. Moore; wounded, Taylor Coffman, Jos. Baldwin, Chas. Schendle, Thos. Walls, Jno. Smith.

Company K—Lieut. Blue in command, who was killed; wounded, Sergeant Binford; captured, Sergeants Taylor and T. Wilson, Jno. Roebuck, J. Williams, P. McCormick, Jno. Henry, Wm. Evans, Jno. Condor, Thos. Bonworth, Thos. Kelly, Jas. Hackett, Hy. Kress, R. W. Goodman and Wm. Kenney.

In this connection, the brief but interesting letter of Thos. L. Doyle, late Principal of the Virginia Institution for the education of the Deaf, Dumb, and of the Blind, at Staunton, will be read with interest:

INSTITUTION DEAF, DUMB, AND THE BLIND, }
May 18, 1882. }

MY DEAR COLONEL: The main body of the troops that fought the battle of Piedmont (on the Confederate side) marched over from the Valley turnpike during the night, between the 4th and 5th of June, crossing the Middle River, I believe, at the ford near the residence of Maj. Walker (deceased).

Imboden's headquarters on the night of June 4th were at Col. Samuel D. Crawford's house ("Bonnie Doon"), four miles below New Hope. The Federal troops came up the Port Republic road, Stahl commanding the cavalry. Frank Imboden, a captain of one of the troops composing the 18th Virginia cavalry (Geo. W. Imboden's regiment), was captured in the turnpike, below Mt. Meridian, during a hand-to-hand contest.

Just before Gen. Jones received his death-wound, he remarked to Capt. Walter K. Martin, his Adjutant-General, that Hunter's army was desperately beaten, and he desired McNeill, the partisan, to be ordered to fall upon his rear.

My father, Col. Brown, of the 60th Virginia infantry, and Gen. Jones, were killed very near to each other, and were buried side by side in a grass lot in the hamlet of Piedmont. My father was shot through the head, the ball entering the cheek and coming out at the base of the skull. He was perfectly conscious after receiving this wound—was set against a tree by his men, and was bayonetted by the Yankees when they came up.

Before the army got to New Hope, a scant two miles away, the rout and panic became universal, save among the artillery. The defile of New Hope—a long, straggling village, was choked with broken infantry, reserves, cavalry, wagons, &c. · The enemy's horse were preparing to charge, which accomplished, would have been the ruin of Jones' broken remnant. Several squadrons, with this view, rode out of the woods southeast of the Tunker church, and formed a column, with troop front, to make the charge. Lieut. Carter Berkeley, commanding a section of McClenechan's battery, saw this movement, and promptly tearing down the fence, moved his two pieces into the field to the west of the road and opened upon this cavalry while in the act of forming. Two or three discharges ran them off, and active pursuit stopped.

This is about what I told you this morning, but I thought it would be more satisfactory to you to have it in this shape.

Very truly yours,

COL. J. LEWIS PEYTON.   T. J. DOYLE.

P. S.—I lost a brother, Robert M. Doyle, at the second battle of Manassas. He was in the seventeenth year of his age, and was one of the color-guard of the 5th regiment.

The Federal loss was 250 killed. Staunton was immediately occupied. The woolen factory of Crawford & Young was burnt, the Staunton steam-mill, the steam distillery, Confederate Government workshops, the stables and house used for storing forage, the stables of Trotter and twenty-six coaches, the railway stations, etc. The railway track was destroyed at intervals to Goshen, with the fine bridges at Swoope's, Craigsville, and Goshen—also the culverts and small bridges. East of Staunton they tore up the track to Christian's Creek, bending the rails, and burning the bridges at the creek and at Fishersville. They broke open and plundered the shops and stores in Staunton, destroyed the shoe factory and newspaper offices, throwing the type of the "Spectator" into the streets.

On the 10th of June the consolidated columns of Gen. Hunter marched from Staunton through Middlebrook to Lexington. Three miles from Staunton, on the Middlebrook road, the Confederates, under Gen. Mc-Causland, were posted behind rail breastworks, designed to delay the Federal advance. They were dislodged by the Federals, and driven ahead. Seventeen miles from Staunton the Confederates made a halt and killed a few Federals, when they were dispersed by cavalry. On the 11th the enemy reached Lexington. We cannot follow them further.

SECOND INVASION OF AUGUSTA.

The most energetic steps were taken to meet another invasion of the county, as appears from the following Circular of the Enrolling Officer of the county of Augusta and the Eleventh Conscription District. See the "Vindicator" of Sept. 23d, 1864:

CIRCULAR No. 12.

In obedience to Circular No. 20, Bureau of Conscription, Sept. 9, 1864, County Officers and Advisory Boards are required to proceed at once and with unremitting vigor to make a registration of all persons between the ages of sixteen and fifty years in their respective counties. This registration will include all exempts from any cause whatever—detailed conscripts, detailed soldiers and foreigners. The registration of youths who will attain the age of seventeen during the next twelve months must be accurately made. Local officers and Advisory Boards are impressed with the importance of registration, and they will devote their entire time and attention to the work till completed. The registration must be completed in each county before the 1st day of October, and the papers returned to this office not later than Oct. 5th, 1864.

CHARLES S. PEYTON, Lieut.-Col.,
Enrolling Officer for Eleventh District of Va.

It was these drastic measures which caused Gen. Grant, when informed of them, to say, with singular phraseology, that the Confederate Government, in order to uphold its cause, "was robbing both the cradle and the grave."

As the people anticipated from the enemy's movements in the neighborhood of Winchester, the Federals advanced, in the month of September, 1864, up the Valley, under Sheridan. His force consisted of the Sixth Federal army corps, 12,000; Nineteenth corps, 9,000; Crooks' corps, 12,000; three divisions of cavalry, 10,000; artillery, 2,000; with twenty-two batteries of six guns each, or a total force of 45,000 men. Opposed to them was the force under Gens. Early and Breckenridge of 20,000 infantry, with fourteen batteries of artillery of six guns each, and an estimated cavalry force of 3,000. On the 22d of September was fought the battle of Fishersville, where the Confederates were in position, and from which they retired with a loss of 1,100 prisoners.

Sheridan pushed on to Staunton, where all the public property was destroyed, including the railroad and two factories. Sheridan's cavalry proceeded to Waynesboro for the purpose of destroying the iron railroad bridge there and of burning all the barns and mills in that portion of Augusta. In the meantime, the force of Gen. Early had retreated through Brown's Gap, with their wagon trains, but on learning of the operations of the Federal cavalry, Kershaw's division of infantry and Fitzhugh Lee's division of cavalry were ordered to march in their rear and cut off the command of Gen. Torbert, at Waynesboro. The Federal General, however, having ravaged the country with fire, retreated during the night by way of Staunton, and by the celerity of his movements, escaped. Gen. Sheridan reported to Gen. Grant, October 7th, from Woodstock, that "The whole country, from the Blue Ridge to the North Mountain, had been made untenable for a rebel army. I have destroyed over two thousand barns filled with wheat, hay, and farming implements; over seventy mills filled with wheat and flour; four herds of cattle have been driven before the army, and not less than three thousand sheep have been killed and issued to the troops. A large number of horses have been obtained, a proper estimate of which I cannot now make. Lieut. Jno. R. Meigs, my engineer officer, was murdered beyond Harrisonburg, near Dayton. For this atrocious act, all houses within an area of five miles were burned."

Such was the account given by Sheridan of his operations in Augusta and the Valley. A correspondent, who was with the army, thus describes the scenes of their march:

"The atmosphere, from horizon to horizon has been black with the smoke of a hundred conflagrations, and at night a gleam, brighter and more lurid than sunset, has shot from every verge. The orders have been to destroy all forage in stacks and barns, and to drive the stock before them (the Federal army) for the subsistence of the army. * * Indiscriminating (for with such swift work discrimination is impracticable), relentless, merciless, the torch has done its terrible business in the Valley. Few barns and stables have escaped. The gardens and corn-fields have been desolated. The cattle, hogs, sheep, cows, oxen, nearly five thousand in all, have been driven from every farm. The wailing of women and children, mingling with the crackling of flames, has sounded from scores of dwellings. I have seen mothers, weeping over the loss of that which was necessary to their children's lives—setting aside their own—their last cow, their last bit of flour pilfered by stragglers, the last morsel they had in the world to eat or drink. Young girls, with flushed cheeks, and pale, with tearful, or tearless eyes, have pleaded with and cursed the men whom the necessities of war have forced to burn the dwellings reared by their fathers, and turn them into paupers in a day. The completeness of the desolation is awful. Hundreds of nearly starving people are going North. Our trains are crowded with them. They line the wayside. Hundreds more are coming. Absolute want is in mansions used in other days to extravagant luxury."

The desolation of the Shenandoah Valley was thus sketched at the time:

"We have conversed with an intelligent friend, who formerly resided at Edinburg, in Shenandoah county, and who has been compelled to bring his family into a more favored locality, to keep them from starving, and he gives a deplorable picture of the sufferings and privations of these unfortunate people. But a small amount of grain is in possession of the inhabitants, and what little they have it is hardly possible to get ground for want of mills, all having been burned except five or six, in the extent of country of which we speak. In many instances corn has been pounded, baked, and consumed in a rough state, and our informant states that he is familiar with instances where the people have mixed middlings with bran and baked it into bread, in order to stretch the food. Cattle, hogs and sheep have been swept away, and but few horses remain with which to cultivate the ground and raise a crop the present season. It is hard to realize and believe that such a state of things exist, but it is nevertheless fearfully true."

Another says: "With the exception of small enclosures of one or two acres, here and there, there is scarcely a fence worthy of the name from the Rapidan to Bull Run; and the fields, once the pride of the farmers' hearts, and shut in by "ten rails and a rider," are now broad commons, with old landmarks obliterated, ditches filled up, quarters, corn-houses and barns in ruins, while the lone and blackened chimneys of the once happy homestead stand like some grim old sentries on guard until the last. The once majestic forests of oak, hickory, chesnut and pine along the line of the Orange & Alexandria Railroad have disappeared, and given place to the rude huts and cabins improvised by the armies of Lee and Meade: and instead of whortleberries, chinquepins and chestnuts, one kicks upon canteens, worn-out knapsacks, old shoes, bread-boxes, suggestive of the inevitable "hard-tack," bayonet-scabbards, with here and there a stand of grape, a ten-pounder Parrott shell, and everywhere almost the hollow-base "little Minnies," whose whistling tones are so familiar to us all. The village of Raccoonford is a village no longer; Stevensburg is Stevensburg only on the military map; and all along the route, crossing and recrossing the railroad, one sees nothing where man's agency is concerned but utter desolation. The people are returning to their once happy homes, after such hardships as only refugees can know, and are patching up any outbuildings at hand for a temporary residence until the "great house" can be rebuilt and former comforts collected around them. The negroes in Orange county can be hired for their food and quarters; but this does not pertain in Culpepper and Fauquier, where labor is scarce and in demand, as nearly every negro,—man, woman and child, left home early in the war with the hope of an improved condition in the crowded streets of Alexandria and Washington. The supply, however, will be equal, and perhaps more than equal, to the demand, when the farmers are once more prepared to cultivate their lands; but just now there is a feeling of oppressive uncertainty hanging over every man's head, and until courts are established, magistrates, sheriffs, surveyors, commissioners, etc., are appointed, this feeling will prevail, and tend materially to retard the development of the agricultural resources of the country and of that desire to do their duty as good and loyal citizens, which is the sincere and hearty wish of nine-tenths of the people of Virginia, now that the terrible struggle is over, and which has been decided finally against them. The farmers need nearly every article necessary to a successful cultivation of their lands, and with but very limited means for purchasing them, no credit, and an entirely new system of labor to contend with, the problem of success seems to be one of difficult solution ; but with industry, skill and integrity, the prolific soil will soon supply their wants, and in a few years one will scarcely be able to recognize this as the classic battle-ground of the two celebrated armies of the Potomac and Northern Virginia."

In a preceding page the reader has had a brief sketch of the inhuman cruelties inflicted on the settlers by the red men. In this chapter we have allowed the Federals to tell their own story—the story of their devastations and cruelties in the Valley. These wanton acts surpass in barbarity those of Turenne in the Palatinate two hundred years ago, when lust and rapine walked hand in hand with fire and sword. If the glory of Turenne was stained by these cruelties and his reputation as a soldier merges into that of a monster, what must posterity think of a captain whose career is unmarked by victories, and whose fame rests solely upon his success in turning a garden into a desert, so that, to use his own coarse figure, "A crow flying over the Valley must take rations with him." The truth and the whole truth of Sheridan's barbarous rapacity and unfeeling violence has not been told, nor does our space admit of its being done here, but to find anything approaching it we must go beyond the age of Dubois and Turenne, of Wallenstein and Tilly, and search for the like among the annals of the fierce barbarians of the north of Europe or the savages of America ; to the records of those rude tribes who, without religion, education, science or art, gloried in horrible devastations and incredible murders. Like the Huns, Sheridan ravaged and destroyed all around him ; made no distinction between what was sacred and what was profane, respected no age, sex or rank, and converted the most fertile and populous region of the south,—the " Garden of America,"—into a desert in which the women and children—there were no men remaining—were left to starve in sight of their burning barns, smouldering granaries and demolished mills. Avenging his failures in the field upon innocent women and children, Sheridan imitated the barbarity of the Goths and Vandals, and has rendered his memory detestable by abusing the rights of conquest in doing violence to humanity and destroying the monuments of industry and art.

But no oppression, no destitution, could break the spirit of the people of the Valley, or abate their zeal. Men came forward to fill the ranks of the army as if from the funeral pyre and from out the heaps of ruins. The government, too, was undismayed, and President Davis declared in his message to Congress, about this time, that " peace is impossible without independence." But we cannot linger over matters of general history.

The surrender of Lee, April 9, 1865, and the disappearance of the Confederate army, left Virginia desolated, her people impoverished, the civil authorities powerless and at the mercy of the Federals. General Halleck

31 ‡

took command of Richmond, and refused to recognize any official authority in the State officers elected during the war.

On May 9th, President Johnson issued a proclamation recognizing F. H. Pierpont, who was originally elected Governor of West Virginia, and upon the organization of a State government for that district, under the name of West Virginia, moved the seat of his government to Alexandria. During the existence of this government at Alexandria, a legislature was elected, designated the Legislature of Virginia. On the 26th of May, Gov. Pierpont removed the government to Richmond, and regarding his government as the restored State government, he proceeded to exercise authority accordingly. The people of Augusta accepted in good faith this government, and lent themselves cheerfully to its support, and the war being over, returned once more to the pursuits of peace.

CHAPTER XV.

The clouds of civil strife dispelled, the people of Augusta resolutely addressed themselves to the work of repairing the damages resulting from the war. The heroism and genius displayed by the people of Augusta and the south during hostilities, astonishing and unequalled as they were, seem destined to be eclipsed by a more brilliant career in peace. During the seventeen years which have elapsed since the battle of Appomattox bridge, results have been obtained in our county which fill one with unbounded astonishment. Trade has revived and is flourishing; a load of private debt has been discharged, and the county is altogether without debt; fences and enclosures have reappeared of a more permanent and substantial character; old fields have been reclaimed and new ones been brought into cultivation; improved agricultural machinery and a more intelligent system of husbandry have been introduced, which has increased the yield per acre, and added largely to our individual and aggregate wealth. Some of our iron and other ores are being mined, and the public attention been directed to our vast mineral resources. In every part of the county new, handsome and durable buildings have been erected, and in Staunton more substantial and elegant houses have gone up than during any previous fifty years of the town's history. A wise man has said that the farmer is a continuous benefactor. He who digs a well, constructs a stone fountain, plants a grove of trees by the road side, plants an orchard, builds a durable house, reclaims a swamp, or so much as puts a stone seat by the wayside, makes the land so far lovely and desirable, makes a fortune which he cannot carry away with him, but which is useful to his country long afterwards. These substantial buildings enhance the value of the soil and create an attachment for the family residence. " Those who have been accustomed to poetry, ancient or modern, need not be told how finely and how impressively the household gods, the blazing hearth, the plenteous board, and the social fireside, figure in poetical imagery. And this is not tying up nonsense for a song." They are realities of life in its most polished states; they are among its best and most rational enjoyments; they associate the little family community in parental and filial affection and duty, in which even the well-clothed child feels its importance, claims and duties.

The amount of attachment to the family mansion furnishes the criterion of the relative amount of virtue in the members of a family. If the head of a family should wander from the path of paternal duty, and become addicted to vicious habits, in proportion as his virtue suffers a declension a love of his home and family abates, until any place, however base and corrupting it may be, is more agreeable to him than his once sweet home. If a similar declension in virtue happens on the part of the maternal chief of the family mansion, the first effect of her deviation from the path of maternal virtue is that " her feet abideth not in her own house." The same observations apply to children. When a young man or woman, instead of manifesting a strong attachment to the family mansion, is " given to outgoing " to places of licentious resort, their moral ruin may be said to be at no great distance.

Architecture is of use even in the important province of religion. Those who build no houses for themselves, build no temples for the service of God, and of course derive the less benefit from the institutions of religion. The very aspect of those sacred edifices,—churches,—fills the mind of the beholder with a religious awe, and as to the most believing and sincere, it serves to increase the fervor of devotion. Patriotism is augmented by the sight of the majestic forum of justice, the substantial highway, and the bridge with its long succession of ponderous arches. Rome and Greece would no doubt have fallen much sooner had it not been for the patriotism inspired by their magnificent public edifices. But for these, their histories would have been less complete and lasting than they have been. To express the idea in a few words, these fine private mansions and public edifices imply the evolution of a highly organized man brought to supreme delicacy of sentiment; are the evidences of an advancing on an advanced civilization, and of the growth of a nation after its own genius. They indicate a mysterious progress. Brutes make no progress; the savage red men are becoming extinct, not civilized; the negro of to-day in Africa is the negro of Herodotus. The effect of a brick or stone house is immense on the tranquility, power and refinement of the builder. A man in a cave or in a camp, a nomad, will die with no more estate than the wolf or the horse leaves. But so simple a labor as a house being achieved, his chief enemies are kept at bay. He is safe from the teeth of wild animals, from frost, sunstroke and weather, and fine faculties begin to yield their rich harvest; invention and art are born, manners and social beauty and delight. The builders of these durable edifices belong to the class of men who have left the world better than they found it, and their names deserve to be held in remembrance. Where there are so many substantial and elegant buildings, as in Staunton, they cannot be mentioned. The most worthy of enumeration beyond the city limits, but near the city, and they give animation, grace and beauty to the suburbs, are—

1. Montgomery Hall, a mile south of the city, and built by the Hon. John H. Peyton, in 1822-'24, from plans presented him by President Jefferson. The Hall is in a style between the Doric and Corinthian, combining the strength of the former with the delicacy of the latter, and marked for its harmony of proportion and beauty of detail.

2. Oak Grove, built in the early English style, about 1810, by the late Jacob Kinney, Esq.

3. Gaymont, built in the same style, by the late John McDowell, Esq.

4. Wheatlands, built in the same style, by the late William Poage, Esq.

5. Bear–Wallow, built in the Gothic style, by Judge David Fultz.

6. Selma, built in the Grecian style, by the late Simpson F. Taylor, Esq.

7. Spring farm house, built in 1777-'80, by Hessian prisoners, and added to by Judge John Brown.

8. Steep-hill, built by J. Lewis Peyton, in the Gothic or Villa-Romana style.

9. Bellevue, built by J. Emmet Guy, Esq.

10. Fair-View Villa, built by William F. Ast, Esq.

11. Edgewood, built by Joseph P. Ast, Esq.

12. Killarney, built by A. M. Bruce, Esq.

13. Glendale, built in the early English style by the late Silas Smith, Esq., on the eastern slope of Betsy Bell.

AUGUSTA AGRICULTURAL SOCIETY.

Shortly after the close of the civil war, an important step was taken to revive our agricultural interests, and a society was formed, the objects and purposes of which the following sketch will explain:

SKETCH OF THE ORIGIN, PROGRESS AND PRESENT CONDITION OF THE BALDWIN-AUGUSTA FAIR.

Our wisest and best citizens in the past, recognizing the importance of agriculture to all the substantial interests of mankind, at an early period in the present century, sought to encourage a more intelligent and scientific mode of cultivation and improvement in the county, by means of united action, and a free interchange of opinions and experiences. Regarding agriculture as the foundation upon which the fabric of our social, moral, and political institutions are based, and upon which they must ever depend for support and prosperity, they organized, in Staunton, on the 8th of November, 1811, " The Augusta Agricultural Society." They sought by this association to increase the pleasures as well as the profits of rural labor, to enlarge the sphere of useful knowledge, and by concentrating their energies, to give to them greater effect in advancing the public good. The promoters of this movement were General Robert Porterfield, who was elected President, Alexander Nelson, James Bell, John H. Peyton, Chapman Johnson, Jno. Brown, Wm. Boys, Thomas Jackson, and James McNutt, who were officers of the society. Little is known of the history of this association beyond its organization, as the file of " The Republican Farmer," the only newspaper then published in Staunton, has not been preserved, but the society probably expired during the exciting scenes of the war of 1812-1815. Every praise, however, is due to the enlightened men who inaugurated the movement, and sought to promote the public good by dedicating a portion of their time and labor to the advancement of the art of theoretical and practical agriculture—in the success of which the welfare of the community is so deeply involved. And it is much to be regretted that such distinguished examples have not been more generally followed. Notwithstanding the acknowledged strides which agriculture has since made in this county and the State, yet no science has been slower in its progress towards perfection; and even admitting numberless existing instances of intelligent and spirited management among farmers of the higher class, it is still an endeniable fact that the great mass of men are of a very opposite description. Thus it is that the average product of Virginia has fallen below that of other States of less natural fertility and less favored by climate. To remedy this evil by spreading abroad that knowledge which is power, a new generation of public-spirited citizens united together about thirteen years since, in the creation of another association as a means of developing the resources of the county and promoting thrift among the people. The leading spirits in this new movement were Cols. John B. Baldwin and Asher W. Harman, James Henderson, Geo. T. Antrim, Philip O. Polmer and others who undertook the task of forming the Augusta County Fair and prosecuted the design to ultimate success.

The General Assembly of which Col. Baldwin was the then Speaker, on the 15th of January, 1867. passed the act for its incorporation. This act is given in full, as it briefly and clearly sets forth the objects and purposes sought to be secured by its originators.

1. Be it enacted by the General Assembly, that the Court of Augusta county, when the justices thereof are next assembled to lay the county levy, shall choose ten citizens of the county to be " Directors of the Augusta County Fair," and shall divide them by lots into five classes, one of which shall go out of office at the expiration of each year. At the same

term in each year thereafter, the said Court shall fill all vacancies in the said Directory. If a vacancy occurs by expiration of a term, the appointment shall be for five years, but in all other cases for the unexpired term, so as to keep up the regular succession by classes.

2. The Directors so appointed shall be a corporation by the name of the Augusta County Fair, for the purpose of establishing and conducting fairs and other exhibitions of the natural and industrial products of Augusta county, as a means of developing the resources of the county and of promoting enterprise, industry, economy and thrift among the people.

3. The Directory shall, from its own number, choose a President of the corporation. They shall pass rules whereby citizens of Augusta county, on contributing one hundred dollars each to the permanent endowment of the corporation, may become life corporators of the Augusta County Fair. Whenever there shall be at least one such corporator for every two hundred inhabitants of the county, as shown by the next preceding census, the lists shall be certified by the Directory to the Court of Augusta county, who shall cause the same to be entered of record; whereupon elections of Directors by the Court shall cease, and thereafter the said corporators shall be the constituent body, from whom and by whom shall be chosen the Directors of the corporation, to fill vacancies, and to keep up the successions as hereinbefore provided.

4. Elections for Directors by the corporators shall be held at the regular annual fair. The voting shall be viva voce, and a plurality of votes shall elect in any case. In all other respects the elections shall be conducted, certified and determined as the rules shall prescribe.

5. The Court of Augusta county, in laying the county levy for any year, may provide a fund, not exceeding five cents for each inhabitant of the county, as shown by the next preceding census; and the Council of the town of Staunton may, in the same manner, provide a fund, subject to a like limitation, to be paid over in each case to the Augusta County Fair, and to be expended in suitable prizes to be offered at the fairs or other exhibitions conducted by the corporation.

6. This act shall be in force from its passage, and shall be subject to modification or repeal, at the pleasure of the General Assembly.

ACTION OF THE COUNTY COURT.

In accordance with the provisions of this act, the County Court, at its June term, 1867, chose ten citizens of the county to be Directors of the Fair, and divided them into five classes, to go out of office annually, as follows:

1st Class—John B. Baldwin and A. W. Harman.
2nd   "   —James Henderson and G. T. Antrim.
3rd   "   —J. M. McCue and P. O. Polmer.
4th   "   —S. B. Finley and James Walker.
5th   "   —W. A. Burke and W. M. Tate.

FIRST MEETING OF THE DIRECTORS.

The Directors thus appointed and classified by the County Court held their first meeting on the 29th of June, 1867, and elected Col. John B. Baldwin, President, and Major J. Hotchkiss, Secretary. Col. Baldwin immediately entered upon the discharge of his duties, and continued in them until his untimely death in 1873. On this melancholy occasion, the Directors paid a handsome tribute to his memory and his successful labors in establishing the Fair, remarking that, "Wholly unaided, almost without sympathy from any quarter in the then depressed condition of the popular heart, Col. Baldwin, whilst in the Legislature, and Speaker of the House, introduced and carried forward to its enactment the charter of incorporation. But this was much the least of his labors. The pinch was to raise the necessary funds. In the existing condition of affairs and of men's minds, it was a difficult task to awaken and keep alive an interest in almost any enterprise. But when this interest was to be at once and prospectively taxed with money contributions, there were few men with nerve to undertake a task so apparently hopeless.

" We believe John B. Baldwin was the only man in Augusta county who could have carried such a project through to a successful issue.

" The Board. therefore, upon a review of the past seven years, say emphatically that John B. Baldwin was the father and founder of the Augusta County Fair. That it was born of his love for his native county, was cherished by him in their interest, that he gave to it his time and talents and means. That he wrote for it, spoke for it, and worked for it, in season and out of season, believing that it would do more than any other instrumentality to cherish and advance the interest of agriculture and the mechanic arts and household arts not only in Augusta, but ultimately, in the State at large."

CHANGE OF NAME.

As a further acknowledgement of his great efforts on behalf of the fair, the directory, after his death, applied to the General Assembly to have the name of the "father and founder" of the fair indissolubly associated with it, and that body by act approved January 20th, 1874, provided that the name of the Augusta County Fair "shall be and the same is hereby changed to the name of the Baldwin-Augusta Fair."

SUBSEQUENT MEETINGS.

At a meeting of the directory on the 29th of June, 1867, a committee was appointed to prepare rules and regulations for the permanent organization and government of the corporation ; also, to select and report on a suitable place for holding the fairs. It was further provided that corporators might pay the $100 prescribed for admission by executing a satisfactory bond.

SCRIP MADE TRANSFERABLE.

On the 29th of May, 1869, it was resolved that the privilege of memberships of the Augusta County Fair, represented by the certificates granted to corporators, shall be transferable at the death of any corporator, as part of his estate, to any white citizen of the County of Augusta, provided such citizen was not before a corporator, and that no one person shall hold more than one membership.

PURCHASE OF LAND, ETC.

On the 10th of October of the preceding year of 1868, twenty-one acres of land lying to the east of the town on Lewis creek, was purchased for the exhibitions for the sum of $6000, and in these grounds the first fair was held on the 27th, 28th and 29th days of October, 1868.

BY-LAWS.

On August 24th, 1868, the Committee on By-Laws reported the following, which were adopted :

1. The officers shall be a President, a Secretary, a Treasurer, a Superintendent of the Grounds and an Executive Committee, to consist of three members.

PRESIDENT.

The President shall preside at all meetings of the Directory and all general meetings of the Corporators. He shall appoint all committees, except such as shall be otherwise provided for by the Directory. He shall fill any vacancy in the offices of the corporation by an appointment to continue until an election by the Directory. He shall countersign all orders on the treasury before they are paid.

SECRETARY.

The Secretary shall be elected by the Directory and shall hold his office during its pleasure. He shall keep a fair record of the proceedings of the Corporators, of the Directory and of the Executive Committee, entering them in succession in the same book, which shall, at all times, be open to any corporator for inspection. He shall draw all orders upon the treasurer for claims audited by the Executive Committee, and shall enter among the proceedings of the said Committee a list of all such claims, preserving all papers relating thereto. He shall preserve all the papers, books, &c., belonging to the corporation according to such rules as shall from time to time be prescribed by the Directory.

TREASURER.

The Treasurer shall be elected by the Directory, and shall hold his office during its pleasure. He shall give bond, with security, in such penalty as the Directory shall, from time, require, which bond shall be payable to the Augusta County Fair, and shall be conditioned for the faithful discharge of his duties. No payment of any money due to the Corporators shall be valid unless made to the Treasurer, except in such cases as shall be specially provided for by the Directory. No money shall be paid out by the Treasurer except on orders drawn by the Secretary and countersigned by the President.

SUPERINTENDENT.

The Superintendent shall be elected by the Directory, and shall hold his office during its pleasure. It shall be his duty to superintend and take care of the fair grounds under the direction of the Executive Committee.

EXECUTIVE COMMITTEE.

The Executive Committee shall be elected by the Directory, except that the President shall be, ex-officio, chairman of the committee. The members shall continue in office during the pleasure of the Directory. The Executive Committee shall be charged with the duty of carrying into execution all the orders of the Directory not otherwise provided for, and shall have a large discretion, subject at all times to the control of the Directory, to do, in the recess of Directory, whatever may be necessary to protect the interests and advance the purposes of the corporation. The Committee was increased to five, October 16th, 1873.

MEETINGS.

The Directory shall meet regularly on the 4th Monday of each month. Special meetings may be appointed by the Directory, by the Executive Committee or by the President, and a meeting shall be called at any time by the President, on the written demand of any three Directors or any ten Corporators. A meeting of the Corporators may be called at any time by the Directory, and there shall be at least one such meeting in each year, to be held at the Annual Fair.

The following by-law was adopted January 14th, 1871:

ELECTIONS.

The annual election of Directors shall be held at the Secretary's office, in the fair grounds, on the 2d day of the Fair, under the superintendence of three commissioners appointed by the Board of Directors from the body of Corporators, whose duty it shall be to return a correct poll, with a certificate of the result of the election, to the Board of Directors within five days after the election.

AWARD OF PREMIUMS.

On the same day it was resolved that in future the Secretary and Treasurer be authorized to settle the award of premiums due Corporators by giving them credit upon their bonds, their consent thereto having been received.

ADMISSION TO THE GROUNDS.

On the 27th of July, 1872: Resolved, That no ticket can be issued to or privilege granted to, or rights be exercised by, a Corporator except on the production of the Treasurer's receipt showing all dues paid.

On the 23d of November, 1872: Resolved, That hereafter six tickets be issued to each Corporator for the use of his family (not transferable) during the Fair, and that the Corporators, as exhibitors, be put on the same footing as other persons.

ADMISSION OF SCHOOLS.

And the privilege of attending the Fairs, at half price, was accorded the teachers and scholars of the ladies' colleges, in Staunton, by resolution of October 10th, 1876.

NO AUCTION OR GAMBLING ALLOWED AT THE FAIRS.

On the 1st of October, 1875, it was ordered that no person shall expose any article for sale, on the Fair grounds, except previously licensed so to do by the Secretary, nor shall any gambling, pool-selling or other game of chance be permitted.

SALE OF OLD AND PURCHASE OF THE PRESENT LANDS.

Previous to the adoption of many of the foregoing rules and regulations, namely, on the 7th of April, 1873, the Fair grounds on Lewis creek were sold to the Valley Railroad Company for $25,000; and on the 17th of the succeeding month the Directory purchased 33½ acres of the Spring farm estate for $10,000. This constitutes the present landed estate of the incorporation, and here the fairs have been since held, with annually increasing success.

This estate, lying in a beautiful valley among the hills, to the northwest of Staunton, possesses great natural charms, and is susceptible of the highest improvement. It abounds in springs, which supply abundance of pure water, and is traversed by a brook having its source on the adjoining property, (Steephill,) and notwithstanding the recent sale of water right to the city, it is thought that the ornamental water, or Fair grounds lake, may in future be kept up to its present level. If the estate were divided into pasture and woodland, well stocked with shade trees and flowers, and every part made accessible by graveled paths and carriage roads, it would become the most attractive spot in the vicinity of the town, a favorite resort of its jaded business men, and of all seeking recreation and enjoyment.

32 ‡

And I cannot close this report without expressing the hope that such a system of improvement may be speedily undertaken.

In accordance with the resolution of the Board, at its meeting of November 8th, 1879, I have the honor to submit the foregoing report or sketch of the origin, progress and present condition of the B. A. F.

Steephill, November 10th, 1879. JOHN L. PEYTON.

DIRECTORS OF BALDWIN AUGUSTA FAIR.

1. A. M. Bowman; 2. W. L. Bumgardner; 3. C. B. Coiner; 4. J. D. Crowle; 5. A. W. Harman; 6. J. Henderson; 7. J. H. Parkins; 8. John L. Peyton; 9. A. A. Sproul; 10. J. H. Waters.

The manufacturing interests of the county have not been fully developed. We have few factories, and such as we have are not so flourishing as could be desired. This has been partly due to the disadvantages arising before the war from slave labor, and since 1865, from the want of capital. The principal part of our capital in Augusta has been invested in flouring mills, which are scattered over the county, in the tanning of hides, the distilling of spirits, manufacture of wagons, carriages and furniture. Since the war, there has been a greater division of labor than formerly, when the entire negro population was engaged in agriculture. We now have in the towns, and even villages, butchers, bakers, brewers, carpenters, joiners, wheelwrights, plough, cart and wagon makers, and other mechanics, and there is a general disposition to barter and trade,—a growing spirit of enterprise. The opening of our iron and coal mines, marble quarries, the diversion of a certain part of our population to the mechanical arts, has given a limited home market to the farmer, and has caused a sensible improvement in our modes of cultivation and in the yield of our lands. Our county has, in a word, been gradually growing into a commercial community. There has been an increasing desire to live in cities and towns, to engage in trade, and the increase and riches of the towns has contributed to the improvement and cultivation of the lands by furnishing a ready market to the farmer. Many orchards and vineyards* have been planted, and some wine of excellent flavor has been made ; a cloth factory is in operation on the head waters of South river, and an iron foundry and machine shop in Staunton. It cannot be said, however, that our manufactories are numerous and flourishing. There is a wide-spread feeling that we should foster manufactures, and with our vast supplies of iron, copper, coal, manganese, kaolin, which makes excellent earthenware, and sand from which the best of plate-glass may be manufactured, and a soil which, in addition to growing grass and all the cereals,—giving us a great wealth in horses, cattle, sheep and swine,—is admirably adapted to the growth of tobacco, hemp, flax, hops, and the vine, there is every reason to believe that factories will soon exist among

---

*One of the vineyards near Staunton is on La Grange, the estate of Mr. Xaupi, and the grapes are equal in size and flavor to the best the writer has eaten in France and Italy. Others in the county, of which he has no personal knowledge, are probably equal to them.

us and pay high dividends. Our climate is particularly adapted to them, the expense of living is moderate, rents are low, and labor at hand and cheap. Let us hope, then, that many years will not have elapsed before we have factories of every kind. Manufactures of iron in all its forms, of brass, copper and lead; of linen, woollen and cotton cloths; of cordage, furniture, wagons, carriages and farming implements; of paper, glass, leather, hats, silks, laces, watches, and other objects of constant and frequent demand. Our grapes will make raisins equal to those of Malaga, and produce wine and brandy not inferior to those of France and Germany. From the sorghum and beet root, we should make our sugar and molasses. Staunton should be the seat of a factory for canning fruits and vegetables; for the making of starch from our corn; oil from the palma christi, which grows luxuriantly in Augusta; from the walnut and from the olive, which would doubtless flourish in our soil and climate, both of which are similar to those of Italy and the south of France. We would then enjoy all the benefits and blessings arising from order and good government; the liberty and security of individuals; an absence of idlers and paupers, of loafers and gamblers. In a country which has neither foreign commerce, says a great writer, nor any of the finer manufactures, a great proprietor, having nothing for which he can exchange the greater part of the produce of his lands, which is over and above the maintenance of the cultivators, consumes the whole in rustic hospitality at home. If this surplus produce is sufficient to maintain a hundred or a thousand men, he can make use of it in no other way than by maintaining a hundred or a thousand men. He is at all times, therefore, surrounded with a multitude of retainers and dependents, who having no equivalent to give in return for their maintenance, but being fed entirely by his bounty, must obey him, for the same reason that soldiers must obey the prince who pays them. Before the existence of commerce and manufactures in Europe, the hospitality of the rich and great, from the sovereign down to the smallest baron, exceeded every thing which in the present times we can easily form a notion of. Westminster Hall was the dining-room of William Rufus, and might frequently not be too large for his company. It was reckoned a piece of magnificence in Thomas Becket, that he strewed the floor of his hall with clean hay in the season, in order that the knights' and squires, who could not get seats, might not spoil their fine clothes when they sat down on the floor to eat their dinner. A hospitality of the same kind was exercised before the civil war in different parts of the southern states, from Maryland to Texas, and in our own county Fort Lewis, Montgomery Hall, Spring farm, Bear-Wallow, Oak Grove, Glendale, Folly, Selma, and other seats of our great proprietors, were famous for it, as will ever be all fertile agricultural and pastoral regions where commerce and manufactures are little known.

Though Augusta continued to be largely composed of staid men at the opening of the nineteenth century, there was a considerable infusion of new comers, principally from Eastern Virginia. Though many of these were professional gentlemen, and distinguished for their learning, they were more cheerful and easy in mixed society than were the earlier settlers of Covenanter stock. Politeness and good manners could soon be traced, though in different proportions, through every rank, and society began to be more gay and vivacious. Private and public balls were introduced, and the fiddler's animating scrape was more frequently heard. These entertainments, if less splendid, when compared with the classical elegance of those of Richmond and New York, were none the less enjoyed. The programme at these fetes was simple enough. After dancing several hours,—and the figures were performed with a high degree of perfection, a light nymphish grace unsurpassed,—the company was conducted to the supper-room, which was decorated with taste and elegance. After partaking of a sumptuous repast, the guests wandered through the open doors and windows to the garden, which was generally of considerable extent, beautifully illuminated with colored lamps. Here, loitering under the trees and among the shrubbery, they were served with lemonade and other iced beverages. But these customs, not yet exploded, are too common to be described. We have before us the list of a company which attanded a fete at Folly, 14th of December, 1814. It is inserted below, and will serve as a kind of directory of our fashionables at that period :

Mr. Abney, Dr. and Mrs. Boys, Miss Jane Boys, Gen., Mrs. and the Misses Brown, Mr. and Mrs. Baldwin, Mr. Bierne, Mr. J. Blakey, Mr. W. H. Brown, Mrs. and the Misses Bryan, Mr. and Miss Cocke, Miss Coalter, Mr. and Mrs. J. Cowan, Mrs. and the Misses Chambers, Dr. and Mrs. Clarke, Mr. S. Clarke, Mr. K. Chambers, Mr. and Mrs. J. Crawford, Mr. Wm. Chambers, Mr. Davis, Mr. Edrington, Mr. Edmundson, Mr. and Mrs. W. S. Eskridge, Mr. Fulton, Mr., Mrs. and the Misses Fulton, Mr., Mrs. and the Misses Jones, Miss Garth, Mr., Mrs. and the Misses Garber, Mrs. Grove, Mr. J. Garber, Mr. G. Holloway, Mr. Hartman, Mr. A. Hall, Mr. J. B. Heil, Mr. Heiskell, Dr. Hanger, Mr. McIntosh, Mr. W. Kinney, Mr. Mr. J. Kenney, Mrs. Lyle and family, Mr. and Mrs. Mathews, Mr. Wm. Mathews, Mr. and Mrs. McDowell, Miss McDowell, Mr. and Mrs. Miller, Miss McCulloch, Mr. R. C. Nicholas, Mr. and Mrs. Peyton, Mrs. and the Misses Perry, Mr. and Mrs. Peck, Mr. and Mrs. Peck, jr., Miss Porterfield, Mr. Reeves, Judge and Mrs. Stuart, Mr. T. J. Stuart, Mr. and Mrs. Stribling, Mr. Stringfellow, Mr. S. Smith, Miss Skelson, Mr. and Mrs. Sowers, Mr. Shomo, Mr. A. St. Clair, Mr. and Mrs. Ab. Smith, Dr., Mrs. and the Misses Telfair, Miss Tapp, Mr. Temple, Mr. Tebbs, Mr. and Mrs. Wayt, Mr. and Mrs. L. Waddell, Mr. and Mrs. A. Waddell, Miss Waddell, Mr. and Mrs. Wright, Capt., Mrs. and Miss Williamson, Mr. and Mrs. Whyte, Dr. Willson, Miss Waterman, Miss Webb.

ALPHABETICAL LIST OF THE JUSTICES OF AUGUSTA, FROM 1790 TO 1860.

We have not attempted to continue the list after 1860, the recurrent elections at short periods having so greatly enlarged the number of justices that space could not be conveniently found for the catalogue of names.

J. T. ANTRIM,
S. F. ABNEY,
W. D. ANDERSON,
W. C. BRUFFY,
JAMES BELL,
D. S. BELL,
WM. A. BELL,
J. WAYT BELL,
WM. BEARD,
R. G. BICKLE,
JAS. BERRY,
J. D. BROWN,
C. BROWN,
R. P. BROWN,
S. B. BROWN,
D. BLACKBURN,
JACOB BAYLOR,
J. B. BRECKINRIDGE,
G. A. BRUCE,
B. CRAWFORD,
JAS. CRAWFORD,
S. D. CRAWFORD,
G. M. COCHRAN,
J. A. COCHRAN,
A. COYNER,
J. T. CLARK,
JNO. CHURCHMAN,
SAM'L CLINE,
WM. CHAPMAN.
HATCH CLARK,
J. T. CLARK,
JOS. D. CRAIG,
WM. DAVIS,
J. A. DAVIDSON,
HY. EIDSON, JR.,
J. S. ELLIS,
S. B. FINLEY,
JNO. G. FULTON,
ROB'T GUY,
WM. GUY,
TH. GAMBLE,
JAS. R. GROVE,
J. R. GROVE,
D. GRIFFITH,
J. N. GENTRY,
WM. GEORGE,
B. F. HAILMAN,

J. N. HUPP,
M. W. D. HOGSHEAD,
ELIJAH HOGSHEAD,
D. B. HOGSHEAD,
KENTON HARPER,
P. A. HEISKELL,
SAM'L HANSBARGER,
ISAAC HALL,
WM. HARRIS,
JAS. HENRY,
J. A. HARMAM,
SAM'L KENNERLY,
J. KEISER,
D. KERR,
D. KUNKLE,
J. M. LILLEY,
JOHN MCCUE,
J. A. MCCUE,
J. M. MCCUE,
W. W. MONTGOMERY,
E. G. MOORMAN,
SAM'L MCCUNE,
ARCH. M. MOORE,
J. K. MOORE,
N. MASSIE,
C. G. MILLER,
JNO. NEWTON,
J. MORRISON,
J. A. PATTERSON,
D. W. PATTISON,
JOHN H. PEYTON,
J. LEWIS PEYTON,
J. PORTERFIELD,
B. F. POINTS,
WM. RAMSEY,
JNO. RIMEL,
J. C. RIVERCOMB,
A. H. ROSS,
WM. G. STERRETT,
G. B. STUART,
GEO. SEAWRIGHT,
JOS. SMITH,
WM. R. SMITH,
J. B. SYCLE,
W. M. TATE,
D. N. VANLEAR,
A. WADDELL,

L. WADDELL,	LEWIS WAYLAND,
JNO. WAYT,	ALEX'R WALKER,
T. P. WILSON,	LUKE WOODWARD,
WM. WILSON,	ROBERT M. WHITE,
JAMES WILSON,	WM. YOUNG.

In 1869–70 certain constitutional amendments were adopted by a popular vote. Among these was one for township organization, another the substitution of a county judge for the old county court system. The first judge was J. N. Hendren. The officers of the county in 1881 were as follows;

J. M. QUARLES . . . . Judge of County Court.
WM. A. BURNETT . . . . Clerk of County Court.
A. B. LIGHTNER . . . . Sheriff.
JNO. G. STOVER . . . . Surveyor.
SAM'L PAUL . . . . Treasurer.

BEVERLY MANOR DISTRICT.

JNO. PARIS . . . . Supervisor.
J. M. KINNEY . . . . Justice.
J. M. LICKLITER . . . . "
DAVID HENKEL . . . . "
JOHN SULLIVAN . . . . Constable.

RIVERHEADS DISTRICT.

WM. T. RUSH . . . . Supervisor.
J. H. RUSH . . . . Justice.
WM. W. CALE . . . . "
JAMES N. MITCHELL . . . . "
THOS. A. BLOWNLEE . . . . Constable.

MIDDLE RIVER DISTRICT.

WM. CRAWFORD . . . . Supervisor.
K. B. KOINER . . . . Justice.
C. S. ROLLER . . . . "
J. H. CRAWFORD . . . . "
S. N. PATTERSON . . . . Constable.

NORTH RIVER DISTRICT.

S. A. EAST . . . . Supervisor.
J. A. HAMRICK . . . . Justice.
J. A. MILLS . . . . "
C. S. BYERS . . . . Constable.

SOUTH RIVER DISTRICT.

JNO. S. ELLIS . . . . Supervisor.
DAVID W. COINER . . . . Justice.
JACOB COINER, JR . . . . "
A. A. ARNOLD . . . . "
JNO. M. HANGER . . . . Constable.

PASTURES DISTRICT.

H. B. SIEG . . . . Supervisor.
B. O. FERGUSON . . . . Justice.
J. S. GUY . . . . "
W. J. EURITT . . . . "
W. T. LIGHTNER . . . . Constable.

CHAPTER XVI.

CITIES, TOWNS AND VILLAGES.

As new-comers arrived in the county after the settlement of Lewis at Bellefonte, they clustered round about the fort. This soon became a source of inconvenience to the Founder, and led to his selection of the site of the present city of Staunton for a town. It was recommended by its numerous advantages, its central position, its many springs, and good, though limited, water-power. Before the organization of the county, Staunton was a considerable hamlet, and was named in honor of Lady Staunton, the accomplished wife of Lieut.-Gov. Gooch. Here the first court-house was built, but for many years subsequent to 1745, the clerk's office remained at Port Republic. Tradition says that the constant presence of the King's attorney, Mr. Gabriel Jones, and his professional brethren travelling to and fro on this road, led to our witty ancestors styling it the "Lawyers' Lane." That "lane," widened, improved and graded, is the present road by the Western Lunatic Asylum to the National Cemetery, and thence through New Hope to the now historical town of Port Republic. No plat of Staunton was made until 1748, when a few streets and lots were laid off. The plat was subsequently confirmed by the Legislature, was presented in court, and admitted to record 27th February, 1749. It is believed by some that Staunton was incorporated by Act of the Assembly in 1748, and Campbell distinctly so states in his History of Virginia. We have seen nothing to establish this fully, but sufficient to justify a belief in its probability. There is a proclamation, of date April 8th, 1752, from Governor Dinwiddie, repealing certain acts of the Assembly, passed at the revisal in 1748. Among these acts is one entitled, "An act for establishing a town in Augusta County, and allowing fairs to be kept there." At this time, Pittsburg and the surrounding country was supposed to be and claimed as a part of Virginia, and it does not appear whether Pittsburg or Staunton, or either, was referred to in the act. It is probable, however, as Staunton was laid out into streets and lots in 1748, that it was Staunton; and if so, she is the oldest town in the Valley.

The first act for its incorporation, which appears in Hening, was passed in November, 1761, and is in the following words:

1. "Whereas, the erecting towns on the frontier of this colony may prove of great benefit and advantage to the inhabitants, by inducing many of them to settle together, which will enable them the better to defend themselves on any sudden incursions of an enemy; and whereas, it has been represented to this present General Assembly that William Beverly, Esq., deceased, did, in his lifetime, lay out a parcel of land in the County of Augusta, at the court-house of the said county, into lots and streets for a town, and did sometime afterwards give to the said county twenty-five acres of land more, adjoining the said former lots, to be added to and made part of said town, which has also been since laid off into lots and streets, most of which are now disposed of, and many families are settled there;

*   *   *   *   *   *

"Be it, therefore, enacted by the Lieutenant-Governor, Council and Burgesses, of this present General Assembly, and it is hereby enacted by the authority of the same, that the lands so laid off by the said William Beverly, in the County of Augusta, shall be called and known by the name of Staunton. *   *   And whereas, it is necessary that trustees should be appointed for said town hereby erected, Be it further enacted, by the authority aforesaid, That William Preston, Israel Christian, David Stewart, John Brown, John Page, William Lewis, William Christian, Eledge McClenechan, Robert Breckenridge and Randal Lockhart, gentlemen, be and they are hereby nominated, constituted and appointed trustees for the said town of Staunton, in the County of Augusta.

"And the said trustees, or any three of them, respectively, shall and may and they are hereby authorized and empowered to make, from time to time, such rules, orders and directions for the regular and orderly building the houses in the said town as to them shall seem expedient, and also to settle all disputes and controversies concerning the bounds of the lots in the said town.

"And for continuing the succession of the said trustees, Be it further enacted, That in case of the death of any of the said trustees, or their refusal to act, the surviving or other trustees, or the major part of them, shall assemble, and are hereby empowered, from time to time, by instrument in writing under their respective hands and seals, to nominate some other person or persons in the place of him so dying or refusing; which new trustees so nominated and appointed, shall from thenceforth have the like power and authority in all things relating to the matters herein contained, as if he or they had been expressly named and appointed in and by this act. And every such instrument and nomination shall, from time to time, be inserted and registered in the books of the said trustees."

Staunton is the only city in the county in 1882, is the seat of Justice, and the commercial metropolis of the county and much adjacent territory. It is situated on both sides of Lewis creek, and on both sides of its two branches,—Peyton's creek and Gum Spring branch,—which unite in the city and make up Lewis creek, which was so called in honor of the Founder. It is about one hundred and twenty miles from Richmond, and about one hundred and eighty from Washington. Its average height above the sea level is 1,450 feet. A glance at the map shows it to be near the geographical centre of the county.

In May, 1779, an act was passed by the General Assembly, by which the trustees of the town were displaced and the sheriff of the county was directed to proceed to take a poll for the election of five trustees in their room. This act defines the powers of the trustees, imposes penalties for misapplication of taxes, &c. The same act prohibited swine from running at large in the town, and provided that "it shall be lawful for any person whatsoever to kill and destroy every such swine going at large." The causes which led to the removal of the trustees does not appear, nor have we been able to get the names of the old or new trustees. This act was so much opposed by the pig-growers, that the portion relating to swine was repealed by the Legislature of 1782, and pigs were allowed to range at large through the streets.

On November 6, 1787, an act was passed for enlarging the town by the addition of twenty-five acres, the property of Alexander St. Clair, which was ordered to be laid off into lots and streets, and made part of the said town. This is that portion of Staunton commonly called New Town, extending from Church street south and northwest. That portion of the town lying north of Academy street is generally known as Gallowstown. It acquired its name thus: About the year 1795, a man by the name of Bullitt was charged with horse stealing, was tried, and condemned to death. He was executed at the forks of the road, the intersection of New and Augusta streets, opposite the residence of Mr. Evans, where the gallows was erected. At the time Bullitt was hung, his brother was holding a court at the Warm Springs, and the family had hitherto been without reproach. We may add that East Main street and the surrounding district is styled Gospel Hill, from the eminent piety of the late Samson Eagan, who long occupied the present residence of D. A. Kayser. Mr. Eagan was a pillar in the Methodist Episcopal Church.

Within recent years, Staunton has been connected with the east and west by railways, and lying midway between the Atlantic and Ohio, occupies a good commercial position.

The corporation consists of a mayor, who exercises the powers of a justice of the peace, twelve councilmen, six justices of the peace, a constable, four policemen, a treasurer, recorder, town clerk, an attorney, a commissioner of the revenue, &c. The mayors, since 1802, have been—

JOHN McDOWELL,	L. L. STEVENSON,
JACOB SWOOPE,	JOHN EAGAN,
JACOB KINNEY,	K. HARPER,
CHESLEY KINNEY,	JEFF. KINNEY,
CHAPMAN JOHNSON,	R. S. BROOKE,
MICHAEL GARBER,	WILLIAM RUFF,
JOHN H. PEYTON,	T. P. ESKRIDGE,
ERAS. STRIBLING,	N. K. TROUT,

33 ‡

SAMUEL CLARK,   W. M. ALLEN,
JAMES CRAWFORD,   R. G. BICKLE,
WILLIAM KINNEY,   WM. L. BALTHIS,
              J. A. COCHRAN.

The charter of the town was amended by act of the Legislature Feb. 20, 1833.

The climate of Staunton is dry, mild and healthy.

The churches of the town are, for the whites—One Methodist Episcopal, which accommodates 900 persons; one Episcopal (Protestant) 800; two Presbyterian, 1,300; one Baptist, 600; one Lutheran, 400; one Roman Catholic, 400; and for the colored population—One Methodist Episcopal, 700; one African Methodist Episcopal, 1,000; two Baptist, 1,300.

No town possesses greater educational advantages than Staunton, whether we consider its public or private schools.

"Its graded or public schools," says Maj. Hotchkiss, "offering complete facilities for a common or high school education or for a preparation for entering college, are free to all between the ages of five and twenty-one; its select school for boys provides intermediate or academic instruction at a moderate charge to those preferring private preparatory schools; its four denominational but not sectarian female colleges, Methodist, Episcopal, Lutheran and Presbyterian, are among the most thorough and prosperous in the country, as is evidenced by the hundreds of young ladies in attendance upon their classes from more than half the States of the Union. Besides, it is less than two hours by rail from the celebrated University of Virginia, at Charlottesville, with its unrivalled facilities for academic or professional training, and its free academic tuition to the young men of Virginia, on the one hand, and only thirty-six miles (now by stage but soon by rail over a railway in progress), to Washington and Lee University, at Lexington, an incorporated institution, conducted upon much the same plan as the University of Virginia, or the Virginia Military Institute, the West Point of Virginia, with free State cadets, on the other hand.

The Free Public Schools of Staunton were organized in 1870, cotemporaneously with their organization in Virginia, and during the school year 1870-71 ten schools, 8 for white children and 2 for colored, were taught by 14 teachers, for 5.81 months, with an average attendance of 277 white and 103 colored children. At that time there was a joint Superintendent for the public schools of the county and city. In 1873 the free public schools of the city were reorganized with four grades of schools for the whites and two for the blacks, and all put in charge of a City Superintendent of Schools, the city having been most efficiently aided in this work from the Peabody Education Fund and by Dr. Barnas Sears, a citizen of Staunton, the learned General Agent of that fund. During the school year 1873-4 there were 13 grades or schools, 9 for whites and 4 for blacks, with 14 teachers, taught for 7 months, with an average attendance of 390 whites and 160 blacks. Since 1873 the same organization has been continued and under the same Superintendent.

During the school year 1876-7, the last reported, there were 15 schools, 12 for whites and 3 for blacks, taught by 17 teachers, 2 males and 15 females, for 10 months, with an average daily attendance of 422 white and 133 black children, 555 in all. These returns show that 30 per cent. of the white and 27 per cent. of the black school population of the city,—all those between the ages of 5 and 21—were, on an average, in daily attendance in the free public schools during the annual session of ten scholastic months of this year. The enrollment for attendance during the year was 576 whites and 250 blacks, a total of 826, which was 42 per cent. of the white and 50 per cent. of the black school population. One hundred of the white pupils were studying the higher branches. The average monthly enrollment to each teacher was 38, and the average age of the pupils 9.6 years.

The average salaries paid to the male teachers were $120.33 a month and to the female teachers $38.62. There were paid during the year, for teachers' wages, $8,653, for other purposes, rent, fuel, &c., $2,632.93, or a total of $11,285.93. The funds were derived, from the State $1,208.35, from city appropriation $7,992.61, from tuition for those from without the corporation $274.50, and from other sources, including $2,000 from the Peabody Education Fund, $2,486.03, aggregating $11,961.49.

At this time, May 1878, there are in operation, for whites, 12 schools, in 5 grades, with 12 teachers; and for blacks, 4 schools, in 2 grades, with 4 teachers. The grades are: First and Second Primary, Intermediate, Grammar School and High School.

The only requirement for the admission of any one between the ages of 5 and 21, living in Staunton, to its public schools of any grade, is the production of a certificate of vaccination from a city physician on application for enrollment.

Those living beyond the corporate limits of the city may attend its schools by paying tuition at the rate of $1 a month in the primary, $1.50 in the intermediate, $2 in the grammar, and $2.50 in the high schools. The county free schools are open, quite near the city limits, without charge to those living without the corporation.

The aim of the public schools is to give a thorough training in the common English branches to all the pupils, teaching each one to think for himself, thus laying the foundation for intellectual improvement while imparting skill in the application of principles in the affairs of life. Vocal music is taught in all the schools by a teacher having no other duty, and all are drilled in singing and the reading of music.

The City Superintendent of Public Schools has supervision of and duly visits all the schools and investigates not only the study work, but all cases of misdemeanors and punishments. He devotes all his time to the schools. The teachers are appointed by the Board of Education of the city, after they have obtained a certificate of qualification, based on an examination by the Superintendent. They are required to meet every Saturday for normal drill and consultation, and in this way the efficiency and unity of the system is preserved.

The discipline maintained requires a prompt and willing obedience from the pupils and the exercise of a firm but kind and parental authority on the part of the teachers. Parents are consulted and their coöperation sought, and corporal punishment is resorted to only in extreme cases, but good order is strictly insisted upon and enforced, and no town can furnish a more orderly and well-behaved set of children and youths.

Separate and wholly distinct schools are, by law, provided for whites and blacks, but equal facilities are furnished to each race.

There are several private schools,—one, St. Francis, under the supervision of the Sisters of Charity, attached to the Roman Catholic Church,—and two for boys, one conducted by Capt. H. L. Hoover, and the other by G. M. Murray.

There are four ladies' colleges in Staunton, where over five hundred young girls from almost every part of the Union are annually instructed and encouraged in everything virtuous and laudable. In all of these schools the course of study is extensive and thorough, and the graduates turned out from them are celebrated for the graces of their hearts, the elegance of their manners, and the improvement of their understandings. The social and religious influences of Staunton are unsurpassed, and special efforts are made to inspire the young ladies of these seminaries with true ideas; to rouse them from a vacant and insipid life, into one of usefulness and laudable exertion; to recall them from visionary novels and romances into solid reading and reflection, and from the criminal absurdities of fashion to the simplicity of nature and the dignity of virtue. The first established of these seats of learning was the Augusta Female Seminary, founded in 1842. It is under the general control of the members of the Presbyterian Church. The course of instruction is modeled after that of the University of Virginia, and it issues certificates of proficiency in each school, and a diploma is conferred upon full graduates—graduates in seven schools. The sessions begin in September and end in June. The expense per session ranges between $260 and $350, without music and the ancient and modern languages, for which an extra charge is made. For nearly twenty years this school has been under the judicious and enlightened control of Miss Mary J. Baldwin, who has a staff of between twenty and thirty assistants, and enjoys great prosperity.

The Virginia Female Institute was established in 1844, and belongs to the Council of the Diocese of the Protestant Episcopal Church of Virginia. The course of instruction is similar to that in the Augusta Female Seminary. The sessions begin and end about the same time, and the expenses are about the same. The school has recently come under the control of Mrs. J. E. B. Stuart, who has a large staff of assistants, and is increasing in public favor.

The third seminary is the Wesleyan Female Institute, founded in 1846 by the Baltimore Conference of the Methodist Episcopal Church, South. The course of instruction, the period of the session, and the expenses, are similar to those of the other schools. The school has been for nearly fifteen years under the Presidency of Rev. Wm. A. Harris. It has a corps of over twenty assistants, and is highly prosperous.

The fourth great school is the Staunton Female Seminary, under the general auspices of the Lutheran Church. It was established in 1870, and is, as to the course of studies, expenses, &c., similar to the previous three mentioned. Until within a recent period, it was under Rev. J. I. Miller as Principal. Since his late resignation, Rev. Jas. Willis has been appointed and has taken charge of the institution. He comes with the best of recommendations, and will, no doubt, maintain the high reputation acquired by the Seminary in the past.

These ladies' colleges are all of them commodious and elegant brick edifices, with the necessary offices, &c., and are replete with the modern improvements,—gas, heating apparatus, ventilation, bath-rooms, &c. The grounds are prettily and highly improved, ornamented with trees, flowers, fountains, jets d'eau, etc.

Staunton is the seat of two great State charities,—the first, the Institution for the education of the Deaf, Dumb, and of the Blind,—the second, the Western Lunatic Asylum. On both the State has expended hundreds of thousands of dollars, and in their respective spheres they are invaluable. The buildings are grand and imposing. In the Deaf and Dumb and Blind Institution, the pupils receive a good common school education, and are taught some trade or art by which they may, after leaving, maintain themselves. All indigent deaf and blind children are here taught, lodged, boarded and clothed at the public expense. The present principal is Dr. W. R. Vaughn.

In 1851, the writer was the youngest member of the Board of Directors of the Deaf, Dumb and Blind Institution, and as such, in accordance with a custom of the Directory, was requested to write the report for that year to the General Assembly. He performed this duty, and in the course of that paper, said: "The Board respectfully suggests to the General Assembly that owing, no doubt, to the healthfulness of our climate, too little regard has been had in the construction of the buildings to hospital purposes. It is indispensable to the comfort, accommodation, and proper nursing of the sick in so large an establishment, that a separate suite of apartments should be appropriated to their exclusive use. The Institution is now filled to its utmost capacity, and in the event of an epidemic or contagious disease, every inmate would be endangered, and the operations of the Institution probably suspended."

[These suggestions in regard to a hospital for the Institution suggest the want of a hospital for the town and county—a want severely felt during the recent prevalence of small-pox. It is hoped that ere long the town and county may unite in the purchase of a suitable piece of ground in the vicinity of the city and the erection of a substantial building, to be used as a hospital for the sick and disabled—strangers and travelers, as well as residents. A special department might be devoted to fever and small-pox cases, to which might be advantageously added a ward for convalescents. The site of such a charity should be where there is plenty of fresh and pure air, not too far from town, and entirely isolated by being in an open field, susceptible of good drainage. The buildings should be constructed after a plan which would insure ventilation, warmth and light, and where an unlimited supply of water could be had for culinary purposes, for bath-rooms, closets, &c. In connection with it there should be a kitchen, laun-dry, dispensary, and a disinfecting chamber, where heat could be applied to clothes and bedding for the destruction of the germs of disease. A separate building, or a wing, might be fitted up for the use of those able to pay for such accommodations.]

The other great State charity is the Western Lunatic Asylum, situated in the eastern suburbs of Staunton. It is one of the largest establishments of the kind in the United States, accommodating about six hundred pa-tients, and has been eminently successful in the treatment of the insane. The grounds are extensive,—about 230 acres of land belong to and are surrounding the buildings, and have been handsomely and expensively improved. The present Superintendent is Dr. R. S. Hamilton.

THE COUNTY BUILDINGS.

As all of the county buildings of any importance are situated within the limits of Staunton, we have deferred till now any particular allusion to them. About the year 1836-'37, the county undertook, and in the course of a year erected, the present handsome brick court-house with two wings. The east wing is used as the clerk's office of the Circuit Court, and the west is the office of the county clerk. Both have fire-proof vaults for the preservation of the records. These vaults were constructed during the year 1881, at a cost of about $6,000. The building occupies the same site, or very nearly so, of the first court-house, and all others which have been built since 1745, up to the present time. The court room is embellished with portraits of some of our distinguished lawyers, and if all of our worthies were hung around its walls it would form a gallery of no small interest, excite the emulation of the young, and improve the taste of all. The room above the circuit clerk's office is used for the sessions of the Supreme Court of Appeals of Virginia, and that over the county office by the su-pervisors. Those above the court-room are used as jury-rooms, for which they are admirably adapted.

On the square south and opposite the court-house the county built, about 1847-'48, the present massive stone prison, on the site of the former brick jail. It is a handsome two-story building. The prisoners are con-fined in the rear rooms. The front ones furnish good accommodations to the jailor and his family. The present turnkey is George Harlan.

Near the village of Arbor Hill there is a county poor-house, with a farm of about three hundred acres. Here the paupers of the county are kept by the superintendent, at present G. W. Fauber, who is appointed by the court. The Overseer of the Poor is elected every four years by the people. The poor-house has few inmates, and these, for the most part, persons unable, from age or bodily disability, to work. There is a distinction between the town and county poor. The town or city supports its own poor, and it is done at moderate expense through the efficient overseer, John Kurtz. There is no city alms-house, and the object is secured by a system of out-door relief. It is the general opinion that it might be done at less expense and more conveniently by the erection, in the suburbs, of a suitable asylum, for those who are reduced to want and dependence. We have no statistics of either the town or county pauperism, but Augusta is believed to have as few poor, in proportion to her population, as any county in the State. She stands equally high as to crime. The criminal courts have little business, and within the last thirty years few persons have been sent to the penitentiary and fewer still have felt the halter draw. During a residence of nearly forty years in the county, the writer only remembers to have seen four executions, and he believes only five have occurred during that long period. The first three hung were William B. Johnson and two negro accomplices in the crime of rape. They were hung in Sandy Hollow, north of Staunton, in the year 1845. The other was Hemphill Trayer, who was hung Friday, 6th of January, 1854, for the murder of an old man named William Coleman. Shortly after the war, a man by name of Hodges was accused of horse stealing, and was taken from the county jail by a disguised band during the night, carried two miles south of Staunton, on the Lexington road, and there executed. This is the only instance of lynch law which has occurred in the county, and was much regretted by the cool and dispassionate part of the community.

There are three weekly papers published in Staunton—the "Spectator," the "Vindicator," and the "Valley Virginian." They are all handsome and prosperous. The "Goodson Gazette" is a neat and sprightly weekly, published by the pupils of the Deaf and Dumb and the Blind Institution, from a fund dedicated to this purpose by a wealthy and benevolent gentleman, Mr. John J. Goodson, of Norfolk. The "Virginias" is a handsomely printed mining, industrial and scientific monthly, ably edited by Maj. Jed. Hotchkiss.

There are two large hotels in Staunton, the Virginia and the American, and many boarding-houses, notably the Mozart House, the Miller House, the Peyton House and Kalorama.

There are two banks, the National Valley, with a capital of $200,000, and the Augusta National, with a capital of $100,000.

An iron foundry and machine shop, called the Staunton Iron Works, is also in successful operation.

There are three military companies—the West Augusta Guards, the Staunton Artillery, and a colored company. There is also a fine band, called the "Stonewall Band," which was organized in 1855, and during the civil war belonged to the brigade of the famous Stonewall Jackson.

The Baldwin Augusta Fair has, as we have seen, extensive and beautiful grounds near the city, with race track, ornamental water, &c.

The population of Staunton, in 1882, is estimated at 8,000, with about 2,000 in the suburbs, but beyond the city limits.

The following is a correct list of the officers of the city in 1882:

J. W. GREEN SMITH . . . . Judge of Hustings Court.
NEWTON ARGENBRIGHT . . . . Clerk of Hustings Court.
EDWARD ECHOLS . . . . Attorney for Commonwealth.
W. D. RUNNELS . . . . Sergeant.
GEORGE HARLAN, }
JOHN R. KURTZ, } . . . . Deputy Sergeants.

J. A. COCHRAN . . . . : . . . . Mayor.
JOHN M. CARROLL . . . . Treasurer.
E. M. CUSHING . . . . Deputy Treasurer.
GEORGE H. HUDSON . . . . Commissioner Revenue.
CHARLES E. HUDSON . . . . . Assistant Commissioner Revenue.
JOHN R. KURTZ . . . . Overseer of Poor.
JAMES H. WATERS . . . . Chief of Police.
M. HOUNIHAN, }
J. A. NEWMAN, } . . . . Police Officers.
WM. M. SIMPSON, }
E. W. HARMAN . . . . Superintendent Water Works.

SCHOOL BOARD.

JOHN W. TODD . . . . President.
WILLIAM J. NELSON . . . . Clerk.
WILLIAM A. BOWLES . . . . Superintendent Schools.
I. WITZ, }
WILLIAM WHOLEY, }
JOSEPH B. WOODWARD, } . . . . Trustees.
JOHN M. CARROLL, }

CITY COUNCIL.

Robert W. Burke . . . . \ . . . . . . President.
Newton Argenbright . . . . Clerk.
John W. Todd . . . . Chairman Committee on Finance.
James C. Marquis . . Chair'n Com'tee on Streets and Retrnch't.
Isaac Witz . . . . Chairman Committee on Water.
J. D. Crowle . . . Chair'n Com'e on Street Lights and Printing.
John Burns . . . . . Chairman Committee on Fire Department.
Dr. N. Wayt . . . . Chairman Committee on Health.
G. M. Cochran, Jr . . Chair'n Com'e on Ordinances and Schools.
G. G. Gooch . . . . Chairman Committee on Police.
F. B. Berkeley . . . . Chairman Committee on Safety.
John W. Alby . . Chairman Committee on Poor and Public
                    Grounds and Buildings.
P. H. Trout . . . . Chairman Auditing Committee.
John R. Kurtz . . . . Messenger of Council.
Dr. J. H. Fultz . . . . City Physician.
William M. Matheny . . . . Weighmaster.
W. G. Paxton . . . . Sealer Weights and Measures.
W. W. Fretwell . . . . Janitor City Hall.

MAGISTRATES.

William B. Kayser,   ⎫
George D. Pearman,   ⎬ . . . . Ward No. 1.
W. D. Anderson,   ⎭

W. Calvin Straughan, ⎫
B. F. Terry,   ⎬ . . .   . Ward No. 2.

FIRE DEPARTMENT.

Thomas J. Crowder . . . . Chief Engineer.
M. Cox . . . . Captain Augusta Fire Company.
R. A. Hamilton . . . . . Captain Newtown Hose Company.
John M. Hardy . . . . . Captain Hook and Ladder Company.

———

By act of the General Assembly, passed March 16, 1838, it was provided that a turnpike road should be constructed from Staunton to Parkersburg. Under this act the road was located by Col. Claude Crozet and constructed, and has added much to the prosperity of the town and to the country through which it passes. The superintendent of this road, in 1882, is Major William H. Peyton, of Augusta County. The act for its establishment is in these words:

Be it enacted by the General Assembly, That the Board of Public Works be, and they are hereby authorized and directed, to cause to be constructed, a turnpike road from Staunton, through the Dry Branch gap, to Parkersburg. The said board shall possess and may exercise all the powers, and shall be subject to all the duties and restrictions in relation to the road herein provided for, as are given to and imposed upon the president and directors of the N. W. turnpike road, except so far as is herein otherwise specially directed.

The said road shall be commenced and completed as speedily as . the same can be done consistently with a due regard to the interest of the State. It shall nowhere exceed a grade of four degrees, nor shall it be more than twenty feet wide, nor less than fifteen feet, exclusive of side ditches, &c.

2. That in order to defray the expense of constructing said road, the said Board of Public Works be and they are hereby empowered to borrow on the credit of the State, from time to time, such sums of money not exceeding in the aggregate $150,000, as may be necessary therefor, agreeably to such provision as may be contained in any general act authorizing loans for purposes of internal improvement, passed at the present session of the General Assembly. But if no such act be passed, then the said loan shall be effected upon the terms and conditions prescribed by the act of March 19, 1831, for the construction of the Northwestern Turnpike Road. In force from its passage.

———

During the session of 1837, the General Assembly passed an act to incorporate the Staunton and Covington turnpike, and ordered books to be opened at Staunton for receiving subscriptions to the same, under John H. Peyton, Benjamin Crawford, Thomas J. Michie, J. C. Sowers and William Kinney.

34 ‡

On the 30th of March, 1837, the Harrisonburg and Staunton Turnpike Company was incorporated, and books for receiving subscriptions were ordered to be opened at Staunton and other places.

At the same session an act was passed to revive an act incorporating the Staunton and Jenning's Gap Turnpike Company, passed February, 1837.

At the same session an act was passed incorporating the Staunton and Iron Works Turnpike Company, for constructing a road from Staunton to or near Miller's, now Forrer's, Iron Works.

Also an act to incorporate the Dry Branch Gap Turnpike Company for constructing a road from Buffalo Gap to some point on the Harrisonburg and Warm Springs turnpike road. Also an act to incorporate the Staunton and Little Kanawha road; also an act to incorporate the Staunton and Potomac railroad. Acts for the incorporation of other roads were passed, but the terms of the acts were never complied with, and it is not necessary to enumerate them.

In 1838, the Valley Turnpike Company was incorporated, the road located, graded and macadamized.

It was this enlightened policy on the subject of public improvements,—the construction of new and improving old roads,—which led to a considerable increase in the trade and prosperity of Staunton shortly after 1840; and there is no better way of measuring the civilization of a people than by the number of their roads. The most enlightened countries in the world,—such as England, France and Germany,—are those in which roads are most numerous, and the most ignorant, benighted land is Africa, the country where there are fewest roads.

The county is now traversed from east to west by the Chesapeake and Ohio railway, extending from the Atlantic seaboard, at Fortress Monroe, to the Ohio river; from north to south by the Shenandoah Valley railroad, which crosses the Potomac near Harper's Ferry, thence pursues the Valley of the Shenandoah to Waynesborough, in Augusta, and thence going south through Rockbridge to Tennessee; and by the Valley Branch of the Baltimore and Ohio railroad, which passes the Potomac at Harper's Ferry, running south through Winchester, and up the Valley west of the Shenandoah river, and generally parallel to the Shenandoah Valley railroad, to Staunton and Lexington. The ordinary roads are the Valley turnpike from Staunton to Winchester, a well-graded and macademized road, which has added much to the comfort of the people living contiguous to it, and enhancing the value of their lands; the Parkersburg road, from Staunton through Buffalo Gap; the Scottsville road, and numerous county roads penetrating every quarter of Augusta. These roads need grading, widening, ditching and macadamizing, as nothing adds more to the comfort of a country, to the value of its lands and the profits of the farmer than good roads; and many plans for securing this end are now under consideration, and ere long some of them will, no doubt, take form and be carried out.

———

AUGUSTA OR STRIBLING SPRINGS, 13 miles from Staunton, on the North Mountain, is a Summer resort of considerable reputation. The improvements consist of a large hotel, proprietor's residence, a number of cottages, &c.

ARBOR HILL is a pretty little hamlet, 6 miles south of Staunton, on the Middlebrook road. There is a mercantile establishment there, churches, &c.

BARTER BROOK is situated about 7 miles southeast from Staunton, in a fertile and beautiful section of the county. The population is about 50. There are two physicians, a flouring-mill, post-office and smithy.

CRAIGSVILLE is situated on the Chesapeake and Ohio railroad, about 23 miles west of Staunton, and is noted for its valuable marble quarries. It contains a population of 117 souls, two stores and a smithy.

CHURCHVILLE is situated on the Jenning's Gap road, 7 miles from Staunton, and has a population of 245; three stores, four churches, a fine graded school, two resident physicians, an organ manufactory, smithy and a large flouring mill. It is an enterprising and prosperous village, situated in the fertile and lovely valley of Jenning's Branch.

DEERFIELD is situated 25 miles from Staunton on the Warm Springs turnpike, on the Calfpasture, and has a population of about 60 souls. It has one church, a smithy, store-house, and a resident physician.

FISHERSVILLE lies 7 miles east of Staunton, on the Chesapeake and Ohio railroad, and has a population of about 175. It has a Methodist church, two stores, a wagon-maker's shop, smithy, and a resident physician. In the vicinity there is a valuable iron mine, and much lime is burnt in the neighborhood and shipped to market. It is situated on the head waters of the " Long Meadows," one of the richest and finest sections of the county.

GREENVILLE is 12 miles south of Staunton, on the Lexington road. It has a population of about 250. It has churches, shops, a flouring-mill, resident physicians, several stores, &c. It is about a mile north of the Shenandoah Valley railroad, and is prosperous and thriving. There is a sprightly weekly paper published at this place, called the "Greenville Banner."

MOSSY CREEK is situated 2½ miles from Mt. Solon, near the Rockingham line. It is a village of about forty souls; has a post-office; a wagonmaker's and blacksmith's shop, a furniture manufactory, a cooper's, and two flouring mills—Kyle's and Forrer's. One of the oldest Presbyterian churches (Mossy Creek) is here.

MT. SOLON—We are indebted to J. T. Clarke, M. D., for the following account of this prosperous and pretty little village:

" The first settlers at the head of Mossy Creek, who located the lands
at and around the site of the present village, were Robert Gregg, W. Mc-
Dougal, and Adam Stephenson. These lands were granted to them by
Lord Botetourt in the year 1769, or prior thereto, and adjoined the lands
of Samuel McPheeters and Col. Stephenson. A log house was built by a
Mr. Cochran, about 1799, which is now standing and occupied as a residence, and a mill to the north of it. The log house was first used as a
store by the firm of Cochran & Cravens—Dr. Joseph Cravens. This
property was afterwards purchased by John and Christian Landes. One
occupied the original log house, and the other built a similar residence on
the north side of the forks of the road, which was subsequently demolished
by Gabriel Judson, of Luray, and on its site the present commodious store-
house built. They also erected a small log house on the site of the present brick mill-house, which was occupied by a Mr. Decker, the grandfather of Capt. J. F. Hottle, now of the village. The two Landes also
erected a distillery on the south side of the dam, and a saw-mill on the
north side of the forebay of the present mill. On the left side of the road,
south of the creek, opposite the Cochran house, was erected a small log
dwelling and smith shop, occupied and carried on by a Mr. Joseph Shuey.
A school-house was about this time, or not long subsequently, built at the
bend of the Staunton road. John Landes built a barn back of the smith
shop. on the side of the hill, and Christ. Landes built his barn a couple of
hundred yards west of his house, on the North River Gap road. About
the year 1818, the Landes sold the mill property and land attached to
Wm. Cave (a brother-in-law of Abram Smith, who owned the farm called
Egypt, on North River), and shortly after the sale the mill was burned
down. Cave employed John and James Elliott and a Mr. Johnson, mill-
wrights, to rebuild the merchant mill and saw-mill, and James Frazier, of
Jenning's Gap, put up a store on the north side of the dam, and employed
a Mr. J H. Bell to carry it on. Afterwards Bell and B. A. Ervine, both
sons-in-law of Cave, bought out Frazier, and erected dwelling-houses on
the lot adjacent to the store-house, and carried on the mercantile business
until 1835. Cave also erected the brick mill-house, about the year 1827.
About the year 1827, Jacob Daggy opened a tan-yard below the mill, and
put up a brick dwelling-house—property now owned by J. E. Bolen. The
village, with its varying fortunes, has continued ever since. In 1835. E.
Stevens, of Rockingham county, and Henry Blakemore, of Miller's iron-
works, bought out the firm of Bell & Ervine, and Mr. Blakemore, who was
postmaster at the iron-works, by consent of the department, removed the
post-office to his store, and the town was thenceforth christened Mt. Solon.
On Friday, the 20th day of March, 1860, the greater part of the village
was burned down. At present the village contains thirty-four dwelling-
houses, one M. E. Church South, ten shops, nine of which are in operation, viz: two shoe-shops, one smith shop, one pump-maker, one wheel-
wright and chair-maker, two cabinet-makers; one tannery and five store-
houses, three occupied and in successful operation; one wagon and agricultural implement maker, one architect and house carpenter, and 150 inhabitants; is seventeen miles from Staunton, fourteen miles from Harrisonburg, five miles from Stribling Springs, and seven miles from the Dora
Coal Mines and Wooddell's Springs. We also have one school-teacher,
two lighting-rod peddlars, numerous nostrum venders, a Commissioner of
Revenue, and the residence of the County Treasurer. and the usual proportion of gentlemen of leisure, and a physician."

MOUNT MERIDIAN is situated about 18 miles northeast from Staunton, on the Port Republic road, and has a population of 40. It has a large flouring-mill, a store, wagon-maker's shop, smithy, resident physician. There is a large builder's and contractor's shop here, and a church.

MOUNT SIDNEY is situated about 10 miles from Staunton, on the Valley turnpike, and has a population of 244. It has a post-office, churches, stores, workshops, physicians, &c., and is a highly prosperous village. The B. & O. Railroad passes on the outskirts, where there is a station.

MIDDLEBROOK is 12 miles south of Staunton, and has a population of 274, and is one of the most enterprising and prosperous villages in the county, having numerous stores, shops, &c.

MINT SPRING is situated 6 miles south of Staunton, on the Lexington road, and has a population of about 75, a church, blacksmith's shop, stores, &c. It is a station on the Valley Railroad.

MIDWAY is half-way between Staunton and Lexington, and has a population of 76. It has a church, two stores, smithy, a resident physician, &c.

NEW HOPE is 10 miles from Staunton, on the road to Weyer's Cave, and has a population of about 200. It has one church, a Tunker church near, two stores, two resident physicians, a graded school, and the usual workshops belonging to a thriving village.

NEWPORT is situated on the Brownsburg road, 18 miles from Staunton, and has a population of 102.

PEYTONSVILLE. On the beautiful grounds at the intersection of Fair Ground avenue and the Parkersburg road, and north of those handsome thoroughfares, a plat of the streets and lots of this village has been made. In the opinion of many, it is destined to become the most attractive place of residence in the neighborhood of Staunton. The present population, on the Steep-hill estate, on which the lots lie, is 30.

PIEDMONT is 2 miles east of New Hope, and famous as the scene of a bloody engagement during the civil war.

STUART'S DRAFT is a post-office and village about 8 miles from Staunton, on the Shenandoah Valley Railroad, with a population of about 50, and is situated in the midst of one of the richest and most prosperous sections of the county.

SPRING HILL is situated 8 miles northwest of Staunton, and has a population of 132. It is a post-office, has two churches, carriage and wagon-maker, blacksmith, physician, and two stores. It is a thriving and advancing village.

SANGERSVILLE is a post-office and village north of Staunton 22 miles. It has a store, blacksmith shop, two churches, and is a thriving little town of 75 to 100 inhabitants.

VERONA is on the Valley turnpike, about 6 miles north of Staunton, and has a population of 63. It is a station on the B. & O. Railroad, a post-office, has a store, extensive flouring mill, blacksmith shop, &c.

WAYNESBOROUGH was first located on lands belonging to James Flack, and named after Gen. Anthony Wayne. In 1798 Samuel and J. Estill made an addition to the town by laying off with streets and alleys a piece of adjoining land containing twenty-one acres. Good schools were early established, and the education of the young engrossed the public attention for many years. The first act for the incorporation of the trustees of the Waynesborough Academy and Town Hall was passed on 19th of December, 1832, or two years before the incorporation of the town. It is in these words:

Be it enacted by the General Assembly, That Richard Henry, Nathaniel Massie, Wm. Clarke, John Wayt, Robt. Guy, Livingston Waddill, and Alex'r Wayland be, and they are hereby constituted a body politic and corporate by the name and style of "The Trustees of the Waynesborough Academy and Town Hall," and by that name shall have perpetual succession; may sue and be sued, and have a common seal, with power to purchase, receive and hold, to them and their successors forever, any lands, tenements, rents, goods and chattels, of what kind soever, which may be purchased or devised, or given to them, for the use of the said Academy and Town Hall; and to lease or rent or otherwise dispose of the same, or any part thereof, in such manner as to them shall seem most conducive to the advantage of the said Academy and Town Hall; Provided, That not less than a majority of the said trustees shall be sufficient to authorize the sale of any real estate belonging to the said Academy and Town Hall. The said trustees, or their successors, or a majority of them, shall constitute a Board, with power to appoint a President, tutors, treasurer, and such other officers as may be necessary, and shall have power, from time to time, to make and establish such by-laws, rules and regulations, not contrary to the laws and Constitution of this State or the United States, as they may judge necessary for the government of the said Academy and Town Hall.

2. The said trustees, or any one of them, shall have power to take and receive subscriptions for the use of the said Academy and Town Hall; and in case any person shall fail to comply with his or her subscription, to enforce the payment thereof, by warrant before a justice of the peace, or by motion in any court of record in this Commonwealth, according to the amount of such subscription, upon giving ten days previous notice of such motion. And in case of the death, resignation, or legal disability of any one or more of the said trustees, the vacancy or vacancies thereby occasioned, may be supplied by the remaining trustees, or a majority of them.

Nothing in this act shall be so construed as to restrain the General Assembly of this Commonwealth from amending, altering or abolishing, at any future time, the said corporation.

This act shall be in force from its passage.

The act for the incorporation of the town was passed February 12th, 1834, and need not be quoted, as it is in the usual form. It provided for the election of trustees, defined their powers, and authorized them to convey water into the town, etc. In 1874, Waynesborough obtained a new charter, the original charter having been in operation until 1858, when it was supposed to have lapsed. (See Session, acts 1874-5.) Under the new charter, William Withrow was elected Mayor; Thos. H. Antrim, Treasurer; and J. H. Schindett, Sargeant. The Mayors have since been: Dr. P. St. G. Gibson, G. A. Bruce, and G. A. Patterson, who is the present Mayor. A handsome prison was erected in 1866-67, with a commodious Clerk's office and Council Chamber above. The population is 484, and the value of real and personal property is $137,209. Since the construction through the village of the Shenandoah Valley Railroad, there has been a considerable increase in business prosperity, and Waynesborough seems destined to become a commercial and manufacturing centre of importance. There is a monthly magazine published in the town called "The Gem," and conducted with spirit by the enterprising firm of Dudley & Booz. A valuable flouring-mill was erected on the South River, at Waynesboro, as early as 1802. "It has been greatly enlarged," says Mr. William Withrow, to whom the writer is much indebted for information as to Waynesborough, the whole of which he regrets that his limited space does not permit him to use, "and has a capacity equal to, if not greater than any other in the county. It is said to grind one hundred barrels every twenty-four hours. To this mill is attached one for grinding plaster of Paris, of which it turns out from six to eight hundred tons annually."

WEST VIEW is 7 miles west of Staunton, on the Parkersburg turnpike, and has a population of about 60. It has a church, store, post-office. blacksmith's shop, flouring-mill, foundry and machine shop—formerly the property of Philip O. Polmer, dec'd.

CHAPTER XVII.

TOPOGRAPHY, METEOROLOGY, SOILS, GEOLOGY, MINERALOGY, FAUNA, FLORA, ETC.

Augusta county lies in what is commonly called the Valley belt, situated between the Blue Ridge and Alleghany Mountains. (The Alleghanies are sometimes called the Apalachian Mountains. European geographers extend the name northwardly as far as the mountains extend. The mountains get the name from the Apalachies, a tribe of Indians formerly residing in the southern portion of the mountains.) Staunton, about the geographical centre of the county, is about 250 miles from the sea coast and about 270 from the Ohio river. The mountains are not solitary and scattered confusedly over the face of the county, but are disposed in ridges on the eastern and western boundaries, running nearly parallel to each other. In the county there are three solitary peaks, Betsy Bell, the Sugar Loaf, and Elliott's Knob, and one of those ridges or divides which separate the waters of the Shenandoah from the James. The North Mountain range passes entirely through the county, and, from its great extent, was called by the Indians the " Endless Mountains."

The county is bound on the east by the summit of the Blue Ridge on the lines of Albemarle and Nelson counties, on the north by Rockingham county, on the west by Bath, Highland and Pendleton counties—the last being in West Virginia—and on the south by Rockbridge. It occupies the entire width of the Shenandoah Valley, and contains the head-springs, or sources of the Shenandoah river. Staunton, in the centre of the county, is in latitude 38° 09' N. and longitude 79° 04' 12" West from Greenwich. The county is about 35 miles long and about 30 wide, with an area of about 1,000 square miles, and has, by the census of 1870, 222,843 acres of improved land and 178,028 acres of unimproved land. In 1882 it is divided into six districts, among which the population is distributed, by the census of 1880, as follows:

1. Beverly Manor, including Staunton, with a population of 10,026
2. Middle River, with a population of 5,549
3. North River,   "   "   4,313
4. Pastures,   "   "   3,991
5. River Heads   "   "   4,757
6. South River,   "   "   5,074

    Total, by the State's census of 1880 35,710

An extensive traveler in foreign lands, the writer has never seen a superior race of men and women to those of Augusta and Virginia.

The Valley of Virginia, in which Augusta county is situated, "is part," says Hotchkiss, "of the great connected belt of Silurian limestone* valleys that extend for 1,500 miles from the mouth of the St. Lawrence through Canada, Vermont, New York, New Jersey, Pennsylvania, Maryland, the Virginias, Tennessee and Georgia into Alabama, forming not only one of the most beautiful, fertile, populous, and everyway desirable portions of the States it crosses, but is the 'garden of America,' as Washington called it." In the grand plateau of the Virginian Valley, and about midway between Harper's Ferry and Bristol, lies Augusta county. Its surface is entirely above the plane of 1,000 feet of altitude above the sea level; its valley portions, proper, range from near 1,000 to over 2,000 feet in elevation, and its mountain lands range to 4,456 feet in Elliott's Knob. The average of the county is not far from 1,500 feet. The general aspect of the country is animated and inviting. In the scenery there is a union of romantic and rural beauty, a bold variety of broken ground, plain, and mountain peak, harmonized by congenial groves and clambering vines; intervening marks of cheerful cultivation, and the quiet presence of herds of cattle, horses and sheep grazing upon the luxuriant pastures.

The climate of Augusta is noted for its salubrity, the air being dry, pure and bracing, altogether without grossness. No malaria exists, and none of those fevers so common to less favored regions. The causes which modify the climate are in Winter the mountain ranges, which shelter the country from cold winds, and prevent, at every season, those cyclones and tornadoes which sweep the Atlantic coast, and are so destructive on the prairies of the West. The elevation of the Valley and the lofty mountains prevent excessive heats in Summer, and give us cool and pleasant nights. Thousands resort to this section annually in pursuit of health and a delightful Summer residence. The mean January temperature of Staunton, in the heart of the county, is 41° Fahr., and that of Jule 75°, according to the Smithsonian observations. The rainfall is 44 to 56 inches, and the rains are well distributed throughout the year. The winds are moderate in velocity, and the prevailing ones are from the southern quarters. The sky is remarkable for its clearness, and consequently, for the cheerfulness of the atmosphere—clear weather being the rule, cloudy the exception.

The soil is generally fertile, and well adapted to the purposes of agriculture. The country on the South River, on the Middle River, on Lewis' Creek, on Baker's Creek, on Christian's Creek, and on the other creeks and water-courses of the county, in richness of soil, is perhaps second to none in America. Wheat is the most important production, and is exten-

---

*Silurian rocks, or strata, is the name given by Sir Robt. I. Murchiston to a series of rocks forming the upper subdivision of the sedimentary strata found below the old red sandstone, and formerly designated the grey wackes. These strata are well developed in Augusta county.

35 ‡

sively cultivated in every part of the county, and its quality is unsurpassed. Indian corn, rye, oats, barley, are also cultivated with success, and every part is well adapted, even the mountain sides, to grazing. The blue grass is indigenous and exuberant in its growth. The forests are composed of a variety of trees, and, above all, oaks, whose woods are valuable for manufacturing purposes, such as the white, Spanish, black, red, scarlet, post, chesnut, rock chesnut, and other species of oaks remarkable for their strength and durability; white and yellow tulip poplar; cucumber tree and the umbrella tree; black walnut, hickory, white pine, yellow pine, black spruce, hemlock, balsam fir, red cedar, juniper, arbor vitæ, sycamore, beech, chesnut, ash, elm, sumac, locust, horn-beam, or iron-wood, dog-wood, persimmon, wild cherry, birch—black and white, sugar maple, red maple, white maple, gum, and mulberry are common. The indigenous plum tree yields a fruit of agreeable flavor. Of shrubs and plants, the most noted are rhododendron, laurel and honeysuckles,—all being beautiful flowering shrubs,—wild hops, fox grapes, ginseng, sarsaparilla, snake-root, spikenard, vanilla grass, mandrake, wild gooseberry, and such European fruits—grapes, peaches, nectarines, pears—as have been introduced, flourish in Augusta, and the fruit is of delicious flavor.

THE RIVERS AND OTHER WATER COURSES.

The water-shed of the Shenandoah or sources of that river are in Augusta; the thousand streams that form the head of the river are here, and consequently Augusta is better watered than counties lower down the Valley, where the creeks have collected into the main stream. Many of these sources are bold, perennial springs, capable of turning a mill or factory a stone's throw from their sources.

BACK CREEK flows from the spurs of the Blue Ridge and along its base 12 miles in a northerly direction, till it enters South river, which from its source, near Old Providence church, flows east 14 miles, receiving many small tributaries, till it joins Back creek, and then continues four miles further to Waynesborough, thence north 14 miles to Port Republic, where it meets Middle river, and with it forms the south fork of the Shenandoah at an elevation of 1,000 feet above the sea.

CHRISTIAN'S CREEK.—Four miles from Old Providence church are the head springs of Christian's creek, which receives many tributaries, until in 15 miles it enters Middle river.

MILL CREEK is the most important tributary to Christian's creek, entering it 8 miles below its source.

LONG MEADOW RUN heads near the Chesapeake and Ohio railway, three miles east of Christian's creek, and enters Middle river near the same point with Christian's creek.

LEWIS CREEK heads near the bend in Mill creek, and flowing north-east, passes through Staunton and enters, after a ten-mile course, Middle river. It receives from the left

PEYTON'S CREEK, having its sources in the Buttermilk and Wagoners' springs, northwest of Staunton, Fanny's run and Gum Spring branch. Poage's run enters Lewis creek from the north four miles below Staunton.

MIDDLE RIVER.—At the foot of the Little North Mountain Middle river rises. It runs 9 miles along the base of the mountain northeast, where it receives another Back creek; near West-view it receives Baker's creek, which has come down about six miles from the south. Two miles from the mouth of Baker's creek, the river receives

BUFFALO BRANCH, heading at the North Mountain Summit, 2,109 feet, and the highest point of the railroad between the James and Ohio rivers. Buffalo Branch receives Dry Run from the northwest.

GROG SPRING.—About two miles west of Buffalo Gap, in the heart of the mountains, on the south side of the Parkersburg road, a bright little stream issues from the hillside. This is called "Grog Spring," and has been walled up and improved by the Sporting Club of Staunton. The water falls into a handsome marble vase or basin. On a slab let into the wall, supporting the vase, are inscribed some words inviting travellers to quench their thirst.

JENNING'S BRANCH, from the northwest, after receiving Whiskey creek and running a ten-mile course, enters Middle river.

BELL'S CREEK also enters Middle river, coming up from the south.

MOFFETT'S BRANCH is another tributary, also Elk run; also Falling Spring run, near Spring Hill. About 9 miles northeast from the mouth of Lewis creek, Middle river is joined by North river, and then joins the South river at Port Republic.

NORTH RIVER.—In the northwest corner of the county, on the Shenandoah Mountains, are the sources of North river; the two principal streams join, and then receive Freemason's run, and pursuing its course, receives Briery branch from Rockingham county; then it receives Mossy creek, and thence lower it receives Dry river, then Long Glade, and thence southeast till it joins Middle river, having four miles before its junction received Naked creek.

Besides these waters, there are in the county the Little Calfpasture and Big Calfpasture rivers, Walker's creek, Moffett's creek, and South river of the James. All these head or have their sources opposite the sources of the North river in the Shenandoah mountains, and they flow southwest into Rockbridge.

MINERALOGY.

The mineral resources of the county have, as yet, been very imperfectly investigated, but such explorations as have been made show the earth to be pregnant with ores. In many places iron has been found in inexhaustible quantities, and has been mined and smelted at numerous places in the county :—

1. Notably at Elizabeth, now known as Ferrol or Grace furnace, about 16 miles west of Staunton; built about 1863.

2. At Mossy creek charcoal cold-blast furnace, 14 miles northwest of Staunton; built in 1760, burnt in 1841.

3. Mount Torry hot-blast charcoal furnace, 15 miles east of Greenville; built in 1800, rebuilt in 1853.

4. Kennedy charcoal furnace ; built 1842.

5. Estaline cold-blast charcoal furnace, 21 miles west of Staunton, on the head waters of the Little Calfpasture river, built 1838—brown hema-tite ore.

6. Cotopaxi hot-blast charcoal furnace, 16 miles southwest of Staunton on South river, built 1836.

7. Vesuvius cold-blast charcoal furnace, 20 miles southwest of Staun-ton, on South river, built 1828—" black rock " hematite ore.

8. McDowell furnace, on South river, 1½ miles above Waynesborough. This furnace is supposed to have been erected between 1755 and 1780, by Samuel Moore, from whom McDowell, of Nelson, is thought to have ac-quired it. At the same place there was a forge, a saw and grist mill and carding machine, " making it," says Major McCue, " a place of consider-able importance."

MARBLE of great beauty and value has been discovered, and the quar-ries are worked to profit at Craigsville—a demand existing for it at Cin-cinnati and Cleveland. In various other portions of the county it has been discovered—notably at Steephill, near Greenville, and on Betsy Bell. The specimens from the county are of a compact texture and beautiful ap-pearance, and susceptible of a good polish.

LIMESTONE abounds in almost every part of the county, and in differ-ent localities there are

SANDSTONE ridges. One of these commences on Montgomery Hall, extends through Steephill, Selma and on to the Middle river, a distance of six or eight miles. The sandstone in this tract is composed of particles of quartz, united by a cement not calcareous or marly, but argillaceous or argillo-ferruginous and silicious. The grains of quartz are sometimes scarcely distinguishable to the naked eye, and sometimes they are equal in size to an egg. The texture of this sandstone is for the most part loose and porous, but hardens on exposure to the air, and of it durable walls are constructed. The four walls, a hundred feet long and about twelve high, of the Montgomery Hall barn were built nearly fifty years ago of this sandstone, and they are now in as good condition as when erected.

SLATE has been discovered in several localities, and has been worked on the Red Bud estate of Capt. Opie, within two miles of Staunton. This slate is of a bluish color and silky lustre, and splits into plates, and must, at a future day, become of marketable value.

Traces of lead and copper are also found in some of the mountain ranges.

KAOLIN AND FIRE-CLAY—the former of pure white—have been found on the South river, at Porcelain, near Sherando Station, on the Shenandoah railroad. Some years since extensive pottery works were erected, which were unfortunately destroyed by fire before insured. This catastrophe, and the panic of 1873, put an end to operations.

GLASS-SAND of the finest description has also been found on the South river, in this neighborhood, and all the raw material exists of excellent quality and in vast quantities for the manufacture of porcelain, glass, fire-brick, terra-cotta, etc.

FLINT, imbedded in limestone, has been found in several localities.

COAL, anthracite. has been discovered in the North Mountain, at Dora.

OCHRES, OR PIGMENTS, exist in different parts of the county, and

MANGANESE is exported in large quantities. The Crimora mines of Augusta have recently received from England orders for considerable quantities of manganese.

Traces of both zinc and lead have been discovered in the Blue Ridge.

MEDICINAL WATERS.

The Augusta or Stribling Springs are situated on the eastern slope of the North Mountain, about thirteen miles from Staunton. The medicinal effects of the waters are acknowledged, and there are several kinds of water here—alum and chalybeate being among them. The water from the principal spring is strongly impregnated with sulphuretted hydrogen, and is said to equal the celebrated springs of Harrowgate, England. This resort is well improved, picturesquely situated, and is a noted sanitarium or mountain watering-place. Near Deerfield, in the Valley of the Calfpasture, there are numerous sulphur springs,—one formerly called the Lebanon White Sulphur,—and in various other localities there are chalybeate springs and other mineral waters,—notably on the eastern slope of the Blue Ridge, about eighteen miles southeast of Staunton, is the Black Rock Spring, which is said to equal the waters of the Rawley Springs. The Black Rock Spring waters contain iron, soda, lime, magnesia, with carbonic acid gas, and has been found efficacious in dyspepsia, scrofula and other diseases.

THE SEAWRIGHT LITHIA SPRING, near the Augusta church, which much resembles the Buffalo Lithia, has been used by many afflicted persons with good effect.

THE VARIETY SPRINGS, sixteen miles west of Staunton, so called from the different medicinal springs on the tract, are well improved, and annually attract many visitors in search of health and recreation.

CRAWFORD SPRINGS, twenty-three miles west of Staunton, are likewise improved, and are popular.

NATURAL CURIOSITIES.

Under this head we might class many of those uncommon views which abound in our county. Some of these prospects, such as that from Elliott's Knob, are sublime and awe-inspiring, and rivet the attention of every beholder. The scenery of the county, except in the plains, such as that about Verona, is grand, diversified and beautiful.

WEYER'S CAVE, in a hill a short distance west of the Blue Ridge, is about sixteen miles north of Staunton, and is so called from the hunter who discovered it in 1804, Bernard Weyer. It has been said that no language can describe the vastness and sublimity of some or the exquisite beauty and grandeur of other of its innumerable apartments, with their snowy white concretions of a thousand various forms. It is ranked among the great natural wonders of the world. The stalactites and stalagmites are large and of slow growth.

FOUNTAIN CAVE is near Weyer's, and possesses many attractions, abounding in stalactites of a conical form, and basins of water of unknown extent.

THE BLOWING CAVES, in Castle Hill, so named prior to 1746, near Mt. Solon. These subterranean caverns give a passage to the waters of Freemason's Run and part of North river through the hill to the head of Mossy creek. There is a great quantity of spar scattered over the hill and encrusted on its edges of limestone. Where the waters of North river and Freemason's Run unite, and undermine Castle Hill, is called the Funnel.

Under this head may be mentioned an immense spring at the head of Mossy creek and the Blue Hole, near Mt. Solon, which has been sounded one hundred and eighty feet without finding the bottom. There are many of the so-called sink holes north of the creek, and extending as far as North river.

CYCLOPEAN TOWERS, near the Augusta Springs, are from sixty to seventy feet high, composed of limestone in strata, and much resemble the palisades on the Hudson river.

NATIVE ANIMALS.

Augusta belongs to the Nearctic region of North America, in which there are 2,291 different species of vertebrata. We must confine ourselves to those of our county. The condition of Augusta and the Valley, and indeed of the whole country previous to its settlement by Europeans, was highly favorable to the increase of animals. The forests gave them shelter, and they fed upon the productions of a fertile soil, and unmolested but by a few unarmed, or badly armed barbarians, they increased and multiplied with astonishing rapidity. The principal quadrupeds were the buffalo, elk, deer, bear, panther, wild cat, wolf, fox, beaver, otter, raccoon, o'possum, martin, hare, red and grey squirrels, porcupine, skunk, weasel, and mouse. The amphibious animals were the beaver, otter, musk rat and mink. We should like to describe some of the more interesting of these, but our limits do not admit of it. It may be remarked, however, that in disposition they are more mild and temperate, and in size, strength and vital energy superior to the same kinds of animals in Europe. This is illustrated by the following table, which gives the average weight of several kinds of animals in America and Europe:

	IN EUROPE.	IN AMERICA.
Bear	153 pounds.	456 pounds.
Wolf	69 "	92 "
Deer	288 "	308 "
Red fox	13 "	20 "
Porcupine	2 "	16 "
Beaver	18 "	63 "
Hare	7 "	8 "
Rabbit	3 "	7 "
Weasel	2 to 3 oz.	12 to 15 oz.
Otter	8	29

FISH—The waters of Augusta present a numerous list of fish, but they are rapidly diminishing. The most common are bass, pike, or pickerel, catfish, mud-suckers, speckled trout, perch, roach, mullet and eels.

BIRDS—The number of birds in our groves and fields, or who visit the county, is surprisingly great—over a hundred kinds. Many of them are of bright plumage, and one of them, the nightingale, the sweetest songster of the American forest. The most common are eagles, hawks, and other birds of prey, pigeons, ducks, geese, snow-birds, blackbirds and crows, larks, pigeons, robins. woodpeckers, jays. The most diminutive is the humming-bird, whose swiftness, vivacity and plumage make it the admiration of all beholders.

INSECTS—The varieties of these is considerable, especially in warm weather, when the earth and atmosphere teem with these specimens of animated nature. They are, however, for the most part. neither venomous nor otherwise injurious.

SERPENTS AND REPTILES—The number of these is small. The most poisonous are the rattlesnake, copperhead, red belly and garter snakes. Their number is rapidly diminishing. The black snake, water-snake, striped snake, green snake, and several others, are inoffensive; lizards, tortoises, turtles.

———

It has long been the warm wish of many to establish in Staunton a technical and paleontological museum and library. The matter was brought before the public in 1877 by the writer, as will be seen in the following correspondence, and was most favorably received. Maj. Jed. Hotchkiss, Mr. Wm. M. Bowron, F. C. S., and other literary and scientific persons promised their hearty coöperation. So far, nothing has been accomplished, owing to the depression following the financial panic of 1873-4, but it is believed that the suggestions made on the subject will ere many years be carried out:

CORRESPONDENCE.

STAUNTON, September 7, 1877.
CAPT. WM. L. BALTHIS, Mayor, &c., of Staunton:

SIR: I take the liberty, owing to your official position, to address you this letter, and to ask thus publicly the coöperation of the people of the town and county in securing the end in view.

You will doubtless agree with me that it is much to be regretted that we have not had, and have not now in our town, a repository, or museum, where things having a relation to literature, art, science, or natural history, may be preserved. Were a suitable building secured, the industry of the antiquarian, the arborist, the genealogist and mineralogist would soon fill the shelves from the vast storehouse of Augusta's wealth. Such a museum, where one might not only gratify an antiquarian taste, but see displayed the products of the soil, fruits, grain, timber, ores, &c., would be one of the most attractive resorts in our community. It would be of the highest practical importance, also, as such a collection of soils, minerals, timber, &c., would enable strangers seeking investments in our county to see in a few hours what it would otherwise require years to obtain a knowledge of. In such a museum, the student might examine specimens in every branch of science relating to organic and inorganic nature, and the value of such an institution, in connection with our schools, public and private, cannot be overestimated. The science of geology has within the memory of the present generation made immense progress. Aided not only by the higher branches of physics, but by recent discoveries in mineralogy and chemistry, in botany, zoology and comparative anatomy, it has extracted from the bowels of the earth records of former conditions of our planet, and deciphered documents which were a sealed book to our ancestors. It has indeed extended its researches into regions more vast and remote than come within the scope of any physical science except astronomy; yet in our county we have no collection of the evidences of the formation of the earth, of native or extraneous fossils, such as minerals, earths, salts, combustibles, metals, or bodies of vegetable or animal origin, such as plants, shells, bones, &c., many of which are petrified and have been buried in the earth accidentally. Virginia, especially Augusta, abounds in these specimens. Our forests alone contain several hundred different kinds of wood, and generally they are valuable for the manufacture of furniture, for house, ship-building, etc. Who among us has seen them, or any considerable number of them brought together, or could name or classify them, if they were? Our soil is rich in minerals, coals, iron, salt, gold, copper, gypsum, yet there is no collection of them to be seen or studied.

When a boy, I remember to have seen in the county many relics of the red men, such as stone arrow-heads, hatchets, and instruments in the shape of an adze, which the barbarians, no doubt, used to fell timber and scoop out their canoes. What an interest a cabinet of these curiosities would now possess! I trust it is not too late to secure many of these memorials, but, to be successful, no time should be lost. I see, with surprise, no mementoes of the late civil war but a few rusty blades, and now and again a dilapidated scabbard or broken gun-barrel. Let us collect these mementoes, also, of that period in our history:

> " When civil discord first grew high,
> And men fell out, they knew not why."

My interest in the subject is doubtless the greater from the fact that I have visited many celebrated museums in Europe, particularly in Italy, which contain innumerable specimens of the three ages into which antiquarians divide the primeval or pagan ages, namely: First, the stone; secondly, the bronze; and thirdly, the iron; each betokening a different degree of advancement and civilization. And collections also of all succeeding ages, with the natural productions, &c., of every country.

With the hope that such a want may be supplied in our prosperous and growing city, I address you this brief and hurried note, and ask your valuable coöperation.   I am, Mr. Mayor,

Very truly yours,
J. L. PEYTON.

———

COL. JOHN LEWIS PEYTON:

DEAR SIR: I have just read with much interest your letter of the 7th inst., in regard to the importance of establishing in Staunton a suitable place for the reception and preservation of specimens secured by the antiquarian, geologist, &c., &c. I think it a matter of peculiar interest to the citizens of this section of country, where the industrious geologist alone could soon supply a cabinet that would not only add to the knowledge, but to the wealth of our community.

I feel, sure, sir, that your experience will enable you to give proper direction to the project, and that you will find many lovers of science who will be glad of an opportunity to give material aid in furtherance of the proposed object.

With the assurances of a hearty coöperation on my part,

I am yours, truly,

Staunton, Sept. 8, 1877.   WM. L. BALTHIS.

36 ‡

APPENDICES.

APPENDICES.

THE DESCENDANTS OF THE FOUNDER.

The following genealogy of the Lewis family, with the prefixed note of explanation, was prepared some years since, with much care, by Howe Peyton Cochran, Esq., of Charlottesville. It is one of the most complete enumerations of the descendants of an ancestor which we have in Virginia or the South.

EXPLANATION.

JOHN LEWIS, the first European settler of Augusta County, Va., is marked A. His children AB, AC, and his grandchildren ABA, ACA, &c., so that two letters show that the person before whose name they appear is a child of said John Lewis, three letters a grandchild, four letters a great-grandchild. If the table were perfectly accurate, and Samuel Lewis had been marked AA instead of AB, as was done inadvertently, the letters would show a person's descent. For example AEBIA will be the first child of the ninth child of the second child of the fourth child of John Lewis *propositus*, e. g., A John Lewis, E William Lewis, B John Lewis, I Margaret Lynn Lewis, A John Lewis Cochran.

To find the relationship between two persons, for example AEBI and AEFC, the first two letters being the same, they had the same grandparents and are first cousins. Again: AEBI and ADDB will make them second cousins, &c.   H. P. C.

The Lewis family were originally French Huguenots, and left France after the revocation of the Edict of Nantes, 1685. Three brothers, namely William, Samuel and John, fled to England. [See Smiles' History of the Huguenots.] Shortly thereafter William removed to the north of Ireland, where he married a Miss McClelland. Samuel fixed his residence in Wales, while John continued in England. Descendants of each of these three brothers are supposed to have settled in Virginia by the late Mrs. Agatha Lewis Towles, who mentioned the fact that Samuel Lewis emigrated from Wales to Portugal, and was never again heard of.

William Lewis, who settled in Ireland, at his death left issue one son—
namely :
Andrew, who m Miss Calhoun and left issue—namely :
    1. John, b 1678.
    2. Samuel, b 1680.

A.   JOHN LEWIS (*propositus*), m Margaret Lynn, d of the Laird of
    Loch Lynn, and left, at his death in Virginia, the following
    issue—namely:
AB.   1. Samuel, b in Ireland 1716.
AC.   2. Thomas, b "   "   1718.
AD.   3. Andrew, b "   "   1720.
AE.   4. William, b "   "   1724.
AF.   5. Margaret,b"   "   1726.
AG.   6. Anne, b   "   "   1728.
AH.   7. Charles, b in Virginia 1736.

AB.   Samuel Lewis served with distinction as a captain in the war be-
    tween the English and French colonists. His brothers, Andrew,
    William and Charles, were members of his company, and all four
    were at Braddock's defeat, and three of them wounded. Samuel
    was afterwards conspicuous in the defence of Greenbrier county
    and the border settlements from the Indians. He died unm.

AC.   Thomas Lewis was short-sighted, and therefore did not figure so
    conspicuously as his brothers as an Indian warrior. He was a
    man of much learning and ability, a member of the House of
    Burgesses, and a member of the Virginia Convention of 1776.
    His library was one of the most extensive and well selected in the
    colony.   Thomas Lewis m Jane, d of William Strother, of Staf-
    ford county, Va., January 26, 1749, and left the following issue:
ACA.   Thomas, b 1749.
ACB.   Margaret Ann, b 1751.
ACC.   Agatha, b 1753.
ACD.   Jane, b 1755.
ACE.   Andrew, b 1757.
ACF.   Thomas, b 1760.
ACG.   Mary, b 1762.
ACH.   Elizabeth, b 1765.
ACI.   Anne, b 1767.
ACJ.   Frances, b 1769.
ACK.   Charles, b 1772.
ACL.   Sophia, b 1775.
ACM.   William Benjamin, b 1778.

AD.   General Andrew Lewis, "the Hero of the Point," m Elizabeth
    Givens, of Augusta County, in 1749, and left issue—viz.:
ADA.   John.
ADB.   Thomas.
ADC.   Samuel.
ADD.   Andrew.
ADE.   Anne,
ADF.   William.

AE.   Col. William Lewis, of the Sweet Springs, called the "Civilizer of the Border," m Anne Montgomery April 8th, 1754. Her father, when a child, was sent to Scotland from Ireland, to avoid persecution. There he married Miss Thomson, a relative of the famous poet, James Thomson, of Roxburgshire, the author of "The Seasons." Col. Wm. Lewis died at the Brick House, near the Sweet Springs, 1811. His wife died at the same place 1808. They had the following issue:

AEA.   Margaret, b 1756.
AEB.   John, b 1758.
AEC.   Thomas, b 1761.
AED.   Alexander, b 1763.
AEE.   William I., b 1766.   M. C. for Campbell district.
AEF.   Agatha, b 1774.
AEG.   Elizabeth Montgomery, b 1777.
AEH.   Charles W., 1780.

AF.   Margaret Lewis, d unm.

AG.   Anne, d unm.

AH.   Col. Charles Lewis, who was killed October 10, 1774, at the battle of Point Pleasant, m Sarah Murray, a half-sister of Col. Cameron, of Bath county, Va., and left the following issue:

AHA.   Elizabeth, b 1762, died unm.
AHB.   Margaret, b 1765
AHC.   John, b 1766.
AHD.   Mary, b 1768.
AHE.   Thomas, b 1771.
AHF.   Andrew, b 1772.
AHG.   Charles, 1774.

ACA.   John Lewis was a captain in Gen. Andrew Lewis' command in 1774, and was at the battle of the Point, where he was dangerously wounded. He was subsequently an officer in the war of the Revolution, and died 1788, leaving the following issue:

ADAA.   Thomas.
ADAB.   John.
ADAC.   Charles.
ADAD.   Elizabeth, who married Col. John Francisco, of Kentucky.

Nothing further is known of John Lewis [ADA] and his descendants, than that they are scattered through West Virginia, Kentucky and Alabama.

ACB.   Margaret Ann Lewis m McClenahan, of Staunton, Va., by whom she left one child. Her husband dying, she afterwards m Col. William Bowyer, of Staunton, by whom at her death, in 1834, she left five children. Her issue were:

ACBA.   John McClenahan.
ACBB.   William C. Bowyer.
ACBC.   Strother Bowyer.
ACBD.   Luke Bowyer.
ACBE.   Peter G. Bowyer.
ACBF.   Malinda Bowyer.

ACC.   Agatha Lewis m first Capt. Frogg, who was killed at the Point,
        Oct. 10, 1774, by whom she left one daughter; second, she m Col.
        John Stuart, of Greenbrier co., by whom she left four children at
        her death in 1836, aged 83, namely:
ACCA.   Eliz. Frogg, b 1773.
ACCB.   Charles A. Stuart, b 1775.
ACCC.   Lewis Stuart, b 1777.
ACCD.   Margaret Stuart, b 1779.
ACCE.   Jane Stuart, b 17—, who m Maj. Robert Crockett, of Wythe co.
        and left the following issue, namely: I. Maria, who m Judge
        James E. Brown, by whom she left issue, namely: I. Wm. Brown,
        who died unm; II. Jane Brown, who died unm; III. Fanny Pey-
        ton Brown, who m Col. Joseph F. Kent and left issue at her
        death in 1861: 1. Betty, who m George M. Harrison, a lawyer of
        Staunton, Va., and they have two children: 1. Fanny, and 2. Kent;
        2. John Kent, unm; 3. Jane Kent m Howe Peyton Cochran; 4.
        Emma Kent, m Jno. O. Yates; 5. Alexander Kent, unm. After
        her death, Col. K. m Virginia, d of Hon. John Howe Peyton,
        [AEBGI] has issue: 1. Joseph; 2. Susan Peyton; 3 Mary. IV.
        Alexander Brown, fourth son of Judge Brown, was a most prom-
        ising young man, who after graduating with distinction at the
        University of Virginia, commenced the law practice in Wythe,
        but died soon after; 2. Agatha Crockett, m James McGavoc and
        left issue; 3. Charles Crockett, who m Mary Bowyer, of Bote-
        tourt, and left issue; 4. Stuart Crockett, m Margaret Taylor, of
        Smythe co., and left issue, names unknown; 5. Frank Crockett,
        m ———; 6. Gustavus Crockett, m Eliza Erskine, and left issue;
        7. Augustine Crockett, died unm.

ACD.   Jane Lewis m Thomas Hughes, and left issue at her death in 1790,
        aged 35, but number and names are unknown.

ACE.   Andrew Lewis, died unm in 1810.

ACF.   Thomas, died unm in 1847.

ACG.   Mary m John McElhany, and died with issue, 1829, names un-
        known.

ACH.   Elizabeth m Thos. Meriwether Gilmer, of Rockingham co., Va.,
        in 1783, and had the following issue:
ACHA.   Peachy Ridgway Gilmer.
ACHB.   Mary Meriwether Gilmer.
ACHC.   Thomas Lewis Gilmer m Nancy Harvie, of Georgia, by whom
        he left six children.
ACHD.   George Rockingham Gilmer was M. C. for Georgia, and Gover-
        nor of that State. He married Eliza Frances, d of Maj. Robt.
        Grattan, of Va., but left no issue.
ACHE.   John Gilmer m first, Lucy Johnson, d of Col. Nicholas Johnson,
        of Louisa co., Va.; second, Miss Barnett, of Oglethorpe, co., Ga.
        He has eight children and several grandchildren.
ACHF.   William Benj. Strother Gilmer m Elizabeth Marks, d of Nicho-
        las Marks, of Ga. No issue.
ACHG.   Charles Lewis Gilmer m first, Nancy Marks; second, Mrs. Kyle;
        has six children and some grandchildren.

ACHH. Lucy Anne Sophia Gilmer m Benegal S. Bill, of Montgomery, Ala. Has five children living and some grandchildren.

ACHI. James Jackson Gilmer m Elizabeth Jordan, of Jasper co., Ga., and has four children.

ACHJ. Walker Gilmer,
ACHK. Eliza Gilmer, } died young.
ACHL. Edward Hampden Gilmer,

ACI. Anne Lewis married first. Mr. Douthat; no issue. Second, Mr. French, of Ky; issue unknown.

ACJ. Frances Lewis m Layton Yancey of Rockingham co,, Va., and at her death, in 1845, left issue, one son, namely:
ACJA. Col. Wm. B. Yancey.

ACK. Charles Lewis m Miss Yancey, and at his death, near Port Republic, Rockingham co., Va., in 1832, left issue:
ACKA. Thomas,
ACKB. Samuel,
ACKC. Charles.
ACKD. Mary, who m Dr. Musco Chambers, of Clinton co., Ohio.
ACKE. Margaret Strother, who m Rev. C. B. Tippett, of Maryland.

ACL. Sophia Lewis m John Carthrae, of Rockingham co., Va., and removed to Missouri; their issue unknown·

ACM. William Benjamin Lewis m M. Hite, and at his death, in 1842, left issue:
ACMA. William H. Lewis, who m Elizabeth, d of Capt. John Lewis [AHC], of Bath co.; issue unknown.
ACMB. Gen. George Lewis m Miss Effinger.
ACMC. Mary Jane Lewis.

Now for the issue of Gen. Andrew Lewis:

ADA. John Lewis m Patsy Love, of Alexandria, Va., and left issue:
ADAA. Andrew Lewis.
ADAB. Samuel Lewis m Miss Whitley, d of Col. Whitley, of Ky.; issue unknown.
ADAC. Charles Lewis m a d of Gen. Abraham Trigg, of Va.; issue unknown.
ADAD. Elizabeth Lewis m first Mr. Luke, of Alexandria, Va.; second, Mr. Ball, of Ky.; and third, Mr. Marshall, of Ky.; issue unknown.

ADB. Thomas Lewis m Miss Evans, of Point Pleasant, Va.; issue unknown.

ADC. Col. Sam'l Lewis, U. S. A., died unm in Greenbrier co., Va.

ADD. Col. Andrew Lewis, U. S. A., of the Bent Mountain, was b 1759. He m Eliza, d of John Madison, of Montgomery co., Va., and left issue:
ADDA. Charles Lewis, d unm.
ADDB. Thomas Lewis, a distinguished lawyer, who killed and was killed by Mr. McHenry in a duel with rifles at the distance of thirty

yards, the first duel at close quarters ever fought with rifles in Virginia. He left no issue.

ADDC. —— Lewis, }
ADDD. —— Lewis, } both died young.

ADDE. Agatha Lewis, b 1778, m Col. Elijah McClanahan, of Botetourt co., Va., end left issue unknown to writer.

ADE. Anne Lewis m Roland Madison, of Ky., and left issue.:
ADEA. John Madison.
ADEB. Eliza Lewis Madison m Mr. Worthington, of Maryland.
ADEC. Andrew Lewis Madison died a captain in U. S. A.
ADED. Roland Madison, jr., who lives, 1873, in Rushville, Indiana.

ADF. William Lewis, b 1764, m Lucy Madison, by whom he had two children   He married Nancy McClenahan, by whom he left the the following issue, viz:
ADFA. Andrew Lewis,
ADFB. Agatha Lewis,
ADFC. Sally Lewis m Mr. Fleming, and d in Huntsville, Ala., 1865, s p.
ADFD. Betty Lewis m Mr. Beale, by whom she had a daughter, who m Mr. Norvell, and resides in Huntsville, Ala.
ADFE. Lucy Madison Lewis m Jno. Bowyer, of Fincastle, Va., and had issue, one son, who died young.
ADFF. William Lewis, who died in Mississippi, leaving six children.
ADFG. John W. Lewis m Susan Bowyer, of Fincastle, September. 1831: removed to Alabama.   He lost two sons in the civil war of 1860-1865.   He has one son living in Texas, and a daughter married to Dr. Wood. Gen. John W. Lewis was a man of considerable ability and a member of the Legislature of Alabama and a General of militia   He removed to Texas in 1842.
ADFH. Charles Lewis, M. D., an successful surgeon, was killed in a rencontre in the streets of Mobile, Ala.
ADFI. Anne Lewis m Mr. Bradley, and in 1873 lives in San Antonio, Texas.   Issue unknown.
ADFJ. Mary Jane Lewis, died young.
ADFK. Pauline Lewis m Mr. Christian, and d in Tuscumbia, Ala., 1876.

AEA. Margaret Lewis m James McFarland, and removed to Pittsburg, Penn., when it was known as Fort Pitt.   She had eleven children, whose names are unknown, except the two first, Margaret and James.

AEB. John Lewis entered the Continental army as Lieutenant and came out a Major. He m first Miss Jane Sophonisba Thomson, d of Col. Wm. Thomson, of Belleville, S. C., 1788, by whom he had two children ; second, Mary Preston, d of Col. William Preston, of Montgomery co., 1793, by whom he had ten children.   He was a man of great firmness, ability and patriotism—a personal friend of Washington, with whom he passed the winter of 1777 at Valley Forge, and of President Jackson. He resided at the Sweet Springs, where he died in 1823   His issue by Mary Preston were :
AEBA. Eugenia Ann, b 1789.
AEBB. Sophia, b 1790, d young.

AEBC. Susannah Preston, b 1794.
AEBD. Mary Sophia, b 1796.
AEBE. William Lynn, b 1799.
AEBF. John Lewis, b 1801, d young.
AEBG. Anne Montgomery, b 1802.
AEGH. Sarah Elizabeth, b 1806, m Col. John Lewis [ADAAA] no issue.
AEBI. Margaret Lynn, b 1808.
AEBJ. John Benjamin, b 1810.
AEBK. Thomas Preston, b 1812, died unm in 1871.
AEBL. Pollydora, b 1817.

AEC. Thomas Lewis, Major U. S. A., (appointed by Washington), was greatly distinguished for gallantry, and was called the modern Chevalier Bayard, "sans peur et sans reproche." He killed Dr. Bell, of S. C., in a duel, and never enjoyed peace of mind afterwards. He died, s p, in 1804.

AED. Alexander Lewis, b 1763, d 1797, leaving one son.
AEDA. James Alexander Lewis.
AEE. Col. Wm. I. Lewis m Elizabeth Cabell, of Nelson co., Va. He died, s p, at his home, Mount Athos, near Lynchburg, in 1828. He was remarkable for his talents and acquirements, aud his friends several times sought to make him Governor of Virginia.

AEF. Agatha Lewis m Col. Oliver Towles, of Campbell co., Va., in 1794, and at her death in 1843, left issue:
AEFA. Anne M. Towles, b 1794.
AEFB. Oliver Montgomery Towles, d unm 1831.
AEFC. Elizabeth Lewis Towles, b 1801.
AEFD. Wm. Beverley Towles m Harriet C. W. Johnson; issue unknown.
AEFE. Margaret Caroline Towles m E. D. Sims and has three children.
AEFF. Thomas Henry Towles d unm 1847.
AEFG. John Towles d unm 1844.
AEFH. Alfred Lewis Towles m Jane Vaughan, of Missouri, and has two children, names unknown.

AEG. Elizabeth Montgomery Lewis m Col. John Trent, of Cumberland co., Va., and at her death, in 1837, left the following issue:
AEGA. Eliza Trent.
AEGB. Ann Trent.
AEGC. John Trent, M. D., m Miss Friend, and had issue; names unknown.

AEH. Dr. Charles W. Lewis m Mary B. Irvine, sister of Gen. Callender Irvine, of Philadelphia, U. S. Quartermaster. and had issue:
AEHA. Wm. Irvine Lewis, killed in the battle of Alamo, Texas, 1836.
AEHB. Thomas Alexander Lewis m Miss Stockton. and has two children, Irvine Lewis and —— Lewis.
AEHC. Ann Callender Lewis m Maj. de Bonneville, U. S. A., and has issue.
AEHD. Agnes Elizabeth Lewis m Archie Campbell, of Philad'a, and has issue; names unknown.
AEHE. Mary B. F. Lewis m Sam'l M. Leiper, and has issue; names unknown.

AEHF. Armstrong J. Lewis.
AEHG. Callender Irvine Lewis.

AHB. Margaret Lewis m Maj. Pryor, and left one child, viz:
AHBA. Eliza Pryor.

AHC. Capt. John Lewis, of Bath co., Va., m Rachel Miller, of Augusta
      co., and left at his death in 1843 the following issue, viz:
AHCA. Sarah.
AHCB. Henry Miller m Miss O'Connor, of Georgetown, Ky., and has
      issue
AHCC. Charles C.
AHCD. Nancy m Gen. Sam'l H. Lewis [ACKB] of Rockingham co., Va.
AHCE. James m Eliza Dickenson, of Bath co., Va.; issue unknown.
AHCF. William m Eliza C. Miller, of Augusta co., Va.; issue unknown.
AHCG. Martha Miller.
AHCH. John Lewis m Mary J Lewis [ACMC], d of Wm. Benjamin Lewis,
      [ACM] of Rockingham co.; issue unknown.
AHCI. Elizabeth m Wm. H. Lewis [ACMA] and has issue unknown.
AHCK. Hannah, unm.
AHCL. Racheal, d unm.

AHF. Col. Andrew Lewis m Margaret Stuart [ACCD] in 1802, and at
      his death, in 1833, left the following issue, viz:
AHFA. Charles Cameron d unm 1836.
AHFB. Agnes, b 1805.
AHFC. John b 1807, d 1811.
AHFD. Elizabeth, d 1812.
AHFE. Mary J, b 1811, m Charles R. Baldwin in 1833, d 1835.
AHFF. John Stuart.
AHFG. Margaret, d 1819.
AHFH. Sarah Frances, b 1817, m Dr. Creigh, of Lewisburg, W. Va.;
      issue unknown.
AHFI. Elizabeth, b 1819.
AHFJ. Andrew, d young.

AHG. Charles Lewis m Jane Dickinson in 1799, and left issue at his
      death, 1803.
AHGA. 1. John D.
AHGB. 2. Charles C.

ACCA. Eliz. Frogg m Maj. Isaac Estill, of Monroe co., and left four
      children.
ACCAA. Wallace Estill.
ACCAB. John Estill.
ACCAC. —— Estill.
ACCAD. —— Estill.

ACCB. Charles A. Stuart m Miss Robertson, of Augusta County, and
      has the following issue:
ACCBA. Robertson Stuart m Miss Bradford, of Orange, and has issue.
ACCBB. John Stuart m Margaret Lewis, [AACCA]; issue unknown.
ACCBC. Elizabeth Stuart, unm.

ACCC. Lewis Stuart m Sarah Lewis [AHCA] and has issue :
ACCCA. 1. Rachael.
ACCCB. 2. Jane.
ACCCC. 3. Agnes.
ACCCD. 4. Charley, unm.

ACCCE. 5. Margaret m James Davis, brother of Gen. Davis, of Miss., husband of her sister.
ACCCF. 6. Lewis, ⎫
ACCCG. 7. Henry, ⎬ unm.
ACCCH. 8. Andrew, ⎭

ACCD. Margaret Stuart m Col. Andrew Lewis, of Point Pleasant [AHF], and has following issue—viz.:
[See AHF ; the descendants of AHF and ACCD will be the same. Hence AHFA same as ACCDA, and so on.]

ACHA. Peachy Ridgeway Gilmer m Mary B. Harris, of Georgia, and has three living children and two who died ; one of them leaving two and the other three children. P. R. G. has nine grandchildren.

ACHB. Mary Meriwether Gilmer m 1st Warner Taliaferro, by whom she has four living children ; one of these has nine, one eight, one seven and one eight children. One of her children died, leaving one child, who is m and has children. 2d. —— Powers, by whom she has six children. Three of these have married, and have issue, and three have none.

ACKA. Thomas Lewis m Delia Fletcher, and has issue:
ACKAA. Anne Lewis.

ACKB. Gen. Sam'l H. Lewis, of Rockingham, m 1st Nancy Lewis, [AHCD], by whom he had eight children. He married, 2nd, Miss Lomax, d of John Tayloe Lomax, LL.D., Judge of the Eighth Judicial District of Virginia, and author of "A Digest of the Laws Respecting Real Estate," 3 vols. 8 vo., Phila., 1839, by whom he had four children. He married, 3d, Mrs. Fry, by whom no issue.

ADKBA. Charles H. Lewis, United States Minister to Portugal, in 1873 m a d of Judge Lomax, and has issue one daughter.

ACKBB. John Francis Lewis, United States Senator for Virginia in 1874, m Serena, d of Dan'l Sheffey, M. C. for Virginia, and has issue :
1. Serena m John Ambler Smith, M. C. for Virginia, in 1874.
2. Daniel Sheffey, who m a d of John Minor Botts, a distinguished M. C. for Virginia, and other minor children.

ACKBC. Samuel H. Lewis m a Miss Dabney, and has issue; unknown.

ACKBD. Elizabeth Rachael Lewis m Rev. J. C. Wheat, M. A., and has issue.
ACKBE. Mary, ⎫
ACKBF. Anne, ⎬ died unm.
ACKBG. Margaret Lynn, ⎭
ACKBH. William Meade Lewis, d unm.
The above are Gen. S. H. Lewis' children by his first wife.

ACKBI. Charlotte Lewis m Beverly Botts, son of John Minor Botts, and has issue.

ACKBJ. Lunsford Lomax Lewis, Judge of the Supreme Court of Appeals of Virginia, m a d of Hon. J. M. Botts.
ACKBK. Cornelia Lewis, d unm.
ACKBL. Anne, d unm.

ACKC. Charles Chambers Lewis m Mary Allen, and has the following issue :
ACKCA. Charles Chambers Lewis.
    B. James.
    C. Andrew.
    D. Mary.
    E. Henry Clay.
    H. William.
ACKCG. George Kemper Lewis.

ADAA. Andrew Lewis, son of John, m Jane McClenahan, d of Col. William Clenahan, of Botetourt county, and left the following issue :
ADAAA. Col. John Lewis, of Kanawha, b 1796, and m 1st Miss Donally, and left issue ; and 2d Sarah E. Lewis [AEBE] by whom he left no issue.
ADAAB. William Lewis.
ADAAC. Samuel m Frances Montague ; no issue.
ADAAD. Emmatine m C. Inglis, and afterward —— Capehart ; no issue of either.
ADAAE. Sally Neally m James S. Wood, of Botetourt.
ADAAF. Eliza m Madison Pitzer, of Roanoke.

ADFA. Dr. Andrew Lewis, son of William, m Maria Walton, and had issue:
    1. Frank.

ADFAA. Dr. Frank William Lewis m Miss McFarland, of Augusta County, and left issue :
    1. Rev. Frank Walton Lewis, who m Bettie Cheney.
    2. Mary Louise, who m Rev. Frank H Gaines, and one son, Lewis McF.
ADFAB. Lucy Lewis m George W. Shanks, of Roanoke.
ADFAC. Mary Lewis m Hon. Henry A. Edmonson, of Montgomery, long a M. C. for Virginia. Four children—
    1. Maria.
    2. Ellen.
    3. Andrew Lewis.
    4. Henry.

ADFB Agatha Lewis m Mr. Adams, of Mississippi, and has issue :
ADFBA. 1. Hon. George Adams, United States Judge for Mississippi.
ADFBB. 2. William Lewis Adams died unm in Texas, in 1844.
    C. 3. Lucy Adams, died young.
    D. 4. George Madison Lynch Adams, died young in Mississippi.
    5. Mary Adams m Samuel A. Maverick, of S. C., and moved to Texas in 1838, and has issue.

6. Andrew Lewis Adams, M. D., living in Mexico.
7. Robert Strother Adams, died in Ala., 1857.
8. Elizabeth Givens Adams m B. J. Clow, of Lavaca, Texas, and has four daughters.

AEBA. Eugenia Ann Lewis m William Sabb Thompson, of S. C., in 1809, and had issue,
AEBAA. William Russell Thompson, ⎫
AEBAB. John Paul Thompson, ⎬ died unm.
AEBAC. John Lewis Thompson. ⎭

AEBC. Susannah Preston Lewis m Capt. Henry Massie, of Nelson county, and has issue as follows:
AEBCA. Sarah Cocke, b 1811, m Rev. Frank Stanley, of N. C.; no issue.
AEBCB. Mary Preston, b 1813.
AEBCC. Henry, jr., b 1816.
AEBCD. Eugenia Sophia, b 1819.
AEBCE. Thomas Eugene, M. D., b 1822.
AEBCF. Susan Lewis, died young.

AEBD. Mary Sophia Lewis m James Littlepage Woodville, and left issue at her death, in 1836, one son:
AEBDA. James Lewis Woodville, M. D., b 1820, m Mary, d of Cary Breckenridge, of Botetourt.

AEBB. Col. William Lynn Lewis m 1st Ann E. Stuart, of S. C., in 1821, and had issue 4 children; 2d Harriet, d of Col. William R. Thompson, and by her had one son; 3d Letitia Preston, d of John Floyd, Governor of Virginia, by whom he had 5 children.

AEBEA. Mary Ellen Lewis m W. H. Colcock, and had three children. She died in Florida:
  1. Elizabeth.
  2. Thomas.
  3. Anna Stuart.

AEBEB. Ann Sabb Lewis m Goddard Bailey, and has a son and daughter
  C. James Stuart Lewis, M. D., b 1854, and has issue.
  D. Clara, died young.
  E. John St Julian, died in his 20th year.
  F Susan Massie m Mr. Fredericks, of S. C., and has three daughters unm.

AEBEG. Letitia Preston m Thomas Lewis Cocke, and left one daughter.
AEBEH. William Lynn Lewis m Florence Dooley, and has three children
AEBEI. Charles Lewis, unm.

AEBG. Anne Montgomery Lewis, was the 2d wife of Hon. John Howe Peyton, an eminent lawyer, orator and statesman of Virginia, and left at her death, which occurred at Montgomery Hall, near Staunton, in July, 1850, the following issue—namely:
AEBGA Susan Madison Peyton, b 1822, m Col John Brown Baldwin, of

Staunton, a distinguished lawyer and member of the Confederate Congress, and during the civil war colonel of the 52d Virginia Regiment. Col. B. at his death, in 1873, left no issue.

AEBGB. John Lewis Peyton, b 1824, m Henrietta E. C., d of Col. John C. Washington, of N. C., and has issue, one son, namely:

AEBGBA. 1. Lawrence Washington Howe Peyton.

C. Anne Eugenia Peyton, d unm.

D. Mary Preston Peyton m R. A. Gray, of Rockingham, and has issue: 1. Susan Baldwin; 2. Robert; 3. Isabella; 4. Howe Peyton; 5. Preston.

E. Lucy Garnet Peyton m Judge Jno. N. Hendren, and has issue: 1. Anne Montgomery; 2. Lucy Peyton; 3. Samuel.

F. Elizabeth Trent Peyton m Wm Boys Telfair, of Ohio, and has issue: 1. Susan; 2. William P.; 3. Baldwin.

G. Margaret Lynn Peyton m Geo. M. Cochran, Jr., of Staunton, and has issue: 1. Susan; 2. Maria; 3. George; 4. Anne Montgomery; 5. John Baldwin; 6. Margaret; 7. Peyton.

H. Yelverton Howe Peyton, unm, a resident of Texas.

I. Virginia Frances Peyton m Col. Jos. F. Kent, of Wythe co., Va., and has issue: 1. Joseph; 2. Susan Peyton; 3. Mary Preston.

J. Cornelia Peyton m Dr. Thomas Brown, of Abingdon, Va., and at Dr. Brown's death, in 1874, had issue, two sons: 1. John Baldwin; 2. Howe Peyton Brown. She m, second, Wm. Hastings Greene, of Augusta, and had issue, but they have no living children.

AEBI. Margaret Lynn Lewis m John Cochran, a merchant of Charlottesville, and has issue:

AEBIA. John L. Cochran, b 1827 at Montgomery Hall, in Augusta, m Mrs. Mary Massie, of Ohio, widow of Waler Massie; and widow also of Dr. Thos. E. Massie [AEBCE], and has a daughter and son, infants.

AEBIB. James Cochran, b 1830, m Elizabeth Brooke, grand-daughter of Joseph Smith, of Folly, and has issue: 1. Anne; 2. John L.; 3. Joseph; 4. James.

AEBIC. Henry King Cochran, M. D., unm.

AEBID. Howe Peyton Cochran, m Nannie, d. of Gen. Edward C. Carrington, of Halifax, and has one son, an infant. He m, second, Virginia, d of Col. J. F. Kent, and has no issue.

AEBIE. George M. Cochran, died 1838, unm.

AEBIF. William Cochran, died unm.

AEBIG. Mary Preston Lewis Cochran, b 1840, m John M. Preston, of Smythe co., Va., and has five children, all infants.

AEBIH. George M. Cochran, unm.

AEBII. Magdalen Cochran d 1863, unm.

AEBIJ. Preston McDowell Cochran d 1849, in infancy.

AEBJ. Dr. John B. Lewis, of the Sweet Springs, m Mrs. Caroline Smith, d of Col. Wm. Russell Thomson, of South Carolina, 1831, and has issue:

AEBJA. Eugenia A. Lewis. unm.

AEBJB. Dr. John Lewis, of Charlottesville, Va., m Miss Parrott.

C. Anne Stuart, m J. M. Preston White, Judge of the Texian Court of Appeals, and has issue.

D. William Thompson, unm.

E. Charles Montgomery, d unm.

F. Andrew, } twins, d in infancy.
G. Mary Preston, }

AEBL. Pollydora E. Lewis m Maj. Jno. W. Gosse, of Albemarle, and at her death, in 1871, left the following issue:

AEBLA. Mary Preston, d 1865.

AEBLB. Jane Walker, m Joseph Carter, and resides in Missouri.

AEBLC. William, d 1863.

AEBLD. Lynn Lewis.

AEBLE. John Preston.

AEBLF. Susan Massie.

AEBLG. Anne Montgomery Peyton.

AEBLH. Charles Thompson·

AEBLI. Eugenia Byrd.

AEBLJ. Lawrence.

AEDA. James A Lewis, of Kanawha, m Prudence Frazier in 1816, and at his death left the following issue:

AEDAA. William A.

B. Susan Massie m Wm. Frazier, and has issue—nine children, viz: James L., Wm. A., Emma L., W. Howard, Edward, Susan, Harry, Mattie, and John W.

1. Emma L. m Richard P. Bell, of Augusta co., and has issue: 1. Jannette; 2. Wm. Frazier; 3. R. P. Bell

2. Susan M. m W. P. Tams, and has issue, a son, W. F. Tams.

3. Harry m Miss Turpin, of Maryland

AEDBC. James Frederick Lewis.

AEDBD. Prudentia, d unm.

AEDBE. Edward Lewis

AEDBF. John Lewis

AEFA. Anne Maria Towles m Dr Landon Rives, of Cincinnati, Ohio, a brother of W. C Rives, U S. Senator for Va , and author of the "History and Times of James Madison "

AEFAA. Margaret Rives m —— King, of Cincinnati.

AEFAB Landon Rives, M. D., m Letitia Gamble, d of Gen. E. Watts, of Roanoke, and at his death left no issue. Dr. Rives' widow m, secondly, Dr Sorrell, of Georgia, and has no issue

AEFAC. Nannie Rives m —— Longworth, of Cincinnati, Ohio.

AEFAD. Edward Rives, unm.

AEFC. Elizabeth Lewis Towles m John Blair Dabney, of Va., and has the following issue, viz:

AEFCA. John Dabney m Miss Langhorne, and has issue.

38 ‡

B. Maria m Wm. Carrington, and has issue.
C. Susan m —— Taylor, and has issue.
D. Elizabeth m Peter Saunders.
E. Kate, unm.
F. Charles, unm
G. Chiswell m d of Col. Ed. Fontaine.
H. Agatha, died unm·

AEGA Eliza Trent m W. Swoope, of Augusta co., and left issue:
　B. Maria A. m Gen E. C. Carrington, and has issue: 1. E. C.
　　Carrington, jr., m, and has one child; 2. Campbell
　C. —— Swoope, m Geo. W. Hull, of Highland co., Va.
　D. Frank Swoope.
　E. Washington Swoope.
　F. Bolling Swoope.

AEGB. Anne Trent m Judge John Robertson, of Richmond, Va., and
　　left issue:
AEGBA. Powhatan.
　B. Elizabeth, who m —— Barkesdale, and has issue.
　C. Bolling, d unm.
　D. Ann.
　E. Gay.

AEBA. Eliza Pryor m Wm. Wagner, and has the following issue;
　B. Margaret.
　C. Hannah, m John Mitchel, and has issue.
　D. William.
　E. Cameron.
　F. Mary Francis. ·
　G Milly.
　H. Allen.
　I. Emily.
　J. Agnes.
　K. Charles
　L. Ann Eliza

AHCA. Sarah Lewis m Lewis Stuart [ACCC.] For the descendants vide
　　[ACCC.]

AHCC. Charles C. Lewis m Sabina Creigh, and has issue:
AHCCA. Margaret Lewis m John Stuart, [ACCBB] of Greenbrier county,
　　Va.
　B. Rachael Lewis m Col. Charles Arbuckle, of Greenbrier.
　C. John Lewis, unm.
　D. Nancy Lewis m Gen. S. H. Lewis. For her descendants, see
　　first eight children of Gen. L. [ACBB.]

AHCG. Martha Lewis m James A. Cochran, of Augusta county, and
　　left the following issue:
AHCGB. John Lewis Cochran removed to Texas, m and has issue
　C. Col. James Cochran m Nannie, d of Benjamin Crawford, of
　　Staunton, and has issue two children:
　　I. Benjamin.

2. Nannie.

D. Magdalen m John B Cochran, of Ky.

E. Rachael m William Van Lear, of Augusta county, and his issue.

F. Henrietta, d unm.

G. Elizabeth, d unm.

H. Robert m Miss Francisco, of Bath county, Va , and has issue.

I. Samuel, d unm.

J. Virginia, unm.

AHFB Agnes Lewis m John L. Sehon in 1823, and left the following issue :

   1. Fanny,

   2 Margaret Lynn, who m Valentine Horton, and has issue.

   3. Andrew Lewis.

   4. John Leicester.

   5. Sarah Eliz.

   6 Stuart.

   7. Columbus.

   8. Edmund.

   9. Agnes.

AHFF John Stuart Lewis m Mary F. Stribling, in 1837, and has issue :

   1 Fanny,

   2 Sarah.

   3 Matilda.

   4 Agnes

AHFI. Elizabeth Lewis m B. S. Thompson, in 1841, and has the following issue :

   1. Charles

   2. Margaret Lynn.

   3. John.

AHGA. John D. Lewis m 1st Miss Shrewsbury, and had the following issue :

   1. Joel Shrewsbury.

   2. Sally.

   He m 2d Miss Dickenson, and had the following issue :

   1. Charles.

   2. ———.

   3. ———.

   He m 3d Miss Daniel ; issue unknown.

AHGB. Charles C. Lewis m Eliza Steinberger in 1826, and had the following issue :

   A. Maria, d 1847.

   B. Caroline, d 1831.

   C. Peter S.

   D. Sarah.

   E. Charles C., d 1842.

ACCAD. Agatha Estill m Henry Erskine, of Greenbrier, and had issue as follows :

A. Elizabeth Erskine m Gustavas Crockett.
Margaret Lewis Erskine m Charles S. Gay, of Richmond,
Va., who removed to Augusta county, and had issue:
1. Charles Gay, killed in the battle of Malvern Hill.
2. Fanny m Richard M. Catlett, a lawyer o: Stáunton.
3. Elizabeth.
4. Erskine, unm.
5. Agatha.
6. William.
7. Carrie, m W. M. Allen, of Staunton.
B. Jane Erskine m William Boyd, a lawyer of Buchanan, in Botetourt county, Va., and has issue:
1. Henry.
2. Alice Boys.
3. William.
4. Andrew.
D. Margaret, William Lewis and John Robertson, children of
Charles S. Gay and wife, died young.

ACCCA. Rachael Stuart m Gen. Davis, of Miss., and had seven children—viz:
1. Runnels.
2. Charles.
3. Sarah.
4. Mary.
5. Alfred.
6 and 7. Unknown.

ACCCB. Jane Stuart m Sam'l Price, of Lewisburg, W. Va., formerly
Lieut.-Gov. of Virginia, and in 1876 United States Senator
for West Virginia, and a'. her death, in 1873, left issue:
1. Margaret Price.
2. Mary.
3. John.
4. Sally.
5. Jennie.
6. Lewis.
C. Agnes Stuart m Charles L. Peyton, son of C. Peyton, and a
great nephew of President Jefferson, of Greenbrier county,
West Virginia, and has issue as follows—viz.:
1. Thomas Peyton.
2. Elizabeth Peyton.
3. Lewis Peyton.
4. Charles Peyton.
5. Harry Peyton.
6 Caroline Peyton,

ADAAA. Col. John Lewis, of Kanawha, left the following issue by his
first wife: he had none by his second, S. E. Lewis [AEBH]:
1. Andrew.
2. Margery, who m ——— Kenna, of Cincinnati, O., and left one
son, Hon. John E. Kenna. M. C. for West Virginia in 1876.
3. John W. Lewis.
4. James Lewis.

ADAAB. William Lewis m Miss Tosh, of Botetourt county, and left five
  sons:
  1. Andrew, d unm.
  2. William.
  3. Thomas.
  4. John.
  5. Charles.

ADAAE. Sally Neally Lewis m J. F. Wood, of Buchanan, and had this
  issue:
  1. Andrew Lewis.
  2. Maj. John Bowyer Wood, U. S. Army.
  3. Edwin N. Wood, M. D., m his cousin, Miss Wood, and after
   her death Eva Allen.
  4. Palemon
  5. Frank Wood.

ADAAF. Eliza Lewis m Madison Pitzer, of Roanoke, by whom she has
  issue as follows:
  1. Andrew Lewis.
  2. Sarah, who m Rev. James McFarland, of Kentucky.
  3. Patsy, who m Prof. Wells, of Roanoke College, Salem, Va.
  4. Emeline, who m C. C. Thompkins.
  5. James
  6. George M.

AEBCB. Mary Preston Massie m John Hampden Pleasants, and at her
  death, in 1837, left issue two children:
  1. James, who m Caroline T Massie, [AEBCCB] and has no issue.
  2. Ann Eliza, who m Douglas Gordon, and has issue.

AEBCC. Henry Massie, jr., m Susan E. Smith, only d of Thomas Bolton
  Smith, of S. C., and has issue;
  1. Henry Lewis.
  2. Caroline m James Pleasants [AEBCBA]
  3. Sarah Lewis, unm.
  4. Thomas Bolton, dead.
  5. William Russell Thompson.
  6. Susan Derby, dead
  7. Charles, dead
  8. Eugene Carter, unm.
  D. Eugenia Sophia Massie m Col. Samuel Gatewood, and left
  issue:
  1. Susan m W. Taliaferro.
  2. Mary m Samuel Goode.
  3. William.
  4. Andrew Cameron.
  5. William Bras.
  6. Fillmore Stanley, dead.

ALBCE. Dr. Thomas E. Massie m the widow of Waller Massie, of Ohio,
  and at his death, in 1863, left three children:
  1. Frank.
  2. Eugenie.
  3. Nita.

THE M'DOWELL FAMILY.

Though the founder of this family settled on Burden's grant, the whole of which lies in the present county of Rockbridge, it is intimately connected with many of our people   The McDowells and Lewises were relatives and lived near each other, previous to 1732, in Ireland. They intermarried so extensively with the McCues, Prestons, Pattons, Cochrans, Moffetts, Bells, Alexanders, &c., of our county, that we take pleasure in inserting the following brief account prepared by our esteemed friend, Judge John H. McCue:

"Ephraim McDowell came to this country and settled in Pennsylvania previous to 1735, and between 1735 and 1740, with his son, John, who had married Magdalene Woods, in Pennsylvania, came to the home of his relative, John Lewis, the Founder. There they met with Burden, and became settlers on his grant near Fairfield, in what is now Rockbridge. John McDowell was Burden's Surveyor. His wife's mother was a Campbell, of the house of the Duke of Argyle. McDowell and eight of his men were killed near Balcony Falls by the Indians on the 25th of December, 1742. John McDowell, oldest child of Ephraim, had two sons, Samuel and James, and one daughter, Sarah. 1st. Samuel was the ancestor of the Reids and Moores of Rockbridge, &c. 2d. James married Eliz. Mc-Clung, and their son, Col. James McDowell, dec'd, of Cherry Grove, near Fairfield, was the father of the late Governor James McDowell, of Mrs. Thos. H. Benton, and of Mrs. Wm. Taylor. Their mother was Sarah Preston, a descendant of the original John Preston, who, at the May term of the County Court of Augusta, 1746, proved the importation, at his own expense, of himself and family from Ireland to Virginia. [See ante, p. 56.]

"The third child of John McDowell and Magdalene Woods was Sarah. She married Col. George Moffett, of Augusta county, the same who drove the Indians from Kerr's Creek, and was ambuscaded and repulsed by them on the Falling Spring farm, in Alleghany county. Col Moffett (not Moffítt, as generally printed,) was distinguished in Indian warfare, at Guilford, Cowpens, King's Mountain, and fought from the beginning to the close of the Revolutionary war. Col. Moffett and wife, Sarah Mc-Dowell, had nine children: 1st. John, died young; 2d. Margaret, married her cousin, Gen. Joseph McDowell, of North Carolina, one of the heroes of King's Mountain, and their son, Gen. Joseph Jefferson McDowell, of Hillsboro, Ohio, who died a few years since, married Sallie McCue, daughter of Rev John McCue, of Long Meadows, Augusta county, Va., who is still living, the only surviving child of her eminent father; 3d. Jas. McDowell Moffett married Hannah Miller (daughter of the founder of Miller's Ironworks on Mossy Creek, the first west of the Blue Ridge) One of their daughters, Hannah Winters Moffett, married John McCue, of the Long Meadow, Augusta county, Va., father and mother of Mrs. Col. D. S. Bell, of Augusta county, Va,: Judge J. H. McCue, Staunton; Mrs. Dr. C. Alexander, Staunton; Mrs. W. B. Dorman, Texas; Mrs. Decatur Hedges, of W. Va.; Jas M. McCue, W. Va.; Wm. A. McCue and Miss Hannah W. McCue, both of Augusta co., Va. The said John McCue was long Presiding Justice of Augusta, and for a number of years represented the county in the Legislature. The fourth child of Col. Moffett, and wife, Sarah, was George, who married Miss Gilkeson, and removed to Fayette, Ky. 5th. William, married a Miss McChesney, and a Jones. 6th. Mary married Dr. Joseph McDowell, of North Carolina, and after his death, she married, secondly,

Col. Jno. Carson, of North Carolina, member of Congress ; their son, Sam'l P. Carson, was also a member of Congress from that State. 7th. The seventh child of Col. George Moffett and wife, Sarah McDowell, was Magdalene, who married James Cochran, of Staunton. Their children were, so far as I am informed, the late John Cochran, of Charlottesville ; Geo M. Cochran, of Staunton ; the late Mrs. Benj. Crawford ; the late J. Addison Cochran ; the descendants of these, are many of them, among the most distinguished professional and business men of the country. 8th Martha, who married Capt. Robert Kirk, of the U. S Navy .9th. Elizabeth, who married James Miller, of Mossy Creek,"

THE PRESTON FAMILY.

The following account of the Preston family, one of the earliest which settled in Augusta, is from the pen of an unknown writer in the Brooklyn "Eagle :"

CONEY ISLAND, September 1, 1879.

DEAR EAGLE:—Charles W. Woolley, of Cincinnati, has been visiting New York, and a glimpse of him here brings up many reminiscences of the Tilden contest for the presidency, and of the impeachment trial of President Andrew Johnson. "Richileu" remembers being one of a dinner party given at Walker's, in Washington, at which the unlucky number thirteen was present, among whom were General Hancock, General Preston, of Louisville, and other celebrities. Benjamin F. Butler got it into his head that some treasonable designs were at the bottom of the dishes of that elegant entertainment, and Mr. Woolley was suspected of knowing all about it. Butler had him summoned as a witness, and on his refusing to answer some questions, had him arrested. Poor Miss Vinnie Ream, who had a studio in a cryptic corner of the basement of the Capitol, was suspected as no better than a Copperhead, and her studio was taken from her and prepared as a prison cell for the contumacious Woolley. William Preston, of Kentucky, one of the guests at that dinner, is a near relative of Mr. Woolley, as is also his wife. He has been a Congressman from that State, a lieutenant-colonel in the Mexican war, United States Minister to the Court of Spain, and a major-general in the Confederate army. He married his relative, Miss Margaret H. Wickliffe, daughter of Robert Wickliffe, of Lexington, who is an aunt of Mr. Woolley. Randal Lee Gibson, member of Congress from Louisiana, is also a relative of Mr Woolley; and thinking of Woolley and Gibson and Preston, "Richelieu" got turning over American genealogies, and thought it might not be uninteresting to your readers to trace the progress of one family in America from its emigration till the present time.

The paterfamilias or original emigrant was John Preston, who was buried in Tinkling Spring Cemetery. He was a native of county Derry, Ireland, and married Miss Elizabeth Patton, of county Donegal. They had five children, all born before emigration. They came to America in 1740, and purchased large possessions in Virginia. To show what a host of heroic men and beautiful women came from this one emigrant, the honors they held, the intermarriages they made, and the prominent influence exerted by them in every department of American society, I propose to group together a few of his descendants under the heads children, grandchildren, great-grandchildren, and great great-grandchildren.

HIS CHILDREN.

William married Miss Susanna Smith. He was a member of the Virginia House of Burgesses, and a zealous patriot in the Revolution.

Letitia married Col. Robert Breckinridge, of Virginia, and after her husband's death, emigrated to Kentucky.

Margaret married Rev. John Brown, a graduate of Princeton College, and a prominent Presbyterian minister in Virginia and Kentucky.

Ann married Francis Smith, of Virginia, and went to Kentucky, where one of her daughters married James Blair, Attorney-General of Kentucky, and father of Francis P. Blair, Sr.

Mary married John Howard, of Virginia, one of whose sons was a member of Congress from Kentucky and Governor of Missouri Territory.

HIS GRANDCHILDREN.

John Breckinridge, a Senator in Congress, and Attorney-General in Jefferson's Cabinet.

James Breckinridge, a member of Congress from Virginia.

Elizabeth Breckinridge married Col. Samuel Meredith, a nephew of Patrick Henry.

John Brown represented Kentucky in the Virginia Legislature; was first (and thrice elected) Senator of the United States from Kentucky, and married to the daughter of the Rev. Dr. John Mason.

James Brown, the first Secretary of State of Kentucky; many years Senator of the United States from Louisiana; United States Minister to France; married to the sister of Mrs. Henry Clay.

John Preston, member of the Legislature of Virginia, and many years Treasurer of that State.

Francis Preston, a member of the Senate of Virginia, a Congressman from that State, and a brigadier-general in the war of 1812; married to a daughter of Gen. William Campbell, the hero of King's Mountain, and a niece of Patrick Henry.

William Preston, a captain in Gen. Wayne's army.

James Patton, President, a member of the Virginia Senate, colonel in the U. S. Army, and Governor of Virginia.

Letitia Preston married to John Floyd, Governor of Virginia, and mother of another Governor (John B. Floyd) of Virginia.

Thomas Lewis Preston, a member of the Virginia Legislature; a major in the war of 1812; married to a daughter of Edmund Randolph, who was a delegate to the Continental Congress, a member of the convention that framed the United States constitution, Governor of Virginia, and Attorney-General and Secretary of State of the United States in Washington's Cabinet.

John Smith, married to the first white child born in Kentucky.

Margaret Howard, married to Robert Wickliffe. of Kentucky.

Letitia Breckinridge, married to Peter B. Porter, of Niagara Falls, Secretary of War in John Quincy Adams' Cabinet, a major-general in the war of 1812, and the only man who ever refused the office of General-in-Chief of the United States army.

HIS GREAT–GRANDCHILDREN.

Joseph Cabell Breckinridge, of the Kentucky House of Representatives and Secretary of State of Kentucky.

John Breckinridge, a professor in Princeton College, and married to a daughter of its President, Dr. Miller.

Robert J. Breckenridge, a distinguished theologian.

William L. Breckinridge, president of Danville College.

John B. Preston, many years a member of the Kentucky Legislature.

William C. Preston, president of South Carolina, United States Senator from South Carolina, and among the foremost orators and statesmen of the United States.

John S. Preston, member of the South Carolina Legislature, brigadier-general in the Confederate army; married a daughter of Major-General Wade Hampton, Sr, then the most wealthy planter of the United States.

Margaret B. Preston married General Wade Hampton, Jr., Governor of South Carolina, now United States Senator.

Elizabeth McDowell married Senator Thomas Hart Benton, the distinguished Senator of Missouri.

James McDowell, member of Congress and Governor of Virginia.

Henrietta Preston, married Albert Sidney Johnson, the great general of the Confederate army.

William Preston, member of Congress from Kentucky, lieutenant-colonel in the Mexican war, United States minister to Spain, and major-general in the Confederate army.

William Ballard Preston, Secretary of the Navy in President Taylor's Cabinet, and senator in the Confederate Congress.

John B. Floyd, Governor of Virginia, Secretary of War in Buchanan's Cabinet, and general in the Confederate army.

Nickettie Floyd married John W. Johnston, United States Senator from Virginia.

John Thomas L. Preston, colonel in the Confederate army, and professor in the Virginia Military Institute.

Francis P. Blair, Sr., the veteran editor of General Jackson's organ.

Thomas F. Marshall, the congressman and eloquent orator of Kentucky.

Alexander K. Marshall, also member of Congress from Kentucky.

Agatha Marshall married Chancellor Caleb Logan, of Kentucky.

Edward C Marshall, member of Congress from California.

Mary W. Parker, married to Thomas L. Crittenden, Secretary of State of Kentucky.

His two great-granddaughters, both daughters of Francis Preston—Susan S. and Sally Buchanan Preston—married their two cousins, James McDowell and John B. Floyd, both Governors of Virginia, one of them a Cabinet minister, and both members of Congress.

Lavallette Floyd married Professor Holmes, of the University of Virginia.

HIS GREAT-GREAT-GRANDCHILDREN.

Peter A. Porter was colonel in the Union army, and fell in the battle of Cold Harbor.

John C. Breckinridge, member of Congress and United States senator from Kentucky, Vice-President of the United States, receiving eight hundred and forty-eight thousand votes. He was also Major-General and Secretary of War in the Confederate States.

Samuel M. Breckinridge, a lawyer and judge in St. Louis.

Margaret M. Breckinridge, devoted to hospital and other charities in the late war.

39 *

William E. P. Breckinridge, colonel in the Confederate army, married to a granddaughter of Henry Clay.

Benjamin Gratz Brown, senator in Congress from Missouri, and Democratic candidate for Vice-President on the ticket with Horace Greeley, receiving two million, eight hundred and thirty-five thousand votes.

John Mason Brown, a colonel of cavalry in the United States army, and a prominent lawyer of Lexington, Ky.

Edward Cabell Carrington was a captain in the Mexican war, member of the Virginia Legislature, brigadier-general in the Union army, and United States attorney for the District of Columbia.

William Campbell Preston Carrington, a Confederate officer, who fell in battle at Baker's creek, near Vicksburg.

Susan Taylor married John B. Weller, member of Congress from Ohio, senator of the United States from California, Governor of California, and United States minister to Mexico.

Jessie Benton married Maj-Gen. John C. Fremont, Republican candidate for President and Governor of Arizona.

Sarah Benton married Richard T. Jacob, Lieutenant-Governor of Kentucky.

Susan V. Benton married Baron Souldree Boilleau, French minister to Peru.

Sally C. P. McDowell married Francis Thomas, Governor of Maryland.

William Preston Johnston, colonel in the Confederate army, confidential aide to President Jefferson Davis, and professor in Washington College, Virginia.

Randall Lee Gibson, brigadier-general in the Confederate service, now member of Congress from Louisiana.

Hart Gibson, member of the Kentucky Legislature. William Preston Gibson, member of the Louisiana Legislature.

Six brothers of these Gibsons, sons of John Preston's granddaughter, Louisiana Hart, named respectively Randall Lee, William Preston, Hart, Claude, Tobias and McKinley Gibson, were all distinguished officers in the Confederate army. William Preston and Claude Gibson gave up their lives for the Southern cause.

Mary Massie married John Hampden Pleasants, the well-known Virginia journalist, killed in a duel by Thos. Ritchie—1846.

Ann M. Lewis married the celebrated lawyer, John Howe Peyton. His son, John Lewis Peyton, the well-known author of " The American Crisis," &c., "Over the Alleghanies and Across the Prairies," &c., " The Adventures of My Grandfather," and other popular works, published in England, was accredited Confederate States agent to England and France during the civil war ; he married Henrietta, daughter of Col. J. C. Washington, and niece of Gov. William A. Graham, of North Carolina, and has issue a son, Lawrence W. H. Peyton. Mr. Peyton's eldest daughter married the late lamented Col. John B. Baldwin, M. C., etc.

Three of his great-great-grandchildren, brothers, named Cochran, were officers in the Confederate service.

Montgomery Blair, Postmaster-General in Lincoln's Cabinet.

James Blair married a daughter of Gen. Thomas Jessup, of the United States army.

Francis P. Blair, Jr., member of Congress and United States senator from Missouri, major-general in the Union army and Democratic candidate for Vice-President on the ticket with Horatio Seymour, receiving two million, seven hundred thousand votes.

Elizabeth Blair married Admiral Lee, of the United States navy.

Ellen Preston married James W. Sheffey.

Mary Sheffey married Prof. W. E. Peters, of the University of Virginia, who was educated in Germany. Prof. Peters married secondly the only sister of his first wife.

Mary T. Payne married Professor Neville, of the University of Kentucky.

Mary W. Packer married Tod Robinson, Judge of the Supreme Court of California.

Alexander Packer Crittenden is a prominent lawyer in San Francisco.

Thomas T. Crittenden, a brigadier-general in the United States army and member of Congress from Missouri.

Robert W. Woolley, secretary of United States legation to Spain, and Charles W. Woolley, who provoked these reminiscences.

LATER GENERATIONS.

Of the children of his great-great-grandchildren I cannot fully speak. Ten years ago several of them were making for themselves positions in society. In 1870 his great-great-grandson, John C. Breckinridge, had seven children, the eldest of whom, Cabell Breckinridge, was married to a daughter of Hon. R. W. Johnson, of Arkansas. His great-great-grandson, B. Gratz Brown, had six children. His great-great-granddaughter, Jessie Benton, had three children, the second of whom, Charles Fremont, was a midshipman in the United States navy. His great-great-granddaughter, Sarah Benton, had a daughter married, and a son, Richard Jacob, jr., a lieutenant in the navy. His great-great-granddaughter, Mary Massie, wife of John Hampden Pleasants, had a son, James Pleasants, a lawyer in Richmond, Va., who had married his cousin, Caroline Massie. and a daughter, Ann Eliza Pleasants, who had married Douglas H. Gordon, of Baltimore, and has four children, who were grandchildren of this great-great-grandchild of this John Preston. His great-grandson, Montgomery Blair, has five children, one of whom had married Gen. Comstock, of the United States army. His great-great-grandson, Francis P. Blair, Jr., had six children, one of whom, Andrew A. Blair, was an ensign in the United States navy.

It is not improbable that at present there are hundreds of grand and great-grandchildren, who, in the not distant future, will sustain the character of this great American family for brains, bravery and beauty in the sixth and seventh generations. But enough for to-night of American genealogies.   RICHELIEU.

THE CAMPBELL FAMILY.

John Campbell emigrated to America from Ireland in 1726, and first settled in Lancaster, Pa. In 1733 he came south to Augusta—then Orange county, and settled near Bellefont. He left two sons, Patrick and David. Patrick left a son Charles, whose son William was born near Staunton 1744, and was the hero of King's Mountain. David Campbell, the youngest son of the original settler, married Mary Hamilton, and left thirteen children. In 1765, John, the eldest son of David Campbell and Mary Hamilton, explored the southwest, and purchased lands on the head-

waters of the Holston, where, soon after, the family settled itself. One of
the daughters, Mary, married Wm. Lochart; a second, Margaret, married
David Campbell. All the Campbells supported the Founder in his early
plans, and shared in the hardships and dangers of the Indian wars. John
Campbell, the eldest son of David, born in Augusta, 1741, was a lieutenant in Wm. Campbell's company, in Col. Christian's regiment, under Gen.
Lewis, in 1774. He commanded a company in the battle of Long Island
Flats of Holston, in July, 1776, defeating the Indians under their famous
chief, Dragon Canoe. He also commanded a company in October, 1776,
in Col. Christian's expedition against the Cherokee towns. In 1778, he
was appointed clerk of Washington county. He died in 1825, in his 85th
year. His younger brother was Col. Arthur Campbell. David, the fourth
brother of those who came to Holston, was educated for the bar. He removed to Tennessee, and was one of the Judges of the Supreme Court.
He died in 1812. Robert, the next brother, born in Augusta, 1752, was a
volunteer under Lewis in 1774, was in all the battles with his brother, and
an ensign at King's Mountain. He was an active, energetic and useful
man. He died 1831, aged 77. Patrick, the youngest brother, was also in
the battle of King's Mountain. He married and left a large family, and
died in his 80th year. Such is a brief sketch of the five brothers, sons of
David Campbell, and grandsons of Jno. C., the original Irish emigrant.
The father of Gen. Wm. Campbell was Charles Campbell, who died in
Augusta. Wm. C., with his mother and sisters, then removed to Holston. Elizabeth, the eldest sister, married Jno. Taylor, from whom Judge
Allen Taylor and the Taylors of Montgomery county are descended.
Jane, the second sister, married Thos. Tate; Margaret, the third sister,
married Arthur Campbell; the fourth sister, Ann, married Richard Pas-
ton. All left families of high respectability.

Another branch of the Campbell family also settled in Augusta. Duncan Campbell, of Invergrary, Argyleshire, Scotland, married in 1612 Mary
McCoy, and the same year emigrated to Ulster county, Ireland, and died
there, leaving descendants, who about 1726 emigrated to Pennsylvania,
and in 1738 they removed to Augusta county, Virginia. Charles Campbell, a descendant in the fifth degree of the original Duncan, settled in
Augusta, near the present Fort Defiance, about four miles northeast of
Fort Lewis, and married Mary Trotter, his brother, William Campbell,
marrying about the same time Elizabeth Wilson, a sister of Rev. Wm.
Wilson, pastor of the Old Stone Church. William Campbell and family
removed to Bourbon co., Ky., in 1790, and in 1800 removed to Brown
co., Ohio, where his son, Charles, married Elizabeth Tweed. Charles
Campbell and Mary Trotter, left a son, John Campbell, who settled in
Lawrence co., Ohio, in 1833, and left issue.

Among our biographical notices will be found sketches of two eminent
members of this family, which is allied by marriage with the Lewis', Prestons, Peytons, Tates, Taylors, and other early and leading families.

THE STUART FAMILY.

The Stuarts are of Scotch origin. During the reign of James I, they
removed to Ireland, where Archibald Stuart married Janet Brown, a sister
of Rev. Jno. Brown, the ancestor of the Browns of Rockbridge and Louisiana. In 1727, A. Stuart emigrated to Pennsylvania, after the birth of
two children, Thomas and Eleanor. In 1738, he removed to Augusta,

and settled on Pratt's farm, near Waynesboro, where he died 1761. He left issue: 1. Thomas; 2. Eleanor; 3. Alexander; 4. Benjamin; all of whom left large families. Archibald Stuart was joined in Augusta some years after 1738 by two brothers, John and David, who came from Ireland, and both of whom married in Augusta and left descendants—the descendants of the one being the Stuarts of Ohio and Illinois, and of the other, the Stuarts of S. C.

Thomas Stuart, who was a man of mark, married Elizabeth Moore, and. had issue nine children: 1. Jane, died unm.; 2. John, died s. p.; James, who removed to Tenn., married Miss Montgomery, and left descendants; 4. Thomas, U. S. A ; 5. Robert, married Miss Roland, of Botetourt; 6. Judy, died unm.; 7. Mary, married James Moffett, of Augusta, and they had issue ten children, viz: 1. John Moffett, who married Eliz. Tate; 2. Betsy, who married J. McClanahan; 3. Robert S., married H. Guthrie; 4. Thomas, died young; 5. Jane, married Dr. J. K. Moore; 6. Wm., married Jane Robertson; 7. Eleanor, married J. C. Moore; 8. Mary, married Alex. T. Barclay; 9. Thomas S., died unm.; 10. Julia, married W. H. Paxton.

Julia, daughter of Thomas Stuart, married Capt. Wm. Lyle, and left issue: Elizabeth, who married Capt. Wm. Paxton, and they left five children.

Eleanor Stuart, daughter of the original emigrant, married Ed. Hall, who emigrated from Ireland to Augusta 1736, and they left issue: six sons and four daughters.

Major Alex. Stuart, second son was born in Pennsylvania, 1733. He was a man of uncommon intellect and energy, and patented large tracts of land in the western counties. He was Major during the Revolution in Col. Samuel McDowell's regiment, and commanded the regiment at the battle of Guilford, where he was dangerously wounded. He was an ardent friend of education, and contributed largely of his private means to the endowment of Liberty Hall Academy, now W. & L. University. Major Stuart married first Mary Patterson, of South river, Augusta co., by whom he left issue: 1. Judge Archibald Stuart, of Staunton; 2. Robert, of Rockbridge; and five daughters: Frances, Jane, Mary, Elizabeth, and Eleanor. He married secondly Mary Moore, by whom he left four children: James, Priscilla, Alexander and Benjamin. He married thirdly Anna Reid, whose maiden name was Miller, but left no issue by her at his death in his 90th year.

Judge Archibald Stuart was born 1757, was educated at Liberty Hall and William and Mary College. In 1781 he joined Gen. Greene's force in N. C., was appointed by him Aid, and he took part in the battle of Guilford. After the war he studied law under the great Jefferson, and returned to Rockbridge. He was now elected under peculiarly flattering circumstances delegate to the Legislature from Botetourt, and after a service of three years, removed to Staunton. He rose so rapidly in popular esteem that he was elected in 1788 as the colleague of Zach. Johnston to represent the county in the Convention to ratify the Constitution of the U. S. In 1791 he m Eleanor Briscoe, d of Col. Gerard Briscoe, of Md. Shortly after this event, he was elected to the Senate of Va., and was subsequently chosen its President. In 1799, he was elected Judge of the General Court of Va., assigned to the Augusta district, and served until 1831. During his career he enjoyed the friendship of such men as Henry, Jefferson, Marshall, Madison, and Monroe. Judge Stuart was distinguished as a

land lawyer, and as a Judge, for his discriminating judgment, and enjoyed
the confidence, respect and esteem of the eminent Bar which practiced at
his Court, among whom were Chapman Johnson, Daniel Sheffey, John H.
Peyton, B. G Baldwin, P. P. Barbour, W. C. Rives, and others. Judge
Stuart was tall of stature and dignified in appearance, an able lawyer and
upright judge. At his death, in 1832, he left four sons: 1. Thomas Jefferson; 2. Archibald P.; 3. Gerard Briscoe; 4. Alex. H. H. Stuart.

Thomas J. m Martha Dabney, and left issue: Col. W. D. Stuart, a gallant and meritorious officer, killed in the battle of Gettysburg. Briscoe
died unm. A. P. Stuart m Josephine Xaupi, by whom he left a large
family, two of whom served in the C. S. A.

Gerard B. Stuart was never married. He has served as J. P. and in the
Legislature, and is a man of ability and great purity of character.

A. H H. Stuart m Frances, eldest d of Gen. B. G. Baldwin, and they
have living issue: one son, Archibald G , and five daughters: 1. Fanny
Peyton, m Prof. J. M. P. Atkinson; 2. Mary, who m Dr. Hunter Mc-
Guire; 3. Susan Baldwin, m Rev. R. A. Gibson; 4. Margaret, m A. F.
Robertson.

Robert Stuart, the second son of Maj. Alex. Stuart, m Elizabeth Mc-
Clung, by whom he left numerous offspring.

Frances Stuart m ——— Lyle, by whom she left one daughter, Isabella,
who m John McDowell, of Staunton, and one son, who died unm.

Jane Stuart m Alex. Walker, of Rockbridge, and they left five children,
who removed to West Va. and Indiana.

Mary P. Stuart m Alex. Hall, of Augusta, and they left issue: Elizabeth died unm. Eleanor m Thos. Walker; they removed to Monroe
county, and left a large family.

James Stuart, eldest son of Maj. S. by his second wife, m Miss Stockton,
of Pittsylvania, and left issue

Priscilla Stuart m Benj. Hall, and removed to Missouri.

Judge Alex. Stuart, youngest son of Maj. S., m first Ann Dabney, and
left issue: two children—Hon. Arch. Stuart, of Patrick, and a daughter,
Ann. He m secondly Mary Gassaway; no issue. He married thirdly
Jane, a sister of Chapman Johnson. He was a man of fine talents and ge-
nial temper, and was greatly regretted at his death, which occurred in
Staunton in 1832.

Hon. Arch. Stuart, of Patrick, was an officer in the war of 1812—a distinguished lawyer and eloquent orator. He m Elizabeth Pannill, by whom
he left issue; 1. Ann, m J. N. Pierce, of Wythe; 2 Bettinia, m Rev. N.
Chevalier; 3. Mary T., m Dr. Headin, of Floyd; 4. David P., died unm.;
5. Wm. A., m Mary, d, of Dale Carter, by whom he had several children. Mrs. S. died in 1862, and W. A. Stuart m Mrs. Alex. S. Brown, by
whom he has a large family. 6. John D. Stuart, M. D., m Anne E. Kent,
and has five children. 7. James E. B. Stuart graduated at West Point
1854, and was commissioned second lieutenant of cavalry; wounded
in battle with Cheyenne Indians, 1858; was at capture of John Brown
in 1859; promoted 1860 to captaincy in United States Army; in 1861 resigned and joined Confederate side, and was made Lieut.-Col. 1st Va.
Cavalry, and rose rapidly to be Major-General, and was placed in command of all the cavalry of the army of Northern Va. Enjoyed the friendship and confidence of Lee, Jackson, and J. E. Johnston, and won the devotion of his men. This enterprising and distinguished officer—the Murat

of the Confederacy—was killed at the age of 29, May, 1864, at the battle of Yellow Tavern. He was the youngest Major-General since the days of Napoleon. He was the idol of the army and of the people of Va. He m Flora, d of Gen. Philip St. George Cooke, U. S. A., by whom he left two children: 1. J. E. B., and 2. Virginia. 8. Columbia, m Peter W. Hairston and they have issue. 9. Virginia, d unm. 10. Victoria, m N. A. Boyden, of N. C.

Annie D. m first W. L. McDowell; second, Judge Ewell Brown

Dr. Chapman J. Stuart m Margaret, d of Judge B. G. Baldwin, and they left issue, one daughter, Mary J, who m Capt. W. L. Clark.

Benjamin Stuart m and left three sons and one daughter by his first wife   By his second, Miss Henderson, he left two children; one died early; the other, Mary, m Samuel H. Steele.

John m Miss Coalter, and removed to Illinois, where their children now live

Nancy m John Alexander, and had seven children, namely: 1. Andrew, m Susan Hunter; 2. Archibald, d young; 3. James, m Miss Sheiry; 4. Eleanor, m Robt. M. White; 5. Martha, m Jos. Scott, M. D.; 6. Dr. Cyrus Alexander, who m Sarah, d of John McCue; 7. Catharine, m W. Hunter.

THE BELL FAMILY.

Joseph Bell came from Lancaster, Penn., to Augusta, about 1740. He was one of several brothers born in Penn., whose father emigrated from the north of Ireland to America some years previously. He settled near the Founder, on the present Valley turnpike, on the farm now owned by Jacob Warwick. The other brothers of Joseph Bell settled in Ohio, Ky., and Tenn., and have left descendants in those States; among them was the late Hon. John Bell, of Tenn., a candidate for the Presidency in 1860 —the Whig ticket being "Bell and Everett."

Joseph Bell m Elizabeth Henderson, of Augusta, and had issue: 1. William; 2. Susan, who m Jno. Wayt, s p; Elizabeth, who m Dr. John Johnston, of Roanoke, and they left a large family; 4. James Bell, who m three times—1st, Sarah Allen, by whom he left issue, Wm. A Bell, and Margaret, who m J. Wayt· He married second Sarah Crawford, d of George Crawford, and left no issue He m third Margaret, d of Wm. Craig, a relative of Rev. John Craig, first minister of Augusta Church, by whom he left issue; 1. John J. Bell; 2. Col. David S. Bell; 3. Mrs J. C. Arbuckle, of Greenbrier; 4. J. Wayt Bell; 5. Mrs. Chesley Kinney; 6. Maj. Henderson M. Bell; 7. Mrs. Frank M. Young, of Staunton; all of whom have families except Mrs. Arbuckle.

Joseph Bell and Wm. Craig were of the original settlers of Augusta, and engaged in building the Old Stone Church, which was erected in 1740.

The late James Bell, Esq., of Prospect Hill, was a magistrate of Augusta from 1796 to a short period before his death, which occurred in 1856, and as such, succeeded to the High Sheriffalty as the oldest magistrate. At the adoption of the Constitution of 1850, was but one term removed from the succession. He was long a consistent and influential member of the Augusta Church, President of the County Court for many years, and served in the Legislature as delegate for Augusta. He was a man of vigorous intellect, great enterprise and industry, and accumulated a large estate.

THE COCHRAN FAMILY.

The first of this family who settled in Augusta about 1745 was John Cochran. who came to Penn., and thence to Augusta. He settled in Staunton as a merchant, and worshiped at the Old Stone Church. He married Susannah Donnelly, likewise of Covenanter stock, and from the north of Ireland. They left issue: James and Robert, and several daughters. He died on his estate, near the Stone Church, now owned by the heirs of Thomas W. McCue, deceased.

James Cochran, the elder son of the original John, m Magdalen, a d of Col. George Moffett, of Revolutionary fame. At his death, which occurred in Staunton in 1836, he left issue: 1. John Cochran, of Charlottesville; 2. George M. Cochran, of Augusta; 3. James A., of Loch Willow, Augusta; 4. Magdalen, wife of Benj. Crawford. It is not necessary to follow out the descendants of James Cochran's children, as they appear in other pedigrees in this volume.

Robert Cochran removed to Ky., m ―― ――, and left issue: one son, John Cochran, who m Ann Buskirk, and has issue: Jno. B. Cochran, a lawyer of Colorado, who m in Va his cousin, Magdalen, a d of Jas. A. Cochran, of Loch Willow. 2. Thomas Cochran, who died circa 1876, Judge of the Louisville (Ky.) Chancery Court. 3. Robert, an officer of the Chancery Court of Louisville, Ky., and daughters,

John Cochran, the emigrant, was a man of great spirit and enterprise, and though he died young, left a handsome inheritance to his children. His son, the late Jas. Cochran, Esq , was distinguished for the soundness of his judgment, the acuteness of his intellect, and the persistency with which he pursued his plans. He accumulated a large estate, was long a magistrate of the county, and died beloved and respected by all.

THE TATE FAMILY.

The Tates came from the north of Ireland to Penn., and thence to Augusta about 1745. The first emigrant left four sons, James, William, John and Robert. The descendants of the first brothers married among the Van Lears, Ewings, Moffetts and Finleys, of Augusta and Rockbridge. Capt. James Tate, the eldest brother, was killed at the battle of Guilford. He was married, and his family removed to Ky and Missouri. He now has a great-grandson, Rev John C. Tate, a Presbyterian minister in Kentucky. William Tate's descendants are settled in Southwestern Va., one of whom is Dr. Thos. Tate, long a State Senator, and afterwards a Federal civil servant, and the. head of one of the bureaux in Washington. John Tate represented Augusta in 1798 in the Legislature, and voted against Madison's celebrated resolutions.

Robert Tate m Margaret, d of John McClung and ―― Alexander, his wife, and they left issue: 1. James; 2. John; 3. William; 4. Elizabeth, who m Col Allen and went to Michigan; 5. Polly, m Sam'l Wallace, of Christian's Creek, Augusta co.; 6. Eleanor, m Sam'l Patterson, of Rockbridge; 7. Phœbe, m Sam'l Wilson, of Rockbridge; 8. Rebecca, m Reid Alexander, of Rockbridge; 9. Isabella, m John B. Christian, of Augusta; 10. Sally, died unm.

James Tate m first Miss Baxter, sister of Dr. Geo. Baxter, and by her had George, Robert, John and Margaret. He m second Mrs. Beale, of Botetourt, whose maiden name was Poage, and by her left several children, the only one of whom survived him was Col. Wm. P. Tate, of Augusta, who m first Miss Kayser, of Alleghany, by whom he left two daughters, Isabella and Margaret. He married second Sarah Christian, and by her left issue: one daughter, Cornelia Tate. His widow m Rev. W. T. Richardson, editor of the "Central Presbyterian," Richmond.

John Tate m Nancy, d and only child of Wm. Moffett, of Augusta, and left issue: 1. Wm. M. Tate; 2. Robt. McC.; 3. John McC.; 4. James M.; 5. Margaret, who m Dr. Steele, of Illinois; 6 Elizabeth, m Jos. Hite, of Illinois; 7. Rebecca, who m —— Blackburn, of Illinois.

Wm. M. Tate m Elizabeth McClung, of Rockbridge, removed to Indiana, and left two children, a son and daughter. Wm. M. Tate, eldest son of John Tate, m first Mattie Frazier, and second Kate, d of Dr. A. Waddell, and has issue by both wives.

This family, like others of the Covenanter stock, was noted for its piety, industry and public spirit, was associated with the early efforts of the Founder to improve the country, and is allied by marriage with some of the principal families of the county.

THE CHRISTIAN FAMILY.

A. G. Christian has kindly furnished the following brief memorandum as to his family. It is made up, principally, from extracts from the family Bible of the late John Christian, of Augusta, who was an elder and clerk of the session in Tinkling Spring and afterwards in Bethel church:

"The Christians long inhabited the Isle of Man, where they were the Dempsters (*i. e.* Judges) in the island. The name was originally McChristian. After 1600 the Mc was dropped, and the name was thence spelled Christian The same family names prevailed then as now—namely: John, Robert, William, James, Isabella, &c. John Christian, of Uncrigg Castle, married Isabella Percy, daughter of the Duke of Northumberland, of Alnwick Castle, and she became famous for her charities, talents and worth. The name was retained long in the family Hutchinson's history of Cumberland county, England, vol. 2, p 148, gives a genealogical table of the Christians from the year A. D. 900 They inhabited Cumberland and Westmoreland counties, England, and for centuries lived in the Isle of Man. The name was first written simply Christian in 1630, by Judge William Christian. The family seat was "Uncrigg," or Uwncrig Castle. Another seat was Ronaldsway. Scott's "Peveril of the Peak" has in the appendix to some additions a note giving some history of the Christian family.

John Christian married Rachael Brownlee on June 21, 1779, and left the following issue: Robert, b September 20, 1781; John Brownlee, b September 1, 1784; Isabella, b December 12, 1786; Sarah, b November 7, 1790; William, b August 21, 1793; James and Israel (twins), b July 21, 1765; Archibald Scott, b October 1st, 1797; Ebenezer, b December 7th, 1801.

Gilbert Christian married Margaret Richardson in Ireland. Their children, who came to America, were: Robert, John, William and Mary. They all settled on Christian's creek about 1733, and took deeds from Beverly (grantee of Crown) about 1736, recorded in Orange county, Va. Robert married Isabella Tiffins, while a recruiting officer in the Indian war, at Winchester, Va. (Their children are the list above.) John Christian and William had large families. Most of their descendants went to Ken-

40 *

tucky and Tennessee. Mary married, first, John Moffett, and they left issue; after the death of John Moffett she married James Trimble, and from this marriage sprung the late Governor of Ohio, Allen Trimble."

THE CRAWFORD FAMILY.

The first of this family, who emigrated from Ireland to Pennsylvania, was Patrick Crawford. He removed from Pennsylvania to Augusta about 1750, and settled on the farm now occupied by Col John H. Crafford. He m and left three sons—1. William; 2. James; 3 John. William m Nancy Smith, a d of Abraham Smith, and left issue—1. Benjamin Crafford; 2. George; 3. James; 4. John; 5. William, and six daughters. James died unm; John m Mary Allen, and they left issue—1. John; 2 George; 3. James, and four daughters, namely: 1. Mrs E. G. Moorman; 2. Mrs. Col. Franklin McCue; 3. Mrs Wm. English, and Mrs Stuart McClung. 1. Benj. Crawford m Magdalen, a d of James Cochran, and they left issue: 1. Elizabeth; 2. James; 3. Nancy, who m Col. James Cochran, of Culpepper, and they have two children—1. Benjamin C.; 2. Patsy. 4. Addison, of Bath, unm, and 5. Benjamin Lewis, M. D., who died in Texas, 1878, unm. James, eldest son of B. C., m Cornelia, a d of Wm. G. Miller, of Rockingham, and they have issue one son, viz.: William B. 1. James (the second son of Patrick Crawford, the emigrant,) m Miss McClung, of Greenbrier, and left issue—1. John H.; 2. Dr. Wm. M. Crawford, of Mt. Sidney; 3. Edward C.; 4. James A.; 5. Marshall; 6. Mrs. Bettie Taylor, who has no issue; 7. Mrs. Minor; 8. Mrs. David Hanger. Col. John H. Crawford m Mrs. Zirkle, whose maiden name was Rice, of Shenandoah, and they have issue one son—a minor. Dr. Wm. M. Crawford m Miss McChesney, of Rockbridge, and they have a large family. Edward Crawford m a d of Wm. Crawford, of the Stone Church, and they have a son and daughter James A. m in Texas, and their descendants are unknown. Marshall Crawford m a d of Alex. Crawford, of Crawford's Springs, Augusta, and they have issue one daughter. Mrs. Minor has a large family, and also her sister, Mrs. David Hanger. Wm. Crawford, fifth son of Patrick, m 1st Margaret, d of James Bouland, and he left issue at his death, in 1881—1. James; 2. Sarah; 3. Ann, unm; 4. George; 5. Benjamin, unm. James m Mary, d of Wm. Miller, and they have three children. Sarah m E. C. Crawford, and they have two children. 4. George m Lillie, a d of Isaac Parkins, and g d of Col. Samuel C. Harnsberger. William C. m secondly Sarah, a sister of his first wife, but left no issue by her. Col. James Crawford, a former lawyer of Staunton, was connected with this family through the Bells. He m first a Miss Stribling, and left issue—1. Erasmus S.; 2. James; 3. Magnus W., and 4. Mrs. Manifee, who has a large family. Magnus m Miss Simms, of Orange, and they have a large family. Col. James Crawford m secondly Peggy, a d of Col. Wm. Bell, of Lewis creek, and left issue at his death, in 1858—1. William Bell; 2. John; 3 Taliaferro, died unm; 4. Mrs. Margaret Burrell, of Lewisburg, and they have issue; 5. Sarah, who m J. Wayt Bell, and they left issue one son—Taliaferro; 6. Fanny, who m John S. Churchman, and they have issue; 7. Mrs. H. P. Dickerson, who has a family; and one daughter who died unm.

Patrick Crawford was a man of sound sense, great energy and persevering industry, and accumulated a good estate. His descendants have intermarried with the principal families of the county, and have long been among our leading men of business.

The late Benjamin Crawford was long a successful Staunton merchant, a bank officer and justice of the peace, in which capacities he was well known by the writer, who served with him in a bank directory and as a member of the county court. Mr. Crawford's powers were useful rather than brilliant; his success the result of patience and perseverance. With a warmer imagination he would probably have been misled by speculative theory like so many of his contemporaries. His industry and his temperance were the sources of his early success, and they nurtured in him the spirit of that independence which was the leading characteristic of his life.

THE M'CUE FAMILY.

We are indebted to Judge John H. McCue for the following very brief account of his grandfather, Rev. John McCue, and his descendants:

" Rev. John McCue's father emigrated from the north of Ireland, and was of the Covenanter stock. He settled in Lancaster co., Penn'a; from thence in a few years he removed to Nelson co., Va., circa 1737. He left a large family, the eldest of whom, Rev. Jno McCue, graduated A. B. at Washington College previous to its charter in 1782, and studied divinity under Rev. Jas. Waddell, whom he succeeded as pastor of Tinkling Spring. He founded the first Presbyterian church west of the Alleghanies in Lewisburg, Greenbrier co., and was succeeded at Lewisburg by Rev. —— McIlhany, D.D. Rev. Jno. McCue was pastor of the Staunton church in 1791, and in the same year took charge of Tinkling Spring. He married a daughter of James Allen, of Augusta, and among his descendants are the Bells, Wayts, Crawfords, Hydes, Kaysers and Franciscoes of Augusta, and the Trimbells of Ohio. Rev. John McCue left five sons, James A., John, William M. D., Franklin and Cyrus, and five daughters, Mrs. Alex'r Barry, Mrs. Gen. Jos. McDowell of N. C., Mrs. Jas. Miller, Mrs. Jos. Matthews, and Mrs. John Porterfield. The Rev. Jno. McCue was distinguished for his piety, strength of character and intellect, learning and eloquence. His grandson, Judge J. H. McCue, possesses an MS. volume of his sermons characterized by learning, deep research and profound thought."

John McCue, Esq. — The writer cannot permit this occasion to pass without paying a slight tribute of respect to the memory of one of the best and purest men he ever knew. It was his good fortune to have known from boyhood the late John McCue, of the Long Meadows—to have spent some time now and again under his hospitable roof, to serve with him on the County Court, and to enjoy his friendship during the early years of his life. He soon learned to esteem and admire him for his sterling worth and many good qualities, and the more he knew of him in after years, the higher was his estimate of his talents and his character. From the sacred calling of his father, the reader will not be surprised to learn that more care was taken to secure his moral and religious principles than to instruct him in professional or general literature, for both of which, however, he exhibited a decided and early liking. His parents sought to make him good rather than great While yet a boy he expressed a wish to engage in agricultural pursuits, a desire heightened by his ardent love for natural scenery and a taste for the seclusion of the country. After he acquired the extensive and valuable estate on the " Long Meadows," he removed there, and there the principal part of his useful and honorable life was spent, and there he died. His social, intellectual, and moral qualities need not be described. To sum up all in a few words: He was a man of vigorous intellect, generous soul, and varied information. Though a Whig by conviction, and decided in his politics, he never was a partizan, and while serving in the General Assembly, of which he was often a popular and influential member, was a laborious and conscientious worker rather than a frequent and ambitious speaker. No man had a higher sense of honor, and he enjoyed the confidence and respect of both parties, wielded much influence, and served to the entire satisfaction of his constituents. In private life, Mr. McCue exhibited an active benevolence and the same Christian piety which marked his public career. His heart overflowed with benevolence and kindly feelings, and this precious quality rendered him even more delightful in the social circle than his strong, bright intellect. His conversation was eagerly sought by the good and wise, who derived both pleasure and profit from his varied stores of original thought and acquired information. To a large extent he lived for others. In all his acts he showed a forgetfulness of self, and in the last scene of his life exhibited the firmness of the philosopher united to the piety of the Christian. Mr. McCue not only paid homage to the Great Source of all good and precious gifts, whether intellectual or material, but made religion his favorite theme—not a religion of mental abstraction, but one of practical efficacy on every feeling of the heart and every action of the life. It was ever his aim to promote glory to God in the highest by advancing " Peace on earth and good will towards men." In his neighborhood and among the congregation of Tinkling Spring, his memory is not only cherished as that of a good and wise man, but venerated as that of a public and private benefactor.

THE HANGER FAMILY.

The first of this family who settled in Augusta, 1750, was Peter Hanger, an emigrant from Penn., whose family had previously settled there, having crossed the ocean from Germany. He married in Penn , and at his death, in 1801, on the farm now owned by the city of Staunton, in connection with the water-works, left issue, a large family, one of whom was Peter Hanger, of the Willow Spout, who m —— Zink, and they left issue: 1. Peter; 2. Dr. John; 3. Wm. S.; 4. David, who died in Missouri; 5. Mrs. Jacob Baylor; 6. Mrs. S. M. Woodward; 7. Mrs. Hannah Allen.

Peter Hanger settled on an estate near Waynesboro, and m Martha, a d of George Crawford, by whom he left issue : 1. George C.; 2. Catharine, who m J H. Evans; 3 Peter; 4. Nancy, who m Col. Alex. R. Robertson; 5. John; 6. H. Miller; 7. William; 8. Marshall Hanger, long a delegate from Augusta county to the General Assembly of Virginia, and for years Speaker of the Lower House; 9. Dr. David W; 10. Edgar, who died young; 11. Norman, unm.

This family, one of the earliest seated in the county, was noted for its spirit and enterprise, and actively seconded the efforts of the Founder in subduing the country, introducing improvements, and advancing the public interests. Another brother, George Hanger, settled on the Middle River, and left numerous descendants.

THE MATHEWS FAMILY.

The Mathews family came originally from Ireland, and settled in Augusta about the year 1739. They took up the land about four miles from the present village of Churchville, and twelve from Staunton, now owned and occupied by Valentine Hupman. The members of the family were: 1. William; 2. Richard; 3. James; 4. John; 5. Sampson.

William Mathews m ―――― ――――, and left issue: 1. Richard; 2. John; 3. Isaac; 4. Kate, died unm.; 5. Mary, m ――――Rankin, of Ky.; 6. Margaret, m Fred Hanger; 7. Jane, died unm; and 8. Elizabeth, b 1774, m Abner Gaines, b 1766, of Orange co., Va., about 1789. They removed to Kentucky and left issue; 1. James Mathews Gaines, b 1793; 2. John P., b 1795; 3. Wm. H., b 1797; 4. Mary W., b 1800; 5. Richard M., b 1802; 6. Benj. F., b 1804; 7. Augusta W., b 1805; 8. Arch'd K., b 1808; 9. Abner, b 1810; 10. Elizabeth, b 1812; 11. Mildred Pollard, b 1815; 12. Harriet B., b 1818.

James M. m Elvira Toussey, and they left one child, now living.

John P. removed to Oregon and became Governor of the Territory. He m Eliza Kinkead, of Ky., and had a large family.

Wm. H. m first Miss Early, a relative of Gen. Jubal A Early, and had five children. He m second Miss Belden, of Arkansas, and has seven children.

Mary W. m Craig Bush, and they left five children.

Richard m Eliza Hutchins, of Miss., and they left three children.

Benjamin P. also m a Miss Kinkead, of Ky., and they have issue living in Florida.

Augustus m Miss Daniel, of Richmond, Ky., and they left a large family.

Archibald m first Miss Dudley, of Georgetown, and they left issue. He m second the sister of his first wife, and they have issue: a large family.

Abner died unm.

Elizabeth m Lewis Hubbell, of N. Y., and left issue living in Boone co., Ky.

Mildred m Anthony H. Davies, of Chicot co., Arkansas, and they have issue, eight children, namely: 1. Anthony, d; 2. Fanny Walker: 3. Walter; 4. Mildred; 5. Robert Geddes Davies; 6. Anthony; 7. Abner; 8. Joseph Davies.

Governor George Mathews, of Georgia, and Sampson Mathews, of Staunton, one of whose daughters m Sam'l Clark, another Gen. Sam'l Blackburn, were of this family, but no list of their descendants in Va. or the South could be procured.

THE PORTERFIELD FAMILY.

The first of this family emigrated from England early in the 18th century, and settled in Penn. Thence two of his sons removed to Va. and settled in Jefferson, namely: Robert and Charles. A third son removed to the West and became a citizen of Ky. Both Robert and Charles were officers during the war of the Revolution, and Charles died unm., from wounds received during the war. After the war, about 1782, Col. Robert Porterfield removed to Augusta and settled on South river, on a farm which he called "Soldiers' Retreat." He m Rebecca Farrar, of Amelia co., by whom he had issue: 1. Charles, who died unm.; 2. Polly; 3. John; 4. Rebecca. Polly m Lewis Wayland, of Augusta, and left a large family, who have removed to Ky. John Porterfield m Betsy McCue, a sister of John and Col. Franklin McCue, and had only one child, Robert Porterfield, who m a daughter of John Wayt, and left one son, Robert Porterfield, of Lewisburg, Greenbrier co., W Va., who m Miss McClung, of Greenbrier and they have three children, namely: Mattie, Herbert and Annie. Rebecca Porterfield m William Kinney, Esq., of Staunton, and they left issue, nine children, viz: 1. Mary, m Alfred Chapman, of Orange, and they have a large family; 2. Jane, who m E. M. Taylor, of N. Y., and they have eight children; 3. Robert Porterfield, who m Isabella, d of L. L. Stevenson, and they have a large family; 4. Rebecca, who m S. A. Richardson, of Mass., and they have three children; 5. William Kinney, M. D., who died unm.; 6. Annie Maria, who m Maj. H. M. Bell, a lawyer of Staunton, and they have three children: 1. Richard P.; 2. Annie; and 3. Henderson M., jr.; 7. Eliza, unm.; 8. Charles N., who died unm.; 9. John C., d unm.

Gen. Porterfield had two sisters: 1. Rebecca, who died unm.; 2. Eleanor, who m Mr. Heath, Attorney-Gen. of Ky., and they left no issue. He was a man of high character, strong sense and martial spirit.

THE WAYT FAMILY.

The first of this family who emigrated from England to Va. was George Wayt, who settled in Orange county, circa 1750. He had three sons, namely: 1. John; 2 William; 3. James. John, the eldest son, removed to Augusta about 1790, and m Susan, a d of Joseph Bell, by whom he left no issue. He was a distinguished Mason, merchant, and Mayor of the town. He was an eminently good and pious man, being an Elder in the Staunton Presbyterian Church. William Wayt m Miss Hodges, of Caroline county, and left one son, John Wayt, and three daughters. John Wayt removed to Augusta in 1811. He married twice: first, Margaret A. Bell, d of James Bell, by whom he left issue, one daughter, who m Robt. J. Porterfield, by whom she left issue, one son. She m secondly Johnston E. Bell, of Lewisburg, and left three children, one son and two daughters. John Wayt m second Sarah A. Bell, d. of Maj. Wm. Bell, of Lewis creek, and left issue at his death in Staunton in 1877, three children: 1. Dr. Newton Wayt; 2. J. Howard Wayt; 3. Mattie, who m Thos. A. Bledsoe, Cashier Nat. V. Bank, Staunton, and they have issue, two daughters, S. Bell and Mary Lou Bledsoe.

Dr. Newton Wayt m Julia B., a d of Wade H. Heiskell, and has issue, two sons and one daughter, viz: 1. Baldwin; 2. Hampton; 3. Mattie. J. Howard Wayt is unmarried.

John Wayt, was long a magistrate of the county, an elder in the churches in Waynesboro and Staunton, and was for years a leading merchant and banker. He had a strong mind, great industry and enterprise. He enjoyed the confidence, respect and esteem of the community, and died beloved and regretted by the entire public.

THE WADDELL FAMILY.

The first person of this name, of whom we have any knowledge, is John Waddell, rector of the University of St. Andrew's, Scotland, in 1527, previous to the Reformation.

The Waddells afterwards became staunch Covenanters, Protestants of the strictest sect   The whole family seems to have participated in the battle of Bothwell Bridge, June 22d, 1679. No less than four of them were taken prisoners there, viz : William and Robert Waddell, of Monkland Parish ; Walter Waddell, of Sprunston, and Alexander Waddell, of Castletown. The sufferings of the prisoners in Grayfriars Churchyard, Edinburg, is a matter of history. Some of them died under the harsh treatment they received; others made their escape; others were set free on signing a declaration never to take arms against the King ; and about two hundred and fifty were banished to the Island of Barbadoes. These were taken away by a merchant of Leith, named Paterson, who contracted with the government to transport the banished men, the four Waddells being among them. After leaving port a storm arose, and the vessel being driven around the Orkney Islands, was wrecked at a place called the Mulehead of Darness. By Paterson's order, the prisoners were shut up beneath the hatches, and two hundred of them were drowned. All the Waddells perished, except William. The fifty prisoners who escaped found their way to the north of Ireland and settled there, the government interfering with them no further.

It is believed that William Waddell was the grandfather of the Rev. James Waddell, DD., widely known as the Blind Preacher. The father of Dr Waddell was named Thomas, and came to America from County Down, Ireland, in 1739. He settled in the southeastern part of Pennsylvania, near the Delaware line. He had three sons, William, Robert and James, and a daughter named Sally. William and Robert moved at an early day to Western Pennsylvania, where Robert reared a large family of children. William and Sally never married.

James Waddell was an infant when the family came to America. His father was a plain man, and the son at first looked forward to nothing better than a life of manual labor. But while a small boy, he and his older brothers chased a hare into a hollow tree, and thrusting his left hand into the hollow to seize the game, it was nearly severed by his brother's axe. The parts adhered, but the hand was permanently disabled. This "accident" led to his being sent to the school of the Rev. Dr. Finley, afterwards President of Princeton College, then one of the most celebrated schools in the country. He rose to be an assistant teacher, and among his pupils was the eminent Dr. Benjamin Rush.

About the year 1758, he started, on horseback, to go to Charleston, South Carolina, where he expected to spend his life in teaching. Passing through Virginia, he encountered, in Hanover county, the Rev. Samuel Davies, who prevailed upon him to remain here. At first, he taught for some time in Louisa county, in association with the Rev. Mr. Todd. Becoming a minister, he located in Lancaster county, where he married Mary Gordon, daughter of Col. James Gordon. When the Revolutionary war began, he removed to Augusta county, and lived during the war on a large farm which he purchased and called Spring Hill. This farm is on South River, some miles above Waynesboro, and part of it was lately owned by Mr. Zachariah McChesney. During his residence here he preached at Tinkling Spring and Staunton. After the war he removed to the place, where he died, near Gordonsville, his dwelling being in Louisa county, but the farm in the three counties of Louisa, Orange and Albemarle.

THE PEYTON FAMILY.

The Peyton family is of high antiquity in the mother country. According to Camden, Du Moulin, and other historians and antiquarians, the founder was William de Malet, one of the great barons who accompanied William I to the conquest of England, and obtained from that monarch many grants of manors and lordships as a recompense for his military services. Among these lordships were Sibton and Peyton Halls, in Norfolk, from the latter of which, Reginald, a nephew of William de Malet, assumed the surname of Peyton, in accordance with the usage of the times.

The name is also one of the earliest connected with the colony of Va. Sir Henry Peyton was knighted by James I, and was gentleman of the Privy Chamber of Prince Henry, 1610, was a member of the London Company to whom King James, May 23d, 1609, granted a charter "to deduce a colony and make habitation in that part of America commonly called Va." Sir Henry Peyton was the fourth son of the Right Hon. Sir Thomas Peyton, M. P. for Dunwich in 1557, and Customer of Plymouth, by his wife, Lady Cecilia Bouchier, daughter of John, second Earl of Bath. He m Lady Mary, d of Edward Seymour, Duke of Somerset. His nephew, son of his brother, Robert, namely: John Peyton, is supposed to have been the first who made the voyage to Va., circa 1622, when in his 26th year, and to have settled in the colony 1644. He m Ellen Pakington, of London, and left two sons:

I. Henry Peyton, of Acquia, Westmoreland county, Va.;

II. Valentine Peyton, of Nominy, Westmoreland county, Va., a colonel in the British army.

The descendants of the two are scattered through Va. and the South and West. From Valentine was descended the gallant and patriotic Col. Harry Peyton, of Revolutionary fame, who, when he heard that his last son, Yelverton, had been killed at the siege of Charleston, S. C., 1780, by a cannon ball from the enemy's fleet, exclaimed: "Would to God I had another to put in his place."* Frances Peyton was a daughter of Col. Harry P., and m the late Judge John Brown, of the Staunton Circuit, and left issue:

I. Judge Jas. E. Brown, of Wytheville, uncle by marriage of Gen. J. E. B. Stuart.

II. Martha Steele, who m Judge B. G. Baldwin, father of Col. J. B. Baldwin, Mrs. A. H. H. Stuart, Mrs. James M. Ranson, and Mrs. Chapman J. Stuart.

III. Margaret Brown m William S. Eskridge, and left issue: Mrs. John Towles, of La., and Mrs. R. T. W. Duke, of Albemarle.

From the elder brother, Henry Peyton, of Acquia, was descended Hon. Balie Peyton, of Tenn., a distinguished lawyer, soldier and statesman. He served as M. C. for Tenn., 1833-37, as colonel of 5th Louisiana regiment in the Mexican war, 1845-48, and was Minister Plenipotentiary to Chili, 1848-1852; Hon Joe Peyton, M. C. for Tenn.; Hon. Francis Peyton, an influential and patriotic member of the H. of D. of Va. from 1777 to 1785—also a member of the Convention of 1776 to frame a Constitution for Va.; Hon. E. G. Peyton, late Chief Justice of the Supreme Court of Miss.; Col. Robert L. Y. Peyton, late Confederate States Senator for Missouri; Hon. Samuel O. Peyton, M. C. for Ky., and others.

---

*Yelverton Peyton, when shot, fell into the arms of the late Gen. Ro. Porterfield, of Augusta, who was standing by his side.

Another branch of the original stock of Peytons settled in Va. circa 1665, namely: Robert Peyton, a grandson of Sir Edward Peyton, Baronet of Isleham co., of Camb. He took up large tracts of land in Gloucester, and made his home at Isleham, in the present county of Matthews. From these early settlers have sprung a numerous progeny settled in almost every part of the U. S., from N. Y. to Georgia and from Minnesota to Texas and California. The earliest Peyton connected with Augusta was Henry J. Peyton, who came up from Prince William to Winchester, and thence to Augusta about 1796. In 1802 he was appointed Clerk of the Chancery Court of this district, and served with great satisfaction to the public until 1814. The second who came to the county was John Howe Peyton, of Montgomery Hall, who settled in Staunton in 1809, on receiving the appointment of Attorney for the Commonwealth. He was the son of John R. Peyton, of Stony Hill, Stafford, who was known and acknowledged in his day as a man of gifted intellect and penetrating good sense. He lived in the seclusion of the country, devoted to rural pursuits and the cultivation of social happiness. He died in 1798, in his 45th year, and now sleeps under the solemn trees of Stony Hill Cemetery side by side with his fathers. " He was one of many thousand such that die betimes, whose story is a fragment, known to few." His father, John Peyton, was a man who combined within himself every noble and generous quality, of whom one of his contemporaries said: " It would require no common pencil to depict the undeviating rectitude of his conduct, the unshaken constancy of his friendship, the unwearied activity of his benevolence and invariable warmth of his affections, the untarnished purity of his habits, and the unabated fervor of his piety." John H. Peyton inherited in a remarkable manner these moral qualities, and was, says Mr. Bezer Blundell, F. S. A.: "A wise and good man, eminent alike for his learning and ability as a jurist, and for the purity of his private morals. Trained in the best principles, and early imbued with a veneration for the noblest characters of antiquity, Mr. Jno. H. Peyton did not seek public favor by courting the populace, or his reputation might have been more extended. His virtue was of another complexion. Content with his profession, and with his own consciousness of rectitude, he always sought to be in reality what he appeared, and might have changed his family motto, ' Patior-Potior,' for that of the late Lord Somers: ' Esse quam videri.' He was noticeable, also, as a fine specimen, doubtless much over the average, of the upper class of our Colonial gentry, at a period when Virginia flourished first under the direct influence of monarchy, and subsequently as a republic, but a republic whose institutions were tempered, and so to speak, toned down by traditionary influences, which still refined, though they no longer controlled them." John H. Peyton m first Susan Madison, d of Wm. Strother Madison, a relative of Bishop Madison, by whom he left issue, one son, the late Col. Wm. M. Peyton, of Roanoke, who m Sally, a d of Judge Allen Taylor, by whom he left issue a large family, of whom there are now living: Mrs. Walter Preston, of Abingdon, whose eldest daughter m Judge Geo. W. Ward; 2. Capt. Wm. M. Peyton, of Kanawha, W. Va., who m Miss Mann, of Gloucester co., Va., and has a large family. 3. Sally, who m T. C. Reed, and left one child, Betty, who m Dr. Wm. Berkeley, of Roanoke, a relative of Lord Botetourt, once Gov. of the colony; 4. Bernadine, who m —— Lewellyn, Esq., of Albemarle, who has a large family. Col. Wm M. Peyton died in 1868 deeply regretted by a numerous circle of friends throughout the State and country. He was a man of ability and

41 *

learning, a ripe scholar, possessing all the essentials of a great writer. His mind was broad, his power of dramatic description remarkable, and in his analysis of character, elaborate and distinct. With his clear, vivid and eloquent style, and love of literature, he would doubtless have risen to the first distinction as a writer, but for a physical malady (vertigo), causing partial paralysis, which early interfered with his labors, and finally put an end to his life. He served at different times in the General Assembly and in other public positions, and was universally respected for the purity of his life, the activity of his benevolence, and the rectitude of his conduct. John H. Peyton m secondly Ann Montgomery, d of Maj. John Lewis, of the Sweet Springs, by whom he left issue at his death at Montgomery Hall in 1847.

I. John Lewis Peyton, who m Henrietta E. C., d of Col. J. C. Washington, of N. C., by whom he has issue: one son, Lawrence W. H.

II. Yelverton, unm, a resident of Texas.

III. Susan Madison m Col J. B. Baldwin; no issue.

IV. Ann Montgomery, d unm.

V. Mary Preston m Robt. Gray, and has issue: 1. Robert; 2. Peyton; 3 Preston; 4. Susan; 5. Isabella.

VI. Lucy Garnett m Judge Jno. N. Hendren, and has issue: one son, Samuel, and two daughters, Annie M. and Lucy Peyton.

VII. Elizabeth, m Wm. Boys Telfair, of Ohio, and they have issue: 1. William; 2. John; 3. Susan.

VIII. Margaret Lynn m Capt. Geo M. Cochran, of Staunton, and they have issue: 1. Susan; 2. Maria; 3. George; 4. Ann; 5. John; 6. Margaret; 7. Peyton.

IX. Virginia, m Col. Jos. F. Kent, of Wythe, and they have issue: 1. Joseph F.; 2. Susan; 3. Mary.

X. Cornelia m first Dr. Thos Brown, and at his death he left issue: two sons, 1. Baldwin; and 2. Peyton. Mrs. Brown m secondly Wm. H. Greene, of Augusta, but they have no living issue.

THE BALDWIN FAMILY.

Dr. Cornelius Baldwin (the great-grandson of John Baldwin, who settled at Milford, Conn., in 1638-9,) was born in Elizabeth City, N. J., in 1751; served as an army surgeon during the Revolution, and at the end of the war settled at Winchester, Va. He married, about 1784, Mary, the youngest daughter of Col. Gerard Briscoe, of "Cloverdale," near Winchester. Colonel Briscoe was from Montgomery county, Md.; his wife, Mary Baker, was born in Annapolis; they had only two children—viz.: Elizabeth Briscoe, who married Judge Hugh Holmes, and Eleanor Briscoe, who married Judge Archibald Stuart, of Staunton, (the father and mother of Hon. A. H. H. Stuart.)

Dr. Cornelius Baldwin's children by his first wife, Mary Briscoe (she was born 1767, died September 26, 1808,) were ten—viz.:

I. Margaret, b 1785, d 1826.

II. Eliza C., b 1787, d December 11, 1844.

III. Briscoe Gerard, b January 17, 1789, d May 18, 1853.

IV. Cornelius E., b 1791, d about 1828.

V. Robert T., b 1793, d 1863.

VI. Archibald Stuart, b 1797, d 1873.

VII. Hugh Holmes; d young.

VIII. Mary Briscoe, b November 18, 1800; living in 1878.

IX. William Daniel, b 1803, d 1830.

X. Alexander G., b 1805, d in 1835, at Fort Towson, Arkansas. He was educated at West Point, and died a lieutenant in the U. S. A.; unmarried

Dr. Cornelius Baldwin married secondly, in May, 1813, Mildred, d of Dr. Throgmorton, of Clarke county, Va. She d in September, 1816, leaving issue.

XI. Cornelia, who married the Rev. William H. Mitchell, of Washington, D. C.

Dr Cornelius Baldwin married thirdly, in 1819, Miss Susan Prichard. No issue.

Margaret Baldwin married, in 1803, Judge William Daniel, Sr., of Lynchburg, b in Cumberland in 1770, d in Lynchburg November 20, 1839. He first entered the State Legislature in 1798-99; served in both of its branches with distinguished ability; was transferred to the Bench, and continued to his death a member of the General Court of Virginia. His children were :

I. Mary C. B., b 1804, d at "Union Hill" in 1843; married, in 1825, Mayo Cabell, Esq., of " Union Hill."

II. William, Jr., judge, b in Cumberland 1808, died at Nelson courthouse in 1873; married first, in 1843, Sarah A., (d in 1846) d of John W. Warwick, of Lynchburg. Their eldest child is John W. Daniel. Judge Wm. Daniel, Jr., married secondly Miss Elizabeth, d of Governor William H. Cabell, president of the Virginia Court of Appeals

III. Eliza, b 1810, d in 1831; married, in 1831, William J. Lewis, M. C. for Lynchburg District. No issue.

IV. Elvira Augusta, b 1817. d June 29, 1862; married, in 1836, Col. Charles Ellet, Jr., of Philadelphia.

V. Martha, married Judge Wood Bouldin, of the Virginia Court of Appeals.

Eliza Cook Baldwin married, in 1810, Capt. Joseph C. Baldwin, who descended from Nathaniel Baldwin, who settled at Milford, Conn., in 1638-9.

I. Cornelius Clarke, b 1811; established the Lexington "Gazette" in 1836; married first, in 1837, Margaret, d of Hugh Paxton; secondly, in 1858, Miss Sue A. Sale.

II. Elizabeth Holmes, b 1813, d 1844; married, 1832, William H. Garber, Esq , of Staunton. Among their children are Judge John Garber, formerly of the Supreme Court of Nevada, Virginia Garber, who married Gen. Reuben Davis, of Mississippi, M. C., &c , and Maj Alexander M. Garber.

III. Joseph Glover, born at Friendly Grove, one mile south of Winchester, January 21, 1815; received his elementary education in Staunton, being a class-mate of the writer, who at that early day discovered his intellectual superiority, and predicted for him a brilliant future; married, in 1839, Miss Sidney, d of Judge Jno. White, of Talledega, Ala. In 1835 he edited the "Buchanan Advocate;" removed to De Kalb county, Miss , in 1836, and to to Gainesville, Ala , in 1838, where he practiced law for twelve years in partnership with J. Bliss, Esq.; represented Sumpter county in the Legislature in 1843-4; removed to Livingston, Ala , in 1850; wrote "The Flush Times of Alabama and Mississippi " in 1853, and "Party Leaders " in 1854; removed to California in 1854; was a judge of the Supreme Court from October

1858, to January, 1862, when he resumed the practice of law in San Francisco; he d September 30, 1864. His eldest son, Judge Alex. White Baldwin, b in 1840, killed in a railroad collision near San Francisco in November, 1868; educated at the University of Virginia; a practicing lawyer at eighteen; a prosecuting attorney at nineteen; a leader of the Nevada Bar at twenty-one; a United States District Judge at twenty-five; one of the most brilliant and promising young men of his day in America. His (J. G. Baldwin's) oldest daughter, Kate Baldwin, married Hon. John B. Fenton, of California.

IV. Cyrus Briscoe, b 1819, d June 25, 1862, in C. S. A.; married, first, Miss Gates; second, a d of Judge Vandegreff, of Gainesville. Ala.

V. Cornelia, married, in 1859, Hon. Edward Stanley, M. C., of North Carolina. He moved to San Francisco, where he died without issue July, 1872.

Gen. B. G. Baldwin married, 1812, Martha Steele (b September 12th, 1791, died January, 1870,) d of Chancellor John Brown and his wife Fanny Peyton (d of Col. Henry Peyton, a distinguished patriot and soldier of 1776.) Gen. B. G. Baldwin was educated at William and Mary College; studied law; frequently a member of the Legislature; a member of the State Constitutional Convention of 1829; appointed a judge of the Court of Appeals 1842. His children were:

I. Frances Cornelia, married August 1, 1833, Hon. A. H. H. Stuart.

II. Mary Eleanor, married July 1, 1841, Col. James M. Ranson.

III. John Brown, b near Staunton January 11, 1820, d September 30, 1873; Speaker of the House of Delegates of Virginia; Inspector-General of the State forces; colonel of the Fifty-second regiment Virginia volunteers, C. S. A.; member Confederate Congress, and filled most acceptably other positions of honor and trust. He married in 1842, Susan M., d of Hon. John H. Peyton, an eminent lawyer of Staunton, Va. No issue.

IV. Margaret, married Dr. Chapman Johnson Stuart.

V. Col. Briscoe G., and VI. James William. Briscoe was chief of ordnance C. S. A. of Northern Virginia. James was drowned in James river, at Richmond, Va., October, 1876.

Dr Cornelius E. Baldwin married Nelly, daughter of Major Isaac Hite, of Belle Grove, near Middletown, whose wife was the sister of President Madison. Mr. Madison left each of Dr. Baldwin's three daughters a handsome legacy. Issue:

I. Eleanor, married Lewis Davidson; moved to Missouri.

II. Mary B., a missionary of the Protestant Episcopal Church at Athens, Greece; d in 1877 at Jaffa, Syria.

III. Dr. Hite, formerly a surgeon U. S. N.

IV. James.

V. Dr. Robert T., a surgeon C. S. N.

VI. Ann, married Mr. Hay, of Missouri, U. S. consul at Jaffa. He d leaving one child, John Baldwin Hay. now (1878) United States consul-general at Constantinople, Turkey. Mrs. Hay has charge of a mission school at Jaffa.

Dr. Robert T Baldwin, a surgeon in the U. S. A. in the war of 1812; married first, Sally Mackey (no issue); second, Portia Hopkins, and had issue:

I. Cornelia, married J. Peyton Clarke.

II. Mary Briscoe, married Rev. J M. P. Atkinson, D. D., president of Hampden-Sidney College.

III. Dr. Robert.

IV. Ludwell.

V. John, d 1877.

Dr. Archibald Stuart Baldwin married Kitty Mackey, sister to his brother Robert's first wife. Issue:

I. Mary, married Mr. Tidball, a lawyer; moved to California.

II. Margaret, married Robert Whitehead, a lawyer of Nelson county, Va.

III. Catherine, married Dr. Sigismund Neil.

IV. Dr. Robert F., superintendent State Lunatic Asylum, Staunton, Va.; a colonel and surgeon in C. S. A.; d 1879.

V. Dr. John, married a d of Hon. Richard W. Barton, M. C. from Virginia, &c. He d in 1862.

VI. Dr. Cornelius, married a d of Marshall Jones, of New Orleans.

VII. Sallie.

VIII. Fannie.

Mary Briscoe Baldwin married William W. Donaghe. Issue:

I. Margaret, D., married Rev. Robert White, D. D.

II. Dr. Briscoe B., married Miss Brooke.

III. Mary A., unm.

IV. Annie, married H. Jouette Gray.

V. William W., married Lucy Callaghan.

William Daniel Baldwin married Margaret, d of John C. Sowers. He d aged twenty-seven, leaving only one child, Mary Julia Baldwin.

THE KOINER FAMILY.

Maj. Absolom Koiner has kindly furnished the following brief account of his family:

"The Koiner family, one of the most numerous in the county, with branches of it settled in nearly all of the states south and west of New England, is of German origin, and has been traced as far back as the year 1650, on the Parish records of Winterlingen, Wurtenburg, where a portion of the family still remains. The family name from 1650 to the 29th of January, 1720, when Michael Koinath, the progenitor of the American family was born, was variously spelled, viz: Koinath, Kaeinath, Konot, Koynat, Keinot, Keinath, Keinodt, Kainath, and Michael's birth is registered Koinath.—Michael emigrated to America between 1740—45, and settled in Lancaster county, Pa. The records of the Lutheran church at New Holland, in said county, contains "the marriage of Michael Keinet or Keined, son of Conrad Keinet, of Wurtenburg, to Margaret Diller, daughter of Casper Diller on the 21st of February, 1749." The Dillers are a numerous family to this day, and are chiefly Lutherans. Tradition has it, that Michael Koiner made repeated trading voyages across the Atlantic, and on his last voyage a sister accompanied him to America. Caught in a storm, he was compelled to throw his goods (firearms) overboard, and his sister was swept into the sea. On his return to Pennsylvania he engaged in smithing trade to restore his lost fortunes. He was a man of medium size, of great energy and firmness. He was one of the first to clear away the brush wood, and build at Millerstown, Pa., where his son Casper was born, and probably others. Subsequently he moved west of the Susquehanna river into that part of Cumberland county which is now Franklin county, and settled on the Yellow-breaches creek. He here became the owner of land. He had ten sons and three daughters, namely, according to seniority: 1,— George Adam; 2, Conrad; 3, George Michael; 4, Mary; 5, Elizabeth; 6, Casper; 7, Catharine; 8, John; 9, Martin; 10, Jacob; 11, Christian; 12, Philip; and 13, Frederick. The daughter's names, after marriage, were Mary Hedabaugh, Elizabeth Balsley, wife of Christian; Catharine Slagle, wife of Jacob. The families of the first and last named daughters have gone to the west. His sons, George Adam and Casper, came to Augusta county, Va., first. About the year 1787 their father came and purchased farms; the first, a tract of 300 acres for £335, conveyed to him on the 22nd Aug., 1787, as Michael Coynant, of Cumberland county, Pa.

On 25th September, 1790, there was conveyed to him 200 acres by Hefflepower. On the 21st October, 1790, 303 acres, on South River, by Archibald Bowling, for £400. The latter is the farm on which he settled and lived for about six years preceding his death. This farm has been in his family to the present, and is now owned and occupied by Casper B. Koiner, his great-grandson. Michael, the patriarch, died 7th of November, 1796. His wife's age was 79 years. Both were buried at Koiner's, now Trinity church, near the South River. He and his family primarily belonged to the Lutheran branch of the Protestant church. All the family of the progenitor came to Virginia except his son Conrad, who remained in Pennsylvania, and reared a numerous family there. His sons George Adam, Casper, Martin, Philip, Frederic and George Michael remained and died in Augusta county, Va. The rest, who came from Pennsylvania, subsequently emigrated to other states,—John, at an early day, to Ohio, and founded a prosperous family; Christian to West Virginia, and Jacob not remembered.

"The farms of these early setlers have, with great uniformity, remained in the hands of their posterity, to wit: The farm of George Adam is still in the possession of his grandson, George K. Keiser; that of Casper in the possession of his son, Simon; that of Martin, on the Glades, in the possession of a daughter descendant of the Bell family; that of Philip in the possession of his son, David W.; and that of George Michael in the possession of his son, Michael A.

"The oldest three sons were soldiers in the Revolutionary war, and Philip, one of the younger, was an officer in the war of 1812, with others of the second generation·

"Casper, one of the first to emigrate from Pennsylvania to Virginia, was the father of the most numerous and prosperous family. He had nine sons and two daughters, viz: 1, Jacob; 2, Michael; 3, John; 4, Philip; 5, David; 6, Samuel; 7, Martin; 8, Simon; and 9, Benjamin. The daughters were, 1, Mary, the wife of George Koiner; and 2, Susan, the wife of Dr. Samuel G. Henkel. Each of these, with scarcely an exception, had large and prosperous families, who are mainly still residents of Augusta county. With a few exceptions, only, agriculture has engaged their attention, attended with uniform development and success."

<hr />

GEN. R. H. LEE.

The following interesting letter to the late Major Robert Grattan, referring to a company of horse composed almost exclusively of Augusta men who marched to Western Pennsylvania to aid in suppressing the whiskey insurrection, will be read with interest by all, more especially by the descendants of those patriotic men:

HARRISONBURG, VA., September 23, 1882:

COL. JOHN L. PEYTON:

Dear Sir,—Enclosed you will find the letter I spoke to you of. I am sorry I could not send it to you sooner. You see it is addressed to Capt. Grattan, who was my grandfather, and was generally known in after years as Major Robert Grattan. The company of cavalry which he commanded was composed of volunteers principally from Augusta county, and I have heard my father say that his father had often spoken to him of the splendid physique of the men. Among them were Millers, Turks, Bells, &c. My grandfather was the smallest man of the company, and he stood six feet in his stockings. The letter of Gen. Lee is wholly in his own handwriting, as you observe, and is quite complimentary in its terms.

Very truly yours,

GEO. G. GRATTAN.

HEADQUARTERS, Nov. 17, 1794.

SIR— PITTSBURG.

As soon as you can make it convenient, after joining your troops, you will please to move by the way of Morgantown to Staunton. Being furnished with means to subsist your men and horses, you will of course take your own measures for that purpose. I prefer your taking a route to Morgantown from McFarland's, on the west side of the Monongehala river, if any can be found convenient. You will deposit your tents, &c, agreeably to general orders, at Winchester. The arms you will retain, provided you hold yourself responsible to the United States for them. If so, favor me with a letter to this effect, enclosing a return of the arms.

I cannot conclude this letter without making my acknowledgments to you, your officers and soldiers in their cheerful and manly demeanor during the expedition. To me they have given great satisfaction; to themselves they have done great honor. I wish you and them a happy meeting with your friends, and shall always take pleasure in manifesting, by every means in my power, the high esteem I entertain of the merit of your troop. Sincerely, RICH'D H. LEE.

CAPT. GRATTAN.

LIST OF DEEDS.

The following is a list of deeds of land made by William Beverly on his manor, the number of acres and the name of the person to whom sold between the years 1738 and 1744:

John Lewis, 2,071 acres, February 20, 1738; William Cathey, 446 acres, September 28, 1738; Samuel Givens, 311 acres, September 27, 1738; George Hutcheson, 380 acres, February 20, 1738; George Hutcheson, 530 acres, February 21, 1738; George Hutcheson, 667 acres, February 20, 1738; Thomas Black, 599 acres, June 4, 1739: James Caldwell, 600 acres, February 20, 1738; George Robinson, 892 acres, February 20, 1738; Jas. Davis, 570 acres, February 20, 1738; Dan. Mahahan, 510 acres, February 20, 1738; P. Campbell, 1,546 acres, February 20, 1738; Th. Henderson, 391 acres, February 20, 1738; John Wilson, 340 acres, June 5, 1739; Wm. Smith, 135 acres, June 5, 1739; John Trimmel, 447 acres, June 5, 1739; John Anderson, 747 acres, June 5, 1738; Samuel Guy, 324 acres, June 5, 1738; John Davison, 785 acres, June 5, 1738; Samuel Davison, 253

James McClure, 408 acres, June 5, 1738; Andrew McClure, 370 acres, February 20, 1738; Fra. McClure, 196 acres, June 5, 1739; John Wilson, 200 acres, June 5, 1739; Joseph Tees, 465 acres, June 5, 1739; Martha Mitchell, 279 acres, October 1, 1739; George Home, 375 acres, October 1, 1739; John Moffett. 396 acres, February 29, 1739; John Robert and William C. Weysties, 1,614 acres, February 29, 1739; and the following between this time and 1744: John Mills, 650 acres; James Desper, 576 acres; Robt. Turk, 1,313 acres; William Sedgerwood, 387 acres; James Carr, 473 acres; Finley McClure, 441 acres; Robt. King, 750 acres; Alexander Breckenridge, 245 acres; Samuel Hughes, 440 acres; Th. Kirkpatrick, 296 acres; James Fulton, 637 acres; Sarah Ramsey, 390 acres; William Johnston, 100 acres; Robert Page, 202 acres; Pat. Martin, 321 acres; John Searight, 413 acres; Wm. Wright, 413 acres; John Hutcheson, 292 acres; David Edmiston, 350 acres; John Hart, 400 acres; James Risk, 800 acres; Pat. Cook, 590 acres; Robt. Campbell, 350 acres; Nat. Patterson, 201 acres; James Robinson, 395 acres; Moses Thompson, 1,040 acres; Moses Thompson, 410 acres; William Vance, 400 acres; Joseph Reid, 454 acres; George Caldwell, 405 acres; R. McDonald, 141 acres; D. Byrne, 567 acres; George Anderson. 411 acres; Robert Patterson, 331 acres; John Pickens, 764 acres; Robert Crockett, 322 acres; Jas. Lesley. 226 acres; D. Campbell, 466 acres; Robert McClenehan, 331 acres; John McCutchen, 920 acres; James Patton, 474 acres; William Hutcheson, 372 acres; Robert Young. 373 acres; Pat. Hays. 600 acres; John Breckenridge, 684 acres; William Robinson, 403 acres; Sam. Doag. 647 acres; Joseph Reed. 100 acres; Fr. Beaty, 588 acres; Ar. Hambreton, 515 acres; J. McUlluck, 230 acres; Robt. Black, 201 acres; Andrew Russell, 496 acres; William Skillim, 635 acres; George and Robert Breckenridge, 761 acres; Jacob Lockart. 436 acres; John Craig. 335 acres; Robert Cunningham. 483 acres; Alex. Campbell, 559 acres; Wm. Thompson, 94 acres.

LONGITUDE AND LATITUDE OF POINTS IN STAUNTON.

"The Virginias" for September contains the following, which will not only prove interesting to hundreds of our readers, but may be of value to some:

We are indebted to Supt. J. E. Hilgard for the exact latitudes and longitudes of points in the city of Staunton, Va , determined by observations of Assistant A. T. Mosman, of the United States Coast and Geodetic Survey:

	N. Latitude.			W. Longitude.			
Astronomical station, Sears Hill.	38°	08'	46°. 54	79°	04'	19''.	08
N. mer. monument, Lushbaugh Hill	38	09	39. 84	79	04	19.	08
Stand-pipe at reservoir.	38	09	12. 89	79	04	44.	52
Station City-view Hill.	38	08	49. 99	79	03	29.	91
S mer. monument, Gaymont.	38	07	57. 53	79	04	19.	09
Baptist churah spire.	38	08	56. 63	79	04	36.	16
Court-house, ball on belfry.	38	08	55. 89	79	04	20.	72
First Presbyterian church, rod on spire.	38	09	01. 89	79	04	17.	46
Western Lunatic Asylum, steam chimney.	38	08	40. 39	70	03	57.	25
Lutheran church, tower ornament.	38	08	58. 21	79	04	25.	29
Second Presbyterian church, S. E. corner tower.	38	09	01. 30	70	04	30.	48
Episcopal church, N. E. corner tower.	38	08	56. 33	79	04	31.	43
Betsy Bell Mountain.	38	08	14	79	03	21	
Mary Grey Mountain.	38	07	51	89	02	55	

Some one will ask of what use is it to have so many accurate determinations of points in one city. We answer that by using these absolutely determined and intervisible points for reference a competent civil engineer can make a survey of lots, etc., that can be .restored at any time even if all local evidence of its corners are destroyed, and by like references an accurate map, impossible without the aid of such geodetic determinations, can be made of the city and its surroundings. The 9-sheet map of Virginia makes the position of Staunton—Lat 38° 08' 30"; Long. 79° 63"; Gray's atlas makes it Lat 38° 09"; Long. 79° 04".

BIOGRAPHICAL NOTICES.

Both justice and decency require that we should bestow on our forefathers an honorable remembrance.—THUCYDIDES.

BIOGRAPHICAL NOTICES.

HON. THOMAS LEWIS.

Thomas Lewis, the eldest son of the Founder, was born in Donegal, Ireland, April 27th, 1718, and died in Augusta, January 31st, 1790. He was a man of strong and cultivated mind, of spirit and enterprise, and during the colonial period and the Revolutionary war rendered important services to the country. In 1746, he was appointed colonial surveyor of Augusta, and much of Washington's great wealth was acquired by surveys of land under his authority and in common with him. He and Col. John Wilson represented the county in the House of Burgesses almost uninterruptedly from 1745 to 1767, and they voted, in 1765, for Patrick Henry's celebrated resolutions declaring that this "general assembly have the only exclusive right and power to lay taxes and impositions upon the inhabitants of this colony; that any efforts in an opposite direction are illegal, unconstitutional and unjust, and have a manifest tendency to destroy British as well as American freedom." In 1775, he was unanimously elected delegate to the Colonial Congress, and was one of the first to enroll his name among the "Sons of Liberty." He was commissioner of the old confederacy of the thirteen colonies, in 1778, to treat with the Indian tribes who had been defeated at the battle of Point Pleasant, and successfully concluded his negotiations, thus setting free from the defence of the western border thousands of our best troops who hastened to join the standard of Washington and fight for the independence of their country. He was a member of the convention which ratified the Constitution of the United States, and by a vote so nearly divided that the patriot yet rejoices at his country's escape from the anarchy which would have been the consequence of a different result. He urged with eloquence and ability the adoption of the Constitution and voted for its ratification. After the Revolution, Washington made him a visit at Lewiston, in Rockingham, and there arranged their land claims. Gov. Gilmer says in his Sketches of Upper Georgia, p. 548: " My father, then a youth of nineteen, returning from my Grandfather Lewis', where he had been visiting my mother, met Washington fording the Shenandoah river in the dusk of the evening.

Washington asked him how he should go to Mr. Lewis'. My father, taking him for some big Dutchman of the neighborhood, who was poking fun at him on account of his frequent visits to the Lewis family, answered, "follow your nose."

It is a noticeable fact in a country of such rapid changes as ours that his descendants still own and reside upon his estate of Lewiston, near Port Republic, in the present county of Rockingham. His great-grandson, Hon. John F. Lewis. is the present Lieut-Governor of Virginia; another great-grandson, Hon. L. L. Lewis, is Judge of the Supreme Court of Appeals of Virginia, and a great-great-grandson, D. S. Lewis, United States Attorney for the Western District of Virginia.

Gen. Samuel H. Lewis, a grandson, in a letter of date April 6th, 1855, addressed to Hon. Samuel Price, of Lewisburg, W. Va., thus speaks of him: "The defective sight of Thomas Lewis prevented him from joining his gallant brothers in the field. With the aid of glasses, which he always used, he was hardly able to tell an Indian from a white man at the distance of twenty paces." The letter alluded to above says further: "I have heard that he was six feet in height, robust but not inclined to corpulency; his eyes and hair were dark; his complexion fair. I have heard him spoken of as a handsome, fine-looking man. The caste of his profile I cannot describe, but I do not think it was Roman or aquiline, as I have heard it said that my elder brother, Thomas, resembled him in features. He was exceedingly near-sighted, and was under the necessity of using glasses habitually. There is no family portrait extant of him that I know of. He was of a grave and serious temper; strict, perhaps rigid, in his notions of moral and religious duty. Though a supporter of and a regular attendant upon the services of the Established Church, he was not a communicant. He was possessed of a liberal education, and was probably one of the best mathematicians of his day in the State. He had a literary taste, and when not engaged in business or occupied with company, was generally to be found in his library. His collection of books was very extensive and valuable, embracing many of the most important works then extant in history, biography, moral philosophy, political economy, national law, theology and poetry. In his theological department were Tillotson, Barrow, South, 'the Boyle Lecturer,' and other standard works of the English church. He was born in Donegal county, Ireland, on the 27th of April, 1718, and died at his residence, in Rockingham county, on the Shenandoah river, three miles from Port Republic, on the 31st day of January, 1790. In his will he fixed the place on his own estate where he wished to be buried, and desired that the burial service might be read from the Book of Common Prayer by his friend, Peachy Gilmer. He died of a cancer in the face. He was, as I have always understood, the eldest son of John Lewis. He married on the 26th of January, 1749, Jane, the daughter of

William Strother, Esq., of Stafford county, whose estate, opposite to Fredericksburg, joined the residence of the father of Gen. Washington, with whom (G. W.) she was a school-mate, and nearly of the same age. She died in September, 1820. Thomas and Jane Lewis brought up a family of thirteen children."

GEN. ANDREW LEWIS, BORN 1720, IN IRELAND, DIED 1781, IN VA.

The following sketch of this distinguished soldier is from the pen of Fred'k Johnston, of Salem:

"Those who have seen the equestrian statue of George Washington near the Capitol of Virginia in Richmond, must have observed among the noble figures placed below and around that of the Father of his Country one marked with the name of Andrew Lewis, the hero of Point Pleasant. His strikingly majestic form and figure never fail to remind me when I look at it, (as I have often done, and each time with increasing admiration) of the memorable remark made by the Governor of the Colony of New York, when General Lewis was a commissioner on behalf of Virginia at the treaty of Fort Stanwix, in New York, in 1768, that "the earth seemed to tremble under him as he walked along." He it was who is the subject of this "sketch."

*   *   *   *   *   *

Andrew, the second son of John Lewis, resided on the Roanoke, in Botetourt county, as did his brother Charles. The will of Andrew Lewis, which is on record in the county court of Botetourt—dated in 1780, and admitted to record in February, 1782, showing that he died between those periods—devises to his son William two thousand acres of land lying on Roanoke river. This embraces the fine body of lands lying west of Salem for many years owned by Dr. John Johnston, on which there is a magnificent spring, which, in years gone by, furnished the water power for a manufacturing mill, that has long since disappeared. It also embraces the very valuable farm know as "Dropmore," containing one thousand acres, bought from Capt. William Lewis by Nathaniel Burwell, and was sold in the 1869 for $100,000—one hundred dollars an acre—probably the largest sale of the same quantity of land that was ever made in Virginia. As will be more particularly stated hereafter, Gen. Andrew Lewis, who owned this land at the time of his death in 1781, was buried on an eminence overlooking the beautiful valley of Roanoke river, spreading out for six miles above and below the spot where the grave is now marked, from which spot I hope his dust will be removed at an early day to the public cemetery near by.

Some of the decendants of Gen. Lewis are now living in Roanoke county. Col. Thomas Lewis and his brother Andrew, and great-grand-children—also Maj. Andrew L. Pitzer, and other children of Madison Pitzer, who married Eliza Lewis, daughter of Capt. Andrew Lewis—also the children of Col. Elijah McClanahan, who married Agatha Lewis, daughter of Col. Andrew Lewis, of Bent Mountain. Mrs. Colin Bass, now residing in Salem, is one of those children. Capt. Andrew Lewis married Jane McClanahan, a sister of Col. Elijah and James McClanahan, and at the close of his life resided on the farm now owned by Capt. Robert B. Moorman, half a mile west of Big Lick Depot.

Col. Andrew Lewis, of Bent Mountain, formerly in Montgomery county, now in Roanoke, was one of the sons of Gen. Andrew Lewis, who died about the year 1844, at an advanced age—about 84. My personal recollections of Col. Lewis are very distinct, having often seen him in my boyhood, at my father's house, and at his own house on Bent mountain, where he owned an immense body of lands that were valuable for pasturage and raising fine cattle in former days. and where, like Alexander Selkirk, he reigned as "monarch of all he surveyed," for a great number of years. I also met with him a few times in the latter part of his life, after religion (which he embraced when near eighty years old) had softened some of the rough points of his character. Like all the Lewises, he was a man of commanding figure and appearance, reminding one of the description given by Stuart in his "Historical Memoir" of General Andrew Lewis:—"He was upwards of six feet high, of uncommon strength and agility, and his form of the most exact symmetry. He had a stern countenance, and was of a reserved and distant deportment, which rendered his presence more awful than engaging."

Col. Andrew Lewis was twice married—first to a daughter of Thomas Madison, by whom he had three children one, Charles, who died unmarried, and Thomas, who was killed by McHenry in a duel fought with rifles. which was fatal to both parties. This event created great interest at the time of its occurrence, not only on account of the high standing and character of the parties, but of its tragical termination. The only daughter of Col. Lewis by this marriage was Agatha, who married Col. Elijah McClanahan and left a large number of descendants. By his second marriage with Miss Bryant. he had one daughter, Kitty, who married Joseph King, and is still living on Bent Mountain with her son, Joseph R. King.

Doctor Andrew Lewis was another member of the Lewis family, who lived and died in Botetourt. He was a son of Capt. Wm. Lewis, who was twice married—first to a daughter of Thomas Madison, and afterwards to Nancy McClanahan. sister of Col. Elijah McClanahan. Dr. Lewis rose to great eminence in his profession—married Maria Walton, who is now living near Salem. and had three children—two daughters and one son.— One of the daughters, Lucy, married George W. Shanks; the other, Mary, married Henry A. Edmundson. The son, Dr. Wm. W. Lewis. married a daughter of Rev. Dr. McFarland, and left a daughter and son, Frank Lewis, who is now at the Seminary, preparing for the ministry, being the only one of the Lewis name (so far as I know) who has devoted himself to that calling. Having thus traced the Botetourt branches of the Lewis family from their ancestor, John Lewis, of Augusta county, I will now return to my first plan of presenting a sketch of Andrew Lewis, commonly known and referred to as the "hero of Point Pleasant," which is gathered in part from "Howe's Historical Collections," page 204, on Botetourt county— but venturing to suggest a correction in one or two particulars, which will be pointed out—also Charles Campbell's "Introduction to the History of the Colony of the Old Dominion"—from the same author's larger work, "History of the Colony and Ancient Dominion of Virginia," and from Foote's "Sketches of Virginia," 2d series, all of which are works of high authority.

(1.) Howe, on page 204 as above, states that "General Andrew Lewis resided on the Roanoke river, in this county. He was one of the six sons [should be five sons and one daughter] of that John Lewis who, with

Mackey and Salling, had been foremost in settling Augusta county, and the most distinguished of a family who behaved so bravely in defending the infant settlements against the Indians. In Braddock's war he was in a company in which were all the brothers, Samuel Lewis, being the captain. On page 182—Augusta county—the same author speaks of but four sons of John Lewis, of whom Thomas is said to be the eldest. Here is obviously a mistake, and an apparent contradiction, since Samuel and Thomas cannot both have been the eldest son. In a note on page 589 of Campbell's larger works, the following statement is made: "Thos. Lewis, eldest son of John Lewis, owing to a defective vision, was not actively engaged in the Indian wars. He married a Miss Strother, of Stafford. The second son, Samuel, died without issue. William, of the Sweet Springs. was distinguished in the frontier wars, and was an officer in the Revolutionary war. The fifth son, Col. Charles Lewis, fell at Point Pleasant." I think it may fairly be concluded that Howe is mistaken in his statement that John Lewis had six sons, and that Sam was the eldest. He only gives the names of four, including Samuel, and omitting Charles. The statement of Charles Campbell is no doubt the correct one. Howe proceeds: "This corps distinguished themselves at Braddock's defeat. They, with some other of the Virginia troops, were in the advance, and first attacked the enemy. Severed from the rest of the army, they cut their way through the enemy to their companions, with the loss of many men. The conduct of Andrew Lewis at Grant's defeat, in his attack on Fort du Quesne. acquired for him the highest reputation for prudence and courage. He was at this time a major. Both Lewis and Grant were made prisoners. While they were prisoners, Grant addressed a letter to Gen. Forbes, attributing their defeat to Lewis. This letter being inspected by the French, who knew the falsehood of the charge, they handed it to Lewis, who waited on Grant and challenged him. Upon his refusing to fight, Lewis spit in his face in the presence of the French officers, and then left him to reflect on his baseness. Major Lewis was with Washington July 4th, 1754, at the capitulation of Fort Necessity, when by the articles agreed upon the garrison was to retire and return without molestation to the inhabited parts of the country; and the French commander promised that no embarrassment should be interposed either by his own men or the savages. While some of the soldiers of each army were intermixed, an Irishman, exasperated by an Indian near him, "cursed the copper-colored scoundrel," and raised his musket. Lewis, who had been twice wounded in the engagement, and was then hobbling on a staff, raised the Irishman's gun as he was in the act of firing, and thus not only saved the life of the Indian, but probably prevented a general massacre of the Virginia troops. He was the commander and general of the Virginia troops at the battle of Point Pleasant, fought the 10th of May, 1774. [This should be the 10th of October, as stated by all the historians except Howe.] In this campaign the Indians were driven west of the Ohio. Washington, in whose regiment Lewis had once been a major, formed so high an opinion of his bravery and military skill that at the commencement of the Revolutionary War he was induced to recommend him to Congress as one of the major-generals of the American army—a recommendation which was slighted in order to make room for Gen. Stephens. It is also said that when Washington was commissioned as commander-in-chief he expressed a wish that the appointment had been given to Gen. Lewis.

43 ‡

Upon this slight in the appointment of Stephens, Washington wrote a letter to Gen. Lewis, which is published in his correspondence, expressive of his regret at the course pursued by Congress, and promised that he should be promoted to the first vacancy. At his solicitation, Lewis accepted the commission of Brigadier-General, and was soon after ordered to the command of a detachment of the army stationed near Williamsburg. He commanded the Virginia troops when Lord Dunmore was driven from Gwynn's Island, in 1776, and announced his orders for attacking the enemy by putting a match to the first gun, which was an eighteen-pounder.

Gen. Lewis resigned his command in 1781, to return home, being seized ill with a fever. He died on his way, in Bedford county, about forty (more correctly twenty-two) miles, from his own house on the Roanoke, lamented by all acquainted with his meritorious services and superior qualities."

HIS WILL.

The following is the full text of the last will and testament of General Lewis, an interesting document in itself, and bearing evidence to the wonderful success of this emigrant Irish boy, who during his brief career in Virginia, when more than half of his life was spent in the public service, acquired and devised to his children over 30,000 acres of land:

" In the name of God, Amen. I, Andrew Lewis, of the county and parish of Botetourt, make this my last will and testament. I resign my soul to its Creator in all humble hopes of its future happiness, as in the disposal of a being infinitely good. As to my body, I leave it to be buried at the discretion of my executors hereinafter named. And as to my worldly estate, I dispose of it in the following manner and form:

First. I give to my beloved wife two negro men and two negro women for her lifetime, with a right to work one-third part of the farm I live on, called and known by the name of Birchfield. Also such part of the stock, not exceeding the sixth part, as she may find it necessary for her support for life.

To my son John I give the tract of land on which he lives, containing 470 acres. Also a tract of land on both sides of Greenbrier river, at the mouth of Ewing's creek, containing 480 acres. Also 1,000 acres on Sinking creek, in the Kentucky county, part of my 5,000 tract, and that he take 1,000 acres in a body, at either end of this tract, as may best please him.

To my son Samuel I give all my lands near Staunton, in Augusta county, there being three distinct tracts, to-wit: the Stone House tract, containing 740 acres, and a tract joining the lower end thereof, on which I lived, containing 680 acres, and the third, joining the southeast side of the two above named tracts containing 185 acres, deeded to me by Robert Beverly. Also a tract of land in Greenbrier county, on the Sink-hole lands, containing 1,200 acres. I also give him my gold watch.

To my son Thomas I give the tract of land joining the upper end of the tract I live on, known by the name of Burks, or Old Place, containing 283 acres, and on the north side of Roanoke river. Also a tract of land on the north side of Greenbrier river, near to Weaver's Nob, and known by the name of Richland, containing 1,170 acres. Also a tract in Greenbrier county, on which John Cook lives, containing 500 acres, and known by the name of Falling Spring tract. Also a tract containing 200 acres, joining the southwest end of the Warm Spring tract, and on both sides of the Warm Spring branch.

To my son Andrew I give the following tracts of land, to-wit: the mill tract, on which he lives, containing 269 acres, formerly Thomas Tash's. Also a tract of land joining the lower end of the above, containing 100 acres, and known by Burk's Spring. Also two tracts adjoining the southeast side of the above tract, one containing 116 acres, the other 63 acres. Also a tract of land in Greenbrier county, on the south side of Greenbrier river, opposite to the mouth of Muddy creek, containing 780 acres. Also a tract of land in the same county, on the branches of Indian creek, known by the name of Fork Survey containing 400 acres.

To my son William I give the following tracts of land, to-wit: the tract on which I live, called Birchfield, containing 112 acres, and a tract joining the north side thereof, containing 625 acres. Also the Red Spring Meadow tract, containing 800 acres or thereabouts. Also a tract containing 400 acres, on the head of Back creek, a branch of Dunlap's creek, and about five miles from the Sweet Springs.

To my daughter Ann, I give, to be sold for her use, the following tracts of land, to-wit: 250 acres on Wolf creek, a branch of Roanoke, and on the north side of the river, and a tract of land on the head branches of Peters' creek, containing 190 acres. Also a tract of land adjoining the northeast end thereof, about 100 or 106 acres, patented in the name of Robert Breckenridge, and by his will Col. Preston is to make me a title. Also my part of the land surveyed in partnership between Breckenridge, Preston and myself, and patented as the last-mentioned tract, and the title made in the same manner by Col. Preston to the lands lying between Peter Evans' and Tinker's creek. Also 280 acres between the Warm and Hot Springs, on which Jeremiah Edwards lives. Also all my rights held by my brother Thomas and myself in two small surveys, containing the Hot Springs. Also a tract of land on the Hot Springs branch, called Cedar Run, and joining the end of Thomas Fitzpatrick's, containing 175 acres.

To my three grandsons, Andrew, Samuel and Charles, sons of John Lewis, I give all my part of the Pocotated tract [intended for Pocotalico, no doubt, but incorrectly spelled in transcribing,] of land, which part, I think, is 2,100 acres, and the whole patented in the name of John Fry, Adam Stephen, Andrew Lewis, Peter Hogg, John Savage, Thos. Butler, ——— Wright, and John Daniel Wilper. All the residue of my lands, to-wit: 1,000 acres, part of the 2,000 on Sinking creek, in Kentucky co., and the 3,000 tract on Elkhorn, and the 9,000 acres in the forks of the rivers Ohio and the Great Kanawha, and a 100 acre tract on Rockcastle creek, near the 9,000, together with 750 entered by warrants, on the Cole river and the Kanawha, be equally divided, having respect to the situation and quality of the land, between my sons, Thomas, Andrew and William.

Any money, negroes, and stock I may die possessed of, after my wife has set apart what is devised her, and even that part after her decease, and after my daughter Ann has made choice of a negro wench, or girl, and man, to be equally divided between my sons, Samuel, Thomas and Andrew, and William and my daughter Ann.

My wearing apparel I give to my son Andrew, and after Samuel, Thomas and Ann has each taken a bed and furniture, all the remainder of the house and kitchen furniture be considered the property of William, his mother having a right to retain the use of such of them as may be absolutely necessary whilst she lives. In case any of my sons and daughter die before her, or without lawful issue, the part of the estate willed to such deceased to be equally divided between the survivors above mentioned. It's my desire that my brother Thomas, Col. William Preston, and my three sons, Samuel, Thomas and Andrew, and I hereby appoint them executors of this my last will and testament, and that each of them, with my brother William and sister Margaret, as well as my other children, wear a mourning ring, to be purchased at the expense of the estate before a division.

I hereby revoke all former wills by me made, ratifying and confirming this, and no other, to be my last will and testament. In witness whereof I have hereunto set my hand and affixed my seal, this 23d day of Jan'y, 1780. Signed, sealed and delivered by the testator in the presence of us as his last will and testament, and on the day and year above mentioned.

ANDREW LEWIS, [L. S.]

James Neily,
William Armstrong,
William Neily.

Proved and admitted to probate on the 14th day of February, 1782. by the County Court of Botetourt.   W. H. ALLEN, D. C.

COLONEL WILLIAM LEWIS.

Col. Wm. Lewis, the Founder's third son, was born in Ireland about 1724. He was remarkably handsome in the face. perfectly well formed in person, tall, robust and vigorous. Fond of books, his great delight from boyhood was the study of literature and philosophy. He thus shunned public employments, and never would have left his retirement but for the stirring times in which he lived. On reaching a proper age, he was entered at a school in Eastern Virginia—the school of Rev. James Waddell. D. D.—and after acquiring a liberal education, proceeded to Philadelphia, where he graduated as a doctor of medicine. It was during his sojourn in that city that he formed the acquaintance and won the heart of Ann Montgomery, of Delaware. who afterwards became his wife. Returning to Virginia, he would gladly have spent his days in the quiet pursuits of his profession, but the war of 1753-'54 coming on, he volunteered for service, and was severely wounded at the battle of Braddock's defeat. Returning to Augusta, he resumed the practice, and soon became conspicuous for his large intelligence, his professional skill and his influence in the community. In this field he sought to promote good fellowship, to inspire a feeling of compassion among the whites for the aborigines, and to protect the Indians from the injustice of unscrupulous and greedy traders. He urged the erection of schools and churches, and was remarkable for his high regard for all things relating to education and religion. Here his life would have been spent but for the Revolution. Imbued with a sense of our wrongs, and a determination to resist the tyranny of Great Britain, he abandoned a second time his peaceful employments in 1776, and accepted a commission as colonel in the old continental line. He was an elder in the Presbyterian church, and his compassionate kindness and many acts of charity drew the eyes of the people upon him, so that he was commonly spoken of as the Civilizer of the Border. He served in the army until 1781, when he returned to his family in Augusta. Gov. Gilmer, in his sketches, thus speaks of him on page 58: "William Lewis, though as powerful in person and brave in spirit as either of his brothers, was less disposed to seek fame by the sacrifice of human life. He was an elder in the Presbyterian church of the old Covenanter sort. His son Thomas was an officer in Wayne's army of high reputation for soldierly conduct. Soon after Tom's return home from the service, he saw some wild ducks on a Sunday morning on the Sweet Spring creek. Taking a fowling piece in his hand, he crept along a zig-zag fence until within shooting distance, and was about firing when he felt the sharp pang of a birch applied to his back. Turning suddenly, he saw the uplifted hand of his father, who exclaimed, ' I'll teach you not to profane the Sabbath here.' " It is not surprising that the old man was styled the Civilizer of the Border. In a book published in Richmond by C. H. Wynne, in 1858, entitled " Recollections, &c., of Lynchburg, by the oldest inhabitant," on pages 316-318, there is an account of the Lewis'. The author says "William Lewis owned a princely estate where Staunton now stands (this should doubtless read near Staunton,) and he with his brothers, Andrew, Thomas, Charles and Samuel, were in the battle of Braddock's defeat. They received their early instruction from the venerable Dr. Waddell, the blind preacher. The names of these distinguished men are all well known in history, so that only a slight mention of them here is necessary, it being only designed to make a brief record of some of the incidents connected with the family of Mrs. Agatha Towles " (neé Lewis.) William Lewis removed from Augusta to the Sweet Spring, circa 1790, where he died in 1812, revered as a patriarch and honored and beloved as a man and citizen.

His son, Hon. William I. Lewis, represented Campbell County District in the United States Congress from 1815 to 1817, and his son, Major John Lewis, a distinguished officer of the Revolution, spent the winter of 1777 at Valley Forge with Washington, between whom and Lewis a warm personal friendship existed, and was in many of the battles of the Revolution. Major Lewis died in 1823. He was a man of lofty character and indomitable spirit.

COL. CHARLES LEWIS,

the fourth son of the Founder, was killed at the battle of the Point, October 10, 1774. " He was esteemed," says Howe, p. 183, " the most skillful of all the leaders of the border warfare, and was as much beloved for his noble and amiable qualities as he was admired for his military talents."

Hon. Alex. H. H. Stuart, M. C. for the Augusta District from 1841 to 1843, and during President Fillmore's administration Secretary of the Interior, 1850-'53, has communicated in the following letter some interesting particulars as to Col. Charles Lewis, who, it seems, was the "Idol of the Army":

STAUNTON, October 18th, 1882.

COL: JOHN L. PEYTON:

Dear Sir,—I regret very much that I cannot give you any detailed account of Col. Charles Lewis, who was killed at the battle of Point Pleasant in 1774. I remember being present at a conversation, about 1830, between my father and the late Andrew Reid (father of Col. Samuel McD. Reid) in regard to him. Mr. Reid had served under Col. Lewis in 1774, and was actively engaged in the battle of Point Pleasant. Col. Charles Lewis was a younger brother of Gen. Andrew Lewis. Gen. Andrew Lewis was represented to have been a man of reserved manners and great dignity of character,—somewhat of the order of George Washington. His vigorous intellect, unquestionable courage and solid virtues inspired unlimited confidence in all who knew him, but there was nothing showy or attractive about him. Charles Lewis, on the other hand, was represented by Mr. Reid as being a man of brilliant talents, of most engaging manners, and, as Mr. Reid expressed it, "the idol of the whole army." My father, who was a much younger man than Mr. Reid, and had no personal acquaintance with Col. Charles Lewis, but was familiar with his character, as described by his cotemporaries, concurred with Mr. Reid in the high estimate which he had formed of his abilities and noble qualities, and they agreed in expressing the belief that if he had not been prematurely cut off he would have been a conspicuous figure in our Revolutionary war. Mr. Reid said the death of Col. Charles Lewis threw gloom over the whole army.		Respectfully yours, &c.,

ALEX. H. H. STUART.

COL. ARTHUR CAMPBELL.

Arthur Campbell was born in Augusta County in 1742. When fifteen years old, he volunteered as a militiaman, to perform duty in protecting the frontier from incursions of the Indians. He was stationed in a fort on the Cowpasture river, near where the road crosses leading from Staunton to the Warm Springs. While engaged in this service, he was captured by the Indians, who loaded him with their packs, and marched seven days into the forests with his captors, who were from Lakes Erie and Michigan, and were on their return. Campbell, at the end of seven days, was so exhausted that he was unable to travel, and was treated by the Indians with great severity. An old chief, taking compassion on him, protected him from further injury, and on reaching the Lakes adopted Campbell, in whose family the young man remained during his three years' captivity.

During this time, Campbell made himself familiar with the Indian language their manners and customs, and soon acquired the confidence of the old chief, who took him on all his hunting excursions. During these they rambled over Michigan and the northern parts of Ohio, Indiana and Illinois. In 1749, a British force marched towards the Upper Lakes, of which the Indians were informed by their scouts. Campbell formed the bold resolution of escaping to this force. While out on one of their hunting excursions, Campbell left the Indians, and after a fortnight's tramp through the pathless wilds reached the British. The British commander was much interested in Campbell's account of his captivity and escape, and with his intelligence, and engaged him to pilot the army, which he did with success. Shortly after he returned to Augusta, after an absence of more than three years. For his services in piloting the army he received a grant of 1,000 acres of land near Louisville, Kentucky.

In 1772, his father, David Campbell, and family, removed to the "Royal Oak," on Holstein river, and in 1776, Arthur Campbell was appointed major in the Fincastle militia, and elected to the General Assembly. He was also a member of the convention for forming the Constitution. When Washington county was formed he was commissioned colonel commandant, and during the time he was in commission commanded several expeditions, particularly that against the Cherokees.

He was tall, of a dignified air, an extensive reader and good talker. He married a sister of Gen. William Campbell, and left issue at his death, in 1816, in Knox county, Kentucky.

GEN. WILLIAM CAMPBELL.

William Campbell was born in Augusta County about the year 1745, and was of Scotch origin. He received a liberal education, and early displayed a taste and genius for military science. He was of well-proportioned and commanding figure, being over six feet high, and of grave and dignified demeanor. In 1775, he joined the first regular troops raised in Virginia, having been commissioned a captain in the first regiment. In 1776, he resigned, owing to the danger to which his family and friends were exposed from Indian hostilities, and returned to Washington county, where he was commissioned lieutenant-colonel of the county militia, and the year following to the colonelcy on the resignation of Col. Evan Shelby, se'r. In this rank he continued until after the battles of King's Mountain and Guilford, when he was appointed by the Legislature of Virginia to the rank of Brigadier-General, and was ordered to join LaFayette in opposing the British in 1781. After the defeat of the British General Furguson, Cornwallis imbibed a personal resentment, and had the temerity to threaten Gen. Campbell with death if he fell into his hands. To these threats Gen. Campbell responded by declaring that if Cornwallis fell into the hands of the Americans he would meet the fate of Ferguson. This, soon after, at the battle of Guilford, had nearly been the case, for had all the militia behaved with the firmness as did the wing commanded by Gen. Campbell, the British army must have met with total defeat.

On forming the army in Virginia, in 1781, under LaFayette, Gen. Camp-

bell became a favorite of Lafayette, who gave him command of the brigade
of light infantry and riflemen. A few weeks before the siege of Yorktown, illness caused him to retire to the country house of a friend, and
there, in the thirty-sixth year of his age, he expired.

To military genius he united moral and social virtues and an exemplary
life. His military career was short but brilliant. With an inferior force of
undisciplined militia, he marched in a few days near two hundred miles,
over rugged mountains, in search of the enemy, who were commanded by
experienced officers, and who had chosen at King's Mountain his field for
battle. It was a strong position, more in the nature of a fortification than
an open field. The assault on the British was impetuous and irresistible,
and their victory glorious. It caused the retreat of the British army, and
broke up their plan of an invasion of Virginia in that year. It also reani-
mated the friends of Liberty in the southern states, and was the prelude
to the final triumph the following year at Yorktown.

The Virginia Legislature voted him a sword, horse and pistols for his
conduct at King's Mountain, and named a county in his honor. Congress
passed in his favor highly complimentary resolutions.

At the time of his death, LaFayette issued an order regretting the decease of " an officer whose services must have endeared him to every citizen and soldier," as one who had "acquired a glory in the affairs of
King's Mountain and Guilford which will do his memory everlasting honor
and ensure him a high rank among the defenders of Liberty in America."

COL. WILLIAM FLEMING.

William Fleming was a native of Scotland, and, while in his minority,
emigrated to Virginia. He was represented as of noble blood, and had
received a liberal education, which he sought to utilize on a broader field
than that of his Caledonian home. Of a bold and adventurous spirit, he
wandered from the early seats of colonization in Virginia to the mountains
of Augusta, and was so much pleased with the beauty of the country, its
fertility, and the hospitable manners and customs of the people, that he
determined to take up his residence among them. He accordingly settled
in that part of Augusta now known as Botetourt, and on the James river,
about 1760. He took up large grants of public lands, which, enhancing
in value, soon made him a man of fortune. He was a man of fine physique, vigorous constitution, enterprising spirit, and fond of athletic sports,
in which he excelled, and of social tastes, which made him popular. When
the war of 1774 was impending, he raised, under the orders of Gen. Andrew Lewis, a regiment. which he commanded at the battle of Point
Pleasant, where he received a wound, from which he only partially recovered, and which hastened his death.

Col. Fleming married and left a family. One of his daughters, Anne, married Rev. George A. Barter, D. D., Rector, in 1798, of Liberty Hall Academy, Professor of Mathematics, Natural Philosophy and Astronomy, and minister of New Monmouth and Lexington churches, and, in 1831, Professor of Theology in Union Theological Seminary.

On page 363 of Howe's History of Virginia, Col. Fleming is mentioned as having been Governor of Virginia during the Revolutionary war. This must be an error. Patrick Henry was Governor from 1776 to 1779; then Thomas Jefferson to 1781; then Thomas Nelson to November, 1781; then Benjamin Harrison to 1784, when Henry was again elected Governor.*

OLD LETTER.

Through the kindness of Mr. D. W. Bernard, in whose possession the original now is, we have been furnished with the following letter, written by the mother of the great Patrick Henry to Mrs. Fleming, wife of Col. Fleming. It is a quaint old document, which we are satisfied will possess for our readers an especial interest:

15TH OCT'R, 1774.

DEAR MADAM:

Kind Providence preserved me and all with me safe to our home in Hanover. Here people have been very sickly, but hope the sickly season is nigh over. My dear Annie has been ailing two or three days with a fever; the dear children are very well.

My son Patrick has been gone to Philadelphia near seven weeks. The affairs of Congress are kept with great secresy—nobody being allowed to be present. I assure you we have our lowland troubles and fears with respect to Great Britain Perhaps our good God may bring good to us out of these many evils which threaten us, not only from the mountains but from the seas. I cannot forget to thank my dear Mrs. Fleming for the great kindness that you showed us when in Botetourt, and assure you that I remember Col. Fleming and you with much esteem and best wishes, and I shall take it very kind if you will let me hear from you.

My daughter, Betty, joins me in kind love to yourself and Miss Rosie, and especially to your dear good mother when you see her.

I am, dear madam,

Your humble serv't,

SARAH HENRY.

REV. JAMES MADISON, D. D.

James Madison was born, August 27, 1749, in that part of Augusta County now embraced within the limits of Rockingham, and near the present town of Port Republic. He obtained his early education in Maryland, and then at William and Mary College, where he matriculated 1768. He was distinguished at college for his diligence and attainments, and received a gold medal, presented by Lord Botetourt, in 1772. He studied law, and was admitted to the Bar, but soon abandoned it to study for the

---

*Col. F. was for a brief period acting Governor.
PUBS.

44 ‡

ministry. In 1773, he was chosen Professor of Mathematics in William and Mary, and in 1775, proceeded to England, was admitted to holy orders, and was licensed by the Bishop of London for the colony of Virginia. On his return to Virginia he resumed his situation in William and Mary, and in 1777, became president of the college. He now returned to England to qualify himself more thoroughly for his position, and remained abroad till 1778. Returning home, he entered upon his college duties with zeal. In 1784, he retired from the mathematical department, and became Professor of Natural and Moral Philosophy, International Law, etc., and retained those positions, with the presidency, until his death, August, 1815.

In 1785, the University of Pennsylvania conferred upon him the degree of Docter of Divinity.

Notwithstanding the Episcopal Church had been in existence for more than a century and a half in Virginia, she never had a Resident-Bishop until 1785—being nominally a part of the Diocese of London. Her first Convention was held in May, 1785, when Bishop Madison presided.

At the period when Bishop Madison entered on his office, the Episcopal Church in Virginia was in a state of extreme depression—the clergy being few in number, and many suffering from poverty, and the Bishop expressed the fear, at this convention, "that the great dereliction sustained by our church hath arisen, in no small degree, from the want of that fervent Christian zeal which her many pious and zealous pastors ought more generally to have inspired."

The Bishop made his first visitation in 1792. At this time he seems to have been intensely interested on uniting all sincere Christians: "There is no one," he says, "but must cordially wish for such a union, provided it did not require a sacrifice of those points which are deemed essential by our church; from them we have no power to retreat." At the New York convention of 1792, he opposed the use of "Articles" altogether, on the "principles of the confessional," and other like books.

His preaching was popular, and his character commanded respect, but his influence did little to revive the languishing interests of the church in Virginia.

His published works are a thanksgiving sermon, 1781; a letter to J. Morse, 1795; an addresss to the Episcopal Church in 1790; a eulogy on Washington, 1800; a discourse at the funeral of Mrs. Ann Semple, sister of President Tyler; a large map of Virginia, and several papers in Barton's journal.

Bishop Madison married, in 1779, Sarah Tate, one of the bright belles who adorned the society of Williamsburg. They left two children: James Catesby Madison, of Roanoke county, Va., and Susan, who married R. G. Scott, of Richmond.

MAJ. SAMUEL M'CULLOCH

was born on Short creek, Augusta, now northwestern West Virginia, about 1752. At a very early age he distinguished himself as a bold and efficient borderer. As an Indian hunter, he had few superiors. He seemed to track the wily red man with a sagacity as remarkable as his efforts were successful. From early boyhood, he was almost constantly engaged in excursions against the enemy, or scouting for the security of the settlements. It was mainly to these energetic operations that the frontier was so often saved from savage depredation, and by cutting off their retreat, attacking their hunting camps, and annoying them in various other ways, he rendered himself an extraordinary object of fear and hatred. For these acts they marked him, and vowed vengeance against his name. In consideration of his services, he was commissioned major in 1775, and in 1777 he performed a remarkable feat. The circumstances connected with this achievement are as follows: During the siege of Wheeling, the Indians drove Major McCulloch to the summit of a lofty hill which overhangs the present city. Knowing their relentless hostility toward himself, he strained every muscle of his noble steed to gain the summit, and then escaped along the brow in the direction of Van Meter's fort. At length he attained the top, and galloping ahead of his pursuers, rejoiced at his lucky escape. As he gained a point on the hill near where a road passes, what should he suddenly encounter but a considerable body of Indians, who were just returning from a plundering excursion among the settlements. In an instant he comprehended the extent of his danger. Escape seemed out of the question, either in the direction of Short creek or back to the bottom. A fierce and revengeful foe completely hemmed him in, cutting off every chance of escape. What was to be done?—Fall into their hands and share the most refined torture? That thought was agony, and in an instant the bold soldier, preferring death among the rocks and brambles, determined to plunge over the precipice before him—full three hundred feet high and almost perpendicular. Without a moment's hesitation, for the savages were pressing upon him, he firmly adjusted himself in the saddle, grasped securely the bridle in his left hand, and supporting his rifle in the right, pushed his unfaltering horse over. A plunge, a crash —crackling timber and tumbling rocks, were all that the wondering savages could see or hear. They looked, chagrined and bewildered, one at another,—and while they inwardly regretted that the fire had been spared its victim, they could not but greatly rejoice that their most inveterate enemy was at length beyond the power of doing further injury. But, lo! ere a single savage had recovered from his amazement, what should they see but the invulnerable major, on his white steed, galloping across the peninsula. Such was the feat of Major McCulloch, certainly one of the most daring and successful ever attempted. The place has become memorable as "McCulloch's Leap," and will remain so long as the hill stands and the recollections of the past have a place in the hearts of the people.

It is to us a matter of regret that more of the stirring incidents in this man's life have not been collected and preserved. We have heard of many daring feats of personal prowess, but they come to us in such a mixed and unsatisfactory form as to render their publication unsafe.

We come now to the most painful duty of the biographer—the catastrophe—the death of his hero. Towards the latter end of July, 1782, indications of Indians having been noticed by some of the settlers, Major McCulloch and his brother John mounted their horses and left Van Metre's fort, to ascertain the correctness of the report. They crossed Short creek, and continued in the direction of Wheeling, but inclining towards the river. They scouted closely but, cautiously; and, not discovering any such "signs" as had been stated, descended to the bottom, at a point on the farm now owned by Alfred P. Woods, about two miles above Wheeling. They then passed up the river to the mouth of Short Creek, and thence up Girty's Point in the direction of Van Metre's. Not discovering any indications of the enemy, the brothers were riding leisurely along (July 30, 1782,) and when a short distance beyond the "Point," a deadly discharge of rifles took place, killing Major McCulloch instantly. His brother escaped, but his horse was killed. Immediately mounting that of his brother, he made off to give the alarm. As yet no enemy had been seen; but, turning in his saddle after riding fifty yards, he said the path was filled with Indians, and one fellow in the act of scalping the unfortunate major. Quick as thought the rifle of John was at his shoulder, and in an instant more the savage was rolling in the agonies of death. John escaped to the fort unhurt, with the exception of a slight hip wound.

On the following day a party of men from Van Metre's went out and gathered up the mutilated remains of Major McCulloch. The savages had disemboweled him, but the viscera all remained except the heart. Some years subsequent to this melancholy affair an Indian, who had been one of the party on this occasion, told some whites that the heart of Maj. McCulloch had been divided and eaten by the party. This was done, said he, that "We be bold, like Major McCulloch." On another occasion an Indian, in speaking of the incident, said, "The whites (meaning John McCulloch) had killed a great captain, but they (the Indians) had killed a greater one."

Before closing this notice, it may, perhaps, be well enough to advert again to the question of identity, for the two brothers have been associated with these deeds. In the first place, then, it seems generally conceded that the person who accomplished the feat was Major McCulloch, and the year of its occurrence 1777. Well, Samuel McCulloch was commissioned major in 1775, John not until 1795. Let the reader decide which must

have been the man. In 1775-'6-'7, etc., Samuel McCulloch was one of
the most active and distinguished borderers in Virginia,—the pride of the
settlements and a terror to the savages. John was born in 1759, and therefore, in 1777, was only eighteen years of age,—quite too young a man to
have rendered himself so odious to the fierce old Shawanese warriors.
But there need be no necessity for depending upon doubtful conjecture or
uncertain data. Without one single exception, all the older citizens agree
in saying that it was Major Samuel. The late Col. Wood said so unhesitatingly and stated positively, that Major John never claimed the credit, although he (W.) often talked to him of the exploit.

Major John McCulloch was, perhaps, quite as brave and true as his
brother. He did ample service in our long struggle for independence, and
a more devoted patriot could not be found. He filled many important
posts of honor and trust, and was greatly respected. The early records of
Ohio county show that he acted a conspicuous part on the bench and
otherwise.

The death of Maj. Samuel McCulloch occurred at the most unfortunate
period of our history. It was in the Summer of that year (1782) so memorable in the annals of the west The united tribes of the north and
west were meditating an attack upon the frontier posts of Virginia, and
many feared that some of the weaker ones might yield. Amid such perilous scenes as these, the death of such a man could not but be greatly deplored.

Major McCulloch married a Miss Mitchell, and had only enjoyed the
wedded life six months at the time of his death.

COL. EBENEZER ZANE.

Ebenezer Zane was born October, 1747, in Augusta, now Berkeley Co.,
W. Va. The family is of Danish origin, but at an early day removed to
England and thence in the 17th century to America. One branch settled
in N. Jersey, the other in Va. The subject of this notice sprung from the
latter branch. In 1770, he wandered to the west with his brothers Silas
and Jonathan, and made his home on the site of the present town of Wheeling. In 1772 his family and a few friends removed from Berkeley to his
new abode on the Ohio. There was not at the time a permanent Anglo-
Saxon settlement from the source to the mouth of the Ohio. The little
band at Wheeling stood alone in the immense solitude. Zane and his associates soon opened a "clearing" and grew a crop of corn. In 1773 many
families joined the settlement. Mr. Zane married a sister of the daring
borderer, McCulloch, by whom he had eleven children. Zane's intercourse
with the Indians was marked by mildness and honorable dealing—hence
his hamlet escaped the fury of the savages until 1777. All three brothers
were men of enterprise, prudence and sound judgment, and the Wheeling

settlement was mainly due to them for its security and preservation during the revolution.

He was conspicuous during the seige of Fort Henry, and brought himself so prominently before the public that he received various marks of distinction from the Colonial State and Federal governments. He was a disbursing officer under Dunmore, and enjoyed under the Commonwealth numerous civil and military distinctions. He always preferred, however, the peace and quietude of his own home to the bustle and pomp of public place. He was as generous as brave ; strictly honorable to all men, and most jealous of his own rights. He possessed, in an eminent degree, the constituents of a true gentleman—the disposition to render unto all their dues, the quick, delicate, accurate perception of others' rights and others' claims. His temperament was nervous-bilious—quick, impetuous, and hard to restrain when excited. He was, in short, a plain blunt man, rude of speech, but true of heart, knowing nothing of the formalities of social life and caring about little else than his family, his friends and his country.

The personal appearance of Col. Zane was somewhat remarkable: dark complexion, piercing black eyes, huge brows, and prominent nose—not very tall, but uncommonly active and athletic, he was a match for almost any man in the settlement, and many are the incidents, in wood and field, told of his prowess and his strength. He was a devoted hunter and spent much of his time in the woods. But few men could out-shoot, and fewer still out-run Zane. In illustration of his skill with the rifle, we will give an incident : About the year 1781, some of the whites in the fort observed an Indian on the island going through certain personal movements for the especial benefit of those within the fort. Colonel Zane's attention having been drawn to the indelicate performances, declared he would spoil the sport, and charging his rifle with an additional ball, patiently waited for the chap to re-appear. In a moment his naked body was seen emerging from behind a large sycamore, and commencing anew his performances, Col. Zane drew upon him a practised aim and the next instant the native harlequin was seen to go through a peculiar gyration, believed not to have been "on the bills."

Col. Zane was a man of true courage, as is exemplified by his almost single-handed defence of his own dwelling, in the fall of 1782.

The government of the United States, duly appreciating his capacity, energy and influence, employed him by an act of Congress, May, 1796, to open a road from Wheeling to Limestone, (Maysville.) This duty he performed in the following year, assisted by his brother Jonathan, and son-in-law, John McIntyre, aided by an Indian guide, Tomepomehala, whose knowledge of the country enabled him to render valuable suggestions. The road was marked through under the eye of Colonel Zane and then committed to his assistants to cut out. As a compensation for opening this road, Congress granted Col. Zane the privilege of locating military warrants upon three sections of land ; the first to be at the crossing of the Muskingum, the second at Hock-hocking, and the third at Scioto. Col. Zane thought of crossing the Muskingum at Duncan's falls, but foreseeing the great value of the hydraulic power created by the falls, determined to cross at the point where Zanesville has since been established, and thus secure this important power. The second section was located where Lancaster now stands, and the third on the east side of the. Scioto opposite Chillicothe. The first he gave, principally, to his two assistants for services rendered. In addition to these fine possessions, Col. Zane acquired large bodies of land throughout Western Virginia, by locating patents for those persons whose fear of the Indians deterred them undertaking personally so hazardous an enterprise.

After a life full of adventure and vicissitudes, the subject of our notice died of jaundice, in 1811, at the age of sixty four.

LEWIS WETZEL.

A singular custom with this borderer was to take an Autumn hunt in the Indian country. On one occasion he penetrated to the Muskingum, and fell upon a camp of four Indians. He waited till midnight, and then glided into the camp, his rifle in one hand, a tomahawk in the other. He rested his gun against a tree, and drawing his knife, approached the four sleeping warriors. Quick as thought he cleft the skull of one, in an instant a second was slain, the third, rising, shared the fate of his comrades, the fourth darted into the darkness and escaped, although Wetzel pursued some distance, uttering horrid yells.

During one of his scouts, he took shelter, on a stormy night, in a deserted cabin. He climbed into the loft to sleep, and had been there only a short time when six savages entered, lit a fire, and commenced preparing a meal. Soon after supper, the Indians fell asleep. Wetzel crawled down quietly, and going out, hid himself behind a log. In the morning one of the savages stepped forth. Wetzel, who had his finger on the trigger, shot him dead, and taking to his heels, escaped. When twenty-five, he entered the service of Gen. Harmer, commanding at Marietta. While thus engaged, he killed a friendly chief. He was arrested and confined in the fort. He requested the general to give him up to the savages, of whom there were a large number present, and let him and them fight it out with their knives—he against all. This the general refused to do, but allowed him to walk about the grounds, handcuffed, for the benefit of his health. Wetzel took advantage of this, and escaped. He made his way to the Ohio, swam the river, though his hands were in heavy iron handcuffs, went to the cabin of a friend, and was released. A large reward was offered by Gen. Harmer for his arrest, but the settlers became incensed at the idea of hanging a white man for killing an Indian, when they were killing the whites every day. Wetzel was afterwards recaptured, but set at liberty. During the career of this man of indomitable courage, energy and skill he killed twenty-seven Indian warriors. He died in 1808. He was five feet ten inches high, erect, broad across the shoulders, deep chest, and limbs denoting great muscular strength. His complexion was dark, eyes black, wild and rolling. His black hair was luxuriant, and when combed out fell below his knees—a rare scalp for the savages could they have secured it. He loved his friends and hated his enemies He was a rude, blunt man of few words. His name and fame will long survive among the backwoodsmen.

ANDREW POE.

Andrew Poe, one of the most formidable warriors of the border, was born about 1760, near Frederick, Md., and removed to northwest Virginia about 1774. He was shrewd, active and courageous, a thorough back-woodsman in every sense of the word. He was tall, muscular and erect, and determined to hold his own against the savages. In 1781, a party of six Indians crossed the Ohio near Poe's residence, and committed many depredations. Capt. Poe, with seven companions, pursued the barbarians, who were soon found to be under command of " Big Foot," one of the most daring, skillful and athletic of all the western warriors. Like Saul of old, Big Foot, who was nearly seven feet high, towered a head above his peers. Poe was delighted with the prospect of testing his strength with such a foe, and urged on the pursuit. Poe separated from his men in search of the savages near the river (Ohio) and soon came upon Big Foot, who was resting under the shade of a willow, talking to a single companion, another warrior. Poe engaged them both in gladatorial contest. During the struggle, Big Foot's companion staggered under a blow into the river, and Poe released himself from the giant grasp of Big Foot. Before the giant could interpose, Poe shot Big Foot's companion, and engaged in a fist fight with the giant, during which both rolled into the river, and each attempted to drown the other. Carried out into the current beyond their depth, each was compelled to relax his hold and swim for his life. Big Foot, on reaching the shore, was shot by Poe's brother, who came up while they were in the water and comprehended the situation. Big Foot's death was a severe blow to his tribe, and enhanced Poe's fame prodigiously. Poe, during his whole life, was an active and useful frontiersman and Indian fighter, and at his death, in 1840, left numerous descendants.

CAPT. SAMUEL BRADY.

Samuel Brady, called the "Marion of the West," was born at Shippens · burg, Pa., 1756, and was the son of Jno. Brady. who was made a captain in the Colonial army for his services in the old French and Indian war. In 1776 Samuel joined the army, was commissioned Lieutenant and marched to Boston. He continued with the army and was in all the principal battles until after that of Monmouth, when he was ordered to the west and joined Gen. Broadhead. Broadhead employed Brady as a spy o ascertain the strength, resources &c. of the savages. Disguised as savages, Brady, Williamson and Wetzel reached the Indian towns on the upper Sandusky. They entered the Indian village at night and made a thorough reconnoissance, and then retreated, traveling all night. In the morning they discovered the savages in pursuit, but finally escaped, having killed one of the enemy. Satisfied with the information brought by Brady and his companions, Broadhead's army moved onward. During all the Indian wars up to 1794, Brady took an active part and no braver or bolder man ever drew a sword or fired a rifle. He married a daughter of Capt. Van Swearengen, of Ohio county, and left descendants.

JESSE HUGHES.

One of the most active, daring and successful Indian hunters in the mountain region of Virginia was Jesse Hughes—sometimes styled the Wetzel of his portion of the State. He was born on the headwaters of the Monongahela, Va., about 1768, and early became skilled in the use of the rifle and tomahawk. He was a man of iron constitution, and could endure extraordinary privations and fatigue. Many anecdotes are told of his encounters with the red men and of the invaluable services he rendered to the white settlements on the Monongahela. Jesse Hughes was more than a match at any time for the most wary savage in the forest. In his ability to anticipate all their artifices, he had few equals and no superiors. He was a great favorite, and no scouting party could be complete unless Jesse Hughes had something to do with it.

REV. JAMES WADDELL, D. D.

James Waddell was born in Ulster, Ireland, July, 1739, of Scotch parentage. Shortly after this event, his parents emigrated to America, and settled, in the Autumn of 1739, in Pennsylvania. Here he remained until 1753, during which period the foundation of a liberal education was laid at the "log college" of a Dr. Finley, at Nottingham. His proficiency in the ancient languages caused him, while yet a lad under fifteen, to be selected as a tutor in the school, and afterwards in that of Dr. Robt. Smith. While a member of Dr. Finley's school, he embraced religion, and " a

45 ‡

constraint was on him to preach the Gospel." When nineteen years of age he left Pennsylvania for South Carolina to open a school, and passing through Virginia, made the acquaintance of Rev. Samuel Davies, of Hanover. They soon became devoted friends, and Waddell abandoned his purpose of going south, and became a teacher in the school of Rev. John Todd, of Louisa, and here commenced the studies preparatory for the sacred ministry. In 1760, he offered himself to Hanover Presbytery as a candidate for the Gospel ministry, then meeting at the Stone church, in Augusta, and was licensed and appointed to preach the Gospel as a candidate for the holy ministry, January, 1761. His ministerial talents were so remarkable that during this year he received numerous calls, among them one from Brown's meeting-house (Hebron), and another from Jenning's Gap, Augusta. All of these he declined. In June, 1762, he was regularly ordained, and accepted a call from Lancaster and Northumberland counties. Colonel James Gordon, a wealthy and influential merchant, whose daughter he subsequently married, was the principal Presbyterian in the community to which Mr. Waddell now removed, and to which he devoted the most active part of his ministerial life. He, in fact, continued here until 1778, when, on account of ill health and the inroads of the Revolutionary war, he removed to Augusta. There was much persecution of Dissenters in those colonial days, and Mr. W. was assailed from the pulpit and by the press, Rev. William Gisberne, of Richmond county and parish, making himself conspicuous by calling Mr. W., in one of his sermons, "a pickpocket, dark lantern, moonlight preacher and enthusiast," at the same time raising a hue and cry for the arrest of "the new light, instigated by folly, impudence, and the devil, and bringing him to the whipping post" (Foote. p. 373.) Mr. Waddell vindicated himself from these scurrilous attacks in a dignified and truly Christian letter, of date July 21st, 1768, addressed to his calumniator, in which he advised him, above all things, to abstain from bitter invectives and scurrilous language against others, and bidding him farewell, assured him, with grim humor, that in all things wherein he, Mr. Gisberne, thought him his enemy, he, Mr. Waddell, was his friend and most humble servant.

In April, 1774, Mr. Waddell was called to Timber Ridge, which call he declined. In 1778, he removed to his estate of Spring Hill, near Waynesboro, Augusta, where he resided seven years, acting continuously as minister of Tinkling Spring and sometimes at Staunton. During this time he animated the soldiers by his patriotic addresses, urging them to go forth in defence of their native or adopted land. To the forces of Campbell, McDowell and Moffett assembled at Midway before marching to North Carolina to oppose Lord Cornwallis, he preached stirring sermons on the great principles of the Gospel, and bade them a pastor's affectionate farewell. In 1785, he returned to his plantation of Belle Grove, in Louisa, where he resided until his death, in 1805. He was first buried at Hope-well farm, his former residence, but in 1881 his remains were removed to the memorial church, which bears his name, near Rapidan Station, on the Virginia Midland railroad. His preaching places were Hopewell, near Gordonsville, the D. S. meeting-house, about five miles from Charlottes-ville, at the Brick church, near Orange Courthouse, and occasionally at other points. Here he opened his classical school, in which so many Augusta boys were educated, and which acquired such a deservedly high and extended reputation. The great affliction of Dr. W.'s life was his blindness, caused by cataract. He suffered also from a nervous complaint, which for some years previous to his blindness deprived him of the use of the pen. He was devoted to books, and after his loss of sight, his wife and other members of the family spent hours daily reading to him. His heavy bodily afflictions did not impair his spirits. He was always not only composed, but cheerful, happy and resigned. His powers of conver-sation were extraordinary, and his sermons rather in the style of a conver-sation than declamation. His voice was melodious, his gestures simple and dignified, and his eloquence irresistible. In 1798, he visited Mary-land, and submitted to an operation for cataract. It was successful, and the blessed light of heaven was restored to him for a brief period. The cataract, however, returned, but the good man stood at his post, like the true minister of Christ, and preached Him crucified faithfully "unto death."

The great lawyer and statesman, William Wirt, thus describes Mr. Waddell in the "British Spy." His description immortalizes the writer and his hero:

"It was one Sunday, as I traveled through the county of Orange, that my eye was caught by a cluster of horses tied near a ruinous, old, wooden house, in the forest, not far from the roadside. Having frequently seen such objects before in traveling through these States, I had no difficulty in understanding that this was a place of religious worship

"Devotion should have stopped, to join in the duties of the congregation; but I must confess, that curiosity to hear the preacher of such a wilderness, was not the least of my motives. On entering, I was struck with the pre-ternatural appearance; he was a tall and very spare old man; his head, which was covered with a white linen cap, his shriveled hands, and his voice, were all shaking under the influence of a palsy; and few minutes ascertained to me that he was perfectly blind.

"The first emotions which touched my breast, were those of mingled pity and veneration. But ah! how soon were all my feelings changed. The lips of Plato were never more worthy of a prognostic swarm of bees, than were the lips of this holy man! It was a day of the administration of the sacrament; and his subject of course, was the passion of our Saviour. I had heard the subject handled a thousand times—I had thought it exhaust-ed long ago. Little did I suppose, that in the wild woods of America, I was to meet with a man whose eloquence would give to this topic a new and more sublime pathos, than I had ever before witnessed.

" As he descended from the pulpit, to distribute the mystic symbols, there was a peculiar, a more than human solemnity in his air and manner which made my blood run cold, and my whole frame shiver.

"He then drew a picture of the sufferings of our Saviour; his trial before Pilate; his ascent up Calvary; his crucifixion, and his death. I knew the whole history; but never, till then, had I heard the circumstanaes so selected, so arranged, so coloured! It was all new: and I seemed to have heard it for the first time in my life. His enunciation was so deliberate, that his voice trembled on every syllable; every heart in the assembly trembled in unison. His peculiar phases had that force of description that the original scene appeared to be, at that moment, acting before our eyes. We saw the very faces of the Jews: the staring frightful distortions of malice and rage. We saw the buffet; my soul kindled with a flame of indignation; and my hands were involuntarily and convulsively clenched.

"But when he came to touch on the patience, the forgiving meekness of our Saviour; when he drew, to the life, his blessed eyes streaming in tears to heaven; his voice breathing to God, a soft and gentle prayer of pardon on his enemies, 'Father, forgive them, for they know not what they do'—the voice of the preacher. which had all along faltered, grew fainter and fainter, until his utterance being entirely obstructed by the force of his feelings, he raised his handkerchief to his eyes, and burst into a loud and irrepressible flood of grief. The effect is inconceivable. The whole house resounded with the mingled groans, and sobs, and shrieks of the congregation.

"It was some time before the tumult had subsided, so far as to permit him to proceed. Indeed, judging by the usual, but fallacious standard of my own weakness, I began to be very uneasy for the situation of the preacher. For I could not conceive how he would be able to let his audience down from the height to which he had wound them, without impairing the solemnity and dignity of his subject, or perhaps shocking them by the abruptness of the fall. But—no; the descent was as beautiful and sublime, as the elevation had been rapid and enthusiastic.

"The first sentence which broke the awful silence, was a quotation from Rousseau,—'Socrates died like a philosopher, but Jesus Christ like a God!'

"I despair of giving you any idea of the effect produced by this short sentence, unless you could perfectly conceive the whole manner of the man, as well as the peculiar crisis in the discourse. Never before did I completely understand what Demosthenes meant by laying stress on delivery. You are to bring before you the venerable figure of the preacher; his blindness constantly recalling to your recollection old Homer, Ossian and Milton, and associating with his performance the melancholy grandeur of their geniuses; you are to imagine that you hear his slow, solemn, well accented enunciation, his voice of affecting trembling melody; you are to remember the pitch of passion and enthusiasm to which the congregation were raised; and then the few minutes of portentous, death-like silence which reigned throughout the house; the preacher removing the white handkerchief from his aged face, (even yet wet with the recent torrent of his tears,) and slowly stretching forth the palsied hand which holds it, begins the sentence,—'Socrates died like a philosopher'—then pausing, raising his other hand, pressing them both clasped together, with warmth and energy to his breast, lifting his 'sightless balls' to heaven, and pouring his whole soul into his tremulous voice—'but Jesus Christ—like a God!' If he had been indeed and in truth an angel of light, the effect could scarcely have been more divine.

"Whatever I had been able to conceive of the sublimity of Massillon, or the force of Bourdaloue, had fallen far short of the power which I felt from the delivery of this simple sentence. The blood, which just before had rushed in a hurricane upon my brain, and in the violence and agony of my feelings, had held my whole system in suspense, now ran back into my heart, with a sensation which I cannot describe—a kind of shuddering, delicious horror! The paroxysm of blended piety and indignation to which I had been transported, subsided into the deepest self-abasement, humility and adoration. I had just been lacerated and dissolved by sympathy for our Saviour as a fellow-creature; but now, with fear and trembling. I adored him as—'a God!'

"If this description give you the impression that this incomparable minister had anything of shallow, theatrical trick in his manner, it does him great injustice. I have never seen, in any orator, such a union of simplicity and majesty. He has not a gesture, an attitude or an accent, to which he does not seem forced, by the sentiment which he is expressing. His mind is too serious, too earnest, too solicitous, and, at the same time, too dignified to stoop to artifice. Although as far removed from ostentation as a man can be, yet it is clear from the train, the style and substance of his thoughts, that he is not only a very polite scholar, but a man of extensive and profound erudition. I was forcibly struck with a short yet beautiful character which he drew of our learned and amiable countryman, Sir Robert Boyle. He spoke of him as if 'his noble mind had, even before death, divested herself of all influence from his frail tabernacle of flesh', and called him. in his peculiarly emphatic and impressive manner, 'a pure intelligence: the link between men and angels.'

"This man has been before my imagination almost ever since. A thousand times, as I rode along, I dropped the reins of my bridle, stretched forth my hand. and tried to imitate his quotation from Rousseau; a thousand times I abandoned the attempt in despair, and felt persuaded that his peculiar manner and power arose from an energy of soul, which nature could give, but which no human being could justly copy. In short, he seems to be altogether a being of a former age, or of a totally different nature from the rest of men.

"Guess my surprise when, on my arrival at Richmond, and mentioning the name of this man, I found not one person who had ever before heard of James Waddell! Is it not strange that such a genius as this, so accomplished a scholar, so divine an orator, should be permitted to languish and die in obscurity, within eighty miles of the metropolis of Virginia?"

HON. DANIEL SHEFFEY.

Daniel Sheffey was born at Frederick, Md., in 1770. He was bred a shoemaker in his father's shop. His educational was inconsiderable, but possessing an ardent desire for knowledge, he passed his leisure in reading, and became particularly fond of astronomy and mathematics. Arriving at manhood, he travelled on foot, with his "kit" on his back, to Winchester. From thence he walked through the Valley of Virginia, earning sufficient money by his trade to pay his expenses, until he arrived in Wythe county. Here he commenced his trade as a shomaker. The novelty and originality of his character, and the flashes of genius which enlivened his conversation, often compelled his new friends to look on the eccentric youth as a wonder. Becoming popular, he studied law in the office of Alex. Smyth, and was admitted to the Bar, and obtained business. After some years he located in Staunton, where he enjoyed a lucrative practice. He often represented Augusta in the House of Delegates, and in 1811, was elected to Congress. His speech in favor of a renewal of the charter of the first United States Bank was a masterly combination of sound judgment and conclusive facts; for three hours profound silence reigned, and all were astonished at his talents. He opposed the war of 1812. On one occasion he gave John Randolph, whose bitter sarcasm few could withstand, a severe retort. In commenting on a speech of Mr. Sheffey, he said, " the shoemaker ought not to go beyond his last." In an instant, Mr. Sheffey retorted, " If that gentleman had ever been on the shoemaker's bench, he never would have left it."

Mr. Sheffey was a plain man; his accent German, his pronunciation not agreeable, yet the most refined audience always paid him profound attention. He died in Staunton in 1830, leaving no son, but five daughters, one of whom married Rev. E. Boyden, of Albemarle, and they have a large family; a second, Oliver P. Baldwin, of Cleveland, Ohio, and they have numerous children, a third, Serena, married Hon. John F. Lewis, and they have a number of children—the eldest son of J. F. Lewis, Hon. D. S. Lewis, being United States Attorney for the Western District of Virginia in 1882, and a daughter, who married Mr. Davis, of Lewisburg, West Virginia. The remaining daughters of Hon. D. Sheffey are Ann E. and Mrs. Celestine Hanson, widow of the late Capt. Hanson, U. S. A.

HON. JOHN HOWE PEYTON,

was born in Stafford county, Virginia, April 3d, 1778, of colonial descendants of the ancient English Peytons of Isleham. After completing his preliminary studies at Fredericksburg, he proceeded, in 1794, to the University of New Jersey (Princeton), where he graduated M. A. in 1797 with distinguished honors, taking the lead in all his classes. — Returning to Virginia, he studied law under Judge Bushrod Washington, one of the Justices of the Supreme Court of the United States, and was admitted to the Bar in 1799. He immediately obtained a considerable practice, to which he devoted himself with laborious assiduity. In 1806, he was elected the representative for Stafford to the House of Delegates of Virginia, and was regarded from the first as a brilliant debater, and at the end of the session it was conceded that he had no superior in the Commonwealth as a parliamentary orator. Popular in the House, he was more so in society, from his agreeable and instructive conversation and many accomplishments. During the years he continued a member of the General Assembly, he was a leading spirit, and his labors were crowned with uniform success. He was the author of the celebrated report and resolutions on the subject of a tribunal for settling disputes between the State and Federal judiciary, adopted by the Senate and House, January 26th, 1810. This report and resolutions terminated the matter of a proposal from the State of Pennsylvania to amend the Constitution of the United States. In this document it was declared that "a tribunal is already provided by the Constitution of the United States—viz.: the Supreme Court—more eminently qualified, from their habits and duties, from the mode of their selection, and from the tenure of their offices to decide the disputes aforesaid in an enlightened manner than any other tribunal which could be created" * * * and that "the creation of a tribunal such as is proposed by Pennsylvania, so far as we are able to form an idea of it, from the description given in the resolutions of the Legislature of the State, would, in the opinion of·the committee, tend rather to invite than prevent collisions between the Federal and State courts."

In 1808-'9, so widespread was his legal reputation, he was appointed public prosecutor for the Augusta district, and removed to Staunton. He now gave his entire energies to the law, and the distinguishing peculiarities of his intellect made themselves more manifest. It was observed that in all of his investigations his philosophical mind rose above the technicalities of the common law to the consideration of general principles, and he was never more eloquent than when expatiating upon those principles which lie at the foundation of all duty and are equally applicable to all its forms. He was not unmindful of other duties which devolve upon the citizen, and in 1812, when war was declared against Great Britain by the United States, was commissioned a major of volunteers and marched with the Augusta troops to Camp Holly, and served until the end of the war, in 1815, when he resumed the practice, and was elected mayor of the city of Staunton. He was at the same time appointed Deputy United States, or Federal, Attorney for the Western District of Virginia. His success at the Bar, and he was now considered one of the most learned and ablest Virginia lawyers, and the ablest criminal lawyer and public prosecutor Virginia had ever known, did not engross his intellectual activity. He contributed to the reviews papers rich in lessons of truth, wisdom and faith; on literary, social and political subjects, and maintained a correspondence with President Jefferson, Gov. Randolph, Chief Justice Marshall, James Monroe, James Madison, John Tyler, and other eminent men of the time.

In 1824, when he had attained the height of his fame, his friends urged him to accept a position on the General Court of Virginia, but as this would have required his removal to another district, he peremptorily declined. In 1836, he was elected Senator for the Augusta and Rockbridge district, and in 1840, was reëlected. In the Senate, he occupied a commanding position of influence, and gave a general support to the Whig party. He opposed the annexation of Texas, a revenue tariff, and a war with England on the question of the Oregon boundary line. In the course of an exhaustive speech on the subject, he said: "In regard to Oregon, while our title to the whole of that vast region, extending westward from the Rocky Mountains to the Pacific Ocean, and from the 42° of north latitude to 54° 40', was certainly as good as that of any other nation, and probably better, we had ourselves, on repeated occasions, virtually admitted that it was not so complete and unqualified as to preclude all other claims to any portion of it; and that, therefore, a war for Oregon, unless an attempt be made to wrest it forcibly from our possession, would be not only a blunder but a crime."

The annexation of Texas he opposed on many grounds: 1. America was already, in 1840, too vast to be national and too rich to be democratic, and any extension of her borders would only increase the evils; 2. He objected to a clause in the Constitution of Texas which refused to the Legislature power to pass laws for the emancipation of slaves. No one had a deeper or more inextinguishable thirst to promote human liberty and happiness. All his ambition for personal, professional or literary success was controlled by this master passion of his nature; 3. He was opposed to the American Government assuming the debt of Texas, and 4. Because he thought annexation would lead to useless wars as to boundary, &c. On the question of the tariff, he held that direct protection was a legitimate object of legislation and he opposed any tariff which gave merely incidental protection. He derived his doctrine on the question both from the justice and necessity of the case, and from the explicit avowal of those who framed the Constitution, and of those who sat in the first Congress under it, that it was designed and desired to lay duties for the encouragement and protection of domestic manufactures, and he would allow no arguments of expediency to induce him to abandon his ground and to fall in with the friends of a tariff for revenue giving incidental protection. This phraseology he denounced as a device of demagogues who were willing to conceal or abandon their principles in order to secure success.

He expressed the opinion that the independence of the American continent from the control, political and physical, of European nations, was of paramount importance, and had any European government aided Spain in her efforts to subdue her revolted American colonies, seeking to secure their independence and establish republican governments, he favored armed intervention by the United States. In other words, he was a supporter of the "Monroe Doctrine." He opposed nullification and secession, favored a United States bank, believing that the success of the thirteen colonies was due largely to the financial facilities afforded by the " Bank of North America," at Philadelphia, and that two banks, chartered by the United States Government—the first in 1791 and the second in 1816—enabled America to pay off the Revolutionary debt, and to pass through the war of 1812–1815, and to restore, in 1816, mercantile credit. He advocated popular education, by means of State aid, and a generous system of internal improvements. On all of these questions his speeches were able and eloquent, exhibiting a soundness of view, an extent of research, a manliness of principle, an accuracy of learning, and a vigor of style never surpassed in Virginia.

In 1840, he was appointed by President Harrison a visitor to the United States Military Academy at West Point, and wrote the interesting and instructive report of the Board of Visitors for that year. In 1844, owing to impaired health, arising from a fall from his horse while hunting on Isleham, one of his estates in Alleghany, he resigned his seat in the Senate, the office of Public Prosecutor, and all public employments.

In person, he was tall and handsome, with large piercing blue eyes, and a countenance of majestic benevolence. Very attentive to his attire, he dressed usually in blue broad cloth with gold buttons. He enjoyed among his contemporaries the reputation of being a metaphysician, a logician, and a political economist of the first order ; a profound and comprehensive lawyer and general scholar ; a man of massive intellect without affectation, and of genius without conceit. He kept up a large establishment at Montgomery Hall, and dispensed a generous hospitality, contributed liberally to all public works, was open as day to melting charity, and left at his death, April 3rd, 1847, the reputation of being a perfect gentleman and one of the best of men.

We follow this outline by interesting sketches, giving more in detail the leading characteristics of Mr. Peyton's mind and heart. These sketches were written by surviving contemporaries, who, from intimacy in daily life, had the best opportunities to know him as a man, a lawyer, statesman and citizen. The first is by Prof. J. T. L. Preston, V. M. I.:

The late John H. Peyton. Esq., of Staunton, Va., was one of the finest specimens that we have ever known of the complete lawyer. During the prime of life he pursued his profession with a laborious assiduity rarely equalled, and though as age advanced upon him he remitted his efforts, he did not discontinue his practice until a short time before his death, which occurred April 3, 1847, in the 69th year of his age. None of his contemporaries secured a more ample reward in either reputation or pecuniary emolument.

We have spoken of Mr. Peyton as a complete lawyer. Law, as a practical profession, has several departments. and it is not unusual to see a lawyer distinguished in some of them, with a compensating deficiency in others. Some practitioners are successful collectors ; some are much esteemed as judicious advisers in matters not strictly legal ; some are favorite

46 ‡

advocates, with a subdivision into those who are influential with the court, and those who are persuasive before a jury; some are designated good judges of law, or, in other words, safe counsellors, and of some the *forte* is Common Law Practice, while others are distinguished as chancery law-yers. The organization of the courts in Virginia, and the nature of the business, at least in the interior, requires every lawyer to enter upon the whole of this miscellaneous practice; and it is not to be wondered at that some, even good lawyers, are not equally strong in every part. Mr. Pey-ton knew every part of his profession thoroughly. He had studied dili-gently as a student; he had known the expectant struggles of the young practitioner; he had practised under the old system before the reorganiza-tion of the judiciary, and afterwards under the new; he had met in contest the strongest men in each department of the profession, and he had made himself a champion in all. We may add that some lawyers who exhibit the highest skill in securing the rights of the clients, are foolishly ignorant of their own; in other words, they let slip the fair, well earned profits of their profession—not so with Mr. Peyton. He knew the value of his pro-fessional services; he gave them to the fullest extent to those who applied for them, and then he insisted upon just remuneration. We notice this point, not at random, but to present a feature belonging to the character of the complete lawyer.

The characteristic of Mr. Peyton's life was efficiency. This efficiency had for its elements native vigor of intellect, great resoluteness of charac-ter and courageous self-confidence, ample and thorough acquirements and the quickness, precision and dexterity of action that belong only to those who have been taught by a varied experience to understand thoroughly human nature. In conversation Mr. Peyton was ready, entertaining and instructive. But conversation was not his *forte*, though he was fond of it. He was not fluent, his manner was sometimes too direct for the highest style of polished social intercourse of a general nature, and besides he had a remarkable way of indulging in a strain of covert satirical banter, when his words would be so much at variance with the expression of his coun-tenance, and particularly with the expression of his mouth, that the hearer was often in an uncomfortable state of uncertainty how to take him. His person was large, and his bearing dignified but not graceful. His manner was unaffected, but not without formality, nor was it perfectly conciliatory. Some styled him aristocratic, while none could deny that his self respect and confident energy gave an imperious cast to his demeanor. We have oftener than once thought applicable to him, in a general way, those lines of Terence:

> "Ellum, confidens, catus,
> Cum faciem videas, videtur esse quantivis preti,
> Tristis severitas inest in voltu, atque in verbis fides."

His voice was true and clear, and capable of sufficient variety, but with-out a single musical intonation, and a little sharper than you would expect to hear from a man of his size and form. If it is asked what was the style of his speaking, it may be replied—just what might be expected to belong to such a man as he has been described, that is to say, never was the speaker a more complete reflection of the man than in his case. We can-not believe that any one who knew him was ever surprised when they heard him speak; what he said was just what they would expect him to say. This is often the case with speakers and writers, but not always. En-ergy, reality and efficiency were his characteristics as a man, and equally so as a speaker. Distinctness of conception lay at the foundation of his excellence. Some great speakers, some even preëminently great speakers, not unfrequently hurl unforged thunderbolts. They feel the maddening impulse of the god, but give forth their utteranee before the true prophetic fury comes on.

Mr. Peyton's mind was no sybil's cave, whence came forth wind-driven leaves inscribed with mighty thoughts disposed by chance, but a spacious castle, from whose wide open portal issued men at arms, orderly arrayed. He had hardly opened his case, when the hearer was aware that he had thought over the whole of it, had a given course to pursue, and would close when he came to the end of it. This distinctness of conception comprehended the subject as a whole, and shed its light upon each detail belonging to it. This ensured the most perfect method in all that he said.— Before he began to speak he had determined in his own mind, not only the order of the different parts of his discourse, but also their relative importance in producing the general impression. Hence he was never led away by the tempting character of any peculiar topic, to expatiate upon it unduly; he did not take up matter irrelevant to the case because it might touch himself personally; he never spoke for those behind the bar, nor did he neglect to secure the fruits of victory in order to pursue an adversary to utter discomfiture. He spoke as a lawyer, he spoke for the verdict, and expected to gain it by showing that he was entitled to it. Some speakers hope to accomplish their object by single, or at least, successive impulses —now a clinching argumentative question, now a burst of brilliant declamation, and now a piece of keen wit, or a rough personality. Such speakers forget, or do not know, that a jury may admire, may be diverted, and even moved, without being won. He that gains the verdict must mould, and sway, and lead, and this is to be effected by continued persistent pressure, rather than by *tours de force*. This Mr. Peyton knew well, and observed it with perfect self-command. His hearers came away satisfied with the whole, rather than treasuring up remarkable points and passages. Let it not be supposed, however, that he was a cold speaker, who treated men as mere intellectual machines, to be set in motion by the pulleys, screws and levers of logic. Far from it; he understood human nature well, and knew the motive power of the feelings; but then he knew, too, that the way to excite the most effective sympathy is not to make a loud outcry, but to make a forcible exhibition of real suffering—that the best way to rouse our indignation against fraud, deceit, or oppression, is not to exhort us to hate it, but to show its hatefulness. One of his most distinguished cotemporaries upon the same circuit was celebrated for his powers as a criminal advocate; his manner was obviously upon the pathetic order, and perhaps a trifle too declamatory. We have seen them in the same cause, and have thought that if the eloquence of Gen. Briscoe G. Baldwin flushed the countenance quicker, the earnestness of Mr. Peyton stirred the heart deeper. Of the oratory of a class of speakers by no means rare (not, however, including in this class the distinguished jurist above alluded to,) it has been well said, "declamation roars while passion sleeps;" of speaking justly characterized by this line, Mr. Peyton's was the precise reverse. With him thought became passionate before the expression became glowing, as the wave swells before it crests itself with foam.

Mr. Peyton's language was forcible, pure and idiomatic. It served well the vehicle of his thoughts, but contributed nothing to them. There is a

real and legitimate advantage belonging to the masterly use of words, of
which many great speakers know well how to avail themselves.

Mr. Peyton attempted nothing of the sort. His diction was thoroughly English, with a marked preference for the Anglo-Saxon branch of the
language, and his sentences came out in the most natural order with unusual clearness and vigor, but not unfrequently with plainness that bordered
upon homliness. His style, however, was always that of speaking as distinguished from mere conversation—a distinction which some of our modern speakers forget, when in order to appear at their ease, they treat with
no little disregard not only the rules of rhetoric, but the rules of grammar
as well, and use words and phrases which are (to take a word from the vocabulary we are condemning) nothing better than slang. On the contrary
there was in Mr. Peyton's style the fruit of early studies and high-bred
association, a classical tinge, extremely pleasant to the scholar, though
perhaps not appreciable by those for whom he generally spoke. It must
not be supposed, from what has been said of his excellent method, that
he resembled in this respect some of our able but greatly tedious lawyers,
who take up in regular succession every possible point in the case, however minute, and worry us by officially offering help where none is needed—so far from it he showed his consummate skill as well in what he omitted as in what he handled, and, as a general thing, his speeches were shorter in duration, and yet fuller of matter than those of his opponent. His
use of figurative language was easy and natural, and not stinted ; but his
figures were always introduced as illustrations and not as arguments. It
is not unusual to meet with a speaker who is unable to enounce distinctly
the general principle he wishes to use, throw out an illustration to enable
himself to pick out the principle from it, or at least to give his hearers a
chance to do it for themselves ; not so with Mr. Peyton. He held up the
torch of illustration, not to throw a light forward to guide himself in his
own investigations, but to enable those following the more readily to tread
the road along with him. He had a very noticeable fondness for recurring to the primary fundamental principles of morals, and doubtless he
was restrained, by his practical judiciousness, from indulging this disposition to the full. One of his favorite books was Lord Bacon's Essays, and
under other circumstances he might himself have been a distinguished
moral essayist.

As may well be supposed, his general strain was grave. The high idea
he entertained of the dignity of his profession, and the earnestness with
which he gave himself to it, alike precluded either levity or carelessness.
However, he was fully able, quite ready upon occasion, to avail himself of
a keen wit, that was all the more effective because it was dry and sarcas-
tic. It occurs to us to mention an instance well known to his circuit, not il-
lustrative of his severity but his pleasantry. In a criminal prosecution, he,
as prosecuting attorney, was opposed by two gentlemen of ability, whose
pathos had been so great as to draw abundant tears from their own eyes.
One of them, a gentleman, who has since filled a distinguished national
position (Hon. A. H. H. Stuart, Secretary of Interior of the United States,
1850-3), was noted for the facility with which he could cover over his
brilliant eloquence with the liquid varnish of his tears. On this occasion
he had been singularly lachrymose, and supported by his colleague in the
same way, the sensation produced was very considerable. Mr. Peyton
commenced his reply by regretting the disadvantage the commonwealth
labored under in being represented by him who was a very poor hand at

crying, and certainly was not able to cry against two at a time. The ludicrousness of the expression completely neutralized the pathos of his opponents. He was not averse either to a bit of farce now and then, as is shown by a story told of him. In a remote part of the circuit a lawyer wished to adorn a moving passage of a part of a speech he was just rising to make, with an apposite example, and applied to Mr. Peyton, setting beside of him, to help him to the name of the man in the Bible who would have his pound of flesh. With imperturbable gravity he answered Absalom! The effect of thus confounding Shakespeare and Scripture may be imagined.

We have said that Mr. Peyton was thoroughly furnished in every part of his profession ; in one department his qualifications were peculiar and unsurpassed. Without disparagement to others, it may be said, we think, that he was the best commonwealth's attorney in the State of Virginia. He was the lawyer of the commonwealth, and he treated the commonwealth as a client, and labored for her with the same industry, zeal, and fidelity that he manifested in behalf of any other client. The oft-quoted merciful maxim of the common law, "better that ninety and nine guilty men should escape than one innocent man suffer," he interpreted as a caution to respect the rights of the innocent, and not as an injunction to clear the guilty, and he labored to reduce the percentage of rogues unwhipt of justice as low as possible With a clearness and force rarely equaled would he point out the necessity of punishing the guilty in order that the innocent might be safe, thus exhibiting the absolute consistency of strict justice with true mercy. So simply and earnestly would he do this, that he not only bound the consciences of the jury, but also made them feel that they were individually interested in the faithful execution of the laws. Here his clear perception of the moral principles upon which rests the penal code, and his fondness for recurring to general principles, stood him in great stead. It was delightful to hear him expatiate upon this theme, for upon no other was he more truly eloquent.

Mr. Peyton served at different times in both branches of the legislature, but we speak not of him as a politician. Our purpose has been solely to exhibit some of the qualities which made him an eminent member and ornament of the legal profession.

The following interesting sketch is from the pen of William Frazier, Esq., who was for ten years intimately associated in business intercourse with Mr. Peyton. It was originally published in the "Valley Virginian," and was thus introduced by the editor :

"Our readers will find Mr. Frazier's recollections of John Howe Peyton, on our first page, a most interesting article. All will derive pleasure from its perusal, but more especially the few surviving cotemporaries in our midst of that great lawyer. To the young, the article possesses a peculiar value. The distinguished men who have passed from the stage of life, and whose names are as "familiar as household words" to the old, or even middle aged, are to the young only historical personages; they require to be informed of what their fathers remember. Other sketches or recollections of Mr. Peyton are being prepared by a few of his professional brethren who survive, and who remember him when in the vigor of his intellect and the fullness of his fame. These, in all probability, will be included in a volume of memoirs, where it is proposed to preserve in a permanent form the story of his useful and honorable life.

"We have heard that Miss Sarah L. Randolph, author of the life of Stonewall Jackson, contemplates a work embracing the lives of many, if not all, eminent Virginia lawyers. It is a much needed work, and we wish her every success in her praiseworthy undertaking."

"My personal acquaintance with Mr. Peyton," says Mr. Frazier, "commenced in October, 1834, when I entered upon the practice of my profession at the Staunton Bar.

He was then, as I learn from his biography, in his fifty-seventh year, and from that circumstance only it might be inferred he had passed his climatric. Certainly nothing in his physical appearance or his forensic display betokened a decay of power, bodily or mental.

Yet having amassed a handsome fortune, he established himself in a beautiful home, and surrounded by a large and interesting family, he felt himself entitled to some relaxation from the arduous demands of his profession—or, at least, from its drudgery. He accordingly relegated to younger members of the bar all minor causes, and to his junior associates the preparation in *pays* of his chancery causes, in the matter of taking depositions and the like vacation duties.

But for ten years following the date of my introduction to him, there was hardly an important or celebrated cause tried at the Staunton Bar, whether in the State Courts or the United States Court, without the aid and illumination of his splendid intellect; whilst also in Albemarle, Rockbridge and Bath counties he largely participated in the like weighty causes.

In the Supreme Court of Appeals of Virginia his reputation throughout the State enlarged the theatre of his professional service much beyond that of his local circuit.

I wish it were in my power to give a just and discriminating analysis of his processes in the investigation and conduct of a great cause, or even a fair description of his style of forensic argument.

This much may be safely said : that he seized, by apparent intuition, upon the strong and dominating points in a case, not infrequently finding these, or some of them, buried out of sight from a scrutiny less searching than his, beneath a mass of irrelevant or conflicting testimony.

Having thus entrenched himself in one or a few strong positions, his array of the facts was so masterly, his presentation of them so luminous, and his arguments from them so logical, that he rarely failed to carry the tribunal with him safely and irresistibly to his conclusions.

Discarding thus the minor points and less material phases of the cause from his examination and discussion, or dismissing them in a few rapid, searching sentences, his debate was conspicuous for its compactness and logical order. Accordingly, his speeches ordinarily did not exceed one hour, and even in the most complex and voluminous causes they rarely went beyond two hours. I can recall but one occasion in which he consumed nearly three hours.

His style was fluent, but not of that fluency which comes of redundant words and phrases, for I have never listened to one so terse and vigorous. I think it can be said there was hardly a superfluous word—and every sentence bore upon the conclusion aimed at. It was, therefore, never a weariness to hear this great advocate, and the promiscuous audience followed his argument, his sarcasm or his invective, with as much apparent interest as did court and jury.

It has been written of him that he was equally versed and at home in every department of the profession (unless admiralty and maritime law be excepted), but I think it was as a common lawyer that he excelled, and that it was in the common law he found his chief delight. He was perfectly conversant with the principles of the Feudal law and immemorial usages of England as expounded by Littleton, Coke, Bacon, and all the fathers and great interpreters of English jurisprudence. Having come to the Bar while special pleading was yet a legal science and carefully practised system, and before popular and not too well informed legislatures sought to "simplify" the practice of the law by Statutes of Jeofails, he was, without doubt, one of the most practised and expert special pleaders of his time. His naturally astute and logical mind, finding its expression through the channels of a terse and luminous style, caused his pleadings in all their stages to be master-pieces of art.

His fame as a prosecutor of the pleas of the Commonwealth has never been surpassed, if equalled, in Virginia. On this field he achieved triumphs of the most brilliant kind. His pride in his profession, and the great principles of right and justice underlying it, no less than his inborn contempt for chicanery and fraud, not to speak of crime in its grosser forms, combined to make him a 'terror to evil-doers.' Some critics, even among the profession, sometimes were disposed to censure him as too harsh and unrelenting towards the prisoner at the bar. But if every circuit throughout our land possessed at this day so able, fearless and conscientious a prosecutor as did the Augusta and the surrounding circuit at that happier day in our history, perhaps we might find less cause to deplore the depreciation of the public morals, which so painfully invest the present era.

It would be a halting and very defective sketch of this eminent jurist which failed to speak of his striking originality. Negatively speaking, there was little or no common-place and hum-drum in his forensic arguments, his debates from the hustings or his addresses to his constituents. In a positive sense his speeches, at least on great occasions and when his powers were thoroughly roused, rarely failed to be marked by some flash of genius. I recall a conversation just after the close of a protracted and laborious June term of the Augusta Circuit Court, in which the late Judge Lucas P. Thompson and Gen. Briscoe G. Baldwin bore the leading parts. The last-named was paying generous tribute to Mr. Peyton's force and originality. Judge Thompson remarked, in substance, that he had never seen Mr. Peyton go through a cause deeply interesting and moving him in which he did not utter some view or sentiment illuminated by genius, or, at the least, some illustration marked by a bold originality ; and he instanced two causes, tried at the late term—one a civil suit and a very heavy will case, in which he made a novel and scorching application of a familiar fable of Æsop. I forbear to give its details, because both the critic and his subject have passed from earth.

In the same cause three signatures were to be identified and proved— that of the testator and also of the two attesting witnesses—all three having died since their attestation. Many witnesses were called to prove the genuineness of the three names. Opposing counsel sought to badger the witnesses by urging them to specify what peculiar marks there were in the handwriting and signatures, whereby they could speak so positively as to their identity and genuineness. This of course, for the most part, they could not do, and in the argument of the cause before the jury the same counsel strove to throw discredit and contempt upon those witnesses (all men of good character) for their failure and inability so to describe the quality and peculiar marks in the calligraphy of the signers as to show they were familiar with their handwriting. In his reply to those sallies of his opponent, Mr. Peyton swept away the whole airy fabric by a single happy illustration:

"Gentlemen," he said, " you have often been assembled in crowds upon some public or festive occasion. Your hats have been thrown pell-mell in a mass with perhaps a hundred other hats, all having a general resemblance. Suppose you had attempted to describe your hat to a friend or servant, so that he might go and pick it out for you. It has as many points for accurate description as a written signature—its color, height of crown, width of brim, its band, lining, &c. Do you think that friend or servant could by any possibility have picked out your hat for you? And yet when you went yourself, the moment your eye would light upon it you instantly recognize it amongst a hundred or five hundred other hats. Familiarity with it has stamped its picture on your mind, and the moment you see it, the hat fills and fits the picture on your mind as perfectly as the same hat fits your head."

The jury were evidently won, and gave full credence to the ridiculed witnesses.

The other instance during the same term (cited by Judge Thompson,) occurred in the celebrated prosecution of Naaman Roberts for forgery—in forging the name of Col. Adam Dickinson to a bond for six hundred dollars.

The body of the bond was confessedly the handwriting of the prisoner at the bar. That was admitted. The signature was a tolerably successful attempt at imitating the peculiar handwriting of Adam Dickinson. But no expert could look at the whole paper and fail to see a general resemblance between the body of the instrument and the signature, raising a strong conviction in the mind that both proceeded from the same hand.

The defense strongly insisted upon excluding the body of the instrument from the view of the witness, by covering it with paper or turning it down, and so confining the view to the signature only—upon the familiar doctrine of the law of evidence forbidding a comparison of various handwritings of the party as a ground for an opinion upon the identity or genuineness of the disputed writing. And this point was ably and elaborately argued by the prisoner's counsel.

The learned prosecutor met it thus:

"Gentlemen, this is one entire instrument, not two or more brought into comparison. Let me ask each one of you, when you meet your friend, or when you meet a stranger, in seeking to identify him, what do you look at? Not his nose, though that is the most prominent feature of the human face; not at his mouth, his chin, his cheek; no, you look him straight in the eye, so aptly called 'the window of the soul.' You look him in the eye, but at the same time you see his whole face. Now, put a mask on that face, leaving only the eyes visible, as the learned counsel would have you mask the face of this bond, leaving to your view only the fatal signature.

" If that human face, so masked, was the face of your bosom friend, could you for a moment identify him, even though permitted to look in at those windows of his soul? No; he would be as strange to you as this accursed bond has ever been strange to that worthy gentleman, Colonel Adam Dickinson, but a glance at whose face traces the guilty authorship direct to the prisoner at the bar."

This most striking illustration seemed to thrill the whole audience, as it virtually carried the jury.

Mr. Peyton never was a politician. His taste and predilection lay not in that direction. But no man was better informed of the course of public affairs, or had a keener insight into the character or motives of public men. Once, and so far as I knew, once only, did he participate in the debates of a Presidential canvass. It was the memorable one of 1840, and the speech was delivered from the Albemarle hustings. His analysis of the political character of Martin Van Buren, and his delineation of his public career from his desertion of De Witt Clinton down to his obsequious ingratiation with Andrew Jackson, was incisive and masterly, and all the more powerful and impressive because pronounced in a judicial rather than a partisan temper. Competent judges, long familiar with the very able harangues and debates on that rostrum, declared it one of the ablest that had been listened to by any Albemarle audience.

Of his services in the Virginia Senate, I need only say, what every one would naturally expect, they were most valuable from that enlightened conservatism in the prevention of crude and vicious legislation. In the last session of his first term in the Senate, a vigorous effort was made for the passage of a stay-law rather than an increase of taxation.

It hardly needs to be said that he opposed the former and sustained the latter measure with all the vigor of his honest and manly nature. Nor could he ever have looked with any patience upon that brood of enactments since his day—the stay of executions, homestead exemptions, limitations upon sales of property, et id omne genus, professedly passed in the interest of the poor and the laboring man, yet in fact more detrimental to that class than to any other, and most damaging to the credit of the state abroad.

Let me say, in conclusion, that the person and figure of Mr. Peyton were fine and commanding. His carriage was always erect, his head well poised on his shoulders, while his ample chest gave token of great vitality. On rising to address court or jury, there was something more than commonly impressive in his personal presence, and whether clad in "Virginia home-spun" or English blue broadcloth with gold buttons (and I have often seen him in both), whenever you saw him button his coat across his breast and slowly raise his spectacles to rest them on the lofty crown, you might confidently expect an intellectual treat of no mean order.

There never was a broader contrast presented in the same person than that between Howe Peyton the lawyer, the public prosecutor, or even the senatorial candidate amongst the people, and the same individual in his own home. Here, in the midst of his family, or surrounded by friends, all the rigor of his manner relaxed, and he was the model of an affectionate husband and father, and the most genial of companions. He was "given to hospitality," and there was perhaps no mansion in all this favored region where it was more generously and elegantly dispensed, through many years, than at "Montgomery Hall."

47 ‡

The following are Judge Jno. H. McCue's recollections:

One of the truest tests of the greatness of a man is very often the impression, as I think, which, without intending, he makes upon the minds of the young with whom he may come in contact. There are few of us who do not remember having met, in our earlier days, with men whose presence filled us with respect and awe, before even, perhaps, we had learned their names and reputations, and who, in after years, seemed to stand out from amid our youthful recollections, apart and distinct from the memories of other men—men who, unconsciously, stamp their individuality not only upon our minds, but who often serve, though we may not perceive it, as models upon which our own conduct is, or ought to be, moulded, and the impress of whose attributes and virtues serve as standards by which we judge of other men.

The impressions I have of John Howe Peyton are those which I formed when a youth, but they were such as to stamp him not only as an able and good man, but as a great man in the truest acceptation of the term.

When a boy at the school in Waynesboro, Augusta county, of the Rev. James C. Wilson, D. D., a famous criminal trial was progressing in the Circuit Superior Court at Staunton. Mr. Peyton was the prosecutor, and was regarded as the ablest prosecuting attorney then or who had ever been in the Commonwealth of Virginia. Everybody was talking of this trial, in which, for various reasons, not necessary to be here detailed, the community was deeply interested. Shortly after, as I remember, while every one was still speaking of the trial, I saw standing in the porch of the hotel at Waynesboro, a gentleman of splendid form, broad shoulders and extended chest, with a magnificent head which was carried erect, and which might be aptly compared to that of Daniel Webster. His eyes were large and bright, his features straight, finely chiseled, forming a face of Grecian lineaments, and expression. I did not then know who he he was. The idea formed on my youthful mind was that he must be a great and famous man. I inquired respecting him, and was told that he was Mr. Howe Peyton, the famous lawyer and prosecutor. I had often heard my father speak of Mr. Peyton as one of the great lawyers of Virginia, then having her Johnson, Wickham, Tazewell, Baldwin, Sheffey, Wirt, Leigh, Tucker, Stannard, and other eminent men, who were his cotemporaries. I had never seen Mr. Peyton until now. There was something, however, in the noble and dignified appearance and bearing of the man now standing before me that at once arrested attention and impressed the beholder. The opinion formed by me of his greatness was afterwards, upon a better acquaintance, fully justified.

I knew little of Mr. Peyton personally until after I entered the University of Virginia, with his son, John Lewis Peyton, in 1842, both of us members of the law class under the late Henry St. George Tucker. Mr. Peyton, at that time Commonwealth's Attorney in Albemarle, and in the other counties composing the circuit of Judge Thompson, when in Charlottesville attending the court, sojourned at the residence of his brother-in-law, John Cochran, Esq., now (1879) surviving in his eighty-sixth year. Upon these occasions, at his request, his son and myself spent much time with him. Mr. Peyton manifested a deep interest, naturally, in the progress of his son, and in my own, because of his warm and intimate friendship for my father. It was during the frequent conversations which it pleased him to hold with us, that I learned to appreciate the great powers of his mind, not perhaps so much as to its capacity but more especially as to the wonderful faculty he possessed of simplyfying and rendering clear the most abstruse subjects. And in this perhaps, as much as in anything else, lay the secret of his success as a lawyer. He could take, for instance, the most difficult and complicated point of law, and in a few well-chosen, pithy sentences, place it clearly and forcibly before the minds of his hearers. As an illustration. I remember, shortly after we had commenced the study of law in the junior department, he made special inquiry as to our progress, examined us upon what we had gone over, and inquired the subject of our next lecture. We replied that it was "Uses and Trusts," frankly confessing that although we had read the text we still felt ignorant of the subject. He then said, 'Listen to me, boys,' and went into a dissertation upon that intricate and difficult subject, and in a conversation of perhaps two hours, gave us a history, accurate in chronology, minute in detail, profound and clear, as an exposition of the whole science, and this without reference to book or note, thus indicating the profoundest learning, and rendering the subject so clear to our minds that when we went to the review the whole field seemed to be laid open before us. In this simple way he demonstrated not only his power before courts and juries, but likewise the rare ability he possessed to impart to others, in the plainest and most comprehensive manner, what he knew and what had heretofore seemed to them insuperably difficult.

It was one of the noticeable traits of his character that he was ever anxious to impart information and knowledge to the young. He rarely lost an opportunity of instructing, and this, in such an easy, unaffected conversational style that it captivated the attention, while it instructed the mind. In the many conversations with his son and myself, during this and the next succeeding term at the University, it seemed to be his constant desire to communicate to us historic and philosophic knowledge, and to lead us insensibly into the deep delights of history and literature. In this connection, I must say that after a longer and more extended acquaintance with Mr. Peyton, I learned to regard him as a man of the profoundest learning, not only in the great principles and science of the common law, but also in general history and literature; and he expressed himself with more precision, condensation, vigor and beauty of language than any man I have ever known. I never heard Mr. Peyton speak at the bar or on the hustings. From what I know and have heard of him, his conception of a great subject and mode of expression were as clear, distinct and demonstrative as that of Edmund Burke. Judge Tucker, who had known him so well and for over forty years, once said to me: "I regard Mr. Peyton as one of the profoundest and most learned of lawyers."

During one of my summer vacations I visited his son, J. L. Peyton, at Montgomery Hall. I had formed an intimate friendship with him which yet continues. On this visit I was a witness and subject of the splendid hospitality of Mr. Peyton and his amiable and accomplished wife. One morning, shortly after sun rise, John Lewis Peyton and myself, leaving our chamber, strolled into the park-like grounds, admiring the venerable and wide-spreading oaks and beautiful scenery. On the porch in front of his office, which contained his law library, and many works on literature and the sciences, was the dignified figure of Mr. Peyton, seated in his accustomed arm chair, book in hand, and a long pipe in his mouth. [He was much addicted to the use of the Virginian weed.] On our approach he rose, and politely exchanging with us the morning salutations, bade us be seated. He then said : "I am looking over, for a second time, the first volume of Allison's history of Europe. Though it has faults of style, and is marred by political prejudices, it is the most remarkable historical work of the century."

The book was closed, his finger between the leaves. In this attitude he proceeded, as was a habit with him, upon a disquisition as to the value and importance of historical study. "It instructed," said he, "the young whose destiny it might be in time to guard the rights or secure the welfare of the community." He declared in general terms that the object of history, the great object, was to make men wiser in themselves and better members of society. By recalling the past it opened up a wider field for observation and reflection than any personal experience could do, and thus prepared a man to act and advise in present contingencies. He continued in this vein, illustrating his views by reference to ancient, medieval and modern history, displaying a soundness of view, an extent of research, a manliness of principle, an accuracy of learning, and a vigor of style, surpassing anything I have ever heard.

There have been few truly great men who were not noted for their courtesy and hospitality. Both of these traits Mr. Peyton possessed in a high degree. His manner to his son and myself was most courteous and ever of such a nature as to impress us with the idea, if possible, that we were men entering upon the great theatre of life, with the prospect before us of attaining eminence in our profession, of rendering ourselves useful to the State, and of service to society at large. There was something in the appearance and manner of the man, when you first came into his presence and under his influence, before he had uttered anything more than the ordinary salutations, that convinced you at once that you were in no ordinary presence, and upon closer intimacy that you felt that you were under the influence and power of a great man—a master spirit. In public, in his intercourse with men generally, as I have seen him, there was a *hauteur*, a dignity and ever a majesty, that repelled rather than attracted men. At his own fireside, that feeling was entirely dispelled, and the boy even was drawn to him, listened to and talked with him, as though he were his equal. Such were the warm sympathies, the tender feelings, the affectionate nature of this, to the world, reserved and haughty man.

Mr. Peyton, as a Legislator and Senator, representing Rockbridge and Augusta, made his mark as one of the leading statesman of Virginia, stamping his genius and learning upon the statute laws of the State, establishing for himself such a reputation as would have placed him, had he been a member of the Senate of the United States by the side of Webster, Clay and Calhoun. But his love for home and family, devotion to his profession, and natural fondness for rural pursuits, suppressed all desire for public life and extended reputation. He was fond of horses, dogs. and all the occupations of the country gentleman. Had he desired and entered public life, his reputation would have been national, and he a noted character in history. It is well here to say, that Mr. Peyton had been thoroughly trained, not only in the classical and mathematical schools of the country in early youth, but was also a graduate, with the degree of Master of Arts, of Princeton College, where his great abilities were early and fully manifested and recognized by the erudite and eminent men under whose charge that institution of learning was then conducted.

Mr. Peyton—then a young man—was a member of the Lower House of Legislature of Virginia in 1808, 1809 and 1810, from the County of Stafford, and wrote and offered a serious of resolutions, as chairman of a committee, raised upon certain resolutions adopted by the Legislature of the State of Pennsylvania, and communicated by the Governor of that State to Governor Tyler (afterwards President of the United States) with reference to an amendment to the Constitution, so as to prevent a collision between the State Governments and the Government of the Union, as to their judicial departments, which preamble and resolutions, drawn by Mr. Peyton, were adopted unanimously by both branches of the Legislature. This important State paper can be seen in the works of Daniel Webster, Vol. III, pages 352, 353 and 354. So able and important were these resolutions at the time, as to attract the attention of the leading statesmen of the country, and guide the other States in the adoption of similar resolutions, thus overthrowing the effort of Pennsylvania to establish a separate and distinct judicial department as arbiter between the Federal and State Governments.

In the great discussion between Daniel Webster and General Hayne, of South Carolina, Mr. Webster, in his second speech in reply to Mr. Hayne, referred to and quoted the preamble and resolution spoken of, as so conclusive of that question as to admit of no further discussion.

Mr. Webster was so much struck with Mr. Peytons's resolutions that he wished to know something of their author. Meeting Daniel Sheffey, long one of the representatives in the Lower House of Congress from Virginia, the following conversation, in substance, occurred. Mr. W. asked:

"Do you know a gentleman in Virginia by the name of Peyton, the author of some resolutions in the House of Delegates in 1810, on the subject of a conflict between the Government of the Union and the State Governments?"

"Yes," replied Mr. Sheffey, "he lives in Staunton, and is the leader of the bar in the circuit."

"I am not surprised to learn it," rejoined Mr. Webster.

"No," said Sheffey. "He is a sound lawyer, who unites to a vigorous judgment and sterling ability, intense study and vast learning."

"Is he a speaker," said Mr. Webster.

"Not in a popular sense," said Sheffey. "He is not a florid speaker, indulges in no meretricious display of rhetoric, but thoroughly armed in the strength of his knowledge, research and cultivated ability, without any effort to show it, he possesses gigantic power, and by it has risen to the head of the profession. And he is not only a great but a good man."

"It is a misfortune to your people and the country that such a man should not have been sent to Washington long ago," said Mr. Webster. "He would have maintained Virginia's proud intellectual supremacy, and by the soundness of his views enhanced her influence."

At the death of Judge Stuart, in 1830, the vacancy occasioned by the death of that able jurist (father of Hon. Alexander H. H. Stuart,) Lucas P. Thompson, of Amherst county, then a young man who had distinguished himself in the Constitutional Convention of 1829 and 1830, became a candidate for the office of Judge. Mr. Peyton was also brought forward by his friends. Thompson had made himself popular on the basis question, and was regarded as one of the most rising men of his contemporaries. He was the junior of Mr. Peyton. My father, at that time, was a member of the House of Delegates from Augusta county. The contest for Judge came off. My father, the ardent advocate of Mr Peyton, was sustained in his opinion of him by some of the ablest jurists of Virginia, amongst them was Benjamin Watkins Leigh, who said to him that "Mr. Peyton was the greatest lawyer west of the Blue Ridge." The then Senator for this district, a personal enemy without just cause, however, of Mr. Peyton, exerted all his popularity and power in favor of Thompson, and on his election boasted that he had accomplished a long cherished wish, that of defeating an ambition of Mr. Peyton. But he signally failed. It is well known that Mr. P. did not wish the office of Judge, much preferred to retain the greatly more lucrative and equally honorable situation of public prosecutor and his large law practice, as well because of the more active character of his duties as prosecutor, as in the interest of a large and growing family.

Major James Garland, now Judge of the Hustings Court of Lynchburg, himself a great lawyer and statesmen, about the time I went to the bar of Nelson county, said in a conversation with me: "I was a member of the Legislature that elected Thompson. But for the course of the Senator from Augusta and Rockbridge, your father would have succeeded in the election of John Howe Peyton, than whom there is no greater lawyer in the Commonwealth."

Mr. Frazier has so well described him as a common lawyer, and the most eminent prosecutor that Virginia has ever had, that I forbear to say anything further with reference to that matter. That is a part of the history of the jurisprudence of this State. I will add, that I have seen his Coke Littleton, (studied by him as a student of law) with the marginal pages filled with annotations and references, indicating the application and devotion he felt for his profession. I am told that he had a grim way of preventing such as had not the ability, from entering into the profession of the law. In his labrary there was a rare old edition of Littleton on Tenures. He considered this book as the basis of the laws of real property in England, and he thought that it should be first read without Coke's Commentary. When a young man desired to study law under him, whom he knew to have no capacity to succeed, he placed this work in his hands, asking him to read it again and again and strive to understand it without recourse to the commentary, and return for examination, after a fortnight or three weeks' perusal, of such part as he had mastered. It rarely happened that the young man did not hand him back the book at the end of a short time. announcing his purpose of seeking a livelihood in some other field. Thus he was instrumental in keeping some from the profession who by entering into the law would have derived no profit to themselves nor reflected credit upon the profession. And on the other hand when he discovered merit in a young man no one was more prompt, active and generous in encouraging it.

His conversation with his son and myself above referred to, on Uses and Trusts, exemplified the fact that he had not forgotten in his maturer what he had learned in his younger years. I have been told that Mr. Peyton had acquired the habit of reading, or at least looking over, Blackstone once a year, and it was rarely the case that he referred to precedents and decisions of the courts, which has become the bane of the profession of this day, but for authority he went down to the deep foundations of the law, treating and regarding it as a fixed and accurate science, not depending upon the opinion of this jurist or that, and thus arriving at just conclusions alike convincing to judge and jury. There have been many men whom the accident of applause or fortune have made great, but few who were great in themselves. Amongst the latter, Mr. Peyton stands in the front rank. As a man, he was true, honest, noble and generous ; despising the low, vulgar and ignoble and valuing only the pure and elevated ; seeking, by genuine courtesy and kindness, to win all hearts, and by stern integrity to retain the golden opinions he had gained. As a father and husband he was active and earnest in his endeavor to fill the picture of a true man ; as a lawyer, he stood second to none, and by the breadth of his learning and knowledge, his clear and comprehensive manner, and his earnest and determined performance of duty as public prosecutor, he has won a position such as few lawyers have ever attained. As a statesman, the high praise which his generation gave him, the deep respect in which he was held by the eminent men of his time, and the undying record which history bears to his genius and achievements, mark him as one of the great men of Virginia, who may be proud of her son, while she can justly regret that he should have sought privacy and retirement in preference to national glory. Modest, sincere, learned and determined, Virginia has had few to equal—none to surpass him. As in the past, he moulded and controlled the opinions and actions of the times, so in the future may he ever serve as a model for the true and the good, and prove an incentive to the ambitious. May the young learn to emulate his life and example, while the old revere and respect his memory.

Sketches of Mr. Peyton have been written by Hon. Geo. W. Thompson, of Wheeling ; Col. D. S. Young, Joseph A. Waddell and others, but space will not admit of their introduction here. They all concur in representing him as a man of extraordinary moral and intellectual endowments. Judge Alex. Rives says of him : " There was no one at the bar, with whom I was associated, for whom I cherish the same admiration, respect and esteem." In the same appreciative terms, Prof. Minor, of the University of Virginia, the late J. D. Davidson, of Lexington, and numerous others have written recently to the author.

JUDGE BRISCOE G. BALDWIN.

We are indebted to Hon. Alex. H. H. Stuart for the following brief sketch of this distinguished lawyer :

Briscoe Gerard Baldwin was the eldest son of Dr. Cornelius Baldwin and his wife Mary, who was a daughter of Col. Gerard Briscoe, of Frederick county, Va. Dr. Cornelius Baldwin was a native of New Jersey, a surgeon in the Revolutionary army, and a member of the Cincinnati Society.

After the close of the war he settled, as a practising physician, in Winchester, Va., where he married and continued to reside until his death, which occurred about 1820.

Briscoe G. Baldwin was born in Winchester, Va., on the 18th day of January, 1789. He received a rudimentary education in a private school, and subsequently was prepared for college at the Winchester Academy. In 1806, he entered William and Mary College, where he was the fellow-student of John Tyler, William S. Archer and others, who afterwards held distinguished public positions.

At the early age of eighteen he had exhibited so many evidences of talent that he was chosen to deliver the oration at the bi-centennial celebration of the settlement of Jamestown, in 1607.

After his return from William and Mary College, by invitation of the late Judge William Daniel, sen., who had married his eldest sister, he went to Cumberland county, where Judge Daniel then resided, and studied law under his direction and advice. He made such rapid progress in his professional studies that he was licensed to practice before he had attained the age of twenty-one. He then returned to Winchester, and remained some months, devoting himself to the study of his profession and general literature.

In 1809, he removed to Staunton, and entered on the practice of his profession, which he continued to pursue, with diligence and success, until 1842, when he was elected a member of the Supreme Court of Appeals of Virginia, a position which he continued to hold until his death, on 18th May, 1852.

In 1811, he intermarried with Martha Steele, youngest daughter of Chancellor John Brown, of Staunton, and sister of Judge Jas. E. Brown, of Wythe. She was a lady of extraordinary intellectual endowments,—full of vivacity and wit, and of singularly attractive manners and colloquial powers.

Judge Baldwin devoted himself exclusively to his profession and polite literature. He had no taste for political life, and although eminently qualified for almost any public trust, and one of the most popular men of his day, he never sought to obtain any political office. He represented the County of Augusta in 1818-'20, and in 1841-'2, in the General Assembly of Virginia. On the first occasion he was elected, during his absence from home, by a spontaneous uprising of the people, who did not wait to ask his consent to serve. In 1841, at the earnest solicitation of the best men of the county, he consented to be voted for as one of their delegates, and was chosen almost by acclamation. Within a few weeks after he took his seat in the Legislature, he was elected to fill a place on the bench of the Court of Appeals of Virginia.

In 1829, Judge Baldwin was chosen by the people of the Senatorial District, of which Augusta was then a part, as the colleague of Chapman Johnson, Gen. William McCoy and Samuel McD. Moore, in the memorable convention of 1829-'30.

At the Bar, Judge Baldwin proved himself to be not only an able lawyer and skillful special pleader, but one of the most eloquent advocates of his day. Half a century ago, the bar of Staunton was one of the ablest in the Commonwealth. The four most distinguished members of it were Chapman Johnson, Daniel Sheffey, John H. Peyton and Briscoe G. Baldwin. In every important civil cause these gentlemen were arrayed—two and two—against each other, and it was an intellectual treat, of a high order, to witness the forensic contests of these giants in their profession. And it may be added that it was refreshing to observe the high-toned courtesy and absence of every thing like personalities which characterized their forensic tilts.

Judge Baldwin possessed high and varied intellectual powers, which had been developed by careful and thorough culture. He was not only a learned lawyer, but an accomplished scholar. In the midst of his professional labors he always found time to keep abreast of the literature of the day. He was familiar with the English classics, and often illustrated his speeches by quotations from Shakspeare, Milton, Pope, and other standard poets.

To great vigor of intellect he united quick and keen perceptions, a rich and poetic imagination and tender sensibilities, which always brought him into close sympathy with the suffering and oppressed. Hence, as an advocate, he was not only a powerful reasoner but a polished rhetorician, and a ready and adroit debater,—master of every weapon useful in assault or defence. His great efforts at the bar often displayed wonderful versatility of talent. While he would instruct and convince his audience by his logic, he would often delight them by brilliant sallies of wit, keen repartee, pungent sarcasm, scorching denunciation of fraud and injustice, splendid declamation and melting pathos.

One of the most remarkable triumphs achieved by Judge Baldwin at the bar is recorded in 9 Leigh, p. 434. In that case Judge Baldwin had advised and taken an appeal from the decree of the Circuit Court of Augusta. He felt so much confidence in the merits of his client's cause that when the case was called he submitted it, on the petition, without argument. To his surprise and dismay, in a few days, the court, by four to one, decided the case against him. His modesty restrained him, for several days, from asking a rehearing of the case, so as to afford him an opportunity of presenting an argument to the court. Finally, his sense of duty to his client triumphed over his personal scruples, and he asked the privilege of being heard, which was granted. He prepared himself for the discussion with great care, and at the appointed time he delivered an argument of so much force and vigor as to satisfy the court that they had made an erroneous decision, and they reversed their previous judgment by a vote of four to one.

But it was during his ten years service on the Bench of the Court of Appeals that Judge Baldwin's talents and learning were most conspicuously displayed.

Shortly after he took his seat on the Bench, he determined that whenever a cause came before the court in which questions were presented in regard to which the law was obscure or in doubt from conflicting decisions, he would endeavor to sift the matter to the bottom and to educe from the mass of unsatisfactory and often clashing opinions of the courts the true principles which should govern in all such cases. He did not live long enough to carry this beneficent purpose into effect, except to a limited extent. But all who have read his able and lucid opinions, in which he expounded the law on the questions of "Fraud per se," "Adverse Possession," "What Decrees are Final," and others to which I need not refer, must admit that the courts, as well as the bar, are under deep obligations to him for his comprehensive, clear and exhaustive treatment of those subjects. If his life and health had continued ten years longer, he would doubtless have erected for himself, by his luminous expositions of intricate questions of law, a monument more durable than marble or bronze.

In all his private relations—as a citizen, a neighbor, a friend, a husband, a father—his character was without spot or blemish, and few men ever lived who were more generally esteemed and beloved, or who died more universally regretted.

48 ‡

HON. CHAPMAN JOHNSON.

We are under obligations to Mrs. A. F. Gifford, the accomplished daughter and only surviving child of the late Chapman Johnson, for the following brief account of her distinguished father:

"Chapman Johnson was the son of Thomas Johnson and Jane Chapman, both of English descent, born on his father's estate, in Louisa county, Va., on the 15th March, 1779.

He was educated at William and Mary College, in Williamsburg, Va., and included the law course in his studies while there, continuing that special study, and beginning his practice at the bar, in Augusta county, about the year 1804. During frequent visits to Richmond, while a student at Williamsburg, he made the acquaintance of Mary Ann Nicolson, orphan daughter of George and Margaret Nicolson, of Richmond, and ward of her uncle, Charles Copeland. This lady became his wife in 1806, when, at the age of twenty-seven, he came to reside in Staunton. Soon after his marriage he purchased the brick building close by the court-house, where he lived until the year 1824. Having been sent to the Legislature in 1822-'23, and impatient of separation from his family, he removed to Richmond to live in 1824, his children having all been born in Staunton, except the youngest, Carter Page, who was born in Richmond.

His strong attachment to the mountain district led him to purchase property near Staunton,—one of the farms, " Bearwallow," becoming his family summer-home from that time. And thus his old friendships and associations were kept up as long as he lived.

He died in Richmond on the 12th of July, 1849, after several years of failing health, his widow surviving him ten years, and dying at the home of her son-in-law, at Blackheath, near Richmond, in May, 1860. They left four children: George Nicolson, the oldest; William Boswell, Mary Ann, and Carter Page. George Nicolson married Margaret, daughter of Adam and Betsy Menzies, of Kentucky, and died in Richmond in March, 1855, leaving a wife and five children: Mary Ann, Marguerite Howard, Chapman, Arthur Nicolson, and Caroline Gifford, all living but Arthur Nicolson, who died about twelve years ago at their present home in Covington, Ky. William Boswell married Margaret Sarah, daughter of John B. Breckinridge, of Staunton, Va., and died on 31st May, 1879. His widow died in June, 1880. They left three children: Carter Page, William Boswell, and Nathalie, all living. Carter Page married Anne Love Forest, daughter of Jane and Richard Forest, of Washington City; was lost in the steamer Arctic on 27th September, 1894; his wife died in April, 1852. They left two children: Jane Forest and Chapman Love, both living. Mary Ann married Adolphus Frederic Gifford, of London, Eng.; they had no children. He was lost at sea in January, 1862. His widow is the only survivor of the four children of Chapman Johnson.

With regard to Mr. Johnson's social habits, he was too hard-working and studious a lawyer to find much leisure for the pleasures of society, but whenever opportunity offered, proved himself highly appreciative of social intercourse with his many warm friends, and enjoyed his seasons of Summer relaxation, as long as health lasted, with the mirthful elasticity of youth. While justly admired for the dignity, courtesy, ease and polish of the true gentleman, on every public occasion, it was in domestic life and around his own fireside that his social qualities were chiefly displayed, and the peculiar graces of both mind and heart revealed.

Mr. Johnson was a sincere believer in the religion of Christ, his faith being manifested in the unfeigned humility, integrity and benevolence of his daily life, as in his moderation, self-control and strict observance of the "Golden Rule." He was earnestly attached to the Episcopal Church, and a regular and earnest attendant of the old Monumental Church, under Bishop Moore's preaching, and, in the latter years of his life, became a member and communicant of that church. His mind was logical and argumentative—not only comprehending the prominent points of a subject with ease, but gifted in power to impart the clear and full understanding of a case to his listeners. His style, as a speaker, was clear, strong, forcible and earnest, his manner gaining in enthusiasm and his voice in energy and strength as his oratory grew in eloquence."

Mr. Johnson served in the Virginia Senate and in the State Convention of 1829 as delegate for the Augusta District and with distinguished ability.

COL. JOHN B. BALDWIN.

The following sketch of this able and distinguished man is from the pen of J. A. Waddell, Esq.:

"John Brown Baldwin was the eldest son of the late Judge Briscoe G. Baldwin, and was born at Spring Farm, near Staunton, on the 11th day of January, 1820. After passing through a course of instruction at several primary schools, he entered the Staunton Academy, where he was prepared for college. At an early age he developed a remarkable talent and fondness for mathematical studies; but, strange to say, considering the distinguished position he afterwards attained as a public speaker, he betrayed during boyhood no special facility in the acquisition of languages. At the age of sixteen, he entered the University of Virginia, where he prosecuted his studies for three consecutive years. During that time he acquired a high standing for masculine talent and all the qualities which win the confidence and affection of associates.

When his collegiate course closed, he returned to Staunton and studied law for two years under his father, then a lawyer in full practice. At the age of twenty-one, he began his professional career as the partner of Hon. A. H. H. Stuart. The partnership continued for nearly three years; he then commenced the practice on his own responsibility. At that time the Bar of Staunton was distinguished for ability and learning, and it required no small amount of talent and industry to ensure success in the face of such formidable competition. But he was not dismayed by the difficulties which stood in his way. Conscious of his own powers, he determined to command success, and nobly did he accomplish his purpose.

On the 20th of September, 1842, he intermarried with Susan Madison Peyton, eldest daughter of the eminent lawyer, John Howe Peyton, Esq. It is not the purpose of the writer to intrude into the privacy of domestic life and relate what there occurred; but having enjoyed the privilege of mingling freely in the scene, he cannot forbear saying that it was one of the utmost felicity. From the time the young couple went to housekeeping in a modest dwelling, near the court-house, until the life of the husband ended in an elegant mansion adorned with all that wealth and taste could provide, their home was a Vale of Tempe, disturbed by no rude wind, and familiar access to it was a source of exquisite enjoyment to the guest. The cheerful greeting, the unaffected kindness, the high converse and sparkling wit, can never be forgotten by any who ever entered there.

The first circumstance that called forth the talent of Col. Baldwin as a debater, and attracted to him a large share of public attention, was his participation in the heated political contest of 1844. The late Greene B. Samuels, of Shenandoah, was the Democratic nominee for the Electoral College, and Mr. Stuart, of Augusta, was the representative of the Whig party. The latter having been called by public business to New York, in the midst of the canvass, Col. Baldwin took his place. He was then only twenty-four years of age, and at first some fear was entertained that he might not contend successfully with his able and experienced antagonist. But, after the first meeting, all apprehension vanished, and men of all parties admitted that the youthful champion was competent for any encounter.

As soon as he attained the age prescribed by the Constitution, he was elected by the people of Augusta a member of the House of Delegates. In the Legislature, although one of the youngest members, he distinguished himself as a debater, and gave ample assurance of future eminence. During the session the question of calling a convention to frame a new Constitution was agitated, and this brought up the issue whether representation in the convention should be upon the "mixed" or the "white basis"—that is, whether persons and property, or persons alone, should be taken into account in adjusting the basis of representation. Col. Baldwin took a decided and prominent stand in favor of the former, which was the basis of representation in the Legislature under the existing Constitution, and contended that any departure from it by the General Assembly would be unconstitutional and revolutionary. He firmly maintained his opinions, although he well knew they were unpopular among his constituents. This was his first public display of that high moral courage and determination not to sacrifice right to expediency which marked his whole future career.

Having, as he anticipated, been defeated for the Legislature at the next election, he turned his attention with renewed energy to his profession, and never afterwards exhibited a desire to return to public life. When he subsequently held representative trusts in the Convention of 1861, in the Confederate Congress, and in the Legislature of 1865-'7, they were not sought by him, but were conferred by the unsolicited suffrages of the people, who had learned to appreciate his talents and moral worth. He acted for several years as captain of the Staunton Light Infantry, a volunteer military company, and subsequently as colonel of the 52d regiment, C. S. A.

In 1859, having already acquired a reputation throughout the State as a leading lawyer, a vacancy occurring on the bench of the Court of Appeals by the death of Judge Samuels, without his agency he was brought before the people by his friends for the position. His successful competitor was Judge William J. Robertson, of Charlottesville, and it may be mentioned 1 a fact creditable to both that the rivalry on that occasion disturbed in no ~ree the life-long and warm friendship which subsisted between the two 'lidates.

While not seeking office, Col. Baldwin was a man of very pronounced political opinions. He was decided in all his convictions, and earnest, as well as able and eloquent, in maintaining them. He, therefore, took an active part in the political contests of 1848–'52–'56 and '60. When the question of secession began to agitate the public mind, in 1860, he came forth as one of the most ardent supporters of the Union, and commenced the canvass on the Bell and Everett side in a speech at the club-house in Richmond city. In the great contest of that year, he supported with burning zeal and matchless ability the Union ticket. His clarion voice rang throughout the State, and he probably contributed more than any other man to turn the scale in Virginia in favor of conciliation and peace between the jarring sections.

Referring to his club-house speech, the Richmond "Whig" of the next day said:

"For over two hours and a-half did the able and distinguished speaker hold that vast concourse of persons spell-bound by the magic of faultless argument and overpowering eloquence. It was a masterly and extraordinary effort, and places Col. Baldwin in the front rank of the debaters, not only of Virginia, but of the entire Union. It was an effort that would have done honor to any deliberative body on earth. Indeed, the delivery of such a speech in the Senate of the United States would have created a profound impression there, and produced a sensation throughout the country. It was a lofty, noble, magnificent effort—a grand and glorious display of high mental power. His unanswerable logic, his wit, his humor, his eloquence—who in all that vast audience but was instructed, elevated, delighted and carried away by his matchless reasoning and the irresistible force of his argument! We are sure that no speech has been delivered here for years which was listened to with more rapt attention, and which produced a more powerful and lasting impression upon a Richmond audience. To attempt even a faint outline of Col. Baldwin's speech on Friday evening would be simply folly on our part, and we therefore forbear."

The State Convention of 1861 being called, Col. Baldwin was elected one of the three representatives of Augusta county. His earnest appeals there in behalf of the Union, and his anxious efforts to avert the civil war, are familiar facts. Every reader will recall the transcendant ability which he displayed in his memorable reply to the speeches of two distinguished gentlemen who were regarded as leaders of the secession party. By common consent that speech was pronounced the ablest and most eloquent that was delivered in the Convention. The writer happens to know, but not from Col. Baldwin himself, that years afterwards, while he was sojourning in a distant city, a gentleman previously unknown to him, sought him out to thank him for the pleasure he had enjoyed in listening to that speech.

It has been stated that Col. Baldwin finally voted for the ordinance of secession. This is a mistake. He voted against it, and resisted every appeal to change his vote, stating that his negative vote was the true record of his opinions. But after the ordinance had been ratified by the people, he signed it as an act of representative duty. During the session of the Convention he was delegated by a portion of the Union members as their commissioner to Washington. He proceeded to the city, and after an interview with President Lincoln, returned to Richmond greatly disappointed and grieved. At one period of the session, when the fact burst upon him that secession and war were inevitable, he retired with a colleague from the hail to his chamber, and his sturdy frame was convulsed with an emotion which nothing could relieve but a flood of tears. Let it not be supposed that there was any unmanly weakness in this. As well upbraid the Hebrew prophet for weeping over the calamities of his people. It merely betrayed the suffering of a great soul, as with the vision of a "seer" he looked over the field of deadly strife, and saw in the back ground the ruined homesteads and desolated firesides of his native land. The die was cast, however; the path of duty was plain to him; his position was taken, and thenceforth, with brave and cheerful front, he carried himself throughout the war. As he himself expressed it, he felt that it only remained for Virginia to show to the world how gallantly a people could meet an issue they had exhausted every honorable effort to avoid.

After the war began, Col. Baldwin resigned his seat in the Convention and accepted the office of Inspector-General of the Virginia forces, which was tendered to him by Governor Letcher. In that position he rendered signal service to the State. When the troops of Virginia had been organized and turned over to the Confederate States, he was appointed colonel of the 52d Virginia Regiment of Infantry, raised at Staunton, and went with his command to West Virginia. He continued in active and arduous service at the Alleghany outposts until illness completely prostrated him, and before he had recovered, was elected to the Confederate Congress from the Augusta District. The illness referred to was caused by a physical ailment from which he never recovered, which repeatedly subjected him to intense suffering, and finally terminated his life.

While a thorough organizer and disciplinarian, Col. B. carried into the field the same personal characteristics of courtesy and kindliness to those in subordinate relations which contributed so much to his popularity in civil life. The sturdy yeomen of West Augusta, whom he commanded, recognized in him, too, the. high soldierly qualities of a worthy leader. His connection with the regiment was severed with mutual regret. Indeed, we hazard nothing in saying that no officer in the army was more universally admired and respected, alike by superiors and inferiors in rank.

As most of the sessions of the Confederate Congress were secret, the public had no opportunity of hearing or seeing reports of the speeches of its members; but we have the concurrent testimony of all who were present, that Col. Baldwin was regarded as one of the ablest debaters in that body so distinguished for talent and statesmanship. His speech in opposition to the suspension of the writ of *habeas corpus* has often been described as one of the noblest defences of the principles of liberty ever pronounced in this country.

During the recesses of Congress, Col. Baldwin acted as Colonel of a regiment of Reserves raised in his county, and repeatedly led out his command to repel the enemy.

Upon the surrender of Gen Lee, when it was manifest that a further continuance of the contest would be fruitless of good, Col. Baldwin was one of the first to counsel the acceptance of the situation and a restoration of peace to the country. He took an active part in the meeting held in Staunton, on the 8th of May, 1865, which had for its objects the preservation of order and the reinstatement of the Government. This, it is believed, was the first meeting of the kind ever held in the Southern States, but it was soon followed by similar meetings elsewhere.

In October, 1865, members of the General Assembly under the restored Government, were elected. Col. Baldwin was absent from home for some weeks, and did not return until a few days before the election; but without having announced himself a candidate, he was elected a member of the House of Delegates. At the convening of the Legislature in December, he was elected Speaker of the House. Almost every page of the journal of that body bears the impress of his talent and patriotism. Nothing was too great and nothing too small to receive his careful consideration. On questions of internal improvement he exhibited wonderful sagacity. He was particularly interested in the Chesapeake and Ohio Railroad, and aided materially to secure its completion. The extension of the road to the Ohio River may almost be said to be due to his efforts. As a praliamentarian he had few equals; and in the midst of other employments, he found time to digest the admirable system of rules by which the House of Delegates is still governed. Among the measures originated by him during the session of this Legislature, was that establishing the Augusta County Fair. On the floor, as well as in the chair, he added every day to his reputation as a man of practical wisdom, of unsurpassed ability in debate, and of unselfish patriotism. His popularity and influence were unrivaled, and there was no office in the gift of the Legislature which he might not have had. Towards the close of the last session he was prominently spoken of for the office of Governor, but, as is generally remembered, through the intervention of the Federal Government, the anticipated election was not held.

The great Convention of the people of Virginia, met in Richmond, in December, 1867, to remonstrate against and organize for the defeat of the "Underwood Constitution," and Col. Baldwin was one of the most influential members. It was then that he proposed the system of political organization, which, being adopted by the Convention, has been productive of the most beneficial results.

In 1868, a Convention of the Conservative party of Virginia was held to nominate candidates for the various State offices filled by popular election. Col. Baldwin was chosen President of the body, and was importuned to accept the nomination for the office of Governor. For reasons purely patriotic, he declined the position; but, notwithstanding his positive refusal, upon counting the votes it was found that he lacked only three of receiving the nomination. Of his speech on this occasion, the Richmond "Enquirer" said: "She eloquent and able address of this gentleman, in declining to allow his name to be used as a candidate for the gubernatorial nomination of the Conservative Convention last Friday, was the master-speech of the occasion, we think. It is no compliment to Col. Baldwin to hold him up to the admiration of the people of Virginia, for he has reached the zenith of their confidence, and stands before them now almost without a peer, *sans peur et sans reproche;* but no one could hear the able speech in question, without perceiving that he was giving another proof of the wisdom of his head and the patriotic love of his heart, which have made him almost the idol of the people. Even while he spoke the charming thought filled the minds of his hearers that such a speech was adding another leaf to the crown of laurels with which his mother State will some day crown his brow, 'when the King shall claim his own again."

He was a member of the National Convention which nominated Seymour and Blair for the Presidency and Vice Presidency of the United States, and chairman of the Virginia delegation.

In December, 1868, the House of Representatives at Washington passed a bill requiring the President to cause the "Underwood Constitution" to be submitted as a whole to the people of Virginia; and it was apparent that unless some steps were taken to arrest it, the bill would become a law, and thereby the Constitution, with its test oaths and disfranchisements, be imposed upon our people. At this crisis, a few gentlemen of Staunton, perceiving the imminence of the danger, agreed on consultation to invite a more general conference in Richmond. About fifty gentlemen accordingly met in that city, on the 31st of December, and after due deliberation determined to make an effort to induce Congress to grant to the people of Virginia the right to vote separately on the objectionable clauses, so as to eliminate them from the Constitution. A "Committee of Nine," of whom Col. Baldwin was one, was appointed to go to Washington for the purpose indicated. The mission was successful, and thus the State escaped the threatened evils. In this service Col. Baldwin displayed marked ability, and contributed largely to the success of the scheme. For a time it was mis-understood, or misrepresented, and opposed by a large portion, if not a majority, of the people. The members of the Committee were assailed by invective and ridicule; but they persevered in their effort, and at this day, few. or none, will deny that the measure was one of consummate states-manship. As remarked by a recent writer, in regard to the matter; "A few gentlemen who preferred the welfare of the State to their own popu-larity, organized a movement that saved their fellow-citizens almost in spite of themselves."

Such was the course of John B. Baldwin on all occasions. He never paused to inquire whether a measure were popular or otherwise; he only sought to know whether it was right. Time and again he confronted the popular sentiment, meeting his opponents singly or in crowds, and plying them with argument, anecdotes and witticism. He has, almost literally, been known to disperse a mob by a timely joke. He was in no degree a demagogue, yet no man was ever more beloved by all classes of the peo-ple, and he never lost his hold upon their affections.

The polictical services so frequently alluded to, were mere episodes in Col. Baldwin's life His great efforts were directed to building up the material interests of his State and native county, for which he cherished a filial affection, and to pursue with fidelity his special calling. Distinction as a lawyer was regarded by him as more vaulable than any other fame. He never was a grasping money-maker;—on the contrary, he was too in-different to the pecuniary emoluments of his profession.

It is common to speak of Col. Baldwin as a self-reliant man, and about most matters he was remarkably so; but there was a class of questions in re-gard to which he was habitually cautious and distrustful of himself. Wher-ever his feelings were implicated and action was required, he sought the counsel of friends. His self-confidence never made him supercilious. He never sought to intimidate or over-shadow any one; but the weakest as-sociate, or opponent, was treated by him with respect; and no inferior in age or intellect came in contect with him without being inspired with a somewhat better opinion of himself. He possessed the art of making such persons feel comfortable in his presence. Hence he was a great favorite with children and servants, the simple and the lowly. He burdened no recipient of his kindness with a sense of gratitude.

For several years Col. Baldwin was a member of the Board of Visitors of the University of Virginia, and he was ever one of the most devoted and active friends and supporters of that institution.

While Col. Baldwin did not become a member of any church, the principles of the Christian religion were deeply imbedded in his heart and exhibited in his daily life. He was a regular and serious attendant at public worship, and a constant reader of the Bible. He felt and always expressed profound reverence for the truths of revelation and regard for Christian people of every name and denomination. It has been truly remarked that in his public speeches he never related a vulgar anecdote or sought to give point to wit by profanity. Although his opinions were proclaimed to the world, he was ever reticent in the expression of his feelings and inner experiences; but those who knew him most intimately are persuaded that during the last year or two of his life the subject of religion had come home to him as a matter of personal concern, and that if he had lived a little longer he would have publicly declared his interest in it. After an illness of several weeks, his active and useful life was terminated September 30, 1873. Never before in this community have the sickness and death of any one caused such interest and sorrow. During his illness our whole population awaited the result with the utmost solicitude; the report of each favorable change in his symptoms was eagerly circulated, and whenever the reverse appeared, sadness was expressed in every countenance; and when, at last, his death was announced, the lamentation was deep and universal. On the occasion of his funeral, all business in the town was suspended, the bells of the various churches were tolled, and the whole people rose up to show honor and love to him who had been to each a wise counsellor and sympathizing friend.

SUPPLEMENT.

From the "Spectator" of December 1866, we derive the following list of early marriages, which were solemnized in Augusta between the years 1785 and 1793. The ceremony was performed in all these cases by Rev. John Brown, once pastor of New Providence, in Rockbridge, who, after serving that congregation for nearly fifty years, removed to Kentucky, and filled the pulpit of a Presbyterian church in Woodford county. He was a strong man in the church, and the father of Hon. James Brown, Minister Plenipotentiary to France, and from him are descended the distinguished Col. J. Mason Brown, of Louisville, Ky., Gov. B. Gratz Brown, of Missouri, and others. The list was obtained from Rev. John Brown's private memorandum book, and will prove of no small interest to the descendants, now scattered through many States, of those early settlers. Many of the names are familiar to us, and they all belong to the class of those who have labored for the advancement of civilization, the support of constitutional authority, and the development of our national resources. They have done their best to encourage every effort for the cause of education, the diffusion of knowledge, the extension of human freedom, and the spread of the Gospel. Many of them have gone forth as pioneers to stimulate by their example, to build up by their enterprise, to enrich by their wealth, and to plant, wherever they set down, schools, colleges, churches and institutions for the welfare of mankind. Let their names be placed on record to impress on the minds of the young the story of their lives, their examples of patriotism, moral worth and Christian benevolence.

The list is as follows:

November 9th, 1785—Jacob Morrell and Elizabeth Brooback.
" 10th, " —Lewis Jordan and Mary Trible.
December 6th, " —Isaac Trencher and Margaret McColmick.
" " " —Arthur Connelly and Jane Dale.
" 14th " —J. Moore and Jennie Steele.
" 19th " —James Risk and Elizabeth Rusk.
" 29th " —Thomas Weles and Carrie White.
January 3d, 1786—Robert Grier and Margaret Campbell.
" 9th, " —William Carpenter and Mary Strickler.
" 12th, " —Michael Kenady and Ellen McCaferty.
" 28th, " —Thomas Broom and Sara Galen.

February 9th, 1786—John Spence and Isabel McCormick.
March 13th, " —Epr. Doly and July Ann Doherty.
" 23d, " —James Paxton and Phebe McClung.
April 13th, " —Sam'l Talford and Eliz'th Call.
" " " —Ed. Crydan and Jannet Ramsey.
" 20th, " —James Grigsby and Reb Wallace.
May 4th, " —James Parks and Jean Buchanan.
" 25th, " —John McCampbell and Martha Bennet.

The above marriages were certified and sent to Andrew Reed, clerk of Rockbridge, June 27th, 1786, by Capt. Andrew Moore.

August 14th, 1788—John Collins and Mary Resner.
September 30th, " —Ralph Wandless and Crispy Nicholas.
January 22d, 1789—James Talford and Jean McCorkery.

The above sent by James Brown, son of widow Brown, June 23, 1789.

September 1st, 1789—James Kelso and Betsy Sittington.
October 6th, " —Robert Cooper and Martha Steel.
November 27th, " —Peter Burns and Jane Miller.
January 11th, 1790—Cawson McCullock and Lidia Vernon.
March 16th, " —William Higginbottom and Polly Shannon.
June 10th, " —William Dowthat and Anna Lewis.

The above returned by myself (Rev. J. Brown) June 11th, 1790.

July 31st, 1790—John Doughady and Agness Davidson.
August 9th, " —Luke Collins and Sarah Miller.
October 14th, " —Alexander Thompson and Sallie Bell.
December 8th, " —Enoch Bogas and Eliz. McCroskry.
February 22d,1791—Joseph Walker and Grizzel McCroskry.
April 5th, " —William Davis and Anis Caldwell. [William D. was father of the late Walter Davis, of Augusta.]
" " " —John Bell and Rachel Foster.
" 7th, " —Michael Miller and Christian Cline.
" 28th, " —Thomas Paxton and Martha Steel.
May 19th, " —David Wilson and Sarah Steel.
June 23d, " —Joseph Shanklin and Phaney Garlon.

The above sent by Samuel Brown, to be recorded by the clerk of Augusta.

Dec'ber 29th, 1791—Robt. Martin and Mary Miller.
January 12th, 1792—Arch'd Musry and Sarah Fulton.
February 15th, " —James Calhoon and Mary Lessly.
May 29th, " —Jacob Calk and Mary McFadden.

The above sent by Preston Brown.

January 21st, 1793—Richard Hay and Rachel Risk.
February 17th, " —Daniel Moore and Martha Barnett.
June 15th, " —William Beard and Margaret McNutt.
" 22d, " —John Weir and Jean Spreil.

The above sent by Mrs. Humphreys.

September 17th, 1793—James Poague and Sarah Henry.
November 23d, " —Samuel McClintock and Susanna King.
" 29th, " —William Alexander and Sarah Henry.

INDEX.

FINIS.